Sales and Marketing

Sales trend analysis	Database querying and reporting	Chapter 1
Customer reservation system	Database querying and reporting	Chapter 3
Improving marketing decisions	Spreadsheet pivot tables	Chapter 14
Customer profiling	Database design	Chapter 6*
	Database querying and reporting	
Customer service analysis	Database design	Chapter 12
	Database querying and reporting	
Sales lead and customer analysis	Database design	Chapter 9
	Database querying and reporting	
Blog creation and design	Blog creation tool	Chapter 4

Internet Skills

Business Problem	Chapter
Using online software tools to calculate shipping costs	Chapter 1
Using online interactive mapping software to plan efficient transportation routes	Chapter 2
Researching product information and evaluating Web sites for auto sales	Chapter 3
Using Internet newsgroups for marketing	Chapter 4
Researching travel costs using online travel sites	Chapter 5
Searching online databases for products and services	Chapter 6
Using Web search engines for business research	Chapter 7
Researching and evaluating business outsourcing services	Chapter 8
Redesigning business processes for Web procurement	Chapter 9
Researching real estate prices	Chapter 10
Researching international markets and pricing	Chapter 11
Researching and evaluating supply chain management services	Chapter 12
Evaluating e-commerce hosting services	Chapter 13
Using online software tools for retirement planning	Chapter 14
Using shopping bots to compare product price, features, and availability	Chapter 15

Analytical, Writing, and Presentation Skills*

Business Problem	Chapter
Management analysis of a business	Chapter 1
Value chain and competitive forces analysis	Chapter 3
Business strategy formulation	
Formulating a corporate privacy policy	Chapter 4
Employee productivity analysis	r 7
Disaster recovery planning	r 8
Identifying international markets	r 11
Locating and evaluating suppliers	12
Developing an e-commerce strategy	r 13
Identifying knowledge management opportunities	Chapter 15

*Hands-On MIS Projects on MyMISLab

For

Erica and Elisabeth

—K.C.L. AND J.P.L.

For J.W. and D.S.,
and other friends and colleagues for their support
and love; for my parents, both now deceased,
who taught me to value teaching and excellence;
and finally, for God, for all his gifts

—M.E.B.

About the Authors

Kenneth C. Laudon is a Professor of Information Systems at New York University's Stern School of Business. He holds a B.A. in Economics from Stanford and a Ph.D. from Columbia University. He has authored twelve books dealing with electronic commerce, information systems, organizations, and society. Professor Laudon has also written over forty articles concerned with the social, organizational, and management impacts of information systems, privacy, ethics, and multimedia technology.

Professor Laudon's current research is on the planning and management of large-scale information systems and multimedia information technology. He has received grants from the National Science Foundation to study the evolution of national information systems at the Social Security Administration, the IRS, and the FBI. Ken's research focuses on enterprise system implementation, computer-related organizational and occupational changes in large organizations, changes in management ideology, changes in public policy, and understanding productivity change in the knowledge sector.

Ken Laudon has testified as an expert before the United States Congress. He has been a researcher and consultant to the Office of Technology Assessment (United States Congress), Department of Homeland Security, and to the Office of the President, several executive branch agencies, and Congressional Committees. Professor Laudon also acts as an in-house educator for several consulting firms and as a consultant on systems planning and strategy to several Fortune 500 firms.

At NYU's Stern School of Business, Ken Laudon teaches courses on Managing the Digital Firm, Information Technology and Corporate Strategy, Professional Responsibility (Ethics), and Electronic Commerce and Digital Markets. Ken Laudon's hobby is sailing.

Jane Price Laudon is a management consultant in the information systems area and the author of seven books. Her special interests include systems analysis, data management, MIS auditing, software evaluation, and teaching business professionals how to design and use information systems.

Jane received her Ph.D. from Columbia University, her M.A. from Harvard University, and her B.A. from Barnard College. She has taught at Columbia University and the New York University Graduate School of Business. She maintains a lifelong interest in Oriental languages and civilizations.

The Laudons have two daughters, Erica and Elisabeth, to whom this book is dedicated.

About the Canadian Adapter

Mary Elizabeth Brabston is Associate Professor of Management Information Systems at the University of Manitoba's I.H. Asper School of Business. Dr. Brabston received her doctorate from Florida State University. Having spent her working life as a banker, political staffer, development officer, and academic, Dr. Brabston brings a comprehensive view to her analysis of how information systems can help organizations to achieve their potential. Her teaching and research interests involve strategic planning and applications of information systems and information resource management, as well as electronic commerce, including ethical and legal issues associated with advancing information technology. Her work has appeared in publications such as the *Journal of Computing and Information Technology*, the *Journal of Computer Information Systems*, the *Journal of Information Systems Education*, and *Human Relations*, and in several books. Dr. Brabston is also faculty advisor to the Asper School's Co-operative Education Program and the school's chapter of Beta Gamma Sigma, the business school honorary. She is also Director of Accreditation for the school and serves on University Senate.

Brief Contents

Contents

CHAPTER 3

Information Systems, Organizations, and Strategy   60

OPENING CASE: EBay Fine-Tunes Its Strategy   60

CHAPTER 6   Databases and Information Management   171

PART III   Developing and Managing Information Systems   277

CHAPTER 9   Developing Information Systems   278

CHAPTER 10   Information Resource Management and Project Management   **309**

CHAPTER 11   Managing Global Systems   **342**

PART IV   How Digital Businesses Use Information and Systems 371

CHAPTER 12   Enterprise Applications to Manage Supply Chains and Respond to Customers 372

CHAPTER 15   Managing Knowledge   457

Preface

We wrote this book for business school students who wanted an in-depth look at how business firms use information technologies and systems to achieve corporate objectives. Information systems are one of the major tools available to business managers for achieving operational excellence, developing new products and services, improving decision making, and achieving competitive advantage.

When interviewing potential employees, business firms often look for new hires who know how to use information systems and technologies for achieving bottom-line business results. Regardless of whether you are an accounting, finance, management, operations/supply chain management, marketing, or information systems major, the knowledge and information you find in this book will be valuable throughout your business career.

We have made every effort to ensure the currency and authority of cases and examples used through this text. The research literature as well as professional publications form an important foundation for our work.

What's New in MIS?

Plenty. In fact, there's a whole new world of doing business using new technologies for managing and organizing business operations. What makes the MIS field the most exciting area of study in schools of business is the continuous change in technology, management, and business processes (Chapter 1 describes these changes in more detail).

A continual stream of information technology innovations is transforming the traditional business world. Examples include the emergence of cloud computing, the growth of a mobile digital business platform, and, not least, the use of social networks by managers to achieve business objectives. Most of these changes have occurred in the past few years. These innovations are enabling entrepreneurs and innovative traditional firms to create new products and services, develop new business models, and transform the day-to-day conduct of business. In the process, some old businesses, even industries, are being destroyed while new businesses are springing up.

For instance, the emergence of online music stores—driven by millions of consumers who prefer iPods and MP3 players—has forever changed the older business model of distributing music on physical devices, such as records and CDs. Online video rentals are similarly transforming the old model of distributing films through theatres and then through DVD rentals at physical stores. New high-speed broadband connections to the home have supported these two business changes.

E-commerce is back, generating more than $305 billion in revenues in 2008, and growing at 15 percent a year. It is forever changing how firms design, produce, and deliver their products and services. E-commerce has reinvented itself again, disrupting the traditional marketing and advertising industry and putting major media and content firms in jeopardy. MySpace and Facebook, along with other social networking sites such as YouTube, Twitter, and Second Life, exemplify the new face of e-commerce in the 21st century. They sell services. When we think of e-commerce we tend to think of selling physical products. While this iconic vision of e-commerce is still very powerful and is the fastest-growing form of retail in North America, growing alongside is a whole new value stream based on selling services, not goods. It is a services model of e-commerce. Information systems and technologies are the foundation of this new e-commerce.

Likewise, the management of business firms has changed: With new mobile phones, high-speed wireless Wi-Fi networks, and wireless laptop computers, remote salespeople on the road are only seconds away from their managers' questions and oversight. Managers on the move are in direct, continuous contact with their employees. The growth of enterprise-wide information systems with extraordinarily rich data means that managers no longer operate in a fog of confusion, but instead have online, nearly instantaneous access to the really important information they need for accurate and timely decisions. In addition to their public uses on the Web, wikis and blogs are becoming important corporate tools for communication, collaboration, and information sharing.

The Fifth Canadian Edition: The Comprehensive Solution for the MIS Curriculum

Since its inception, this text has helped to define the MIS course around the globe. This edition continues to be authoritative and exceptionally up to date, but it is also more customizable, flexible, and geared to the needs of different colleges, universities, and instructors. The book is now part of a complete learning package that includes the core text and an extensive MyMISLab.

The core text consists of 15 chapters with hands-on projects covering the most essential topics in MIS. The MyMISLab provides more in-depth coverage of chapter topics, career resources, additional case studies, supplementary chapter material, interactive quizzes, and data files for hands-on projects.

The Core Text

The core text provides an overview of fundamental MIS concepts using an integrated framework for describing and analyzing information systems. This framework shows information systems composed of management, organization, and technology elements and is reinforced in student projects and case studies.

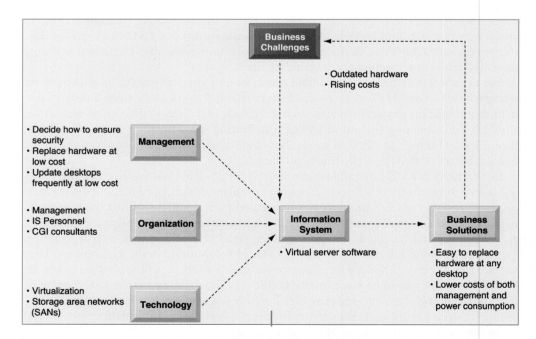

A diagram accompanying each chapter-opening case graphically illustrates how management, organization, and technology elements work together to create an information system solution to the business challenges discussed in the case.

Chapter Organization

Each chapter contains the following elements:

- A chapter-opening case describing a real-world organization to establish the theme and importance of the chapter
- A diagram analyzing the opening case in terms of the management, organization, and technology model used throughout the text
- A series of Learning Objectives
- Two Window On boxes on Management, Organizations, or Technology using real-world companies with To Think About questions and MIS in Action projects
- A chapter Summary keyed to the Learning Objectives
- A list of Key Terms and their page references
- Review Questions for students to test their comprehension of chapter material
- Discussion Questions raised by the broader themes of the chapter
- A Collaboration and Teamwork project to develop teamwork and presentation skills, with options for using open source collaboration tools
- A Learning Track Modules section identifying supplementary material to be found on the MyMISLab
- A Hands-On MIS Projects section featuring two Management Decision Problems, a hands-on application software project, and a project to develop Internet skills
- A chapter-ending case study for students to apply chapter concepts
- A part-ending CBC Canadian Case Study for students to further explore chapter concepts

Key Features

We have enhanced the core text to make it more interactive, instructor-friendly, and leading-edge. The fifth Canadian edition includes the following new features:

Business-Driven Content, Cases, and Examples The text helps students see the direct connection between information systems and business performance. It describes the main business objectives driving the use of information systems and technologies in corporations all over the world: operational excellence; new products and services; customer and supplier intimacy; improved decision making; competitive advantage; and survival. In-text examples and case studies show students how specific companies use information systems to achieve these objectives.

We use examples and cases from business and public organizations throughout the text to illustrate the important concepts in each chapter. The case studies describe well-known companies and organizations that are familiar to students, such as Google, Facebook, Toyota, Walmart, Bell Canada, Procter & Gamble, and Zellers.

Student Learning-Focus Student Learning Objectives are organized around a set of study questions to focus student attention. Each chapter concludes with a Summary and Review Questions organized around these study questions.

Interactivity There is no better way to learn about MIS than by doing MIS. We provide different kinds of hands-on projects in which students can work with real-world business scenarios and data and learn first-hand what MIS is all about. These projects heighten student involvement in this exciting subject.

- **Window On Management, Organizations, and Technology Boxes.** Two of these features appear in each chapter and have been designed to be used in the classroom or on Internet discussion boards to stimulate student interest and active learning. Each feature uses a real-world company and concludes with two types of activities: To Think About questions and MIS in Action Projects. The To Think About questions provide topics for class discussion, Internet discussion, or written assignments. The MIS in Action hands-on Web activities give students the opportunity to explore issues discussed in the case more thoroughly.

WINDOW ON TECHNOLOGY

Air Canada Takes Off with Maintenix

Air Canada is Canada's most prominent airline. It is the largest provider of scheduled passenger services in the Canadian market, the Canada–U.S. transborder market, and the international market to and from Canada. The airline serves more than 33 million customers annually and provides direct passenger service to more than 170 destinations on five continents. But the company's information systems had plenty of room for improvement. When Air Canada technicians worked on planes, they used several different legacy software packages installed over the past 15 years. The systems weren't able to interact with one another or with finance and inventory systems. The inefficiencies of these systems were costing Air Canada the time of its engineers and money that could have been used on maintaining its planes, instead of needlessly maintaining excess inventory.

Air Canada turned to Mxi Technologies for help in addressing these problems. Mxi is renowned in the airline industry for its Maintenix software package, which provides integrated, intelligent aviation MRO (maintenance, repair, and operations) software to aviation organizations hoping to improve productivity. The benefits of Maintenix that interested Air Canada were enhanced visibility of fleet-wide data, timelier

since aviation technicians, equipment, and parts are always on the move.

The Maintenix software package consists of six different modules, which are separate segments of the product that interconnect. Airlines deploying Maintenix can choose which modules they want to use as well as whether they want full or partial installation of those modules. The six modules are maintenance engineering, line maintenance, materials management, heavy maintenance, shop maintenance, and finance. Air Canada chose to fully implement the maintenance engineering, line maintenance, and materials management modules. The airline chose to only partially implement the heavy maintenance, shop maintenance, and finance modules because a separate contractor that also maintains Air Canada planes handles those tasks.

The maintenance engineering module is the foundation of the Maintenix system. It is used to establish the configuration hierarchy, rules, and maintenance program that all of the other modules depend upon. Through this module, the airline can set up a "logical configuration," which describes aircraft components, part relationships, and compatibility rules.

Each chapter contains two Window On boxes on Management, Organizations, or Technology using real-world companies to illustrate chapter concepts and issues.

- **New Collaboration and Teamwork Projects.** Each chapter features a collaborative project that encourages students working in teams to use Google Sites, Google Docs, and other open source collaboration tools. The first team project in Chapter 1 asks students to build a collaborative Google Site.
- **Hands-On MIS Projects.** Each chapter concludes with a Hands-On MIS Projects section containing three types of projects: two Management Decision Problems, a hands-on application software exercise using Microsoft Excel or Access, and a project that develops Internet business skills.

HANDS-ON MIS Projects

The projects in this section give you hands-on experience evaluating and selecting communications technology, using spreadsheet software to improve selection of telecommunications services, and using Web search engines for business research.

Management Decision Problems

1. Your company supplies ceramic floor tiles to Rona, Home Depot, and other home improvement stores. You have been asked to start using radio frequency identification tags on each case of the tiles you ship to help your customers improve the management of your products and those of other suppliers in their warehouses. Use the Web to identify the cost of hardware, software, and networking components for an RFID system for your company. What factors should be considered? What are the key decisions that have to be made in determining whether your firm should adopt this technology?

2. Fictional BestMed Medical Supplies Corporation sells medical and surgical products and equipment from over

700 different manufacturers to hospitals, health clinics, and medical offices. The company employs 500 people at seven different locations across Canada, including account managers, customer service and support representatives, and warehouse staff. Employees communicate via traditional telephone voice services, e-mail, instant messaging, and cell phones. Management is inquiring about whether the company should adopt a system for unified communications. What factors should be considered? What are the key decisions that have to be made in determining whether to adopt this technology? Use the Web, if necessary, to find out more about unified communications and its costs.

Two real-world business scenarios per chapter provide opportunities for students to apply chapter concepts and practise management decision making.

Achieving Operational Excellence: Building a Job Database and Web Page for an International Consulting Firm

Software skills: Database and Web page design
Business skills: Human resources internal job postings

Companies with many overseas locations need a way to inform employees about available job openings in these locations. In this project, you will use database software to design a database for posting internal job openings and a Web page for displaying this information.

Fictional KTP Consulting operates in various locations around the world. KTP specializes in designing, developing, and implementing enterprise systems for medium- to large-size companies. KTP offers its employees opportunities to travel, live, and work in various locations throughout Canada, the United States, Europe, and Asia. The firm's

human resources department has a simple database that enables its staff to track job vacancies. When an employee is interested in relocating, he or she contacts the human resources department for a list of KTP job vacancies. KTP also posts its employment opportunities on the company Web site.

What type of data should be included in the KTP job vacancies database? What information should not be included in this database? Based on your answers to these questions, build a job vacancies database for KTP. Populate the database with at least 20 records. You should also build a simple Web page that incorporates job vacancy data from your newly created database. Send a copy of the KTP database and Web page to your professor.

Students practise using software in real-world settings for achieving operational excellence and enhancing decision making.

- **Canadian and International Companies Featured in This Edition.** We feature numerous real-world companies and organizations in our examples, cases, and Window On boxes. For a complete listing of these Canadian and international business firms and associations, see the Organization Index on page I-2 at the end of this book.

Achieving Operational Excellence: Evaluating E-Commerce Hosting Services

Software skills: Web browser software
Business skills: Evaluating e-commerce hosting services

This project will help develop your Internet skills in commercial services for hosting an e-commerce site for a small startup company.

You would like to set up a Web site to sell towels, linens, pottery, and tableware from Portugal and are examining services for hosting small business Internet storefronts. Your Web site should be able to take secure credit card payments

and to calculate shipping costs and taxes. Initially, you would like to display photos and descriptions of 40 different products. Visit Yahoo! Small Business, GoDaddy, and Volusion and compare the range of e-commerce hosting services they offer to small business, their capabilities, and costs. Also examine the tools they provide for creating an e-commerce site. Compare these services and decide which you would use if you were actually establishing a Web store. Write a brief report indicating your choice and explaining the strengths and weaknesses of each.

Each chapter features a project to develop Internet skills for accessing information, conducting research, and performing online calculations and analysis.

New Leading-Edge Topics

This edition includes new coverage of the following leading-edge topics:

- Cloud computing
- Web 2.0 and Web 3.0
- Collaboration systems and tools
- SaaS (software as a service)
- Globalization
- Virtual worlds
- Widgets
- Web mining and text mining
- Unified communications
- Unified threat management
- Business uses of wikis, blogs, and social networking
- Service level agreements
- Software localization

Globalization

This edition has even more global emphasis than previous editions. New material on globalization (Chapter 1), global workgroup collaboration (Chapter 2), global security threats (Chapter 8), global supply chains (Chapter 9), global marketplaces (Chapter 10), offshore outsourcing (Chapter 11), and software localization (Chapter 15), accompanied by numerous examples of multinational and non–North American companies, show how to use IS in a global business environment.

Assessment and AACSB Assessment Guidelines

The Association to Advance Collegiate Schools of Business (AACSB) is a not-for-profit corporation of educational institutions, corporations and other organizations that seeks to improve business education primarily by accrediting university business programs. As part of its accreditation activities, the AACSB has developed an Assurance of Learning Program designed to ensure that schools do in fact teach students what they promise. Schools are required to state a clear mission, develop a coherent business program, identify student learning objectives, and then prove that students do in fact achieve the objectives.

We have attempted in this book to support AACSB efforts to encourage assessment-based education. The front end papers of this edition identify student learning objectives and anticipated outcomes for our Hands-On MIS Projects. On the MyMISLab is a more inclusive and detailed assessment matrix that identifies the learning objectives of each chapter and lists the available assessment tools for ensuring students do in fact achieve the learning objectives. But because every school is different and might have its own mission and learning objectives, no document can deal with all situations. The authors will provide custom advice on how to use this text in colleges with different missions and assessment needs. Please e-mail the Canadian author or contact your local Pearson Canada representative for contact information.

For more information on the AACSB Assurance of Learning Program and how this text supports assessment-based learning, please visit the Web site for this book.

Customization and Flexibility: New Learning Track Modules

Our Learning Tracks feature gives instructors the flexibility to provide in-depth coverage of the topics they choose. A Learning Tracks section at the end of each chapter directs students to short essays or additional chapters on the MyMISLab. This supplementary content takes students deeper into MIS topics, concepts and debates; reviews basic technology concepts in hardware, software, database design, telecommunications, and other areas; and provides additional hands-on software instruction. The fifth Canadian edition includes new Learning Tracks titled Business Process Management, Cloud Computing, Web 2.0, The Booming Job Market in IT Security, Hot New Careers in E-Commerce, Computer Forensics, C-SOX, Service-Level Agreements, Building a Web Page, Excel Pivot Tables, and Capital Budgeting for Information Systems, and additional coverage of Computer Hardware and Software technology.

MyMISLab

Supplied with every new copy of this textbook, MyMISLab provides students with access to a wealth of resources. Personal access codes can also be purchased separately at **www.pearsoned.ca/mymislab**. Incuded in MyMISLab are the following features:

- Pearson's MyITLab technology, the next generation of online assessment and training for Microsoft Office 2007. A realistic, open simulation of Microsoft Office 2007 allows students to complete an activity using most if not all accepted methods to completion. MyITLab includes Grader, a live-in-the-application project grading tool that will enable you to assign projects that students can complete live in Excel and Access and then submit for immediate grading.
- Pearson eText gives you access to the text wherever you can access the Internet. eText pages look exactly like the printed text, offering powerful new functionality for students and instructors.

- Two pre-loaded sample tests for each chapter so you can self-assess your understanding of the material.
- A personalized study plan that tells you where you need to study based on your results. You can find the key topics you need to review to improve.
- Additional quiz material for practice.
- Video Cases that illustrate chapter concepts and include questions that help students apply what they have learned in the case.

Instructional Support Materials

MyMISLab Pearson Canada's online resource, MyMISLab, offers instructors all of their resources in one place. With MyMISLab, you will be able to enliven your lectures with a variety of material. Your students will be able to prepare and perform better on assignments and exams with customized study plans. MyMISLab is available to instructors by going to **www.pearsoned.ca/mymislab** and by following the instructions on the opening screen. Students receive access to MyMISLab when they purchase their new text.

Image Library The Image Library is an impressive resource to help instructors create vibrant lecture presentations. Almost every figure and photo in the text is provided and organized by chapter for convenience. These images and lecture notes can be imported easily into Microsoft PowerPoint to create new presentations or to add to existing ones.

Instructor's Manual The Instructor's Manual features not only answers to review, discussion, case study, and collaboration and teamwork project questions but also an in-depth lecture outline, teaching objectives, key terms, teaching suggestions, and Internet resources. This supplement can be downloaded from the secure faculty section of the MyMISLab and is also available on the Instructor's Resource CD-ROM.

Computerized Test Item File in TestGen Test-Generating Software Pearson TestGen is a special computerized test item file that enables instructors to view and edit existing questions, add questions, generate tests, and print tests in a variety of formats. This test bank, created by James Clark of the University of Lethbridge, contains approximately 1400 questions, and includes a comprehensive collection of true/false, multiple-choice, fill-in-the-blank, and essay questions. The questions are rated by difficulty level, and the answers are referenced by section. An electronic version of the Test Item File is available in TestGen, and TestGen conversions are available for Blackboard or WebCT course management systems. All TestGen files are available for download at the Instructor Resource Centre.

MyTest MyTest from Pearson Canada is a powerful assessment-generation program that helps instructors easily create quizzes, tests, exams, and homework or practice handouts. Instructors can author questions and tests online, which allows ultimate flexibility and efficiency in managing their marking and assessments. MyTest for *Management Information Systems,* Fifth Canadian Edition, includes more than 1400 multiple-choice, true/false, and short essay questions. The questions are also available in TestGen format on the Instructor's Resource CD-ROM.

Annotated PowerPoint Slides Electronic colour slides created by Dale Foster of Memorial University of Newfoundland are available in Microsoft PowerPoint. The slides are annotated using the Notes section of PowerPoint slides. The notes provide teaching hints for instructors and conceptual background. The slides illuminate and build on key concepts in the text. Faculty can download the slides from the Web site, and they are also provided on the Instructor's Resource CD-ROM.

Instructor's Resource CD-ROM The CD includes the Instructor's Manual, Lecture Notes, TestGen, PowerPoint slides, and the helpful lecture tool, Image Library.

Microsoft Office Tutorial Software

For instructors seeking application software training to use with this text, Pearson Canada is pleased to offer student training in Microsoft Office 2007. This item is not available as a stand-alone item, but it can be packaged with this text at an additional charge. Contact your local Pearson Education representative for more details.

Acknowledgments

The production of any book involves valued contributions from a number of persons. We would like to thank all of our editors for encouragement, insight, and strong support for many years. We thank Don Thompson for guiding the development of this edition and Eleanor MacKay for her role in managing the project.

We praise Madhu Bhardwaj at Glyph International and Marisa D'Andrea at Pearson Canada for overseeing production for this project. Our special thanks go to our supplement authors for their work. We are indebted to Megan Miller for her help during production.

Special thanks to my colleague Professor Fang Chen at the Asper School of Business at the University of Manitoba, who provided suggestions for improvement. A thank-you goes to Zach Zahradnik for his review and keen eye in seeing this text to final edit.

We also want to especially thank all our reviewers whose suggestions helped improve our texts. Reviewers for this edition include the following:

Peter Bierman, Humber College

David Chan, University of Toronto

Danny Cho, Brock University

James D. Clark, University of Lethbridge

Franca Giacomelli, Humber College

Dr. Andy Igonor, NAIT

Michael Kauk, Conestoga College

Francisco Moro, University of Windsor

Roy Sinn, Langara College

Cameron Welsh, University of Calgary

Part I

Organizations, Management, and the Networked Enterprise

PART I

CANADIAN CASE STUDY

Can Canadians Make Money on the Web?

CHAPTER 1

Information Systems in Global Business Today

LEARNING OBJECTIVES

After reading this chapter, you will be able to answer the following questions:

1. How are information systems transforming business, and what is their relationship to globalization?

2. Why are information systems so essential for running and managing a business today?

3. What exactly is an information system? How does it work? What are its management, organization, and technology components?

4. What are complementary assets? Why are complementary assets essential for ensuring that information systems provide genuine value for an organization?

5. What academic disciplines are used to study information systems? How does each contribute to an understanding of information systems? What is a sociotechnical systems perspective?

OPENING CASE

Smart Systems and Smart Ways of Working Help Toyota Become Number One

Toyota Motor Corporation is about to surpass GM as the world's largest automaker, projected to sell more than 10 million vehicles in 2009. Toyota is also considered the world's best automaker. The quality and reliability of Toyota vehicles are the gold standards of the industry, even among the company's lower-priced models. Customer loyalty is so high that Toyota can make sales without heavy discounting.

Toyota stands head and shoulders above fierce competition because it has been so skilful at combining quality with efficiency. One key to Toyota's success is its vaunted Toyota Production System, which is based on lean production—eliminating waste while optimizing value. Toyota has based its business processes and information systems on the principles of just-in-time delivery, quality, and continuous improvement.

By organizing its business processes and information systems around these principles, Toyota delivers value to the customer at a competitive price. As Ludo Vandervelden, vice president of Finance and Accounting, Information Systems, and Vehicle Logistics for Toyota Motor Europe, points out, "You can achieve cost reductions and, at the same time, make your customers happy through implementation of smarter business processes."

Toyota Motor Europe and other Toyota divisions around the world use information systems to support these business processes. Vehicle production is based on actual customer orders rather than "best guesses" of what to stock in dealer showrooms, so the company builds only cars that customers want, when they want them, without additional delays or quality problems.

Toyota Motor Europe uses a vehicle orders management system based on Oracle E-Business Suite software to reduce the time it takes between placing a customer order and delivering the vehicle to the customer. The software integrates easily with the company's existing systems and also with those of Toyota's independent dealerships and national marketing and sales companies, which run their own separate information systems based on a variety of technologies.

This system encompasses several business processes. It starts with the customer selecting a car and various options, such as tinted windows or a navigation system. The dealer uses the system to configure a car with all of the selected options in front of the customer and then locates the best available car and options in the Toyota supply chain, including vehicles scheduled for production in the future. The dealer then uses the system to place the order through national distributors, which consolidate the order with those of their other retailers and place an order through Toyota Motors Europe. Toyota Motor Europe consolidates orders from the national distributors and places an order with Toyota's factories. Each car is then shipped and invoiced from the factory to headquarters to national distributors to retailers, triggering all related accounting processes at each step. National distributors can use the system to monitor their orders and those of different dealers and even "swap" cars with various retailers.

The vehicle order management system has helped Toyota reduce production time and the cost of maintaining materials and finished cars in inventory, while increasing customer service and satisfaction. According to Vandervelden, "with improved information transparency, we would be able to better readjust . . . our allocation of available product to markets that would be in high demand . . . and to reduce stock."

Sources: Katheryn Potterf, "Ready to Roll," *Profit Magazine*, May 26; Ian Rowley, "No Traffic Ahead for Toyota," *BusinessWeek*, February 6, 2006, and "Triumphs & Trip-Ups in 2004," *Baseline Magazine*, December 20, 2004; Frank Filipponio, "Toyota Aims to Sell 10.4M Vehicles in 2009," **www.autoblog.com/2007/08/22/ toyotal-aims-to-sell-10-4m-vehicles-in-2009/ print** (accessed July 26, 2009).

Toyota has flourished in a highly competitive environment because it has created a set of finely tuned business processes and information systems that simultaneously promote agility, efficiency, and quality. It can respond instantly to customers and changes in the marketplace as events unfold while working closely with suppliers and retailers. The experience of Toyota and other companies described in this text will help you learn how to make your own business more competitive, efficient, and profitable.

The chapter-opening diagram highlights important points raised by this case and this chapter. As part of its ongoing effort to monitor quality, efficiency, and costs, Toyota management saw an opportunity to use information systems to improve business performance. Technology alone would not have provided a solution; Toyota had to carefully revise its business processes to support a build-to-order production model that based vehicle production on actual customer orders rather than "best guesses"

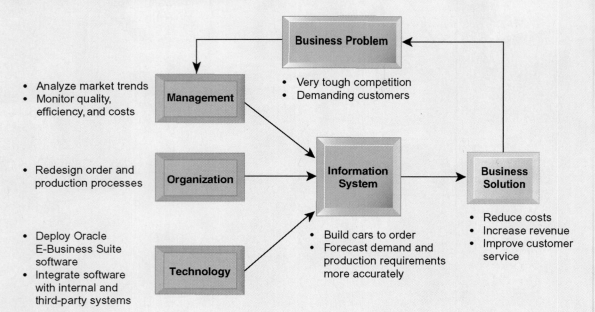

- Analyze market trends
- Monitor quality, efficiency, and costs

Management

Business Problem

- Very tough competition
- Demanding customers

- Redesign order and production processes

Organization

Information System

Business Solution

- Reduce costs
- Increase revenue
- Improve customer service

- Deploy Oracle E-Business Suite software
- Integrate software with internal and third-party systems

Technology

- Build cars to order
- Forecast demand and production requirements more accurately

of customer demand. Once that was accomplished, Oracle E-Business software was useful for coordinating the flow of information among disparate internal production, ordering, and invoicing systems within the company and with systems of retailers and suppliers.

By helping Toyota build only the cars customers have ordered, its vehicle order management system reduces inventory costs because the company and its dealers do not have to pay for making and storing vehicles customers did not want. The system also increases customer satisfaction by making it easier for customers to buy exactly the model, make, and options they desire. Information provided by the system helps management monitor trends and forecast demand and production requirements more accurately.

1.1   The Role of Information Systems in Business Today

It is not business as usual in Canada anymore or in the rest of the global economy. In 2008, the information and communication technologies (ICT) sector of the Canadian economy totalled $59.2 billion (see Figure 1-1).

As managers, most of you will work for firms that are intensively using information systems and making large investments in information technology. You will certainly want to know how to invest this money wisely. If you make wise choices, your firm can outperform competitors. If you make poor choices, you will be wasting valuable capital. This book is dedicated to helping you make wise decisions about information technology and information systems.

How Information Systems Are Transforming Business

You can see the results of this massive spending around you every day by observing how people conduct business. More wireless cell phone accounts were opened in 2008 than telephone land lines installed. Cell phones, BlackBerrys, iPhones, e-mail, and online conferencing over the Internet have all become essential tools of business. By June 2008, more than 80 million businesses worldwide had dot-com Internet sites registered (Versign, 2008). In 2007, Canadian e-commerce sales were $62.7 billion, with business-to-business sales accounting for 62 percent of that amount. In 2008, more than 42 percent of Canadian businesses had dot-com Internet sites registered. Fully 81 percent of Canadian Internet users shop online while 56 percent actually buy online (eMarketer, 2006).

FIGURE 1-1   Distribution of Canadian GDP at basic prices by ICT industry, 2008.

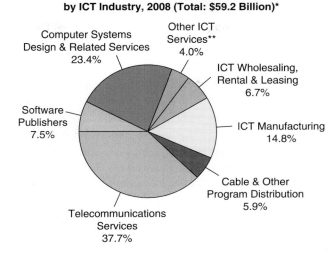

**Distribution of GDP at Basic Prices
by ICT Industry, 2008 (Total: $59.2 Billion)***

Computer Systems
Design & Related Services
23.4%

Other ICT
Services**
4.0%

ICT Wholesaling,
Rental & Leasing
6.7%

Software
Publishers
7.5%

ICT Manufacturing
14.8%

Cable & Other
Program Distribution
5.9%

Telecommunications
Services
37.7%

* In 2002 constant dollars.
** Aggregation of NAICS 51811, 51821, and 5191.

The Canadian information and communication technologies sector grew to more than $59.2 billion in 2008.

Source: Industry Canada, 2008 **www.ic .gc.ca/eic/site/ict-tic.nsf/vwimages/o\ 0105864eng.gif** (accessed July 26, 2009). Reproduced with the permission of the Minister of Public Works and Government Services, 2010.

In 2007, FedEx moved more than 100 million packages in the United States, mostly overnight, and the United Parcel Service (UPS) moved 3.7 billion packages worldwide. Businesses sought to sense and respond to rapidly changing customer demand, reduce inventories to the lowest possible levels, and achieve higher levels of operational efficiency. Supply chains have become more fast paced, with companies of all sizes depending on just-in-time inventory to reduce their overhead costs and get to market faster.

As newspaper readership continues to decline, in North America, more than 64 million people receive their news online. About 67 million Americans now read blogs, and 21 million write blogs, creating an explosion of new writers and new forms of customer feedback that did not exist five years ago (Pew, 2008). Social networking sites such as MySpace and Facebook attract more than 70 and 30 million visitors a month, respectively, and businesses are starting to use social networking tools to connect their employees, customers, and managers worldwide.

E-commerce and Internet advertising are booming: Google's online ad revenues surpassed $20 billion in 2007, and Internet advertising continues to grow at more than 25 percent a year, reaching more than $34 billion in revenues in 2008.

Federal and provincial security and accounting laws requiring many businesses to keep e-mail messages for five years, coupled with existing occupational and health laws requiring firms to store employee chemical exposure data for up to 60 years, are spurring the growth of digital information now estimated to be 5 exabytes annually, or 5 billion billion bytes.

What Is New in Management Information Systems?

What makes management information systems the most exciting topic in business is the continual change in technology, management use of the technology, and the technology's impact on business success. Old systems are being creatively destroyed, and entirely new systems are taking their place. New industries appear, old ones decline, and successful firms are those that learn how to use the new technologies. Table 1-1 summarizes the major new themes in business uses of information systems. These themes will appear throughout the book in all the chapters, so it might be a good idea to take some time now and discuss these with your professor and other students. You may even want to add to the list.

TABLE 1-1 What is new in MIS.

CHANGE	BUSINESS IMPACT
TECHNOLOGY	
Cloud computing platform emerges as a major business area of innovation	A flexible collection of computers on the Internet begins to perform tasks traditionally performed on corporate computers.
More powerful, energy-efficient computer processing and storage devices	Intel's new PC processor chips consume 50 percent less power, generate 30 percent less heat, and are 20 percent faster than the previous models, packing more than 400 million transistors on a dual-core chip.
Growth in software as a service (SaaS)	Major business applications are now delivered online as an Internet service rather than as boxed software or custom systems.
Netbooks emerge as a growing presence in the PC marketplace, often using open-source software	Small, lightweight, low-cost, energy-efficient, net-centric sub-notebooks use Linux, Google Docs, open-source tools, flash memory, and the Internet for their applications, storage, and communications.
A mobile digital platform emerges to compete with the PC as a business system	Apple opens its iPhone software to developers and then opens an Applications Store on iTunes where business users can download hundreds of applications to support collaboration, location-based services, and communication with colleagues.
MANAGEMENT	
Managers adopt online collaboration and social networking tools to improve coordination, collaboration, and knowledge sharing	Google Apps, Google Sites, Microsoft's Office Sharepoint, and IBM's Lotus Connections are used by more than 100 million business decision makers worldwide to support blogs, project management, online meetings, personal profiles, social bookmarks, and online communities.
Business intelligence applications accelerate	More powerful data analytics and interactive dashboards provide real-time performance information to managers to enhance management control and decision making.
Managers adopt millions of mobile tools such as smartphones and mobile Internet devices to accelerate decision making and improve performance	The emerging mobile platform greatly enhances the accuracy, speed, and richness of decision making as well as responsiveness to customers.
Virtual meetings proliferate	Managers adopt telepresence video conferencing and Web conferencing technologies to reduce travel time and cost while improving collaboration and decision making.
ORGANIZATIONS	
Web 2.0 applications are widely adopted by firms	Web-based services enable employees to interact as online communities using blogs, wikis, e-mail, and instant messaging services. Facebook, MySpace, and Twitter create new opportunities for businesses to collaborate with customers and vendors.
Telework gains momentum in the workplace	The Internet, wireless laptops, iPhones, and BlackBerrys make it possible for growing numbers of people to work away from the traditional office.
Outsourcing production	Firms learn to use the new technologies to outsource production work to low-wage countries.
Co-creation of business value	Sources of business value shift from products to solutions and experiences, and from internal sources to networks of suppliers and collaboration with customers. Supply chains and product development become more global and collaborative; customer interactions help firms define new products and services.

In the technology area, there are three interrelated changes: (1) the emerging mobile digital platform (think iPhones, BlackBerrys, and tiny Web-surfing netbooks), (2) the growth of online software as a service, and (3) the growth in "cloud computing" where more and more business software runs over the Internet. Of course, these changes depend on other building-block technologies described in Table 1-1, such as faster processor chips that use much less power.

YouTube, iPhones and Blackberrys, and Facebook are not just gadgets or entertainment outlets. They represent new emerging computing platforms based on an array of new hardware and software technologies and business investments. Besides being successful products in their own right, these emerging technologies are being adopted by corporations as business tools to improve management and achieve competitive advantages. We call these developments the "emerging mobile platform."

Managers routinely use so-called "Web 2.0" technologies like social networking, collaboration tools, and wikis in order to make better, faster decisions. Millions of managers rely heavily on the mobile digital platform to coordinate vendors, satisfy customers, and manage their employees. For many if not most managers, a business day without their cell phones or Internet access is unthinkable.

As management behaviour changes, how work gets organized, coordinated, and measured also changes. By connecting employees working on teams and projects, the social network is where works gets done, where plans are executed, and where managers manage. Collaboration spaces are where employees meet one another—even when they are separated by continents and time zones. The strength of cloud computing and the growth of the mobile digital platform mean that organizations can rely more on telework, remote work, and distributed decision making. Think decentralization. This same platform means firms can outsource more work, and rely on markets (rather than employees) to build value. It also means that firms can collaborate with suppliers and customers to create new products or make existing products more efficiently.

All of these changes contribute to a dynamic new global business economy. In fact, without the changes in management information systems just described, the global economy would not succeed.

Globalization Challenges and Opportunities: A Flattened World

In 1492, Columbus reaffirmed what astronomers were long saying: the world was round, and the seas could be safely sailed. As it turned out, the world was populated by peoples and languages living in near total isolation from one another, with great disparities in economic and scientific development.

The world trade that ensued after Columbus's voyages has brought these peoples and cultures closer. The Industrial Revolution was really a world-wide phenomenon energized by expansion of trade among nations.

In 2005, journalist Thomas Friedman wrote an influential book declaring the world was now "flat," by which he meant that the Internet and global communications had greatly reduced the economic and cultural advantages of developed countries. North American and European countries were in a fight for their economic lives, competing for jobs, markets, resources, and even ideas with highly educated, motivated populations in low-wage areas in the less-developed world (Friedman, 2006). This "globalization" presents both challenges and opportunities.

A growing percentage of the economy of North America and other advanced industrial countries in Europe and Asia depends on imports and exports. Many firms derive half their revenues from foreign operations. It is not just goods that move across borders. So too do jobs, some of them high-level jobs that pay well and require a post-secondary degree. In the past decade, Canada lost many manufacturing jobs to offshore, low-wage producers. But manufacturing is now a very small part of Canadian employment (less than 10 percent) (Statistics Canada). In a normal year, a number of service jobs move offshore to lower-wage countries, many of them in less-skilled information system occupations, but also including "tradable service" jobs in architecture, financial services, customer call centres, consulting, engineering, and even radiology.

On the plus side, the Canadian economy appears to have stabilized after months of job losses, and employment in information systems and the other service occupations listed above has expanded in sheer numbers, wages, productivity, and quality of work (Statistics Canada). Outsourcing has actually accelerated the development of new systems in North America and worldwide.

The challenge for you as a business student is to develop high-level skills through education and on-the-job experience that cannot be outsourced. The challenge for your business is to avoid markets for goods and services that can be produced offshore much less expensively. The opportunities are equally immense. You will find throughout this book examples of companies and individuals who either failed or succeeded in using information systems to adapt to this new global environment.

What does globalization have to do with management information systems? That is simple: everything. The emergence of the Internet into a full-blown international communications system has drastically reduced the costs of operating and transacting on a global scale. Communication between a factory floor in Shanghai and a distribution centre in Winnipeg, Manitoba, is now instant and virtually free. Customers now can shop in a worldwide marketplace, obtaining price and quality information reliably 24 hours a day. Firms producing goods and services on a global scale achieve extraordinary cost reductions by finding low-cost suppliers and managing production facilities in other countries. Internet service firms, such as Google and eBay, are able to replicate their business models and services in multiple countries without having to redesign their expensive fixed-cost information systems infrastructure. Half of the revenue of eBay in 2009 originates outside North America. Briefly, information systems enable globalization.

The Emerging Digital Firm

All of the changes we have just described, coupled with equally significant organizational redesign, have created the conditions for a fully digital firm. A digital firm can be defined along several dimensions. A **digital firm** is one in which nearly all of the organization's *significant business relationships* with customers, suppliers, and employees are digitally enabled and mediated. Core **business processes** are accomplished through digital networks spanning the entire organization or linking multiple organizations.

Business processes refer to the set of logically related tasks and behaviours that organizations develop over time to produce specific business results and the unique manner in which these activities are organized and coordinated. Developing a new product, generating and fulfilling an order, creating a marketing plan, and hiring an employee are examples of business processes, and the ways organizations accomplish their business processes can be a source of competitive strength. (A detailed discussion of business processes can be found in Chapter 2.)

Digital firm
Business processes

Management WINDOW ON MANAGEMENT

Virtual Meetings: Smart Management

For many businesses, including investment banking, accounting, law, technology services, and management consulting, extensive travel is a fact of life. The expenses incurred by business travel have been steadily rising in recent years, primarily due to increasing energy costs. In an effort to reduce travel expenses, many companies, both large and small, are using videoconferencing and Web conferencing technologies.

A June 2008 report issued by the Global e-Sustainability Initiative and the Climate Group estimated that up to 20 percent of business travel could be replaced by virtual-meeting technology. A videoconference allows individuals at two or more locations to communicate through two-way video and audio transmissions at the same time.

The critical feature of videoconferencing is the digital compression of audio and video streams by a device called a codec. Those streams are then divided into packets and transmitted over a network or the Internet. The technology has been plagued by poor audio and video performance in the past, usually related to the speed at which the streams were transmitted, and its cost was prohibitively high for all but the largest and most powerful corporations. Most companies viewed videoconferencing as a poor substitute for face-to-face meetings.

However, vast improvements in videoconferencing and associated technologies have renewed interest in this way of working. Videoconferencing is now growing at an annual rate of 30 percent. Proponents of the technology claim that it does more than simply reduce costs. It allows for "better"' meetings as well: it is easier to meet with partners, suppliers, subsidiaries, and colleagues from within the office or around the world on a more frequent basis, which in most cases simply cannot be reasonably accomplished through travel. You can also meet with contacts that you would not be able to meet at all without videoconferencing technology.

The top-of-the-line videoconferencing technology is known as telepresence. Telepresence strives to make users feel as if they are actually present in a location different from their own. Telepresence products provide the highest-quality videoconferencing available on the market to date. Only a handful of companies, such as Cisco, HP, and Polycom, supply these products. Prices for fully equipped telepresence rooms can run to $500 000.

Companies able to afford this technology report large savings. For example, technology consulting firm Accenture reports that it eliminated expenditures for 240 international trips and 120 domestic flights in a single month. The ability to reach customers and partners is also dramatically increased. Other business travellers report tenfold increases in the number of customers and partners they are able to reach for a fraction of the previous price per person. Cisco has more than 200 telepresence rooms and predicts that it saves $122 million in travel costs each year. In a personal interview with the author, John Schwarz, a member of the executive board of the leading enterprise software company in the world, stated that his company, SAP, had saved at a minimum tens of millions of dollars through the use of telepresence.

Videoconferencing products have not traditionally been feasible for small businesses, but another company, LifeSize, has introduced an affordable line of products as low as $6000. Reviews of the LifeSize product indicate that when a great deal of movement occurs in a frame, the screen blurs and distorts somewhat. But overall, the product is easy to use and will allow many smaller companies to use a high-quality videoconferencing product.

There are even some free Internet-based options such as Skype videoconferencing and ooVoo. These products are of lower quality than traditional videoconferencing products, and they are proprietary, meaning they can only talk to others using the same system. Most videoconferencing and telepresence products are able to interact with a variety of other devices. Higher-end systems include features like multi-party conferencing, video mail with unlimited storage, no long-distance fees, and a detailed call history.

Companies of all sizes are finding Web-based online meeting tools such as WebEx, Microsoft Office Live Meeting, and Adobe Acrobat Connect especially helpful for training and sales presentations. These products enable participants to share documents and presentations in conjunction with audioconferencing and live video via Webcam. Activision, publisher of popular video games like Guitar Hero, Call of Duty 4, and Tony Hawk's Proving Ground, uses HD video to link international developers creating next-generation games, reduce travel, and accelerate its business cycle.

Before setting up videoconferencing or telepresence, it is important for a company to make sure it really needs the technology to ensure that it will be a profitable venture. Companies should determine how their employees conduct meetings, how they communicate and with what technologies, how much travel they do, and their network's capabilities. There are still plenty of times when face-to-face interaction is more desirable, and often travelling to meet a client is essential for cultivating clients and closing sales.

Videoconferencing figures to have an impact on the business world in other ways, as well. More employees may be able to work closer to home and balance their work and personal lives more efficiently; traditional office environments and corporate headquarters may shrink or disappear; and freelancers, contractors, and workers from other countries will become a larger portion of the global economy.

To Think About

1. One consulting firm has predicted that video and Web conferencing will make business travel extinct. Do you agree? Why or why not?

2. What is the distinction between videoconferencing and telepresence?

3. What are the ways in which videoconferencing provides value to a business? Would you consider it smart management? Explain your answer.

4. If you were in charge of a small business, would you choose to implement videoconferencing? What factors would you consider in your decision?

MIS in Action

Explore the WebEx Web site (**www.webex.com**) and note all of its capabilities for both small and large businesses, then answer the following questions:

1. List and describe its capabilities for small-medium and large businesses. How useful is WebEx? How can it help companies save time and money?

2. Compare WebEx video capabilities with the videoconferencing capabilities described in this case.

3. Describe the steps you would take to prepare for a Web conference as opposed to a face-to-face conference.

Sources: Steve Lohr, "As Travel Costs Rise, More Meetings Go Virtual," *The New York Times*, July 22, 2008; Karen D. Schwartz, "Videoconferencing on a Budget," *eWeek*, May 29, 2008; Jim Rapoza, "Videoconferencing Redux," *eWeek*, July 21, 2008; Mike Fratto, "High-Def Conferencing at a Low Price," *Information Week*, July 14, 2008; Marianne Kolbasuk McGee, "Looking into the Work-Trend Crystal Ball," *Information Week*, June 24, 2008; Eric Krapf, "What's Video Good For?," *Information Week*, July 1, 2008; "Activision Uses LifeSize HD Video to Accelerate Game Development," www.lifesize.com/files/Activision_Case_Study.pdf (accessed July 26, 2009).

Key corporate assets—intellectual property, core competencies, and financial and human assets—are managed through digital means. In a digital firm, any piece of information required to support key business decisions is available at any time and anywhere in the firm.

Digital firms sense and respond to their environments far more rapidly than traditional firms, giving them more flexibility to survive in turbulent times. Digital firms offer extraordinary opportunities for more flexible global organization and management. In digital firms, both time shifting and space shifting are the norm. *Time shifting* refers to business being conducted continuously, 24/7, rather than in narrow "work day" time bands of 9 a.m. to 5 p.m. *Space shifting* means that work takes place in a global workshop, as well as within national boundaries. Work is accomplished physically wherever in the world it is best accomplished.

A few firms, such as Cisco Systems and Dell Computers, are close to becoming digital firms, using the Internet to drive every aspect of their business. Most other companies are not fully digital, but they are moving toward close digital integration with suppliers, customers, and employees. Many firms, for example, are replacing traditional face-to-face meetings with "virtual" meetings using videoconferencing and Web conferencing technology. The Window on Management on pages 8 and 9 provides more detail on this topic.

Strategic Business Objectives of Information Systems

What makes information systems so essential today? Why are businesses investing so much in information systems and technologies? Entire sectors of the economy are nearly inconceivable without substantial investments in information systems. E-commerce firms such as Chapters.Indigo.ca, eBay, Google, and E*Trade simply would not exist. Today's service industries—finance, insurance, and real estate, as well as personal services such as travel, medicine, and education—could not operate without information systems. Similarly, retail firms such as Walmart and Canadian Tire and manufacturing firms such as Bombardier and RIM require information systems to survive and prosper. Just as offices, telephones, filing cabinets, and efficient tall buildings with elevators were once the foundations of business in the 20th century, information technology is a foundation for business in the 21st century.

There is a growing interdependence between a firm's ability to use information technology and its ability to implement corporate strategies and achieve corporate goals (see Figure 1-2). What a business would like to do in five years often depends on what its systems will be able to do. Increasing market share, becoming the high-quality or low-cost producer, developing new products, and increasing employee productivity depend more and more on the kinds and quality of information systems in the organization. The more you understand about this relationship, the more valuable you will be as a manager.

FIGURE 1-2   The interdependence between organizations and information systems.

In contemporary systems, there is a growing interdependence between a firm's information systems and its business capabilities. Changes in strategy, rules, and business processes increasingly require changes in hardware, software, databases, and telecommunications. Often, what the organization would like to do depends on what its systems will permit it to do.

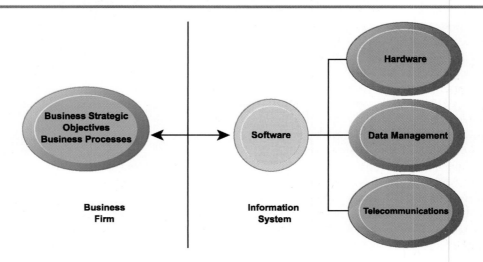

Specifically, business firms invest heavily in information systems to achieve six strategic business objectives: operational excellence; new products, services, and business models; customer and supplier intimacy; improved decision making; competitive advantage; and survival.

Operational Excellence Businesses continuously seek to improve the efficiency of their operations in order to achieve higher profitability. Information systems and technologies are some of the most important tools available to managers for achieving higher levels of efficiency and productivity in business operations, especially when coupled with changes in business practices and management behaviour.

Walmart, the largest retailer on Earth, exemplifies the power of information systems coupled with brilliant business practices and supportive management to achieve world-class operational efficiency. In 2008, Walmart achieved close to US$458 billion in sales in large part because of its RetailLink system, which digitally links its suppliers to every one of Walmart's stores. As soon as a customer purchases an item, the supplier monitoring the item knows to ship a replacement to the shelf.

Walmart is the most efficient retail store in the industry, achieving sales of more than US$34 per square foot, compared to its closest competitor, Target, at US$28 a square foot, with other retail firms producing less than US$15 a square foot.

New Products, Services, and Business Models Information systems and technologies are a major enabling tool for firms to create new products and services, as well as entirely new business models. A **business model** describes how a company produces, delivers, and sells a product or service to create wealth.

Today's music industry is vastly different from the industry in 2000. Apple Inc. transformed an old business model of music distribution based on vinyl records, tapes, and CDs into an online, legal distribution model based on its own iPod technology platform. Apple has prospered from a continuing stream of iPod innovations, including the iPod, the iTunes music service, and the iPhone.

Customer and Supplier Intimacy When a business really knows its customers, and serves them well, the customers generally respond by returning and purchasing more. This raises revenues and profits. Likewise with suppliers: the more a business engages its suppliers, the better the suppliers can provide vital inputs. This lowers costs. How to really know your customers or suppliers is a central problem for businesses with millions of offline and online customers.

The Mandarin Oriental in London, England, and other high-end hotels exemplify the use of information systems and technologies to achieve customer intimacy. These hotels use computers to keep track of guests' preferences, such as their preferred room temperature, check-in time, frequently dialled telephone numbers, and television programs, and store these data in a giant data repository. Individual rooms in the hotels are networked to a central network server computer so that they can be remotely monitored or controlled. When a customer arrives at one of these hotels, the system automatically changes the room conditions, such as dimming the lights, setting the room temperature, or selecting appropriate music, based on the customer's digital profile. The hotels also analyze their customer data to identify their best customers and to develop individualized marketing campaigns based on customers' preferences.

With its stunning multi-touch display, full Internet browsing, digital camera, and portable music player, Apple's iPhone set a new standard for mobile phones. Other Apple products have transformed the music and entertainment industries.

Nygård, a Canadian-based clothing manufacturer, informs its suppliers electronically of its needs and expects just-in-time delivery of inventory from halfway around the world. In other words, Nygård's material inventory is near zero, as is the cost of storing it.

Business model

FIGURE 1-3   An example of a digital dashboard.

Information Builders' digital dashboard delivers comprehensive and accurate information for decision making. The graphical overview of key performance indicators helps managers quickly spot areas that need attention.

Improved Decision Making Many business managers operate in an information fog bank, never really having the right information at the right time to make an informed decision. Instead, managers rely on forecasts, best guesses, and luck. The result is over- or underproduction of goods and services, misallocation of resources, and poor response times. These poor outcomes raise costs and lose customers. In the past decade, information systems and technologies have made it possible for managers to use real-time data from the marketplace when making decisions.

For instance, Trimac, a large Canadian trucking firm, uses an assessment of key performance indicators that Trimac has labelled its "dashboard project." The idea is to create consistent reporting across every level of the organization so that when a manager wants to know the effectiveness of any particular tool, person, or function, she can more easily identify the necessary data on a company-wide or divisional level. An example of a digital dashboard is shown in Figure 1-3.

Competitive Advantage When firms achieve one or more of these business objectives—operational excellence; new products, services, and business models; customer/supplier intimacy; and improved decision making—chances are they have already achieved a competitive advantage. Doing things better than your competitors, charging less for superior products, and responding to customers and suppliers in real time all add up to higher sales and higher profits that your competitors cannot match.

Perhaps no other company exemplifies all of these attributes leading to competitive advantage more than Toyota Motor Company, discussed in the chapter-opening case. Toyota has become the world's largest automaker because of its high level of efficiency and quality. Competitors struggle to keep up. Toyota's legendary Toyota Production System (TPS) focuses on organizing work to eliminate waste, making continuous improvements, and optimizing customer value. Information systems help Toyota implement its TPS and produce vehicles based on what customers have actually ordered.

Survival Business firms also invest in information systems and technologies because they are necessities of doing business. Sometimes these "necessities" are driven by industry-level changes. For instance, after Citibank introduced the first automatic teller machines (ATMs) in the New York region in 1977 to attract customers through higher service levels, its competitors rushed to provide ATMs to their customers to keep up with Citibank. Today, virtually all banks have ATMs and link to national and international ATM networks, such as CIRRUS. Providing ATM services to retail banking customers is simply a requirement of being in and surviving in the retail banking business.

There are many federal and provincial statutes and regulations that create a legal duty for companies and their employees to retain records, including digital records. The *Canadian Rules on the Sarbanes-Oxley Act*, more commonly known as the *C-SOX Act*, which was intended to improve the accountability of public firms and their auditors, requires certified public accounting firms that audit public companies to retain audit working papers and records, including all e-mails, for a number of years. Many other pieces of federal and provincial legislation in health care, financial services, education, and privacy protection impose significant information retention and reporting requirements on Canadian businesses and other organizations. Firms turn to information systems and technologies to provide the capability to respond to these requirements.

1.2   Perspectives on Information Systems

So far we have used *information systems* and *technologies* informally without defining the terms. **Information technology (IT)** consists of all the hardware and software that a firm needs to use in order to achieve its business objectives. This includes not only computer machines, disk drives, and handheld mobile devices, but also software, such as the Windows or Linux operating systems, the Microsoft Office desktop productivity suite, and the many thousands of computer programs and applications that can be found in a typical large firm. "Information systems" are more complex and can be best be understood by looking at them from both a technology and a business perspective.

What Is an Information System?

An **information system** can be defined technically as a set of interrelated components that collect (or retrieve), process, store, and distribute information to support decision making and control in an organization. In addition to supporting decision making, coordination, and control, information systems may also help managers and workers analyze problems, visualize complex subjects, and create new products.

Information systems contain information about significant people, places, and things within the organization or in the environment surrounding it. By **information,** we mean data that have been shaped into a form that is meaningful and useful to humans. Data, in contrast, are streams of raw facts representing events occurring in organizations or the physical environment before they have been organized and arranged into a form that people can understand and use.

A brief example contrasting information and data may prove useful. Supermarket checkout counters scan millions of pieces of data from bar codes, which describe each product. This data can be totalled and analyzed to provide meaningful information, such as the total number of bottles of dish detergent sold at a particular store, which brands of dish detergent were selling the most rapidly at that store or sales territory, or the total amount spent on that brand of dish detergent at that store or sales region (see Figure 1-4).

Information technology (IT)
Information system
Information

FIGURE 1-4   Data and information.

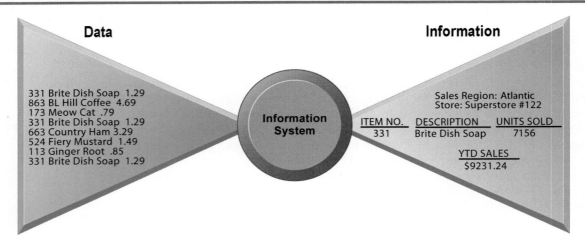

Raw data from a supermarket checkout counter can be processed and organized to produce meaningful information, such as the total unit sales of dish detergent or the total sales revenue from dish detergent for a specific store or sales territory.

Four activities in an information system produce the information that organizations need to make decisions, control operations, analyze problems, and create new products or services. These activities are input, processing, output, and feedback (see Figure 1-5). **Input** captures or collects raw data from within the organization or from its external environment. **Processing** converts this raw input into a meaningful form. **Output** transfers the processed information to the people who will use it or to the activities for which it will be used. Information systems also require **feedback,** which is output that is returned to appropriate members of the organization to help them evaluate or correct the input and processing stages.

In Toyota's vehicle orders management system (see the chapter opening case), the raw input consists of customer order data including the dealer identification number,

Input
Processing
Output
Feedback

FIGURE 1-5   Functions of an information system.

An information system contains information about an organization and its surrounding environment. Three basic activities—input, processing, and output—produce the information organizations need. Feedback is output returned to appropriate people or activities in the organization to evaluate and refine the input. Environmental actors, such as customers, suppliers, competitors, stockholders, and regulatory agencies, interact with the organization and its information systems.

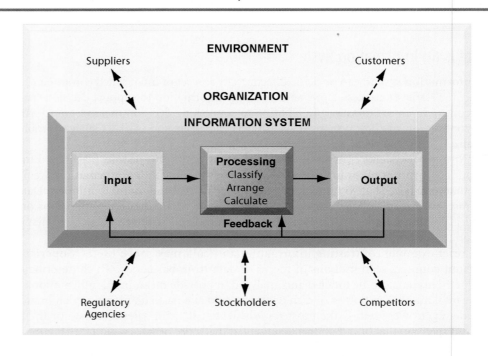

model, colour, and optional features of each car ordered. Toyota's computers store this data and process it to locate the models with options specified by the customer that are either in inventory or under production, to place orders to national distributors, to consolidate the orders, and then to transmit them to factories. Toyota's production systems then tell its factories how many vehicles to manufacture for each model, colour, and option package; how much to bill for each vehicle; and where to ship the vehicles. The output consists of shipping instructions, invoices, and production reports. The system provides meaningful information, such as which models, colours, and options are selling in which locations, the most popular models and colours, and which dealers sell the most cars.

Although computer-based information systems use computer technology to process raw data into meaningful information, there is a sharp distinction between a computer and a computer program on the one hand and an information system on the other. Electronic computers and related software programs are the technical foundation, tools, and materials of modern information systems. Computers provide the equipment for storing and processing information. Computer programs, or software, are sets of operating instructions that direct and control computer processing. Knowing how computers and computer programs work is important in designing solutions to organizational problems, but computers are only part of an information system.

A house is an appropriate analogy. Houses are built with hammers, nails, and wood, but these do not make a house. The architecture, design, setting, landscaping, and all of the decisions that lead to the creation of these features are part of the house and are crucial for solving the problem of putting a roof over one's head. Computers and programs are the hammer, nails, and lumber of computer-based information systems, but alone they cannot produce the information a particular organization needs. To understand information systems, you must understand the problems they are designed to solve, their architectural and design elements, and the organizational processes that lead to these solutions.

Dimensions of Information Systems

To fully understand information systems, you must understand the broader organization, management, and information technology dimensions of systems (see Figure 1-6) and their power to provide solutions to challenges and problems in the business environment. We refer to this broader understanding of information systems, which encompasses an understanding of the management and organizational dimensions of systems as well as

FIGURE 1-6   Information systems are more than computers.

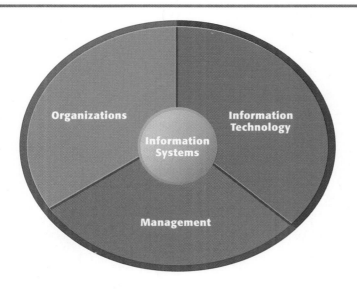

Using information systems effectively requires an understanding of the organization, management, and information technology shaping the systems. An information system creates value for the firm as an organizational and management solution to challenges posed by the environment.

the technical dimensions of systems, as **information systems literacy. Computer literacy,** in contrast, focuses primarily on knowledge of information technology.

The field of management information systems (MIS) tries to achieve this broader information systems literacy. MIS deals with behavioural issues as well as technical issues surrounding the development, use, and impact of information systems used by managers and employees in the firm.

Let us examine each of the dimensions of information systems—organizations, management, and information technology.

Organizations Information systems are an integral part of organizations. Indeed, for some companies, such as credit reporting firms, without an information system, there would be no business. The key elements of an organization are its people, structure, business processes, politics, and culture. We introduce these components of organizations here and describe them in greater detail in Chapters 2 and 3.

Organizations have a structure that is composed of different levels and specialties. The structures reveal a clear-cut division of labour. Authority and responsibility in a business firm are organized as a hierarchy or a pyramid structure. The upper levels of the hierarchy consist of managerial, professional, and technical employees while the lower levels consist of operational personnel.

Senior management makes long-range strategic decisions about products and services and ensures the financial performance of the firm. **Middle management** carries out the programs and plans of senior management, and **operational management** is responsible for monitoring the daily activities of the business. **Knowledge workers,** such as engineers, scientists, or architects, design products or services and create new knowledge for the firm while **data workers,** such as secretaries or clerks, assist with paperwork at all levels of the firm. **Production or service workers** actually produce the product and deliver the service (see Figure 1-7).

Experts are employed and trained for different business functions. The major **business functions,** or specialized tasks performed by business organizations, consist of sales and marketing, manufacturing and production, finance and accounting, and human resources (see Table 1-2). Chapter 2 provides more detail on these business functions and the ways in which they are supported by information systems.

An organization coordinates work through its hierarchy and through its business processes, which are logically related tasks and behaviours for accomplishing work. Developing a new product, fulfilling an order, or hiring a new employee are examples of business processes.

Most organizations' business processes include formal rules that have been developed over a long time for accomplishing tasks. These rules guide employees in a variety of procedures, from writing an invoice to responding to customer complaints.

Information systems literacy
Computer literacy
Senior management
Middle management
Operational management
Knowledge workers
Data workers
Production or service workers
Business functions

FIGURE 1-7   Levels in a firm.

Business organizations are hierarchies consisting of three principal levels: senior management, middle management, and operational management. Information systems serve each of these levels. Scientists and knowledge workers often work with middle management.

TABLE 1-2 Major business functions.

FUNCTION	PURPOSE
Sales and marketing	Selling the organization's products and services
Manufacturing and production	Producing and delivering products and services
Finance and accounting	Managing the organization's financial assets and maintaining the organization's financial records
Human resources	Attracting, developing, and maintaining the organization's labour force; maintaining employee records

Some of these business processes have been written down, but others are informal work practices, such as a requirement to return telephone calls from co-workers or customers, that are not formally documented. Information systems automate many business processes. For instance, how a customer receives credit or how a customer is billed is often determined by an information system that incorporates a set of formal business processes.

Each organization has a unique **culture,** or fundamental set of assumptions, values, and ways of doing things, that has been accepted by most of its members. You can see organizational culture at work by looking around your university or college. Some bedrock assumptions of university life are that professors know more than students, the reasons students attend post-secondary institutions is to learn, and that classes follow a regular schedule.

Parts of an organization's culture can always be found embedded in its information systems. For instance, UPS's concern with placing service to the customer first is an aspect of its organizational culture that can be found in the company's package tracking systems, which we describe later in this section.

Different levels and specialties in an organization create different interests and points of view. These views often conflict over how the company should be run and how resources and rewards should be distributed. Conflict is the basis for organizational politics. Information systems come out of this cauldron of differing perspectives, conflicts, compromises, and agreements that are a natural part of all organizations. In Chapter 3, we examine these features of organizations and their role in the development of information systems in greater detail.

Management Management's job is to make sense out of the many situations faced by organizations, make decisions, and formulate action plans to solve organizational problems. Managers perceive business challenges in the environment, set the organizational strategy for responding to those challenges, and allocate the human and financial resources to coordinate the work and achieve success. Throughout, they must exercise responsible leadership. The business information systems described in this book reflect the hopes, dreams, and realities of real-world managers.

But managers must do more than manage what already exists. They must also create new products and services and even re-create the organization from time to time. A substantial part of management responsibility is creative work driven by new knowledge and information. Information technology can play a powerful role in helping managers design and deliver new products and services and redirecting and redesigning their organizations. Chapter 14 treats management decision making in detail.

Information Technology Information technology is one of many tools managers use to cope with change. **Computer hardware** is the physical equipment used for input, processing, and output activities in an information system. It consists of the following: computers of various sizes and shapes (including mobile handheld devices); various input, output, and storage devices; and telecommunications devices that link computers together.

Computer software consists of the detailed, preprogrammed instructions that control and coordinate the computer hardware components in an information system. Chapter 5

Culture
Computer hardware
Computer software

describes the contemporary software and hardware platforms used by firms today in greater detail.

Data management technology consists of the software governing the organization of data on physical storage media. More detail on data organization and access methods can be found in Chapter 6.

Networking and telecommunications technology, consisting of both physical devices and software, links the various pieces of hardware and transfers data from one physical location to another. Computers and communications equipment can be connected in networks for sharing voice, data, images, sound, and video. A **network** links two or more computers to share data or resources, such as a printer.

The world's largest and most widely used network is the Internet. The **Internet** is a global "network of networks" that uses universal standards (described in Chapter 7) to connect millions of different networks with more than 1.4 billion users in more than 230 countries around the world.

The Internet has created a new "universal" technology platform on which to build new products, services, strategies, and business models. This same technology platform has internal uses, providing the connectivity to link different systems and networks within the firm. Internal corporate networks based on Internet technology are called **intranets.** Private intranets extended to authorized users outside the organization are called **extranets.** Firms use extranets to coordinate their activities with other firms for making purchases, collaborating on design, and other interorganizational work. For most business firms today, using Internet technology is both a business necessity and a competitive advantage.

The **World Wide Web** is a service provided by the Internet that uses universally accepted standards for storing, retrieving, formatting, and displaying information in a page format on the Internet. Web pages contain text, graphics, animations, sound, and video and are linked to other Web pages. By clicking on highlighted words or buttons on a Web page, you can link to related pages to find additional information and links to other locations on the Web. The Web can serve as the foundation for new kinds of information systems such as UPS's Web-based package tracking system described in the following Window on Technology

All of these technologies, along with the people required to run and manage them, represent resources that can be shared throughout the organization and constitute the firm's **information technology (IT) infrastructure.** The IT infrastructure provides the foundation, or *platform,* on which the firm can build its specific information systems. Each organization must carefully design and manage its information technology infrastructure so that it has the set of technology services it needs for the work it wants to accomplish with information systems. Chapters 5 through 8 of this text examine each major technology component of information technology infrastructure and show how they all work together to create the technology platform for the organization.

The Window on Technology describes some of the typical technologies used in computer-based information systems today. United Parcel Service (UPS) invests heavily in information systems technology to make its business more efficient and customer oriented. It uses an array of information technologies including bar code scanning systems, wireless networks, large mainframe computers, handheld computers, the Internet, and many different pieces of software for tracking packages, calculating fees, maintaining customer accounts, and managing logistics.

Let us identify the organization, management, and technology elements in the UPS package tracking system we have just described. The organization element anchors the package tracking system in UPS's sales and production functions (the main product of UPS is a service—package delivery). It specifies the required procedures for identifying packages with both sender and recipient information, taking inventory, tracking the packages en route, and providing package status reports for UPS customers and customer service representatives.

The system must also provide information to satisfy the needs of managers and workers. UPS drivers need to be trained in both package pickup and delivery procedures and in how to use the package tracking system so that they can work efficiently and effectively.

Data management technology

Networking and telecommunications technology

Network

Internet

Intranets

Extranets

World Wide Web

Information technology (IT) infrastructure

UPS customers may need some training to use UPS in-house package tracking software or the UPS Web site.

UPS's management is responsible for monitoring service levels and costs and for promoting the company's strategy of combining low cost and superior service. Management decided to use computer systems to increase the ease of sending a package using UPS and of checking its delivery status, thereby reducing delivery costs and increasing sales revenues.

The technology supporting this system consists of handheld computers, bar code scanners, wired and wireless communications networks, desktop computers, UPS's central computer, storage technology for the package delivery data, UPS in-house package tracking software, and software to access the World Wide Web. The result is an information system solution to the business challenge of providing a high level of service with low prices in the face of mounting competition.

Technology

WINDOW ON TECHNOLOGY

UPS Competes Globally with Information Technology

United Parcel Service (UPS) started out in 1907 in a closet-sized basement office. Jim Casey and Claude Ryan—two teenagers from Seattle with two bicycles and one phone—promised the "best service and lowest rates." UPS has used this formula successfully for more than 90 years to become the world's largest ground and air package-distribution company. It is a global enterprise with more than 425 000 employees, 93 000 vehicles, and the world's ninth largest airline. Today UPS delivers more than 15 million parcels and documents each day in North America and more than 200 countries and territories.

The firm has been able to maintain leadership in small-package delivery services despite stiff competition from FedEx and other package delivery services by investing heavily in advanced information technology. UPS spends more than $1 billion each year to maintain a high level of customer service while keeping costs low and streamlining its overall operations.

It all starts with the scannable bar-coded label attached to a package, which contains detailed information about the sender, the destination, and when the package should arrive. Customers can download and print their own labels using special software provided by UPS or by accessing the UPS Web site. Before the package is even picked up, information from the "smart" label is transmitted to one of UPS's two computer centres and sent to the distribution centre nearest its final destination. Dispatchers at this centre download the label data and use special software to create the most efficient delivery route for each driver that considers traffic, weather conditions, and the location of each stop. UPS estimates its delivery trucks save 28 million miles and burn 3 million fewer gallons of fuel each year as a result of using this technology.

The first thing a UPS driver picks up each day is a handheld computer called a Delivery Information Acquisition Device (DIAD), which can access one of the wireless networks cell phones rely on. As soon as the driver logs on, his or her day's route is downloaded onto the handheld. The DIAD also automatically captures customers' signatures along with pickup and delivery information. Package tracking information is then transmitted to UPS's computer network for storage and processing. From there, the information can be accessed worldwide to provide proof of delivery to customers or to respond to customer queries. It usually takes fewer than 60 seconds from the time a driver presses "complete" on a DIAD for the new information to be available on the Web.

Through its automated package tracking system, UPS can monitor and even reroute packages throughout the delivery process. At various points along the route from sender to receiver, bar code devices scan shipping information on the package label and feed data about the progress of the package into the central computer. Customer service representatives are able to check the status of any package from desktop computers linked to the central computers and respond immediately to inquiries from customers. UPS customers can also access this information from the company's Web site using their own computers or wireless devices such as cell phones.

Anyone with a package to ship can access the UPS Web site to track packages, check delivery routes, calculate shipping rates, determine time in transit, print labels, and schedule a pickup. The data collected at the UPS Web site are transmitted to the UPS central computer and then back to the customer after processing. UPS also provides tools that enable customers, such Cisco Systems, to embed UPS functions, such as tracking and cost calculations, into their own Web sites so that they can track shipments without visiting the UPS site.

UPS is now leveraging its decades of expertise managing its own global delivery network to manage logistics and supply chain activities for other companies. It created a UPS Supply Chain Solutions division that provides a complete bundle of standardized services to subscribing companies at a fraction of what it would cost to build their own systems and infrastructure.

These services include supply chain design and management, freight forwarding, customs brokerage, mail services, multi-modal transportation, and financial services, in addition to logistics services.

Hired Hand Technologies, a manufacturer of agricultural and horticultural equipment, uses UPS Freight services not only to track shipments but also to build its weekly manufacturing plans. UPS provides up-to-the-minute information about exactly when parts are arriving within 20 seconds.

To Think About

1. What are the inputs, processing, and outputs of UPS's package tracking system?

2. What technologies are used by UPS? How are these technologies related to UPS's business strategy?

3. What problems do UPS's information systems solve? What would happen if these systems were not available?

MIS in Action

Explore the UPS Web site (www.ups.com), and answer the following questions:

1. What kind of information and services does the Web site provide for individuals, small businesses, and large businesses? List these services and write several paragraphs describing one of them, such as UPS Trade Direct or Automated Shipment Processing. Explain how you or your business could benefit from the service.

2. Explain how the Web site helps UPS achieve some or all of the strategic business objectives we described earlier in this chapter. What would be the impact on UPS's business if this Web site were not available?

Sources: United Parcel Service, "Powering Up the Supply Chain," *UPS Compass*, Winter 2008 and "LTL's High-Tech Infusion," *UPS Compass*, Spring 2007; Claudia Deutsch, "Still Brown, but Going High Tech," *The New York Times*, July 12, 2007; and www.ups.com (accessed July 26, 2008).

It Is Not Just Technology: A Business Perspective on Information Systems

Managers and business firms invest in information technology and systems because they provide real economic value to the business. The decision to develop or maintain an information system assumes that the returns on this investment will be superior to other investments in buildings, machines, or other assets. These superior returns will be expressed as increases in productivity, as increases in revenues (which will increase the firm's stock market value), or perhaps as superior long-term strategic positioning of the firm in certain markets (which produce superior revenues in the future).

From a business perspective, we can see that an information system is an important instrument for creating value for the firm. Information systems enable the firm to increase its revenue or decrease its costs by providing information that helps managers make better decisions or that improves the execution of business processes. For example, the information system for analyzing supermarket checkout data illustrated in Figure 1-4 can increase firm profitability by helping managers make better decisions on which products to stock and promote in retail supermarkets.

Every business has an information value chain, illustrated in Figure 1-8, in which raw information is systematically acquired and then transformed through various stages that add value to that information. The value of an information system to a business, as well as the decision to invest in any new information system, is, in large part, determined by the extent to which the system will lead to better management decisions, more efficient business processes, and higher firm profitability. Although there are other reasons that systems are developed, their primary purpose is to contribute to corporate value.

From a business perspective, information systems are part of a series of value-adding activities for acquiring, transforming, and distributing information

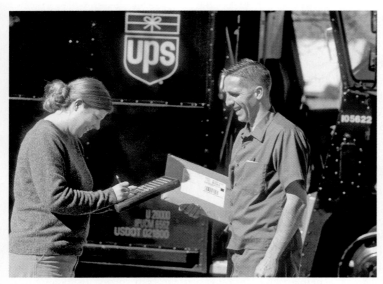

Using a handheld computer called a Delivery Information Acquisition Device (DIAD), UPS drivers automatically capture customers' signatures along with pickup, delivery, and time card information. UPS information systems use these data to track packages while they are being transported.

FIGURE 1-8   The business information value chain.

From a business perspective, information systems are part of a series of value-adding activities for acquiring, transforming, and distributing information that managers can use to improve decision making, enhance organizational performance, and, ultimately, increase firm profitability.

that managers can use to improve decision making, enhance organizational performance, and, ultimately, increase firm profitability.

The business perspective calls attention to the organizational and managerial nature of information systems. An information system represents an organizational and management solution, based on information technology, to a challenge or problem posed by the environment. Every chapter in this book begins with a short case study that illustrates this concept. A diagram at the beginning of each chapter illustrates the relationship between a business challenge and resulting management and organizational decisions to use IT as a solution to challenges generated by the business environment. You can use these diagrams as a starting point for analyzing any information system or information system problem you encounter.

Review the diagram at the beginning of the chapter that reflects this expanded definition of an information system. The diagram shows how Toyota's vehicle orders management system solves the business challenge presented by fierce competition and rapidly changing consumer preferences. The system creates value for Toyota by making its ordering and production processes more efficient and effective. The diagram also illustrates how management, technology, and organizational elements work together to create the system.

1.3   Complementary Assets: Organizational Capital and the Right Business Model

Awareness of the organizational and managerial dimensions of information systems can help us understand why some firms achieve better results from their information systems than others. Studies of returns from information technology investments show that there is considerable variation in the returns firms receive (see Figure 1-9). Some firms invest a

FIGURE 1-9 Variation in returns on information technology investment.

Although, on average, investments in information technology produce returns far above those returned by other investments, there is considerable variation across firms.

Source: Based on Brynjolfsson and Hitt (2000).

IT Capital Stock (relative to industry average)

great deal and receive a great deal (quadrant 2); others invest an equal amount and receive few returns (quadrant 4). Still other firms invest little and receive much (quadrant 1) while others invest little and receive little (quadrant 3). This suggests that investing in information technology does not by itself guarantee good returns. What accounts for this variation among firms?

The answer lies in the concept of complementary assets. Information technology investments alone cannot make organizations and managers more effective unless they are accompanied by supportive values, structures, and behaviour patterns in the organization and other complementary assets. Business firms need to change how they do business before they can really reap the advantages of new information technologies.

Some firms fail to adopt the right business model that suits the new technology or seek to preserve an old business model that is doomed by new technology. For instance, recording label companies refused to change their old business model, which was based on physical music stores for distribution rather than adopt a new online distribution model. As a result, online legal music sales are dominated not by record companies but by a technology company called Apple Computer.

Complementary assets are those assets required to derive value from a primary investment (Teece, 1988). For instance, realizing value from automobiles requires substantial complementary investments in highways, roads, gasoline stations, repair facilities, and a legal regulatory structure to set standards and control drivers.

Recent research on business information technology investment indicates that firms that support their technology investments with investments in complementary assets, such as new business models, new business processes, management behaviour, organizational culture, and training, receive superior returns while those firms failing to make these complementary investments receive fewer or no returns on their information technology investments (Brynjolfsson, 2003; Brynjolfsson and Hitt, 2000; Davern and Kauffman, 2000; Laudon, 1974). These investments in organization and management are also known as **organizational and management capital.**

Table 1-3 lists the major complementary investments that firms need to make to realize value from their information technology investments. Some of this investment involves tangible assets, such as buildings, machinery, and tools. However, the value of investments in information technology depends to a large extent on complementary investments in management and organization.

Key organizational complementary investments are a supportive business culture that values efficiency and effectiveness, an appropriate business model, efficient business processes, decentralization of authority, highly distributed decision rights, and a strong information system (IS) development team.

Complementary assets

Organizational and management capital

TABLE 1-3 Complementary social, managerial, and organizational assets required to optimize returns from information technology investments.

ORGANIZATIONAL ASSETS	Supportive organizational culture that values efficiency and effectiveness
	Appropriate business model
	Efficient business processes
	Decentralized authority
	Distributed decision-making rights
	Strong IS development team
MANAGERIAL ASSETS	Strong senior management support for technology investment and change
	Incentives for management innovation
	Teamwork and collaborative work environments
	Training programs to enhance management decision skills
	Management culture that values flexibility and knowledge-based decision making
SOCIAL ASSETS	The Internet and telecommunications infrastructure
	IT-enriched educational programs raising labour force computer literacy
	Standards (both government and private sector)
	Laws and regulations creating fair, stable market environments
	Technology and service firms in adjacent markets to assist implementation

Important managerial complementary assets are strong senior management support for change, incentive systems that monitor and reward individual innovation, an emphasis on teamwork and collaboration, training programs, and a management culture that values flexibility and knowledge.

Important social investments (not made by the firm but by society at large, other firms, governments, and other key market actors) are the Internet and the supporting Internet culture, educational systems, network and computing standards, regulations and laws, and the presence of technology and service firms.

Throughout this book, we emphasize a framework of analysis that considers technology, management, and organizational assets and their interactions. Perhaps the single most important theme in the book, reflected in case studies and exercises, is that managers need to consider the broader organization and management dimensions of information systems to understand current problems as well as to derive substantial above-average returns from their information technology investments. As you will see throughout the text, firms that can address these related dimensions of the IT investment are, on average, richly rewarded.

1.4   Contemporary Approaches to Information Systems

The study of information systems is a multidisciplinary field. No single theory or perspective dominates. Figure 1-10 illustrates the major disciplines that contribute problems, issues, and solutions in the study of information systems. In general, the field can be divided into technical and behavioural approaches. Information systems are sociotechnical systems. Though they are composed of machines, devices, and "hard" physical technology, they require substantial social, organizational, and intellectual investments to make them work properly.

The study of information systems deals with issues and insights contributed from technical and behavioural disciplines.

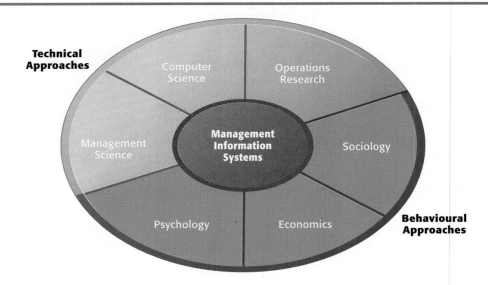

Technical Approach

The technical approach to information systems emphasizes mathematically based models to study information systems as well as the physical technology and formal capabilities of these systems. The disciplines that contribute to the technical approach are computer science, management science, and operations research.

Computer science is concerned with establishing theories of computability, methods of computation, and methods of efficient data storage and access. Management science emphasizes the development of models for decision making and management practices. Operations research focuses on mathematical techniques for optimizing selected parameters of organizations, such as transportation, inventory control, and transaction costs.

Behavioural Approach

An important part of the information systems field is concerned with behavioural issues that arise in the development and long-term maintenance of information systems. Issues such as strategic business integration, design, implementation, utilization, and management cannot be explored usefully with the models used in the technical approach. Other behavioural disciplines contribute important concepts and methods.

For instance, sociologists study information systems with an eye toward how groups and organizations shape the development of systems and also how systems affect individuals, groups, and organizations. Psychologists study information systems with an interest in how human decision makers perceive and use formal information. Economists study information systems with an interest in understanding the production of digital goods, the dynamics of digital markets, and understanding how new information systems change the control and cost structures within the firm.

The behavioural approach does not ignore technology. Indeed, information systems technology is often the stimulus for a behavioural problem or issue. But the focus of this approach is generally not on technical solutions. Instead, it concentrates on changes in attitudes, management and organizational policy, and behaviour.

Approach of This Text: Sociotechnical Systems

Throughout this book, you will find a rich story with four main actors: suppliers of hardware and software (the technologists); business firms making investments and seeking to obtain value from the technology; managers and employees seeking to achieve business value (and other goals); and the contemporary legal, social, and cultural context (the firm's environment). Together these actors produce what we call *management information systems.*

The study of management information systems (MIS) arose in the 1970s to focus on the use of computer-based information systems in business firms and government agencies. MIS combines the work of computer science, management science, and operations research with a practical orientation toward developing system solutions to real-world problems and managing information technology resources. It is also concerned with behavioural issues surrounding the development, use, and impact of information systems, which are typically discussed in the fields of sociology, economics, and psychology.

Our experience as academics and practitioners leads us to believe that no single approach effectively captures the reality of information systems. The successes and failures of information are rarely all technical or all behavioural. Our best advice to you is to understand the perspectives of many disciplines. Indeed, the challenge and excitement of the information systems field is that it requires an appreciation and tolerance of many different approaches.

The view we adopt in this book is best characterized as the **sociotechnical view** of systems. In this view, optimal organizational performance is achieved by jointly optimizing both the social and technical systems used in production.

Adopting a sociotechnical systems perspective helps to avoid a purely technological approach to information systems. For instance, the fact that information technology is rapidly declining in cost and growing in power does not necessarily or easily translate into productivity enhancement or bottom-line profits. The fact that a firm has recently installed an enterprise-wide financial reporting system does not necessarily mean that it will be used—or used effectively. Likewise, the fact that a firm has recently introduced new business procedures and processes does not necessarily mean that employees will be more productive in the absence of investments in new information systems to enable those processes.

In this book, we stress the need to optimize the firm's performance as a whole. Both the technical and behavioural components need attention. This means that technology must be changed and designed in such a way as to fit organizational and individual needs. Sometimes, the technology may have to be "de-optimized" to accomplish this fit. For instance, mobile phone users adapt this technology to their personal needs, and as a result, manufacturers quickly seek to adjust the technology to conform with user expectations. Organizations and individuals must also be changed through training, learning, and planned organizational change to allow the technology to operate and prosper. Figure 1-11 illustrates this process of mutual adjustment in a sociotechnical system.

Sociotechnical view

FIGURE 1-11   A sociotechnical perspective on information systems.

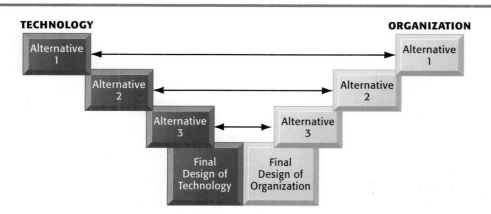

In a sociotechnical perspective, the performance of a system is optimized when both the technology and the organization mutually adjust to one another until a satisfactory fit is obtained.

SUMMARY

1. *How are information systems transforming business, and what is their relationship to globalization?*

   E-mail, online conferencing, and cell phones have become essential tools for conducting business. Information systems are the foundation of fast-paced supply chains. The Internet allows many businesses to buy, sell, advertise, and solicit customer feedback online. Organizations are trying to become more competitive and efficient by digitally enabling their core business processes and evolving into digital firms. The Internet has stimulated globalization by dramatically reducing the costs of producing, buying, and selling goods on a global scale. New information system trends include the emerging mobile digital platform, online software as a service, and cloud computing.

2. *Why are information systems so essential for running and managing a business today?*

   Information systems are a foundation for conducting business today. In many industries, survival and the ability to achieve strategic business goals are difficult without extensive use of information technology. Businesses today use information systems to achieve six major objectives: operational excellence; new products, services, and business models; customer/supplier intimacy; improved decision making; competitive advantage; and day-to-day survival.

3. *What exactly is an information system? How does it work? What are its management, organization, and technology components?*

   From a technical perspective, an information system collects, stores, and disseminates information from an organization's environment and internal operations to support organizational functions and decision making, communication, coordination, control, analysis, and visualization. Information systems transform raw data into useful information through four basic activities: input, processing, output, and feedback.

   From a business perspective, an information system provides a solution to a problem or challenge facing a firm and represents a combination of management, organization, and technology elements. The management dimension of information systems involves issues such as leadership, strategy, and management behaviour. The technology dimension consists of computer hardware, software, data management technology, and networking/telecommunications technology (including the Internet). The organizational dimension of information systems involves issues such as the organization's hierarchy, functional specialties, business processes, culture, and political interest groups.

4. *What are complementary assets? Why are complementary assets essential for ensuring that information systems provide genuine value for an organization?*

   In order to obtain meaningful value from information systems, organizations must support their technology investments with appropriate complementary investments in organizations and management. These complementary assets include new business models and business processes, supportive organizational culture and management behaviour, appropriate technology standards, regulations, and laws. New information technology investments are unlikely to produce high returns unless businesses make the appropriate managerial and organizational changes to support the technology.

5. *What academic disciplines are used to study information systems? How does each contribute to an understanding of information systems? What is a sociotechnical systems perspective?*

   The study of information systems deals with issues and insights contributed from both technical and behavioural disciplines. The disciplines that contribute to the technical approach focusing on formal models and capabilities of systems are computer science, management science, and operations research. The disciplines contributing to the behavioural approach focusing on the design, implementation, management, and business impact of systems are psychology, sociology, and economics. A sociotechnical view of systems considers both technical and social features of systems and solutions that represent the best fit between them.

Key Terms

Business functions, 16	Feedback, 14	Network, 18
Business model, 11	Information, 13	Networking and telecommunications technology, 18
Business processes, 8	Information system, 13	
Complementary assets, 22	Information systems literacy, 16	Operational management, 16
Computer hardware, 17	Information technology (IT), 13	Organizational and management capital, 22
Computer literacy, 16	Information technology (IT) infrastructure, 18	
Computer software, 17		Output, 14
Culture, 17	Input, 14	Processing, 14
Data management technology, 18	Internet, 18	Production or service workers, 16
Data workers, 16	Intranets, 18	Senior management, 16
Digital firm, 8	Knowledge workers, 16	Sociotechnical view, 25
Extranets, 18	Middle management, 16	World Wide Web, 18

Review Questions

1. *How are information systems transforming business, and what is their relationship to globalization?*
   - *Describe how information systems have changed the way businesses operate and their products and services.*
   - *Identify three major new information system trends.*
   - *Describe the characteristics of a digital firm.*
   - *Describe the challenges and opportunities of globalization in a "flattened" world.*

2. *Why are information systems so essential for running and managing a business today?*
   - *List and describe six reasons that information systems are so important for business today.*

3. *What exactly is an information system? How does it work? What are its management, organization, and technology components?*
   - *Define the term information system, and describe the activities it performs.*
   - *List and describe the organizational, management, and technology dimensions of information systems.*
   - *Distinguish between data and information and between information systems literacy and computer literacy.*

   - *Explain how the Internet and the World Wide Web are related to the other technology components of information systems.*

4. *What are complementary assets? Why are complementary assets essential for ensuring that information systems provide genuine value for an organization?*
   - *Define complementary assets and describe their relationship to information technology.*
   - *Describe the complementary social, managerial, and organizational assets required to optimize returns from information technology investments.*

5. *What academic disciplines are used to study information systems? How does each contribute to an understanding of information systems? What is a sociotechnical systems perspective?*
   - *List and describe each discipline that contributes to a technical approach to information systems*
   - *List and describe each discipline that contributes to a behavioural approach to information systems.*
   - *Describe the sociotechnical perspective on information systems.*

Discussion Questions

1. *Information systems are too important to be left to computer specialists. Do you agree? Why or why not?*

2. *If you were setting up Web sites for NBA teams, what management, organization, and technology issues might you encounter?*

Collaboration and Teamwork: Creating a Web Site for Team Collaboration

Form a team with three or four classmates. Then use the tools at Google Sites to create a Web site for your team. You will need to a create a Google account for the site and specify the collaborators (your team members) who are allowed to access the site and make contributions. Specify your professor as the viewer of the site so that he or she can evaluate your work. Assign a name to the site. Select a theme for the site, and make any changes you wish to colours and fonts. Add features for project announcements and a repository for team documents, source materials, illustrations, electronic presentations, and Web pages of interest. You can add other features if you wish. Use Google to create a calendar for your team. After you complete this exercise, you can use this Web site and calendar for your other team projects.

 Visit the MyMISLab website at **www.pearsoned.ca/mymislab**. This online homework and tutorial system puts you in control of your own learning with study and practice tools directly correlated to this chapter's content.

Learning Track Modules

The following Learning Tracks provide content relevant to topics covered in this chapter:

1. How Much Does IT Matter?
2. Information Systems and Your Career

HANDS-ON MIS   Projects

The projects in this section give you hands-on experience in analyzing financial reporting and inventory management problems, using data management software to improve management decision making about increasing sales, and using Internet software for developing shipping budgets.

Management Decision Problems

1. The Dollar Store operates deep discount stores in Canada offering housewares, cleaning supplies, clothing, health and beauty aids, and packaged food, with most items selling for $1. Its business model calls for keeping costs as low as possible. Although the company uses information systems (such as a point-of-sale system to track sales at the register), it deploys them very sparingly to keep expenditures to the minimum. The company has no automated method for keeping track of inventory at each store. Managers know approximately how many cases of a particular product the store is supposed to receive when a delivery truck arrives, but the stores lack technology for scanning the cases or verifying the item count inside the cases. Merchandise losses from theft or other mishaps have been rising and now represent more than 3 percent of total sales. What decisions have to be made before investing in an information system solution?

2. Snyders of Hanover, which sells more than 78 million bags of pretzels, snack chips, and organic snack items each year, had its financial department use spreadsheets and manual processes for much of its data gathering and reporting. Hanover's financial analyst would spend the entire final week of every month collecting spreadsheets from the heads of more than 50 departments worldwide. She would then consolidate and re-enter all the data into another spreadsheet, which would serve as the company's monthly profit-and-loss statement. If a department needed to update its data after submitting the spreadsheet to the main office, the analyst had to return the original spreadsheet and wait for the department to resubmit its data before finally submitting the updated data in the consolidated document. Assess the impact of this situation on business performance and management decision making.

Improving Decision Making: Using Databases to Analyze Sales Trends

Software skills: Database querying and reporting
Business skills: Sales trend analysis

Effective information systems transform data into meaningful information for decisions that improve business performance. On the MyMISLab for Chapter 1, you can find a Store and Regional Sales Database with raw data on weekly store sales of computer equipment in various sales regions. A sample is shown on the next page, but the MyMISLab may have a more recent version of this database for this exercise. The database includes fields for store identification number, sales region number, item number, item description, unit price, units sold, and the weekly sales period when the sales were made. Develop some reports and queries to make this information more useful for running the business. Try to use the information in the database to support decisions on which products to restock, which stores and sales regions would benefit from additional marketing and promotional campaigns, which times of the year products should be offered at full price, and which times of the year products should be discounted. Modify the database table, if necessary, to provide all of the information you require. Print your reports and results of queries.

Achieving Operational Excellence: Using Internet Tools to Budget for Shipping Costs

Software skills: Internet-based software
Business skills: Shipping cost budgeting

In this exercise, you will use the same online software tools that businesses use to calculate and budget for shipping costs. Using these tools, you will choose the "best" shipper for your business. "Best" does not necessarily mean lowest cost but includes a consideration of other factors, such as scheduling, ease of use, and compatibility with your business schedule.

Assume you are the shipping clerk of a small firm that prints, binds, and ships popular books for a mid-level publisher. Your production facilities are located in Kitchener, Ontario (postal code N2M 2Y4). Your customers' warehouses are located in Calgary, Alberta (T2E 0B3); Halifax, Nova Scotia (B3P 2L5); Richmond, British Columbia (V7E 3M1); Montréal, Québec (H1Y 2G5); and St. John's, Newfoundland (A1E 2X1). The production facility operates 250 days per year. Your books are usually shipped in one of two package sizes:

- A: 9 inches tall by 13 inches long by 17 inches wide, weighing 20 kilograms

- B: 10 inches tall by 6 inches long by 12 inches wide, weighing 7 kilograms

The company ships about four of the A boxes to each of the warehouses on an average day and about eight B boxes daily.

1. What is the best shipper for your company? Go on the Web and compare three shippers, such as FedEx (**www.fedex.com**), UPS (**www.ups.com**), and Canada Post (**www.canadapost.ca**). Consider not only costs but also issues such as delivery speed, pickup schedules, drop-off locations, tracking ability, and ease of use of the Web site. Which service did you select? Explain why.

CASE STUDY

How the Royal Canadian Golf Association Cut Costs and Improved Customer Service

The Royal Canadian Golf Association (RCGA) supports more than 375 000 members at 1650 golf clubs across Canada and supervises more than 20 golf tournaments annually. The RCGA publishes the Rules of Golf and handicapping and course ratings. It supports turfgrass and environmental research, the Canadian Golf Hall of Fame and Museum, and Canada's junior golf program. Golf tournaments supervised by the RCGA include the Canadian Open, the CN Canadian

Women's Open, along with 6 regional and 10 amateur tournaments, and the CN Canadian Women's Tour. The RCGA was founded in 1895 and has very traditional roots and a very traditional culture.

Until 2003, the RCGA used a local computer located at national headquarters in Oakville, Ontario, to manage all of its tournaments. After organizers entered players' names, the system would generate the foursomes and choose their starting times for each tournament. If there were changes, such as the year Tiger Woods dropped out of the Canadian Open the week before the tournament, or delayed starting times, changes could be made only in Oakville on the local PC. "Anything, from a player who drops out due to bad weather, can affect a tournament. With our previous system, nothing was live, and we had no ability to accommodate changes on-site, where the action was taking place," says Brent McLaughlin, RCGA director of amateur competitions. Players also had to apply by filling out paper forms and either faxing or mailing them to the Oakville office, where each application was entered into the system by hand.

Realizing the lack of efficiency in this system, the RCGA contracted with Martron, Inc., which has offices in Kitchener, Ontario, and Winnipeg, Manitoba. The RCGA realized that its Web site was also inadequate and wanted a more sophisticated, user-friendly, Web site that was easy to update and to find information on.

"Our first step was to take the scores from a local application to a Web site. Then we proposed the development of a Web-based application," says Peter Gingrich, senior account manager with Martron, Inc. Using the .NET framework (discussed in Chapter 5), the new application allows the RCGA to manage its tournaments from a single, Web-based application. A live scoring module permits the RCGA to upload players' scores to the Web site in real time. Kyocera smartphones can be used to access the application and upload scores from the golf course.

The RCGA can make changes to the tournament on the fly. For example, organizers can cancel a round due to a rain delay and reschedule the players, posting the new starting times on the Web in real time. "We now have the ability to be in Newfoundland and operate a tournament in Vancouver using this system and make changes accordingly," says McLaughlin. The RCGA can now also offer online player registration, enabling immediacy in correspondence and response between players and the RCGA. All of this results in lower costs and better player and fan service.

"From a customer service standpoint, the answers are immediate now. Everything has been streamlined, and it filters all the way through the process, down to our volunteers. We employ approximately 12 000 volunteers over the course of a year, and because they all have access to the application via our Web site, they all have the most current data, at all times," says McLaughlin.

The system also more than halved printing and mailing costs for entry forms that would be mailed out. Now the entry forms are available on the Web. Overall, the new Web site for the RCGA is very user-friendly, with easy to find information. The RCGA also hosts other Web sites, such as those devoted to golfers who travel in Canada (**www.rcganetworktravel.org**), to junior golfers (**www.future-links.org**), and to RCGA member clubs and their members (**www.rcganetwork.org**). Each of these Web sites stands on its own but is run by the RCGA, which has developed the capability to develop and manage these sophisticated Web sites.

CASE STUDY QUESTIONS:

1. Why did the RCGA invest in information technology?

2. What were the disadvantages of the old system?

3. What do you think might have been the obstacles to overcome in developing the new tournament application?

4. How do you think the new Web site(s) help the RCGA to fulfill its mission and strategy?

Sources: "Stephen Ross Fired as RCGA Executive Director," March 9, 2007, **www.fairwaysgolf.ca/news.php?id=290&what=news** (accessed September 3, 2009); "RCGA Case Study," **www.martron.com** (accessed June 1, 2007); "RCGA Cuts Costs and Improves Customer Service with Microsoft® .NET-based Online Tournament Program, April 21, 2005, **www.microsoft.com/canada/casestudies/rcga.mspx?pf=true** (accessed September 3, 2009).

CHAPTER 2

How Businesses Use Information Systems

LEARNING OBJECTIVES

After reading this chapter, you will be able to answer the following questions:

1. What are business processes? How are they related to information systems?

2. How do information systems serve the various levels of management in a business?

3. How do enterprise applications, intranets, and collaboration and communication systems improve organizational performance?

4. What is the difference between e-business, e-commerce, and e-government?

5. What is the role of the information systems function in a business?

OPENING CASE

The Tata Nano Makes History Using Digital Manufacturing

On January 10, 2008, India's Tata Motors unveiled its Nano car. It was an historic moment, because the Nano was the cheapest car ever made at that time, with a price tag around $3000. The Nano joined Ford's Model T as a car within reach of millions of people who previously could not afford one.

Tata Motors started its Nano project in 2003, when a team was charged with creating a car that would cost no more than about $3000 without compromising on safety, aesthetics, or value to the customer. It was a Herculean task. Tata met the challenge by using digital manufacturing systems to dramatically shorten the time required to design the new product and bring it to market. The ability to develop and produce new products with many different variations within a very short time span is a key competitive advantage in the automotive industry.

Until a few years ago, it would have been impossible to design and produce the Nano at this price. Tata Motors had outdated manufacturing processes. Manual effort was required to create and maintain processes, plants, and product design, resulting in longer lead times to choose the appropriate tools for an operation. The company had to create programs manually for assembly-line robots, a process that was error-prone and time consuming. These delays had a number of negative consequences: Data used to plan a vehicle became useless over time, and the company was unable to easily change its product mix, roll out a new product on an existing production line, or schedule the assembly of two different products on the same line.

All that changed in July 2005 when Tata Motors switched to digital manufacturing using Dassault Systems' Digital Enterprise Lean Manufacturing Interactive Application (DELMIA). Digital manufacturing automates processes in product design and production engineering planning, enabling Tata to plan manufacturing processes, design plant layouts, and then simulate the repercussions of those plans, including the impact of new manufacturing techniques and changes of products on existing production lines. Digital manufacturing provides data to Tata's SAP enterprise resource planning system, which costs out a product, an assembly or a subassembly. Digital manufacturing also simulates the movements of people working on the shop floor so that planners can design more efficient work processes. Companies using digital manufacturing can model products and operations and make changes to them on the computer. This cuts down on the use of expensive physical prototypes, which must be rebuilt each time a design changes.

According to T.N. Umama-heshwaran, who headed Tata Motors' digital manufacturing program, "We can't imagine what would take place at a new plant if we did not have DM Tools. Two years before the first stone of a plant is

31

laid, we already start working on it. We don't even know where the site will be, but we know what it will take to make 750 cars a day."

As a result of adopting digital manufacturing, Tata Motors has reduced time-to-market for new passenger cars by at least six months. The company can now rapidly identify areas of "work overload" and constraints while quickly adapting assembly lines to accommodate multiple automobile variations. The ability to simulate facilities and processes has reduced the cost of physical rework. Manufacturing and facilities planning now take 30 percent less time, with a 20 percent reduction in the cost of the manufacturing planning process. For certain functions, the time to design an entire process end-to-end has been reduced by more than 50 percent.

Sources: Gunjan Trivedi, "Driving Down Cost," *CIO Asia,* February 2008; Richard Chang, "Nano's Price Is under Pressure," *The New York Times,* August 10, 2008; and **www.tatapeoplescar.com** (accessed July 31, 2008).

The experience of Tata Motors illustrates how much companies today rely on information systems to run their businesses and drive innovation, growth, and profitability. It also shows how much information systems make a difference in a company's ability to innovate, execute, and improve overall business performance.

The chapter-opening diagram calls attention to important points raised by this case and this chapter. Management identified an opportunity to use information systems to improve business performance and radically reduce costs.

Tata Motors was confronted with both a problem and an opportunity. The company operates in a highly competitive industry where manufacturers are expected to bring new car models with many different variations to market very quickly, but Tata Motors was slowed by relying too much on manual processes. Tata management also saw an opportunity to enter a new marketspace, specifically consumers in India and other developing countries who wanted cars but could not afford them. Management decided to design and develop a car for this market and to switch to digital manufacturing for all of its car production. Technology alone would not have provided a solution. The company had to revise many of its manufacturing processes to support digital manufacturing. Once that was accomplished, Dassault's DELMIA software proved invaluable for modelling designs, factories, and production processes and for coordinating information between processes. Digital manufacturing systems increased flexibility and efficiency while decreasing production costs, and made it possible to pioneer in low-cost cars such as the Nano.

2.1 Business Processes and Information Systems

In order to operate, businesses must deal with many different pieces of information about suppliers, customers, employees, invoices, and payments, and of course their products and services. They must organize work activities that use this information to operate efficiently and enhance the overall performance of the firm. Information systems make it possible for firms to manage all their information, make better decisions, and improve the execution of their business processes.

Business Processes

Business processes, which we introduced in Chapter 1, refer to the manner in which work is organized, coordinated, and focused to produce a valuable product or service. Business processes are concrete workflows of material, information, and knowledge—sets of activities. Business processes also refer to the unique ways in which organizations coordinate work, information, and knowledge and the ways in which management chooses to coordinate work.

To a large extent, the performance of a business firm depends on how well its business processes are designed and coordinated. A company's business processes can be a source of competitive strength if they enable the company to innovate or to execute better than its rivals. Business processes can also be liabilities if they are based on outdated ways of working that impede organizational responsiveness and efficiency. The chapter-opening case on Tata Motors' product development and manufacturing processes clearly illustrates these points.

Every business can be seen as a collection of business processes. Some of these processes are part of larger encompassing processes. (In the chapter-opening case, for instance, designing a new car model, manufacturing components, and assembling the finished car are all part of the overall production process.) Many business processes are tied to a specific functional area. For example, the sales and marketing function would be responsible for identifying customers, and the human resources function would be responsible for hiring employees. Table 2-1 describes some typical business processes for each of the functional areas of business.

Other business processes cross many different functional areas and require coordination across departments. For instance, consider the seemingly simple business process of fulfilling a customer order (see Figure 2-1). Initially, the sales department would receive a sales order. The order will pass first to accounting to ensure the customer can pay for

TABLE 2-1   Examples of functional business processes.

FUNCTIONAL AREA	BUSINESS PROCESS
Manufacturing and production	Assembling the product
	Checking for quality
	Producing bills of materials
Sales and marketing	Identifying customers
	Making customers aware of the product
	Selling the product
Finance and accounting	Paying creditors
	Creating financial statements
	Managing cash accounts
Human resources	Hiring employees
	Evaluating employees' job performance
	Enrolling employees in benefits plans

the order either by a credit verification or request for immediate payment prior to shipping. Once the customer credit is established, the production department has to pull the product from inventory or produce the product. Then the product will need to be shipped (which may require working with a logistics firm, such as UPS or DHL). A bill or invoice will then have to be generated by the accounting department, and a notice will be sent to the customer indicating that the product has shipped. Sales will have to be notified of the shipment and prepare to support the customer by answering calls or fulfilling warranty claims.

What at first appears to be a simple process, fulfilling an order, turns out to be a very complicated series of business processes that require the close coordination of major functional groups in a firm. Moreover, efficiently performing all these steps in the order fulfillment process requires a great deal of information. The required information must flow rapidly both within the firm—with business partners, such as delivery firms—and to and from the customer. Computerized information systems make this possible.

FIGURE 2-1   The order fulfillment process.

Fulfilling a customer order involves a complex set of steps that requires the close coordination of the sales, accounting, and manufacturing functions.

How Information Technology Enhances Business Processes

Exactly how do information systems enhance business processes? Information systems automate many steps in business processes that were formerly performed manually, such as checking a client's credit, or generating an invoice and shipping order. But today information technology can do much more. New technology can actually change the flow of information, making it possible for many more people to access and share information, replacing sequential steps with tasks that can be performed simultaneously, and eliminating delays in decision making. It can even transform the way the business works and drive new business models. Ordering a book online from chapters. indigo.ca or downloading a music track from iTunes are entirely new business processes based on new business models that would be inconceivable without information technology.

That is why it is so important to pay close attention to business processes, both in your information systems course and in your future career. By analyzing business processes, you can achieve a very clear understanding of how a business actually works. Moreover, by conducting a business process analysis, you will also begin to understand how to change the business to make it more efficient or effective. Throughout this book, we examine business processes with a view to understanding how they might be changed, or replaced, by using information technology to achieve greater efficiency, innovation, and customer service.

2.2   How Information Systems Serve Management

Now that you understand business processes, it is time to look more closely at how information systems support the business processes of a firm. Because a business may have hundreds or even thousands of different business processes and because there are different interests, specialties, and levels in an organization, there are different kinds of systems. No single system can provide all the information an organization needs.

A typical business organization will have systems supporting processes for each of the major business functions—systems for sales and marketing, manufacturing and production, finance and accounting, and human resources. You can find examples of systems for each of these business functions in the Learning Tracks for this chapter. Functional systems that operate independently of each other are becoming a thing of the past because they cannot easily share information to support cross-functional business processes.

They are being replaced with large-scale cross-functional systems that integrate the activities of related business processes and organizational units. We describe these integrated cross-functional applications in Section 2.3.

A typical business firm will also have different systems supporting the decision-making needs of each of the main management groups we described earlier. Operational management, middle management, and senior management each use a specific type of system to support the decisions they must make to run the company. Let us look at these systems and the types of decisions they support.

Transaction Processing Systems

Operational managers need systems that keep track of the elementary activities and transactions of the organization, such as sales, receipts, cash deposits, payroll, credit decisions, and the flow of materials in a factory. **Transaction processing systems (TPS)** provide this kind of information. A transaction processing system is a computerized system that performs and records the daily routine transactions necessary to conduct business, such as sales order entry, hotel reservations, payroll, employee record keeping, and shipping.

The principal purpose of systems at this level is to answer routine questions and to track the flow of transactions through the organization. How many parts are in inventory? What happened to Mr. Williams's payment? To answer these kinds of questions, information generally must be easily available, current, and accurate.

Transaction processing
systems (TPS)

FIGURE 2-2   A payroll TPS.

A TPS for payroll processing captures employee payment transaction data (such as a time card). System outputs include online and hard-copy reports for management and employee paycheques.

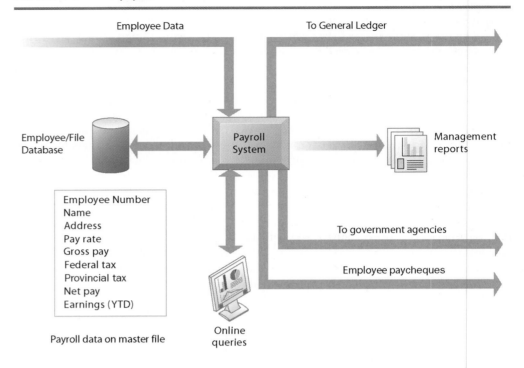

At the operational level, tasks, resources, and goals are predefined and highly structured. The decision to grant credit to a customer, for instance, is made by a lower-level supervisor according to predefined criteria. All that must be determined is whether the customer meets the criteria.

Figure 2-2 illustrates a TPS for payroll processing. A payroll system keeps track of money paid to employees. An employee time card with the employee's name, social insurance number, and number of hours worked per week represents a single transaction for this system. Once this transaction is input into the system, it updates the system's file or database (see Chapter 6) that permanently maintains employee information for the organization. The data in the system are combined in different ways to create reports of interest to management and government agencies and to send paycheques to employees.

Managers need TPS to monitor the status of internal operations and the firm's relations with the external environment. TPS are also major producers of information for the other types of systems. For example, the payroll system illustrated in Figure 2-2, along with other accounting TPS, supplies data to the company's general ledger system, which is responsible for maintaining records of the firm's income and expenses and for producing reports such as income statements and balance sheets. It also supplies employee payment history data for insurance, pension, and other benefits calculations to the firm's human resource systems and employee payment data to government agencies.

Transaction processing systems are often so central to a business that TPS failure for a few hours can lead to a firm's demise and perhaps that of other firms linked to it. Imagine what would happen to UPS if its package tracking system were not working. What would the large retailers do without their computerized systems? (See the chapter-ending case study on Zellers.)

Management Information Systems and Decision-Support Systems

Middle management needs systems to help with monitoring, controlling, decision-making, and administrative activities. The principal question addressed by such systems is this: Are things working well?

In Chapter 1, we defined management information systems as the study of information systems in business and management. The term **management information systems (MIS)**

Management information systems (MIS)

FIGURE 2-3 How management information systems obtain their data from the organization's TPS.

In the system illustrated by this diagram, three TPS supply summarized transaction data to the MIS reporting system at the end of the time period. Managers gain access to the organizational data through the MIS, which provides them with the appropriate reports.

also designates a specific category of information systems serving middle management. MIS provide middle managers with reports on the organization's current performance. This information is used to monitor and control the business and predict future performance.

MIS summarize and report on the company's basic operations using data supplied by transaction processing systems. The basic transaction data from TPS are compressed and usually presented in reports that are produced on a regular schedule. Today, many of these reports are delivered online.

Figure 2-3 shows how a typical MIS transforms transaction-level data from inventory, production, and accounting into MIS files that are used to provide managers with reports. Figure 2-4 shows a sample report from this system.

MIS serve managers primarily interested in weekly, monthly, and yearly results although some MIS enable managers to drill down to see daily or hourly data if required. MIS generally provide answers to routine questions that have been specified in advance and have a predefined procedure for answering them. For instance, MIS reports might list the total pounds of lettuce used this quarter by a fast-food chain or, as illustrated in Figure 2-4, compare total annual sales figures for specific products to planned targets. These systems generally are not flexible and have little analytical capability. Most MIS use simple routines,

FIGURE 2-4 Sample MIS report.

This report, showing summarized annual sales data, was produced by the MIS in Figure 2-3.

Consolidated Consumer Products Corporation Sales by Product and Sales Region: 2009

PRODUCT CODE	PRODUCT DESCRIPTION	SALES REGION	ACTUAL SALES	PLANNED	ACTUAL versus PLANNED
4469	Carpet Cleaner	Maritimes	4 066 700	4 800 000	0.85
		ON/QC	3 778 112	3 750 000	1.01
		Prairies	4 867 001	4 600 000	1.06
		BC	4 003 440	4 400 000	0.91
	TOTAL		16 715 253	17 550 000	0.95
5674	Room Freshener	Northeast	3 676 700	3 900 000	0.94
		South	5 608 112	4 700 000	1.19
		Midwest	4 711 001	4 200 000	1.12
		West	4 563 440	4 900 000	0.93
	TOTAL		18 559 253	17 700 000	1.05

such as summaries and comparisons, as opposed to sophisticated mathematical models or statistical techniques.

Decision-support systems (DSS) support nonroutine decision making for middle management. They focus on problems that are unique and rapidly changing, for which the procedure for arriving at a solution may not be fully predefined in advance. They try to answer questions such as these: What would be the impact on production schedules if we were to double sales in the month of December? What would happen to our return on investment if a factory schedule were delayed for six months?

Although DSS use internal information from TPS and MIS, they often bring in information from external sources, such as current stock prices or product prices of competitors. These systems use a variety of models to analyze data, or they condense large amounts of data into a form in which decision makers can analyze them. DSS are designed so that users can work with them directly; these systems explicitly include user-friendly software.

An interesting, small, but powerful DSS is the voyage-estimating system of a subsidiary of a Canadian metals company that exists primarily to carry bulk cargoes of coal, oil, ores, and finished products for its parent company. The firm owns some vessels, charters others, and bids for shipping contracts in the open market to carry general cargo. A voyage-estimating system calculates financial and technical voyage details. Financial calculations include ship/time costs (fuel, labour, capital), freight rates for various types of cargo, and port expenses. Technical details include a myriad of factors, such as ship cargo capacity, speed, port distances, fuel and water consumption, and loading patterns (location of cargo for different ports).

The system can answer questions such as the following: Given a customer delivery schedule and an offered freight rate, which vessel should be assigned at what rate to maximize profits? What is the optimal speed at which a particular vessel can optimize its profit and still meet its delivery schedule? What is the optimal loading pattern for a ship bound for Vancouver from Malaysia? Figure 2-5 illustrates the DSS developed for this company. The system operates on a powerful desktop personal computer, providing a system of menus that makes it easy for users to enter data or obtain information.

This voyage-estimating DSS draws heavily on analytical models. Other types of DSS are less model-driven, focusing instead on extracting useful information to support decision making from massive quantities of data. For example, Intrawest—the largest ski operator in North America—collects and stores vast amounts of customer data from its Web site, call centre, lodging reservations, ski schools, and ski equipment rental stores.

Decision-support systems (DSS)

FIGURE 2-5 Voyage-estimating decision-support system.

This DSS operates on a powerful PC. It is used daily by managers who must develop bids on shipping contracts.

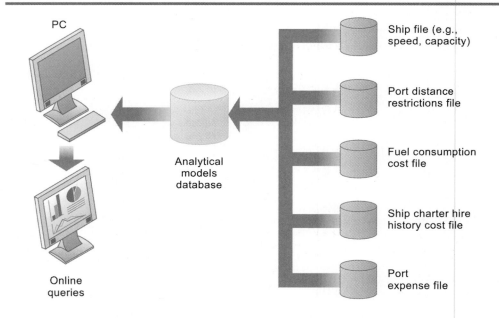

It uses special software to analyze these data to determine the value, revenue potential, and loyalty of each customer so managers can make better decisions on how to target their marketing programs. The system segments customers into seven categories based on needs, attitudes, and behaviours, ranging from "passionate experts" to "value-minded family vacationers." The company then e-mails video clips that would appeal to each segment to encourage more visits to its resorts.

Sometimes you will hear DSS referred to as business intelligence systems because they focus on helping users make better business decisions. You will learn more about them in Chapters 6 and 14.

The Window on Technology describes another example of a system for decision support. Air Canada adopted Maintenix software for its aviation maintenance program to help schedule and organize aircraft maintenance work. Try to identify the decision-support applications detailed in the case and the kinds of decisions they support.

Technology

WINDOW ON TECHNOLOGY

Air Canada Takes Off with Maintenix

Air Canada is Canada's most prominent airline. It is the largest provider of scheduled passenger services in the Canadian market, the Canada–U.S. transborder market, and the international market to and from Canada. The airline serves more than 33 million customers annually and provides direct passenger service to more than 170 destinations on five continents. But the company's information systems had plenty of room for improvement. When Air Canada technicians worked on planes, they used several different legacy software packages installed over the past 15 years. The systems weren't able to interact with one another or with finance and inventory systems. The inefficiencies of these systems were costing Air Canada the time of its engineers and money that could have been used on maintaining its planes, instead of needlessly maintaining excess inventory.

Air Canada turned to Mxi Technologies for help in addressing these problems. Mxi is renowned in the airline industry for its Maintenix software package, which provides integrated, intelligent aviation MRO (maintenance, repair, and operations) software to aviation organizations hoping to improve productivity. The benefits of Maintenix that interested Air Canada were enhanced visibility of fleet-wide data, timelier decision making, support of its currently existing business model, and increased operational efficiencies.

Maintenix provides a system platform that is accessible via the Web and easy to deploy to all stations around the world. Mxi claims that its software reduces repetitive tasks and time spent chasing missing or incomplete information by allowing maintenance, engineering, and finance divisions to easily share information. Maintenix can supply data to the company's existing enterprise resource planning (see Section 2.3) and financial software, and Air Canada plans to link it up with its PeopleSoft finance and human resource applications. Wireless deployment also makes Maintenix more effective

since aviation technicians, equipment, and parts are always on the move.

The Maintenix software package consists of six different modules, which are separate segments of the product that interconnect. Airlines deploying Maintenix can choose which modules they want to use as well as whether they want full or partial installation of those modules. The six modules are maintenance engineering, line maintenance, materials management, heavy maintenance, shop maintenance, and finance. Air Canada chose to fully implement the maintenance engineering, line maintenance, and materials management modules. The airline chose to only partially implement the heavy maintenance, shop maintenance, and finance modules because a separate contractor that also maintains Air Canada planes handles those tasks.

The maintenance engineering module is the foundation of the Maintenix system. It is used to establish the configuration hierarchy, rules, and maintenance program that all of the other modules depend upon. Through this module, the airline can set up a "logical configuration," which describes aircraft components, part relationships, and compatibility rules.

Line maintenance involves matching a dynamic list of maintenance work requirements against finite resources at varying locations within a flight schedule that is constantly undergoing change.

The module includes line station planning applications, which are designed to schedule maintenance and allocate work, based on the capabilities of the line station facilities as well as the aircrafts' scheduled locations. For example, this module allows Air Canada to ensure that qualified technicians are available before scheduling maintenance.

The materials management module deals with the logistically complex process of ensuring availability of parts without overstocking. Maintenix ensures that the minimum amount of each part is always in inventory without causing engineers to be short on parts at any time. Maintaining this delicate balance is critical in order to maximize revenue and achieve greater operational efficiencies. Maintenix allows wireless, real-time management of inventory, automates routine activities, and integrates fully with Air Canada's existing inventory management systems.

The biggest advantage of the system is that all of this information provided by Maintenix's various modules is located in one place. This results in more rapid scheduling and avoids pitfalls of poorly organized information systems, such as scheduling work to a station that lacks the proper qualifications to accomplish it.

One example of how Maintenix will increase Air Canada's efficiency might be as follows. An Air Canada technician requests a part she needs for maintenance from supply. Maintenix automatically processes the request. If the required part is available, Maintenix automatically reserves it, and the appropriate personnel are immediately informed that the part is ready to be picked for issue. In the meantime, the technician is easily able to track the status of the part requests and is made aware once the part is ready to be collected. If any change happens and the part is unavailable, Maintenix will notify the technician. As a result, technicians can accomplish more maintenance work as opposed to managing details that Maintenix is now handling via automation. This leads to increased productivity and increased profitability. The system is expected to be fully implemented in 2010.

To Think About

1. What problems does Air Canada hope that Maintenix will solve?
2. How does Maintenix improve operational efficiency and decision making?
3. Give examples of three decisions supported by the Maintenix system. What information do the Maintenix modules provide to support each of these decisions?

MIS in Action

Visit the Mxi Technologies Web site (**www.mxi.com**), and examine the Maintenix modules for heavy maintenance, shop maintenance, and finance modules. Then answer the following questions:

1. How could an airline benefit from implementing these modules?
2. Give an example of a decision that each of these modules supports.

Sources: Greg Meckbach, "Air Canada to Overhaul Maintenance Software," *ComputerWorld Canada*, April 18, 2008; "Air Canada Selects Maintenix for Fleetwide Implementation," Reuters, April 15, 2008; "Maintenix Product Overview," www.mxi.com (accessed September 24, 2009).

Executive Support Systems for Senior Management

Senior managers need systems that address strategic issues and long-term trends, both in the firm and in the external environment. Senior managers are concerned with questions such as these: What will employment levels be in five years? What are the long-term industry cost trends, and where does our firm fit in? What products should we be making in five years? What new acquisitions would protect us from cyclical business swings?

Executive support systems (ESS) help senior management make these decisions. ESS address nonroutine decisions requiring judgment, evaluation, and insight because there is no agreed-on procedure for arriving at a solution. ESS present graphs and data from many sources through an interface that is easy for senior managers to use. Often the information is delivered to senior executives through a **portal**, which uses a Web interface to present integrated personalized business content. You will learn more about other applications of portals in Chapters 13 and 15.

ESS are designed to incorporate data about external events, such as new tax laws or competitors, but they also draw summarized information from internal MIS and DSS. They filter, compress, and track critical data, displaying the data of greatest importance to senior managers. For example, the CEO of Leiner Health Products, the largest manufacturer of private-label vitamins and supplements in the United States, has an ESS that provides on his desktop a minute-to-minute view of the firm's financial performance as measured by working capital, accounts receivable, accounts payable, cash flow, and inventory. The information is presented in the form of a digital dashboard, which displays on a single screen graphs and charts of key performance indicators for managing a company. **Digital dashboards** are becoming an increasingly popular feature of ESS.

Executive support systems (ESS)
Portal
Digital dashboards

FIGURE 2-6   Model of an executive support system.

This system pools data from diverse internal and external sources and makes them available to executives in an easy-to-use form.

Figure 2-6 illustrates a model of an ESS. It consists of workstations with menus, interactive graphics, and communications capabilities that can be used to access historical and competitive data from internal corporate systems and external databases such as Dow Jones News/Retrieval or Gallup. More details on leading-edge applications of DSS and ESS can be found in Chapter 14.

The Window on Organizations section on the next page describes Kia's quality improvement system that not only informs management of quality problems but also helps identify sources of defects in Kia automobiles. Kia uses the information from the system to improve its production processes to eliminate or reduce defects. Improving vehicle quality lowers Kia's costs for warranty repairs while increasing customer satisfaction. As you read this case, try to identify the problems facing this company, how information systems are helping it solve them, and the management, organization, and technology issues it must address.

Note the types of systems illustrated by this case and the role they play in improving both operations and decision making.

2.3   Systems That Span the Enterprise

Reviewing all the different types of systems we have just described, you might wonder how a business can manage all the information in these different systems. In fact, getting all the different kinds of systems in a company to work together has proven to be a major challenge. There are several solutions to this problem.

Enterprise Applications

One solution is to implement **enterprise applications,** which are systems that span functional areas, focus on executing business processes across the business firm, and include all levels of management. Enterprise applications help businesses become more flexible and productive by coordinating their business processes more closely and integrating groups of processes so they focus on efficient management of resources and customer service.

Enterprise applications

Information Systems Help Kia Solve Its Quality Problems

A decade ago, few Canadians had heard of Korean car maker Kia Motors. The company started selling cars in North America in 1994, promising high-quality vehicles at prices well below the competition. That year, Kia sold 12 163 vehicles. Kia Canada's sales increased almost 8 percent in 2008 to 37 500 units; Kias are 10 to 15 percent cheaper than comparable vehicles by competitors.

From a marketing and sales standpoint, Kia has been a phenomenal success. But until 2002, Kia ranked at the bottom of J.D. Power and Associates' annual initial-quality survey of new vehicle owners. In 1997, when the average North American car had 1.1 defects per vehicle, Kia had 2.75. In 2002, Kia had improved to 2.12 defects per vehicle, but the industry average was 1.33. Kia had a long way to go, and this was affecting its ability to sell cars, retain customers, and keep operational costs down.

Kia has tried to keep customers happy despite its quality problems by offering a 5 year/100,000 kilometre warranty program, which provides coverage until either the yearly or total mileage figure is reached, whichever occurs first. That means that Kia must pay for repairs on all warrantied items in its vehicles for many more years than its competitors are willing to do for their products, which raises operating costs and eats into profits.

Like all manufacturers of vehicles sold in the United States, Kia had to create a system by December 1, 2003, to report any defects, accidents, or injuries involving its vehicles to the U.S. National Highway Traffic Safety Administration (NHTSA). This was a major challenge for the company. The information Kia had to report was stored in at least seven different systems run by Kia's warranty, parts, consumer, and legal affairs departments.

Fragmentation of this information in different systems prevented Kia from getting a complete picture of defects. Parts sales are the first indicator of a defect, warranty claims the second, and consumer complaints the third. Looking at parts sales alone will not provide an answer. A sudden increase in brake pad orders from Kia dealers making repairs indicates there might be a problem with a particular pad.

By examining warranty claims, Kia might discover that brake pads were being ordered only for four-wheel drive models of one of its vehicles and not for two-wheel drive models. This additional information might show that the problem was actually a result of excess vibration caused by the vehicle's design rather than the brake pads.

Kia could have created a series of stopgap software programs to extract the required information from these various computer systems and collate it manually. But this would have been time consuming and would not provide any other benefits to the company. So Kia's management decided instead to create a defect early warning system that could identify potential problems, such as faulty brake parts, by combining warranty claims, parts orders, field reports, and consumer complaints.

Kia enlisted Infogain, a Los Gatos, California, software consulting firm to help it design a new system solution. Infogain created a software "engine" that examines six Kia systems for warranty claims, parts sales, vehicle identification number master storage files, and vehicle inventories and stores the essential information in a single common data repository. The system automatically breaks down and categorizes reports based on individual components, such as steering assemblies or headlights, and links to Kia's Clarify customer relationship management system, tracking consumer complaints received by phone, e-mail, or postal mail.

Once the data have been stored in a single place, Kia can use Crystal Analysis software to analyze them, highlighting events, such as spikes in warranty claims related to a particular vehicle model, unusual increases in parts orders, or high numbers of accidents resulting in serious injury or death, on an early-warning dashboard. Managers are able to analyze the data by daily, weekly, or monthly reporting periods and by specific car models, model years, and components. They also can break down the data in detail to see how many complaints or warranty claims are associated with a specific item, such as a steering assembly.

Information from this system is helping Kia pinpoint the sources of defects and determine what percentage of its vehicles is likely to have problems. The company can then improve its production processes before the problems become more widespread, thus lowering costs for warranty repairs. This information also helps Kia determine the most cost-effective strategy for dealing with its quality problems. For example, should Kia recall all batteries if battery defects occur in extreme heat or limit recalls to vehicle sold in hotter climes?

Kia's quality has indeed improved. In quality rankings released on May 18, 2005, J.D. Power reported that Kia had 1.40 problems per vehicle, finishing second for quality in the compact-car category behind the Toyota Prius. According to Hirofumi Yokoi, an analyst with auto industry consulting firm CSM Worldwide, today "Kia quality is relatively comparable" with more established automakers.

To Think About

1. Why was it so difficult for Kia to identify sources of defects in the cars it produced?

2. What was the business impact of Kia's not having an information system to track defects? What other business processes besides manufacturing and production were affected?

3. How did Kia's new defect-reporting system improve the way it ran its business?

4. What management, organization, and technology issues did Kia have to address when it adopted its new quality control system?

5. What new business processes were enabled by Kia's new quality control system?

MIS in Action

1. Visit the Autobytel Web site (**www.autobytel.com**—or check out **Canadacar.com,** and select a Kia model for your research. Investigate the retail price, warranties, and any relevant reviews and safety data. Select a comparable model (suggested by Autobytel) from another automobile manufacturer, and gather the same data for that make and model.

2. Visit the J.D. Power Web site (**www.jdpower.com**), and explore the Ratings section under the Autos tab. Examine Kia's overall quality rating and the quality ratings for overall quality manufacturing, mechanical quality manufacturing,

and body and interior quality manufacturing. Compare Kia's quality ratings to the quality ratings for the competing automaker you have been researching.

3. Create a table comparing the two cars you have selected on the basis of price, warranties, and quality. Would you select the Kia? Why or why not?

There are four major enterprise applications: enterprise systems, supply chain management systems, customer relationship management systems, and knowledge management systems. Each of these enterprise applications integrates a related set of functions and business processes to enhance the performance of the organization as a whole. Figure 2-7 shows that the architecture for these enterprise applications encompasses processes spanning the entire organization and, in some cases, extending beyond the organization to customers, suppliers, and other key business partners.

Sources: Craig Simons, "Kia Makes U.S. Inroads and Builds for Future Growth," Cox News Service, March 14, 2006; Mel Duvall, "Kia Motors America: Lemon Aid," *Baseline Magazine,* June 2005; and **www.kia.com** (accessed June 18, 2006).

FIGURE 2-7   Enterprise application architecture.

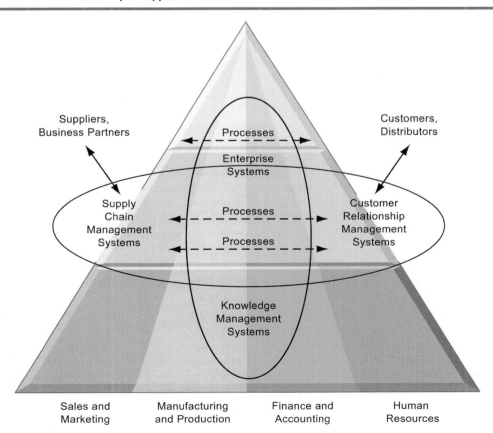

Enterprise applications automate processes that span multiple business functions and organizational levels and may extend outside the organization.

FIGURE 2-8   Enterprise systems.

Enterprise systems integrate the key business processes of an entire firm into a single software system that enables information to flow seamlessly throughout the organization. These systems focus primarily on internal processes but may include transactions with customers and vendors.

Enterprise Systems A large organization typically has many different kinds of information systems built around different functions, organizational levels, and business processes that cannot automatically exchange information. This fragmentation of data in hundreds of separate systems ("silos of information") degrades organizational efficiency and business performance. For instance, sales personnel might not be able to tell at the time they place an order whether the ordered items are in inventory, and manufacturing cannot easily use sales data to plan for new production.

Enterprise systems, also known as *enterprise resource planning (ERP)* systems, solve this problem by collecting data from various key business processes in manufacturing and production, finance and accounting, sales and marketing, and human resources, and storing the data in a single central data repository. Information that was previously fragmented in different systems can be easily shared across the firm to help different parts of the business work more closely together (see Figure 2-8).

For example, when a customer places an order, the data flow automatically to other parts of the company that are affected by them. The order transaction triggers the warehouse to pick the ordered products and schedule shipment. The warehouse informs the factory to replenish whatever has depleted. The accounting department is notified to send the customer an invoice. Customer service representatives track the progress of the order through every step to inform customers about the status of their orders. Improved coordination between these different parts of the business lowers costs while increasing customer satisfaction.

Air Liquide, the world's leading supplier of industrial and medical gases, operates more than 500 production sites worldwide, 250 of which are in Europe. Over the years, the company had implemented a large variety of systems to serve these sites. Acquisitions of new subsidiaries added to the number of systems the company maintained; at one time, the company had 800 individual applications running across Europe. This patchwork of uncoordinated local systems prevented Air Liquide from easily shipping products across European national borders. Implementing mySAP ERP software allowed the company to centralize business processes that had previously been handled locally or nationally and replace its tangled legacy systems with centralized integrated software supporting the activities of the company as a whole. Air Liquide now has a common set of applications, consistent business processes, and integrated master data while still allowing international subsidiaries some measure of flexibility to adapt to local conditions (SAP AG, 2007).

Supply Chain Management Systems **Supply chain management (SCM) systems** help businesses manage relationships with their suppliers. These systems help suppliers, purchasing firms, distributors, and logistics companies share information about orders,

Enterprise systems
Supply chain management (SCM) systems

production, inventory levels, and delivery of products and services so that they can make better decisions about how to organize and schedule sourcing, production, and distribution. The ultimate objective is to get the right amount of their products from their source to their point of consumption with the least amount of time and with the lowest cost.

Supply chain management systems are one type of **interorganizational system** because they automate the flow of information across organizational boundaries. You will find examples of other types of interorganizational information systems throughout this text because these systems make it possible for firms to link electronically to customers and to outsource their work to other companies.

For example, until it implemented a supply chain management system from SAP, Montréal-based Alcan Packaging had trouble fulfilling customer orders for its packaging materials for food, pharmaceuticals, and cosmetics. It did not have the information to make good decisions about how much to produce, how to allocate personnel, or how to meet the delivery dates requested by customers. It would go from working employees overtime one month to cutting back staff the next. It could not accurately project when it would meet shipment requirements (SAP, 2005).

Customer Relationship Management Systems **Customer relationship management (CRM) systems** help firms manage their relationships with their customers. CRM systems provide information to coordinate all of the business processes that deal with customers in sales, marketing, and service to optimize revenue, customer satisfaction, and customer retention. This information helps firms identify, attract, and retain the most profitable customers; provide better service to existing customers; and increase sales.

CRM systems consolidate and integrate customer information from multiple communication channels—telephone, e-mail, wireless devices, retail outlets, and the Web. Detailed and accurate knowledge of customers and their preferences helps firms increase the effectiveness of their marketing campaigns and provide higher-quality customer service and support. Figure 2-9 illustrates some of the functions of Salesforce.com, a leading vendor of software-as-a-service customer relationship management systems.

Interorganizational system

Customer relationship management (CRM) systems

FIGURE 2-9   Salesforce.com is one of the leading vendors of CRM software.

Illustrated here are some of the capabilities of Salesforce.com, a market-leading provider of on-demand customer relationship management (CRM) software. CRM systems integrate information from sales, marketing, and customer service.

For example, Saab U.S.A., which imports and distributes vehicles to U.S. dealerships, used CRM applications for automotive dealers from Oracle-Siebel Systems to integrate data that were distributed among systems supporting its dealer network, a customer service assistance centre, and a lead management centre. The CRM systems provide a 360-degree view of each Saab customer, including prior service-related questions and all the marketing communication the customer has ever received. The systems provide detailed information to measure the sales results of specific leads, and target leads are directed more precisely to the right salespeople at the right dealerships. Since the CRM applications were implemented, Saab's follow-up rate on sales leads has increased from 38 to 50 percent, and customer satisfaction rose from 69 to 75 percent.

Knowledge Management Systems The value of a firm's products and services is based not only on its physical resources but also on intangible knowledge assets. Some firms perform better than others because they have better knowledge about how to create, produce, and deliver products and services. This firm knowledge is difficult to imitate, is unique, and can be leveraged into long-term strategic benefits. **Knowledge management systems (KMS)** enable organizations to better manage processes for capturing and applying knowledge and expertise. These systems collect all relevant knowledge and experience in the firm and make it available wherever and whenever it is needed to improve business processes and management decisions. They also link the firm to external sources of knowledge.

KMS support processes for acquiring, storing, distributing, and applying knowledge, as well as processes for creating new knowledge and integrating it into the organization. They include enterprise-wide systems for managing and distributing documents, graphics, and other digital knowledge objects; systems for creating corporate knowledge directories of employees with special areas of expertise; office systems for distributing knowledge and information; and knowledge work systems to facilitate knowledge creation. Other knowledge management applications use intelligent techniques that codify knowledge for use by other members of the organization and tools for knowledge discovery that recognize patterns and important relationships in large pools of data.

We examine enterprise systems and systems for supply chain management and customer relationship management in greater detail in Chapter 12 and cover knowledge management applications in Chapter 15.

Intranets and Extranets

Enterprise applications create deep-seated changes in the way the firm conducts its business, and they are often costly to implement. To coordinate their activities, many different departments and employees must change the way they work and the way they use information. Companies that do not have the resources to invest in enterprise applications can still achieve some measure of information integration by using intranets and extranets, which we introduced in Chapter 1.

Intranets and extranets are really more technology platforms than specific applications, but they deserve mention here as one of the tools firms use to increase integration and expedite the flow of information within the firm, and with customers and suppliers. Intranets are internal networks built with the same tools and communication standards as the Internet and are used for the internal distribution of information to employees, and as repositories of corporate policies, programs, and data. Extranets are intranets extended to authorized users outside the company. We describe the technology for intranets and extranets in more detail in Chapter 7.

An intranet typically centres on a portal that provides a single point of access to information from several different systems and to documents using a Web interface. These portals can be customized to suit the information needs of specific business groups and individual users if required. They may also feature e-mail, collaboration tools, and tools for searching internal corporate systems and documents.

For example, SwissAir's corporate intranet for sales provides its salespeople with sales leads, fares, statistics, libraries of best practices, access to incentive programs, discussion

Knowledge management
systems (KMS)

groups, and collaborative workspaces. The intranet includes a Sales Ticket capability that displays bulletins about unfilled airplane seats around the world to help the sales staff work with colleagues and with travel agents who can help them fill those seats.

Companies can connect their intranets to internal company transaction systems, enabling employees to take actions central to a company's operations, such as checking the status of an order or granting a customer credit. SwissAir's intranet connects to its reservation system.

Extranets expedite the flow of information between the firm and its suppliers and customers. SwissAir uses an extranet to provide travel agents with fare data from its intranet electronically. GUESS Jeans allows store buyers to order merchandise electronically from ApparelBuy.com. The buyers can use this extranet to track their orders through fulfillment or delivery.

Collaboration and Communication Systems: "Interaction" Jobs in a Global Economy

With all these systems and information, you might wonder how it is possible to make sense out of them. How do people working in firms pull it all together, work toward common goals, and coordinate plans and actions? Information systems cannot make decisions, hire or fire people, sign contracts, agree on deals, or adjust the price of goods to the marketplace.

The number of people who perform these tasks in a firm is growing. Blue-collar production jobs are now down to 15 percent of the labour force, and transactional jobs—filling out forms or reports or accepting payments—are now 25 percent of the labour force. Moreover, the "interaction" jobs are the fastest growing: 70 percent of all new jobs created since 1998 are "interaction" jobs.

With globalization, firms have teams around the globe in different time zones working on the same problem, so the need for continuous interaction and communication around the clock has greatly expanded. Working 24/7 is not just a problem for call centres, but involves a much larger group of managers and employees than in the past.

Jobs such as sales representative, marketing manager, stock analyst, corporate lawyer, business strategist, or operations manager require sharing information and interacting with other people. Here are some business decisions that require knowledge based on collaboration and interaction:

- How much should we charge for this service?
- What kind of discount should we give a customer who is considering our competitor?
- Should we sign a three-year contract with a vendor, or would we be safer with a one-year contract?
- Should we make a special deal with our largest distributor, or work with all distributors on an equal basis?
- Should we put our price list on the Web site where our competitors can see it?
- Where should we be looking for new lines of business?

The answers to these questions generally cannot be found in structured information systems such as those we have described earlier in this chapter. True, these systems help managers and employees by making essential information available. But what is needed to complete these decisions is face-to-face interaction with other employees, managers, vendors, and customers, along with systems that allow them to communicate, collaborate, and share ideas.

We now briefly introduce some of the enterprise-wide information system solutions used by business firms for this purpose. They include Internet-based collaboration environments, e-mail and instant messaging (IM), communication via cell phones and other mobile devices, social networking, wikis, and virtual worlds. Chapters 7, 13, and 15 describe these solutions in greater detail.

In the past, these collaboration and communication systems were not considered an essential part of the information systems field or even an IT management concern. Today this has changed, and our view of information systems is extended to include these vital management tools.

Internet-Based Collaboration Environments Teams of employees who work together from many different locations around the world need tools to support workgroup collaboration. These tools provide storage space for team documents, a space separate from corporate e-mail for team communications, group calendars, and an audio-visual environment where members can "meet" face to face in a live video conference (see the Chapter 1 Window on Management on page 8). Products such as IBM's Lotus Sametime and Internet conferencing systems such as WebEx, Microsoft Office Live Meeting, and Adobe Acrobat Connect are especially helpful.

E-mail and Instant Messaging (IM) Worldwide, there are an estimated 210 billion legitimate e-mail messages sent each day. One in six people in the world use e-mail. There are also about 12 billion instant messages sent every day, 8 billion of which originate in business networks. E-mail and instant messaging have been embraced by corporations as a major communication and collaboration tool to support interaction jobs.

Cell Phones and Smartphones Chapter 1 has described new mobile platforms that have emerged for coordinating and running businesses, including cell phones and smartphones such as iPhones and BlackBerrys. More than 12 million BlackBerry subscribers use wireless devices made by Canada's Research in Motion for e-mail, text messaging, instant messaging, phone, and wireless Internet connections. Cell phones are today a basic part of a firm's telecommunications infrastructure for supporting professionals and other employees whose primary job is talking with one another, with customers and vendors, and with their managers. Cell phones, iPhones, and BlackBerrys are digital devices, and the data generated by their communications may be stored in large corporate systems for later review and use in legal proceedings.

Social Networking We have all visited social networking sites such as MySpace and Facebook, which feature tools to help people share their interests and interact. Social networking sites such as LinkedIn.com provide networking services to business professionals while other niche sites have sprung up to serve lawyers, doctors, engineers, and dentists. IBM has built a Connections component into its Lotus collaboration software to add social networking features. Users are able to set up profiles, blog, tag documents of interest, and use online forums to communicate with other co-workers about their interests and projects. Social networking tools are quickly becoming a corporate tool for sharing ideas and collaborating among interaction-based jobs in the firm.

Wikis Wikis are a type of Web site that makes it easy for users to contribute and edit text content and graphics without any knowledge of Web page development or programming techniques. The most well-known wiki is Wikipedia, one of the largest collaboratively edited reference projects in the world. It relies on volunteers, makes no money, accepts no advertising, and is used by 35 million people in the United States alone. It has become the world's most successful online encyclopedia, with more than 20 percent of the online reference market.

Wikis are ideal tools for storing and sharing company knowledge and insights. Enterprise software vendor SAP AG has a wiki that acts as a base of information for people outside the company, such as customers and software developers who develop programs that interact with SAP software. In the past, those people asked and sometimes answered questions in an informal way on SAP online forums, but that was an inefficient system, with people asking and answering the same questions over and over.

At Intel Corporation, employees developed their own internal wiki in 2006, and it has been edited about 100 000 times and viewed more than 27 million times by Intel employees. The most common search is for the meaning of Intel acronyms such as EASE for "employee access support environment" and POR for "plan of record." Other popular resources include a page about software-engineering processes at the company. Wikis are destined to become a major repository for unstructured corporate knowledge in part because they are so much less costly than formal knowledge management systems and they can be much more dynamic and current.

Virtual Worlds The case study concluding Chapter 15 features a detailed description of Second Life, an online 3-D **virtual world** where 14 million "residents" have established lives by building graphical representations of themselves known as avatars. Organizations such as IBM and Insead, an international business school with campuses in France and Singapore, are using this virtual world to house online meetings, training sessions, and "lounges." Canada Post has a "shopping island" in Second Life. Real-world people represented by avatars meet, interact, and exchange ideas at these virtual locations. Communication takes place in the form of text messages similar to instant messages.

E-Business, E-Commerce, and E-Government

The systems and technologies we have just described are transforming firms' relationships with customers, employees, suppliers, and logistic partners into digital relationships by using networks and the Internet. So much business is now enabled by or based upon digital networks that we use the terms *electronic business* and *electronic commerce* frequently throughout this text. **Electronic business,** or **e-business,** refers to the use of digital technology and the Internet to execute the major business processes in the enterprise. E-business includes activities for the internal management of the firm and for coordination with suppliers and other business partners. It also includes **electronic commerce,** or **e-commerce.** E-commerce is the part of e-business that deals with the buying and selling of goods and services over the Internet. It also encompasses activities supporting those market transactions, such as advertising, marketing, customer support, security, delivery, and payment.

The technologies associated with e-business have also brought about similar changes in the public sector. Governments on all levels are using Internet technology to deliver information and services to citizens, employees, and businesses with which they work. **E-government** refers to the application of the Internet and networking technologies to digitally enable government and public sector agencies' relationships with citizens, businesses, and other arms of government. In addition to improving delivery of government services, e-government can make government operations more efficient and also empower citizens by giving them easier access to information and the ability to network electronically with government agencies and with other citizens. For example, Canadian citizens can conduct most of their passport application process online. The Internet has become a powerful tool for instantly mobilizing interest groups for political action and fund raising.

2.4   The Information Systems Function in Business

We have seen that businesses need information systems to operate today and that they use many different kinds of systems. But who is responsible for running these systems? Who is responsible for making sure the hardware, software, and other technologies used by these systems are running properly and are up to date? End users manage their systems from a business standpoint, but managing the technology requires a special information systems function. Chapter 10 provides more detail on this critical business area, but a brief introduction is needed here.

In all but the smallest of firms, the **information systems department** is the formal organizational unit responsible for information technology services. The information systems department is responsible for maintaining the hardware, software, data storage, and networks that comprise the firm's IT infrastructure. We describe IT infrastructure in detail in Chapter 5.

Virtual world
Electronic business
E-business
Electronic commerce
E-commerce
E-government
Information systems department

The Information Systems Department

The information systems department consists of specialists, such as programmers, systems analysts, project leaders, and information systems managers. **Programmers** are highly trained technical specialists who write the software instructions for computers. **Systems analysts** constitute the principal liaisons between the information systems groups and the rest of the organization. It is the systems analyst's job to translate business problems and requirements into information requirements and systems. **Information systems managers** are leaders of teams of programmers and analysts, project managers, physical facility managers, telecommunications managers, or database specialists. They are also managers of computer operations and data entry staff. In addition, external specialists, such as hardware vendors and manufacturers, software firms, and consultants, frequently participate in the day-to-day operations and long-term planning of information systems.

In many companies, the information systems department is headed by a **chief information officer (CIO)**. The CIO is a senior manager who oversees the use of information technology in the firm. Today's CIOs are expected to have a strong business background as well as information systems expertise and to play a leadership role in integrating technology into the firm's business strategy. Large firms today also have positions for a chief security officer, chief privacy officer, and chief knowledge officer, all of whom work closely with the CIO.

The **chief security officer (CSO)** is in charge of information systems security for the firm and is responsible for enforcing the firm's information security policy (see Chapter 8). (Sometimes this position is called the chief information security officer (CISO) where information systems security is separated from physical security.) The CSO is responsible for educating and training users and information systems specialists about security, keeping management aware of security threats and breakdowns, and maintaining the tools and policies chosen to implement security.

Information systems security and the need to safeguard personal data have become so important that corporations collecting vast quantities of personal data have established positions for a **chief privacy officer (CPO)**. The CPO is responsible for ensuring that the company complies with existing data privacy laws.

The **chief knowledge officer (CKO)** is responsible for the firm's knowledge management program. The CKO helps design programs and systems to find new sources of knowledge or to make better use of existing knowledge in organizational and management processes.

End users are representatives of departments outside the information systems group for whom applications are developed. These users are playing an increasingly large role in the design and development of information systems.

In the early years of computing, the information systems group was composed mostly of programmers who performed very highly specialized but limited technical functions. Today, a growing proportion of staff members are systems analysts and network specialists, with the information systems department acting as a powerful change agent in the organization. The information systems department suggests new business strategies and new information-based products and services, and coordinates both the development of the technology and the planned changes in the organization.

In the past, firms generally developed their own software and managed their own computing facilities. Today, many firms are turning to external vendors to provide these services (see Chapters 5 and 9) and are using their information systems departments to manage these service providers.

Organizing the Information Systems Function

There are many types of business firms, and there are many ways in which the IT function is organized within the firm (see Figure 2-10). A very small company will not have a formal information systems group. It might have one employee who is responsible for keeping its networks and applications running, or it might use consultants for these services. Larger companies will have a separate information systems department, which may be organized along several different lines, depending on the nature and interests of the firm.

Programmers

Systems analysts

Information systems managers

Chief information officer (CIO)

Chief security officer (CSO)

Chief privacy officer (CPO)

Chief knowledge officer (CKO)

End users

FIGURE 2-10   Organization of the information systems function.

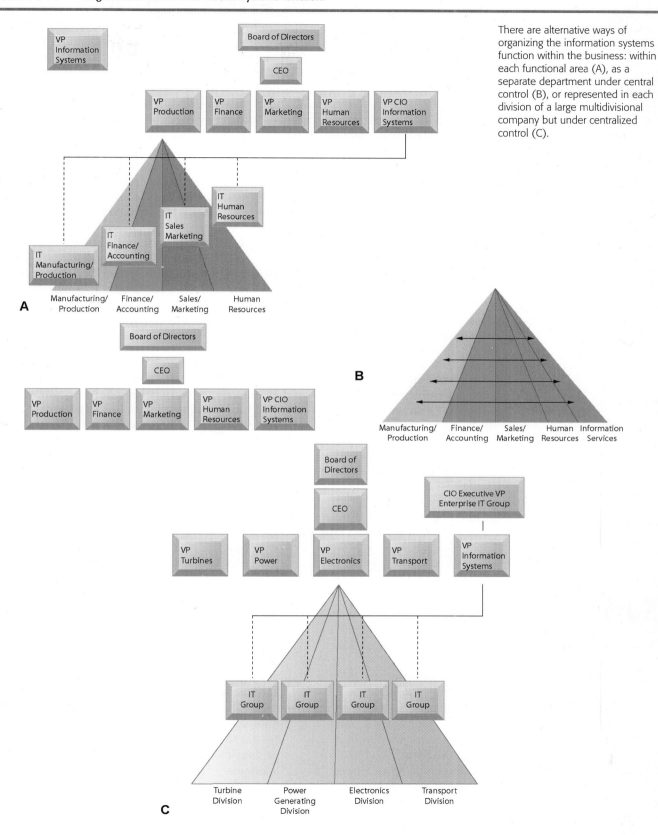

There are alternative ways of organizing the information systems function within the business: within each functional area (A), as a separate department under central control (B), or represented in each division of a large multidivisional company but under centralized control (C).

Sometimes you will see a decentralized arrangement where each functional area of the business has its own information systems department and management that typically reports to a senior manager or chief information officer. In other words, the marketing department would have its own information systems group as would manufacturing and each of the other business functions. The job of the CIO is to review information technology investments and decisions in the functional areas. The advantage of this approach is that systems are developed that directly address the business needs of the functional areas. However, central guidance is weak and the danger is high that many incompatible systems will be developed, increasing costs as each group makes its own technology purchases.

In another arrangement, the information systems function operates as a separate department similar to the other functional departments with a large staff, a group of middle managers, and a senior management group that fights for its share of the company's resources. You will see this approach in many large firms. This central information systems department makes technology decisions for the entire company, which is more likely to produce more compatible systems and more coherent long-term systems development plans.

Very large firms with multiple divisions and product lines might allow each division (such as the Power Generating Division or the Electronics Division) to have its own information systems group. All of these divisional information systems groups report to a high-level central information systems group and CIO. The central IS group establishes corporate-wide standards, centralizes purchasing, and develops long-term plans for evolving the corporate computing platform. This model combines some divisional independence with some centralization.

IT Governance How much should the information systems function be centralized? How much power should information systems management and business management be given to determine what systems to develop and how to manage them? Each organization will have its own set of answers. The question of how the information systems department should be organized is part of the larger issue of **IT governance.** IT governance includes the strategy and policies for using information technology within an organization. It specifies the decision rights and framework for accountability to ensure that the use of information technology supports the organization's strategies and objectives. What decisions must be made to ensure effective management and use of information technology, including the return on IT investments? Who should make these decisions? How will these decisions be made and monitored? Firms with superior IT governance will have clearly thought out the answers (Weill and Ross, 2004).

IT governance

SUMMARY

1. *What are business processes? How are they related to information systems?*

   A business process is a logically related set of activities that defines how specific business tasks are performed, and it represents a unique way in which an organization coordinates work, information, and knowledge. Managers need to pay attention to business processes because they determine how well the organization can execute its business, and they may be a source of strategic advantage. There are business processes specific to each of the major business functions, but many business processes are cross-functional. Information systems automate parts of business processes, and they can help organizations redesign and streamline these processes.

2. *How do information systems serve the various levels of management in a business?*

   Systems serving operational management are transaction processing systems (TPS), such as payroll or order processing, that track the flow of the daily routine transactions necessary to conduct business. Management information systems (MIS) and decision-support systems (DSS) support middle management. Most MIS reports condense information from TPS and are not highly analytical. DSS support management decisions that are unique and rapidly changing using advanced analytical models and data analysis capabilities. Executive support systems (ESS) support senior management by providing data that are often in the form of graphs and charts delivered via portals using many sources of internal and external information.

3. How do enterprise applications, intranets, and collaboration and communication systems improve organizational performance?

Enterprise applications (enterprise systems, supply chain management systems, customer relationship management systems, and knowledge management systems) are designed to coordinate multiple functions and business processes. Enterprise systems integrate the key internal business processes of a firm into a single software system to improve coordination, efficiency, and decision making. Supply chain management systems help the firm manage its relationship with suppliers to optimize the planning, sourcing, manufacturing, and delivery of products and services. Customer relationship management uses information systems to coordinate all of the business processes surrounding the firm's interactions with its customers to optimize firm revenue and customer satisfaction. Knowledge management systems enable firms to optimize the creation, sharing, and distribution of knowledge. Jobs where interaction is the primary value-adding activity benefit from collaboration and communication systems. Intranets and extranets use Internet technology and standards to assemble information from disparate systems and present it to the user in a Web page format. Extranets make portions of private intranets available to outsiders.

4. What is the difference between e-business, e-commerce, and e-government?

E-business (electronic business) refers to the use of digital technology and the Internet to execute a firm's business processes. It includes internal business processes and processes for coordination with suppliers and other external entities. E-commerce (electronic commerce) is the part of e-business dealing with the purchase and sale of goods and services over the Internet, including support activities such as marketing and customer support. E-government refers to the application of the Internet and networking technologies to digitally enable government and public-sector agencies' relationships with citizens, businesses, and other governmental bodies.

5. What is the role of the information systems function in a business?

The information systems department is the formal organizational unit responsible for information technology services. It is responsible for maintaining the hardware, software, data storage, and networks that comprise the firm's IT infrastructure. The department consists of specialists, such as programmers, systems analysts, project leaders, and information systems managers and is often headed by a CIO.

Key Terms

Chief information officer (CIO), 50
Chief knowledge officer (CKO), 50
Chief privacy officer (CPO), 50
Chief security officer (CSO), 50
Customer relationship management (CRM) systems, 45
Decision-support systems (DSS), 38
Digital dashboard, 40
Electronic business (e-business), 49

Electronic commerce (e-commerce), 49
E-government, 49
End users, 50
Enterprise applications, 41
Enterprise systems, 44
Executive support systems (ESS), 40
Information systems department, 49
Information systems managers, 50
Interorganizational system, 45

IT governance, 52
Knowledge management systems (KMS), 46
Management information systems (MIS), 36
Portal, 40
Programmers, 50
Supply chain management (SCM) systems, 44
Systems analysts, 50
Transaction processing systems (TPS), 35
Virtual world, 49

Review Questions

1. *What are business processes? How are they related to information systems?*

- *Define business processes, and describe their relationship to business performance.*

- *Describe the relationship between information systems and business processes.*

2. *How do systems serve the various levels of management in a business?*

- *Describe the characteristics of TPS and the role they play in a business.*

- *Describe the characteristics of MIS, and explain how MIS differ from TPS and from DSS.*

- *Describe the characteristics of DSS, and explain how DSS differ from ESS.*

- *Describe the relationship between TPS, MIS, DSS, and ESS.*

3. *How do enterprise applications, collaboration and communication systems, and intranets improve organizational performance?*

- *Explain how enterprise applications improve organizational performance.*
- *Define enterprise systems, and describe how they change the way an organization works.*
- *Define supply chain management systems, and describe how they benefit businesses.*
- *Define customer relationship management systems, and describe how they benefit businesses.*
- *Describe the role of knowledge management systems in the enterprise.*
- *List and describe the various types of collaboration and communication systems.*
- *Explain how intranets and extranets help firms integrate information and business processes.*

4. *What is the difference between e-business, e-commerce, and e-government?*
   - *Distinguish between e-business and e-commerce.*
   - *Define and describe e-government.*
5. *What is the role of the information systems function in a business?*
   - *Describe how the information systems function supports a business.*
   - *Compare the roles played by programmers, systems analysts, information systems managers, the CIO, CSO, and CKO.*

Discussion Questions

1. *How could information systems be used to support the order fulfillment process illustrated in Figure 2-1? What are the most important pieces of information these systems should capture? Explain your answer.*

2. *Adopting an enterprise application is a key business decision as well as a technology decision. Do you agree? Why or why not? Who should make this decision?*

Collaboration and Teamwork: Identifying Management Decisions and Systems

With a team of three or four other students, find a description of a manager in a corporation in *The Globe and Mail*, the *National Post*, *Maclean's*, *BusinessWeek*, *Forbes*, *Fortune*, or another business publication or do your research on the Web. Gather information about what the manager does and the role he or she plays in the company. Identify the organizational level and business function where this manager works. Make a list of the kinds of decisions this manager has to make and the kind of information the manager would need for those decisions. Suggest how information systems could supply this information. If possible, use Google Sites to post links to Web pages, team communication announcements, and work assignments; to brainstorm; and to work collaboratively on project documents. Try to use Google Docs to develop a presentation of your findings for the class.

 Visit the MyMISLab Web site at **www.pearsoned.ca/mymislab**. This online homework and tutorial system puts you in control of your own learning with study and practice tools directly correlated to this chapter's content.

Learning Track Modules

The following Learning Tracks provide content relevant to topics covered in this chapter.

1. Systems from a Functional Perspective
2. Challenges of Using Business Information Systems

HANDS-ON MIS   Projects

The projects in this section give you hands-on experience analyzing opportunities to improve business processes with new information system applications, using a spreadsheet to improve decision making about suppliers and using Internet software to plan efficient transportation routes.

Management Decision Problems

1. Ben's Lumber Company in Saskatoon is one of the oldest retail lumber yards in Saskatchewan. It features a large selection of materials for flooring, decks, mouldings, windows, siding, and roofing. The prices of lumber and other building materials are constantly changing. When a customer inquires about the price on pre-finished wood flooring, sales representatives consult a manual price sheet and then call the supplier for the most recent price. The supplier in turn consults a manual price sheet, which has been updated each day. Often the supplier must call back Don's sales representatives because the supplier does not have the newest pricing information immediately on hand. Assess the business impact of this situation, describe how this process could be improved with information technology, and identify the decisions that would have to be made to implement a solution. Who would be making those decisions?

2. David's Hardware is a mom-and-pop business in Halifax, Nova Scotia. Store space is limited, and the rent has doubled over the past five years. The owners, David and Kathleen Nelson, are under pressure to use every square foot of space as profitably as possible. The Nelsons have never kept detailed records of stock in inventory or of their sales. As soon as a shipment of goods arrives, the items are immediately placed on store shelves to be sold. Invoices from suppliers are kept for tax purposes only. When an item is sold, the item number and price are rung up at the cash register. The Nelsons use their own judgment in identifying items that need to be reordered. Many times, however, they are caught short and lose a sale. What is the business impact of this situation? How could information systems help David and Kathleen run their business? What data should these systems capture? What reports should the systems produce? What decisions could the systems improve?

Improving Decision Making: Use a Spreadsheet to Select Suppliers

Software skills: Spreadsheet date functions, data filtering, DAVERAGE function
Business skills: Analyzing supplier performance and pricing

In this exercise, you will learn how to use spreadsheet software to improve management decisions about selecting suppliers. You will start with raw transactional data about suppliers organized as a large spreadsheet list. You will use the spreadsheet software to filter the data based on several different criteria to select the best supplies for your company.

You run a company that manufactures aircraft components. You have many competitors that are trying to offer lower prices and better service to customers, and you are trying to determine whether you can benefit from better supply chain management. On the MyMISLab for Chapter 2, you will find a spreadsheet file that contains a list of all of the items that your firm has ordered from its suppliers during the past three months. A sample is shown on the next page, but the MyMISLab may have a more recent version of this spreadsheet for this exercise. The fields in the spreadsheet file include vendor name, vendor identification number, purchaser's order number, item identification number, item description (for each item ordered from the vendor), cost per item, number of units of the item ordered (quantity), total cost of each order, vendor's accounts payable terms, order date, and actual arrival date for each order.

Prepare a recommendation of how you can use the data in this spreadsheet database to improve your decisions about selecting suppliers. Some criteria to consider for identifying preferred suppliers include the supplier's track record for on-time deliveries, suppliers offering the best accounts payable terms, and suppliers offering lower pricing when the same item can be provided by multiple suppliers. Use your spreadsheet software to prepare reports to support your recommendations.

Achieving Operational Excellence:
Using Internet Software to Plan Efficient Transportation Routes

In this exercise, you will use the same online software tool that businesses use to map out their transportation routes and select the most efficient route. The MapQuest (www.mapquest.com) Web site includes interactive capabilities for planning a trip. The software on this Web site can calculate the distance between two points and provide itemized driving directions to any location.

You have just started working as a dispatcher for Cross-Country Transport, a new trucking and delivery service based in Winnipeg, Manitoba. Your first assignment is to

plan a delivery of office equipment and furniture from Montreal, Quebec (at the corner of Rue Stanley and Rue Ste.-Catherine O) to Lethbridge, Alberta (corner of 3rd Avenue South and 6th Street South). To guide your trucker, you need to know the most efficient route between the two cities. Use MapQuest to find the route that is the shortest distance between the two cities. Use MapQuest again to find the route that takes the least time. Compare the results. Which route should Cross-Country use?

CASE STUDY

Zellers Merchandises Better through Information Systems and Business Intelligence

In the Canadian retail landscape, staying ahead of the pack requires intelligence. Margins are often razor-thin, and profits can be found in the details of knowing your business. For businesses in Canada, the ability to "see" into operations has become increasingly crucial to success, and many

retailers are now taking a look at technology as a way to provide them with that insight. Hudson's Bay Company is just such an organization.

Hudson's Bay Company (HBC) is Canada's oldest corporation, leading department store retailer, and one of the country's largest employers. Established in 1670 as a fur-trading company, HBC today employs 70 000 people and has an extensive array of goods and services available through its 98 Bay stores, 302 Zellers stores, and 45 Home Outfitters stores.

At Zellers, HBC's mass merchandise retail chain, technology is changing the way it conducts daily business, especially in inventory management. An ongoing challenge for Zellers staff is knowing when to restock merchandise and being sure they know what is in inventory. Until just a few years ago, inventory management for the stockroom was done using a pen, paper, and a spreadsheet. Throughout the day, sales associates would walk around the sales floor, examine shelf contents, write down what merchandise needed to be refilled, and then go to the stockroom to find the merchandise and replenish the shelves. Any changes in stock levels, such as when new stock arrived, were captured by entering the information manually into a spreadsheet.

Recognizing that each store in the chain was likely following similar procedures and that there were a number of inefficiencies with this method, the IT department decided to develop an inventory application to reside at each of the Zellers stores. The system, named Listed Inventory Database System 2 (LID 2), enabled employees to keep better track of the flow of merchandise from the backroom to the sales floor. However, LID 2 was still an inefficient, time-consuming system that did not provide management a clear view of store operations. With LID 2, an associate still had to physically walk the sales floor, record merchandise that was running low, go to the stockroom, and then print out reports that would indicate which items needed to be replenished.

LID 2's reporting functionality was also limited. When reports were created for management at headquarters, they were often outdated and did not provide an accurate snapshot of how the store or even the chain was operating. The database was also not centralized, resulting in silos of information. This meant information needed by management to make decisions was not easily accessible.

"LID 2 was an improvement over the previous system but it was still an inefficient system," says Chris Marinis, senior manager, Development Services, Hudson's Bay Company. "Sales associates still had to manually input the information, which is time consuming. From a management perspective, reports were not easy to obtain, and they often had to approach the IT team to produce these reports. Since many reports had to be printed on the weekend and did not reflect the flow of inventory on those days, reports were also not as accurate as they could be. That meant that the information our management team received per store was not reflective of the activity during the weekend, which is typically the busiest time of the week."

HBC management knows that inventory levels in the backroom must be closely aligned with sales to minimize inventory-holding costs. In addition, HBC management needed to know which merchandise was selling well to avoid stockouts and lost sales. Consolidating data from point-of-sale terminals and stockroom inventory data was key to the proposed new system.

Recognizing that it needed to improve inventory management and gain better insight into its operations at Zellers stores, HBC worked with Microsoft Canada and T4G Ltd. to develop a new version of its LID application, which included the reporting capabilities of Microsoft SQL Server 2000 Reporting Services. IBM's Data Integration Facility also helped to manage the integration of the data so that store personnel receive twice-a-day reports on what merchandise is running low on the floor. These reports include a picking list so that personnel can efficiently find and take merchandise from the stockroom to the floor; the software even takes into account shelf capacity and location.

Dubbing it LID 3, the application is a proprietary wireless, integrated replenishment, and stockroom management system that includes shift productivity reporting. LID 3 integrates with the supply chain and point-of-sale systems using a centralized database. The system leverages RF Symbol technology used by Zellers while the application and data are at HBC's central computing facility. The system enables HBC to ensure product is always in stock by automating shelf replenishment; optimize inventory allocation among stores by monitoring stockroom inventory from a central database; allocate more store labour to the sales floor to serve customers; and achieve cost savings of $5 million per year.

HBC knew that the business intelligence (BI) capabilities of SQL Server Reporting Services would provide LID 3 with the means to gain insight into its Zellers operations. With this capability, management gets a clearer picture of the flow of inventory within the chain, helping them to make better business decisions. Since implementing the inventory management system at Zellers, HBC has realized many benefits including time savings and improved productivity.

"Working together with HBC's internal IT team, we were able to deploy the application with minimal disruption to day-to-day operations, which is crucial in the competitive retail environment," says Geoff Flood, president, T4G Ltd.

HBC launched the LID 3 pilot project at five Zellers stores across Canada in April 2004. Today, the application has been fully deployed across all Zellers stores and ompany headquarters and supports up to 2000 users.

LID 3 enables Zellers to track inventory the moment it arrives and when it leaves the store. The system is integrated with the point-of-sale systems as well as with wireless devices used by sales associates to track inventory on the floor and in the stockroom. LID 3 captures all the information in real time and sends it to the centralized database.

"As soon as a truck arrives at the store, the system knows what merchandise is getting there before we actually slot that merchandise in the stockroom," says Marinis. "As we begin selling merchandise, those pieces of information are integrated into the system so that we can replenish the shelves and always keep them full for customers. That's key to our business. . . . But what's really critical to the whole system is the fact that we can now take the information that is captured in the centralized database and use that information more effectively through the creation of reports."

With the reporting capability, HBC can aggregate data coming in from the supply chain and point-of-sale systems to give users specialized reports based on their specific needs. Reports can also be delivered to key personnel in a format with which they are comfortable, making it easy for them to access the information they need to make decisions; reports can be sent as an e-mail attachment, viewed using a Web browser, or even exported to a Microsoft Excel spreadsheet.

There are basically two types of Zellers reports. At the store level, sales associates starting a shift, for example, can obtain a report indicating what is currently on the sales floor, what has been moved to the sales floor during the last shift, and what is still in the stockroom. Sales associates now have the information they need to know what merchandise is available to make sure the sales floor is well stocked.

Store managers access these reports to give them an accurate picture of the flow of merchandise inside the store throughout the day, week, or month. Better decisions can now be made about purchasing and staffing, and this information can easily be sent to district and regional managers.

The second type of report is for management at headquarters, giving them a clear picture of Zellers operations, whether at the level of the individual store, a specific district, an entire region, or the whole chain. Management can now identify trends within Zellers and make better decisions.

"Our senior vice president of stores would probably look at a total Zellers point of view while the regional vice president would care more about the region. District managers are only interested in their district. All of these levels, from the store hierarchy to the merchandise hierarchy, are reflected in our new reports," says Marinis.

"With this system, because the data is centralized, we can create reports in real time. If management says they need it in an hour, we can deliver it. Our business has definitely become more agile as a result of implementing SQL Server Reporting Services."

The reporting capability has helped to improve the productivity of both IT and non-IT staff. With LID 3's ability to provide a near real-time snapshot of inventory on the shelves and in the backroom, Zellers is able to save time and improve productivity for sales associates. Sales associ-

ates no longer have to walk the floors to learn what is available and what needs to be replenished. With a centralized database permitting users to create reports quickly and easily, sales associates and store management can get the information they need.

"Thanks to SQL Server Reporting Services, this system is far more efficient," says Marinis. "On a daily basis, you're taking away a couple of hours of work on a per-store basis. Multiply that by 313 stores, seven days a week, and all of sudden, you can see the efficiency coming in."

The ease with which reports can be created has also helped to boost the productivity of IT staff. Users can easily access reports using the LID 3 system; employees no longer have to contact IT to provide the information they need, freeing up the IT team's time to manage more critical tasks.

"In the past, management had little visibility into operations. What visibility they did have was always outdated," says Marinis. "Since we had data in 300 locations, we would only go and pull this data once a week. We would pull it on Friday night and develop the report over the weekend. On Monday morning, when head office came in, they would have some visibility as to what was happening in the stores. However, of course by then, the picture had changed, and therefore, the information was never totally up to date." With 300 stores, there were at least 600 reports.

"With SQL Server Reporting Services, the picture is virtually instantaneous. Any transaction the store generates is reflected in real time, and that is valuable to our business. For example, if I took 10 units from the back and brought them to the sales floor, the removal of these 10 units is reflected instantly in real time because our database is centrally located," says Marinis.

According to Marinis, feedback from users at the stores and at head office has been positive. "They are pleased with what they can do with information now. That's what matters," says Marinis. "They have online query capabilities where they can drill down and access information they need. They are able to turn data into actionable information. That's key to our ongoing success."

"Obviously customers can only find merchandise on the sales floor, not in the stockroom. From a presentation point of view, as a store, you have more merchandise to sell or available for sale on the sales floor. What this system translates to is fuller shelves and better services for customers," says Marinis.

According to Marinis, his team has received positive feedback about the system across the board from the stores to head office. "At the store level, we're getting statements like 'our sales floor has never looked fuller.' And we have that empirical evidence to suggest that that statement is absolutely accurate."

Even better is the payback for the system. In financial terms, the system paid for itself during its first year of operation, with return on investment calculated at 100 percent the first year of LID 3's operations.

CASE STUDY QUESTIONS:

1. Describe and diagram the previous process for inventory control and the new process. What are the differences between the new and old processes?

2. What improvement may be seen with the implementation of LID 3? How do wireless devices and wireless transmission help this process?

3. Should all retail stores switch to inventory management control systems such as LID 3? Why or why not?

4. What management, organization, and technical factors would you want to take into account before implementing a new inventory control system?

Sources: Ryan Patrick, "HBC Puts LID Technology on Zellers Inventory," IT World Canada, **www.itworldcanada.com/Mobile/ViewArticle. aspx?title=&id=idgml-2726a919-81bd-4628&s=395692** (accessed September 3, 2009); Neil Sutton, "HBC Puts IT Smarts into Its Merchandising Strategy," IT Business Canada, **www.itbusiness.ca,it/ client/en/Home/News.asp?id=40143&bsearch=True** (accessed September 3, 2009); "Hudson's Bay Company Creates an Award-Winning Inventory Solution," **www.xtremeretail.com/studies/hbcfinal. pdf** (accessed September 3, 2009); "Hudson's Bay Company Gains More Accurate Business Snapshot of Its Zellers Operations with Microsoft SQL Server 2000 Reporting Services," **www.microsoft.com/ canada/casestudies/hbc.mspx** (accessed September 3, 2009).

CHAPTER 3

Information Systems, Organizations, and Strategy

LEARNING OBJECTIVES

After reading this chapter, you will be able to answer the following questions:

1. Which features of organizations do managers need to know about to develop and use information systems successfully? What is the impact of information systems on organizations?

2. How does Porter's competitive forces model help companies develop competitive strategies using information systems?

3. How do the value chain and value web models help businesses identify opportunities for strategic information system applications?

4. How do information systems help businesses use synergies, core competencies, and network-based strategies to achieve competitive advantage?

5. What are the challenges posed by strategic information systems, and how should they be addressed?

OPENING CASE

EBay Fine-Tunes Its Strategy

EBay has been synonymous with Internet auctions. It started out as one of the first successful Internet auction businesses, mushrooming into a gigantic electronic marketplace hosting more than 532 000 online storefronts all over the world. In 2007, eBay's marketplaces generated nearly $94 billion in revenue. Hundreds of thousands of people support themselves by selling on eBay, and millions more use eBay to supplement their income. EBay now boasts 83 million active users.

EBay derives the bulk of its revenue from fees and commissions associated with its sales transactions. A portion of eBay's revenue comes from direct advertising on the site, and some comes from end-to-end service providers such as PayPal whose services increase the ease and speed of eBay transactions.

Not long ago, eBay's growth strategy focused on expansion in geography and scope and on continuing innovation to enhance the variety and appeal of products on its sites. EBay has been developing and acquiring new products and services that encompass all the activities people perform on the Internet. It has been fashioning a diversified portfolio of companies with a hand in each of the Internet's big cash pots: shopping, communicating, search, and entertainment.

In 2002, eBay bought PayPal for $1.5 billion. PayPal, whose service enables the exchange of money between individuals over the Internet, brings additional transaction-based fee revenue. EBay is banking on PayPal being the standard payment method for online transactions. The service already receives 40 percent of its business from payment transactions not associated with eBay.

In 2005, eBay acquired Shopping.com, an online shopping comparison site, and Skype Technologies, which provides a service for free or low-cost voice calls over the Internet. Markets that eBay traditionally had trouble penetrating, such as real estate, travel, new-car sales, and expensive collectibles, require more communication among buyers and sellers than eBay currently offers, and Skype provides voice communication services to help.

EBay also acquired the ticket-reselling Web site StubHub, bought a 25-percent stake in classified ad site Craigslist, and purchased Kurant, now ProStores, whose technology helps users set up online stores. Some analysts report that while many of eBay's individual acquisitions appear successful, they have not created the synergy that was intended, and diversification has detracted from eBay's core business, auctions.

But eBay's auction business is changing, too. EBay sells many items at a fixed price, and fixed sales already account for 40 percent of marketplace revenue. In Canada, eBay occasionally offers fee-free fixed price sales to vendors. This side of the business is growing much more rapidly than online auctions. Amazon.com and other rivals are attracting more shoppers with fixed-price listings. To shift toward that model, eBay struck a deal with giant Web retailer Buy.com to sell millions of DVDs, electronics, books, and other items on eBay

at lower fees than would be charged individual sellers. In August 2008, eBay lowered its listing fees for all sellers offering fixed-priced items under its "Buy It Now" format.

Mom and pop dealers have objected vociferously, but eBay says that hosting fixed-price sales by reliable retailers makes shopping more customer-friendly and predictable. "We are challenging some of the core assumptions we have made about our business," observes Stephanie Tilenius, general manager of eBay North America. "Instead of focusing on being an auction business, we are looking at what it takes to create the best

marketplace out there." Will bringing large sellers to its site dilute eBay's brand and reputation as a dynamic flea market? Or will it steer eBay toward the fastest part of e-commerce growth? The e-commerce world is watching.

Sources: Laurie J. Flynn, "EBay Is Planning to Emphasize Fixed-Price Sales Format over Its Auction Model," *The New York Times*, August 20, 2008; Brad Stone, "Buy.com Deal with EBay Angers Sellers," *The New York Times*, July 14, 2008, "Profit Climbs for eBay, but Auction Growth Is Slowing," *The New York Times*, July 17, 2008, and "EBay's Leader Moves Swiftly on a Revamping," *The New York Times*, January 24, 2008; Catherine Holahan, "EBay's Changing Identity," *BusinessWeek*, April 23, 2007; and Associated Press, "EBay Rethinks Its Ways as It Enters Middle Age" (accessed via **CNN.com**, June 18, 2007).

The story of eBay illustrates some of the ways that information systems help businesses compete and the interdependence of business processes, information systems, and the organization's surrounding environment. It also illus-

trates the challenges of sustaining a competitive advantage.

The chapter-opening diagram calls attention to important points raised by this case and this chapter. EBay was able to take advantage of the

opportunities created by the Internet. It pioneered in online auctions where individuals could sell to other individuals. This strategy catapulted eBay to become one of the first—and largest—Internet retailers. Today its name is still synonymous with Internet auctions.

But eBay operates in a very rapidly changing environment where customers can easily switch to other online retailers that offer more value and convenience. As time went on, eBay's original strategy was not enough to keep it profitable and growing. EBay started losing market share to Amazon and other online retailers that were able to offer the convenience of goods sold at a fixed price and with better service. EBay has had to continually fine-tune its strategy and business processes to remain competitive. EBay revised its strategy by acquiring other Internet businesses and then de-emphasizing online auctions in favour of fixed price sales by large companies such as Buy.com. Today it is a large but highly diversified online platform where many different types of businesses engage in e-commerce.

3.1 Organizations and Information Systems

Information systems and organizations influence one another. Information systems are developed by managers to serve the interests of the business firm. At the same time, the organization must be aware of and open to the influences of information systems to benefit from new technologies.

The interaction between information technology and organizations is complex and is influenced by many mediating factors, including the organization's structure, business processes, politics, culture, surrounding environment, and management decisions (see Figure 3-1). You will need to understand how information systems can change social and work life in your firm. You will not be able to design new systems successfully or understand existing systems without understanding your own business organization.

As a manager, you will be the one to decide which systems will be developed, what they will do, and how they will be implemented. You may not be able to anticipate all of the consequences of these decisions. Some of the changes that occur in business firms because of new information technology (IT) investments cannot be foreseen and have results that may or may not meet your expectations. Who would have imagined 15 years ago, for instance, that e-mail and instant messaging would become a dominant form of business communication and that many managers would be inundated with more than 200 e-mail messages each day?

What Is an Organization?

An **organization** is a stable, formal social structure that takes resources from the environment and processes them to produce outputs. This technical definition focuses on three elements of an organization. Capital and labour are primary production factors provided by

FIGURE 3-1   The two-way relationship between organizations and information technology.

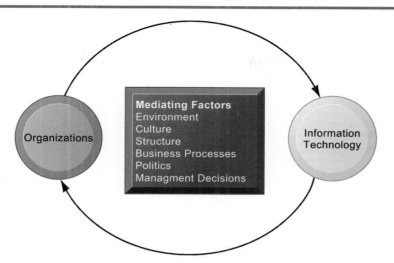

This complex two-way relationship is mediated by many factors, not the least of which are the decisions made—or not made—by managers. Other factors mediating the relationship include the organizational culture, structure, politics, business processes, and environment.

the environment. The organization (the firm) transforms these inputs into products and services in a production function. The products and services are consumed by environments in return for supply inputs (see Figure 3-2).

An organization is more stable than an informal group (such as a group of friends that meets every Friday for lunch) in terms of longevity and routineness. Organizations are formal legal entities with internal rules and procedures that must abide by laws. Organizations are also social structures because they are a collection of social elements, much as a machine has a structure—a particular arrangement of valves, cams, shafts, and other parts.

This definition of organizations is powerful and simple, but it is not very descriptive or even predictive of real-world organizations. A more realistic behavioural definition of an organization is that it is a collection of rights, privileges, obligations, and responsibilities that is delicately balanced over a period of time through conflict and conflict resolution (see Figure 3-3).

In this behavioural view of the firm, people who work in organizations develop customary ways of working; they gain attachments to existing relationships; and they make arrangements with subordinates and superiors about how work will be done, the amount of work that will be done, and under what conditions work will be done. Most of these arrangements and feelings are not discussed in any formal rulebook.

How do these definitions of organizations relate to information systems technology? A technical view of organizations encourages us to focus on how inputs are combined to create outputs when technology changes are introduced into the company. The firm is seen as infinitely malleable, with capital and labour substituting for each other quite easily. But the more realistic behavioural definition of an organization suggests that developing new

FIGURE 3-2   The technical microeconomic definition of the organization.

In the microeconomic definition of organizations, capital and labour (the primary production factors provided by the environment) are transformed by the firm through the production process into products and services (outputs to the environment). The products and services are consumed by the environment, which supplies additional capital and labour as inputs in the feedback loop.

FIGURE 3-3   The behavioural view of organizations.

The behavioural view of organizations emphasizes group relationships, values, and structures.

information systems, or redeveloping old ones, involves much more than a technical rearrangement of machines or workers—that some information systems change the organizational balance of rights, privileges, obligations, responsibilities, and feelings that have been established over a long period of time.

Changing these elements can take a long time, be very disruptive, and require more resources to support training and learning. For instance, the length of time required to effectively implement a new information system is much longer than usually anticipated simply because there is a lag between implementing a technical system and teaching employees and managers how to use the system.

Technological change requires changes in who owns and controls information, who has the right to access and update that information, and who makes decisions about whom, when, and how. This more complex view forces us to look at the way work is designed and the procedures used to achieve outputs.

The technical and behavioural definitions of organizations are not contradictory. Indeed, they complement each other: The technical definition tells us how thousands of firms in competitive markets combine capital, labour, and information technology while the behavioural model takes us inside the individual firm to see how that technology affects the organization's inner workings. Section 3.2 describes how each of these definitions of organizations can help explain the relationships between information systems and organizations.

Features of Organizations

All modern organizations have certain characteristics. They are bureaucracies with clearcut divisions of labour and specialization. Organizations arrange specialists in a hierarchy of authority in which everyone is accountable to someone and authority is limited to specific actions governed by abstract rules or procedures. These rules create a system of impartial and universal decision making. Organizations try to hire and promote employees on the basis of technical qualifications and professionalism (not personal connections). The organization is devoted to the principle of efficiency: maximizing output using limited inputs. Other features of organizations include their business processes, organizational culture, organizational politics, surrounding environments, structure, goals, constituencies, and leadership styles. All of these features affect the kinds of information systems used by organizations.

Routines and Business Processes All organizations, including business firms, become very efficient over time because individuals in the firm develop **routines** for producing goods and services. Routines—sometimes called *standard operating procedures*—are

Routines

FIGURE 3-4   Routines, business processes, and firms.

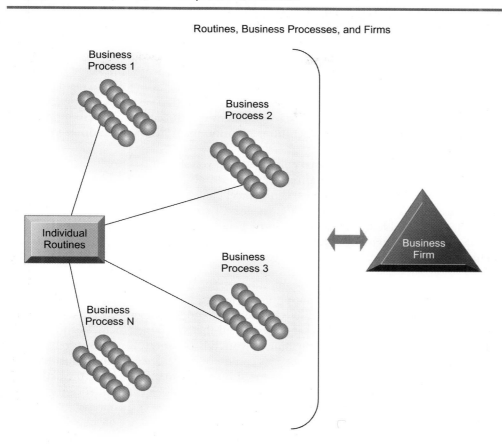

Routines, Business Processes, and Firms

Business Process 1

Business Process 2

Individual Routines

Business Process 3

Business Process N

Business Firm

All organizations are composed of individual routines and behaviours, a collection of which make up a business process. A collection of business processes make up the business firm. New information system applications require that individual routines and business processes change to achieve high levels of organizational performance.

precise rules, procedures, and practices that have been developed to cope with virtually all expected situations. As employees learn these routines, they become highly productive and efficient, and the firm is able to reduce its costs over time as efficiency increases. For instance, when you visit a doctor's office, receptionists have a well-developed set of routines for gathering basic information from you; nurses have a different set of routines for preparing you for an interview with a doctor; and the doctor has a well-developed set of routines for diagnosing you. *Business processes*, which we introduced in Chapters 1 and 2, are collections of such routines. A business firm in turn is a collection of business processes (Figure 3-4).

Organizational Politics People in organizations occupy different positions with different specialties, concerns, and perspectives. As a result, they naturally have divergent viewpoints about how resources, rewards, and punishments should be distributed. These differences matter to both managers and employees, and they result in political struggle for resources, competition, and conflict within every organization. Political resistance is one of the great difficulties of bringing about organizational change—especially the development of new information systems. Virtually all large information systems investments by a firm that bring about significant changes in strategy, business objectives, business processes, and procedures become politically charged events. Managers who know how to work with the politics of an organization will be more successful than less-skilled managers in implementing new information systems. Throughout this book, you will find many examples of instances in which internal politics defeated the best-laid plans for an information system.

Organizational Culture All organizations have bedrock, unassailable, unquestioned (by the members) assumptions that define their goals and products. Organizational culture encompasses this set of assumptions about what products the organization should produce, how it should produce them, where, and for whom. Generally, these cultural assumptions are taken totally for granted and are rarely publicly announced or spoken about. Business processes—the actual way business firms produce value—are usually ensconced in the organization's culture.

You can see organizational culture at work by looking around your university or college. Some bedrock assumptions of university life are that professors know more than students, the reason students attend college is to learn, and classes follow a regular schedule. Organizational culture is a powerful unifying force that restrains political conflict and promotes common understanding, agreement on procedures, and common practices. If we all share the same basic cultural assumptions, agreement on other matters is more likely.

At the same time, organizational culture is a powerful restraint on change, especially technological change. Most organizations will do almost anything to avoid making changes in basic assumptions. Any technological change that threatens commonly held cultural assumptions usually meets a great deal of resistance. However, there are times when the only sensible way for a firm to move forward is to employ a new technology that directly opposes an existing organizational culture. When this occurs, the technology is often stalled while the culture slowly adjusts.

Organizational Environments Organizations reside in environments from which they draw resources and to which they supply goods and services. Organizations and environments have a reciprocal relationship. On the one hand, organizations are open to and dependent on the social and physical environment that surrounds them. Without financial and human resources—people willing to work reliably and consistently for a set wage or revenue from customers—organizations could not exist. Organizations must respond to legislative and other requirements imposed by government as well as the actions of customers and competitors. On the other hand, organizations can influence their environments. For example, business firms form alliances with other businesses to influence the political process; they advertise to influence customer acceptance of their products.

Figure 3-5 illustrates the role of information systems in helping organizations perceive changes in their environments and also in helping organizations act on their environments. Information systems are key instruments for *environmental scanning*, helping managers identify external changes that might require an organizational response.

Environments generally change much faster than organizations. New technologies, new products, and changing public tastes and values (many of which result in new government

FIGURE 3-5   Environments and organizations have a reciprocal relationship.

Environments shape what organizations can do, but organizations can influence their environments and decide to change environments altogether. Information technology plays a critical role in helping organizations perceive environmental change and in helping organizations act on their environment.

The Organization and Its Environment

Environmental Resources and Constraints

The Firm

Governments
Competitors
Customers
Financial Institutions
Culture

Knowledge
Technology

Information Systems

TABLE 3-1 Disruptive technologies: Winners and losers

TECHNOLOGY	DESCRIPTION	WINNERS AND LOSERS
Microprocessor chips (1971)	Thousands and eventually millions of transistors on a silicon chip	Microprocessor firms win (Intel, Texas Instruments) while transistor firms (GE) decline.
Personal computers (1975)	Small, inexpensive, but fully functional desktop computers	PC manufacturers (HP, Apple, IBM) and chip manufacturers prosper (Intel) while mainframe (IBM) and minicomputer (DEC) firms lose.
PC word processing software (1979)	Inexpensive, limited but functional text editing and formatting for personal computers	PC and software manufacturers (Microsoft, HP, Apple) prosper while the typewriter industry disappears.
World Wide Web (1989)	A global database of digital files and "pages" instantly available	Owners of online content and news benefit while traditional publishers (newspapers, magazines, and broadcast television) lose.
Internet music services (1998)	Repositories of downloadable music on the Web with acceptable fidelity	Owners of online music collections (MP3.com, iTunes), telecommunications providers that own Internet backbone (ATT, Verizon), and local Internet service providers win while record label firms and music retailers lose (Tower Records).
PageRank algorithm	A method for ranking Web pages in terms of their popularity to supplement Web search by key terms	Google wins (it owns the patent) while traditional keyword search engines (AltaVista) lose.
Software as a service	Using the Internet to provide remote access to online software	Online software services companies (Salesforce.com) win while traditional "boxed" software companies (Microsoft, SAP, Oracle) lose.

regulations) put strains on any organization's culture, politics, and people. Most organizations are unable to adapt to a rapidly changing environment. Inertia built into an organization's standard operating procedures, the political conflict raised by changes to the existing order, and the threat to closely held cultural values inhibit organizations from making significant changes. Young firms typically lack resources to sustain even short periods of troubled times. It is not surprising that few companies that existed in the early 20th century still exist today.

Disruptive Technologies: Riding the Wave Technology's impact on organizations is especially noteworthy because it has become such a disruptive force. Sometimes a new technology comes along like a tsunami and destroys everything in its path. Some firms are able to create these tsunamis and ride the wave to profits; others learn quickly and are able to swim with the current; still others are obliterated because their products, services, and business models are obsolete. They may be very efficient at doing what no longer needs to be done. There are also cases where no firms benefit, and all the gains go to consumers (firms fail to capture any profits). Business history is filled with examples of **disruptive technologies.** Table 3-1 describes just a few disruptive technologies from the past and some from the likely near-term future.

Disruptive technologies are tricky. Firms that invent disruptive technologies as "first movers" do not always benefit if they lack the resources to really exploit the technology or fail to see the opportunity. The MITS Altair 8800 is widely considered the first PC, but its inventors did not take advantage of their first mover status. Second movers, so-called "fast followers" such as IBM and Microsoft, reaped the rewards.

Disruptive technologies

TABLE 3-2 Organizational structures.

ORGANIZATIONAL TYPE	DESCRIPTION	EXAMPLES
Entrepreneurial structure	Young, small firm in a fast-changing environment. It has a simple structure and is managed by an entrepreneur serving as its single chief executive officer.	Small start-up business
Machine bureaucracy	Large bureaucracy existing in a slowly changing environment, producing standard products. It is dominated by a centralized management team and centralized decision making.	Midsize manufacturing firm
Divisionalized bureaucracy	Combination of multiple machine bureaucracies, each producing a different product or service, all topped by one central headquarters.	Power Corporation, Hudson's Bay Company
Professional bureaucracy	Knowledge-based organization in which goods and services depend on the expertise and knowledge of professionals. Dominated by department heads with weak centralized authority.	Law firms, school systems, hospitals
Adhocracy	Task force organization that must respond to rapidly changing environments. Consists of large groups of specialists organized into short-lived multidisciplinary teams and with weak central management.	Consulting firms, such as the Rand Corporation

ATMs revolutionized retail banking, but the inventor, Citibank, was copied by other banks, and ultimately all banks used ATMs with the benefits going mostly to the consumers. Google was not a first mover in search, but rather an innovative follower that was able to maintain rights to a powerful new search algorithm called PageRank. So far it has been able to hold onto its lead while most other search engines have faded down to small market shares.

Organizational Structure Organizations all have a structure or shape. Mintzberg's classification, described in Table 3-2, identifies five basic kinds of organizational structure (Mintzberg, 1979).

The kind of information systems you find in a business firm—and the nature of problems with these systems—often reflects the type of organizational structure. For instance, in a professional bureaucracy such as a hospital, it is not unusual to find parallel patient record systems operated by the administration, by doctors, and by other professional staff such as nurses and social workers. In small entrepreneurial firms, you will often find poorly designed systems developed in a rush that often outgrow their usefulness quickly. In huge multidivisional firms operating in hundreds of locations, you will often find there is not a single integrating information system, but instead each locale or each division has its set of information systems.

Other Organizational Features Organizations have goals and use different means to achieve them. Some organizations have coercive goals (e.g., prisons); others have utilitarian goals (e.g., businesses). Still others have normative goals (e.g., universities, religious groups). Organizations also serve different groups or have different constituencies, some primarily benefiting their members, others benefiting clients, stockholders, or the public. The nature of leadership differs greatly from one organization to another; some organizations may be more democratic or authoritarian than others. Another way organizations differ is by the tasks they perform and the technology they use. Some organizations perform primarily routine tasks that can be reduced to formal rules that require little judgment (such as manufacturing auto parts) while others (such as consulting firms) work primarily with nonroutine tasks.

3.2 How Information Systems Impact Organizations and Business Firms

Information systems have become integral, online, interactive tools deeply involved in the minute-to-minute operations and decision making of large organizations. Over the last decade, information systems have fundamentally altered the economics of organizations and greatly increased the possibilities for organizing work. Theories and concepts from economics and sociology help us understand the changes brought about by IT.

Economic Impacts

From the point of view of economics, IT changes both the relative costs of capital and the costs of information. Information systems technology can be viewed as a factor of production that can be substituted for traditional capital and labour. As the cost of information technology decreases, it is substituted for labour, which historically has been a rising cost. Hence, information technology should result in a decline in the number of middle managers and clerical workers as information technology substitutes for their labour (Laudon, 1989).

As the cost of information technology decreases, it also substitutes for other forms of capital such as buildings and machinery, which remain relatively expensive. Therefore, over time, we should expect managers to increase their investments in IT because of its declining cost relative to other capital investments.

IT also obviously affects the cost and quality of information and changes the economics of information. Information technology helps firms contract in size because it can reduce transaction costs—the costs incurred when a firm buys on the marketplace what it cannot make itself. According to **transaction cost theory,** firms and individuals seek to economize on transaction costs, much as they do on production costs. Using markets is expensive (Coase, 1937; Williamson, 1985) because of costs such as locating and communicating with distant suppliers, monitoring contract compliance, buying insurance, obtaining information on products, and so forth. Traditionally, firms have tried to reduce transaction costs through vertical integration, by getting bigger, hiring more employees, and buying their own suppliers and distributors, as both General Motors and Ford used to do.

Information technology, especially the use of networks, can help firms lower the cost of market participation (transaction costs), making it worthwhile for firms to contract with external suppliers instead of using internal sources. As a result, firms can shrink in size (numbers of employees) because it is far less expensive to outsource work to a competitive marketplace rather than hire employees. Information systems make it possible for companies such as Cisco Systems and Dell Inc. to outsource their production to contract manufacturers such as Flextronics instead of making their products themselves.

Figure 3-6 shows that as transaction costs decrease, firm size (the number of employees) should shrink because it becomes easier and cheaper for the firm to contract for the purchase of goods and services in the marketplace rather than to make the product or offer the service itself. Firm size can stay constant or contract even as the company increases its revenues. For example, when Eastman Chemical Company split off from Kodak in 1994, it had $4 billion in revenue and 24 000 full-time employees. In 2007, it generated $8 billion in revenue with only 11 000 employees.

Information technology also can reduce internal management costs. According to **agency theory,** the firm is viewed as a "nexus of contracts" among self-interested individuals rather than as a unified, profit-maximizing entity (Jensen and Meckling, 1976). A principal (owner) employs "agents" (employees) to perform work on his or her behalf. However, agents need constant supervision and management; otherwise, they will tend to pursue their own interests rather than those of the owners. As firms grow in size and scope, agency costs or coordination costs rise because owners must expend more and more effort supervising and managing employees.

Transaction cost theory
Agency theory

FIGURE 3-6   The transaction cost theory of the impact of information technology on the organization.

Firms traditionally grew in size to reduce transaction costs. IT potentially reduces the transaction costs for a given size, opening up the possibility of revenue growth without increasing size or even revenue growth accompanied by shrinking size.

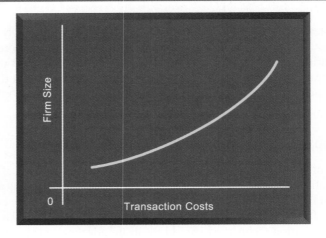

By reducing the costs of acquiring and analyzing information, information technology permits organizations to reduce agency costs because it becomes easier for managers to oversee a greater number of employees. Figure 3-7 shows that by reducing overall management costs, information technology enables firms to increase revenues while shrinking the number of middle managers and clerical workers. We have seen examples in earlier chapters where information technology expanded the power and scope of small organizations by enabling them to perform coordinating activities such as processing orders or keeping track of inventory with very few clerks and managers.

Because IT reduces both agency and transaction costs for firms, we should expect firm size to shrink over time as more capital is invested in IT. Firms should have fewer managers, and we expect to see revenue per employee increase over time.

Organizational and Behavioural Impacts

Theories based in the sociology of complex organizations also provide some understanding about how and why firms change with the implementation of new IT applications.

IT Flattens Organizations Large, bureaucratic organizations, which primarily developed before the computer age, are often inefficient, slow to change, and less competitive than

FIGURE 3-7   The agency cost theory of the impact of information technology on the organization.

As firms grow in size and complexity, traditionally they experience rising agency costs. IT makes it possible to increase the number of employees who can be managed by a single manager, reducing the overall costs of management (agency costs). This creates the possibility that firms can shrink in managerial ranks and still increase revenues as management becomes more efficient.

FIGURE 3-8   Flattening organizations.

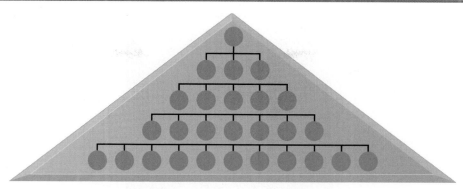

A traditional hierarchical organization with many levels of management

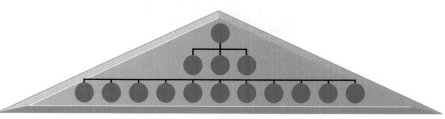

An organization that has been "flattened" by removing layers of management

Information systems can reduce the number of levels in an organization by providing managers with information to supervise larger numbers of workers and by giving lower-level employees more decision-making authority.

newly created organizations. Some of these large organizations have downsized, reducing the number of employees and the number of levels in their organizational hierarchies.

Behavioural researchers have theorized that information technology facilitates flattening of hierarchies by broadening the distribution of information to empower lower-level employees and increase management efficiency (see Figure 3-8). IT pushes decision-making rights lower in the organization because lower-level employees receive the information they need to make decisions without supervision. (This empowerment is also possible because of higher educational levels among those in the workforce, which give employees the capabilities to make intelligent decisions.) Because managers now receive so much more accurate information on time, they become much faster at making decisions, so fewer managers are required. Management costs decline as a percentage of revenues, and the hierarchy becomes much more efficient.

These changes mean that the management span of control has also been broadened, enabling high-level managers to manage and control more workers spread over greater distances. Many companies have eliminated thousands of middle managers as a result of these changes.

Post-industrial Organizations Post-industrial theories based more on history and sociology than economics also support the notion that IT should flatten hierarchies. In post-industrial societies, authority increasingly relies on knowledge and competence, not merely on formal positions. Therefore, the shape of organizations flattens because professional workers tend to be self-managing, and decision making should become more decentralized as knowledge and information become more widespread throughout the firm (Drucker, 1988).

Information technology may encourage task-force-networked organizations in which groups of professionals come together—face to face or electronically—for short periods of time to accomplish a specific task (e.g., designing a new automobile); once the task is accomplished, the individuals join other task forces. The global consulting service Accenture is an example. It has no operational headquarters and no formal branches. Many of its 186 000 employees move from location to location to work on projects at client locations in 49 different countries.

FIGURE 3-9   Organizational resistance and the mutually adjusting relationship between technology and the organization.

Implementing information systems has consequences for task arrangements, structures, and people. According to this model, to implement change, all four components must be changed simultaneously.

Source: Leavitt (1965).

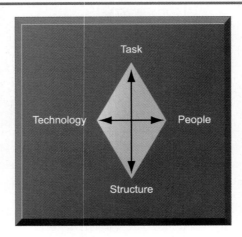

Who makes sure that self-managed teams do not head off in the wrong direction? Who decides which person works on which team and for how long? How can managers evaluate the performance of someone who is constantly rotating from team to team? How do people know where their careers are headed? New approaches for evaluating, organizing, and informing workers are required, and not all companies can make virtual work effective.

Understanding Organizational Resistance to Change Information systems inevitably become bound up in organizational politics because they influence access to a key resource—namely, information. Information systems can affect who does what to whom, when, where, and how in an organization. Many new information systems require changes in personal, individual routines that can be painful for those involved and require retraining and additional effort that may or may not be compensated. Because information systems potentially change an organization's structure, culture, business processes, and strategy, there is often considerable resistance to them when they are introduced.

There are several ways to visualize organizational resistance. Leavitt (1965) used a diamond shape to illustrate the interrelated and mutually adjusting character of technology and organization (see Figure 3-9). Here, changes in technology are absorbed, deflected, and defeated by the arrangement of organizational tasks, structures, and people. In this model, the only way to bring about change is to change the technology, tasks, structure, and people simultaneously. Other authors have spoken about the need to "unfreeze" organizations before introducing an innovation, quickly implementing it, and "refreezing" or institutionalizing the change (Alter and Ginzberg, 1978; Kolb, 1970). This is known as the Lewin/Schein theory of change.

Because organizational resistance to change is so powerful, many information technology investments flounder and do not increase productivity. Indeed, research on project implementation failures demonstrates that the most common reason for failure of large projects to reach their objectives is not the failure of the technology, but organizational and political resistance to change. Chapter 10 treats this issue in detail. Therefore, as a manager involved in future IT investments, your ability to work with people and organizations is just as important as your technical awareness and knowledge.

The Internet and Organizations

The Internet, especially the World Wide Web, has an important impact on the relationships between many firms and external entities and even on the organization of business processes inside a firm. The Internet increases the accessibility, storage, and distribution of information and knowledge for organizations. In essence, the Internet is capable of dramatically lowering the transaction and agency costs facing most organizations. For instance, brokerage firms and banks can now deliver their internal operations procedures manuals to their employees at distant locations by posting them on their corporate Web sites, saving millions of dollars in printing and distribution costs.

A global sales force can receive nearly instant price product information updates using the Web or instructions from management sent by e-mail. Vendors of some large retailers can access retailers' internal Web sites directly to find up-to-the-minute sales information and to initiate replenishment orders instantly.

Businesses are rapidly rebuilding some of their key business processes based on Internet technology and making this technology a key component of their IT infrastructures. If prior networking is any guide, one result will be simpler business processes, fewer employees, and much flatter organizations than in the past.

Implications for the Design and Understanding of Information Systems

To deliver genuine benefits, information systems must be developed with a clear understanding of the organization in which they will be used. In our experience, the central organizational factors to consider when planning a new system are the following:

- The environment in which the organization must function
- The structure of the organization: hierarchy, specialization, routines, and business processes
- The organization's culture and politics
- The type of organization and its style of leadership
- The principal interest groups affected by the system and the attitudes of workers who will be using the system
- The kinds of tasks, decisions, and business processes that the information system is designed to assist

Understanding all of these organizational factors and the relationships among them can help us to understand why some information systems and technology are easier to implement in certain organizations than in others (see also Chapter 10).

3.3 Using Information Systems to Achieve Competitive Advantage

In almost every industry you examine, you will find that some firms do better than most others. There is almost always a stand-out firm. In the automotive industry, Toyota is considered a superior performer. In pure online retail, Amazon is the leader; in off-line retail Walmart, the largest retailer on earth, is the leader. In online music, Apple's iTunes is considered the leader with more than 75 percent of the downloaded music market, and in the related industry of digital music players, the iPod is the leader. In Web search, Google is considered the leader.

Firms that "do better" than others are said to have a competitive advantage over others. They either have access to special resources that others do not, or they are able to use commonly available resources more efficiently—usually because of superior knowledge and information assets. In any event, they do better in terms of revenue growth, profitability, or productivity growth (efficiency), all of which in the long run translate into higher stock market valuations than their competitors.

But why do some firms do better than others and how do they achieve competitive advantage? How can you analyze a business and identify its strategic advantages? How can you develop a strategic advantage for your own business? And how do information systems contribute to strategic advantages? One answer to that question is Michael Porter's competitive forces model.

FIGURE 3-10   Porter's competitive forces model.

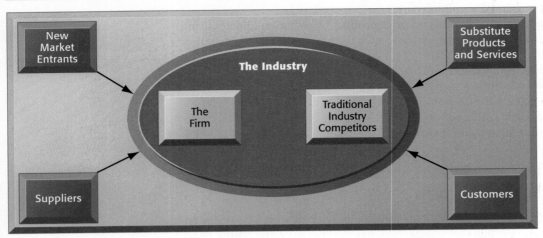

In Porter's competitive forces model, the strategic position of the firm and its strategies are determined not only by competition with its traditional direct competitors but also by four other forces in the industry's environment: new market entrants, substitute products and services, customers, and suppliers.

Porter's Competitive Forces Model

Arguably, the most widely used model for understanding competitive advantage is Michael Porter's **competitive forces model** (see Figure 3-10). This model provides a general view of the firm, its competitors, and the firm's environment. Earlier in this chapter, we described the importance of a firm's environment and the dependence of firms on environments. Porter's model is all about the firm's general business environment. In this model, five competitive forces shape the fate of the firm.

Traditional Competitors All firms share market space with other competitors who are continually devising new, more efficient ways to produce by introducing new products and services and attempting to attract customers by developing their brands and imposing switching costs on their customers.

New Market Entrants In a free economy with mobile labour and financial resources, new companies are always entering the marketplace. In some industries, there are very low barriers to entry while in other industries, entry is very difficult. For instance, it is fairly easy to start a pizza business or just about any small retail business, but it is much more expensive and difficult to enter the computer chip business, which has very high capital costs and requires significant expertise and knowledge that is hard to obtain. New companies have several possible advantages: They are not locked into old plants and equipment, they often hire younger workers who are less expensive and perhaps more innovative, they are not encumbered by old worn-out brand names, and they are "more hungry" (more highly motivated) than traditional occupants of an industry. These advantages are also their weakness. They depend on outside financing for new plants and equipment, which can be expensive; they have a less-experienced workforce; and they have little brand recognition.

Substitute Products and Services In just about every industry, there are substitutes that your customers might use if your prices become too high. New technologies create new substitutes all the time. Even oil has substitutes. Ethanol can substitute for gasoline in cars; vegetable oil for diesel fuel in trucks; and wind, solar, coal, and hydro power for industrial electricity generation. Likewise, the Internet telephone service can substitute for traditional telephone service, and fibre optic telephone lines to the home can substitute for cable TV lines. And, of course, an Internet music service that allows you to download music tracks to an iPod is a substitute for CD-based music stores. The more substitute products and services in your industry, the less you can control pricing and the lower your profit margins.

Competitive forces model

Customers A profitable company depends in large measure on its ability to attract and retain customers (while denying them to competitors) and charge high prices. The power of customers grows if they can easily switch to a competitor's products and services, or if they can force a business and its competitors to compete on price alone in a transparent marketplace where there is little product differentiation and all prices are known instantly (such as on the Internet). For instance, in the used textbook market on the Internet, students (customers) can find multiple suppliers of just about any current textbook. In this case, online customers have extraordinary power over used-book firms.

Suppliers The market power of suppliers can have a significant impact on firm profits, especially when the firm cannot raise prices as fast as suppliers can. The more different suppliers a firm has, the greater control it can exercise over suppliers in terms of price, quality, and delivery schedules. For instance, manufacturers of laptop PCs almost always have multiple competing suppliers of key components, such as keyboards, hard drives, and display screens.

Information System Strategies for Dealing with Competitive Forces

What is a firm to do when it is faced with all these competitive forces? And how can the firm use information systems to counteract some of these forces? How do you prevent substitutes and inhibit new market entrants? There are four generic strategies, each of which often is enabled by using information technology and systems: low-cost leadership, product differentiation, focus on market niche, and strengthening customer and supplier intimacy.

Low-Cost Leadership A firm can use information systems to achieve the lowest operational costs and the lowest prices. The classic example is Walmart. By keeping prices low and shelves well stocked using a legendary inventory replenishment system, Walmart became the leading retail business in North America. Walmart's continuous replenishment system sends orders for new merchandise directly to suppliers as soon as consumers pay for their purchases at the cash register. Point-of-sale terminals record the bar code of each item passing the checkout counter and send a purchase transaction directly to a central computer at Walmart headquarters. The computer collects the orders from all Walmart stores and transmits them to suppliers. Suppliers can also access Walmart's sales and inventory data using Web technology.

Walmart's continuous replenishment system is also an example of an efficient customer response system. An efficient customer response system directly links consumer behaviour to distribution and production and supply chains. Walmart's continuous replenishment system provides such an efficient customer response. Dell Inc.'s assemble-to-order system, described below, is another example of an efficient customer response system.

Because the system replenishes inventory with lightning speed, Walmart does not need to spend much money on maintaining large inventories of goods in its own warehouses. The system also enables Walmart to adjust purchases of store items to meet customer demands. Competitors, such as Sears, have been spending 24.9 percent of sales on overhead. But by using systems to keep operating costs low, Walmart pays only 16.6 percent of sales revenue for overhead. (Operating costs average 20.7 percent of sales in the retail industry.)

Walmart's continuous inventory replenishment system uses sales data captured at the checkout counter to transmit orders to restock merchandise directly to its suppliers. The system enables Walmart to keep costs low while fine-tuning its merchandise to meet customer demands.

Product Differentiation A firm can use information systems to produce **product differentiation**, that is, to enable new products and services or greatly change the customer convenience in using your existing products and services. For instance, Google continuously introduces new and unique search services on its Web site, such as Google Maps. By purchasing PayPal, an electronic payment system, in 2003, eBay made it much easier for customers to pay sellers and expanded use of its auction marketplace. Apple created the iPod, a unique portable digital music player, plus a unique online Web music service where songs can be purchased for 99 cents. Continuing to innovate, Apple introduced a portable iPod video player and a multimedia smartphone that includes iPod capabilities.

Manufacturers and retailers are using information systems to create products and services that are customized and personalized to fit the precise specifications of individual customers. Dell Inc. sells directly to customers using assemble-to-order manufacturing. Individuals, businesses, and government agencies can buy computers directly from Dell, customized with the exact features and components they need. They can place their orders directly using a toll-free telephone number or by accessing Dell's Web site (see Figure 3-11). Once Dell's production control receives an order, it directs an assembly plant to assemble the computer using components from an on-site warehouse based on the configuration specified by the customer.

Lands' End customers can use its Web site to order jeans, dress pants, chino pants, and shirts custom-tailored to their own specifications. Customers enter their measurements into a form on the Web site, which then transmits each customer's specifications

Product differentiation

FIGURE 3-11   Dell Inc.'s Web site.

On the Dell Inc. Web site, customers can select the options they want and order their computer custom built to these specifications. Dell's assemble-to-order system is a major source of competitive advantage.

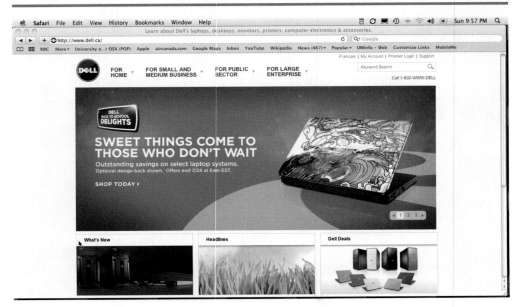

TABLE 3-3 IT-enabled new products and services providing competitive advantage.

One-click shopping: Amazon	Amazon holds a patent on one-click shopping that it licenses to other online retailers.
Online music: Apple iPod and iTunes	An integrated handheld player backed up with an online library of over 6 million songs.
Search engine advertising: Google	Online search engine integrated with online advertising using text ads; more than 10 billion searches per month; Google holds several patents on its PageRank method of search response.
Golf club customization: Ping	Customers can select from more than 1 million different golf club options; a build-to-order system ships their customized clubs within 48 hours.
Online bill payment: epost.ca	Almost 3 million households were registered at epost.ca, as of 2006.
Online person-to-person payment: PayPal.com	Enables transfer of money between individual bank accounts and between bank accounts and credit card accounts.

over a network to a computer that develops an electronic made-to-measure pattern for that customer. The individual patterns are then transmitted electronically to a manufacturing plant where they are used to drive fabric-cutting equipment. There are almost no extra production costs because the process does not require additional warehousing, production overruns, and inventories, and the cost to the customer is only slightly higher than that of a mass-produced garment. Fourteen percent of Lands' End shirt and pants sales are now customized. This ability to offer individually tailored products or services using the same production resources as mass production is called **mass customization.**

Table 3-3 lists a number of companies that have developed IT-based products and services that other firms have found difficult to copy or at least take a long time to copy.

Focus on Market Niche A firm can use information systems to enable a specific market focus and serve this narrow target market better than competitors. Information systems support this strategy by producing and analyzing data for finely tuned sales and marketing techniques. Information systems enable companies to analyze customer buying patterns, tastes, and preferences closely so that they efficiently pitch advertising and marketing campaigns to smaller and smaller target markets.

The data come from a range of sources—credit card transactions, demographic data, purchase data from checkout counter scanners at supermarkets and retail stores, and data collected when people access and interact with Web sites. Sophisticated software tools find patterns in these large pools of data and infer rules from them to guide decision making. Analysis of this data drives one-to-one marketing that creates personal messages based on individualized preferences. For example, Hilton Hotels' OnQ system analyzes detailed data collected on active guests in all of its properties to determine the preferences of each guest and each guest's profitability. Hilton uses this information to give its most profitable customers additional privileges, such as late checkouts. Contemporary customer relationship management (CRM) systems feature analytical capabilities for this type of intensive data analysis (see Chapters 2 and 12).

The Window on Technology section on the next page shows how 7-Eleven improved its competitive position by wringing more value out of its customer data. This company's early growth and strategy had been based on face-to-face relationships with its customers and intimate knowledge of exactly what they wanted to purchase. As the company grew over time, it was no longer able to discern customer preferences through personal face-to-face relationships. A new information system helped it obtain intimate knowledge of its customers once again by gathering and analyzing customer purchase transactions.

Mass customization

WINDOW ON TECHNOLOGY

7-Eleven Stores Ask the Customer by Asking the Data

There is probably a 7-Eleven store in your neighbourhood, and it is a convenient place for picking up a can of Coke or a quick ham-and-cheese sandwich. It is the largest convenience retailer in the world and the number-one convenience store chain in North America, with 7100 stores.

This company started out about 75 years ago as an ice-dock operator. When refrigerators started replacing iceboxes, the manager of each store asked customers one-by-one what items they would like to stock in their new appliances. By asking customers directly and stocking only the items customers most wanted, the company grew and prospered.

Over time, the company moved away from its roots, losing touch with customers along the way. It had no means of knowing what sold in each store and allowed vendors to decide what to stock on its shelves. Although large vendors, such as Coca-Cola and Frito-Lay, had powerful information systems for analyzing what they sold in individual stores, other vendors did not have such systems. Moreover, the vendors' systems were designed to maximize opportunities for their businesses, not for 7-Eleven.

7-Eleven stores are not all alike. What their customers want depends a great deal on the neighbourhood and region of the country where they are located. What sells well in Charlottetown may not work in Whistler.

Without detailed knowledge of its customer and sales patterns, 7-Eleven was unable to determine which items were selling well or which items were most profitable to sell in the first place. This made a difference to the company's bottom line because of missed sales opportunities, lower profits, and excess store inventory, some of which consisted of perishable goods that had a very short shelf life. Profit margins are very thin in the convenience store business, so a quarter-point increase in sales volume can spell the difference between success and failure.

In 2004, 7-Eleven installed Hewlett-Packard servers and networking switches in all its U.S. stores to implement a Retail Information System. This system collects data from point-of-sale terminals in every store about each purchase made daily by its 6 million North American customers and transmits the information in real time to a 7-terabyte Oracle database operated by Electronic Data Systems (EDS).

With this database, 7-Eleven keeps track of its purchase transactions and analyzes them to amass information about customer demand, pricing, and interest in new products, such as the Diet Pepsi Slurpee. Analysis of the data shows which items are selling well in which stores, which items customers are most interested in, seasonal demand for items, and which items are most profitable to sell in the first place.

Management uses this information to identify sales trends, improve product assortment, eliminate slow-moving products from inventory, and increase same-store sales by stocking products that are high in demand. Insights gleaned from the data also help 7-Eleven develop new products such as its fresh food offerings that attract new customers and increase transaction size.

The system provides store managers with information on daily, weekly, and monthly sales of each item to help them determine which items to order and the exact quantities they will need for their stores. Managers use this information plus their on-the-spot knowledge of the neighbourhood to make final ordering decisions.

Store managers enter orders into workstations or handheld computers by 10 a.m. each day. The system consolidates these orders and transmits them to 7-Eleven's suppliers. Orders are consolidated four times daily, one for each U.S. time zone in which 7-Eleven stores operate. 7-Eleven's orders for fresh food items are aggregated at 7-Eleven headquarters and transmitted to fresh food suppliers and bakeries for preparation and delivery the next day.

Thanks to information technology, 7-Eleven has come full circle in its ability to respond to the needs of the customer. By tracking and analyzing its data, it knows its customers as intimately as it did when store owners talked to each customer face to face. According to 7-Eleven President and CEO James Keyes, "Now we can use technology as a surrogate for being able to talk to every customer who walks in the door."

To Think About

1. Why is knowing about the customer so important to a company such as 7-Eleven?

2. What are the benefits of 7-Eleven's Retail Information System?

3. In terms of Porter's model, what strategic forces does the Retail Information System seek to address?

4. Which of the strategies described in the chapter does the Retail Information System support?

MIS in Action

Visit a nearby 7-Eleven store. You can find your nearest 7-Eleven store by logging on to **www.7-eleven.com** and using the site's store locator. Observe the items available for sale and the sales process at the store.

1. What technologies does the store use to process a purchase? Do you see any other technologies being used at the store?

2. Do you think the selection of items for sale is appropriate for the neighbourhood and location of the particular 7-Eleven store you are visiting? What items might the Retail Information System have suggested for this store? Do you see any items that appear to be selling poorly at this store?

3. How well do you think 7-Eleven's Retail Information System works in stocking items for this store?

Sources: Oracle Corporation, "Streamlining Convenience," 2006 Shared Strategy Study and "7-Eleven Inc.," **www.oracle.com** (accessed July 15, 2006); Christopher Koch, "Who's Mining the Store?" *CIO*, May 15, 2005; James Keyes, "Data on the Fly," *Baseline*, August 2005; Laurie Sullivan, "Fine-Tuned Pricing," *InformationWeek*, August 15/22, 2005; "About 7-Eleven," **www.7-eleven.com/about/history.asp** (accessed May 11, 2007); and Steven Marlin, "The 24-Hour Supply Chain," *InformationWeek*, January 26, 2004.

Strengthen Customer and Supplier Intimacy A firm can use information systems to tighten linkages with suppliers and develop intimacy with customers. Chrysler Corporation uses information systems to facilitate direct access by suppliers to production schedules, and even permits suppliers to decide how and when to ship supplies to Chrysler factories. This allows suppliers more lead time in producing goods. On the customer side, Chapters.Indigo.ca keeps track of user preferences for book and CD purchases and can recommend titles purchased by others to its customers. Strong linkages to customers and suppliers increase **switching costs** (the cost of switching from one product to a competing product) and loyalty to the firm.

Table 3-4 summarizes the competitive strategies we have just described. Some companies focus on one of these strategies, but you will often see companies pursuing several of them simultaneously. For example, Dell tries to emphasize low cost as well as the ability to customize its personal computers.

The Internet's Impact on Competitive Advantage

The Internet has nearly destroyed some industries and has severely threatened more. The Internet has also created entirely new markets and formed the basis for thousands of new businesses. The first wave of e-commerce transformed the business world of books, music, and air travel. In the second wave, eight new industries are facing a similar transformation scenario: telephone services, movies, television, jewellery, real estate, hotels, bill payments, and software. The breadth of e-commerce offerings continues to grow, especially in travel, information clearinghouses, entertainment, retail apparel, appliances, and home furnishings.

For instance, the printed encyclopedia industry and the travel agency industry have been nearly decimated by the availability of substitutes over the Internet. Likewise, the Internet has had a significant impact on the retail, music, book, brokerage, and newspaper industries. At the same time, the Internet has enabled new products and services, new business models, and new industries to spring up every day—from eBay and Amazon, to

Switching costs

TABLE 3-4 Four basic competitive strategies.

STRATEGY	DESCRIPTION	EXAMPLE
Low-cost leadership	Use information systems to produce products and services at a lower price than competitors while enhancing quality and level of service.	Walmart
Product differentiation	Use information systems to differentiate products, and enable new services and products.	Google, eBay, Apple, Lands' End
Focus on market niche	Use information systems to enable a focused strategy on a single market niche; specialize.	Hilton Hotels, Harrah's
Customer and supplier intimacy	Use information systems to develop strong ties and loyalty with customers and suppliers.	Chrysler Corporation, Chapters.Indigo.ca

TABLE 3-5 Impact of the Internet on competitive forces and industry structure.

COMPETITIVE FORCE	IMPACT OF THE INTERNET
Substitute products or services	Enables new substitutes to emerge with new approaches to meeting needs and performing functions.
Customers' bargaining power	Availability of global price and product information shifts bargaining power to customers.
Suppliers' bargaining power	Procurement over the Internet tends to raise bargaining power over suppliers; suppliers can also benefit from reduced barriers to entry and from the elimination of distributors and other intermediaries standing between them and their users.
Threat of new entrants	The Internet reduces barriers to entry, such as the need for a sales force, access to channels, and physical assets; it provides a technology for driving business processes that makes other things easier to do.
Positioning and rivalry among existing competitors	Widens the geographic market, increasing the number of competitors, and reducing differences among competitors; makes it more difficult to sustain operational advantages; puts pressure to compete on price.

iTunes and Google. In this sense, the Internet is "transforming" entire industries, forcing firms to change how they do business.

Because of the Internet, the traditional competitive forces are still at work, but competitive rivalry has become much more intense (Porter, 2001). Internet technology is based on universal standards that any company can use, making it easy for rivals to compete on price alone and for new competitors to enter the market. Because information is available to everyone, the Internet raises the bargaining power of customers, who can quickly find the lowest-cost provider on the Web. Profits have been dampened. Some industries, such as the travel industry and the financial services industry, have been more impacted than others. Table 3-5 summarizes some of the potentially negative impacts of the Internet on business firms identified by Porter.

However, contrary to Porter's somewhat negative assessment, the Internet also creates new opportunities for building brands and building very large and loyal customer bases that are willing to pay a premium for the brand, for example, Yahoo!, eBay, Air Miles, RedEnvelope, Chapters.Indigo.ca, Google, and many others. In addition, as with all IT-enabled business initiatives, some firms are far better at using the Internet than other firms are, which creates new strategic opportunities for the successful firms.

The Business Value Chain Model

Although the Porter model is very helpful for identifying competitive forces and suggesting generic strategies, it is not very specific about what exactly to do, and it does not provide a methodology to follow for achieving competitive advantages. If your goal is to achieve operational excellence, where do you start? This is where the business value chain model is helpful.

The **value chain model** highlights specific activities in the business where competitive strategies can best be applied (Porter, 1985) and where information systems are most likely to have a strategic impact. This model identifies specific, critical leverage points where a firm can use information technology most effectively to enhance its competitive position. The value chain model views the firm as a series or chain of basic activities that add a margin of value to a firm's products or services. These activities can be categorized as either primary activities or support activities (see Figure 3-12).

Primary activities are most directly related to the production and distribution of the firm's products and services, which create value for the customer. Primary activities include inbound logistics, operations, outbound logistics, sales and marketing, and service. Inbound logistics includes receiving and storing materials for distribution to production. Operations transforms inputs into finished products. Outbound logistics entails storing and distributing finished products. Sales and marketing includes promoting and selling the firm's products. The service activity includes maintenance and repair of the firm's goods and services.

Value chain model
Primary activities

FIGURE 3-12   The value chain model.

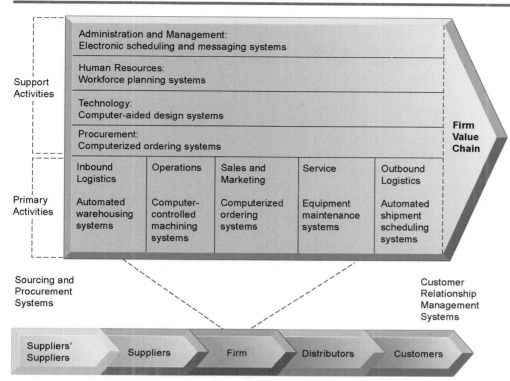

This figure provides examples of systems for both primary and support activities of a firm and of its value partners that can add a margin of value to a firm's products or services.

Support activities make the delivery of the primary activities possible and consist of organization infrastructure (administration and management), human resources (employee recruiting, hiring, and training), technology (improving products and the production process), and procurement (purchasing input).

Now you can ask at each stage of the value chain, "How can we use information systems to improve operational efficiency and improve customer and supplier intimacy?" This will force you to critically examine how you perform value-adding activities at each stage and how the business processes might be improved. You can also begin to ask how information systems can be used to improve the relationship with customers and with suppliers that lie outside the firm's value chain but belong to the firm's extended value chain where they are absolutely critical to your success. Here, supply chain management systems that coordinate the flow of resources into your firm and customer relationship management systems that coordinate your sales and support employees with customers are two of the most common system applications that result from a business value chain analysis. We discuss these enterprise applications in detail later in Chapter 12.

Using the business value chain model will also cause you to consider benchmarking your business processes against your competitors or others in related industries, and identifying industry best practices. **Benchmarking** involves comparing the efficiency and effectiveness of your business processes against strict standards and then measuring performance against those standards. Industry **best practices** are usually identified by consulting companies, research organizations, government agencies, and industry associations as the most successful solutions or problem-solving methods for consistently and effectively achieving a business objective.

Once you have analyzed the various stages in the value chain at your business, you can come up with candidate applications of information systems. Then, once you have a list of candidate applications, you can decide which to develop first. By making improvements in your own business value chain that your competitors might miss, you can achieve competitive advantage by attaining operational excellence, lowering costs, improving profit margins, and forging a closer relationship with customers and suppliers.

Support activities
Benchmarking
Best practices

If your competitors are making similar improvements, then at least you will not be at a competitive disadvantage—the worst of all cases.

Extending the Value Chain: The Value Web Figure 3-12 shows that a firm's value chain is linked to the value chains of its suppliers, distributors, and customers. After all, the performance of most firms depends not only on what goes inside a firm but also on how well the firm coordinates with direct and indirect suppliers, delivery firms (logistics partners, such as DHL or UPS), and, of course, customers.

How can information systems be used to achieve strategic advantage at the industry level? By working with other firms, industry participants can use information technology to develop industry-wide standards for exchanging information or business transactions electronically, which force all market participants to subscribe to similar standards. These efforts increase efficiency, making product substitution less likely and perhaps raising entry costs—thus discouraging new entrants. Also, industry members can develop industry-wide, IT-supported consortia, symposia, and communications networks to coordinate activities concerning government agencies, foreign competition, and competing industries.

Looking at the industry value chain encourages you to think about how to use information systems to link up more efficiently with your suppliers, strategic partners, and customers. Strategic advantage derives from your ability to relate your value chain to the value chains of other partners in the process. For instance, if you are Amazon.com, you want to build systems that

- Make it easy for suppliers to display goods and open stores on the Amazon site
- Make it easy for customers to pay for goods
- Develop systems that coordinate the shipment of goods to customers
- Develop shipment tracking systems for customers

In fact, this is exactly what Amazon has done to become one of the Web's most satisfying online retail shopping sites. The Window on Organizations section discusses how Amazon.com developed and executes this business strategy. It also shows that Amazon.com had to revise its strategy several times in order to remain competitive.

Internet technology has made it possible to create highly synchronized industry value chains called value webs. A **value web** is a collection of independent firms that use information technology to coordinate their value chains to produce a product or service for a market collectively. A value web is more customer-driven and operates in a less linear fashion than the traditional value chain.

Value web

Organizations

WINDOW ON ORGANIZATIONS

Amazon.com: An Internet Giant Fine-Tunes Its Strategy

Amazon.com made Internet history as one of the first large-scale retail companies to sell over the Web: in 2004 it hit $4.6 billion in online revenues, and by 2006 its sales hit $11 billion in revenue. It has grown to become one of the largest Internet retailers on earth. But the real significance of Amazon for this chapter is Amazon's continuous innovation in business strategy and information systems. In fact, the two are closely connected at Amazon: Its business innovations are all driven by huge investments in information systems.

In 1995, former investment banker Jeff Bezos took advantage of new business opportunities created by the Internet by setting up a Web site to sell books directly to customers online.

There were 3 million titles in print, and any one physical bookstore could only stock a fraction of them.

A "virtual" bookstore offers a much larger selection of titles. Bezos believed consumers did not need to actually "touch and feel" a book before buying it, and Amazon.com provided online synopses, tables of contents, and reviews to help with selection. Amazon.com was able to charge lower prices than physical bookstores because it maintained very little of its own inventory (relying instead on distributors) and did not have to pay for maintaining physical storefronts or a large retail sales staff.

Amazon tried to provide superior customer service through e-mail and telephone customer support, automated order confirmation, online tracking and shipping information, and the ability to pay for purchases with a single click of the mouse using credit card and personal information a customer had provided during a previous purchase. This was called "1-Click" express shopping, and it made the shopping experience even more convenient. Amazon even received a patent for its 1-Click technology.

In 1998, Amazon started selling music, CDs, videos, and DVDs, revising its business strategy "to become the best place to buy, find, and discover any product or service available online"—the online Walmart. Its offerings grew to include electronics, toys, home improvement products, video games, apparel, gourmet food, travel services, personal care, and jewellery. It also introduced Amazon.com Auctions (similar to those offered by eBay), Amazon Marketplace (online store-fronts for small retailers).

To service these new product lines, Amazon significantly expanded its warehouse and distribution capabilities and hired large numbers of employees. These moves strained its ability to adhere to its original vision of being a "virtual" retailer with lean inventories, low head count, and significant cost savings over traditional bookstores.

In 2001 and 2002, Amazon tried to increase revenue by cutting prices, offering free shipping, and leveraging its technology infrastructure to provide e-commerce services to other businesses. Amazon's Merchants@ and Amazon Marketplace allow other businesses to fully integrate their Web sites into Amazon's site to sell their branded goods using Amazon's fulfillment and payment systems. Nordstrom, Gap, and Target stores use Amazon to sell their goods and then pay Amazon commissions and fees. In the Amazon Marketplace program, individuals are encouraged to sell their used or new goods on Amazon's Web site even when they compete directly with Amazon's sales of the same goods. Sales by third parties now represent 25 percent of Amazon's revenues.

Amazon refined its business model further to focus more on efficient operations while maintaining a steady commitment to keeping its 49 million customers satisfied. In early 2001, Amazon closed two of its eight warehouses, laid off 15 percent of its workforce, and consolidated orders from around the country prior to shipping to reduce shipping costs. Amazon used six sigma quality measures to reduce errors in fulfillment. These measures reduced fulfillment costs from 15 percent of revenue in 2000 to 10 percent by 2003.

Amazon finally became profitable in 2003 and remains an online retailing powerhouse growing at over 60 percent a year. It continues to innovate with IT-enabled services: free unlimited two-day shipping for $79 a year (Amazon Prime). Amazon entered the dry goods grocery business in 2006. These innovations increased its costs and reduced its profits, much to the disappointment of the stock market, which has depressed Amazon's stock from a high of $100 in 2000 down to the mid-$20 range in 2006 and back to the mid-upper $80 range in 2009 as this text was going to print.

But Amazon faces powerful online retail competitors such as eBay and Yahoo!, which also are very adept at using information systems to develop new products and services. Google

is emerging as a competitor because so many consumers use its search engine—more than 10 billion searches are performed each month at Google—and in the process are exposed to search engine ads. Google is expanding into other shopping services: Google Base offers free classified listings of goods for sale, and Google Checkout provides an online service that stores users' financial information to facilitate purchases from participating Internet vendors. Amazon is countering with new offerings, such as a digital mapping service with street-level photographs, a grocery store for nonperishable items sold in bulk, and selling short stories online for 49 cents apiece, along with additional expenditures to improve customer convenience and the shopping experience.

Like Google, eBay, Yahoo!, AOL, and other Web giants, Amazon has a Canadian Web site, Amazon.ca, which includes almost identical elements, products, and services as its U.S.-based site. The Canadian site is, of course, offered in both English and French, and shipping charges are for within-Canada shipping, a true benefit for Canadian customers.

After about 15 years riding the wave as the largest online retailer in North America, if not the world, the question is whether Amazon can turn its leadership in e-commerce into genuine long-term success. Can Amazon keep adapting its strategy to remain profitable and powerful?

To Think About

1. Analyze Amazon.com using the competitive forces and value chain models. How has it responded to pressures from its competitive environment? How does it provide value to its customers?

2. Describe Amazon's evolving business strategy.

3. Why did the company change its strategy?

4. Do you think Amazon can continue to be successful? Explain your answer.

MIS in Action

Search for an iPod nano on Amazon.ca, eBay.ca, and Yahoo! Shopping (**http://ca.shopping.yahoo.com**). Compare the shopping experience at these sites to answer the following questions.

1. Evaluate how each site offers information about a product, including information about the reliability of the vendor.

2. Evaluate each of the sites in terms of how many sources for the product they offer.

3. Evaluate the sites in terms of pricing and availability of the product you have selected.

4. Which site would you choose for shopping for your nano? Why?

Sources: Mary Crane, "Child's Play? Amazon Takes On Toys," Forbes.com, July 5, 2006; "Amazon Adds Groceries to Its Site," *The Wall Street Journal*, June 15, 2006; Randall Stross, "Trying to Get a Read on Amazon's Books," *The New York Times*, February 12, 2006; Bob Tedeschi, "Making Several Stops at Shops Online, but Paying All at Google," *The New York Times*, July 17, 2006; Gary Rivlin, "A Retail Revolution Turns 10," *The New York Times*, July 10, 2005; and Shaheen Pasha, "Amazon Has New Stories to Tell," *CNN Money*, August 22, 2005.

Jeff Bezos is the founder, president, CEO, and chairman of the board of Amazon.com. Amazon.ca, which was launched in 2002, is an early e-commerce leader that has adjusted its strategy multiple times. It is trying to become a one-stop source for online shoppers.

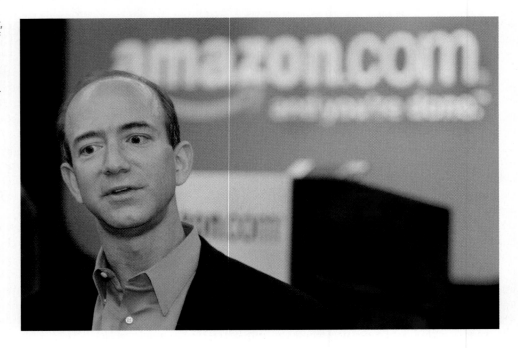

Figure 3-13 shows that this value web synchronizes the business processes of customers, suppliers, and trading partners among different companies in an industry or in related industries. These value webs are flexible and adaptive to changes in supply and demand. Relationships can be bundled or unbundled in response to changing market conditions. Firms will accelerate time to market and to customers by optimizing their value web relationships to make quick decisions about who can deliver the required products or services at the right price and location.

FIGURE 3-13   The value web.

The value web is a networked system that can synchronize the value chains of business partners within an industry to respond rapidly to changes in supply and demand.

Synergies, Core Competencies, and Network-Based Strategies

A large corporation is typically a collection of businesses. Often, the firm is organized financially as a collection of strategic business units, and the returns to the firm are directly tied to the performance of all the strategic business units. Information systems can improve the overall performance of these business units by promoting synergies and core competencies.

Synergies The idea of synergies is that when the output of some units can be used as inputs to other units, or two organizations pool markets and expertise, these relationships lower costs and generate profits. Recent bank and financial firm mergers, such as the merger of Toronto Dominion Bank and Canada Trust as well as Great West Life and Canada Life, occurred precisely for this purpose.

One use of information technology in these synergy situations is to tie together the operations of disparate business units so that they can act as a whole. For example, when Air Canada and Canadian Airlines merged, Air Canada not only eliminated the competition but also gained access to airport landing gates and customers, including the customers' profiles and loyalty card (i.e., frequent flyer program) data. After an initial problematic implementation of the information systems of these two Canadian giants, the loyalty card programs were merged, with Canadian's flyers having Air Canada miles. For other companies, it is not so easy. Both Great West Life Assurance and Investors Group are owned by the Power Corporation, but they cannot take advantage of the synergies that could be possible due to privacy issues. There is no mechanism to merge their information systems since doing so would open customer files of one company to the other company and its representatives—without their customers' permission.

Enhancing Core Competencies Yet another way to use information systems for competitive advantage is to think about ways that systems can enhance core competencies. The argument is that the performance of all business units will increase insofar as these business units develop or create a central core of competencies. A **core competency** is an activity for which a firm is a world-class leader. Core competencies may involve being the world's best miniature parts designer, the best package delivery service, or the best thin-film manufacturer. In general, a core competency relies on knowledge that is gained over many years of experience and a first-class research organization or simply key people who follow the literature and stay abreast of new external knowledge.

Any information system that encourages the sharing of knowledge across business units enhances competency. These systems might encourage or enhance existing competencies and help employees become aware of new external knowledge; they might also help a business leverage existing competencies to related markets.

For example, Procter & Gamble (P&G), a world leader in brand management and consumer product innovation, uses a series of systems to enhance its core competencies. P&G uses an intranet called InnovationNet to help people working on similar problems share ideas and expertise. The system connects those working in research and development (R&D), engineering, purchasing, marketing, legal affairs, and business information systems around the world, using a portal to provide browser-based access to documents, reports, charts, videos, and other data from various sources. It includes a directory of subject matter experts who can be tapped to give advice or collaborate on problem solving and product development and links to outside research scientists and entrepreneurs who are searching for new, innovative products worldwide.

P&G sells more than 300 different branded products, with separate lines of business for Fabric and Home Care, Baby and Family Care, Beauty Care, Health Care, and Snacks, Coffee, and Pet Care. It now uses custom-developed marketing management software to help all these groups share marketing ideas and data for marketing campaigns. This system supports strategic planning, research, advertising, direct mail, and events, and is able to analyze the impact of marketing projects on the business.

Network-Based Strategies The availability of Internet and networking technology have inspired strategies that take advantage of firms' abilities to create networks or network

Core competency

with each other. Network-based strategies include the use of network economics, a virtual company model, and business ecosystems.

Network Economics   Business models based on a network may help firms strategically by taking advantage of **network economics.** In traditional economics—the economics of factories and agriculture—production experiences diminishing returns. The more any given resource is applied to production, the lower the marginal gain in output until a point is reached where the additional inputs produce no additional outputs. This is the law of diminishing returns, and it is the foundation for most of modern economics.

In some situations, the law of diminishing returns does not work. For instance, in a network, the marginal costs of adding another participant are about zero while the marginal gain is much larger. The larger the number of subscribers in a telephone system or the Internet, the greater the value to all participants because each user can interact with more people. It is not much more expensive to operate a television station with 1000 subscribers than with 10 million subscribers. The value of a community of people grows with size while the cost of adding new members is inconsequential.

From this network economics perspective, information technology can be strategically useful. Internet sites can be used by firms to build communities of users—like-minded customers who want to share their experiences. This builds customer loyalty and enjoyment, and builds unique ties to customers. EBay and iVillage, an online community for women, are examples. Both businesses are based on networks of millions of users, and both companies have used the Web and Internet communication tools to build communities. The more people offer products on eBay, the more valuable the eBay site is to everyone because more products are listed, and more competition among suppliers lowers prices. Network economics also provides strategic benefits to commercial software vendors. The value of their software and complementary software products increases as more people use them, and there is a larger installed base to justify continued use of the product and vendor support.

Virtual Company Model   Another network-based strategy uses the model of a virtual company to create a competitive business. A **virtual company,** also known as a virtual organization, uses networks to link people, assets, and ideas, enabling it to ally with other companies to create and distribute products and services without being limited by traditional organizational boundaries or physical locations. One company can use the capabilities of another company without being physically tied to that company. The virtual company model is useful when a company finds it cheaper to acquire products, services, or capabilities from an external vendor or when it needs to move quickly to exploit new market opportunities and lacks the time and resources to respond on its own.

Fashion companies, such as GUESS, Ann Taylor, Levi Strauss, and Reebok, enlist Hong Kong–based Li & Fung to manage production and shipment of their garments. Li & Fung handles product development, raw material sourcing, production planning, quality assurance, and shipping. Li & Fung does not own any fabric, factories, or machines, outsourcing all of its work to a network of more than 7500 suppliers in 37 countries all over the world. Customers place orders to Li & Fung over its private extranet. Li & Fung then sends instructions to appropriate raw material suppliers and factories where the clothing is produced. The Li & Fung extranet tracks the entire production process for each order.

Working as a virtual company keeps Li & Fung flexible and adaptable so that it can design and produce the products ordered by its clients in short order to keep pace with rapidly changing fashion trends.

Business Ecosystems: Keystone and Niche Firms   The Internet and the emergence of digital firms call for some modification of the industry competitive forces model. The traditional Porter model assumes a relatively static industry environment; relatively clear-cut industry boundaries; and a relatively stable set of suppliers, substitutes, and customers, with the focus on industry players in a market environment. Instead of participating in a single industry, some of today's firms are much more aware that they participate in industry sets—collections of industries that provide related services and products (see Figure 3-14).

Network economics
Virtual company

FIGURE 3-14   An ecosystem strategic model.

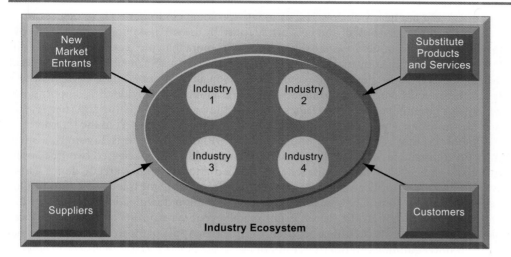

Industry Ecosystem

The digital firm era requires a more dynamic view of the boundaries among industries, firms, customers, and suppliers, with competition occurring among industry sets in a business ecosystem. In the ecosystem model, multiple industries work together to deliver value to the customer. IT plays an important role in enabling a dense network of interactions among the participating firms.

Business ecosystem is another term for these loosely coupled but interdependent networks of suppliers, distributors, outsourcing firms, transportation service firms, and technology manufacturers (Iansiti and Levien, 2004).

The concept of a business ecosystem builds on the idea of the value web described earlier, the main difference being that cooperation takes place across many industries rather than many firms. For instance, both Microsoft and Walmart provide platforms composed of information systems, technologies, and services that thousands of other firms in different industries use to enhance their own capabilities. Microsoft has estimated that more than 40 000 firms use its Windows platform to deliver their own products, support Microsoft products, and extend the value of Microsoft's own firm. Walmart's order entry and inventory management system is a platform used by thousands of suppliers to obtain real-time access to customer demand, track shipments, and control inventories.

Business ecosystems can be characterized as having one or a few keystone firms that dominate the ecosystem and create the platforms used by other niche firms. Keystone firms in the Microsoft ecosystem include Microsoft and technology producers such as Intel and IBM. Niche firms include thousands of software application firms, software developers, service firms, networking firms, and consulting firms that both support and rely on the Microsoft products.

Information technology plays a powerful role in establishing business ecosystems. Obviously, many firms use information systems to develop into keystone firms by building IT-based platforms that other firms can use. As the chapter-opening case notes, eBay has created a platform for auctions and online stores used by over 500 000 small businesses every day. In the digital firm era, we can expect greater emphasis on the use of IT to build industry ecosystems because the costs of participating in such ecosystems will fall and the benefits to all firms will increase rapidly as the platform grows.

Individual firms should consider how their information systems will enable them to become profitable niche players in larger ecosystems created by keystone firms. For instance, in making decisions about which products to build or which services to offer, a firm should consider the existing business ecosystems related to these products and how it might use IT to enable participation in these larger ecosystems.

A powerful, current example of a rapidly expanding ecosystem is the mobile Internet platform. In this ecosystem there are four industries: device makers (Apple iPhone, RIM BlackBerry, Motorola, Palm, LG, and others), wireless telecommunication firms (Rogers, Primus, SaskTel, Telus, and others), independent software applications providers (generally small firms selling games, applications, and ring tones), and Internet service providers (which participate as providers of Internet service to the mobile platform).

Each of these industries has its own history, interests, and driving forces. But these elements come together in a sometimes cooperative, and sometimes competitive, new industry

Business ecosystem

we refer to as the mobile digital platform ecosystem. More than other firms, Apple has managed to combine these industries into a system. It is Apple's mission to sell physical devices (iPhones) that are nearly as powerful as today's personal computers. These devices work only with a high-speed broadband network supplied by the wireless phone carriers. In order to attract a large customer base, the iPhone had to be more than just a cell phone. Apple differentiated this product by making it a "smartphone," one capable of running thousands of different, useful applications. Apple could not develop all these applications itself. Instead it relies on generally small, independent software developers to provide these applications, which can be purchased at the iTunes store. In the background is the Internet service provider industry, which makes money whenever iPhone users connect to the Internet.

One of the most successful developers for the iPhone platform is Tapulous, a small start-up company in Silicon Valley. Tapulous has developed and released two free applications, a game called Tap Tap Revenge, modelled after a popular arcade dance game, and Twinkle, an application that lets iPhone users send messages over Twitter or Tapulous's own system. The game has attracted 1.2 million downloads while Twinkle has 100 000 users. Although the firm has not made a cent yet from its applications, it will someday charge for its premium services. Meanwhile, Apple plans to earn an additional $439 million in annual revenue as a result of the App Store. Apple keeps about 30 percent of the revenues.

3.4 Using Systems for Competitive Advantage: Management Issues

Strategic information systems often change the organization as well as its products, services, and operating procedures, driving the organization into new behavioural patterns. Successfully using information systems to achieve a competitive advantage is challenging and requires precise coordination of technology, organizations, and management.

Sustaining Competitive Advantage

The competitive advantages strategic systems confer do not necessarily last long enough to ensure long-term profitability. Because competitors can retaliate and copy strategic systems, competitive advantage is not always sustainable. Markets, customer expectations, and technology change; globalization has made these changes even more rapid and unpredictable. The Internet can make competitive advantage disappear very quickly because virtually all companies can use this technology. Classic strategic systems, such as American Airlines's SABRE computerized reservation system, Citibank's ATM system, and FedEx's package tracking system, benefited by being the first in their industries. Then rival systems emerged. Amazon.com, discussed earlier in this chapter, was an e-commerce leader but now faces competition from Chapters, eBay, Yahoo!, and Google. Information systems alone cannot provide an enduring business advantage. Systems originally intended to be strategic frequently become tools for survival, required by every firm to stay in business, or they may inhibit organizations from making the strategic changes essential for future success.

Aligning IT with Business Objectives

The research on IT and business performance has found that (1) the more successfully a firm can align information technology with its business goals, the more profitable it will be and (2) only one-quarter of firms achieve alignment of IT with the business. About half of a business firm's profits can be explained by alignment of IT with business (Luftman, 2003).

Most businesses get it wrong. Information technology takes on a life of its own and does not serve management and shareholder interests very well. Instead of business people taking an active role in shaping IT to the enterprise, they ignore it, claim not to understand IT, and tolerate failure in the IT area as just a nuisance to work around. Such firms pay a hefty price in poor performance. Successful firms and managers understand what IT can do and how it works, take an active role in shaping its use, and measure its impact on revenues and profits.

Performing a Strategic Systems Analysis   To align IT with the business and use information systems effectively for competitive advantage, managers need to perform a strategic systems analysis. To identify the types of systems that provide a strategic advantage to their firms, managers should ask the following questions:

1. What is the structure of the industry in which the firm is located?
   - What are some of the competitive forces at work in the industry? Are there new entrants to the industry? What is the relative power of suppliers, customers, and substitute products and services over prices?
   - Is the basis of competition quality, price, or brand?
   - What are the direction and nature of change within the industry?
   - From where are the momentum and change coming?
   - How is the industry currently using information technology? Is the organization behind or ahead of the industry in its application of information systems?
2. What are the business, firm, and industry value chains for this particular firm?
   - How is the company creating value for the customer—through lower prices and transaction costs or higher quality? Are there any places in the value chain where the business could create more value for the customer and additional profit for the company?
   - Does the firm understand and manage its business processes using the best practices available? Is it taking maximum advantage of supply chain management, customer relationship management, and enterprise systems?
   - Does the firm leverage its core competencies?
   - Are the industry supply chain and customer base changing in ways that benefit or harm the firm?
   - Can the firm benefit from strategic partnerships and value webs?
   - Where in the value chain will information systems provide the greatest value to the firm?
3. Have we aligned IT with our business strategy and goals?
   - Have we correctly articulated our business strategy and goals?
   - Is IT improving the right business processes and activities to promote this strategy?
   - Are we using the right metrics to measure progress toward those goals?

Managing Strategic Transitions

Adopting the kinds of strategic systems described in this chapter generally requires changes in business goals, relationships with customers and suppliers, and business processes. These sociotechnical changes, affecting both social and technical elements of the organization, can be considered **strategic transitions**—a movement between levels of sociotechnical systems.

These changes often entail blurring of organizational boundaries, both external and internal. Suppliers and customers must become intimately linked and may share each other's responsibilities. Managers will need to devise new business processes for coordinating their firms' activities with those of customers, suppliers, and other organizations. The organizational change requirements surrounding new information systems are so important that they merit attention throughout this text. Chapter 10 examines organizational change issues in more detail.

SUMMARY

1. *Which features of organizations do managers need to know about to develop and use information systems successfully? What is the impact of information systems on organizations?*

    All modern organizations are hierarchical, specialized, and impartial, using explicit routines to maximize efficiency. All organizations have their own cultures and politics arising from differences in interest groups, and they are affected by their surrounding environment. Organizations differ in goals, groups served, social roles, leadership styles, incentives, types of tasks performed, and type of structure. These features help explain differences in organizations' use of information systems.

    Information systems and the organizations in which they are used interact with and influence each other. The introduction of a new information system will affect organizational structure, goals, work design, values, competition between interest groups, decision making, and day-to-day behaviour. At the same time, information systems must be designed to serve the needs of important organizational groups and will be shaped by the organization's structure, business processes, goals, culture, politics, and management. Information technology can reduce transaction and agency costs, and these changes have been accentuated in organizations using the Internet. New systems disrupt established patterns of work and power relationships, so there is often considerable resistance to them when they are introduced.

2. *How does Porter's competitive forces model help companies develop competitive strategies using information systems?*

    In Porter's competitive forces model, the strategic position of the firm, and its strategies, are not only determined by competition with its traditional direct competitors, but also greatly affected by new market entrants, substitute products and services, suppliers, and customers. Information systems help companies compete by maintaining low costs, differentiating products or services, focusing on market niche, strengthening ties with customers and suppliers, and increasing barriers to market entry with high levels of operational excellence.

3. *How do the value chain and value web models help businesses identify opportunities for strategic information system applications?*

    The value chain model highlights specific activities in the business where competitive strategies and information systems will have the greatest impact. The model views the firm as a series of primary and support activities that add value to a firm's products or services. Primary activities are directly related to production and distribution while support activities make the delivery of primary activities possible. A firm's value chain can be linked to the value chains of its suppliers, distributors, and customers. A value web consists of information systems that enhance competitiveness at the industry level by promoting the use of standards and industry-wide consortia and by enabling businesses to work more efficiently with their value partners.

4. *How do information systems help businesses use synergies, core competencies, and network-based strategies to achieve competitive advantage?*

    Because firms consist of multiple business units, information systems achieve additional efficiencies or enhance services by tying together the operations of disparate business units. Information systems help businesses leverage their core competencies by promoting the sharing of knowledge across business units. Information systems facilitate business models based on large networks of users or subscribers who take advantage of network economics. A virtual company strategy uses networks to link to other firms so that a company can use the capabilities of other companies to build, market, and distribute products and services. In business ecosystems, multiple industries work together to deliver value to the customer. Information systems support a dense network of interactions among the participating firms.

5. *What are the challenges posed by strategic information systems, and how should they be addressed?*

    Implementing strategic systems often requires extensive organizational change and a transition from one sociotechnical level to another. These changes are called strategic transitions and are often difficult and painful to achieve. Moreover, not all strategic systems are profitable, and they can be expensive to develop. Many strategic information systems are easily copied by other firms so that strategic advantage is not always sustainable.

Key Terms

Agency theory, 69
Benchmarking, 81
Best practices, 81

Business ecosystem, 87
Competitive forces model, 74
Core competency, 85

Disruptive technologies, 67
Mass customization, 77
Network economics, 86

Review Questions

1. *Which features of organizations do managers need to know about to develop and use information systems successfully? What is the impact of information systems on organizations?*

   - *Define an organization, and compare the technical definition of organizations with the behavioural definition.*
   - *Identify and describe the features of organizations that help explain differences in organizations' use of information systems.*
   - *Describe the major economic theories that help explain how information systems affect organizations.*
   - *Describe the major behavioural theories that help explain how information systems affect organizations.*
   - *Explain why there is considerable organizational resistance to the introduction of information systems.*
   - *Describe the impact of the Internet and disruptive technologies on organizations.*

2. *How does Porter's competitive forces model help companies develop competitive strategies using information systems?*

   - *Define Porter's competitive forces model, and explain how it works.*
   - *Describe what the competitive forces model explains about competitive advantage.*
   - *List and describe four competitive strategies enabled by information systems that firms can pursue.*
   - *Describe how information systems can support each of these competitive strategies and give examples.*
   - *Explain why aligning IT with business objectives is essential for strategic use of systems.*

3. *How do the value chain and value web models help businesses identify opportunities for strategic information system applications?*

   - *Define and describe the value chain model.*
   - *Explain how the value chain model can be used to identify opportunities for information systems.*
   - *Define the value web, and show how it is related to the value chain.*
   - *Explain how the value web helps businesses identify opportunities for strategic information systems.*
   - *Describe how the Internet has changed competitive forces and competitive advantage.*

4. *How do information systems help businesses use synergies, core competences, and network-based strategies to achieve competitive advantage?*

   - *Explain how information systems promote synergies and core competencies.*
   - *Describe how promoting synergies and core competencies enhances competitive advantage.*
   - *Explain how businesses benefit by using network economics.*
   - *Define and describe a virtual company and the benefits of pursuing a virtual company strategy.*

5. *What are the challenges posed by strategic information systems, and how should they be addressed?*

   - *List and describe the management challenges posed by strategic information systems.*
   - *Explain how to perform a strategic systems analysis.*

Discussion Questions

1. *It has been said that there is no such thing as a sustainable strategic advantage. Do you agree? Why or why not?*

2. *It has been said that the advantage that leading-edge retailers such as Dell and Walmart have over their competition isn't technology; it's their management. Do you agree? Why or why not?*

Collaboration and Teamwork: Identifying Opportunities for Strategic Information Systems

With your team of three or four students, select a company described in *The Globe and Mail*, the *National Post*, *Fortune*, *Forbes*, or another business publication. Visit the company's Web site to find additional information about that company and to see how the firm is using the Web. On the basis of this information, analyze the business. Include a description of the organization's features, such as important business processes, culture, structure, and environment, as well as its business strategy. Suggest strategic information systems appropriate for that particular business, including those based on Internet technology, if appropriate. If possible, use Google Sites to post links to Web pages, team communica- tion announcements, and work assignments; to brainstorm; and to work collaboratively on project documents. Try to use Google Docs to develop a presentation of your findings for the class.

 Visit the MyMISLab website at **www.pearsoned.ca/mymislab.** This online homework and tutorial system puts you in control of your own learning with study and practice tools directly correlated to this chapter's content.

Learning Track Modules

The following Learning Track provides content relevant to topics covered in this chapter.

1. The Changing Business Environment for Information Technology

HANDS-ON MIS   Projects

The projects in this section give you hands-on experience identifying information systems to support a business strat- egy, analyzing organizational factors affecting the information systems of merging companies, using a database to improve decision making about business strategy, and using Web tools to configure and price an automobile.

Management Decision Problems

1. HBC, Inc., through its subsidiaries, operates approximately 600 retail stores in Canada. Its retail stores sell a range of merchandise, including men's, women's, and children's apparel; accessories; cosmetics; home furnishings; and housewares. Senior management has decided that HBC needs to tailor merchandise more to local tastes, that the colours, sizes, brands, and styles of clothing and other merchandise should be based on the sales patterns in each individual HBC store. For example, stores in Newfoundland might stock clothing in larger sizes and brighter colours than those in Regina, or the HBC in Vancouver's OakRidge Centre might include a greater variety of makeup shades to attract trendier shoppers. How could information systems help HBC's management implement this new strategy? What pieces of data should these systems collect to help management make mer- chandising decisions that support this strategy?

2. Today's US Airways is the result of a merger between US Airways and America West Airlines. Before the merger, US Airways dated back to 1939 and had very traditional business processes, a lumbering bureaucracy, and a rigid information systems function that had been outsourced to Electronic Data Systems. America West was formed in 1981, had a younger workforce and a more freewheel- ing entrepreneurial culture, and managed its own infor- mation systems. The merger was designed to create synergies from US Airways' experience and strong net- work on the east coast of the United States with America West's low-cost structure, information systems, and routes in the western United States. What features of organizations should management have considered as it merged the two companies and their information sys- tems? What decisions need to be made to make sure the strategy works?

Improving Decision Making: Using a Database to Clarify Business Strategy

Software skills: Database querying and reporting; database design
Business skills: Reservation systems; customer analysis

In this exercise, you will use database software to analyze the reservation transactions for a hotel and use that information to fine-tune the hotel's business strategy and marketing activities.

The Queen's Inn is a small three-story hotel on the Atlantic Ocean in St. John's, Newfoundland. Ten rooms overlook side

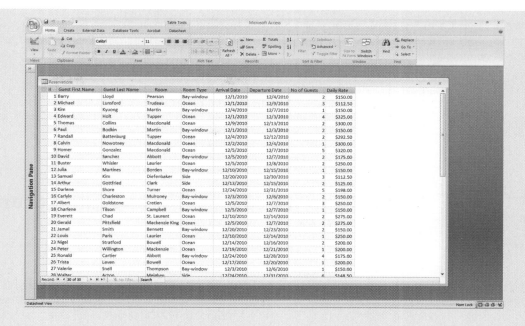

streets, 10 rooms have bay windows that offer limited views of the ocean, and the remaining 10 rooms in the front of the hotel face the ocean. Room rates are based on room choice, length of stay, and number of guests per room. Room rates are the same for one to four guests. Fifth and sixth guests must pay an additional $20 charge each per day. Guests staying for seven days or more receive a 10 percent discount on their daily room rates.

Business has grown steadily during the past 10 years. Now totally renovated, the inn uses a romantic weekend package to attract couples, a vacation package to attract young families, and a weekday discount package to attract business travellers. The owners currently use a manual reservation and bookkeeping system, which has caused many problems. Sometimes two families have been booked in the same room at the same time. Management does not have immediate data about the hotel's daily operations and income.

On the MyMISLab for Chapter 3, you will find a database for hotel reservation transactions developed in Microsoft Access. A sample is shown above, but the MyMISLab may have a more recent version of this database for this exercise.

Develop some reports that provide information to help management make the business more competitive and profitable. Your reports should answer the following questions:

1. What is the average length of stay per room type?
2. What is the average number of visitors per room type?
3. What is the base income per room (i.e., length of visit multiplied by the daily rate) during a specified period of time?
4. What is the strongest customer base?

After answering these questions, write a brief report describing what the database information reveals about the current business situation. Which specific business strategies might be pursued to increase room occupancy and revenue? How could the database be improved to provide better information for strategic decisions?

Improving Decision Making: Using Web Tools to Configure and Price an Automobile

Software skills: Internet-based software
Business skills: Researching product information and pricing

In this exercise, you will use software at Web sites for selling cars to find product information about a car of your choice and use that information to make an important purchase decision. You will also evaluate two of these sites as selling tools.

You are interested in purchasing a new Ford Focus. (If you are personally interested in another car, domestic or foreign, investigate that one instead.)

Go to the Web site of CarsDirect (**www.carsdirect.com**) and begin your investigation. Locate the Ford Focus.

Research the various specific automobiles available in that model, and determine which you prefer. Explore the full details about the specific car, including pricing, standard features, and options. Locate and read at least two reviews if possible. Investigate the safety of that model based on the U.S. government crash tests performed by the National Highway Traffic Safety Administration if those test results are available. You should also look at the Consumer Reports online car guide to see what it (offers **www.crcanadacars. org**). Unfortunately, the Consumer Reports site requires a fee to give you information. Explore the features for locating a vehicle in inventory and purchasing directly. Finally, explore the other capabilities of the CarsDirect site or a Canadian site for financing.

Having recorded or printed the information you need from CarsDirect for your purchase decision, surf the Web site of the manufacturer, in this case Ford (**www.ford.com**). Compare the information available on Ford's Web site with that of CarsDirect for the Ford Focus. Be sure to check the price and any incentives being offered (which may not agree with what you found at CarsDirect). Next, find a local dealer on the Ford site (**www.ford.ca**) so that you can view the car before making your purchase decision. Explore the other features of Ford's Web site.

Try to locate the lowest price for the car you want in a local dealer's inventory. Which site would you use to purchase your car? Why? Suggest improvements for the sites of CarsDirect and Ford.

CASE STUDY   YouTube, the Internet, and the Future of Movies

The Internet has transformed the music industry. Sales of CDs in retail music stores have been declining while sales of songs downloaded through the Internet to iPods and other portable music players are skyrocketing. And the music industry is still contending with millions of people illegally downloading songs for free. (See Chapter 4 for reasons that music piracy is not nearly the problem it is in the United States.) Will the motion picture industry have a similar fate?

Increased levels of high-speed Internet access, powerful PCs with DVD readers and writers, portable video devices, and leading-edge file-sharing services have made downloading of video content faster and easier than ever. Free and often illegal video downloads are currently outpacing paid video downloads by four to one. But the Internet is also providing new ways for movie and television studios to distribute and sell their content, and they are trying to exploit that opportunity.

In early 2006, major movie studios reached agreements with sites such as CinemaNow and Movielink, which has since been acquired by Blockbuster, to sell movies online via download. Until that time, those sites had offered movie downloads as rentals, which, like the video-on-demand model, the customer could watch for only 24 hours. Warner Brothers also expanded its presence by entering into relationships with video-downloading services Guba.com and BitTorrent. The studios moved to build on the momentum created by the success of the iTunes music store, which demonstrated that consumers were very willing to pay for legal digital downloads of copyrighted material. At the same time, they hoped that entering the download sales market would enable them to preemptively confront the piracy issue in their industry to avoid the fate of the music industry.

What remained a question was whether the studios could replicate the success of iTunes. The initial pricing schemes certainly did not offer the same appeal as Apple's $0.99 per song or $9.99 per CD. Movielink set the price for new movies at $20 to $30. Older movies were discounted to $10. Movielink was counting on the fact that customers would pay more for the immediacy of downloading a movie in their homes, as opposed to visiting a bricks-and-mortar store such as HMV or an online store such as Chapters.Indigo.ca, both of which sell new DVDs for less than $20.

However, even if customers were willing to pay a little extra, they were getting less for their money. Most movie downloads did not come with the extra features that are common with DVD releases. Moreover, the downloaded movies were programmed for convenient viewing on computer screens, but transporting them from the computer to the TV screen involved a more complicated process than most consumers were willing to tackle. Neither Movielink nor CinemaNow offered a movie format that could be burned to a DVD and played on a regular DVD player.

Right around the time that the studios were making their foray into Web distribution, a new challenge emerged. YouTube, which started up in February 2005, quickly became the most popular video-sharing Web site in the world. Even though YouTube's original mission was to provide an outlet for amateur filmmakers, digital rights management issues immediately emerged.

Sure enough, video clips of copyrighted Hollywood movies and television shows soon proliferated on YouTube right alongside the video diaries created by teenagers with Webcams and the amateur films created by film students. YouTube's measures to discourage its users from posting illegal clips included limiting the length of videos to 10 minutes and removing videos at the request of the copyright owner. It was, however, a losing battle. Clips from popular movies and shows were often posted by multiple users, and they could be reposted as quickly as they were removed. And watching a two-hour movie in twelve 10-minute pieces proved to be a small price to pay to view the movie for free.

It is difficult to gauge how much Hollywood-derived content is submitted to YouTube without the studios' permission. Academics and media executives estimate it ranges from 30 to 70 percent. Viacom claimed in a 2008 lawsuit that more than 150 000 unauthorized clips of its copyrighted television programs had appeared on YouTube. The media conglomerate is seeking $1.25 billion in damages from YouTube.

When Google purchased YouTube in 2006 for $2 billion, the site gained considerable clout in the media world. With YouTube reporting 100 million video views per day and becoming one of the most visited sites on the Web, the major production studios were not going to stand idly by while someone else profited from movies that cost them an average of more than $129 million to make. NBC Universal, for example, assigned three employees to search YouTube every day for property that had been posted without permission.

Of course, in the end, the chase probably is not worthwhile. Rather than pursue an unachievable goal, some of the major studios, including NBC Universal, Time Warner's Warner Brothers Entertainment, and News Corporation's Twentieth Century Fox, sought more constructive solutions. They entered into negotiations with YouTube to establish licensing agreements that would make copyrighted content available legally. The licensing model was already in place between YouTube and several major music companies. Furthermore, YouTube had already engineered successful arrangements with major studios to market movies on the site.

The studios clearly recognize the value of getting exposure for their movies on such a heavily trafficked Web site. Marc Shmuger, chairman of Universal Pictures, noted that his company's marketing team distributed promotional video clips of all its new films to Web sites such as YouTube. It made sense for the movie industry to follow the lead of the music industry, where the focus shifted from killing off illegal uploads to taking advantage of digital music as a new source of revenue.

In early 2007, YouTube revealed its intention to explore a revenue-sharing model with content creators. YouTube developed filtering and digital fingerprinting technology called Video ID to make this possible. Video ID allows copyright owners to compare the digital fingerprints of their videos with material on YouTube and then flag infringing material. Using this technology, VideoID is able to filter many unauthorized videos before they appear on the YouTube Web site. If infringing videos do make it online, they can be tracked using Video ID.

YouTube does not remove all the infringing material. Instead, it has arranged with CBS, Universal Music, Lionsgate, Electronic Arts, and other media companies that have the copyrights to "claim" their videos and start showing ads alongside them. YouTube and the copyright owners share the revenue. The revenue so far is minimal, with ads appearing with only a fraction of YouTube's millions of videos. But the media companies feel that these YouTube ads help get their customers excited about their content.

Whatever the motion picture studios' relationship to YouTube, it remains to be seen whether streaming video can actually be profitable. Screen Digest, a London research firm, forecasts that 55 percent of the video content watched in North America in 2010 will be in the form of video streams—more than 44 billion of them. However, that 55 percent of the video content will account for only 15 percent of the revenues produced by video content. A large part of the problem is that the videos that are most popular online are the least attractive to advertisers due to inappropriate or objectionable material or because they are simply dull. For all of the players in the movie game—studios, video-sharing sites, rental companies—partnerships and revenue sharing seem the best choice for maximizing the revenue streams made possible by new technology.

The developments in online movie distribution have come at a difficult time for the movie industry. DVD sales in 2008 were sharply down from previous years and marked the first time that DVD sales actually decreased from the previous year, dropping to $19.4 billion from $20.1 billion. Distributing movies online offers movie studios some cost-cutting benefits, including avoiding expenses from handling distribution themselves and from returned products. Equally as important, it may allow movie studios to earn revenues where their products might otherwise have been distributed illegally.

The studios continue to seek out more partners for movie downloads. The six major studios reached an agreement with Walmart to allow the discount-shopping giant to sell movie downloads from its Web site. Walmart joined iTunes, CinemaNow, Amazon, and others that already had such deals. All will now compete on pricing and ease-of-use of their Web sites. Two things are certain. Technology will continue to advance, and lawyers will continue to argue concepts such as liability and fair use.

CASE STUDY QUESTIONS:

1. What competitive forces have challenged the movie industry? What problems have these forces created? What changes have these problems caused the movie and televisions studios to make?

2. Describe the impact of disruptive technology on the companies discussed in this case.

3. How have the movie studios responded to YouTube? What is the goal of the response? What can the movie studios learn from the music industry's dealings with online digital music and copyright infringement?

4. Should motion picture companies continue to use YouTube to promote their new films? Why or why not?

5. Go to YouTube (www.youtube.com)and search for videos from your favourite movie or television show. What do you find on the site? Do you see any advertisements attached to the video? Do you feel this way of advertising is effective? Why or why not?

Sources: Brian Steller, "Now Playing on YouTube: Clips with Ads," *The New York Times*, August 16, 2008; Brooks Barnes, "Warner Tries a New Tactic to Revive Its DVD Sales," *The New York Times*, May 26, 2008; Larry Neumeister, "Viacom Alleges YouTube Copyright Infringement," *USA Today*, May 27, 2008; "Hollywood Asks YouTube: Friend or Foe?" *The New York Times*, January 15, 2007; Catherine Holahan, "Google and YouTube: A Catch-22," *BusinessWeek*, January 26, 2007 and "Upload Video, Download Cash on YouTube?" *BusinessWeek*, January 30, 2007; Eric Benderoff, "Web Sites Begin to Pay for Content," *The Baltimore Sun*, January 31, 2007; Greg Sandoval, "Does YouTube Have a Control Problem?" *CNET News*, February 5, 2007; and Jennifer LeClaire, "YouTube.com Stirs Napster Memories in Digital Movie Era," *TechNewsWorld*, February 5, 2007.

CHAPTER 4

Social, Ethical, and Legal Issues in the Digital Firm

LEARNING OBJECTIVES

After reading this chapter, you will be able to answer the following questions:

1. What ethical, social, and legal issues are raised by information systems?

2. What specific principles for conduct can be used to guide ethical decisions?

3. Why do contemporary information systems technology and the Internet pose challenges to the protection of individual privacy and intellectual property?

4. How have information systems affected everyday life?

OPENING CASE

CASE STUDY: Tech Data Helps to Fight Software Piracy

What is the cost of software piracy in Canada? With the piracy rate pegged at 38 percent, there are more than 30 000 jobs that have been lost, resulting in about $1 billion in wages and salaries lost and more than $255 million in tax revenues lost.

Putting the hard numbers to what seems an innocent—although illegal and unethical—practice makes it real. Software piracy is bad for business.

Today most companies in North America have computer usage policies that tell employees to use only software that has been properly leased or purchased; by implication, this also tells managers not to purchase software that they believe may be pirated for use by their employees. It would be good if we could rely on our fellow employees and managers—as well as our friends and students and even children—to use only valid software, but unfortunately, that is not the case. It is this author's feeling that as students pirate software—both

for its affordability and because most of their friends do so—they will continue these practices as they enter the workplace. We need to educate our students on the facts: Piracy costs businesses and customers money in the long run, and in the short run, it is simply the wrong thing to do.

The Canadian Alliance against Software Theft (CAAST) has conducted surveys on piracy and attitudes toward software piracy in Canada. Fully half of all Canadians think that pirating software for individual use is acceptable, but three-quarters of all Canadians think that it is unacceptable for organizations to pirate software, an interesting paradox. Still, more than 85 percent of Canadians believe that "there is something wrong with downloading illegal software." CAAST conducts an annual survey of software piracy. In the 2008 survey of 110 countries, 52 percent reportedly reduced their rate of piracy from the previous year, with one-third of the

countries reporting the same level or piracy. However, 71 percent of the countries surveyed reported a piracy rate of 50 percent or higher, an astounding statistic. Even though China has taken great steps to reduce its piracy rate, it still has a piracy rate of 80 percent. The so-called BRIC countries (Brazil, Russia, India, and China, whose economies are the fastest growing) have a piracy rate of 73 percent.

Worldwide, for every $2 worth of software that was purchased legitimately, $1 was purchased illegally. Yet, in more than half the countries in the CAAST survey, the reverse was the case: For every $1 purchased legitimately, $2 of software was purchased illegally. Again, an astounding statistic. Fortunately, for those of us living in Canada, Canada was ranked 17th of the 20 countries with the lowest piracy rates, with a rate of 32 percent in this survey. Still, here in Canada, piracy accounted for losses of $1.5 billion. For those with an eye for the absurd, Armenia had the highest piracy rate: 92 percent!

To truly understand the impact of piracy, consider the following. According to IDC, a leading IT research organization, for every $1 that is spent on software, there is at least an additional $1.25 spent on software services to design, create, install, and support the software; most of the $1.25 goes to local firms, not the big software firms.

In its annual Report on Piracy, the International Intellectual Property Alliance (IIPA) recommended that Canada be included once again on the U.S. Trade Representative's watch list of countries considered to be a haven for pirated and counterfeit goods. The IIPA estimates that piracy was responsible for a loss of $40 billion globally in 2005. While it is not clear what Canada's specific share of that loss is, it is nonetheless an amount that demands the urgent attention of Canadian government and business leaders. The IIPA urges Canada to adopt copyright reform legislation and to adopt stricter enforcement as well.

The negative impact of a sullied reputation within the business community could be devastating. Legitimate companies and Canadian consumers stand to suffer the consequences—a stunted software industry's impact on the job market and potential trade sanctions by the United States, which could cost the Canadian economy millions each year, to start.

According to a survey conducted on behalf of the Entertainment Software Association of Canada by Nielsen Interactive in 2005, 34 percent of video game consumers admitted to having acquired, either through purchase and/or download, a video game that was knowingly copied or pirated. This number is up by 6 percent over 2004. Compared to countries like the United States, where piracy rates decreased, it is clear that if we are to remain competitive, Canada must take strong action to curb piracy.

One company in Canada that provides hardware and software throughout Canada is trying to fight software piracy.

Tech Data Canada is a leading IT distributor of hardware and software to more than 9000 value-added results (VAR) accounts and resellers across Canada. Tech Data employs more than 500 people in Canada and includes technical support, e-business applications, and financial and credit services for its customers.

Founded 33 years ago, Tech Data Corporation is ranked 105th on the Fortune 500 list for 2009. The company and its subsidiaries (of which Tech Data Canada is one) serves more than 100 000 technology resellers around the world in more than 100 countries. The company generated $23.4 billion in sales for the fiscal year ended January 31, 2008, a record for the technology giant. Tech Data employs more than 8000 staff worldwide and ships more than 70 000 shipments in a year. Tech Data Canada was established in 1989; it sells thousands of products from major manufacturers, including components, such as mass storage, enterprise storage, networking, peripherals, software, supplies, and systems. Tech Data Canada sells to only qualified computer resellers and retailers, not to individual customers.

With that kind of a background, even for such a large company, how can Tech Data Canada (TDC) fight software piracy? TDC decided that many of its customers may not understand software piracy and how to recognize it, thereby leaving customers open to commit piracy unknowingly, perhaps by buying from an unscrupulous vendor of pirated software. "We would receive calls from customers who said they could get, for example, a Microsoft software product for a considerable amount less than the actual cost," said Irene Buchan, Director, Product Management and Software Business Unit at TDC. "It was important for us to make our customers realize how software piracy affected their businesses and what they could do to help reduce it."

TDC wanted both its customers and its employees to be able to recognize pirated software and to know how to report it appropriately. Toward this end, TDC launched an anti-piracy program to educate its customers and its sales representatives.

Learning of TDC's desire to launch its anti-piracy program, Microsoft—one of the companies most severely affected by piracy—pledged to help with both finan-

cial support and material for the information seminars that TDC wanted to run across Canada. TDC also conducted sales team training sessions for its sales representatives with Microsoft's help. Microsoft also helped provide questions for TDC's software piracy customer checklist.

The anti-piracy program included distributing a 16-page guide sponsored by vendors like Microsoft to more than 20 000 resellers across Canada. The guide details the impact of piracy on the Canadian economy and businesses, featuring articles from several vendors. TDC also published a one-page question-and-answer checklist for resellers and placed the checklist on its Web site. The questions were used as a sort of warning guide. The checklist also published the contact information for the Canadian Alliance against Software Theft (CAAST) as well as Microsoft's toll-free tip-line so that resellers could report suspected acts of piracy.

As part of the sales representatives' training, a "mystery caller" would telephone sales representatives to offer them supposedly pirated software. This helped to educate the sales representatives on how to recognize a call offering pirated software and how to respond to such a call. "Our anti-piracy program really focuses on bringing greater awareness to our customers and employees by providing them with the skills needed

to identify pirated software," said Buchan. "We will definitely renew our program each year."

The TDC anti-piracy program has seen results. Not only do both TDC customers and sales representatives claim to be more knowledgeable about piracy, but also TDC's customers have seen revenues increased and losses decreased. According to Buchan, "Sales reps have the knowledge to tell resellers, 'That price is too good to be true, I think you bought pirated software.' And resellers can easily reach CAAST or call the toll-free hotline if they believe they have pirated software. Our program benefits everyone in the industry."

Sources: Danielle Labossiere, "The Hidden Cost of Piracy in Canada," *The Globe and Mail*, May 5, 2006; The Canadian Alliance against Software Theft, "Canadians Find Falsified Resumes a Bigger Offence Than Using Pirated Software," **www.caast.com/resources/2006_national_study.pdf** (accessed June 1, 2007); "Sixth Annual BSA–IDC Global Software Piracy Study," **http://global.bsa.org/globalpiracy2008/studies/globalpiracy2008.pdf**; "About CAAST," **www.caast.com/about/default.asp?load=content** (accessed June 1, 2007); "Tech Data Canada Equips Its Resellers and Employees with Tools to Help Fight Software Piracy," **www.microsoft.com/canada/casestudies/techdata.mspx** (accessed June 1, 2007); "Welcome to Tech Data," **www.techdata.com/content/cen/about/companyinfo.main.aspx** (accessed July 23, 2009); "Tech Data Ranks 109th on 2007 Fortune 500," **www.portfolio.com/resources/company-profiles/TECD/press/2007/04/16/tech-data-ranks-109th-on-2007-fortune-500r** (accessed June 1, 2007).

Piracy of software described in the chapter-opening case shows that technology costs organizations worldwide billions of dollars. Managers need to develop appropriate guidelines and policies within their own organizations and to push governments to likewise adopt strict copyright legislation and then to enforce the law.

The chapter-opening diagram calls attention to important points raised by

this case and this chapter. Tech Data Canada was looking for a way to make it easier for its customers to know when they were being offered pirated software. Tech Data hopes its anti-piracy program will help its customers recognize pirated software and pursue purchasing legitimate software. It is a win-win for Tech Data; not only will the vendors it uses, such as Microsoft, make more money, but also Tech Data will, as

its customers purchase legitimate software from Tech Data rather than pirated software from a different vendor. As a manager, you will need to be aware of the negative impacts of information systems and their use, and you need to balance the negative consequences with the positive ones.

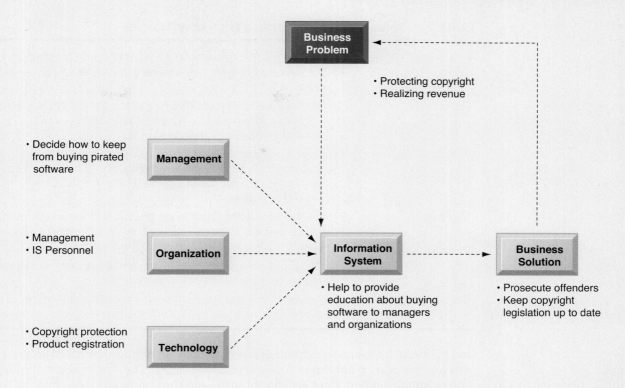

4.1   Understanding Social, Legal, and Ethical Issues Related to Systems

In the past 10 years, we have witnessed, arguably, one of the most ethically challenging periods for Canadian and global business. Table 4-1 provides a small sample of recent cases demonstrating failed ethical judgment by senior and middle managers. These lapses in management ethical and business judgment occurred across a broad spectrum of industries.

In today's new legal environment, managers who violate the law and are convicted will most likely spend time in prison. Although in the past, business firms would often pay for the legal defence of their employees enmeshed in civil charges and criminal investigations, now firms are encouraged to cooperate with prosecutors to reduce charges against the entire firm for obstructing investigations. These developments mean that, more than ever, as a manager or an employee, you will have to decide for yourself what constitutes proper legal and ethical conduct.

Although these major instances of failed ethical and legal judgment were not masterminded by information systems departments, information systems were instrumental in many of these frauds. In many cases, the perpetrators of these crimes artfully used financial reporting information systems to bury their decisions from public scrutiny in the vain hope they would never be caught.

We deal with the issue of control in information systems in Chapter 8. In this chapter, we talk about the ethical dimensions of these and other actions based on the use of information systems.

Ethics refers to the principles of right and wrong that individuals, acting as free moral agents, use to make choices to guide their behaviours. Information systems raise new ethical questions for both individuals and societies because they create opportunities for intense social change and thus threaten existing distributions of power, money, rights, and obligations. Like other technologies, such as steam engines, electricity, the telephone,

TABLE 4-1 Recent examples of failed ethical judgment by managers.

Government of Canada	Sponsorship Scandal, wherein the government apparently paid favoured marketing firms for services that were either not needed or not provided.
Enron	Top three executives convicted for misstating earnings using illegal accounting schemes and making false representations to shareholders. Bankruptcy declared in 2001.
WorldCom	Second-largest U.S. telecommunications firm. Chief executive convicted for improperly inflating revenue by billions using illegal accounting methods. Bankruptcy declared in July 2002 with $41 billion in debts.
Merrill Lynch	Indicted for assisting Enron in the creation of financial vehicles that had no business purpose, enabling Enron to misstate its earnings.
Parmalat	Italy's eighth-largest industrial group indicted for misstating more than $5 billion in revenues, earnings, and assets over several years; senior executives indicted for embezzlement.
Bristol-Myers Squibb	Pharmaceutical firm agreed to pay a fine of $150 million for misstating its revenues by $1.5 billion and inflating its stock value.

and the radio, information technology can be used to not only achieve social progress, but also commit crimes and threaten cherished social values. The development of information technology will produce benefits for many and costs for others.

Ethical issues in information systems have been given new urgency by the rise of the Internet and electronic commerce. Internet and digital firm technologies make it easier than ever to assemble, integrate, and distribute information, unleashing new concerns about the appropriate use of customer information, the protection of personal privacy, and the protection of intellectual property.

Other pressing ethical issues raised by information systems include establishing accountability for the consequences of information systems, setting standards to safeguard system quality that protects the safety of the individual and society, and preserving values and institutions considered essential to the quality of life in an information society. When using information systems, it is essential to ask, "What is the ethical and socially responsible course of action?"

A Model for Thinking about Ethical, Social, and Political Issues

Ethical, social, and legal or political issues are closely linked. The ethical dilemma you may face as a manager of information systems typically is reflected in social and political debate. One way to think about these relationships is given in Figure 4-1. Imagine society as a more or less calm pond on a summer day, a delicate ecosystem in partial equilibrium with individuals and with social and political institutions. Individuals know how to act in this pond because social institutions (family, education, organizations) have developed well-honed rules of behaviour, and these are supported by laws developed in the political sector that prescribe behaviour and promise sanctions for violations. Now toss a rock into the centre of the pond. But imagine, instead of a rock, that the disturbing force is a powerful shock of new information technology and systems hitting a society more or less at rest. What happens? Ripples, of course.

Suddenly, individual actors are confronted with new situations often not covered by the old rules. Social institutions cannot respond overnight to these ripples—it may take years to develop etiquette, expectations, social responsibility, politically correct attitudes, or approved rules. Political institutions also require time before developing new laws and often require the demonstration of real harm before they act. In the meantime, you may have to act. You may be forced to act in a legal grey area.

We can use this model to illustrate the dynamics that connect ethical, social, and political issues. This model is also useful for identifying the main moral dimensions of the information society, which cut across various levels of action—individual, social, and political.

FIGURE 4-1   The relationship between ethical, social, and political issues in an information society.

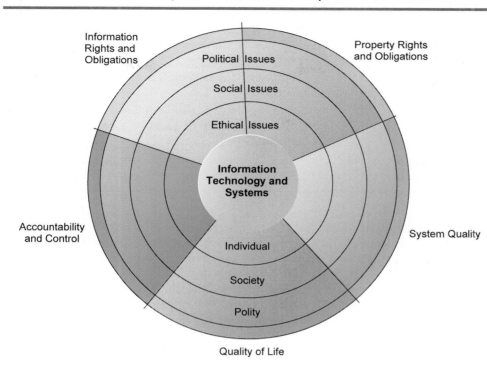

The introduction of new information technology has a ripple effect, raising new ethical, social, and political issues that must be dealt with on the individual, social, and political levels. These issues have five moral dimensions: information rights and obligations, property rights and obligations, system quality, quality of life, and accountability and control.

Five Moral Dimensions of the Information Age

The major ethical, social, and political issues raised by information systems include the following moral dimensions:

Information rights and obligations. What **information rights** do individuals and organizations possess with respect to themselves? What can they protect? What obligations do individuals and organizations have concerning this information?

Property rights and obligations. How will traditional intellectual property rights be protected in a digital society in which tracing and accounting for ownership are difficult and ignoring such property rights is so easy?

Accountability and control. Who can and will be held accountable and liable for the harm done to individual and collective information and property rights?

System quality. What standards of data and system quality should we demand to protect individual rights and the safety of society?

Quality of life. What values should be preserved in an information- and knowledge-based society? Which institutions should we protect from violation? Which cultural values and practices are supported by the new information technology?

We explore these moral dimensions in detail in Section 4.3.

Key Technology Trends That Raise Ethical Issues

Ethical issues long preceded information technology. Nevertheless, information technology has heightened ethical concerns, taxed existing social arrangements, and made some laws obsolete or severely crippled. There are four key technological trends responsible for these ethical stresses and they are summarized in Table 4-2.

The doubling of computing power every 18 months has made it possible for most organizations to use information systems for their core production processes. As a result,

Information rights

TABLE 4-2 Technology trends that raise ethical issues.

TREND	IMPACT
Computing power doubles every 18 months	More organizations depend on computer systems for critical operations.
Data storage costs rapidly declining	Organizations can easily maintain detailed databases on individuals.
Data analysis advances	Companies can analyze vast quantities of data gathered on individuals to develop detailed profiles of individual behaviour.
Networking advances and the Internet	Copying data from one location to another and accessing personal data from remote locations are much easier.

our dependence on systems and our vulnerability to system errors and poor data quality have increased. Social rules and laws have not yet adjusted to this dependence. Standards for ensuring the accuracy and reliability of information systems (see Chapter 8) are not universally accepted or enforced.

Advances in data storage techniques and rapidly declining storage costs have been responsible for the growing databases on individuals—employees, customers, and potential customers—maintained by private and public organizations. These advances in data storage have made the routine violation of individual privacy both cheap and effective. Already massive data storage systems are cheap enough for regional and even local retailing firms to use in identifying customers.

Advances in data analysis techniques for large pools of data are another technological trend that heightens ethical concerns because companies and government agencies are able to find out much detailed personal information about individuals. With contemporary data management tools (see Chapter 6), companies can assemble and combine the myriad pieces of information about individuals stored on computers much more easily than in the past.

Think of all the ways you generate computer information about yourself—credit card purchases; telephone calls; magazine subscriptions; video rentals; mail-order purchases; banking records; municipal, provincial, and federal government records (including court and police records); and visits to Web sites. Put together and mined properly, this

Credit card purchases can make personal information available to market researchers, telemarketers, and direct-mail companies. Advances in information technology facilitate the invasion of privacy.

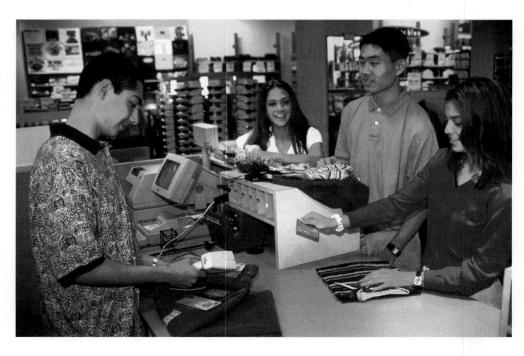

information could reveal not only your credit information but also your driving habits, your tastes, your associations, and your political interests.

Companies with products to sell purchase relevant information from these sources to help them more finely target their marketing campaigns. Chapters 3 and 6 describe how companies can analyze large pools of data from multiple sources to rapidly identify buying patterns of customers and suggest individual responses. The use of computers to combine data from multiple sources and create electronic dossiers of detailed information on individuals is called **profiling.**

For example, hundreds of Web sites allow DoubleClick (**www.doubleclick.net**), an Internet advertising broker, to track the activities of their visitors in exchange for revenue from advertisements based on visitor information DoubleClick gathers. DoubleClick uses this information to create a profile of each online visitor, adding more detail to the profile as the visitor accesses an associated DoubleClick site. Over time, DoubleClick can create a detailed dossier of a person's spending and computing habits on the Web that is sold to companies to help them target their Web ads more precisely.

ChoicePoint gathers data from police, criminal, and motor vehicle records; credit and employment histories; current and previous addresses; professional licences; and insurance claims to assemble and maintain electronic dossiers on almost every adult in the United States. The company sells this personal information to businesses and government agencies. Demand for personal data is so enormous that data broker businesses such as ChoicePoint are flourishing.

A new data analysis technology called **nonobvious relationship awareness (NORA)** has given both the government and the private sector even more powerful profiling capabilities. NORA can take information about people from many disparate sources, such as employment applications, telephone records, customer listings, and "wanted" lists, and correlate relationships to find obscure hidden connections that might help identify criminals or terrorists (see Figure 4-2).

Profiling

Nonobvious relationship awareness (NORA)

FIGURE 4-2   Nonobvious relationship awareness (NORA).

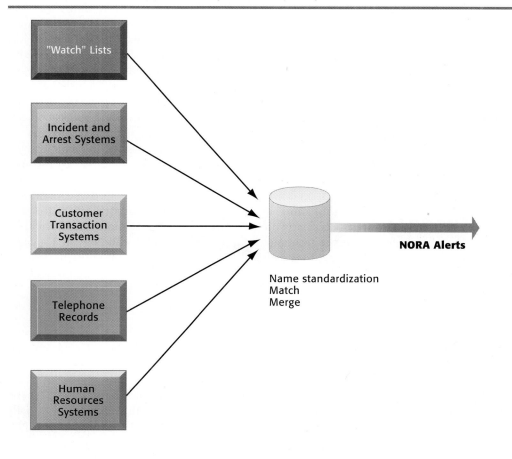

NORA technology can take information about people from disparate sources and find obscure, nonobvious relationships. It might discover, for example, that an applicant for a job at a casino shares a telephone number with a known criminal and issue an alert to the hiring manager.

NORA technology scans data and extracts information as the data are being generated so that it could, for example, instantly discover a man at an airline ticket counter who shares a phone number with a known terrorist before that person boards an airplane. The technology is considered a valuable tool for airport, but does have privacy implications because it can provide such a detailed picture of the activities and associations of a single individual.

Finally, advances in networking, including the Internet, promise to reduce greatly the costs of moving and accessing large quantities of data and open the possibility of mining large pools of data remotely using small desktop machines, permitting an invasion of privacy on a scale and with a precision heretofore unimaginable.

The development of global digital superhighway communication networks widely available to individuals and businesses poses many ethical and social concerns. Who will account for the flow of information over these networks? Will you be able to trace information collected about you? What will these networks do to the traditional relationships between family, work, and leisure? How will traditional job designs be altered when millions of "employees" become subcontractors using mobile offices for which they themselves must pay? In the next section, we consider some ethical principles and analytical techniques for dealing with these kinds of ethical and social concerns.

4.2   Ethics in an Information Society

Ethics is a concern of humans who have freedom of choice. Ethics is about individual choice: When faced with alternative courses of action, what is the correct ethical choice? What are the main features of ethical choice?

Basic Concepts: Responsibility, Accountability, and Liability

Ethical choices are decisions made by individuals who are responsible for the consequences of their actions. **Responsibility** is a key element of ethical action. Responsibility means that you accept the potential costs, duties, and obligations for the decisions you make. **Accountability** is a feature of systems and social institutions: It means that mechanisms are in place to determine who took responsible action and who is responsible. Systems and institutions in which it is impossible to find out who took what action are inherently incapable of ethical analysis or ethical action. **Liability** extends the concept of responsibility further to the area of laws. Liability is a feature of political systems in which a body of laws is in place that permits individuals to recover the damages done to them by other actors, systems, or organizations. **Due process** is a related feature of law-governed societies and is a process in which laws are known and understood and there is an ability to appeal to higher authorities to ensure that the laws are applied correctly.

These basic concepts form the underpinning of an ethical analysis of information systems and those who manage them. First, information technologies are filtered through social institutions, organizations, and individuals. Systems do not have impacts by themselves. Whatever information system impacts exist are products of institutional, organizational, and individual actions and behaviours. Second, responsibility for the consequences of technology falls clearly on the institutions, organizations, and individual managers who choose to use the technology. Using information technology in a socially responsible manner means that you can and will be held accountable for the consequences of your actions. Third, in an ethical, political society, individuals and others can recover damages done to them through a set of laws characterized by due process.

Ethical Analysis

When confronted with a situation that seems to present ethical issues, how should you analyze it? The following five-step process should help.

1. *Identify and describe clearly the facts.* Find out who did what to whom, and where, when, and how. In many instances, you will be surprised at the errors in the initially reported facts, and often you will find that simply getting the facts straight helps

Ethics
Responsibility
Accountability
Liability
Due process

define the solution. It also helps to get the opposing parties involved in an ethical dilemma to agree on the facts.

2. *Define the conflict or dilemma, and identify the higher-order values involved.* Ethical, social, and political issues always reference higher values. The parties to a dispute all claim to be pursuing higher values (e.g., freedom, privacy, protection of property, and the free enterprise system). Typically, an ethical issue involves a dilemma: two diametrically opposed courses of action that support worthwhile values.

3. *Identify the stakeholders.* Every ethical, social, and political issue has stakeholders: players in the game who have an interest in the outcome, who have invested in the situation, and who usually have vocal opinions. Find out the identity of these groups and what they want. This will be useful later when designing a solution.

4. *Identify the options that you can reasonably take.* You may find that none of the options satisfy all the interests involved but that some options do a better job than others. Sometimes arriving at a good or ethical solution may not always be a balancing of consequences to stakeholders.

5. *Identify the potential consequences of your options.* Some options may be ethically correct but disastrous from other points of view. Other options may work in one instance but not in other similar instances. Always ask yourself, "What if I choose this option consistently over time?"

Candidate Ethical Principles

Once your analysis is complete, what ethical principles or rules should you use to make a decision? What higher-order values should inform your judgment? Although you are the only one who can decide which among many ethical principles you will follow, and how you will prioritize them, it is helpful to consider some ethical principles with deep roots in many cultures that have survived throughout recorded history.

1. Do unto others as you would have them do unto you (the **Golden Rule**). Putting yourself into the place of others and thinking of yourself as the object of the decision can help you think about fairness in decision making.

2. If an action is not right for everyone to take, it is not right for anyone (**Immanuel Kant's categorical imperative**). Ask yourself, "If everyone did this, could the organization or society survive?"

3. If an action cannot be taken repeatedly, it is not right to take at all (**Descartes' rule of change**). This is the slippery-slope rule: An action may bring about a small change now that is acceptable, but if it is repeated, it would bring unacceptable changes in the long run. In the vernacular, it might be stated as "once started down a slippery path, you may not be able to stop."

4. Take the action that achieves the higher or greater value (**utilitarian principle**). This rule assumes you can prioritize values in a rank order and understand the consequences of various courses of action.

5. Take the action that produces the least harm or the least potential cost (**risk aversion principle**). Some actions have extremely high failure costs of very low probability (e.g., building a nuclear generating facility in an urban area) or extremely high failure costs of moderate probability (speeding in a car). Avoid these high-failure-cost actions, paying greater attention to the high-failure-cost potential of moderate to high probability.

6. Assume that virtually all tangible and intangible objects are owned by someone else unless there is a specific declaration otherwise. (This is the **ethical "no free lunch" rule**.) If something someone else has created is useful to you, it has value, and you should assume the creator wants compensation for this work.

Golden Rule

Immanuel Kant's categorical imperative

Descartes' rule of change

Utilitarian principle

Risk aversion principle

Ethical "no free lunch" rule

Although these ethical rules cannot be guides to action, actions that do not easily pass these rules deserve some very close attention and a great deal of caution. The appearance of unethical behaviour may do as much harm to you and your company as actual unethical behaviour.

Professional Codes of Conduct

When groups of people claim to be professionals, they take on special rights and obligations because of their special claims to knowledge, wisdom, and respect. Professional codes of conduct are promulgated by associations of professionals, such as the Canadian Medical Association (CMA), the Canadian Bar Association (CBA), the Canadian Information Processing Society (CIPS), and the Association of Computing Machinery (ACM). These professional groups take responsibility for the partial regulation of their professions by determining entrance qualifications and competence. Codes of ethics are promises by professions to regulate themselves in the general interest of society. For example, avoiding harm to others, honouring property rights (including intellectual property), and respecting privacy are among the General Moral Imperatives of the ACM's Code of Ethics and Professional Conduct.

Some Real-World Ethical Dilemmas

Information systems have created new ethical dilemmas in which one set of interests is pitted against another. For example, many large telephone companies are using information technology to reduce the sizes of their workforces. Voice recognition software reduces the need for human operators by enabling computers to recognize a customer's responses to a series of computerized questions. Many companies monitor what their employees are doing on the Internet to prevent them from wasting company resources on nonbusiness activities (see the Chapter 7 Window on Management).

In each instance, you can find competing values at work, with groups lined up on either side of a debate. A company may argue, for example, that it has a right to use information systems to increase productivity and reduce the size of its workforce to lower costs and stay in business. Employees displaced by information systems may argue that employers have some responsibility for their welfare. Business owners might feel obligated to monitor employee e-mail and Internet use to minimize drains on productivity. Employees might believe they should be able to use the Internet for short personal tasks in place of the telephone. A close analysis of the facts can sometimes produce compromised solutions that give each side "half a loaf." Try to apply some of the principles of ethical analysis described to each of these cases. What is the right thing to do?

4.3 The Moral Dimensions of Information Systems

In this section, we take a closer look at the five moral dimensions of information systems first described in Figure 4-1. For each dimension, we identify the ethical, social, and political levels of analysis and use real-world examples to illustrate the values involved, the stakeholders, and the options chosen.

Information Rights: Privacy and Freedom in the Internet Age

Privacy is the claim of individuals to be left alone, free from surveillance or interference from other individuals or organizations, including the state. Claims to privacy are also involved at the workplace: Millions of employees are subject to electronic and other forms of high-tech surveillance (Ball, 2001). Information technology and systems threaten individual claims to privacy by making the invasion of privacy cheap, profitable, and effective.

The claim to privacy is protected in the Canadian, U.S., and German constitutions in a variety of different ways and in other countries through various statutes. In Canada, the claim to privacy is protected primarily by the right to be secure against unreasonable search or seizure found in the *Charter of Rights and Freedoms*. In addition, in 2000, Parliament passed the *Personal Information Protection and Electronic Documents Act* (PIPEDA), Canada's modern privacy law. PIPEDA establishes the following principles to

Privacy

govern the collection, use, and disclosure of personal information: accountability, identifying the purposes for the collection of personal information, obtaining consent, limiting collection, limiting use, disclosure and retention, ensuring accuracy, providing adequate security, making information management policies readily available, providing individuals with access to information about themselves, and giving individuals a right to challenge an organization's compliance with these principles.

PIPEDA further provides for the Privacy Commissioner to receive complaints concerning contraventions of the principles, conduct investigations, and attempt to resolve such complaints. Unresolved disputes relating to certain matters can be taken to the Federal Court for resolution. This act complements the 1983 *Privacy Act*, which imposes rules on how federal government departments and agencies collect, use, and disclose personal information.

Every Canadian province and territory has enacted legislation parallel to the federal *Privacy Act* and the *Access to Information Act*. These laws prevent the unnecessary distribution of one's personal information and guarantee access to unrestricted government information.

Some of the provincial laws apply only to information held by the public sector. "Public-sector" organizations under the privacy laws include public or private companies that are regulated by the government, such as financial institutions, air transportation companies, and broadcast media. Right now Quebec is the only province with privacy laws for the private sector that meet European Union standards. That is significant for international trade, which increasingly concerns information, not hard products. The United States does not meet those standards either.

Due process has become a key concept in defining privacy. Due process requires that a set of rules or laws exist that clearly define how information about individuals will be treated and what appeal mechanisms are available. Perhaps the best statement in Canada of due process in record keeping is given by the Canadian Standards Association's Model Privacy Code. Published in March 1996, the Code establishes 10 basic principles for all organizations that collect or use personal information. Retailers, direct marketers, financial institutions, telecommunications companies, product manufacturers, service providers, schools, universities, hospitals, personnel departments, and government agencies are potential users.

By choosing to adopt the voluntary Code, organizations demonstrate that they are following fair, nationally accepted principles. The Code is also an important resource for consumers, employees, patients, and other "data subjects," says Professor Jim Savary, former vice president of Policy and Issues at the Consumers' Association of Canada. "The Code is a vehicle for challenging an organization's behaviour. You can refer to these principles if you are uneasy about the information you are asked to supply or how it will be used" (Canadian Standards Association International, 1996).

The 10 practices in the Code, very similar to what was enacted in PIPEDA, are

- Accountability
- Identifying purposes
- Consent
- Limiting collection
- Limiting use, disclosure, and retention
- Accuracy
- Safeguards
- Openness
- Individual access
- Challenging compliance

Most North American and European privacy law is based on a regime called **Fair Information Practices (FIP)** first set forth in a report written in 1973 by a U.S. federal government advisory committee (U.S. Department of Health, Education, and Welfare, 1973).

Fair Information Practices (FIP)

TABLE 4-3 Federal Trade Commission fair information practice principles.

1. *Notice/awareness* (core principle). Web sites must disclose their information practices before collecting data. Includes identification of collector; uses of data; other recipients of data; nature of collection (active/inactive); voluntary or required status; consequences of refusal; and steps taken to protect confidentiality, integrity, and quality of the data.

2. *Choice/consent* (core principle). There must be a choice regime in place allowing consumers to choose how their information will be used for secondary purposes other than supporting the transaction, including internal use and transfer to third parties.

3. *Access/participation*. Consumers should be able to review and contest the accuracy and completeness of data collected about them in a timely, inexpensive process.

4. *Security*. Data collectors must take responsible steps to assure that consumer information is accurate and secure from unauthorized use.

5. *Enforcement*. There must be in place a mechanism to enforce FIP principles. This can involve self-regulation, legislation giving consumers legal remedies for violations, or federal statutes and regulations.

FIP is a set of principles governing the collection and use of information about individuals. FIP principles are based on the notion of a mutuality of interest between the record holder and the individual. The individual has an interest in engaging in a transaction, and the record keeper—usually a business or government agency—requires information about the individual to support the transaction. Once information is gathered, the individual maintains an interest in the record, and the record may not be used to support other activities without the individual's consent. In 1998, the U.S. Federal Trade Commission (FTC) restated and extended the original FIP to provide guidelines for protecting online privacy. Table 4-3 describes the FTC's Fair Information Practice principles.

The European Directive on Data Protection In Europe, privacy protection is much more stringent than in many non-European countries. European countries do not allow businesses to use personally identifiable information without consumers' prior consent. On October 25, 1998, the European Commission's Directive on Data Protection went into effect, broadening privacy protection in the European Union (EU) nations. The directive requires companies to inform people when they collect information about them and disclose how it will be stored and used. Customers must provide their informed consent before any company can legally use data about them, and they have the right to access that information, correct it, and request that no further data be collected. **Informed consent** can be defined as consent given with knowledge of all the facts needed to make a rational decision. EU member nations must translate these principles into their own laws and cannot transfer personal data to other countries that do not have similar privacy protection regulations.

Working with the European Commission, the U.S. Department of Commerce developed a safe harbour framework for U.S. firms. A **safe harbour** is a private, self-regulating policy and enforcement mechanism that meets the objectives of government regulators and legislation but does not involve government regulation or enforcement. Businesses outside Europe would be allowed to use personal data from EU countries if they develop privacy protection policies that meet EU standards. Enforcement would occur in the home country using self-policing, regulation, and government enforcement of fair trade statutes. In 2002, Canada became only the third non-European country to gain safe harbour status.

Internet Challenges to Privacy Internet technology has posed new challenges for the protection of individual privacy. Information sent over this vast network of networks may pass through many different computer systems before it reaches its final destination. Each of these systems is capable of monitoring, capturing, and storing communications that pass through it.

Informed consent
Safe harbour

It is possible to record many online activities, including what searches have been conducted, which Web sites and Web pages have been visited, the online content a person has accessed, and what items that person has inspected or purchased over the Web. Much of this monitoring and tracking of Web site visitors occurs in the background without the visitor's knowledge. It is conducted not just by individual Web sites but by advertising networks such as DoubleClick that are capable of tracking all browsing behaviour at thousands of Web sites. Tools to monitor visits to the World Wide Web have become popular because they help businesses determine who is visiting their Web sites and how to better target their offerings. (Some firms also monitor the Internet usage of their employees to see how they are using company network resources.) The commercial demand for this personal information is virtually insatiable.

Web sites can learn the identities of their visitors if the visitors voluntarily register at the site to purchase a product or service or to obtain a free service, such as information. Web sites can also capture information about visitors without their knowledge using cookie technology.

Cookies are tiny files deposited on a user's computer hard drive when a user visits certain Web sites. Cookies identify the visitor's Web browser software and track visits to the Web site. When the visitor returns to a site that has stored a cookie, the Web site software will search the visitor's computer, find the cookie, and know what that person has done at the site in the past. It may also update the cookie, depending on the activity during the visit. In this way, the site can customize its contents for each visitor's interests. For example, if you purchase a book on the Chapters.Indigo.ca Web site and return later from the same browser, the site will welcome you by name and recommend other books of interest based on your past purchases. DoubleClick, described earlier in this chapter, uses cookies to build its dossiers with details of online purchases and to examine the behaviour of Web site visitors. Figure 4-3 illustrates how cookies work.

Web sites using cookie technology cannot directly obtain visitors' names and addresses. However, if a person has registered at a site, that information can be combined with cookie data to identify the visitor. Web site owners can also combine the data they have gathered from cookies and other Web site monitoring tools with personal data from other sources, such as offline data collected from surveys or paper catalogue purchases, to develop very detailed profiles of their visitors.

There are now even more subtle and surreptitious tools for surveillance of Internet users. Marketers use Web bugs as another tool to monitor online behaviour. **Web bugs** are tiny graphic files embedded in e-mail messages and Web pages that are designed to monitor who is reading the e-mail message or Web page and transmit that information to another computer. Other **spyware** can secretly install itself on an Internet user's computer

Cookies
Web bugs
Spyware

FIGURE 4-3   How cookies identify Web visitors.

User   **Server**

Cookies are written by a Web site on a visitor's hard drive. When the visitor returns to that Web site, the Web server requests the ID number from the cookie and uses it to access the data stored by that server on that visitor. The Web site can then use these data to display personalized information.

1. The Web server reads the user's Web browser and determines the operating system, browser name, version number, Internet address, and other information.
2. The server transmits a tiny text file with user identification information called a cookie, which the user's browser receives and stores on the user's computer hard drive.
3. When the user returns to the Web site, the server requests the contents of any cookie it deposited previously in the user's computer.
4. The Web server reads the cookie, identifies the visitor, and calls up data on the user.

by piggybacking on larger applications. Once installed, the spyware calls out to Web sites to send banner ads and other unsolicited material to the user, and it can also report the user's movements on the Internet to other computers. More information is available about Web bugs, spyware, and other intrusive software in Chapter 8.

Google has started using behavioural targeting to help it display more relevant ads based on users' search activities. One of its programs enables advertisers to target ads based on the search histories of Google users, along with any other information the user submits to Google or Google can obtain, such as age, demographics, region, and other Web activities (such as blogging). An additional program allows Google to help advertisers select keywords and design ads for various market segments based on search histories, such as helping a clothing Web site create and test ads targeted at teenage females.

Google has also been scanning the contents of messages received by users of its free Web-based e-mail service called Gmail. Ads that users see when they read their e-mail are related to the subjects of these messages. Profiles are developed on individual users based on the content in their e-mail. Google's Chrome Web browser, introduced in 2008, has a Suggest feature that automatically suggests related queries and Web sites as the user enters a search. Critics pointed out this was a key-logger device that would record every keystroke of users forever. Google subsequently announced it would anonymize the data in 24 hours.

While the United States has allowed businesses to gather transaction information generated in the marketplace and then use that information for other marketing purposes without obtaining the informed consent of the individual whose information is being used, PIPEDA changed that practice in Canada. While U.S. e-commerce sites are largely content to publish statements on their Web sites informing visitors about how their information will be used, Canadian firms must not only publish their privacy statements, but also have contact information for individuals to inquire about the privacy policy and their own data, as well as a method for individual **opt-in** to the company's data collection about the individual. Some U.S. companies have added opt-out selection boxes to these information policy statements. An opt-out model of informed consent permits the collection of personal information until the consumer specifically requests that the data not be collected. Privacy advocates would like to see wider use of an opt-in model of informed consent in which a business is prohibited from collecting any personal information unless the consumer specifically takes action to approve information collection and use. The Privacy Commissioner of Canada has ruled that in most situations opt-in must be used in Canada.

The online industry has preferred self-regulation to privacy legislation for protecting consumers. In 1998, the online industry formed the Online Privacy Alliance to encourage self-regulation to develop a set of privacy guidelines for its members. The group promotes the use of online seals, such as that of TRUSTe, certifying Web sites adhering to certain privacy principles (see Figure 4-4). Members of the advertising network industry, including DoubleClick, have created an additional industry association called the Network Advertising Initiative (NAI) to develop its own privacy policies to help consumers opt out of advertising network programs and provide consumers redress from abuses.

Individual firms such as AOL, Yahoo!, and Google have recently adopted policies on their own in an effort to address public concern about tracking people online. AOL established an **opt-out** policy that allows users of its site to not be tracked. Yahoo! follows NAI guidelines and also allows opt-out for tracking and Web beacons (Web bugs). Google has reduced retention time for tracking data.

Technical Solutions In addition to legislation, new technologies are available to protect user privacy during interactions with Web sites. Many of these tools are used for encrypting e-mail, for making e-mail or surfing activities appear anonymous, for preventing client computers from accepting cookies, or for detecting and eliminating spyware.

There are now tools to help users determine the kind of personal data that can be extracted by Web sites. The **Platform for Privacy Preferences,** known as **P3P** provides a standard for automatically communicating a Web site's privacy policy to Internet users and for comparing that policy to the user's preferences or to other standards, such as the European Directive on Data Protection. Users can use P3P to select the level of privacy they wish to maintain when interacting with the Web site.

opt-in
opt-out
P3P (Platform for Privacy
  Preferences)

FIGURE 4-4   Use of the TRUSTe seal.

Web sites are now posting their privacy policies for visitors to review. The TRUSTe seal designates Web sites that have agreed to adhere to TRUSTe's established privacy principles of disclosure, choice, access, and security.

The P3P standard allows Web sites to publish privacy policies in a form that computers can understand. Once it is codified according to P3P rules, the privacy policy becomes part of the software for individual Web pages (see Figure 4-5). Users of Microsoft Internet Explorer Web browsing software can access and read the P3P site's privacy policy and a list of all cookies coming from the site. Internet Explorer enables users to adjust their computers to screen out all cookies or let in selected cookies based on specific levels of privacy. For example, the "medium" level accepts cookies from first-party host sites that have opt-in or opt-out policies but rejects third-party cookies that use personally identifiable information without an opt-in policy.

However, P3P works only with Web sites of members of the World Wide Web Consortium that have translated their Web site privacy policies into P3P format. The technology will display cookies from Web sites that are not part of the consortium, but users will not be able to obtain sender information or privacy statements. Many users may also need to be educated about interpreting company privacy statements and P3P levels of privacy.

Property Rights: Intellectual Property

Contemporary information systems have severely challenged existing law and social practices that protect private intellectual property. **Intellectual property** is considered to be intangible property created by individuals or corporations. Information technology has made it difficult to protect intellectual property because computerized information can be so easily copied or distributed on networks. Intellectual property is subject to a variety of protections under three different legal traditions: trade secrets, copyright, and patent law.

Trade Secrets Any intellectual work product—a formula, device, pattern, or compilation of data—used for a business purpose can be classified as a **trade secret,** provided it is not based on information in the public domain. Trade secret law has arisen out of the

Intellectual property

Trade secret

FIGURE 4-5   The P3P standard.

P3P enables Web sites to translate their privacy policies into a standard format that can be read by the user's Web browser software. The browser software evaluates the Web site's privacy policy to determine whether it is compatible with the user's privacy preferences.

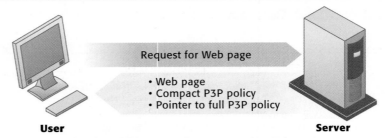

1. The user with P3P Web browsing software requests a Web page.
2. The Web server returns the Web page along with a compact version of the Web site's policy and a pointer to the full P3P policy. If the Web site is not P3P-compliant, no P3P data are returned.
3. The user's Web browsing software compares the response from the Web site with the user's privacy preferences. If the Web site does not have a P3P policy or the policy does not match the privacy levels established by the user, it warns the user or rejects the cookies from the Web site. Otherwise, the Web page loads normally.

broad "duty of good faith" and the principle of equity that whoever "has received information in confidence shall not take unfair advantage of it." The Supreme Court of Canada has stated that the test for whether there has been a breach of confidence consists of three elements:

1. The information conveyed must be confidential (that is, it must not be public knowledge);

2. The information must have been communicated in confidence; and

3. The information must have been misused by the party to whom it was communicated.

As trade secret law in Canada is a matter of provincial jurisdiction, the drafting and interpretation of agreements that contain trade secret provisions must be carried out by a lawyer in the province that governs the agreement in question. Similarly, the assessment of whether a breach of confidence has occurred must be carried out by a lawyer in the province that governs the obligation of confidence. In general, trade secret laws grant a monopoly on the ideas behind a work product, but it can be a very tenuous monopoly.

Software that contains novel or unique elements, procedures, or compilations can be included as a trade secret. Trade secret law protects the actual ideas in a work product, not only their manifestation. To make this claim, the creator or owner must take care to bind employees and customers with nondisclosure agreements and to prevent the secret from falling into the public domain.

The limitation of trade secret protection is that, although virtually all software programs of any complexity contain unique elements of some sort, it is difficult to prevent the ideas in the work from falling into the public domain when the software is widely distributed.

Copyright **Copyright** is a statutory grant that protects creators of intellectual property from having their work copied by others for any purpose for a period of at least 50 years. The Copyright Office registers copyrights and enforces copyright law in Canada. Parliament has extended copyright protection to books, periodicals, lectures, dramas, musical compositions, maps, drawings, artwork of any kind, and motion pictures. The intent behind copyright laws has been to encourage creativity and authorship by ensuring that creative people receive the financial and other benefits of their work. Most industrial nations have their own copyright laws, and there are several international conventions and bilateral agreements through which nations coordinate and enforce their laws.

Copyright law in Canada is one of the principal means of protecting computer software in Canada. Canadian copyright law is governed by the *Copyright Act*, which protects

Copyright

original literary, artistic, musical, and dramatic works. Computer software is protected in Canada as a literary work. Canadian copyright comes into existence automatically, and, in the case of software, it comes into existence at the time the software was created and continues until the end of the calendar year in which the author of the software dies (regardless of whether the author has sold or assigned the copyright in the software or not) and continues for an additional period of 50 years following the end of that calendar year.

"Moral" rights are also protected under Canadian copyright law. Moral rights in Canada include the right of the author of a piece of software to be associated with the software by name or pseudonym and the right to remain anonymous. They also include the author's right to the integrity of the software (that is, the author's right to stop the software from being distorted, mutilated or modified, to the prejudice of the author's honour or reputation, or from being used in association with a product, service, cause, or institution).

Moral rights remain with the author of a piece of software, even where the software, or the copyright in the software, has been sold or assigned, regardless of whether the author created the software in the employ of someone else or created it under contract or otherwise.

Copyright protection is clear-cut: It protects against copying of entire programs or their parts. Damages and relief are readily obtained for infringement. The drawback to copyright protection is that the underlying ideas behind a work are not protected, only their manifestation in a work. A competitor can use your software, understand how it works, and develop new software that follows the same concepts without infringing on a copyright.

"Look and feel" copyright infringement lawsuits are precisely about the distinction between an idea and its expression. Most of this type of copyright infringement has occurred in the United States. For instance, in the early 1990s, Apple Computer sued Microsoft Corporation and Hewlett-Packard Inc. for infringement of the expression of Apple's Macintosh interface. Among other claims, Apple claimed that the defendants copied the expression of overlapping windows. The defendants counterclaimed that the idea of overlapping windows can be expressed only in a single way and, therefore, was not protectable under the "merger" doctrine of copyright law. When ideas and their expression merge, the expression cannot be copyrighted. In general, courts appear to be following the reasoning of a 1989 U.S. case—*Brown Bag Software vs. Symantec Corp.*—in which the court dissected the elements of software alleged to be infringing. The court found that neither similar concept, function, general functional features (e.g., drop-down menus), nor colours are protected by copyright law (*Brown Bag vs. Symantec Corp.*,1992).

Patents A **patent** grants the owner an exclusive monopoly on the ideas behind an invention for between 17 and 20 years. The intent behind patent law is to ensure that inventors of new machines, devices, or methods receive the full financial and other rewards of their labour and yet still make widespread use of the invention possible by providing detailed diagrams for those wishing to use the idea under license from the patent's owner. The granting of a patent is determined by the Patent Office and relies on court rulings.

The key concepts in patent law are originality, novelty, and invention. The Canadian Patent Office does not accept applications for software patents because software is considered to fall under Canadian copyright law. In the United States, the U.S. Patent Office did not routinely issue patents on software until a 1981 Supreme Court decision that held that computer programs could be a part of a patentable process. Since that time, hundreds of U.S. software patents have been granted, and thousands await consideration.

The strength of patent protection is that it grants a monopoly on the underlying concepts and ideas of software. The difficulty is passing stringent criteria of nonobviousness (e.g., the work must reflect some special understanding and contribution), originality, and novelty as well as years of waiting to receive protection.

Challenges to Intellectual Property Rights Contemporary information technologies, especially software, pose severe challenges to existing intellectual property regimes and, therefore, create significant ethical, social, and political issues. Digital media differ from books, periodicals, and other media in terms of ease of replication; ease of transmission; ease of alteration; difficulty in classifying a software work as a program, book, or even music; compactness—making theft easy; and difficulties in establishing uniqueness.

Patent

The proliferation of electronic networks, including the Internet, has made it even more difficult to protect intellectual property. Before widespread use of networks, copies of software, books, magazine articles, or films had to be stored on physical media, such as paper, computer disks, or videotape, creating some hurdles to distribution. Using networks, information can be more widely reproduced and distributed. As stated in the chapter-opening case study, worldwide, for every two dollars of software purchased legitimately, one dollar's worth was obtained illegally (Business Software Alliance, 2009).

The Internet was designed to transmit information freely around the world, including copyrighted information. With the World Wide Web in particular, you can easily copy and distribute virtually anything to thousands and even millions of people around the world, even if they are using different types of computer systems. Information can be illicitly copied from one place and distributed through other systems and networks even though these parties do not willingly participate in the infringement.

Individuals have been illegally copying and distributing digitized MP3 music files on the Internet for a number of years. File-sharing services such as Napster, and later Grokster, Kazaa, and Morpheus sprang up to help users locate and swap digital music files, including those protected by copyright. Illegal file sharing became so widespread that it threatened the viability of the music recording industry. The recording industry won some legal battles for shutting these services down but has not been able to halt illegal file sharing entirely. As more and more homes adopt high-speed Internet access, illegal file sharing of videos will pose similar threats to the motion picture industry (see the case study concluding Chapter 3).

Mechanisms are being developed to sell and distribute books, articles, and other intellectual property legally on the Internet, and the U.S. **Digital Millennium Copyright Act (DMCA)** of 1998 is providing some copyright protection. The DMCA implemented a World Intellectual Property Organization Treaty that makes it illegal to circumvent technology-based protections of copyrighted materials. Internet service providers (ISPs) are required to take down sites of copyright infringers that the ISPs are hosting, once they are notified of the problem.

What effect did the DMCA have on Canadian copyright legislation? The DMCA set the agenda for copyright discussions in Canada on

- Technological tampering—"devices" or "conduct"
- ISP liability
- Library provisions to be examined
- Database protection

The Speech from the Throne in the fall of 2002 sought to establish policy to bring Canada into alignment with the World Intellectual Property Organization (WIPO) and also to look at some other long-term aims of copyright legislation in Canada. Compliance with WIPO would include short-term goals of technological measures protection and digital rights management as well as the liability of the Internet service provider when copyright is infringed by its users. The government also planned to look at the blank recording levy—a levy incorporated in the price of blank media that is aggregated and split among various recording industry publishers, artists, etc.—that is currently in place and to examine the fair-use part of the *Copyright Act* and whether it could or should be expanded. In the medium term, Canadian lawmakers will be looking at the duration of copyright and whether it should be increased to life plus 70 as has taken place in the United States.

Microsoft, IBM, and other major software and information content firms are represented by the Software and Information Industry Association (SIIA), which lobbies for new laws and enforcement of existing laws to protect intellectual property around the world. The SIIA runs an anti-piracy hotline for individuals to report piracy activities and educational programs to help organizations combat software piracy and has published guidelines for employee use of software.

Digital Millennium Copyright
Act (DMCA)

Accountability, Liability, and Control

Along with privacy and property laws, new information technologies are challenging existing liability law and social practices for holding individuals and institutions accountable. If a person is injured by a machine controlled, in part, by software, who should be held accountable and, therefore, held liable? Should a public bulletin board or an electronic service, such as America Online, permit the transmission of pornographic or offensive material (as broadcasters), or should it be held harmless against any liability for what users transmit (as is true of common carriers, such as the telephone system)? What about the Internet? If you outsource your information processing, can you hold the external vendor liable for injuries done to your customers? Some real-world examples may shed light on these questions.

Computer-Related Liability Problems On November 28, 2000, a double failure in Sprint Canada's network shut down trading on Vancouver's Canadian Venture Exchange for more than two hours. Three hundred thousand Rogers@Home cable customers were left without service recently when a rodent chewed through cables that were exposed during routine repairs. In November 1998, a railway backhoe operator accidentally cut an AT&T Canada fibre cable along the rail line between Toronto and Windsor, crashing computers, knocking out phone lines, and generally disrupting communications in southern Ontario. The main branch of the Scotiabank was computerless.

During the weekend of March 15, 2002, tens of thousands of Bank of America customers in California, Arizona, and Nevada were unable to use their paycheques and social security payments that had just been deposited electronically. Cheques bounced. Withdrawals were blocked because of insufficient funds. Because of an operating error at the bank's computer centre in Nevada, a batch of direct-deposit transactions was not processed. The bank lost track of money that should have been credited to customers' accounts, and it took days to rectify the problem (Carr and Gallagher, 2002). Who is liable for any economic harm caused to individuals or businesses that could not access their full account balances in this period?

These cases reveal the difficulties faced by information systems executives who ultimately are responsible for any harm done by systems developed by their staffs. In general, insofar as computer software is part of a machine, and the machine injures someone physically or economically, the producer of the software and the operator can be held liable for damages. Insofar as the software acts like a book, storing and displaying information, courts have been reluctant to hold authors, publishers, and booksellers liable for contents (the exception being instances of fraud or defamation), and hence courts have been wary of holding software authors liable for book-like software.

In general, it is very difficult (if not impossible) to hold software producers liable for their software products when those products are considered like books, regardless of the physical or economic harm that results. Historically, print publishers, books, and periodicals have not been held liable because of fears that liability claims would interfere with rights guaranteeing freedom of expression.

What about software as a service? ATM machines are a service provided to bank customers. Should this service fail, customers will be inconvenienced and perhaps harmed economically if they cannot access their funds in a timely manner. Should liability protections be extended to software publishers and operators of defective financial, accounting, simulation, or marketing systems?

Software is very different from books. Software users may develop expectations of infallibility about software; software is less easily inspected than a book, and it is more difficult to compare with other software products for quality; software claims actually to perform a task rather than describe a task, as a book does; and people come to depend on services essentially based on software. Given the centrality of software to everyday life, the chances are excellent that liability law will soon extend its reach to include software even when the software merely provides an information service.

Telephone systems have not been held liable for the messages transmitted because they are regulated common carriers. In return for their right to provide telephone service, they must provide access to all, at reasonable rates, and achieve acceptable reliability. But broadcasters and cable television systems are subject to a wide variety of federal and local constraints on content and facilities. Organizations can be held liable for offensive content on their Web sites; and online services, such as Yahoo!, might be held liable for postings by their users. Although courts have increasingly exonerated Web sites and ISPs for posting material by third parties, the threat of legal action still has a chilling effect on small companies or individuals who cannot afford to take their cases to trial.

System Quality: Data Quality and System Errors

The debate over liability and accountability for unintentional consequences of system use raises a related but independent moral dimension: What is an acceptable, technologically feasible level of system quality? At what point should system managers say, "Stop testing, we've done all we can to perfect this software. Ship it!" Individuals and organizations may be held responsible for avoidable and foreseeable consequences, which they have a duty to perceive and correct. And the grey area is that some system errors are foreseeable and correctable only at very great expense, an expense so great that pursuing this level of perfection is not feasible economically—no one could afford the product.

For example, although software companies try to debug their products before releasing them to the marketplace, they knowingly ship buggy products because the time and cost of fixing all minor errors would prevent these products from ever being released. What if the product was not offered on the marketplace? Would social welfare as a whole not advance and perhaps even decline? Carrying this further, just what is the responsibility of a producer of computer services—should it withdraw the product that can never be perfect, warn the user, or forget about the risk (let the buyer beware)?

Three principal sources of poor system performance are (1) software bugs and errors, (2) hardware or facility failures caused by natural or other causes, and (3) poor input data quality. A Chapter 8 Learning Track discusses why zero defects in software code of any complexity cannot be achieved and why the seriousness of remaining bugs cannot be estimated. Hence, there is a technological barrier to perfect software, and users must be aware of the potential for catastrophic failure. The software industry has not yet arrived at testing standards for producing software of acceptable but not perfect performance.

Although software bugs and facility catastrophes are likely to be widely reported in the press, by far the most common source of business system failure is data quality. Few companies routinely measure the quality of their data, but individual organizations report data error rates ranging from 0.5 to 30 percent.

Quality of Life: Equity, Access, and Boundaries

The negative social costs of introducing information technologies and systems are beginning to mount along with the power of the technology. Many of these negative social consequences are not violations of individual rights or property crimes. Nevertheless, these negative consequences can be extremely harmful to individuals, societies, and political institutions. Computers and information technologies potentially can destroy valuable elements of our culture and society even while they bring us benefits. If there is a balance of good and bad consequences of using information systems, whom do we hold responsible for the bad consequences? Next, we briefly examine some of the negative social consequences of systems, considering individual, social, and political responses.

Balancing Power: Centre versus Periphery An early fear of the computer age was that huge, centralized mainframe computers would centralize power at corporate headquarters and in the nation's capital, resulting in a Big Brother society, as was suggested in George Orwell's novel *1984*. The shift toward highly decentralized computing, coupled with an ideology of empowerment of thousands of workers, and the decentralization of decision making to lower organizational levels have reduced the fears of power centralization in institutions. Yet much of the empowerment described in popular business magazines is trivial. Lower-level employees may be empowered to make minor decisions, but the key policy decisions may be as centralized as in the past.

Rapidity of Change: Reduced Response Time to Competition Information systems have helped to create much more efficient national and international markets. The now-more-efficient global marketplace has reduced the normal social buffers that permitted businesses many years to adjust to competition. Time-based competition has an ugly side: The business you work for may not have enough time to respond to global competitors and may be wiped out in a year, along with your job. We stand the risk of developing a "just-in-time society" with "just-in-time jobs" and "just-in-time" workplaces, families, and vacations.

Although some people enjoy the convenience of working at home, the "do anything anywhere" computing environment can blur the traditional boundaries between work and family time.

Maintaining Boundaries: Family, Work, and Leisure Parts of this book were produced on trains and planes, as well as on vacations and during what otherwise might have been "family" time. The danger to ubiquitous computing, telecommuting, nomad computing, and the "do anything anywhere" computing environment is that it might actually come true. If so, the traditional boundaries that separate work from family and just plain leisure will be weakened.

Although authors have traditionally worked just about anywhere (typewriters have been portable for nearly a century), the advent of information systems, coupled with the growth of knowledge-work occupations, means that more and more people will be working when traditionally they would have been playing or communicating with family and friends. The work umbrella now extends far beyond the eight-hour day.

Even leisure time spent on the computer threatens these close social relationships. Extensive Internet use, even for entertainment or recreational purposes, takes people away from their family and friends. Among middle-school and teenage children as well as adults, it can lead to harmful anti-social behaviour. The Window on Organizations explores this topic.

Weakening these institutions poses clear-cut risks. Family and friends historically have provided powerful support mechanisms for individuals, and they act as balance points in a society by preserving private life, providing a place for people to collect their thoughts, allowing people to think in ways contrary to their employer, and dream.

Organizations # WINDOW ON ORGANIZATIONS

What Should We Do about Cyberbullying?

The Internet offers a variety of benefits for people of all ages, and young and even older children are no exception. Information is readily available and accessible for school assignments. Kids can more easily keep in touch with their friends by communicating online. Music, games, and other interactive activities abound. Easy access to all of these types of media creates opportunities for unique learning experiences that would not be available otherwise.

However, the same features of the Internet that allow kids—even university students—to chat with friends, do research for a project, play the latest games, and download music also allow bullies and other types of Internet predators to more easily find and affect their victims. Cyberbullying in particular has been on the rise as bullies become more creative in their use of the Internet to humiliate their peers. Bullies use social networking sites, e-mail, instant messaging, cell phone cameras, and other digital technologies to insult and embarrass their targets. Controlling cyberbullying has thus far proven to be a challenge, since policing content on the Internet is a daunting task.

The recent suicide of Megan Meier, a 13-year-old girl from O'Fallon, Missouri, illustrates just how devastating the effects of cyberbullying can be on young children. Megan was the victim of persistent and hateful MySpace bullying, much of which was masterminded by a local parent, 49-year-old Lori Drew, who has been charged with one count of conspiracy and three counts of accessing a computer without authorization and via interstate commerce to obtain information to inflict emotional distress. Ms. Drew was eventually found not guilty of all charges because U.S. law does not yet apply to such a case.

Canadian high school student David Knight was teased, taunted, and bullied at school for years. But it was the abusive Web site that was created specifically to permit others to taunt him that was the final straw. David spent his final school year being home-schooled. "Rather than just some people, say 30 in a cafeteria, hearing them all yell insults at you, it's up there for 6 billion to see. Anyone with a computer can see it," says David. "And you can't get away from it. It doesn't go away when you come home from school. It made me feel even more trapped."

David's case is only one of thousands. According to a recent survey by the University of Toronto, one in five Canadian students who were surveyed reported that they have been bullied online in the last three months. An Alberta study revealed that one-third of students who had committed cyberbullying had also been victims of it. Those who cyberbully feel that they are safe because others cannot see them committing these acts and because they believe they can be anonymous online.

In British Columbia, one in four young people claim to have been the victims of cyberbullying while one in five claim they have bullied others online. According to a survey by Microsoft Canada and Youthography Internet, almost 80 percent of those surveyed feel that others bully online because it is easier than bullying in person and 70 percent believe they will never be caught. Sixty percent of respondents felt that people bully because it is "cool."

It is not only elementary through high school students who commit cyberbullying. In 2007, a prominent Canadian university experienced an episode of cyberbullying when more than 200 students used Facebook to post disparaging comments about a fellow student. Thirty-four students were sanctioned by the school.

Cyberbullying can take many forms. But the law has not yet caught up with this crime. Civil law can try to address cyberbullying, provided the bullying takes the form of libel, slander, or defamation. Others believe that cyberbullies can best be prosecuted using laws about providing a safe workplace and applying that to schools as well. But those laws would prosecute the schools for not providing a safe workplace rather than the students who are doing the bullying. Criminal law regarding harassment may apply.

Interestingly, the *Charter of Rights and Freedoms* guarantees freedom of expression. But the right is "subject only to such reasonable limits prescribed by law as can be demonstrably justified in a free and democratic society" and must be mitigated by Section 7, which guarantees "the right to life, liberty, and security of the person."

In May 2009, a bill was introduced in Parliament to amend the Canadian *Criminal Code* to incorporate cyberbullying in the three existing laws that outline harassment, defamatory libel, and spreading false messages through telecommunications. The bill was deemed necessary because current Canadian law does not stipulate modern technologies such as cell phones, text messages, and social networking sites as ways to commit these crimes. It will be interesting to see if this bill receives royal assent.

Unlike traditional bullying, which tends to happen mostly at school, cyberbullying can occur at any and all times. According to Dr. Walter Roberts, professor of counsellor education at Mankato State University in Minnesota, "The harassment is not limited to the portion of the day when the kids are in school. The targeted kids have no escape."

Many schools are trying to make changes locally to avoid any situations as grim as that of Megan Meier or David Knight. More schools are providing counsellors to speak with students during downtime. Parents are being encouraged to take a more active role in the Internet activities of their children.

Even so, cyberbullying is likely to remain a widespread problem. Bullies have been around for a much longer time than the Internet, and they are unlikely to relinquish their new-found abilities to insult, hurt, and embarrass that social networks and other new methods of communication provide.

To Think About

1. What are some of the technologies and communication methods used by cyberbullies? Why are they so effective?

2. What measures have been taken by school districts and governments to combat cyberbullying? How helpful are they? Can you think of any other ways to effectively control cyberbullying?

3. Should there be stronger laws outlawing cyberbullying? Why or why not?

4. Does a social networking site catering to teens such as Facebook or MySpace represent an ethical dilemma? Why or why not?

MIS in Action

Visit MySpace, at **www.myspace.com,** and click on Safety Tips. Explore the features for parents and educators, for teens, more resources, and safety tips and settings. Describe the capabilities and tools available to educate users about cyberbullying and to combat this practice. Compare this with Facebook; go to **www.facebook.com,** and click on Help, Help Center, then Safety. How effective is this Web site in dealing with cyberbullying?

Sources: Juli S. Charkes, "Cracking Down on the Cyberbully," *The New York Times,* March 30, 2008; Christopher Maag, "When the Bullies Turned Faceless," *The New York Times,* December 16, 2007; and Jennifer Steinhauer, "Woman Indicted in MySpace Suicide Case," *The New York Times,* May 16, 2008; "Missouri: Cyberbullying Law Is Signed," The Associated Press, July 1, 2008; Joan Leishman, "Cyber-bullying," CBC News, **www.cbc.ca/news/background/bullying/cyber_bullying.html**

(accessed July 26, 2009); Media Awareness Network, "Cyberbullying and the Law Fact Sheet, **www.media-awareness.ca/english/resources/educational/teaching_backgrounders/cyberbullying/cyberbullying_law2_h4.cfm?RenderforPrint=1** (accessed October 7, 2009); Gillian Shaw, "Majority of Canadian Kids Say Cyberbullying Seen as "Cool," *The Vancouver Sun*, February 25, 2009; Canadian Press, "U of M Students Disciplined for Cyberbullying," *The Globe and Mail*, March 30, 2009; Nick Martin, "U of M Probes Cyberbullying on Student Site," *The Winnipeg Free Press*, March 1, 2007; Kiwi Commons, "Canadian Bill Proposed to Make Cyberbullying a Crime," May 6, 2009, **www.kiwicommons.com/2009/05/Canadian-bill-proposed-to-make-cyberbullying-a-crime** (accessed July 26, 2009).

Dependence and Vulnerability Today, our businesses, governments, schools, and private associations, such as religious institutions, are incredibly dependent on information systems and are, therefore, highly vulnerable if these systems fail. With systems now as ubiquitous as the telephone system, it is startling to remember that there are no regulatory or standard-setting forces in place that are similar to telephone, electrical, radio, television, or other public utility technologies. The absence of standards and the criticality of some system applications will probably call forth demands for national standards and perhaps regulatory oversight.

Computer Crime and Abuse New technologies, including computers, create new opportunities for committing crime by creating new valuable items to steal, new ways to steal them, and new ways to harm others. **Computer crime** is the commission of illegal acts through the use of a computer or against a computer system. Computers or computer systems can be the object of the crime (destroying a company's computer centre or a company's computer files), as well as the instrument of a crime (stealing computer lists by illegally gaining access to a computer system using a home computer). Simply accessing a computer system without authorization or with intent to do harm, even by accident, is now a federal crime.

Computer abuse is the commission of acts involving a computer that may not be illegal but that are considered unethical. The popularity of the Internet and e-mail has turned one form of computer abuse—spamming—into a serious problem for both individuals and businesses. **Spam** is junk e-mail sent by an organization or individual to a mass audience of Internet users who have expressed no interest in the product or service being marketed. Spammers tend to market pornography, fraudulent deals and services, outright scams, and other products not widely approved in most civilized societies. Some countries have passed laws to outlaw spamming or to restrict its use. In the United States, spam is still legal if it does not involve fraud and the sender and subject of the e-mail are properly identified.

Spamming has mushroomed because it costs only a few cents to send thousands of messages advertising wares to Internet users. According to Sophos, a leading vendor of security software, spam accounted for 92.3 percent of all e-mail traffic during the first quarter of 2008 (Sophos, 2008). Spam costs for businesses are very high (an estimated $61 billion per year) because of the computing and network resources consumed by billions of unwanted e-mail messages and the time required to deal with them.

Internet service providers and individuals can combat spam by using spam-filtering software to block suspicious e-mail before it enters a recipient's e-mail inbox. However, spam filters may block legitimate messages. Spammers know how to skirt around filters by continually changing their e-mail accounts, by incorporating spam messages in images, by embedding spam in e-mail attachments and electronic greeting cards, and by using other people's computers that have been hijacked by botnets (see Chapter 8). Many spam messages are sent from one country while another country hosts the spam Web site.

Spamming is more tightly regulated in Europe than in North America. On May 30, 2002, the European Parliament passed a ban on unsolicited commercial messaging. Now electronic marketing can be targeted only to people who have given prior consent.

Computer crime
Computer abuse
Spam

The U.S. *CAN-SPAM Act* of 2003, which went into effect on January 1, 2004, does not outlaw spamming but does ban deceptive e-mail practices by requiring commercial e-mail messages to display accurate subject lines, identify the true senders, and offer recipients an easy way to remove their names from e-mail lists. It also prohibits the use of fake return addresses. A few people have been prosecuted under the law, but it has had a negligible impact on spamming.

Employment: Trickle-Down Technology and Re-engineering Job Loss Re-engineering work is typically hailed in the information systems community as a major benefit of new information technology. It is much less frequently noted that redesigning business processes could potentially cause millions of middle-level managers and clerical workers to lose their jobs. One economist has raised the possibility that we will create a society run by a small "high tech elite of corporate professionals . . . in a nation of the permanently unemployed" (Rifkin, 1993).

Other economists are much more sanguine about the potential job losses. They believe relieving bright, educated workers from re-engineered jobs will result in these workers moving to better jobs in fast-growth industries.

Missing from this equation are unskilled, blue-collar workers and older, less well-educated middle managers. It is not clear that these groups can be retrained easily for high-quality (high-paying) jobs. Careful planning and sensitivity to employee needs can help companies redesign work to minimize job losses.

The Window on Management explores another consequence of re-engineered jobs. In this case, Walmart's changes in job scheduling for more efficient use of its employees did not cause employees to lose their jobs directly. But it did impact their personal lives and forced them to accept more irregular part-time work. As you read this case, try to identify the problem this company is facing, what alternative solutions are available to management, and whether the chosen solution was the best way to address this problem.

Equity and Access: Increasing Racial and Social Class Cleavages Does everyone have an equal opportunity to participate in the digital age? Will the social, economic, and cultural gaps that exist in most societies be reduced by information systems technology? Or will the cleavages be increased, permitting the better off to become even more better off relative to others?

These questions have not yet been fully answered because the impact of systems technology on various groups in society has not been thoroughly studied. What is known is that information, knowledge, computers, and access to these resources through educational institutions and public libraries are inequitably distributed along ethnic and social class lines, as are many other information resources. Several studies have found that certain ethnic and income groups in both Canada and the United States are less likely to have computers or online Internet access even though computer ownership and Internet access have soared in the past five years. Although the gap is narrowing, higher-income families in each ethnic group are still more likely to have home computers and Internet access than lower-income families in the same group.

A similar **digital divide** exists in both Canadian and U.S. schools, with schools in high-poverty areas less likely to have computers, high-quality educational technology programs, or Internet access availability for their students. Left uncorrected, the digital divide could lead to a society of information haves, computer literate and skilled, versus a large group of information have-nots, computer illiterate and unskilled. Public interest groups want to narrow this digital divide by making digital information services—including the Internet—available to virtually everyone, just as basic telephone service is now. In addition, in both Canada and the United States, individuals with higher levels of education are more likely to access the Internet, creating another digital divide based on educational level.

Health Risks: RSI, CVS, and Technostress The most common occupational disease today is **repetitive stress injury (RSI)**. RSI occurs when muscle groups are forced through repetitive actions often with high-impact loads (such as tennis) or tens of thousands of repetitions under low-impact loads (such as working at a computer keyboard).

Digital divide
Repetitive stress injury (RSI)

Flexible Scheduling at Walmart: Good or Bad for Employees?

With nearly 1.4 million workers domestically, Walmart is the largest private employer in North America. Walmart is also the continent's number-one retailer in terms of sales, registering nearly $463 billion in sales revenue for the fiscal year ending January 31, 2008. Walmart achieved its lofty status through a combination of low prices and low operational costs, enabled by a superb continuous inventory replenishment system.

Now Walmart is trying to lower costs further by changing its methods for scheduling the work shifts of its employees. In early 2007, Walmart revealed that it was adopting a computerized scheduling system, a move that has been roundly criticized by workers' rights advocates for the impact it may have on employees' lives.

Traditionally, scheduling employee shifts at big box stores such as Walmart was the domain of store managers who arranged schedules manually. They based their decisions in part on current store promotions as well as on weekly sales data from the previous year. Typically, the process required a full day of effort for a store manager. Multiply that labour intensity by the number of stores in a chain and you have an expensive task with results that are marginally beneficial to the company.

By using a computerized scheduling system, such as the system from Kronos that Walmart adopted, a retail enterprise can produce work schedules for every store in its chain in a matter of hours. Meanwhile, store managers can devote their time to running their individual stores more effectively.

The Kronos scheduling system tracks individual store sales, transactions, units sold, and customer traffic. The system logs these metrics over 15-minute increments for seven weeks at a time and then measures them against the same data from the previous year. It can also integrate data such as the number of in-store customers at certain hours or the average time required to sell a television set or unload a truck and predict the number of workers needed at any given hour.

A typical result of this type of scheduling might call for a sparse staff early in the day, a significant increase for the midday rush, scaling back toward the end of the afternoon, and then fortifying the staff once again for an evening crowd. However, for a chain like Walmart, which operates thousands of 24-hour stores and has also run into trouble previously for its labour practices, the transition to a computerized scheduling system has resulted in controversy.

For Walmart, using Kronos translates to improved productivity and customer satisfaction. Management reported a 12 percent gain in labour productivity in the quarter ending January 31, 2008. For Walmart employees, known to the company as associates, the change may decrease the stability of their jobs and, possibly, create financial hardship.

The scheduling generated by Kronos can be unpredictable, requiring associates to be more flexible with their work hours.

Stores may ask them to be on call in case of a rush or to go home during a slow spell. Irregular hours and inconsistent paycheques make it more difficult for employees to organize their lives, from scheduling babysitters to paying bills. Alerts from the system may also enable store managers to avoid paying overtime or full-time wages by cutting back the hours of associates who are approaching the thresholds that cause extra benefits to kick in. Associates are almost always people who need all the work they can get.

According to Paul Blank of the Web site WakeUpWalMart.com, which is supported by the United Food and Commercial Workers union, "What the computer is trying to optimize is the most number of part-time and least number of full-time workers at lower labour costs, with no regard for the effect that it has on workers' lives." Sarah Clark, speaking on behalf of Walmart, insists the system's goal is simply to improve customer service by shortening checkout lines and better meeting the needs of shoppers.

To assist in the deployment of its computerized scheduling system in all of its stores, Walmart requests that its associates submit "personal availability" forms. Language on the form instructs associates: "Limiting your personal availability may restrict the number of hours you are scheduled." Anecdotal evidence suggests that some workers have indeed seen their hours cut and their shifts bounced around. Experienced associates with high pay rates have expressed concern that the system enables managers to pressure them into quitting. If they are unwilling to work nights and weekends, managers have a justification for replacing them with new workers who will make much less per hour. Sarah Clark denies that the system is used in this manner.

Critics of the system can cite the *Clayton Antitrust Act* of 1914, which states, "The labour of a human being is not a commodity or article of commerce." No legal battles over computerized scheduling appear imminent, so interpreting whether Walmart's strategy equals treating its labour force as a commodity will have to wait.

In the meantime, Walmart is once again at the forefront of technology trends in its industry. Ann Taylor Stores, Limited Brands, Gap, Williams-Sonoma, and GameStop have all installed similar workforce scheduling systems.

To Think About

1. What is the ethical dilemma facing Walmart in this case? Do Walmart's associates also face an ethical dilemma? If so, what is it?

2. What ethical principles apply to this case? How do they apply?

3. What are the potential effects of computerized scheduling on employee morale? What are the consequences of these effects for Walmart?

MIS in Action

Visit the Web site at **www.WakeUpWalMart.com**, and then answer the following questions:

1. What are this group's major points of contention with Walmart?

2. How well does the Web site serve their cause? Does the site help their cause or hurt it?

3. What other approach could the organization take to bring about change?

   Using Walmart's Web site and Google for research, answer the following questions:

4. How does Walmart address the issues raised by organizations such as **WakeUpWalMart.com?**

5. Are the company's methods effective?

6. If you were a public relations expert advising Walmart, what suggestions would you make for handling criticism?

Sources: Vanessa O'Connell, "Retailers Reprogram Workers in Efficiency Push," *The Wall Street Journal,* September 10, 2008; Kris Maher, "Wal-Mart Seeks New Flexibility in Worker Shifts," *The Wall Street Journal,* January 3, 2007; **www.kronos.com,** (accessed July 15, 2008); Bob Evans, "Wal-Mart Latest 'Orwellian' Technology Move: Get over It," InformationWeek, April 6, 2007 and "More Opinions on Wal-Mart's Flexible Scheduling," *InformationWeek,* April 17, 2007.

The single largest source of RSI is computer keyboards. The most common kind of computer-related RSI is **carpal tunnel syndrome (CTS),** in which pressure on the median nerve through the wrist's bony structure, called a carpal tunnel, produces pain. The pressure is caused by constant repetition of keystrokes: In a single shift, a data entry clerk using a word processor may perform 23 000 keystrokes. Symptoms of carpal tunnel syndrome include numbness, shooting pain, inability to grasp objects, and tingling. Millions of workers have been diagnosed with carpal tunnel syndrome.

RSI is avoidable. Designing workstations for a neutral wrist position (using a wrist rest to support the wrist), proper monitor stands, and footrests all contribute to proper posture and reduced RSI. New, ergonomically correct keyboards are also an option. These measures should be supported by frequent rest breaks and rotation of employees to different jobs.

Carpal tunnel syndrome (CTS)

Computer vision syndrome (CVS)

Technostress

RSI is not the only occupational illness computers cause. Back and neck pain, leg stress, and foot pain also result from poor ergonomic designs of workstations. **Computer vision syndrome (CVS)** refers to any eyestrain condition related to computer display screen use. Its symptoms, which are usually temporary, include headaches, blurred vision, and dry and irritated eyes.

The newest computer-related malady is **technostress,** which is stress induced by computer use. Its symptoms include aggravation, hostility toward others, impatience, and fatigue. According to experts, individuals working continuously with computers come to expect other people and institutions to behave like computers, providing instant responses, attentiveness, and an absence of emotion. Technostress is thought to be related to high levels of job turnover in the computer industry, high levels of early retirement from computer-intense occupations, and elevated levels of drug and alcohol abuse.

The incidence of technostress is not known but is thought to be in the millions and growing rapidly. Computer-related jobs now top the list of stressful occupations based on health statistics in several industrialized countries.

To date, the role of radiation from computer display screens in occupational disease has not been proved. Video display terminals (VDTs) emit nonionizing electric and magnetic fields at low frequencies. These rays enter the body and have unknown effects on

Repetitive stress injury (RSI) is the leading occupational disease today. The single largest cause of RSI is computer keyboard work.

enzymes, molecules, chromosomes, and cell membranes. Long-term studies are investigating low-level electromagnetic fields and birth defects, stress, low birth weight, and other diseases. All manufacturers have reduced display screen emissions since the early 1980s, and European countries, such as Sweden, have adopted stiff radiation emission standards.

The computer has become a part of our lives—personally as well as socially, culturally, and politically. It is unlikely that the issues and our choices will become easier as information technology continues to transform our world. The growth of the Internet and the information economy suggests that all the ethical and social issues we have described will be heightened further as we move into the first digital century.

SUMMARY

1. **What ethical, social, and political issues are raised by information systems?**

   Information technology is introducing changes for which laws and rules of acceptable conduct have not yet been developed. Increasing computing power, storage, and networking capabilities—including the Internet—expand the reach of individual and organizational actions and magnify their impacts. The ease and anonymity with which information is now communicated, copied, and manipulated in online environments pose new challenges to the protection of privacy and intellectual property. The main ethical, social, and political issues raised by information systems centre around information rights and obligations, property rights and obligations, accountability and control, system quality, and quality of life.

2. **What specific principles for conduct can be used to guide ethical decisions?**

   Six ethical principles for judging conduct include the Golden Rule, Immanuel Kant's categorical imperative, Descartes' rule of change, the utilitarian principle, the risk aversion principle, and the ethical "no free lunch" rule. These principles should be used in conjunction with an ethical analysis: identify and describe clearly the facts; define the conflict or dilemma, and identify the higher-order values involved; identify the stakeholders; identify the options that you can reasonably take; and identify the potential consequences of your options.

3. **Why do contemporary information systems technology and the Internet pose challenges to the protection of individual privacy and intellectual property?**

   Contemporary data storage and data analysis technology enables companies to easily gather personal data about individuals from many different sources and analyze these data to create detailed electronic profiles about individuals and their behaviours. Data flowing over the Internet can be monitored at many points. Cookies and other Web monitoring tools closely track the activities of Web site visitors. Not all Web sites have strong privacy protection policies, and they do not always allow for informed consent regarding the use of personal information. Traditional copyright laws are insufficient to protect against software piracy because digital material can be copied so easily and transmitted to many different locations simultaneously over the Internet.

4. **How have information systems affected everyday life?**

   Although computer systems have been sources of efficiency and wealth, they have some negative impacts. Computer errors can cause serious harm to individuals and organizations. Poor data quality is also responsible for disruptions and losses for businesses. Jobs can be lost when computers replace workers, or tasks become unnecessary in re-engineered business processes. The ability to own and use a computer may be exacerbating socioeconomic disparities among different racial groups and social classes. Widespread use of computers increases opportunities for computer crime and computer abuse. Computers can also create health problems, such as RSI, computer vision syndrome, and technostress.

Key Terms

Accountability, 104
Carpal tunnel syndrome (CTS), 122
Computer abuse, 119
Computer crime, 119

Computer vision syndrome (CVS), 122
Cookies, 109
Copyright, 112
Descartes' rule of change, 105

Digital divide, 120
Digital Millennium Copyright Act (DMCA), 114
Due process, 104

Review Questions

1. *What ethical, social, and political issues are raised by information systems?*

   - *Explain how ethical, social, and political issues are connected and give some examples.*
   - *List and describe the key technological trends that heighten ethical concerns.*
   - *Differentiate between responsibility, accountability, and liability.*

2. *What specific principles for conduct can be used to guide ethical decisions?*

   - *List and describe the five steps in an ethical analysis.*
   - *Identify and describe six ethical principles.*

3. *Why do contemporary information systems technology and the Internet pose challenges to the protection of individual privacy and intellectual property?*

   - *Define privacy and fair information practices.*
   - *Explain how the Internet challenges the protection of individual privacy and intellectual property.*

   - *Explain how informed consent, legislation, industry self-regulation, and technology tools help protect the individual privacy of Internet users.*
   - *List and define the three different regimes that protect intellectual property rights.*

4. *How have information systems affected everyday life?*

   - *Explain why it is so difficult to hold software services liable for failure or injury.*
   - *List and describe the principal causes of system quality problems.*
   - *Name and describe four quality-of-life impacts of computers and information systems.*
   - *Define and describe technostress and RSI, and explain their relationship to information technology.*

Discussion Questions

1. *Should producers of software-based services, such as ATMs, be held liable for economic injuries suffered when their systems fail?*

2. *Should companies be responsible for unemployment caused by their information systems? Why or why not?*

Collaboration and Teamwork: Developing a Corporate Ethics Code

With three or four of your classmates, develop a corporate ethics code on privacy that addresses both employee privacy and the privacy of customers and users of the corporate Web site. Be sure to consider e-mail privacy and employer monitoring of worksites, as well as corporate use of information about employees concerning their off-the-job behaviour

(e.g., lifestyle, marital arrangements, and so forth). If possible, use Google Sites to post links to Web pages, team communication announcements, and work assignments; to brainstorm; and to work collaboratively on project documents. Try to use Google Docs to develop your solution and presentation for the class.

Visit the MyMISLab Web site at **www.pearsoned.ca/mymislab.** This online homework and tutorial system puts you in control of your own learning with study and practice tools directly correlated to this chapter's content.

Learning Track Modules

The following Learning Tracks provide content relevant to the topics covered in this chapter:

1. Developing a Corporate Code of Ethics for Information Systems
2. Creating a Web Page

HANDS-ON MIS   Projects

The projects in this section give you hands-on experience in analyzing the privacy implications of using online data brokers, developing a corporate policy for employee Web usage, using blog creation tools to create a simple blog, and using Internet newsgroups for market research.

Management Decision Problems

1. USAData's Web site is linked to massive databases that consolidate personal data on millions of people. Anyone with a credit card can purchase marketing lists of consumers broken down by location, age, income level, and interests.

   If you click on Consumer Leads to order a consumer mailing list, you can find the names, addresses, and sometimes phone numbers of potential sales leads residing in a specific location and purchase the list of those names. You could use this capability to obtain a list, for example, of everyone in Peekskill, New York, making $150 000 or more per year. Do data brokers such as USAData raise privacy issues? Why or why not? If your name and other personal information were in this database, what limitations on access would you want in order to preserve your privacy? Consider the following data users: government agencies, your employer, private business firms, other individuals.

2. As the head of a small insurance company with six employees, you are concerned about how effectively your company is using its networking and human resources. Budgets are tight, and you are struggling to meet payroll because employees are reporting many overtime hours. You do not believe that the employees

   have a sufficiently heavy workload to warrant working longer hours and are looking into the amount of time they spend on the Internet. Each employee uses a computer with Internet access on the job. You requested the following weekly report of employee Web usage from your information systems department.

   Web Usage Report for the Week Ending January 9, 2010:

User Name	Minutes Online	Web Site Visited
Kelleher, Claire	45	**www.doubleclick.net**
Kelleher, Claire	107	**www.yahoo.com**
Kelleher, Claire	96	**www.insweb.com**
McMahon, Patricia	83	**www.itunes.com**
McMahon, Patricia	44	**www.insweb.com**
Milligan, Robert	112	**www.youtube.com**
Milligan, Robert	43	**www.travelocity.com**
Olivera, Ernesto	40	**www.CNN.com**
Talbot, Helen	125	**www.etrade.com**
Talbot, Helen	27	**www.nordstrom.com**

Talbot, Helen	35	**www.yahoo.com**
Talbot, Helen	73	**www.ebay.com**
Wright, Steven	23	**www.facebook.com**
Wright, Steven	15	**www.autobytel.com**

- Calculate the total amount of time each employee spent on the Web for the week and the total amount of time that company computers were used for this purpose.

Rank the employees in the order of the amount of time each spent online.

- Do your findings and the contents of the report indicate any ethical problems employees are creating? Is the company creating an ethical problem by monitoring its employees' use of the Internet?

- Use the guidelines for ethical analysis presented in this chapter to develop a solution to the problems you have identified.

Achieving Operational Excellence: Creating a Simple Blog

Software skills: Blog creation
Business skills: Blog and Web page design

In this project, you will learn how to build a simple blog of your own design using the online blog creation software available at Blogger.com. Pick a sport, hobby, or topic of interest as the theme for your blog. Name the blog, give it a title, and choose a template for the blog. Post at least four entries to the blog, adding a label for each posting. Edit your posts, if necessary. Upload an image, such as a photo, from your hard drive or the Web to your blog. (Google recommends Open Photo, Flickr, Creative Commons, or Creative Commons Search as sources for photos. Be sure to credit the source for your image.) Add capabilities for other registered users, such as team members, to comment on your blog. Briefly describe how your blog could be useful to a company selling products or services related to the theme of your blog. List the tools available to Blogger (including Gadgets) that would make your blog more useful for business and describe the business uses of each. Save your blog and show it to your instructor.

Improving Decision Making: Using Internet Newsgroups for Online Market Research

Software skills: Web browser software and Internet newsgroups
Business skills: Using Internet newsgroups to identify potential customers

This project will help develop your Internet skills in using newsgroups for marketing. It will also ask you to think about the ethical implications of using information in online discussion groups for business purposes.

You are producing hiking boots that you sell through a few stores at this time. You think your boots are more comfortable than those of your competition. You believe you can undersell many of your competitors if you can significantly increase your production and sales. You would like to use Internet discussion groups interested in hiking, climbing, and camping both to sell your boots and to make them well known. Visit Groups.Google.com, which stores discussion postings from many thousands of newsgroups. Through this site, you can locate all relevant newsgroups and search them by keyword, author's name, forum, date, and subject. Choose a message and examine it carefully, noting all the information you can obtain, including information about the author.

- How could you use these newsgroups to market your boots?

- What ethical principles might you be violating if you use these messages to sell your boots? Do you think there are ethical problems in using newsgroups this way? Explain your answer.

- Next use Google or Yahoo.com to search the hiking boots industry and locate sites that will help you develop other new ideas for contacting potential customers.

- Given what you have learned in this and previous chapters, prepare a plan to use newsgroups and other alternative methods to begin attracting visitors to your site.

CASE STUDY | Should Google Organize Your Medical Records?

During a typical trip to the doctor, you will see shelves full of folders and papers devoted to the storage of medical records. Every time you visit, your records are created or modified, and often duplicate copies are generated throughout the course of a visit to the doctor or a hospital. The majority of medical records are currently paper-based, making effective communication and access to the records difficult. Canadians and Americans made well over a billion visits to doctors and hospitals over the past year, with each individual making approximately four visits on average. As a result, there are millions of paper medical records lining the corridors of thousands of local medical practices, and for the most part, they cannot be systematically examined, and they are difficult to share. Though the challenge of updating this antiquated system is enormous, companies such as Google appear to be taking up the task.

In March 2008, Google announced an application that it hopes will alleviate the inefficiency of the current medical record storage system: Google Health. Google Health will allow consumers to enter their basic medical data into an online repository and invite doctors to send relevant information to Google electronically. The service is free to users. Features will include a "health profile" for medications, conditions, and allergies; reminder messages for prescription refills or doctor visits; directories for nearby doctors, and personalized health advice.

The application will also be able to accept information from many different record-keeping technologies currently in use by hospitals and other institutions. The intent of the system is to make patients' records easily accessible and more complete and to streamline record keeping.

Google's mission is "to organize the world's information and make it universally accessible and useful." It is hard to disagree with the worthiness of this goal, and as the undisputed leader in Web search, Google has proven that it is very good at what it does. But what if Google were seeking personal information about you? You might not feel as good about Google's quest to organize the world's information when you consider that some of that information is information that you would prefer remain private.

Google's development of its Google Health application illustrates the conflict between its self-avowed mission and the individual's right to privacy. As with similar cases such as government surveillance and data aggregation, the question is whether or not the privacy risks posed by information systems are significant enough to abandon or curtail the collection of useful information. If information gathering should be curtailed—but not eliminated—how will this be decided, and who should decide? Google is no stranger to this conflict of values; this is merely one example of many where Google has clashed with privacy advocates regarding its information collection practices and handling of that information.

With the launch of Google Health, Google aims to be the catalyst for the process of digitizing and standardizing the nation's medical records in an easy-to-use format. Currently only a small fraction, under 15 percent, of American medical practices keep their medical records online, making it difficult for patients and other doctors to quickly and easily access them. When a patient changes doctors, begins seeing a new doctor, or moves, the absence of online medical records can be a source of needless hassle and effort on the part of both patient and practice. Sometimes, access to medical records can even be a life-or-death matter in the rare cases when power failure prevents access to local data storage systems.

But the added convenience of easily accessible medical records is just one potential benefit of going electronic. As the health care industry continues to face budget pressures from both federal and provincial governments, digitizing patient records has become increasingly attractive as a cost-cutting measure. Although many practices consider the costs of implementing new software to be prohibitive, the potential benefits for the industry as a whole are significant. One survey found that 26 percent of health care technology professionals cited lack of financial support as the most important factor preventing them from digitizing their record keeping. But once practices make the initial investment in new technology, the increase in efficiency is likely to reduce future costs by more than enough to make the switch worthwhile.

Google Health and other efforts to convert to electronic health records stand to provide much-needed organization and efficiency to the health care industry, one of the largest segments of Canada's gross domestic product (GDP)—at about 10 percent of GDP. But concerned individuals and privacy advocates argue that electronic health records will be stored in such a way that increases the likelihood of privacy invasions. Some potential users of the system are concerned that Google will make their medical information accessible to advertisers in a manner similar to the targeted advertisements Gmail users currently see based on the content of their e-mail.

These privacy concerns are far from unfounded. Most federal and provincial privacy regulation in Canada refers to data located in Canada. If Google's servers are located outside Canada, then the server location's regulations and laws take precedence, meaning that generally there would be less privacy mandated by regulation than in Canada. This provides very limited protections for personal medical records that might be held by Google outside Canada. (Likely, only information flowing between health care providers, health insurers, and clearinghouses for payment processing would be covered.) There are currently no U.S. federal privacy protections for patients who set up personal health records online. Even hospitals and practices in the United States that currently use electronic storage formats report a high incidence of security breaches, with a quarter of health care technology professionals reporting at least one security breach in the past year. According to a 2006 U.S. Federal Trade Commission study, about 249 000 Americans had their personal information misused for the purpose of obtaining medical treatment, supplies, or services. But breaches and other forms of medical identity theft are not the biggest concern surrounding electronic health records.

Most people are more worried that sensitive information legitimately accessible via electronic health records might lead to their losing supplemental health insurance or job opportunities. For instance, if employers knew that you had a chronic heart condition, would they want to hire you?

Though the health care industry argues that these privacy concerns are for the most part misplaced, there is evidence that these fears are justified. There are "horror stories" of people whose privacy has been breached with serious consequences for the victims of these breaches. People fear that a switch to electronic medical records could be even more vulnerable to security breaches and privacy violations.

Proponents of electronic health records argue that computer technology, once fully implemented, would enhance security rather than threaten it. They also believe that it is more important to first get the system up and running than to worry about privacy matters. Some experts disagree with that stance, saying that unless an electronic system has sufficient privacy controls from the outset, it is less likely to become universally used. Even if the system's security controls are sufficient, it is important that consumers are aware of those controls and confident that they can use the system without fear of their records being accessed by unauthorized parties. Creating an electronic health system without the proper security controls would be not only an unacceptable privacy risk, but also doomed to failure because potential users would be unwilling to cooperate with the information requirements of the system.

Google has tried to reassure the public that its security is iron-tight and that businesses and individuals should have confidence in its ability to store and protect their data. According to Google Senior Security Manager Eran Feigenbaum, "We've taken an in-depth approach to security, with lots of different layers that build on each other." However, Google has not provided much detail about its security practices—where its computer centres are located, how many people it employs in its security department, and how it protects its army of servers against attack—for fear of opening itself up to attacks.

"Businesses are hoping Google will pick the right tools to secure the infrastructure, but they have no assurances and no say in what it will pick," notes Randall Gamby, security analyst for Burton Group, a Midvale, Utah, research and advisory firm. Feigenbaum adds that Google relies on its own security system and applications for its day-to-day business operations, and that should be proof that its security works.

Google is not the only company to set its sights on online medical records. Microsoft and Revolution Health Group LLC, founded by AOL co-founder Steve Case, among others, are also launching similar sites where users can maintain online health profiles. It is too early to tell whether any of these ventures will be successful in the long term, but Revolution Health Group was forced to fire a quarter of its employees in the face of lower-than-expected earnings in 2007. Microsoft's venture, HealthVault, is still in its infancy along with Google Health. Privacy concerns are not likely to halt the shift toward digitizing our records entirely, but will continue to be arguably the most significant obstacle for these ventures as they work toward creating a standardized, digital system for medical record keeping.

CASE STUDY QUESTIONS:

1. What concepts in the chapter are illustrated in this case? Who are the stakeholders in this case?

2. What are the problems with Canada's current medical record-keeping system? How would electronic medical records alleviate these problems?

3. What management, organization, and technology factors are most critical to the creation and development of electronic medical records?

4. What are the pros and cons of electronic patient records? Do you think the concerns over digitizing medical records are valid? Why or why not?

5. Should people trust Google with their electronic medical records? Why or why not?

6. If you were in charge of designing an electronic medical record-keeping system, what are some features you would include? What are features you would avoid?

Sources: Ericka Chickowski, "Are Google's Security Practices Up to Snuff?" Baselinemag.com, May 23, 2008; Chris Gonsalves, "Google, Microsoft Take Health Care IT Pulse," Baselinemag.com, March 31, 2008, and "Securing, Digitizing Medical Records Remain Priorities in Healthcare IT," Baselinemag.com, February 26, 2008; Bob Brewin, "National Health Records Network to Hook Up With Google, Microsoft," govexec.com, March 27, 2008; Kristen Gerencher, "As More of Our Health Records Move Online, Privacy Concerns Grow," FoxBusiness.com, March 26, 2008; "Preying on Patients," *MarketWatch*, June 19, 2008; and "To Trust or Not to Trust Personal Health Records?" *MarketWatch*, March 26, 2008; Christopher Lawton and Ben Worthen, "Google to Offer Health Records on the Web," *The Wall Street Journal,* February 28, 2008; and Lissa Harris, "Google Health Heads to the Hospital," *Technology Review*, May 28, 2008.

Part I CANADIAN CASE STUDY:
Can Canadians Make Money on the Web?

Everyone acknowledges that use of the Internet, the World Wide Web, and Web 2.0 technologies is rapidly increasing. Sales on eBay continue to increase by double digits every year while global online sales are expected to grow to $9 trillion. With 60 percent of Canadian households having high-speed Internet access, Canadian online sales are also growing.

But the question is: Can Canadians make money on the Web? Can a Canadian start a successful business on the Web? We will profile several online entrepreneurs and discuss whether or not they are being successful and why. Perhaps one of the students who is using this textbook is the next Pierre Omidyar, founder of eBay, or Ali de Bold, founder of ChickAdvisor.

Torontonian Stuart Macdonald ran Marketing at Signature Vacations and subsequently started up and made successful Expedia.ca in Canada and was a senior vice president of Expedia.com. He then started TripHarbor.com and TripHarbour.ca, sister Web sites to help vacationers plan cruises and connect in a community of cruise lovers. He is also Chairman of the Canadian Internet Registration Authority and co-founder of Mesh, Canadian's leading Web conference. Like many entrepreneurs, Stuart sees opportunities and takes risks on starting up not just one business, but several different businesses over time. Today Stuart spends his time investing independently and advising other entrepreneurs.

Three residents of Kelowna—Lance Priebe, Lane Merrifield, and David Krysko—saw the need for a social networking community for kids. They started Club Penguin in 2005. In 2007, after only two years in business, they sold the business to Disney for $350 million—not a bad payday for only two years of work. At the time of the sale to Disney, Club Penguin had 12 million users, 700 000 of whom were paid subscribers, and annual revenues of $40 million. Disney continues the Club Penguin operation out of Kelowna with Web sites in several other countries and offices in England, Australia, and Brazil as well. In 2009, Club Penguin opened a Francophone site for French-speaking kids in both Canada and Europe (and presumably elsewhere).

Ten years after receiving a degree from the University of Toronto and an MBA from Stanford University, Montreal native Jeff Skoll met Pierre Omidyar, who hired Skoll as eBay's first full-time employee and president of the Internet company. He is still the company's second-largest shareholder. Skoll is now producing movies, including recent films *North Country* and *Syriana* (which won several Oscars).

Still another successful Canadian Internet entrepreneur is Albert Lai, who founded mydesktop.com and bubbleshare.com. Lai was a teenager when he founded his first venture and sold it for more than $1 million. Lai has a mentor, Marty Keast, who works with him on some of the business angles, but it is Lai who runs the show. He sold his most recent, photo networking site BubbleShare, in January 2007, to Kaboose Inc. for US$2.25 million. "I've done more startups than most people I know in Toronto," he says. "I get a huge amount of satisfaction building great teams to build great products that people love." Lai is now involved in starting another Web-enabled business using technologies he expects will be called Web 3.0. "People joke about an Internet-enabled toaster, or an Internet-enabled chair," Lai says. "But it's evolving to the point where the sorts of things we used to joke about are actually more practical." Startups are something Lai's good at, says industry veteran Paul Kedrosky, venture partner at Vancouver-based Ventures West. "He's a really creative guy, but he knows how to focus and get things done. And he's a good salesman, which is crucial, because you want to have investors feel like they're signing on to an adventure." Lai's new venture is Kontagent, a Facebook-funded viral analytics platform venture. While Kontagent can provide data analysis for Facebook today, the plan is to have Kontagent provide analysis for many social networking sites.

But are all Canadian Web entrepreneurs successful? We have just looked at a few of the success stories, and we will likely never hear about most of the failures. But what about those who are in limbo, who have started their Web-based companies but have not yet become profitable or achieved the kind of success Albert Lai has?

Ali and Alex de Bold, a husband-and-wife entrepreneurial team in Toronto, founded ChickAdvisor.com in 2006. ChickAdvisor.com is targeted at women in their 20s and 30s who would like advice on where to shop and what to buy; by establishing a community of like-minded individuals, ChickAdvisor provides that forum. Modelled after TripAdvisor.com, which has 5 million users, ChickAdvisor.com serves to support the overall shopping experience, just as TripAdvisor.com supports the overall travel experience. ChickAdvisor earns its revenue from advertisers and retailers that pay a fee for banners or category sponsorship; e-mail, video, or event sponsorship; participation in a product review club, or list their businesses through ChickAdvisor.com's sister site ChickAdvisor.biz. Social shopping is one of the latest Web 2.0 phenomena (or perhaps only a fad) to surface, gaining business from users who want support in their shopping.

In 2008, Ali graduated from Ryerson University, where she has also been a guest speaker to business students. Ali has said that she is glad she has been able to turn her passion (shopping) into a business that combines social networking and e-commerce. Ali and Alex fund their business from their own salaries, what they call the "Bank of Ali and Alex," and by asking their programmers to work for free for the potential of a larger paycheque or stock when ChickAdvisor.com becomes profitable. Unfortunately, at least two of those programmers have complained online about not being paid.

Meanwhile, Ali and Alex continue to promote ChickAdvisor.com. Ali is the creator and host of two original video series, *Where'd You Get That?* and *ChickChat TV*, both of which are sponsored by major Canadian media corporations. These videos also help to promote ChickAdvisor.com. As this was being written, ChickAdvisor.com sponsored another of its Shop Crawls, which also promotes the site to both retailers and shoppers.

But what is ahead for ChickAdvisor.com? After three years, Ali and Alex should be close to showing a profit. While it took eBay eight years to make a profit, a much smaller operation like ChickAdvisor.com should be able to show a profit after three years. Ali and Alex are likely finding it hard to get subscribers to ChickAdvisor.com and to efficiently obtain more and more retail sponsorships. Going door to door for sponsorships is not efficient. What will be the future for ChickAdvisor.com?

David Verlee and two friends thought they understood what all men need. Clean socks! They developed Monthly Socks.com, a site where subscribers can have socks shipped to them on a regular basis, just like a magazine subscription. The socks are available in three sizes, three colours, and only one style.

Verlee, who is also a runner, decided to create a sock that felt like a sports sock—with a double layer at the bottom—but that looks like a dress sock. "Men always say they don't care what they wear. But the truth is, they want to wear something comfortable. And men's dress socks are quite cold. They are usually pretty thin. My feet were always uncomfortable and cold especially in the winter. But you can't wear a sports sock to a meeting," says Verlee.

Since launching in November 2006, with no advertising, he says the service has already broken even. "At first it was just our friends signing up. But then all these subscriptions started pouring in, and we had no idea who these people were or how they found out about it. But obviously it was something people wanted." Verlee says that 80 percent of the people who have signed up for monthly socks have been women, buying the subscriptions as gifts for the men in their lives. "One woman bought a subscription for her brother and the gift note read, 'I've been sick of looking at your socks for the last 10 years,'" says Verlee.

While MonthlySocks.com may be paying the bills, we do not know how successful it is. It is obvious looking at MonthlySocks.com's Web site that the partners do not spend much money on site development, focusing instead on minimizing costs.

During the dot-com bubble of the late 1990s, it was frequently said that "If you build it [a Web site], they [the

visitors] will come." Today we know that is not true. No matter what else is true of a Web site, without a good business model and appropriate content, a Web site will not be successful. We have only to look at Webvan.com (which spent $1 billion in its 18 months of operation) or Pets.com (in operation less than two years) to see that erroneous business models spell disaster for Web entrepreneurs. Shoppers did not want to wait at home for groceries to be delivered and preferred to actually see and even touch the food products they were paying; animal owners needed pet food immediately and did not want to wait for it to be shipped, and while prices at Pets.com were low, the shipping charges made the total bill larger than buying at the local store.

When it comes to social networking Web businesses, "Without users, you have no content. Without content, you have no users." Which comes first, the users or the content? A good business model would detail how to obtain both users and content, how to earn revenue, characteristics and issues of potential users, and how to build the site. Whatever size your business, whether a large corporation or a fledgling Web business, you need an appropriate, well-thought-out business model for your Web site.

CASE STUDY QUESTIONS

1. Do you think the Canadian market for Web-based entrepreneurial businesses is different from the market in other areas of the world? Explain your answer.

2. What do you think made our list of successful Canadian Web entrepreneurs successful? Do they share any personal characteristics, education, or vision?

3. Do you think Web entrepreneurs are the same as other types of entrepreneurs? Explain your answer.

4. What is holding ChickAdvisor.com back from achieving major success? Visit the ChickAdvisor.com Web site, and explain what, if anything, in your view should be done differently on the Web site. Do the same with MonthlySocks.com. What does this tell you?

Sources: Rebecca Eckler, "The Joy of Socks," Maclean's, March 5, 2007, **www.macleans.ca/homepage/magazine/article.jsp?content=2007 0305_103060_103060** (accessed August 3, 2009); Andrea Jezovit, "Welcome to Web 3.0," *Canadian Business Online*, June 18, 2007, - **www.canadianbusiness.com/technology/trends/article. jsp?content=20070618_85496_85496** (accessed August 3, 2009); "Jeffrey Skoll," *Forbes*, **www.forbes.com/lists/2006/10/PB9U.html** (accessed August 3, 2009); "Stuart MacDonald," **www.stuartm acdonald.ca** (accessed August 3, 2009).

Part II

Information Technology Infrastructure

PART II

CANADIAN CASE STUDY

Wi-Fi in Canada: The Good, the Bad, and the Ugly

CHAPTER 5

IT Infrastructure and Emerging Technologies

LEARNING OBJECTIVES

After reading this chapter, you will be able to answer the following questions:

1. What is IT infrastructure, and what are its components?

2. What are the stages and technology drivers of IT infrastructure evolution?

3. What are the current trends in computer hardware platforms?

4. What are the current trends in software platforms?

5. What are the challenges of managing IT infrastructure, and what are management solutions?

OPENING CASE

Bell Canada Uses Virtual Desktop IT Infrastructure to Connect 1700 Desktops

By 2004, Bell Canada employed 8000 call centre agents, one of the largest such staffs in Canada. These agents served more than 27 million customer connections throughout Canada. As the largest subsidiary of Bell Canada Enterprises (BCE), the company was facing outdated hardware and rising costs in its call centres.

By 2004, Bell Canada offered a number of services, including local, mobile, and long-distance telephone service; Internet access; and satellite television, all to both business and residential customers. It continues to offer these services. Today the company employs 44 000 people. With its current desktop systems, Bell faced hardware that was quickly becoming outdated and would need replacing along with rising costs of maintaining its current infrastructure environment.

For its call centre agents, Bell Canada needed a "lockdown" environment that

could accommodate "fat clients" (a fat client is a client computer with most of its resources, e.g., processing power, software, and data on the fat client instead of the server). What this means is that the company needed to be able to extend its own local area network (LAN) to the client's building and enable a few people to work in a locked room to meet the security needs of the client. (A LAN is a network that is housed in one building or on one floor of a building; it has a limited geographic scope.) Because Bell Canada used multiple protocols for security, it was a complex environment to try to function in. Explained Martin Quigley, a senior technical consultant to Bell Canada, who worked at CGI Group, Inc., "You couldn't install programs, you couldn't install anything on the hard drive because they used file sharing. So they had to keep it in a locked room. It was difficult to manage, and it was expensive."

CGI had been providing consulting services for Bell Canada since 1993 when Bell Canada decided to outsource its IT operations, and CGI was contracted to provide IT solutions for the company. Quigley explained the current situation: "Bell Canada came to us with a project to provision, connect, and securely deploy 400 desktop environments within three weeks." Bell Canada and CGI evaluated several possible solutions before deciding to use virtual servers. They determined that using many different physical servers is difficult to manage centrally while virtual servers by definition enable multiple servers to run on one computer because updates and security must be managed on only one computer instead of several different computers. Using virtual servers is also less expensive than using the many computers required by physical servers. Users connect to a virtual server just as they do to any server, using the local area network.

Using this virtualization technology, Bell Canada lowered its total cost of ownership by using a single server to replace several desktops and by employing a single network connection instead of multiple, more expensive network connections. By using the servers "off-site," Bell Canada also reduced the number of site visits by staff to deal with computer problems or upgrades. By using virtual servers, Bell Canada also eliminated the need to ship hardware and applications to remote teleworkers and to have couriers ship and return older hardware from remote locations.

By using virtual servers, Bell Canada has been able to hire more people to work from remote locations who can telecommute on a daily basis. "We don't have to worry about security or the difficulty of setting up their environments," said Quigley. Neither developers nor users can tell the difference between the use of virtual servers and physical

servers since, to them, they are simply connecting to "a server"; regardless of the type of server, it looks the same to everyone except the server administrator. Management of the computing environment has been greatly simplified, and it is both easy and fast to deploy additional desktops.

Since the virtual servers are attached to storage area networks (SANs) which house data physically at various locations but with networked access to the data (see Chapter 6) established by Bell Canada, backup and disaster recovery are easier and faster. Their additional backup servers can take over the load within 25 minutes of a server crashing.

When Bell Canada began this project more than 15 years ago, the company wanted to place 400 desktops in a virtual server environment. By partnering with CGI Group and its partner, VMware, Bell Canada now uses its virtual server environment for 1700 desktops, which has led to further cost savings. VMware is a company that specializes in software

to consolidate physical servers into a virtual server.

It is interesting to note that a year after CGI helped Bell Canada to implement its virtual server environment in 2004, BCE decided to sell its stake in CGI, which it had acquired in 1995; the sale amounted to close to US $1 billion. BCE had purchased its 100 million shares in CGI in 1995, after Bell Canada's first consulting contract with CGI, and was considered a "friendly" buy-back. This could be said to represent an interesting use of "insider" consulting.

Sources: John D. Blau, "BCE to Sell Stake in Canadian IT Service Provider CGI," *Infoworld*, December 19, 2005, **www.infoworld.com/article/05/12/19/HNbcestake_1.html?IP%20TELEPHONY** (accessed February 13, 2009); VMware, "VMware Virtual Desktop Infrastructure Connects Bell Canada for Optimized Customer Care," 2006, **www.vmware.com/files/pdf/customers/06Q3_cs_vmw_Bell_Canada_English.pdf** (accessed February 13, 2009; CGI, "CGI Provides HR Self-Service Solution to Bell Canada's Employees, **www.cgi.com/web/en/library/case_studies/71182.htm** (accessed February 13, 2009). Source for diagram: Kusnetzky Group LLC.

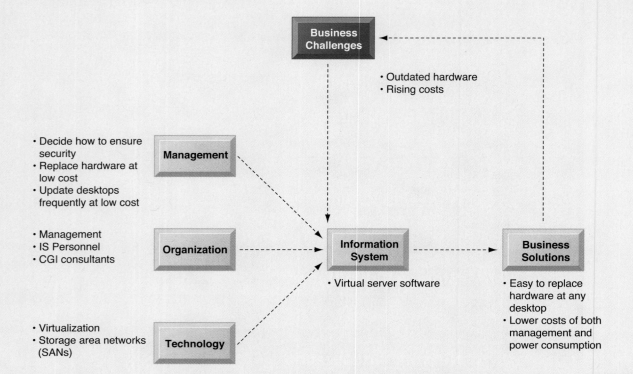

Bell Canada has an enviable track record as a successful telecommunication business. Unfortunately, its growth plans and daily operations were hampered by unmanageable and outdated server technology. Bell Canada's management felt the best solution was to replace its antiquated server infrastructure with new computer hardware and software technologies and to standardize using the technology of a single vendor—VMware. This case highlights the critical role that hardware and software investments can play in improving business performance.

The chapter-opening diagram calls attention to important points raised by this case and this chapter. Management decided that the best way to make technology promote business objectives was to overhaul and standardize IT infrastructure. Bell Canada now uses a more efficient and easily managed server environment that makes it much easier to deploy additional desktops while maintaining security and control. The entire infrastructure is easier to manage and capable of scaling up to accommodate additional desktops, growing transaction loads, and new business opportunities.

5.1 IT Infrastructure

In Chapter 1, we defined *information technology (IT)* infrastructure as the shared technology resources that provide the platform for the firm's specific information system applications. IT infrastructure includes investment in hardware, software, and services—such as consulting, education, and training—that are shared across the entire firm or across entire business units in the firm. A firm's IT infrastructure provides the foundation for serving customers, working with vendors, and managing internal firm business processes (see Figure 5-1).

In 2008, supplying firms around the world with IT infrastructure was a $2.09 trillion industry when telecommunications, networking equipment, and telecommunications services (Internet, telephone, and data transmission) are included. In 2009, with the global economic crisis, global IT spending is expected to decline by about 6 percent to $1.97 trillion. This is the first decline in global IT spending since 2002, immediately after the "dot-com bubble" burst. However, future predictions are that global IT spending, by 2010, will increase by between 6 percent and 15 percent (Woodie, 2009; Ortutay, 2009; Ogg, 2008). Investments in infrastructure account for between 25 and 35 percent of information technology expenditures in large firms (Weill et al., 2002).

FIGURE 5-1   Connection between the firm, IT infrastructure, and business capabilities.

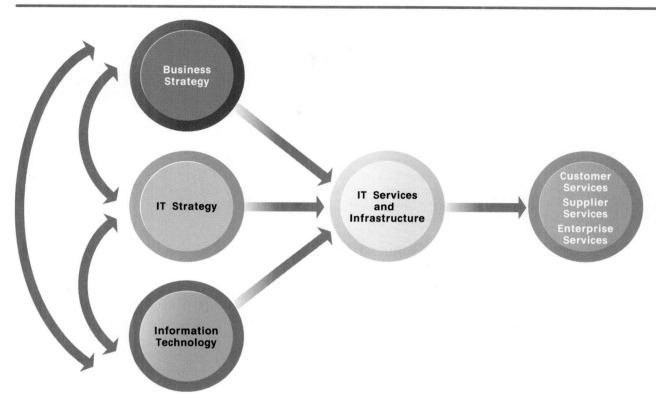

The services a firm is capable of providing to its customers, suppliers, and employees are a direct function of its IT infrastructure. Ideally, this infrastructure should support the firm's business and information systems strategy. New information technologies have a powerful impact on business and IT strategies, as well as the services that can be provided to customers.

Defining IT Infrastructure

IT infrastructure consists of a set of physical devices and software applications that are required to operate the entire enterprise. But IT infrastructure is also a set of firm-wide services budgeted by management and comprising both human and technical capabilities. These services include the following:

- Computing platforms used to provide computing services that connect employees, customers, and suppliers into a coherent digital environment, including large mainframes, desktop and laptop computers, personal digital assistants (PDAs), and Internet "appliances."

- Telecommunications services that provide data, voice, and video connectivity to employees, customers, and suppliers.

- Data management services that store and manage corporate data and provide capabilities for analyzing the data.

- Application software services that provide enterprise-wide capabilities such as enterprise resource planning, customer relationship management, supply chain management, and knowledge management systems that are shared by all business units.

- Physical facilities management services that develop and manage the physical installations required for computing, telecommunications, and data management services.

- IT management services that plan and develop the infrastructure, coordinate IT services with the business units, manage accounting for IT expenditures, and provide project management services.

- IT standards services that provide the firm and its business units with policies that determine which information technology will be used, and where, when, how, and by whom they will be used.

- IT education services that provide training in system use to employees and offer managers training in how to plan for and manage IT investments.
- IT research and development services that provide the firm with research on potential IT projects and investments that could help the firm differentiate itself in the marketplace.

This "service platform" perspective makes it easier to understand the business value provided by infrastructure investments. For instance, the real business value of a fully loaded personal computer operating at 3 gigahertz that costs about $1000 or a high-speed Internet connection is hard to understand without knowing who will use it and how it will be used. When we look at the services provided by these tools, however, their value becomes more apparent: The new PC makes it possible for a high-cost employee making $100 000 a year to connect to all the company's major systems and the Internet. The high-speed Internet service saves this employee about one hour per day in reduced wait time for Internet information. Without this PC and Internet connection, the value of this one employee to the firm might be cut in half.

Evolution of IT Infrastructure

The IT infrastructure in organizations today is an outgrowth of over 50 years of evolution in computing platforms. There have been five stages in this evolution, each representing a different configuration of computing power and infrastructure elements (see Figure 5-2). The five eras are general-purpose mainframe and minicomputer computing, personal computers, client/server networks, enterprise/Internet computing, and cloud computing.

Technologies that characterize one era may also be used in another time period for other purposes. For example, some companies, such as the Bank of Montreal, which employs an IBM z Series mainframe, still run traditional mainframe or minicomputer systems. Mainframe computers today are used as massive servers supporting large Web sites and corporate enterprise applications.

General-Purpose Mainframe and Minicomputer Era (1959 to Present) The introduction of the IBM 1401 and 7090 transistorized machines in 1959 marked the beginning of widespread commercial use of **mainframe** computers.

In 1965 the mainframe computer truly came into its own with the introduction of the IBM 360 series. The 360 was the first commercial computer with a powerful operating system that could provide time sharing, multitasking, and virtual memory in more advanced models. IBM dominated mainframe computing from this point on.

Mainframe computers eventually became powerful enough to support thousands of online remote terminals connected to the centralized mainframe using proprietary communication protocols and proprietary data lines. The first airline reservation systems appeared in 1959 and became the prototypical online, real-time interactive computing system that could scale up to service the whole world.

The mainframe era was a period of highly centralized computing under the control of professional programmers and systems operators (usually in a corporate data centre), with most elements of infrastructure provided by a single vendor, the manufacturer of the hardware and the software. This pattern began to change with the introduction of **minicomputers** produced by Digital Equipment Corporation (DEC) in 1965. DEC minicomputers offered powerful machines at far lower prices than IBM mainframes, making possible decentralized computing, customized to the specific needs of individual departments or business units rather than necessitating time sharing on a single huge mainframe across the organization.

Personal Computer Era (1981 to Present) Although the first truly personal computers (PCs) appeared in the 1970s (the Xerox Alto, MITS' Altair, and the Apple I and II, to name a few), these machines had only limited distribution to computer enthusiasts. The appearance of the IBM PC in 1981 is usually considered the beginning of the PC era because this machine was the first to be widely adopted by U.S. businesses. At first using the DOS operating system, a text-based command language, and later the Microsoft Windows

Mainframe
Minicomputers

FIGURE 5-2 Eras in IT infrastructure evolution.

Stages in IT Infrastructure Evolution

Illustrated here are the typical computing configurations characterizing each of the five eras of IT infrastructure evolution.

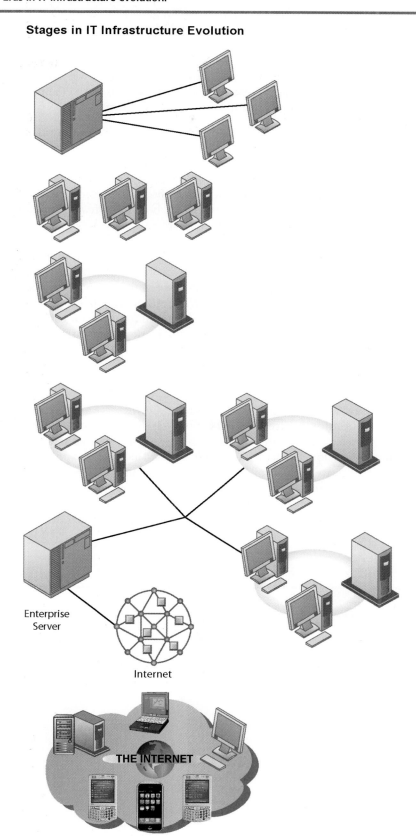

Mainframe/
Minicomputer
(1959–present)

Personal
Computer
(1981–present)

Client Server
(1983–present)

Enterprise/
Internet
(1992–present)

Enterprise
Server

Internet

Cloud
Computing
(2000–present)

THE INTERNET

operating system, the **Wintel PC** computer (Windows operating system software on a computer with an Intel microprocessor) became the standard desktop personal computer. Today, 95 percent of the world's estimated 1 billion computers use the Wintel standard.

Proliferation of PCs in the 1980s and early 1990s launched a spate of personal desktop productivity software tools—word processors, spreadsheets, electronic presentation software, and small data management programs—that were very valuable to both home and corporate users. These PCs were stand-alone systems until PC operating system software in the 1990s made it possible to link them into networks.

Client/Server Era (1983 to Present) In **client/server computing,** desktop or laptop computers called **clients** are networked to powerful **server** computers that provide the client computers with a variety of services and capabilities. Computer processing work is split between these two types of machines. The client is the user point of entry, whereas the server typically processes and stores shared data, serves up Web pages, or manages network activities. The term *server* refers to both the software application and the physical computer on which the network software runs. The server could be a mainframe, but today server computers typically are more powerful versions of personal computers, based on inexpensive Intel chips and often using multiple processors in a single computer box. The simplest client/server network consists of a client computer networked to a server computer, with processing split between the two types of machines. This is called a *two-tiered client/server architecture.* While simple client/server networks can be found in small businesses, most corporations have more complex, **multitiered** (often called **N-tier**) **client/server architectures** in which the work of the entire network is balanced over several different levels of servers, depending on the kind of service being requested (see Figure 5-3). For example, CMS, an enterprise-wide software company headquartered in Toronto, uses a multitiered client/server architecture to manage access by headquarters and global staff as well as customers and developers.

For instance, at the first level, a **Web server** will serve a Web page to a client in response to a request for service. Web server software is responsible for locating and managing stored Web pages. If the client requests access to a corporate system (a product list or price information, for instance), the request is passed along to an **application server.** Application server software handles all application operations between a user and an organization's back-end business systems. The application server may reside on the same computer as the Web server or on its own dedicated computer. Chapters 6 and 7 provide more detail on other pieces of software that are used in multitiered client/server architectures for e-commerce and e-business.

Wintel PC
Client/server computing
Clients
Server
Multitiered
N-tier
Client/server architectures
Web server
Application server

FIGURE 5-3 A multitiered client/server network (N-tier).

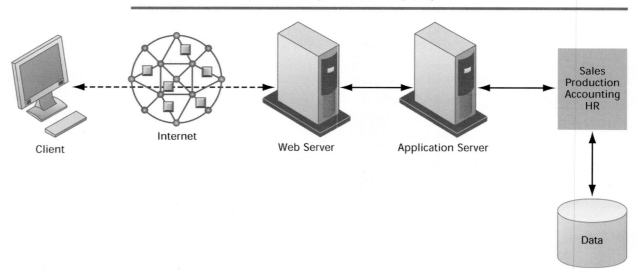

Client — Internet — Web Server — Application Server — Sales Production Accounting HR — Data

In a multitiered client/server network, client requests for service are handled by different levels of servers.

Client/server computing enables businesses to distribute computing work across a series of smaller, less expensive machines that cost much less than minicomputers or centralized mainframe systems. The result is an explosion in computing power and applications throughout the firm.

Novell Netware was the leading technology for client/server networking at the beginning of the client/server era. Today Microsoft is the market leader with its **Windows** operating systems (Windows Server, Windows Vista, Windows XP).

Enterprise/Internet Computing Era (1992 to Present) In the early 1990s, firms turned to networking standards and software tools that could integrate disparate networks and applications throughout the firm into an enterprise-wide infrastructure. As the Internet developed into a trusted communications environment after 1995, more and more business firms began using the *Transmission Control Protocol/Internet Protocol (TCP/IP)* networking standard to tie their disparate networks together. We discuss TCP/IP in detail in Chapter 7.

The resulting IT infrastructure links different pieces of computer hardware and smaller networks into an enterprise-wide network so that information can flow freely across the organization and between the firm and other organizations. It can link different types of computer hardware, including mainframes, servers, PCs, mobile phones, and other handheld devices, and it includes public infrastructures such as the telephone system, the Internet, and public network services. Enterprise infrastructure also requires software to link disparate applications and enable data to flow freely among different parts of the business, such as enterprise applications (see Chapters 2 and 12) and Web services (discussed in Section 5.4).

Cloud Computing Era (2000 to Present) The growing bandwidth power of the Internet has pushed the client/server model one step further, toward what is called the "Cloud Computing Model." **Cloud computing** refers to a model of computing in which firms and individuals obtain computing power and software applications over the Internet, rather than purchasing their own hardware and software. Currently, cloud computing is the fastest growing form of computing, with an estimated market size in 2009 of $9.7 billion, and a projected size of $195 billion in 2012 (Gartner, 2008; Merrill Lynch, 2008).

Hardware firms IBM, HP, and Dell are building huge, scalable cloud computing centres that provide computing power, data storage, and high-speed Internet connections to firms that rely on the Internet for business software applications. Software firms such as Google, Microsoft, SAP, Oracle, and Salesforce.com sell software applications as services delivered over the Internet. For instance, more than 500 000 firms in 2009 will use Google Apps, a suite of Internet-based desktop software applications such as word processing, spreadsheets, and calendars (Hamm, 2008; King, 2008). In 2009, more than 43 000 firms worldwide will be using Salesforce.com's customer relationship management software, some on their iPhones (see this chapter's Window on Organizations).

Table 5-1 compares each era on the infrastructure dimensions introduced.

Technology Drivers of Infrastructure Evolution

The changes in IT infrastructure we have just described have resulted from developments in computer processing, memory chips, storage devices, telecommunications and networking hardware and software, and software design that have exponentially increased computing power while exponentially reducing costs. Let us look at the most important developments.

Moore's Law and Microprocessing Power In 1965, Gordon Moore, the co-founder of Intel Corporation, the leading computer chip manufacturer, wrote in *Electronics Magazine* that since the first microprocessor chip was introduced in 1959, the number of components on a chip with the smallest manufacturing costs per component (generally transistors) had doubled each year. This assertion became the foundation of **Moore's Law.** Moore later reduced the rate of growth to a doubling every two years.

Windows
Cloud computing
Moore's Law

TABLE 5-1   Stages in IT infrastructure evolution.

INFRASTRUCTURE DIMENSION	MAINFRAME ERA (1959 TO PRESENT)	PC ERA (1981 TO PRESENT)	CLIENT/SERVER ERA (1983 TO PRESENT)	ENTERPRISE/INTERNET ERA (1992 TO PRESENT)	CLOUD COMPUTING ERA (2000 TO PRESENT)
SIGNATURE FIRM(S)	IBM	Microsoft/Intel Dell HP IBM	Novell Microsoft	SAP Oracle PeopleSoft	Google Salesforce.com IBM
HARDWARE PLATFORM	Centralized mainframe	Wintel computers	Wintel computers	Multiple: • Mainframe • Server • Client	Remote servers Clients (PCs, netbooks, cell phones, smartphones)
OPERATING SYSTEM	IBM 360 IBM 370 Unix	DOS/Windows Linux IBM 390	Windows 3.1 Windows Server Linux	Multiple: • Unix/Linux • OS 390 • Windows Server	Linux Windows Mac OS X
APPLICATION AND ENTERPRISE SOFTWARE	Few enterprise-wide applications; departmental applications created by in-house programmers	No enterprise connectivity; boxed software	Few enterprise-wide applications; boxed software applications for workgroups and departments	Enterprise-wide applications linked to desktop and departmental applications: • mySAP • Oracle E-Business Suite • PeopleSoft Enterprise One	Google Apps Salesforce.com
NETWORKING/ TELECOMMUNICATIONS	Vendor provided: • Systems Network Windows Architecture (IBM) • DECNET (Digital) • AT&T voice	None or limited	Novell NetWare Windows 2003 Linux AT&T voice	LAN Enterprise-wide area network (WAN) TCP/IP Internet standards–enabled	Internet Wi-Fi Wireless broadband cellular networks
System Integration	Vendor-provided	None	Accounting and consulting firms Service firms	Software manufacturer Accounting and consulting firms System integration firms Service firms	SaaS (Software as a Service) firms
Data Storage and Database Management	Magnetic storage Flat files Relational databases	Dbase II and III Access	Multiple database servers with optical and magnetic storage	Enterprise database servers	Remote enterprise database servers
Internet Platforms	Poor to none (1959–1995)	None at first Later browser - enabled clients	None at first Later • Apache server • Microsoft IIS	None in the early years Later: • Intranet-and Internet-delivered enterprise services • Large server farms	Larger server farms

FIGURE 5-4   Moore's Law and microprocessor performance.

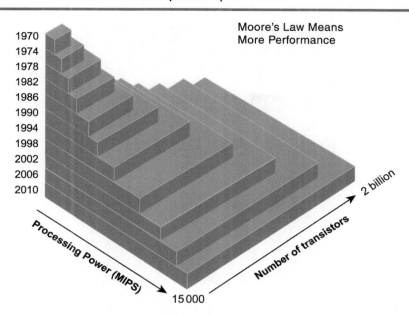

Packing more transistors into a tiny microprocessor has exponentially increased processing power.

Source: Intel, 2004, updated by the authors.

This law would later be interpreted in multiple ways. There are at least three variations of Moore's Law, none of which Moore ever stated: (1) the power of microprocessors doubles every 18 months; (2) computing power doubles every 18 months; and (3) the price of computing falls by half every 18 months.

Figure 5-4 illustrates the relationship between the number of transistors on a microprocessor and millions of instructions per second (MIPS), a common measure of processor power. Figure 5-5 shows the exponential decline in the cost of transistors and rise in computing power.

FIGURE 5-5   Falling cost of chips.

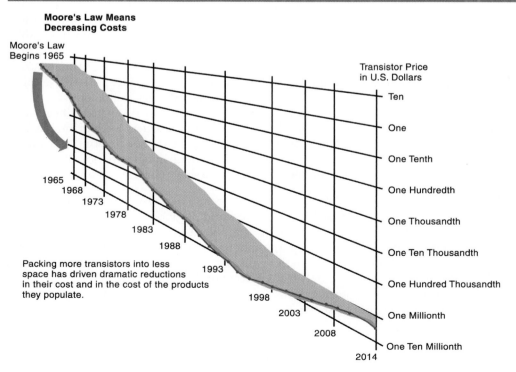

An Intel® processor today can contain as many as 1.72 billion transistors, deliver more than 10 000 MIPS, at a cost of less than 1/10 000th of a cent. That is a little less than the cost of one printed character in this book.

Source: © Intel 2004, updated by the authors.

FIGURE 5-6   Examples of nanotubes.

Nanotubes are tiny tubes about 10 000 times thinner than a human hair. They consist of rolled up sheets of carbon hexagons. Discovered in 1991 by researchers at NEC, they have the potential uses as minuscule wires or in ultrasmall electronic devices and are very powerful conductors of electrical current.

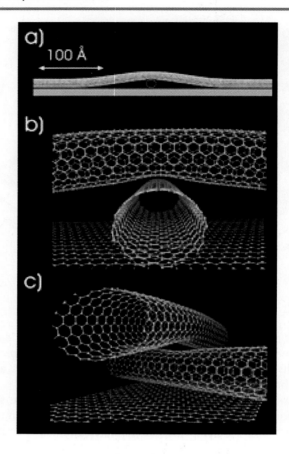

Exponential growth in the number of transistors and the power of processors coupled with an exponential decline in computing costs is likely to continue. Chip manufacturers continue to miniaturize components. Today's transistors should no longer be compared to the size of a human hair but rather to the size a virus, the smallest form of organic life.

By using nanotechnology, chip manufacturers can even shrink the size of transistors down to the width of several atoms. **Nanotechnology** uses individual atoms and molecules to create computer chips and other devices that are thousands of times smaller than current technologies permit. Chip manufacturers are trying to develop a manufacturing process that could produce nanotube processors economically (Figure 5-6). IBM has just started making microprocessors in a production setting using this technology.

As processor speeds increase, heat is generated that cannot be dissipated with air fans. Consumers are pressing for lower power consumption, longer battery life, and lower weight to increase laptop and handheld computer portability. For this reason, Intel and other firms are designing the next generation of chips to be less power-hungry and lower in weight. Other options include putting multiple processors on a single chip (see Section 5-3).

The Law of Mass Digital Storage A second technology driver of IT infrastructure change is the Law of Mass Digital Storage. The world produces as much as 5 exabytes of unique information per year (an exabyte is a billion gigabytes, or 1018 bytes). The amount of digital information is roughly doubling every year (Lyman and Varian, 2003). Almost all of this information growth involves magnetic storage of digital data, and printed documents account for only 0.003 percent of the annual growth.

Fortunately, the cost of storing digital information is falling at an exponential rate of 100 percent a year. Figure 5-7 shows that PC hard drive capacity has experienced a compound annual growth rate of 25 percent in the early years to more than 60 percent a year since 1990. Today's PC hard drives have storage densities approaching 1 gigabyte per square inch and total capacities of over 600 gigabytes.

Nanotechnology

FIGURE 5-7   The capacity of hard disk drives grows exponentially, 1980–2008.

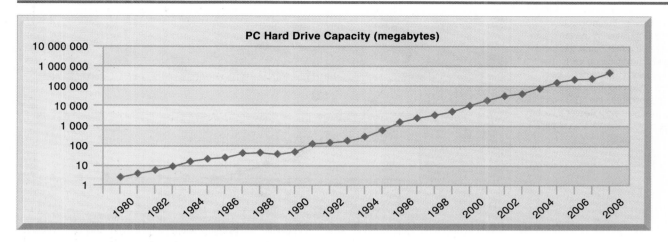

From 1980 to 1990, hard disk drive capacities for PCs experienced a rate of 25 percent annual compound growth, but after 1990, growth accelerated to more than 65 percent each year.

Source: Kurzweil (2003), updated by authors.

Figure 5-8 shows that the number of kilobytes that can be stored on magnetic disks for one dollar from 1950 to the present roughly doubled every 15 months.

Metcalfe's Law and Network Economics Moore's Law and the law of mass storage help us understand why computing resources are now so readily available. But why do people want more computing and storage power? The economics of networks and the growth of the Internet provide some answers.

Robert Metcalfe—inventor of Ethernet local area network technology—claimed in 1970 that the value or power of a network grows exponentially as a function of the

FIGURE 5-8   The cost of storing data declines exponentially, 1950–2010.

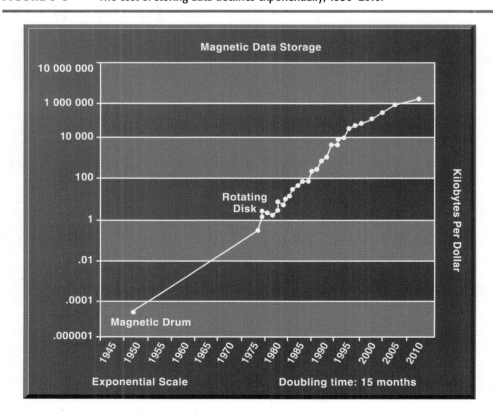

Since the first magnetic storage device was used in 1955, the cost of storing a kilobyte of data has fallen exponentially, doubling the amount of digital storage for each dollar expended every 15 months on average.

Source: Kurzweil (2003) and authors.

FIGURE 5-9   Exponential declines in Internet communication costs.

One reason for the growth in the Internet population is the rapid decline in Internet connection and overall communication costs. The cost per kilobit of Internet access has fallen exponentially since 1995. Digital Subscriber Line (DSL) and cable modems now deliver a kilobit of communication for a retail price of around 2 cents.

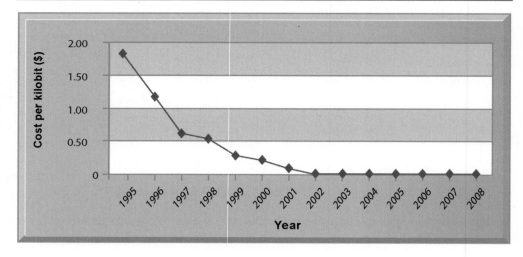

number of network members. Metcalfe and others point to the *increasing returns to scale* that network members receive as more and more people join the network. As the number of members in a network grows linearly, the value of the entire system grows exponentially and continues to grow forever as members increase. Demand for information technology has been driven by the social and business value of digital networks, which rapidly multiply the number of actual and potential links among network members.

Declining Communications Costs and the Internet A fourth technology driver transforming IT infrastructure is the rapid decline in the costs of communication and the exponential growth in the size of the Internet. An estimated 1.5 billion people worldwide now have Internet access. Figure 5-9 illustrates the exponentially declining cost of communication both over the Internet and over telephone networks (which increasingly are based on the Internet). As communication costs fall toward a very small number and approach 0, utilization of communication and computing facilities explodes.

To take advantage of the business value associated with the Internet, firms must greatly expand their Internet connections, including wireless connectivity, and greatly expand the power of their client/server networks, desktop clients, and mobile computing devices. There is every reason to believe these trends will continue.

Standards and Network Effects Today's enterprise infrastructure and Internet computing would be impossible—both now and in the future—without agreements among manufacturers and widespread consumer acceptance of **technology standards.** Technology standards are specifications that establish the compatibility of products and the ability to communicate in a network (Stango, 2004).

Technology standards unleash powerful economies of scale and result in price declines as manufacturers focus on the products built to a single standard. Without these economies of scale, computing of any sort would be far more expensive than is currently the case. Table 5-2 describes important standards that have shaped IT infrastructure.

Beginning in the 1990s, corporations started moving toward standard computing and communications platforms. The Wintel PC with the Windows operating system and Microsoft Office desktop productivity applications became the standard desktop and mobile client computing platform. Widespread adoption of Unix as the enterprise server operating system of choice made possible the replacement of proprietary and expensive mainframe infrastructure. In telecommunications, the Ethernet standard enabled PCs to connect together in small local area networks (LANs; see Chapter 7), and the TCP/IP standard enabled these LANs to be connected into firm-wide networks, and ultimately, to the Internet.

Technology standards

TABLE 5-2 Some important standards in computing.

STANDARD	SIGNIFICANCE
American Standard Code for Information Interchange (ASCII) (1958)	A code that made it possible for computers from different manufacturers to exchange data; later used as the universal language linking input and output devices such as keyboards and mice to computers. Adopted by the American National Standards Institute in 1963.
Common Business-Oriented Language (COBOL) (1959)	An easy-to-use software language that greatly expanded the ability of programmers to write business-related programs and reduced the cost of software. Sponsored by the U.S. Defense Department in 1959.
Unix (1969–1975)	A powerful multitasking, multiuser, portable operating system initially developed at Bell Labs (1969) and later released for use by others (1975). It operates on a wide variety of computers from different manufacturers. Adopted by Sun, IBM, HP, and others in the 1980s, it became the most widely used enterprise-level operating system.
Transmission Control Protocol/Internet Protocol (TCP/IP) (1974)	A suite of communications protocols and a common addressing scheme that enables millions of computers to connect in one giant global network (the Internet). In the last decade, it has become the default networking protocol suite for local area networks and intranets. Developed in the early 1970s for the U.S. Department of Defense by computer scientist Vinton Cerf.
Ethernet (1973)	A network standard for connecting desktop computers into local area networks that enabled the widespread adoption of client/server computing and local area networks and further stimulated the adoption of personal computers.
IBM/Microsoft/Intel Personal Computer (1981)	The standard Wintel design for personal desktop computing based on standard Intel processors and other standard devices, Microsoft DOS, and later Windows software. The emergence of this standard, low-cost product laid the foundation for a 25-year period of explosive growth in computing throughout all organizations around the globe. Today, more than 1 billion PCs power business and government activities every day.
World Wide Web (1989–1993)	Standards for storing, retrieving, formatting, and displaying information as a worldwide web of electronic pages incorporating text, graphics, audio, and video that enabled the creation of a global repository of billions of Web pages by 2004.

5.2 Infrastructure Components

IT infrastructure today is composed of seven major components. Figure 5-10 illustrates these infrastructure components and the major vendors within each component category. These components constitute investments that must be coordinated with one another to provide the firm with a coherent infrastructure.

In the past, technology vendors supplying these components were often in competition with one another, offering purchasing firms a mixture of incompatible, proprietary, partial solutions. But increasingly the vendor firms have been forced by large customers to cooperate in strategic partnerships with one another. For instance, a hardware and services provider such as IBM cooperates with all the major enterprise software providers, has strategic relationships with system integrators (often accounting firms), and promises to work with whichever database products its client firms wish to use (even though it sells its own database management software called DB2). Let us examine the size and dynamics of each of these infrastructure components and their markets, as depicted in Figure 5-10.

Computer Hardware Platforms

In 2008, 285 million PCs were shipped worldwide, with a market value of $308 billion. This component includes client machines (desktop PCs, mobile computing devices such as iPhones and BlackBerrys, and laptops) and server machines. The client machines use primarily Intel or AMD microprocessors (Gartner, 2008; Metrics 2.0, 2008).

FIGURE 5-10   The IT infrastructure ecosystem.

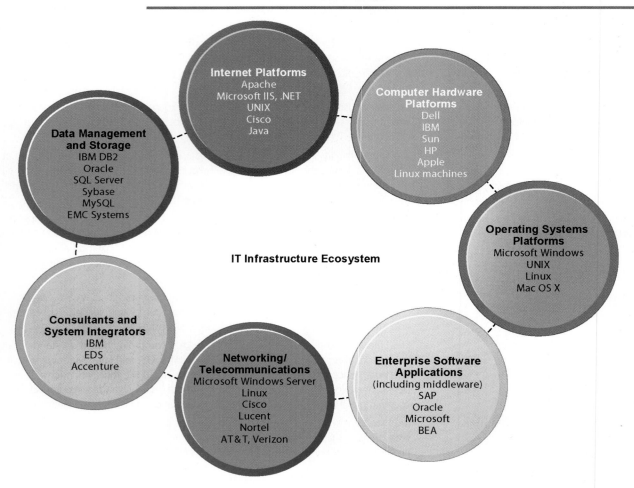

IT Infrastructure Ecosystem

There are seven major components that must be coordinated to provide the firm with a coherent IT infrastructure. Listed here are major technologies and suppliers for each component.

The server market is more complex, using mostly Intel or AMD processors in the form of blade servers in racks, but also includes Sun SPARC microprocessors and IBM PowerPC chips specially designed for server use. **Blade servers** are ultra-thin computers consisting of a circuit board with processors, memory, and network connections that are stored in racks. They take up less space than traditional box-based servers. Secondary storage may be provided by a hard drive in each blade server or by external very large mass-storage drives.

The supply of computer hardware has increasingly become concentrated in top firms such as IBM, HP, Dell, and Sun Microsystems, and three chip producers, Intel, AMD, and IBM. The industry has collectively settled on Intel as the standard processor, with major exceptions in the server market for Unix and Linux machines, which might use Sun or IBM Unix processors.

Mainframes have not disappeared. The mainframe market has actually grown steadily over the last decade although the number of providers has dwindled to one: IBM. IBM has also repurposed

Blade servers

A blade server is a thin, modular processing device that is intended for a single dedicated application (such as serving Web pages). It can be easily inserted into a space-saving rack with many similar servers as shown here.

its mainframe systems so they can be used as giant servers for massive enterprise networks and corporate Web sites. A single IBM mainframe can run up to 17 000 instances of Linux or Windows server software and is capable of replacing thousands of smaller blade servers (see the discussion of virtualization in Section 5.3).

Operating System Platforms

At the client level, 95 percent of PCs and 45 percent of handheld devices use some form of Microsoft Windows **operating system** (such as Windows Vista, Windows XP, or Windows Mobile) to manage the resources and activities of the computer. Windows comprises 70 percent of the server operating market, with 30 percent of corporate servers using some form of the **Unix** operating system or **Linux,** an inexpensive and robust open source relative of Unix. Microsoft Windows Server 2008 is capable of providing enterprise-wide operating system and network services and appeals to organizations seeking Windows-based IT infrastructures.

Unix and Linux are scalable (meaning you can increase capacity at relatively minimal expense), reliable (meaning these operating systems do not often crash), and much less expensive than mainframe operating systems. They can also run on many different types of processors. The major providers of Unix operating systems are IBM, HP, and Sun, each with slightly different and partially incompatible versions.

Enterprise Software Applications

In addition to software for applications used by specific groups or business units, global firms spent much more than $300 billion in 2008 on software for enterprise applications that are treated as components of IT infrastructure. The largest providers of enterprise application software are SAP and Oracle (which acquired PeopleSoft). Also included in this category is middleware software supplied by vendors such as BEA (also acquired by Oracle in 2008) for achieving firm-wide integration by linking a firm's existing application systems.

Microsoft is attempting to move into the lower ends of this market by focusing on small and medium-sized businesses that have not yet implemented enterprise applications. In general, most large firms already use enterprise applications and have developed long-term relationships with their providers. Once a firm decides to work with an enterprise vendor, switching can be difficult and costly, though not impossible.

Data Management and Storage

There are few choices for enterprise database management software, which is responsible for organizing and managing the firm's data so that it can be efficiently accessed and used. Chapter 6 describes this software in detail. The leading database software providers are IBM (DB2), Oracle, Microsoft (SQL Server), and Sybase (Adaptive Server Enterprise), which together supply more than 90 percent of the North American database software marketplace. A growing new entrant is MySQL, a Linux open source relational database product available for free on the Internet and increasingly supported by HP and others. MySQL has a 25 percent share of the database software market (Evans Data Corporation, 2007).

The physical data storage market is dominated by EMC Corporation for large-scale systems and a small number of PC hard disk manufacturers led by Seagate, Maxtor, and Western Digital. In addition to traditional disk arrays and tape libraries, large firms are turning to network-based storage technologies. **Storage area networks (SANs)** connect multiple storage devices on a separate high-speed network dedicated to storage. The SAN creates a large central pool of storage that can be rapidly accessed and shared by multiple servers.

The amount of new digital information in the world is doubling every three years, driven in part by e-commerce and e-business and by statutes and regulations requiring firms to invest in extensive data storage and management facilities. Consequently, the market for digital data storage devices has been growing at more than 15 percent annually over the last five years.

Operating system
Unix
Linux
Storage area networks (SANs)

Networking/Telecommunications Platforms

Globally, firms spend more than $250 billon a year on networking and telecommunications hardware and more than a trillion dollars on networking services (consisting mainly of telecommunications and telephone company charges for voice lines and Internet access; these are not included in this discussion). Chapter 7 is devoted to an in-depth description of the enterprise networking environment, including the Internet and wireless technologies. Windows Server is the predominant local area network operating system, followed by Linux and Unix. Large enterprise-wide area networks primarily use some variant of Unix. Most local and wide area networks use the TCP/IP protocol suite as their networking standard (see Chapter 7).

The leading networking hardware providers are Cisco, Lucent, Nortel, and Juniper Networks. Telecommunications platforms are typically provided by telecommunications/ telephone services companies that offer voice and data connectivity, wide area networking, and Internet access. Leading telecommunications service vendors include Bell Canada, Primus, and provincial telecommunications companies, such as SaskTel and MTS. As noted in Chapter 7, this market is exploding with new providers of cellular wireless, Wi-Fi, and Internet telephone services.

Consulting and System Integration Services

Although 20 years ago it might have been possible for a large firm to implement all its own IT infrastructure, today this is far less common. Even large firms do not have the staff, skills, budget, or necessary experience to do so. Implementing new infrastructure requires (as noted in Chapters 9 and 10) significant changes in business processes and procedures, training and education, and software integration. Leading consulting firms providing this expertise include Accenture, IBM Global Services, Electronic Data Systems, HP Technology Solutions, Infosys, and Wipro Technologies.

Software integration means ensuring the new infrastructure works with the firm's older, so-called legacy systems and ensuring the new elements of the infrastructure work with one another. **Legacy systems** are generally older transaction processing systems created for mainframe computers that continue to be used to avoid the high cost of replacing or redesigning them. Replacing these systems is cost-prohibitive and generally not necessary if these older systems can be integrated into a contemporary infrastructure.

Internet Platforms

Internet platforms overlap with, and must relate to, the firm's general networking infrastructure and hardware and software platforms. Globally, firms spend billions on Internet-related infrastructure, such as hardware, software, and management services to support a firm's Web site—including Web hosting services—and for intranets and extranets. A **Web hosting service** maintains a large Web server, or series of servers, and provides fee-paying subscribers with space to maintain their Web sites.

The Internet revolution of the late 1990s led to a veritable explosion in server computers, with many firms collecting thousands of small servers to run their Internet operations. Since then, there has been a steady push toward server consolidation, reducing the number of server computers by increasing the size and power of each. The Internet hardware server market has become increasingly concentrated in the hands of Dell, HP/ Compaq, and IBM as prices have fallen dramatically.

The major Web software application development tools and suites are supplied by Microsoft (the Microsoft. NET family of development tools used to create Web sites using Active Server Pages for dynamic content), Sun (Sun's Java is the most widely used tool for developing interactive Web applications on both the server and client sides), IBM (WebSphere is IBM's suite of electronic business tools and applications), and a host of independent software developers, including Macromedia (Flash), media software (Real Media), and text tools (Adobe Acrobat). Chapter 7 describes the components of a firm's Internet platform in greater detail.

Legacy systems
Web hosting service

5.3 Contemporary Hardware Platform Trends

Although the cost of computing has fallen exponentially, the cost of the IT infrastructure has actually expanded as a percentage of corporate budgets. Why? The costs of computing services (consulting, systems integration) and software are high, and the intensity of computing and communicating has increased as other costs have declined. For instance, employees now use much more sophisticated applications, requiring more powerful and expensive hardware of many different types (laptop, desktop, mobile handheld computers).

Firms face a number of other challenges. They need to integrate information stored in different applications and even on different platforms (telephone, legacy systems, intranet, Internet sites, desktop, and mobile devices). Firms also need to build resilient infrastructures that can withstand huge increases in peak loads and routine assaults from hackers and viruses while conserving electrical power. Firms need to increase their service levels to respond to growing customer and employee expectations for service. The trends in hardware and software platforms we now describe address some or all of these challenges.

The Emerging Mobile Digital Platform

As computing increasingly takes place over the network, new mobile digital computing platforms have emerged. Communication devices such as cell phones and smartphones such as the BlackBerry and iPhone have taken on many functions of handheld computers, including transmission of data, surfing the Web, transmitting e-mail and instant messages, displaying digital content, and exchanging data with internal corporate systems. The new mobile platform also includes small, low-cost lightweight subnotebooks called **netbooks,** optimized for wireless communication and Internet access, with core computing functions such as word processing, and digital e-book readers such as Amazon's Kindle with some Web access capabilities. More and more business computing is moving from PCs and desktop machines to these mobile devices; managers increasingly use these devices to coordinate work and communicate with employees.

Netbooks

The Eee PC netbook designed by ASUS weighs only two pounds and uses a Linux-based operating system to provide wireless Internet access and a series of open source desktop productivity tools. Portability, ease of use, and low cost have made netbooks increasingly popular computing platforms.

Grid Computing

Grid computing involves connecting geographically remote computers into a single network to create a virtual supercomputer by combining the computational power of all computers on the grid. Grid computing takes advantage of the fact that most computers in the United States use their central processing units on average only 25 percent of the time for the work they have been assigned, leaving these idle resources available for other processing tasks. Grid computing was impossible until high-speed Internet connections enabled firms to connect remote machines economically and move enormous quantities of data across the connection.

Grid computing requires software programs to control and allocate resources on the grid. Client software communicates with a server software application. The server software breaks data and application code into chunks that are then parcelled out to the grid's machines. The client machines can perform their traditional tasks while running grid applications in the background.

The business case for using grid computing involves cost savings, speed of computation, and agility. For example, Royal Dutch/Shell Group is using a scalable grid computing platform that improves the accuracy and speed of its scientific modelling applications to find the best oil reservoirs. This platform, which links 1024 IBM servers running Linux, in effect creates one of the largest commercial Linux supercomputers in the world. The grid adjusts to accommodate the fluctuating data volumes that are typical in this seasonal business. Royal Dutch/Shell Group claims the grid has enabled the company to cut processing time for seismic data while improving output quality and helping its scientists pinpoint problems in finding new oil supplies.

Cloud Computing and the Computing Utility

Earlier in this chapter, we introduced cloud computing, in which hardware and software capabilities are provided as services over the Internet (also referred to as "the cloud"). Data are permanently stored in remote servers in massive data centres and accessed and updated over the Internet using clients that include desktops, notebooks, netbooks, entertainment centres, and mobile devices. For example, Google Apps provides common business applications online that are accessed from a Web browser, while the software and user data are stored on the servers.

Since organizations using cloud computing generally do not own the infrastructure, they do not have to make large investments in their own hardware and software. Instead, they purchase their computing services from remote providers and pay only for the amount of computing power they actually use (or are billed on a subscription basis). You will hear the terms **on-demand computing** or **utility computing** used to describe these services. The Window on Organizations on Salesforce.com on page 159 and the chapter-ending case on Amazon.com describe examples of cloud computing hardware and software services providers.

Some analysts believe that cloud computing represents a sea change in the way computing will be performed by corporations as business computing shifts out of private data centres into "the cloud" (Carr, 2008). This remains a matter of debate. Cloud computing is more immediately appealing to small and medium-size businesses that lack resources to purchase and own their own hardware and software. However, large corporations have huge investments in complex proprietary systems supporting unique business processes, some of which give them strategic advantages. The most likely scenario is a hybrid computing model in which firms will use their own infrastructure for their most essential core activities and adopt cloud computing for less critical systems. Cloud computing will gradually shift firms from having a fixed infrastructure capacity toward a more flexible infrastructure, some of it owned by the firm and some of it rented from giant computer centres owned by computer hardware vendors.

Autonomic Computing

Computer systems have become so complex that some experts believe they may not be manageable in the future. With operating systems, enterprise, and database software

Grid computing
On-demand computing
Utility computing

weighing in at millions of lines of code, and large systems encompassing many thousands of networked devices, the problem of managing these systems is both complex and expensive.

It is estimated that one-third to one-half of a company's total IT budget is spent preventing or recovering from system crashes. About 40 percent of these crashes are caused by operator error. The reason is not that operators are not well trained or do not have the right capabilities; rather, it happens because the complexities of today's computer systems are too difficult to understand, and IT operators and managers are under pressure to make decisions about problems in seconds.

One approach to dealing with this problem from a computer hardware perspective is to employ autonomic computing. **Autonomic computing** is an industry-wide effort to develop systems that can configure themselves, optimize and tune themselves, heal themselves when broken, and protect themselves from outside intruders and self-destruction. Imagine, for instance, a desktop PC that could know it was invaded by a computer virus. Instead of blindly allowing the virus to invade, the PC would identify and eradicate the virus or, alternatively, turn its workload over to another processor and shut itself down before the virus destroyed any files.

A few of these capabilities are present in desktop operating systems. For instance, virus and firewall protection software can detect viruses on PCs, automatically defeat the viruses, and alert operators. These programs can be updated automatically as the need arises by connecting to an online virus protection service such as McAfee. IBM and other vendors are starting to build autonomic features into products for large systems.

Virtualization and Multicore Processors

As companies deploy hundreds or thousands of servers, many have discovered that they are spending almost as much on electricity to power and cool their systems as they did on purchasing the hardware. Energy consumed by data centres more than doubled between 2000 and 2008. In a 2008 survey of North American executives and IT managers regarding their data centres, energy conservation was the most difficult issue to resolve with their current tools. Respondents felt that managing the total cost of power was the second most difficult task, and many of the respondents noted that their interest and work with virtualization technology were influenced by the hope of ultimate energy savings. Some of the survey results regarding energy usage:

- 33 percent of companies have implemented server virtualization for energy-saving goals.
- 55 percent of companies can measure power usage in their data centre, primarily at the UPS level.
- 83 percent consider the ability to measure power consumption at the entire data centre level as "valuable" or "extremely valuable" ("Green IT," 2009; "White Paper," 2006).

Cutting power consumption in data centres is now a major business challenge. The Window on Technology: Computing Goes Green, examines this problem. As you read this Window on Technology, try to identify the alternative solutions for this problem and the advantages and disadvantages of each.

Autonomic computing

Technology # WINDOW ON TECHNOLOGY

Computing Goes Green

Computer rooms are becoming too hot to handle. Data-hungry tasks such as video on demand, music downloads, exchanging photos, and maintaining Web sites require more and more power-hungry machines. The number of servers in corporate data centre servers increased to 29 million worldwide. During the same period, the total annual cost of electricity for data centres jumped from $3.9 billion to $8.8 billion across the world.

What's more, the heat generated from all of these servers is causing equipment to fail. Firms are forced to spend even more on cooling their data centres or to find other solutions. Some organizations spend more money to keep their data centres cool than they spend to lease the property itself. Cooling costs have helped raise the average annual utility bill of a 9000 square metre data centre to $7.2 million. It is a vicious cycle, as companies must pay to power their servers and then pay again to keep them cool and operational. Cooling a server requires roughly the same number of kilowatts of energy as running one. All of this additional power consumption has a negative impact on the environment as well as on corporate operating costs. A major data centre can have power consumption costs that run into the millions of dollars. Saving a large proportion of these costs can have a significant effect on the bottom line for these companies.

BT Global Services, an international company specializing in a variety of IT consulting and other professional services that has offices in Canada, has managed over the last several years to cut its data centre power consumption costs by between 60 and 70 percent and managed to reduce costs as well. According to Steve O'Donnell, global head of Data Centre and Customer Experience Management at BT, "We're really very far ahead in thought leadership on this. We want the market to follow and reduce the global carbon footprint for IT services." BT even wants to increase its savings on power consumption to 80 percent by 2016.

In Kingston, Ontario, Queen's University sent out a bulletin to bring peoples' attention to computer usage and practices, including turning computers off at night and using the energy savings settings on terminals to save money. "There are about 8500 computers on the Queen's campus, and there's significant energy savings to be had if they were turned off in the evenings and if staff and students used the energy [saving] settings on their computers," said John Witjes, engineering director of physical plant services at Queen's.

Another cooling solution comes from Degree Controls Inc., based in Milford, New Hampshire. Degree Controls installs floor tiles equipped with powerful fans that blow cool air directly onto servers. The tiles cost $2200 each.

Some of the world's most prominent firms are tackling their power consumption issues with one eye toward saving the environment and the other toward saving dollars. Google, Microsoft, and HSBC are all building data centres that will take advantage of hydroelectric power. Salesforce.com plans to offset its carbon footprint by investing in renewable energy projects and alternative energy sources.

Hewlett Packard is working on a series of technologies to reduce the carbon footprint of data centres by 75 percent, replace the copper wiring on microprocessors with light pulses, and develop new software and services to measure energy use and carbon emissions. It reduced its power costs by 20 to 25 percent through a consolidation of servers and data centres. None of these companies claim that their efforts will save the world, but they do demonstrate recognition of a growing problem and the commencement of the **green computing** era.

IT managers also have hardware and software options that conserve power. Some organizations are choosing to use thin client computers, which are very basic terminal machines that connect directly to servers and consume significantly less power than normal desktop clients. A call centre operated by Verizon Wireless in Chandler, Arizona, replaced 1700 PCs with thin clients from Sun Microsystems and saw its power consumption go down by one-third. Sun states that on average its thin clients use less than half of the electricity that PCs require. Enterprise Rent-A-Car expects a move from PCs to HP thin clients will cut energy consumption by 5 million kilowatt-hours, save about $500 000 annually, and reduce CO_2 emissions by 6.5 million pounds per year, *Computerworld* reports. The network of more than 45 000 thin client terminals—operated through 743 terminal servers—connects Enterprise rental offices throughout Canada, the United States, the United Kingdom, Ireland, Germany, and Puerto Rico. Thin clients use only 13.6 watt-hours and 2.4 watt-hours of electricity in active and passive states, respectively, compared with the 77.1 watt-hours and 1.8 watt-hours consumed by PCs.

Microsoft's Windows Vista operating system has enhanced sleep features that reduce power consumption by much greater margins than the standby modes in previous versions of Windows. In sleep mode, computers may draw as little as 3 to 4 watts of power versus 100 watts for an idle computer that is not asleep. Businesses also have the option of using more efficient chips in their servers. Virtualization is a highly effective tool for more cost-effective greener computing because it reduces the number of servers required to run a firm's applications. As we saw in the chapter-opening case about Bell Canada, virtualization yields cost reductions and better management as well as the power savings associated with the virtual server environment.

Going green is more than saving power though. It also refers to the need to reduce the use of hazardous materials in computing devices, maximize energy efficiency during the product's lifetime, and promote recyclability or biodegradability of defunct products and factory waste. Many of the components that go into computers are either harmful, such as mercury and lead, or hard to recycle. The Silicon Valley Technology Coalition believes that there are more than 500 million obsolete computers in North America with an additional 130 million cell phones being disposed of annually.

What happens to these devices? Some are, of course, given to organizations and individuals who may or may not be able to use the outdated technology. Others are sent away to be de-composed and recycled. The Silicon Valley Toxics Coalition estimates that 80 percent of the post-consumer e-waste collected for recycling is shipped abroad to countries such as China, India, and Pakistan. Still others are simply left as garbage. Movements are under way to reduce, reuse, and recycle computers, their components, and their packaging in a safe environment.

A variety of government and industry initiatives have been implemented to help move manufacturers and others toward green computing. These include the Energy Star Program adopted by Canada, the European Union's directives 2002/95/EC (RoHS) on the reduction of hazardous substances, the Green Grid consortium of major industry manufacturers, and the International Professional Practice Partnership promulgated by the International Federation for Information Processing (IFIP) which includes certification processes. It is hoped that these and additional initiatives will progress toward global green computing.

To Think About

1. What business and social problems does data centre power consumption cause?
2. What solutions are available for these problems? Which are the most environment-friendly?
3. What are the business benefits and costs of these solutions?
4. Should all firms move toward green computing? Why or why not?

MIS in Action

Perform an Internet search on the phrase *green computing* and then answer the following questions:

1. How would you define green computing?
2. Who are some of the leaders of the green computing movement? Which corporations are leading the way?

Which environmental organizations are playing an important role?

3. What are the latest trends in green computing? What kind of impact are they having?
4. What can individuals do to contribute to the green computing movement? Is the movement worthwhile?

Sources: Jennifer Pritchett, "Queen's University Saving Green by Going Green," *The Kingston Whig Standard*, November 21, 2007; "Green IT Comes of Age: Data Centres That Use 60% percent Less Power," **www.biggerthinking .com/en/efficient_data_centres.aspx** (accessed February 13, 2009); Scott Ferguson, "Cooling the Data Center," *eWeek*, June 9, 2008; Rob Bernard, "Microsoft's Green Growth," *eWeek*, April 7, 2008; Eric Chabrow, "The Wild, Wild Cost of Data Centers," *CIO Insight*, May 2008; Jim Carlton, "IT Managers Make a Power Play," *The Wall Street Journal*, March 27, 2007; "IT Managers Find Novel Ways to Cool Powerful Servers," *The Wall Street Journal*, April 10, 2007; and Marianne Kolbasuk McGee, "Data Center Electricity Bills Double," *Information Week*, February 17, 2007.

The Window on Technology described organizations curbing hardware proliferation and power consumption by using virtualization to reduce the number of computers required for processing. A virtual server uses the hardware of one physical computer to provide the appearance, services, and capabilities of multiple servers, each of which appear to be running their own operating system and providing a unique operating environment. Server virtualization enables companies to run more than one operating system at the same time on a single machine. **Virtualization** means that servers can be accessed in ways that are not restricted by physical configuration or geographic location. Most servers run at just 10 to 15 percent of capacity, and virtualization can boost utilization server utilization rates to 70 percent or higher. Higher utilization rates translate into fewer computers required to process the same amount of work. As we saw in the opening case, it is possible to solve a number of management problems and save costs by using virtualization.

For example, Liverpool Women's NHS Foundation Trust, England's largest specialist in providing health care services for women, saved more than 70 percent of its power consumption costs by combining 30 physical servers into only 4 physical servers through virtualization. Administrative costs of server management also fell by 70 percent. Server virtualization software runs between the operating system and the hardware, masking server resources, including the number and identity of physical servers, processors, and operating systems, from server users. VMware is the leading server virtualization software vendor for Windows and Linux systems. Microsoft offers its own Virtual Server product and has built virtualization capabilities into the newest version of Windows Server.

In addition to reducing hardware and power expenditures, virtualization allows businesses to run their legacy applications on older versions of an operating system on the same server as newer applications. Virtualization also facilitates centralization of hardware administration.

Multicore Processors Another way to reduce power requirements and hardware sprawl is to use multicore processors. A **multicore processor** is an integrated circuit to which two or more processors have been attached for enhanced performance, reduced power consumption, and more efficient simultaneous processing of multiple tasks. This technology enables two processing engines with reduced power requirements and heat dissipation to perform tasks faster than a resource-hungry chip with a single processing core. Today you will find dual-core processors in PCs and quad-core processors in servers. Sun Microsystems' UltraSPARC T2 chip for managing Web applications has eight processors and will soon be followed by a 16-core processor.

Green computing

Virtualization

Multicore processor

5.4 Contemporary Software Platform Trends

There are five major themes in contemporary software platform evolution:

- Linux and open source software
- Java and Ajax
- Web services and service-oriented architecture
- Software mashups and Web 2.0 applications
- Software outsourcing

Linux and Open Source Software

Open source software is software produced by a community of several hundred thousand programmers around the world. According to the leading open source professional association, OpenSource.org, open source software is free and can be modified by users. Works derived from the original code must also be free, and the software can be redistributed by the user without additional licensing. Open source software is by definition not restricted to any specific operating system or hardware technology although most open source software is currently based on a Linux or Unix operating system.

Open source software is based on the premise that it is superior to commercially produced proprietary software because thousands of programmers around the world working for no pay can read, perfect, distribute, and modify the source code much faster, and with more reliable results, than small teams of programmers working for a single software company. The open source movement has been evolving for more than 30 years and has demonstrated after many years of effort that it can produce commercially acceptable, high-quality software.

Now many thousands of open source programs are available from hundreds of Web sites. Popular open source software tools include the Linux operating system, the Apache HTTP Web server, the Mozilla Firefox Web browser, and the OpenOffice desktop productivity suite. Open source tools are being used on netbooks as inexpensive alternatives to Microsoft Office. Major hardware and software vendors, including IBM, Hewlett-Packard, Dell, Oracle, and SAP, now offer Linux-compatible versions of their products. You can find out more out more about the Open Source Definition from the Open Source Initiative, a group that was founded 20 years ago to promote the use of open source software. You can also learn about the history of open source software at the Learning Tracks for this chapter.

Linux Perhaps the most well-known open source software is Linux, an operating system related to Unix. Linux was created by the Finnish programmer Linus Torvalds and first posted on the Internet in August 1991. Linux applications are embedded in cell phones, smartphones, netbooks, and other handheld devices. Linux is available in free versions downloadable from the Internet or in low-cost commercial versions that include tools and support from vendors such as Red Hat.

Linux is currently a small but rapidly growing presence on the desktop, especially as an operating system for Internet-enabled netbooks. It plays a major role in the back office running local area networks, Web servers, and high-performance computing work, with 20 percent of the server operating system market. IBM, HP, Intel, Dell, and Sun have made Linux a central part of their offerings to corporations. More than two dozen countries in Asia, Europe, and Latin America have adopted open source software and Linux.

The rise of open source software, particularly Linux and the applications it supports, has profound implications for corporate software platforms: cost reduction, reliability and resilience, and integration because Linux works on all the major hardware platforms from mainframes to servers to clients.

Software for the Web: Java and Ajax

Java is an operating system–independent, processor-independent, object-oriented programming language that has become the leading interactive programming environment for the

Open source software
Java

Web. Java was created by James Gosling and the Green Team at Sun Microsystems in 1992. Nearly all Web browsers come with a Java platform built in. More recently, the Java platform has migrated into cellular phones, smartphones, automobiles, music players, game machines, and finally, into set-top cable television systems serving interactive content and pay-per-view services. Java software is designed to run on any computer or computing device, regardless of the specific microprocessor or operating system the device uses. For each of the computing environments in which Java is used, Sun has created a Java Virtual Machine that interprets Java programming code for that machine. In this manner, the code is written once and can be used on any machine for which there exists a Java Virtual Machine.

Java is a very robust language that can handle text, data, graphics, sound, and video, all within one program if needed. Java enables PC users to manipulate data on networked systems using Web browsers, reducing the need to write specialized software. A **Web browser** is an easy-to-use software tool with a graphical user interface for displaying Web pages and for accessing the Web and other Internet resources. Microsoft's Internet Explorer, Mozilla Firefox, Apple Safari, and Google Chrome are examples. At the enterprise level, Java is being used for more complex e-commerce and e-business applications that require communication with an organization's back-end transaction processing systems.

The rapid deployment of Java was hindered in the past because of disagreements between Sun Microsystems and Microsoft over Java standards. In April 2004, under pressure from major customers such as General Motors, Microsoft agreed to stop distributing the Microsoft Java Virtual Machine (MSJVM) it had developed for its proprietary version of Java and to cooperate with Sun in the development of new technologies, including Java.

Ajax Have you ever filled out a Web order form, made a mistake, and then had to start all over again after a long wait for a new order form page to appear on your computer screen? Or visited a map site, clicked the North arrow once, and waited for an entire new page to load? **Ajax** (Asynchronous Java Script and XML) is another Web development technique for creating interactive Web applications that prevents all of this inconvenience.

Ajax allows a client and server to exchange small pieces of data behind the scenes so that an entire Web page does not have to be reloaded each time the user requests a change. So if you click North on a map site, such as Google Maps, the server downloads just that part of the application that changes with no wait for an entirely new map. You can also grab maps in map applications and move the map in any direction without forcing a reload of the entire page. Ajax uses JavaScript programs downloaded to your client to maintain a near continuous conversation with the server you are using, making the user experience more seamless.

Web Services and Service-Oriented Architecture

Web services refer to a set of loosely coupled software components that exchange information with each other using universal Web communication standards and languages. They can exchange information between two different systems regardless of the operating systems or programming languages on which the systems are based. They can be fused to build open standard Web-based applications linking systems of two different organizations, and they can also be used to create applications that link disparate systems within a single company. Web services are not tied to any one operating system or programming language, and different applications can use them to communicate with each other in a standard way without time-consuming custom coding.

The foundation technology for Web services is **XML,** which stands for **Extensible Markup Language.** This language was developed in 1996 by the World Wide Web Consortium (W3C, the international body that oversees the development of the Web) as a more powerful and flexible markup language than hypertext markup language (HTML) for Web pages. **Hypertext Markup Language (HTML)** is a page description language for specifying how text, graphics, video, and sound are placed on a Web page document. While HTML is limited to describing how data should be presented in the form of Web pages, XML can perform presentation, communication, and storage of data. In XML, a number is not simply a number; the XML tag specifies whether the number represents a price, a date, or a postal code. Table 5-3 illustrates some sample XML statements.

Web browser

Ajax

Web services

XML

Extensible Markup Language

Hypertext Markup Language (HTML)

TABLE 5-3 Examples of XML.

PLAIN ENGLISH	XML
Subcompact	<AUTOMOBILETYPE="Subcompact">
4 passenger	<PASSENGER UNIT="PASS">4</PASSENGER>
$16 800	<PRICE CURRENCY="USD">$16 800</PRICE>

By tagging selected elements of the content of documents for their meanings, XML makes it possible for computers to manipulate and interpret data automatically and perform operations on the data without human intervention. Web browsers and computer programs, such as order processing or enterprise resource planning (ERP) software, can follow programmed rules for applying and displaying the data. XML provides a standard format for data exchange, enabling Web services to pass data from one process to another.

Web services communicate through XML messages over standard Web protocols. *SOAP*, which stands for *Simple Object Access Protocol*, is a set of rules for structuring messages that enables applications to pass data and instructions to one another. *WSDL* stands for *Web Services Description Language*; it is a common framework for describing the tasks performed by a Web service and the commands and data it will accept so that the Web service can be used by other applications. *UDDI*, which stands for *Universal Description, Discovery, and Integration*, enables a Web service to be listed in a directory of Web services so that the Web service can be easily located. Companies discover and locate Web services through this directory much as they would locate services in the Yellow Pages. Using these protocols, a software application can connect freely to other applications without custom programming for each different application with which it wants to communicate. All computers share the same standards.

The collection of Web services that are used to build a firm's software systems constitutes what is known as a service-oriented architecture. A **service-oriented architecture (SOA)** is set of self-contained services that communicate with each other to create a working software application. Business tasks are accomplished by executing a series of these services. Software developers reuse these services in other combinations to assemble other applications as needed.

Virtually all major software vendors provide tools and entire platforms for building and integrating software applications using Web services. IBM includes Web service tools in its WebSphere e-business software platform, and Microsoft has incorporated Web services tools in its Microsoft. NET platform.

Here is a real-world example of an interorganizational SOA at work. Dollar Rent A Car's systems use Web services for its online booking system with Southwest Airlines' Web site. Although both companies' systems are based on different technology platforms, a person booking a flight on SouthwestAir.com can reserve a car from Dollar without leaving the airline's Web site. Instead of struggling to get Dollar's reservation system to share data with Southwest's information systems, Dollar uses Microsoft. NET Web services technology as an intermediary. Reservations from Southwest are translated into Web services protocols, which are then translated into formats that can be understood by Dollar's computers.

Other car rental companies have linked their information systems to airline companies' Web sites before, but, without Web services, these connections had to be built one at a time. Web services provide a standard way for Dollar's computers to "talk" to other companies' information systems without having to build special links to each one. Dollar is now expanding its use of Web services to link directly to the systems of a small tour operator and a large travel reservation system as well as a wireless Web site for mobile phones and PDAs. It does not have to write new software code for each new partner's information systems or each new wireless device (see Figure 5-11).

Service-oriented architecture (SOA)

FIGURE 5-11 How Dollar Rent A Car uses Web services.

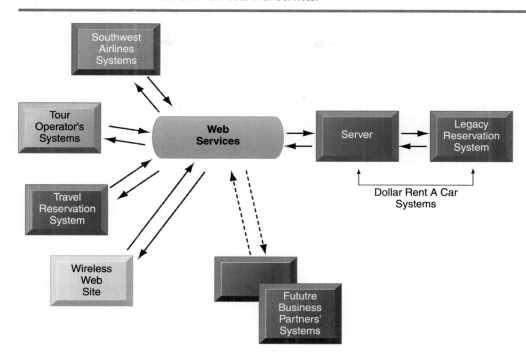

Dollar Rent A Car uses Web services to provide a standard intermediate layer of software to "talk" to other companies' information systems. Dollar Rent A Car can use this set of Web services to link to other companies' information systems without having to build a separate link to each firm's systems.

Mashups and Widgets

In the past, software such as Microsoft Word or Adobe Illustrator came in a box and was designed to operate on a single machine. Increasingly, software is downloadable from the Internet and composed of interchangeable components that integrate freely with other applications on the Internet. Individual users and entire companies mix and match these software components to create their own customized applications and to share information with others. The resulting software applications are called **mashups.** The idea is to take software from different sources and combine it in order to produce a application that is "greater than" the sum of its parts.

Part of the movement called Web 2.0 (see Chapter 7), and in the spirit of musical mashups, Web mashups combine the capabilities of two or more online applications to create a kind of hybrid that provides more customer value than the original sources alone. One area of great innovation is the mashup of mapping and satellite image software with local content. For instance, Zoocasa is a new real estate search engine in Canada that is using Google Maps to display real estate listings. The Zoocasa home page is a simple search box in which the user enters a city or neighbourhood and can define search criteria by price, number of bedrooms, and number of bathrooms. The Zoocasa search results are then presented on a Google Map and listed in a sidebar beside the map. One innovative feature of the map is that if you click on a property marker, the sidebar automatically scrolls to display the property details. Google, Yahoo!, and Microsoft now offer tools to allow other applications to pull in information from their map and satellite images with relatively little programming.

You have performed a mashup if you have ever personalized your Facebook profile or your blog with a capability to display videos or slide shows. The small pieces of software code that enable users to embed content from one site into a Web page or another Web site are called widgets. **Widgets** are small software programs that can be added to Web pages or placed on the desktop to provide additional functionality. For example, the Flixter widget on Facebook profiles transports users to a place where they can list the films they have seen along with their ratings and reviews, view their friends' ratings and reviews, and what is playing in theatres.

Web widgets run inside a Web page or blog. Desktop widgets integrate content from an external source into the user's desktop to provide services such as a calculator, dictionary,

Mashups
Widgets

or display of current weather conditions. The Apple Dashboard, Microsoft Windows Vista Sidebar, and Google Desktop Gadgets are examples of desktop widgets.

Widgets also provide storefront windows for advertising and selling products and services. Random House Inc. has a widget that enables visitors to its Web site to click through to purchase new book releases from its online store. Amazon.com and Walmart have toolbar widgets that enable surfers to search their Web stores while staying on their social network or another personal page. Widgets have become so powerful and useful that Facebook and Google launched programs to attract developers of widgets for their Web sites.

Software Outsourcing

Today most business firms continue to operate legacy systems that continue to meet a business need and that would be extremely costly to replace. But they will purchase most of their new software applications from external sources. There are three external sources for software: software packages from a commercial software vendor, software services from an online service provider, and outsourcing custom application development to an outside software firm, often offshore firms in low-wage areas of the world.

Software Packages and Enterprise Software We have already described software packages for enterprise applications as one of the major types of software components in contemporary IT infrastructures. A **software package** is a prewritten commercially available set of software programs that eliminates the need for a firm to write its own software programs for certain functions, such as payroll processing or order handling. Enterprise application software vendors such as SAP and Oracle-PeopleSoft have developed powerful software packages that can support the primary business processes of a firm worldwide from warehousing, customer relationship management, supply chain management, and finance to human resources. These large-scale enterprise software systems provide a single, integrated, worldwide software system for firms at a cost much less than they would pay if they developed it themselves. Chapter 12 discusses enterprise systems in detail.

Software as a Service (SaaS) It is clear that software will increasingly be delivered and used over networks as a service. Earlier in this chapter, we described cloud computing, in which software is delivered as a service over the Internet. In addition to free or low-cost tools for individuals and small businesses provided by Google or Yahoo!, enterprise software and other complex business functions are available as services from the major commercial software vendors. Instead of buying and installing software programs, subscribing companies rent the same functions from these services, with users paying on either a subscription or per transaction basis. Services for delivering and providing access to software remotely as a Web-based service are now referred to as **Software as a Service (SaaS).**

A leading example is Salesforce.com, which provides on-demand software services for customer relationship management, including salesforce automation, partner relationship management, marketing, and customer service. It includes tools for customization, integrating its software with other corporate applications, and integrating new applications to run other parts of the business. The Window on Organizations provides more detail on these capabilities.

Companies considering the SaaS model need to carefully assess the costs and benefits of the service, weighing all people, organizational, and technology issues, including the ability to integrate with existing systems and deliver a level of service and performance that is acceptable for the business. In some cases, the cost of renting software will add up to more than purchasing and maintaining the application in-house. Yet there may be benefits to paying more for software as a service if this decision allows the company to focus on core business issues instead of technology challenges.

Software package

Software as a Service (SaaS)

Outsourcing

Software Outsourcing A third external source of software is **outsourcing,** in which a firm contracts custom software development or maintenance of existing legacy programs to outside firms, frequently firms that operate offshore in low-wage areas of the world.

According to the Gartner Group, worldwide outsourcing totalled over $539 billion in 2008, and it is growing at about 8 percent a year (Gartner, 2008). The largest expenditure here is paid to North American firms providing middleware, integration services, and other software support that are often required to operate larger enterprise systems. IBM has the largest share of this global market (8 percent) followed by EDS (5 percent) and ADP (3 percent). About 50 percent of all global outsourcing originates in the financial services sector.

For example, in March 2008, Royal Dutch Shell PLC, the world's third-largest oil producer, signed a five-year, $4.88 billion outsourcing deal with T-Systems International GmbH, AT&T, and Electronic Data Systems (EDS). The agreement assigned AT&T responsibility for networking and telecommunications, T-Systems for hosting and storage, and EDS for end-user computing services and integration of the infrastructure services. Outsourcing this work will help Shell cut costs and focus on systems that improve its competitive position in the oil and gas market.

Offshore outsourcing firms have primarily provided lower-level maintenance, data entry, and call centre operations. However, with the growing sophistication and experience of offshore firms, particularly in India, more and more new-program development is taking place offshore. Chapter 9 discusses offshore software outsourcing in greater detail.

In order to manage their relationship with an outsourcer or technology service provider, firms will need a contract that includes a **service-level agreement (SLA).** The SLA is a formal contract between customers and their service providers that defines the specific responsibilities of the service provider and the level of service expected by the customer. SLAs typically specify the nature and level of services provided, criteria for performance measurement, support options, provisions for security and disaster recovery, hardware and software ownership and upgrades, customer support, billing, and conditions for terminating the agreement. The MyMISLab features a Learning Track on this topic.

Service-level agreement (SLA)

WINDOW ON ORGANIZATIONS

Salesforce.com: Software as a Service Goes Mainstream

Salesforce.com has been considered one of the most disruptive technology companies of the past few years and is credited with single-handedly shaking up the software industry with its innovative business model and resounding success. This company provides CRM solutions in the form of software as a service leased over the Internet, as opposed to software bought and installed on machines locally. It was founded in 1999 by former Oracle executive Marc Benioff and has since grown to 2600 employees and earned $913 million in revenue in 2007. Salesforce.com has more than 43 000 corporate customers and well over 1 million subscribers.

The company attributes its success to the many benefits of its on-demand model of software distribution. The on-demand model eliminates the need for large upfront capital investments in systems and lengthy implementations on corporate computers. Subscriptions start as low as $11 per month per user for the pared-down Group version for small sales and marketing teams, with monthly subscriptions for more advanced versions for large enterprises starting

around $80 per user. Salesforce.com implementations take up to three months. There is no hardware for subscribers to purchase, scale, and maintain; no operating systems, database servers, or application servers to install; no consultants and staff; and no expensive licensing and maintenance fees. The system is accessible via a standard Web browser, and Salesforce.com continually updates its software behind the scenes. There are tools for customizing some features of the software to support a company's unique business processes. Salesforce.com's solutions offer better scalability than those provided by large enterprise software vendors because they eliminate the cost and complexity of managing multiple layers of hardware and software.

Benioff believes that all of these advantages will inevitably lead to "the end of software," or, more appropriately, a new future of software in which the software-as-a-service model will supplant the current model and become the new paradigm. However, it is still too soon to tell whether this prediction will turn out to be true. Salesforce faces significant challenges as it continues to grow and refine its business.

The first challenge comes from increased competition, both from traditional industry leaders and new challengers hoping to replicate Salesforce's success. Microsoft, SAP, and Oracle have rolled out subscription-based versions of their CRM products in response to Salesforce. Smaller competitors like NetSuite also have made some inroads against Salesforce's market share. In addition, Siebel Systems, the world's leading CRM supplier bought in 2005 by Oracle, has been a major competitor since Salesforce.com was founded.

Analysts predict that Microsoft has a chance to compete with Salesforce by developing merely an acceptable on-demand CRM product because of the average customer's already-established familiarity with Microsoft applications. Also Microsoft plans to offer its product at half the price of Salesforce.com, using a tactic it has employed with great effect in other marketplaces to pressure competitors. Salesforce.com still has plenty of catching up to do to reach the size and market share of its larger competitors. As of 2007, SAP's CRM market share was 25.7 percent, compared to only 7 percent for Salesforce.com. IBM's customer base includes 9000 software companies that run their applications on their software and that are likelier to choose a solution offered by IBM over Salesforce.com.

Another challenge for Salesforce.com is to expand its business model into other areas. Salesforce is currently used mostly by sales staff needing to keep track of leads and customer lists. One way the company is trying to provide additional functionality is through a partnership with Google and more specifically Google Apps. Salesforce.com is combining its services with Gmail, Google Docs, Google Talk, and Google Calendar to allow its customers to accomplish more tasks via the Web.

The partnership between Salesforce.com and Google represents a united front against Microsoft intended to cut into the popularity of Microsoft Office. Currently, Salesforce.com describes the partnership as "primarily a distribution deal," but it could grow stronger based on the idea that businesses prefer to manage CRM in one place. Salesforce.com and Google both hope that their Salesforce.com for Google Apps initiative will galvanize further growth in on-demand software.

Salesforce opened up its Force.com application development platform to other independent software developers and listed their programs on its AppExchange. Using AppExchange, small businesses can go online and easily download more than 800 software applications, some add-ons to Salesforce.com and others that are unrelated. 24 Hour Fitness, the world's largest privately owned and operated fitness chain, uses App Exchange along with Salesforce.com's Enterprise edition for companywide salesforce automation and customer service. One of its App Exchange applications integrates Hoover's database of up to 21 million companies

and 28 million executives with Salesforce, and another allows users to easily create and distribute on-demand surveys and response forms.

The question is whether the audience for the App Exchange application platform will prove large enough to deliver the level of growth Salesforce wants. Some analysts believe the platform may not be attractive to larger companies for their application needs.

A third challenge is availability. Salesforce.com subscribers depend on the service being available 24/7. But occasional outages have occurred (see the Chapter 8 Window on Technology), making some companies rethink their dependency on software as a service. Salesforce.com provides tools to assure customers about its system reliability and also offers PC applications that tie into its services so users can work offline.

To Think About

1. What are the advantages and disadvantages of the software-as-a-service model?
2. What are some of the challenges facing Salesforce as it continues its growth? How well will it be able to meet those challenges?
3. What kinds of businesses could benefit from switching to Salesforce and why?
4. What factors would you take into account in deciding whether to use Saleforce.com for your business?

MIS in Action

Explore the Salesforce.com Web site. Go to the App Exchange portion of the site, and examine the applications available for each of the categories listed. Then answer the following questions:

1. What are the most popular applications on App Exchange? What kinds of processes do they support?
2. Could a company run its entire business using Salesforce.com and App Exchange? Explain your answer.
3. What kinds of companies are most likely to use App Exchange? What does this tell you about how Salesforce.com is being used?

Sources: J. Nicholas Hoover, "Service Outages Force Cloud Adopters to Rethink Tactics," *InformationWeek*, August 16, 2008, www.informationweek.com/news/services/saas/showArticle.jhtml?articleID=210004236 (accessed November 19, 2009); Jay Greene, "Google and Salesforce: A Tighter Bond," *BusinessWeek*, April 15, 2008; Mary Hayes Weier, "Salesforce, Google Show Fruits of Their Collaboration," *InformationWeek*, April 21, 2008; John Pallatto and Clint Boulton, "An On-Demand Partnership," *eWeek*, April 21, 2008; Gary Rivlin, "Software for Rent," *The New York Times*, November 13, 2007; Steve Hamm, "A Big Sales Job for Salesforce.com," *BusinessWeek*, September 24, 2007; Mary Hayes Weier, "Salesforce.com" and Marianne Kolbasuk McGee, "Salesforce as B-to-B Broker," *InformationWeek*, December 10, 2007; and Salesforce.com, report on Form 10-K for the fiscal year ended January 31, 2008, filed with the SEC on 2/29/08.

5.5   Management Issues

Creating and managing a coherent IT infrastructure raises multiple challenges: dealing with platform and technology change, management and governance, and making wise infrastructure investments.

Dealing with Platform and Infrastructure Change

As firms grow, they can quickly outgrow their infrastructure. As firms shrink, they can get stuck with excessive infrastructure purchased in better times. How can a firm remain flexible when most of the investments in IT infrastructure are fixed-cost purchases and licences? How well does the infrastructure scale? **Scalability** refers to the ability of a computer, product, or system to expand to serve a large number of users without breaking down. New applications, mergers and acquisitions, and changes in business volume all impact computer workload and must be considered when planning hardware capacity.

Firms using mobile computing and cloud computing platforms will require new policies and procedures for managing these new platforms. They will need to inventory all of their mobile devices in business use and develop policies and tools for tracking, updating, and securing them and for controlling the data and applications that run on them. Firms using cloud computing and SaaS will need to fashion new contractual arrangements with remote vendors to make sure that the hardware and software for critical applications are always available when needed. It is up to business management to determine acceptable levels of computer response time and availability for the firm's mission-critical systems to maintain the level of business performance they expect.

Management and Governance

A long-standing issue among information system managers and CEOs has been the question of who will control and manage the firm's IT infrastructure. Chapter 2 introduced the concept of IT governance and described some issues it addresses. Other important questions about IT governance include: Should departments and divisions have the responsibility of making their own information technology decisions, or should IT infrastructure be centrally controlled and managed? What is the relationship between central information systems management and business unit information systems management? How will infrastructure costs be allocated among business units? Each organization will need to arrive at answers based on its own needs.

Making Wise Infrastructure Investments

IT infrastructure is a major investment for the firm. If too much is spent on infrastructure, it lies idle and constitutes a drag on firm financial performance. If too little is spent, important business services cannot be delivered, and the firm's competitors (who spent just the right amount) will outperform the underinvesting firm. How much should the firm spend on infrastructure? This question is not easy to answer.

A related question is whether a firm should purchase its own IT infrastructure components or rent them from external suppliers. As we discussed earlier, a major trend in computing platforms—both hardware and software—is to outsource to external providers. The decision either to purchase your own IT assets or rent them from external providers is typically called the *rent versusbuy* decision.

Competitive Forces Model for IT Infrastructure Investment Figure 5-12 illustrates a competitive forces model you can use to address the question of how much your firm should spend on IT infrastructure. Although similar to Porter's competitive forces model, which we discussed in Chapter 3, this model has six components as compared to Porter's original five forces. The following section describes these six forces or factors and their impact on the firm's IT services and infrastructure.

Scalability

FIGURE 5-12 Competitive forces model for IT infrastructure.

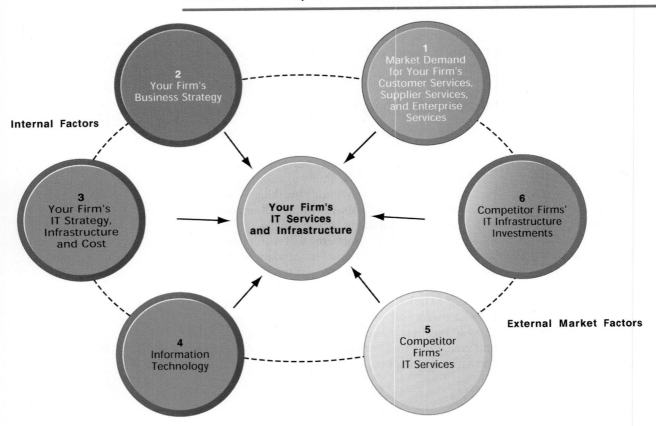

There are six factors you can use to answer the question, "How much should our firm spend on IT infrastructure?"

Market Demand for Your Firm's Services Make an inventory of the services you currently provide to customers, suppliers, and employees. Survey each group, or hold focus groups to find out if the services you currently offer are meeting the needs of each group. For example, are customers complaining of slow responses to their queries about price and availability? Are employees complaining about the difficulty of finding the right information for their jobs? Are suppliers complaining about the difficulties of discovering your production requirements?

Your Firm's Business Strategy Analyze your firm's five-year business strategy, and try to assess what new services and capabilities will be required to achieve strategic goals.

Your Firm's Information Technology (IT) Strategy, Infrastructure, and Cost Examine your firm's information technology plans for the next five years, and assess its alignment with the firm's business plans. Determine total IT infrastructure costs. You will want to perform a total cost of ownership analysis (see the discussion later). If your firm has no IT strategy, you will need to devise one that takes into account the firm's five-year strategic plan.

Information Technology Assessment Is your firm behind the technology curve or at the bleeding edge of information technology? Both situations are to be avoided. It is usually not desirable to spend resources on advanced technologies that are still experimental, often expensive, and sometimes unreliable. You want to spend on technologies for which standards have been established and IT vendors are competing on cost, not design, and where there are multiple suppliers. However, you do not want to put off investment in new technologies or allow competitors to develop new business models and capabilities based on the new technologies.

TABLE 5-4 Total cost of ownership (TCO) cost components.

INFRASTRUCTURE COMPONENT	COST COMPONENTS
Hardware acquisition	Purchase price of computer hardware equipment, including computers, terminals, storage, and printers
Software acquisition	Purchase or license of software for each user
Installation	Cost to install computers and software
Training	Cost to provide training for information systems specialists and end users
Support	Cost to provide ongoing technical support, help desks, and so forth
Maintenance	Cost to upgrade the hardware and software
Infrastructure	Cost to acquire, maintain, and support related infrastructure, such as networks and specialized equipment (including storage backup units)
Downtime	Cost of lost productivity if hardware or software failures cause the system to be unavailable for processing and user tasks
Space and energy	Real estate and utility costs for housing and providing power for the technology

Competitor Firms' IT Services   Try to assess what technology services competitors offer to customers, suppliers, and employees. Establish quantitative and qualitative measures to compare them to those of your firm. If your firm's service levels fall short, your company is at a competitive disadvantage. Look for ways your firm can excel at service levels.

Competitor Firm IT Infrastructure Investments   Benchmark your expenditures for IT infrastructure against your competitors. Many companies are quite public about their innovative expenditures on IT. If competing firms try to keep IT expenditures secret, you may be able to find IT investment information in public companies' annual reports to the federal government when those expenditures impact a firm's financial results.

Your firm does not necessarily need to spend as much as, or more than, your competitors. Perhaps it has discovered much less expensive ways of providing services, and this can lead to a cost advantage. Alternatively, your firm may be spending far less than competitors and experiencing commensurate poor performance and losing market share.

Total Cost of Ownership of Technology Assets In benchmarking your firm's expenditures on IT infrastructure with that of your competitors, you will need to consider a wide range of costs. The actual cost of owning technology resources includes the original cost of acquiring and installing hardware and software, as well as ongoing administration costs for hardware and software upgrades, maintenance, technical support, training, and even utility and real estate costs for running and housing the technology. The **total cost of ownership (TCO)** model can be used to analyze these direct and indirect costs to help firms determine the actual cost of specific technology implementations. Table 5-4 describes the most important TCO components to consider in a TCO analysis. Figure 5-13 illustrates the concept of TCO.

When all these cost components are considered, the TCO for a PC might run up to three times the original purchase price of the equipment. Hidden costs for support staff, downtime, and additional network management can make distributed client/server architectures—especially those incorporating mobile wireless devices—more expensive than centralized mainframe architectures. Hardware and software acquisition costs account for only about 20 to 40 percent of TCO, so managers must pay close attention to administration costs to understand the full cost of the firm's hardware and software. It is possible to reduce some of these administration costs through better management. Many large firms are saddled with redundant, incompatible hardware and software because their departments and divisions have been allowed to make their own technology purchases.

These firms could reduce their TCO through greater centralization and standardization of their hardware and software resources, as did Bell Canada, described in the

Total cost of ownership (TCO)

FIGURE 5-13   The Iceberg Model for total cost of ownership

An iceberg illustrates the concept of TCO, where most of the content is hidden.

TCO
"Iceberg Model"
(*there's always more that lies beneath the surface*)

Hardware—23%

Software Licensing—10%

Customization and Implementation—33%

IT Personnel Training—11%

User Training—9%

Annual Maintenance—14%

Total—100%

chapter-opening case. Companies could reduce the size of the information systems staff required to support their infrastructure if the firm minimizes the number of different computer models and pieces of software that employees are allowed to use. In a centralized infrastructure, systems can be administered from a central location and troubleshooting can be performed from that location.

SUMMARY

1. *What is IT infrastructure, and what are its components?*

IT infrastructure is the shared technology resources that provide the platform for the firm's specific information system applications. IT infrastructure includes hardware, software, and services that are shared across the entire firm. Major IT infrastructure components include computer hardware platforms, operating system platforms, enterprise software platforms, networking and telecommunications platforms, database management software, Internet platforms, and consulting services and systems integrators.

2. *What are the stages and technology drivers of IT infrastructure evolution?*

The five stages of IT infrastructure evolution are the mainframe era, the personal computer era, the client/server era, the enterprise/Internet computing era, and the cloud computing era. Drivers include Moore's Law, the law of mass data storage, and Metcalfe's Law. Moore's Law deals with the exponential increase in processing power and decline in the cost of computer technology, stating that every 18 months the power of microprocessors doubles, implying that the price of computing falls in half. The Law of Mass Digital Storage deals with the exponential decrease in the cost of storing data, stating that the number of kilobytes of data that can be stored on magnetic media for $1 roughly doubles every 15 months.

Metcalfe's Law helps shows that a network's value to participants grows exponentially as the network takes on more members. Also driving exploding computer use is the rapid decline in costs of communication and growing agreement in the technology industry to use computing and communications standards.

3. *What are the current trends in computer hardware platforms?*

The emerging trends in mobile digital computing platform, grid computing, mobile platforms, on-demand cloud computing, and autonomic computing demonstrate that, increasingly, computing is taking place over a network. Grid computing involves connecting geographically remote computers into a single network to create a computational grid that combines the computing power of all the computers on the network with which to attack large computing problems. Cloud computing is a model of computing in which firms and individuals obtain computing power and software applications over the Internet, rather than purchasing and installing the hardware and software on their own computers. In autonomic computing, computer systems have capabilities for automatically configuring and repairing themselves.

Virtualization organizes computing resources so that their use is not restricted by physical configuration or geographic location. Server virtualization enables companies to run more than one operating system at the same time on one computer. A multicore processor is a microprocessor to which two or more processors have been attached for enhanced performance, reduced power consumption, and more efficient simultaneous processing of multiple tasks.

4. What are the current trends in software platforms?

Contemporary software platform trends include the growing use of Linux, open source software, Java and Ajax, Web services, mashups and widgets, and software outsourcing. Open source software is produced and maintained by a global community of programmers and is downloadable for free. Linux is a powerful, resilient open source operating system that can run on multiple hardware platforms and is used widely to run Web servers. Java is an operating-system and hardware-independent programming language that is the leading interactive programming environment for the Web. Ajax allows a client and server to exchange small pieces of data behind the scenes so that an entire Web page does not have to be reloaded each time the user requests a change.

Web services are loosely coupled software components based on open Web standards that are not product-specific and can work with any application software and operating system. They can be used as components of Web-based applications linking the systems of two different organizations or to link disparate systems of a single company. Mashups and widgets are the building blocks of new software applications and services based on the cloud computing model. Companies are purchasing their new software applications from outside sources, including software packages, by outsourcing custom application development to an external vendor (that may be offshore) or by renting software services (SaaS).

5. What are the challenges of managing IT infrastructure, and what are management solutions?

Major challenges include dealing with platform and infrastructure change, infrastructure management and governance, and making wise infrastructure investments. Solution guidelines include using a competitive forces model to determine how much to spend on IT infrastructure and where to make strategic infrastructure investments and establishing the total cost of ownership (TCO) of information technology assets. The total cost of owning technology resources includes not only the original cost of computer hardware and software but also costs for hardware and software upgrades, maintenance, technical support, and training.

Key Terms

Ajax, 155
Application server, 138
Autonomic computing, 151
Blade servers, 146
Clients, 138
Client/server computing, 138
Cloud computing, 139
Extensible Markup Language (XML), 155
Green computing, 153
Grid computing, 150
Hypertext Markup Language (HTML), 155
Java, 154
Legacy systems, 148
Linux, 147
Mainframe, 136
Mashups, 157

Minicomputers, 136
Moore's Law, 139
Multicore processor, 153
Multitiered (N-tier) client/server architectures, 138
Nanotechnology, 142
Netbooks, 149
On-demand computing, 150
Open source software, 154
Operating system, 147
Outsourcing, 158
Scalability, 161
Service-level agreement (SLA), 159
Server, 138
Service-oriented architecture (SOA), 156
Software as a Service (SaaS), 158

Software package, 158
Storage area networks (SANs), 147
Technology standards, 144
Total cost of ownership (TCO), 163
Unix, 147
Utility computing, 150
Virtualization, 153
Web browser, 155
Web hosting service, 148
Web server, 138
Web services, 155
Widgets, 157
Windows, 139
Wintel PC, 138

Review Questions

1. What is IT infrastructure and what are its components?

- Define IT infrastructure from both a technology and a services perspective.
- List and describe the components of IT infrastructure that firms need to manage.

2. What are the stages and technology drivers of IT infrastructure evolution?

- List each of the eras in IT infrastructure evolution, and describe its distinguishing characteristics.

- Define and describe the following: Web server, application server, multitiered client/server architecture.
- Describe Moore's Law and the Law of Mass Digital Storage. What is Metcalfe's Law?
- Describe how network economics, declining communications costs, and technology standards affect IT infrastructure.

3. What are the current trends in computer hardware platforms?
   - Describe the evolving mobile platform, grid computing, and cloud computing.
   - Explain how businesses can benefit from autonomic computing, virtualization, and multicore processors.

4. What are the current trends in software platforms?
   - Define and describe open source software and Linux, and explain their business benefits.

- Define Java and Ajax, and explain why they are important.
- Define and describe Web services and the role played by XML.
- Define and describe software mashups and widgets.
- Name and describe the three external sources for software.

5. What are the challenges of managing IT infrastructure, and what are management solutions?
   - Name and describe the management challenges posed by IT infrastructure.
   - Explain how using a competitive forces model and calculating the total cost of ownership (TCO) of technology assets help firms make good infrastructure investments.

Discussion Questions

1. Why is selecting computer hardware and software for the organization an important management decision? What management, organization, and technology issues should be considered when selecting computer hardware and software?

2. Should organizations use software service providers for all their software needs? Why or why not? What management, organization, and technology factors should be considered when making this decision?

Collaboration and Teamwork: Evaluating Server Operating Systems

Form a group with three or four of your classmates. One group should research and compare the capabilities and costs of Linux versus the most recent version of the Windows operating system for servers. Another group should research and compare the capabilities and costs of Linux versus Unix. If possible, use Google Sites to post links to Web pages, team communication announcements, and work assignments; to brainstorm; and to work collaboratively on project documents. Try to use Google Docs to develop a presentation of your findings for the class.

 Visit the MyMISLab Web site at **www.pearsoned.ca/mymislab.** This online homework and tutorial system puts you in control of your own learning with study and practice tools directly correlated to this chapter's content.

Learning Track Module

The following Learning Tracks provide content relevant to topics covered in this chapter:

1. How Computer Hardware and Software Work

2. Service-Level Agreements
3. The Open Source Software Initiative

HANDS-ON MIS Projects

The projects in this section give you hands-on experience in developing solutions for managing IT infrastructures and IT outsourcing, using spreadsheet software to evaluate alternative desktop systems and using Web research to budget for a sales conference.

Management Decision Problems

1. The University of Vancouver Medical Centre (UVMC)—a fictional medical centre—relies on information systems to operate 19 hospitals, a network of other care sites, and international and commercial ventures. Demand for additional servers and storage technology has been growing by 20 percent each year. UVMC was setting up a separate server for every application, and its servers and other computers were running a number of different operating systems, including several versions of Unix and Windows. UVMC had to manage technologies from many different vendors, including Hewlett-Packard (HP), Sun Microsystems, Microsoft, and IBM. Assess the impact of this situation on business performance. What factors and management decisions must be considered when developing a solution to this problem?

2. Qantas Airways, Australia's leading airline, faces cost pressures from high fuel prices and lower levels of global airline traffic. To remain competitive, the airline must find ways to keep costs low while providing a high level of customer service. Qantas had a 30-year-old data centre. Management had to decide whether to replace its IT infrastructure with newer technology or outsource it. What factors should be considered by Qantas' management when deciding whether to outsource? If Qantas decides to outsource, list and describe points that should be addressed in a service-level agreement.

Improving Decision Making: Using a Spreadsheet to Evaluate Hardware and Software Options

Software skills: Spreadsheet formulas
Business skills: Technology pricing

In this exercise, you will use spreadsheet software to calculate the cost of alternative desktop systems.

You have been asked to obtain pricing information on hardware and software for an office of 30 people. Using the Internet, get pricing for 30 PC desktop systems (monitors, computers, and keyboards) manufactured by Lenovo, Dell, and HP/Compaq as listed at their respective corporate Web sites. (For the purposes of this exercise, ignore the fact that desktop systems usually come with preloaded software packages.) Also obtain pricing on 15 desktop printers manufactured by Hewlett-Packard, Canon, and Dell. Each desktop system must satisfy the minimum specifications shown in the following table:

Minimum Desktop Specifications

Processor speed	Dual-core 2 GHz
Hard drive	250 GB
RAM	3 GB
DVD-ROM drive	16 x
Monitor (diagonal measurement)	17 inches

Each desktop printer must satisfy the minimum specifications shown in the following table:

Minimum Monochrome Printer Specifications

Print speed (black and white)	20 pages per minute
Print resolution	600 × 600
Network-ready?	Yes
Maximum price/unit	$700

After pricing the desktop systems and printers, obtain pricing on 30 copies of the most recent versions of Microsoft Office, Lotus SmartSuite, and Sun Star Office desktop productivity packages and on 30 copies of Microsoft Windows Vista Business. The application software suite packages come in various versions, so be sure that each package contains programs for word processing, spreadsheet analysis, database analysis, graphics preparation, and e-mail.

Prepare a spreadsheet showing your research results for the desktop systems, printers, and software. Use your spreadsheet software to determine the desktop system, printer, and software combination that will offer both the best performance and pricing per worker. Because every two workers will share one printer (15 printers/30 systems), assume only half a printer cost per worker in the spreadsheet. Assume that your company will take the standard warranty and service contract offered by each product's manufacturer.

Improving Decision Making: Using Web Research to Budget for a Sales Conference

Software skills: Internet-based software
Business skills: Researching transportation and lodging costs

In this exercise, you will use software at various online travel sites to arrange transportation and lodging for a large sales force to attend a sales conference at two alternative locations. You will use that information to calculate total travel and lodging costs and decide where to hold the conference.

The fictional Foremost Composite Materials Company is planning a two-day sales conference for October 15–16, starting with a reception on the evening of October 14. The conference consists of all-day meetings that the entire sales force, numbering 125 sales representatives and their 16 managers, must attend. Each sales representative requires his or her own room, and the company needs two common meeting rooms, one large enough to hold the entire sales force plus a few visitors (200) and the other able to hold half the force. Management has set a budget of $105 000 for the representatives' room rentals. The hotel must also have such services as overhead and computer projectors as well as a business centre and banquet facilities. It also should have facilities for the company representatives to be able to work in their rooms and to enjoy themselves in a swimming pool or gym facility. The company would like to hold the conference in either Whistler, BC or Montreal, QC.

Foremost usually likes to hold such meetings in Hilton- or Marriott-owned hotels. Use the Hilton and Marriott Web sites to select a hotel in whichever of these cities would enable the company to hold its sales conference within its budget.

Link to the two sites' home pages, and search them to find a hotel that meets Foremost's sales conference requirements. Once you have selected the hotel, locate flights arriving the afternoon prior to the conference because the attendees will need to check in the day before and attend your reception the evening prior to the conference. Your attendees will be coming from Toronto (54), Vancouver (32), Quebec City (22), Edmonton (19), and Winnipeg (14). Determine costs of each airline ticket from these cities. When you are finished, create a budget for the conference. The budget will include the cost of each airline ticket, the room cost, and $60 per attendee per day for food.

1. What was your final budget?
2. Which did you select as the best hotel for the sales conference and why?

CASE STUDY | Amazon's New Store: Utility Computing

Looking for a good deal on that DVD box set of *The West Wing* or the last *Harry Potter* book? Since opening as an online bookstore in 1995, Amazon.com has morphed into a virtual superstore with product offerings in 36 categories, including furniture, jewellery, clothing, and groceries. But what if what you really need is a place to store several terabytes of data? Or the computing power of 100 Linux servers? Now you can get those from Amazon too.

Over its first 12 years, Amazon.com committed $2 billion to refine the information technology infrastructure that was largely responsible for making it the top online retailer in the world. Following the burst of the dot-com bubble in 2001, Amazon focused heavily on modernizing its data centres and software so that it could add new features to its product pages such as discussion forums and software for audio and video.

In March 2006, Amazon introduced the first of several new services that founder Jeff Bezos hoped would transform its future business. With Simple Storage Service (S3) and later Elastic Compute Cloud (EC2), Amazon entered the cloud utility computing market. The company had realized that the benefits of its $2 billion investment in technology could also be valuable to other companies.

Amazon had tremendous computing capacity, but like most companies, used only a small portion of it at any one time. Moreover, the Amazon infrastructure was considered by many to be among the most robust in the world. So, the one-time bookseller exposed the guts of its entire system over the Internet to any developer who could make use of it. Amazon began to sell its computing power on a per-usage basis, just as a power company sells electricity.

S3 is a data storage service that is designed to make Web-scale computing easier and more affordable for developers. Customers pay 15 cents per gigabyte of data stored per month on Amazon's network of disk drives. There is also a charge of 20 cents per gigabyte of data transferred. The service has neither a minimum fee nor a startup charge. Customers pay for exactly what they use and no more. Data may be stored as objects ranging in size from 1 byte to 5 gigabytes, with an unlimited number of objects permitted. Using S3 does not require any client software, nor does it require the user to set up any hardware. Amazon designed S3 to provide a fast, simple, and inexpensive method for businesses to store data on a system that is scalable and reliable. S3 promises 99.99 percent availability through a mechanism of fault tolerance that fixes failures without any downtime.

Working in conjunction with S3, EC2 enables businesses to utilize Amazon's servers for computing tasks, such as testing software. Using EC2 incurs charges of 10 cents per instance-hour consumed. An instance supplies the user with the equivalent of a 1.7 GHz x86 processor with 1.75 GB of RAM, a 160 GB hard drive, and 250 megabits per second of bandwidth on the network. The service also includes 20 cents per GB of data traffic inbound and outbound per month, as well as the standard S3 pricing for storing an Amazon Machine Image (AMI), which contains the applications, libraries, data, and configuration settings that a business uses to run its processes.

According to Adam Selipsky, vice president of product management and developer relations for Amazon Web Services (AWS), Amazon is really a technology company that can bring a wealth of engineering prowess and experience to independent developers and corporations by allowing them to run their processes on Amazon's computer systems. Selipsky also emphasizes that AWS is not simply about providing great amounts of storage capacity and server time. AWS creates the opportunity for others to work at Web scale without making the mistakes that Amazon has already made and learned from. *Simplicity* and *ease of use* are not generally terms that go along with building a Web-scale application, but they are major selling points for AWS. Users build on the services through Application Programming Interfaces (APIs) made available by Amazon.

From the very beginning, customers have responded strongly to S3 and EC2. Bezos targeted micro-sized businesses and Web startups as customers for AWS, but the services have also attracted some mid-size businesses and potential big players in e-business.

MileMeter Inc. is a Dallas-based startup that plans to sell auto insurance by the mile. It initially ran its own server in a data centre but moved most of its applications onto "virtual" computers in Amazon's EC2. CEO Chris Gay said, "I don't need to have a systems administrator or a network administrator. I don't have to worry about hardware becoming irrelevant."

Webmail.us provides e-mail management services for thousands of companies around the world from its

Blacksburg, Virginia, headquarters. When the company needed to increase its short-term storage capacity and the redundancy of its primary data backups, it selected S3 as its storage provider. Webmail.us sends more than a terabyte of data to Amazon to store with S3 every week. Bill Boebel, cofounder and chief technology officer of Webmail.us, was very pleased that his company was able to create a simple interface with which Amazon can accept the abundant small files that his company manages. Other backup systems have had difficulty handling the typical Webmail.us backup load, and most hosting companies would require a custom application to handle such data. Webmail.us even used EC2 to develop its storage interface. According to CEO Pat Matthews, Amazon immediately reduced his company's data backup costs by 75 percent.

Powerset is an up-and-coming search engine company based in San Francisco that wants to focus its time and the $15.25 million it has raised on its core business, natural language search technology. By using S3 and EC2, Powerset saves upfront cash expenditures and eliminates the risk that building an infrastructure will take longer than expected. Many of the traditional utility computing suppliers charge around one dollar per CPU hour, or ten times what Amazon charges.

Powerset's CEO Barney Pell says that the pay-as-you go model is very important because his company does not know how fast it will grow. What he does know is that the demand for Powerset's service will come in bursts, and trying to predict hardware needs is a dangerous game. If Powerset overestimates its peak usage capacity, the company will waste money on unnecessary hardware. If the company underestimates peak usage, it could fail to meet its users' expectations and damage its business. With AWS in place, Powerset never has to worry about being unable to add computing power when a spike in usage occurs.

SmugMug Inc., an online photo-sharing startup, was immediately drawn to the ease with which it could back up photos on Amazon's S3. Storing its users' photos on Amazon's devices prevents SmugMug from having to purchase its own additional storage and saved the company $1 million during the first year it used Amazon's services.

As with any large business initiative, there are issues for Amazon to confront before anyone can declare AWS to be a successful venture. Larger businesses may be more inclined to use a more established company, especially one with more experience hosting core applications and data. Currently, Amazon's flexible, pay-as-you-go model gives the company a competitive advantage over companies that require service contracts.

However, according to Daniel Golding, vice president of Tier 1 Research, the established companies, such as IBM, Hewlett-Packard, and Sun Microsystems, may follow Amazon's lead and offer utility computing without service-level agreements (SLAs). Complicating the matter is that some companies are wary of using a supplier that does not offer SLAs, which guarantee the availability of services in terms of time. Golding suggests that Amazon may have launched a major shift in the industry, but others may reap the rewards while Amazon may suffer for it.

One more challenge for Amazon is the viability of AWS itself. Will the services actually function as planned? The company's track record with new technology projects is mixed. Amazon launched its A9.com search site with much fanfare, but the site never really caught on with users. Moreover, the growth of AWS could be harmful to Amazon's Web services line as well as to its retail line if Amazon does not position itself to handle a dramatic increase in demand on its infrastructure. AWS customers could drop the service, and Amazon.com could falter.

In January 2007, February 2008, and July 2008, Amazon's S3 servers experienced significant outages, with service lost for eight hours in July. The January 2007 problem was caused by faulty hardware installed during an upgrade, and it was resolved quickly. The July 2008 outage was more problematic. Amazon reported that components were unable to interact properly due to a problem with "internal system communications." Amazon promised to provide a fuller explanation once it determined the root cause. Some users were critical and questioned whether Amazon was capable of being their solution for hosted storage going forward.

AWS has charmed some high-profile clients. Microsoft uses S3 to increase software download speeds for its users. Linden Lab, creator of the online virtual world Second Life, uses the service to alleviate the pounding its servers take when the company releases its frequent software upgrades. The Nasdaq stock exchange uses S3 to host data for Nasdaq Market Replay, an application that lets companies play back historical market data in real time. However, Nasdaq is reluctant to use an online service for transactional or highly secure data.

For Canadians wishing to use Amazon's Web services and S3 architecture and applications, Amazon presents a double-edged sword. The services appear to have great potential, but issues such as currency and tax conversion and transborder data laws (see Chapter 4) and regulations may prevent Canadian companies from using Amazon's service because its servers and services are all resident in the United States, not in Canada.

To better support large accounts, Amazon started round-the-clock phone support and credits if S3 availability falls below 99.99 percent in a single month. For now, the potential of AWS is being converted into performance mostly by tech-savvy developers with financial backing. More than 370 000 developers, ranging from individuals to large companies, have signed up. As more developers contribute and the services evolve, Amazon hopes one day to make it possible for anyone with an idea and an Internet connection to begin to put together the next Amazon.com.

CASE STUDY QUESTIONS:

1. What technology services does Amazon provide? What are the business advantages to Amazon and to subscribers of these services? What are the disadvantages to each? What kinds of businesses are likely to benefit from these services?

2. How do the concepts of capacity planning, scalability, and TCO apply to this case? Apply these concepts both to Amazon and to subscribers of its services.

3. Search the Internet for companies that supply utility computing. Select two or three such companies, and compare them to Amazon. What services do these companies provide? What promises do they make about availability? What is their payment model? Who is their target client? If you were launching a Web startup business, would you choose one of these companies over Amazon for Web services? Why or why not? Would your answer change if you were working for a larger company and had to make a recommendation to the CTO?

4. Name three examples of IT infrastructure hardware components and software components that are relevant to this case. Describe how these components fit into or are used by Amazon's Web services and/or the customers that subscribe to these services.

5. Think of an idea for a Web-based startup business. Explain how this business could utilize Amazon's S3 and EC2 services.

6. What are the legal, ethical, and privacy issues for Canadian businesses that might want to use the AWS and S3 services offered by Amazon? How would that affect the potential for these services in Canada? Is there a solution to this problem?

Sources: Thomas Claburn, "Amazon's S3 Cloud Service Turns into a Puff of Smoke," *InformationWeek*, July 28, 2008; Chris Preimesberger, "Perils in the Cloud," *eWeek*, August 4, 2008; Jessica Mintz, "Amazon's Hot New Item: Its Data Center," Associated Press, February 1, 2008; J. Nicholas Hoover, "Ahead in the Cloud: Google, Others Expand Online Services," *InformationWeek*, April 14, 2008; J. Nicholas Hoover and Richard Martin, "Demystifying the Cloud," *InformationWeek*, June 23, 2008; Edward Cone, "Amazon at Your Service," *CIO Insight*, January 7, 2007; Robert D. Hof, "So You Wanna Be a Web Tycoon? Amazon Can Help," **www.webworkerdaily.com**, January 24, 2007; and Thomas Claburn, "Open Source Developers Build on Amazon Web Services," TechWeb.com, January 12, 2007.

CHAPTER 6

Databases and Information Management

LEARNING OBJECTIVES

After reading this chapter, you will be able to answer the following questions:

1. What are the problems of managing data resources in a traditional file environment, and how are they solved by a database management system?

2. What are the major capabilities of database management systems (DBMS), and why is a relational DBMS so powerful?

3. What are some important principles of database design?

4. What are the principal tools and technologies for accessing information from databases to improve business performance and decision making?

5. Why are information policy, data administration, and data quality assurance essential for managing a firm's data resources?

OPENING CASE

Can HP Mine Success from an Enterprise Data Warehouse?

Hewlett-Packard (HP) is one of the world's largest vendors of information technology, including personal computers, server computers, printers, and consulting services. Although the company had considerable systems expertise to sell to other companies, it was bedeviled by information technology problems of its own. HP had plenty of data, but they were stored in multiple applications and data repositories across departments, business units, and geographic locations. HP's numerous systems and applications were unable to deliver the information the company needed for a complete and consistent picture of its business operations.

CEO Mark Hurd had difficulty collecting and analyzing "consistent, timely data spanning different parts of the business." Some systems tracked sales and pricing by product, while others tracked sales

information geographically. Commonly used financial information such as gross margins to measure profitability were calculated differently from business unit to business unit. Corporate management was obtaining information from more than 750 separate sources of data throughout the company.

Lack of data consistency dragged down sales and profits. Compiling information about the business from various systems could take up to a week, so managers had to make decisions based on relatively stale data. Seemingly simple questions, such as how much the company was spending on marketing across its different businesses, were difficult to answer. Without a consistent view of the enterprise, senior executives struggled with decisions on matters such as the size of sales and service teams assigned to particular systems.

Management clearly needed better information.

HP management decided the solution was to build a data warehouse with a single global enterprise-wide database of shareable information that delivers a unified, accurate vision of the business. The data warehouse replaces 17 different database technologies and unites 14 000 databases currently in use, giving HP's workforce access to data in real time with no departmental or geographic boundaries.

In November 2005, HP CIO Randy Mott created a team to model the enterprise-wide database that would be the foundation of the data warehouse. They developed a way of modeling data across the entire company and ensuring that the data would always be up to date, consistent for the entire enterprise, and complete. HP developed its own proprietary

HP Neoview enterprise data warehouse platform
— the future of Business Intelligence

» Large Enterprise Business

» Business & IT services
» Solutions
» Technologies
» Partners
» Support & Drivers
» Business Technology
» TV, News & Library
» HP-UX 11i

Improving merchandise performance and customer satisfaction are the core objectives of the company. IT must apply technology wisely, to serve the business and support those objectives. That's why we chose the Neoview platform—and so far, it has exceeded our expectations.

Jim Lance, CIO, Bon-Ton Stores

» Learn more

Teradata Transition Program
»» Learn more

»» Seize the gold.
BI on HP Neoview

HP CIO and Neoview = better business outcomes
»» See the video

News and announcements

Capitalizing on information for better business outcomes

Lower cost: HP delivers massive scale, complex mixed workload, high concurrency and continuous availability to help you keep your competitive advantage

Mitigate risk: HP is a trusted BI partner leveraging industry-standards, proven techniques and pre-packaged solutions

Drive revenue: by turning data into usable, shareable information available in real time

» Teradata Transition Program
» Press release and virtual press kit
» Media coverage
» What the analysts are saying
» HP Neoview webcasts
» Business Technology

New product, solutions, services and partners

Platform	Solutions	Services and partners
» HP Neoview platform	» Business Intelligence	» HP Neoview Services
» See the data sheet	» Communications	» HP BI Services
» Download the brochure	» Financial Services	» HP Neoview BI Partners

platform for the warehouse, consisting of an integrated set of servers, storage, operating system, database management system (DBMS) and software for querying and reporting, all optimized for data warehousing. HP's data warehouse platform proved so successful that the company decided to sell it to other companies as a "data warehouse appliance" product called Neoview. Upon completion, HP's data warehouse contained over 400 terabytes of data and was being utilized by 50 000 HP workers. All of HP's financial data are accessible via the data warehouse.

HP's efforts appear to be paying off. The company is now able to perform 12 times the number of data queries, updates, and other transactions in its financial database over a three-month period than before it implemented the data warehouse. (One month's transactions peaked at nearly 50 billion.) HP can track how much it spends on marketing across all of its business units, spending by media sector and customer segment, worldwide, or by country. The company was unable to do these things before. The information helps HP management make better decisions about where to spend to get the biggest bang.

Sources: Doug Henschen,"HP Upgrades Neoview Data Warehouse Appliance," *Intelligent Enterprise,* June 2008; "HP Neoview Enterprise Data Warehouse," **www.hp.com**, accessed June 8, 2008; Christopher Lawton, "Data, Data Everywhere," *The Wall Street Journal,* September 24, 2007; and John Foley, "Inside Hewlett-Packard's Data Warehouse Gamble," *InformationWeek,* January 6, 2007.

HP's experience illustrates the importance of data management and database systems for business. The company was unable to fully understand how it was performing as a company or how to make timely decisions because its data were redundant, inconsistent, and fragmented among many different systems and applications. How businesses store, organize, and manage their data has a tremendous impact on organizational effectiveness.

The chapter-opening diagram calls attention to important points raised by this case and this chapter. HP's corporate data had been stored in a number of different databases where they could not be easily retrieved and analyzed. Management determined that profitability and efficiency were curtailed because it could not obtain consistent, company-wide information for measuring business performance. It authorized a team to develop a company-wide model of its data using company-wide standards and business rules for defining, organizing, and accessing the data. It chose to develop its own data warehousing technology for integrating the data from all of its disparate sources into a single comprehensive database, storing the data, organizing the data, and providing tools for making the data easily accessible to large numbers of employees for querying and reporting. By creating a data model for a single view of the company and a database reflecting this model for company-wide querying and reporting, HP has become much more efficient and its managers are making better decisions.

6.1 Organizing Data in a Traditional File Environment

An effective information system provides users with accurate, timely, and relevant information. Accurate information is free of errors. Information is timely when it is available to decision makers when it is needed. Information is relevant when it is useful and appropriate for the types of work and decisions that require it.

You might be surprised to learn that many businesses do not have timely, accurate, or relevant information because the data in their information systems have been poorly organized and maintained. That is why data management is so essential. To understand the problem, let us look how information systems arrange data in computer files and traditional methods of file management.

File Organization Terms and Concepts

A computer system organizes data in a hierarchy that starts with bits and bytes and progresses to fields, records, files, and databases (see Figure 6-1). A bit represents the smallest unit of data a computer can handle. A group of bits, called a byte, represents a single character, which can be a letter, a number, or another symbol. A grouping of characters into a word, a group of words, or a complete number (such as a person's name or age) is called a **field**. A group of related fields, such as a student's name, the course taken, date, and grade, comprises a **record**; a group of records of the same type is called a **file**.

For example, the records in Figure 6-1 could constitute a student course file. A group of related files makes up a **database**. The student course file illustrated in Figure 6-1 could be grouped with files on students' personal histories and financial backgrounds to create a student database.

A record describes an entity. An **entity** is a person, place, thing, or event about which we store and maintain information. Each characteristic or quality describing a particular entity is called an **attribute**. For example, Student_ID, Course, Date, and Grade are attributes of the entity COURSE. The specific values that these attributes can have are found in the fields of the record describing the entity COURSE.

Field
Record
File
Database
Entity
Attribute

FIGURE 6-1   The data hierarchy.

A computer system organizes data in a hierarchy that starts with the bit, which represents either a 0 or a 1. Bits can be grouped to form a byte to represent one character, number, or symbol. Bytes can be grouped to form a field, and related fields can be grouped to form a record. Related records can be collected to form a file, and related files can be organized into a database.

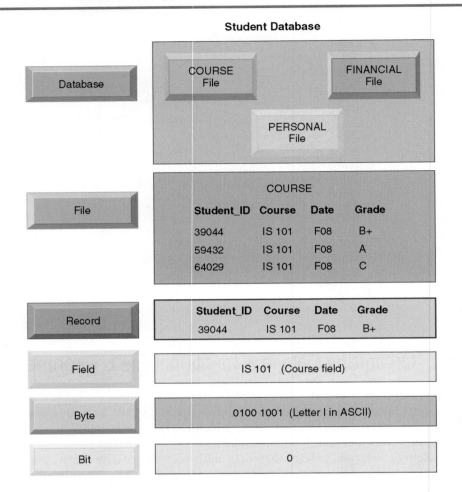

Problems with the Traditional File Environment

In most organizations, systems tended to grow independently without a company-wide plan. Often, accounting, finance, manufacturing, human resources, and sales and marketing each developed their own systems and data files. Figure 6-2 illustrates the traditional approach to information processing.

Each application, of course, required its own files and its own computer program to operate. For example, the human resources functional area might have a personnel master file, a payroll file, an extended health insurance file, a pension file, a mailing list file, and so forth until tens, perhaps hundreds, of files and programs existed. In the company as a whole, this process led to multiple master files created, maintained, and operated by separate divisions or departments. As this process continues for five or ten years, the organization is saddled with hundreds of programs and applications that are very difficult to maintain and manage. The resulting problems are data redundancy and inconsistency, program-data dependence, inflexibility, poor data security, and an inability to share data among applications.

Data Redundancy and Inconsistency **Data redundancy** is the presence of duplicate data in multiple data files so that the same data are stored in more than one place or location. Data redundancy occurs when different groups in an organization independently collect the same piece of data and store it independently of each other. Data redundancy wastes storage resources and also leads to **data inconsistency**, where the same attribute

Data redundancy

Data inconsistency

FIGURE 6-2   Traditional file processing.

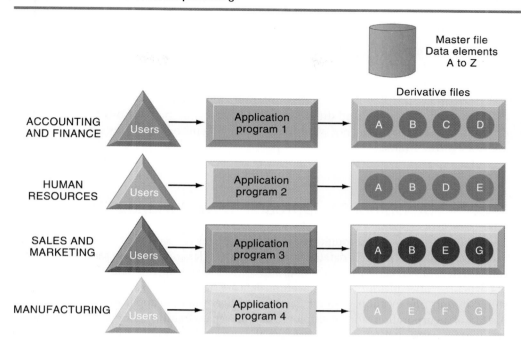

The use of a traditional approach to file processing encourages each functional area in a corporation to develop specialized applications. Each application requires a unique data file that is likely to be a subset of the master file. These subsets of the master file lead to data redundancy and inconsistency, processing inflexibility, and wasted storage resources.

may have different values. For example, in instances of the entity COURSE illustrated in Figure 6-1, the Date field may be updated in some systems but not in others. The same attribute, Student_ID, may also have different names in different systems throughout the organization. Some systems might use Student_ID, and others might use ID, for example.

Additional confusion might result from using different coding systems to represent values for an attribute. For instance, the sales, inventory, and manufacturing systems of a clothing retailer might use different codes to represent clothing size. One system might represent clothing size as "extra large" while another might use the code "XL" for the same purpose. The resulting confusion would make it difficult for companies to create customer relationship management, supply chain management, or enterprise systems that integrate data from different sources.

Program-Data Dependence **Program-data dependence** refers to the coupling of data stored in files and the specific programs required to update and maintain those files so that changes in programs require changes to the data. Every traditional computer program has to describe the location and nature of the data with which it works. In a traditional file environment, any change in a software program could require a change in the data accessed by that program. One program might be modified from a six-character postal code to a seven-character postal code to incorporate the space between the first three characters and the last three. If the original data file were changed from six character to seven character codes, then other programs that required the six-character postal code would no longer work properly. These changes could cost millions of dollars to implement properly.

Lack of Flexibility A traditional file system can deliver routine scheduled reports after extensive programming efforts, but it cannot deliver ad hoc reports or respond to unanticipated information requirements in a timely fashion. The information required by ad hoc requests is somewhere in the system but may be too expensive to retrieve. Several programmers might have to work for weeks to put together the required data items in a new file.

Program-data dependence

Poor Security Because there is little control or management of data, access to and dissemination of information may be out of control. Management may have no way of knowing who is accessing or even making changes to the organization's data.

Lack of Data Sharing and Availability Because pieces of information in different files and different parts of the organization cannot be related to one another, it is virtually impossible for information to be shared or accessed in a timely manner. Information cannot flow freely across different functional areas or different parts of the organization. If users find different values of the same piece of information in two different systems, they may not want to use these systems because they cannot trust the accuracy of their data.

6.2 The Database Approach to Data Management

Database technology cuts through many of the problems of traditional file organization. A more rigorous definition of a database is a collection of data organized to serve many applications efficiently by centralizing the data and controlling redundant data. Rather than storing data in separate files for each application, data are stored so as to appear to users as being stored in only one location. A single database services multiple applications. For example, instead of a corporation storing employee data in separate information systems and separate files for personnel, payroll, and benefits, the corporation could create a single common human resources database.

Database Management Systems

A **database management system (DBMS)** is software that permits an organization to centralize data, manage them efficiently, and provide access to the stored data by application programs. The DBMS acts as an interface between application programs and the physical data files. When the application program calls for a data item, such as gross pay, the DBMS finds this item in the database and presents it to the application program. Using traditional data files, the programmer would have to specify the size and format of each data element used in the program and then tell the computer where they were located.

The DBMS relieves the programmer or end user from the task of understanding where and how the data are actually stored by separating the logical and physical views of the data. The *logical view* presents data as they would be perceived by end users or business specialists while the *physical view* shows how data are actually organized and structured on physical storage media.

The database management software makes the physical database available for different logical views required by users. For example, for the human resources database illustrated in Figure 6-3, a benefits specialist might require a view consisting of the employee's name, social insurance number, and extended health insurance coverage. A payroll department member might need data such as the employee's name, social insurance number, gross pay, and net pay. The data for all these views are stored in a single database where they can be more easily managed by the organization.

How a DBMS Solves the Problems of the Traditional File Environment A DBMS reduces data redundancy and inconsistency by minimizing isolated files in which the same data are repeated. The DBMS may not enable the organization to eliminate data redundancy entirely, but it can help control redundancy. Even if the organization maintains some redundant data, using a DBMS eliminates data inconsistency because the DBMS can help the organization ensure that every occurrence of redundant data has the same value. The DBMS uncouples programs and data, enabling data to stand on their own. Access and availability of information will be increased, and program development and maintenance costs will be reduced because users and programmers can perform ad

Database management
system (DBMS)

FIGURE 6-3   Human resources database with multiple views.

A single human resources database provides many different views of data, depending on the information requirements of the user. Illustrated here are two possible views, one of interest to a benefits specialist and one of interest to a member of the company's payroll department.

hoc queries of data in the database. The DBMS enables the organization to centrally manage data, their use, and their security.

Relational DBMSs Contemporary DBMSs use different database models to keep track of entities, attributes, and relationships. The most popular type of DBMS today for PCs as well as for larger computers and mainframes is the **relational DBMS**. Relational databases represent data as two-dimensional tables (called *relations* or *tuples*). Tables are also referred to as *files*. Each table contains data on an entity and its attributes. Microsoft Access is a relational DBMS for desktop systems while DB2, Oracle Database, and Microsoft SQL Server are relational DBMSs for large mainframes and mid-range computers. MySQL is a popular open source DBMS, and Oracle Database Lite is a DBMS for small handheld computing devices.

Let us look at how a relational database organizes data about suppliers and parts (see Figure 6-4). The database has separate tables for the entity SUPPLIER and for the entity PART. Each table consists of a grid of columns and rows of data. Each individual element of data for each entity is stored as a separate field, and each field represents an attribute for that entity. Fields in a relational database are also called columns. For the entity SUPPLIER, the supplier name, street, city, province, and postal code are stored as a separate fields within the SUPPLIER table, and each field represents an attribute for the entity SUPPLIER.

The actual information about a single supplier that resides in a table is called a *row*. Rows are commonly referred to as *records*, or in technical terms, as **tuples**. Data for the entity PART have their own separate table.

The field for Supplier_Number in the SUPPLIER table uniquely identifies each record so that so the record can be retrieved, updated, or sorted, This is called a **key field**. Each table in a relational database has one field that is designated as its **primary key**. This key field is the unique identifier for all the information in any row of the table, and this primary key cannot be duplicated. Supplier_Number is the primary key for the SUPPLIER table, and Part_Number is the primary key for the PART table. Note that Supplier_Number appears in both the SUPPLIER and PART tables. In the SUPPLIER table, Supplier_Number is the primary key. When the field Supplier_Number appears in the PART table, it is called a **foreign key** and is essentially a lookup field to look up data about the supplier of a specific part.

Operations of a Relational DBMS Relational database tables can be combined easily to deliver data required by users, provided that any two tables share a common data element. Suppose we wanted to find in this database the names and addresses of suppliers that

Relational DBMS
Tuples
Key field
Primary key
Foreign key

FIGURE 6-4   Relational database tables.

A relational database organizes data in the form of two-dimensional tables. Illustrated here are tables for the entities SUPPLIER and PART showing how they represent each entity and its attributes. Supplier_Number is a primary key for the SUPPLIER table and a foreign key for the PART table.

could provide us with part number 137 or part number 150. We would need information from two tables: the SUPPLIER table and the PART table. Note that these two files have a shared data element: Supplier_Number.

In a relational database, three basic operations, as shown in Figure 6-5, are used to develop useful sets of data: select, join, and project. The *select* operation creates a subset consisting of all records in the file that meet stated criteria. Select creates, in other words, a subset of rows that meet certain criteria. In our example, we want to select records (rows) from the PART table where the Part_Number equals 137 or 150. The *join* operation combines relational tables to provide the user with more information than is available in individual tables. In our example, we want to join the now-shortened PART table (only parts 137 or 150 will be presented) and the SUPPLIER table into a single new table.

The *project* operation creates a subset consisting of columns in a table, permitting the user to create new tables that contain only the information required. In our example, we want to extract from the new table only the following columns: Part_Number, Part_Name, Supplier_Number, and Supplier_Name.

Object-Oriented DBMSs Many newer applications require databases that can store and retrieve not only structured numbers and characters but also drawings, images, photographs, audio, and full-motion video. DBMSs designed for organizing structured data

FIGURE 6-5   The three basic operations of a relational DBMS.

PART

Part_Number	Part_Name	Unit_Price	Supplier_Number
137	Door latch	22.00	8259
145	Side mirror	12.00	8444
150	Door moulding	6.00	8263
152	Door lock	31.00	8259
155	Compressor	54.00	8261
178	Door handle	10.00	8259

Select Part_Number = 137 or 150

SUPPLIER

Supplier_Number	Supplier_Name	Supplier_Street	Supplier_City	Supplier_Province	Supplier_PC
8259	CBM Inc.	74 5th Avenue	Saint John	NB	E2M 5T3
8261	B. R. Molds	1277 Gandolly Street	Calgary	AB	T2E 0B3
8263	Jackson Components	8233 Micklin Street	Hamilton	ON	L9H 7M4
8444	Bryant Corporation	4315 Mill Drive	Richmond	BC	V7E 3M1

Join by Supplier_Number

Part_Number	Part_Name	Supplier_Number	Supplier_Name
137	Door latch	8259	CBM Inc.
150	Door moulding	8263	Jackson Components

Project selected columns

The select, join, and project operations enable data from two different tables to be combined and only selected attributes to be displayed.

into rows and columns are not well suited to handling graphics-based or multimedia applications; object-oriented databases are better suited for this purpose.

An **object-oriented DBMS** stores the data and procedures that act on those data as objects that can be automatically retrieved and shared. Object-oriented database management systems (OODBMSs) are becoming popular because they can be used to manage the various multimedia components or Java applets used in Web applications, which typically integrate pieces of information from a variety of sources.

Although object-oriented databases can store more complex types of information than relational DBMSs, they are relatively slow compared with relational DBMSs for processing large numbers of transactions. Hybrid **object-relational DBMSs** are now available to provide the capabilities of both object-oriented and relational DBMSs.

Capabilities of Database Management Systems

A DBMS includes capabilities and tools for organizing, managing, and accessing the data in the database. The most important are its data definition language, data dictionary, and data manipulation language.

DBMSs have a **data definition** capability to specify the structure of the content of the database. It is used to create database tables and to define the characteristics of the fields in each table. This information about the database is documented in a **data dictionary**, an automated or manual file that stores definitions of data elements and their characteristics.

Microsoft Access has a rudimentary data dictionary capability that displays information about the name, description, size, type, format, and other properties of each field in a table (see Figure 6-6). Data dictionaries for large corporate databases may capture additional information, such as usage; ownership (who in the organization is responsible for maintaining the data); authorization; security; and the individuals, business functions, programs, and reports that use each data element.

Querying and Reporting DBMSs include tools for accessing and manipulating information in databases. Most DBMSs have a specialized language called a **data manipulation language** that is used to add, change, delete, and retrieve the data in the database. This language contains commands that permit end users and programming specialists to extract data from the database to satisfy information requests and develop applications. The most prominent data manipulation language today is **Structured Query Language**,

Object-oriented DBMS
Object-relational DBMS
Data definition
Data dictionary
Data manipulation language
Structured Query Language (SQL)

FIGURE 6-6   Microsoft Access data dictionary features.

Microsoft Access has a rudimentary data dictionary capability that displays information about the size, format, and other characteristics of each field in a database. Displayed here is the information maintained in the SUPPLIER table. The small key icon to the left of Supplier_Number indicates that it is a key field.

or **SQL**. Figure 6-7 illustrates the SQL query that would produce the table resulting from our query in Figure 6-8. You can find out more about how to perform SQL queries in our Learning Tracks for this chapter.

Users of DBMSs for large and mid-range computers, such as DB2, Oracle, or SQL Server, employ SQL to retrieve information they need from the database. Microsoft Access also uses SQL, but it provides its own set of user-friendly tools for querying databases and for organizing data from databases into more polished reports.

In Microsoft Access, you will find the Query Wizard and Query Design View features that enable users to create queries by identifying the tables and fields they want and the results, and then selecting the rows from the database that meet particular criteria. These actions in turn are translated behind the scenes into SQL commands. Figure 6-7 illustrates how the same query as the SQL query to select parts and suppliers would be constructed using the Query Design View.

Microsoft Access and other DBMSs include capabilities for report generation so that the data of interest can be displayed in a more structured and polished format than would be possible just by querying. Crystal Reports is a popular report generator for large corporate DBMSs although it can also be used with Access. Access also has capabilities for developing desktop system applications. These include tools for creating data entry screens, reports, and developing the logic for processing transactions.

FIGURE 6-7   Example of an SQL query.

Illustrated here are the SQL statements for a query to select suppliers for parts 137 or 150. They produce a list with the same results as Figure 6-4.

SELECT PART.Part_Number, PART.Part_Name, SUPPLIER.Supplier_Number, SUPPLIER.Supplier_Name
FROM PART, SUPPLIER
WHERE PART.Supplier_Number = SUPPLIER.Supplier_Number AND
Part_Number = 137 OR Part_Number = 150;

FIGURE 6-8   An access query.

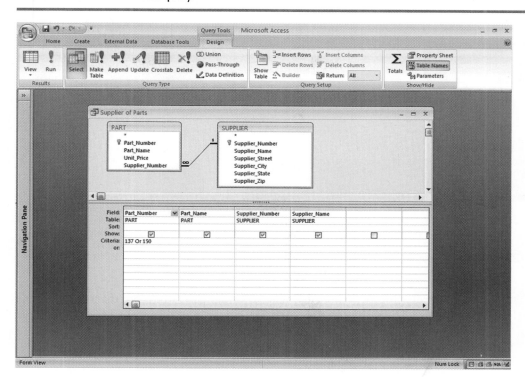

Illustrated here is how the query in Figure 6-7 would be constructed using Microsoft Access query-building tools. It shows the tables, fields, and selection criteria used for the query.

Designing Databases

To create a database, you must understand the relationships among the data, the type of data that will be maintained in the database, how the data will be used, and how the organization will need to change to manage data from a company-wide perspective. The database requires both a conceptual design and a physical design. The conceptual, or logical, design of a database is an abstract model of the database from a business perspective while the physical design shows how the database is actually arranged on direct-access storage devices.

Normalization and Entity-Relationship Diagrams The conceptual database design describes how the data elements in the database are to be grouped. The design process identifies relationships among data elements and the most efficient way of grouping data elements together to meet business information requirements. The process also identifies redundant data elements and the groupings of data elements required for specific application programs. Groups of data are organized, refined, and streamlined until an overall logical view of the relationships among all the data elements in the database emerges.

To use a relational database model effectively, complex groupings of data must be streamlined to minimize redundant data elements and awkward many-to-many relationships. The process of creating small, stable, yet flexible and adaptive data structures from complex groups of data is called **normalization**. Figures 6-9 and 6-10 illustrate this process.

Normalization

FIGURE 6-9   An unnormalized relation for order.

ORDER (Before Normalization)

Order_Number	Order_Date	Part_Number	Part_Name	Unit_Price	Part_Quantity	Supplier_Number	Supplier_Name	Supplier_Street	Supplier_City	Supplier_Province	Supplier_PC

An unnormalized relation contains repeating groups. For example, there can be many parts and suppliers for each order. There is only a one-to-one correspondence between Order_Number and Order_Date.

FIGURE 6-10   Normalized tables created from order.

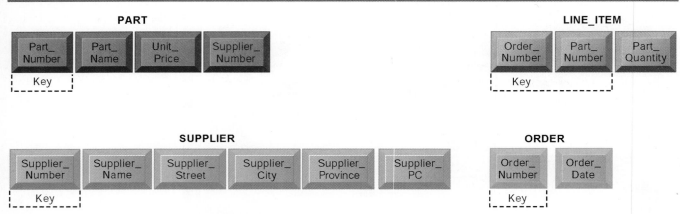

After normalization, the original relation ORDER has been broken down into four smaller relations. The relation ORDER is left with only two attributes and the relation LINE_ITEM has a combined, or concatenated, key consisting of Order_Number and Part_Number.

In the particular business modelled here, an order can have more than one part, but each part is provided by only one supplier. If we build a relation called ORDER with all the fields included here, we would have to repeat the name and address of the supplier for every part on the order, even though the order is for parts from a single supplier. This relationship contains what are called **repeating data groups** because there can be many parts on a single order to a given supplier. A more efficient way to arrange the data is to break down ORDER into smaller relations, each of which describes a single entity. If we go step by step and normalize the relation ORDER, we emerge with the relations illustrated in Figure 6-9. You can find out more about normalization, entity-relationship diagramming, and database design in the Learning Tracks for this chapter.

Relational database systems try to enforce **referential integrity** rules to ensure that relationships between coupled tables remain consistent. When one table has a foreign key that points to another table, you may not add a record to the table with the foreign key unless there is a corresponding record in the linked table. In the database we examined earlier in this chapter, the foreign key Supplier_Number links the PART table to the SUPPLIER table. We may not add a new record to the PART table for a part with Supplier_Number 8266 unless there is corresponding record in the SUPPLIER table for Supplier_Number 8266. We must also delete the corresponding record in the PART table if we delete the record in the SUPPLIER table for Supplier_Number 8266. In other words, we should not have parts from nonexistent suppliers!

Database designers document their data model with **entity-relationship diagrams**, illustrated in Figure 6-11. This diagram illustrates the relationship between the entities ORDER, LINE_ITEM, PART, and SUPPLIER. The boxes represent entities. The lines connecting the boxes represent relationships. A line connecting two entities that ends in two short marks designates a one-to-one relationship. A line connecting two entities that ends with a crow's foot topped by a short mark indicates a one-to-many relationship. Figure 6-11 shows that one ORDER can contain many LINE_ITEMs. (A PART can be ordered many

Repeating data groups

Referential integrity

Entity-relationship diagrams

FIGURE 6-11   An entity-relationship diagram.

This diagram shows the relationships between the entities ORDER, LINE_ITEM, PART, and SUPPLIER that might be used to model the database in Figure 6-9.

times and appear many times as a line item in a single order.) Each PART can have only one SUPPLIER, but many PARTs can be provided by the same SUPPLIER.

It cannot be emphasized enough: If the business does not get its data model right, the system will not be able to serve the business well. The company's systems will not be as effective as they could be because they will have to work with data that may be inaccurate, incomplete, or difficult to retrieve. Understanding the organization's data and how they should be represented in a database is one of the most important lessons you can learn from this course.

For example, Famous Footwear, a shoe store chain with more than 800 locations in 49 US states, could not achieve its goal of having "the right style of shoe in the right store for sale at the right price" because its database was not properly designed for rapidly adjusting store inventory. The company had an Oracle relational database running on an IBM AS/400 midrange computer, but the database was designed primarily for producing standard reports for management rather than for reacting to marketplace changes. Management could not obtain precise data on specific items in inventory in each of its stores. The company had to work around this problem by building a new database where the sales and inventory data could be better organized for analysis and inventory management.

Distributing Databases Database design also considers how the data are to be distributed. Information systems can be designed with a centralized database that is used by a single central processor or by multiple processors in a client/server network. Alternatively, the database can be distributed. A **distributed database** is one that is stored in more than one physical location.

There are two main methods of distributing a database (see Figure 6-12). In a *partitioned* database, parts of the database are stored and maintained physically in one location and other parts are stored and maintained in other locations (see Figure 6-12a) so that each remote processor has the necessary data to serve its local area. Changes in local files can be justified with the central database on a batch basis, often at night. Another strategy is to *replicate* (i.e., duplicate in its entirety) the central database (Figure 6-12b) at all remote locations.

For example, Lufthansa Airlines replaced its centralized mainframe database with a replicated database to make information more immediately available to flight dispatchers. Any change made to Lufthansa's Frankfort DBMS is automatically replicated in New York and Hong Kong. This strategy also requires updating the central database during off-hours.

Distributed systems reduce the vulnerability of a single, massive central site. They increase service and responsiveness to local users and often can run on smaller, less expensive computers. However, local databases can sometimes depart from central data standards and definitions, and they pose security problems by widely distributing access to sensitive data. Database designers need to weigh these factors in their decisions.

Distributed database

FIGURE 6-12   Distributed databases.

There are alternative ways of distributing a database. The central database can be partitioned (a) so that each remote processor has the necessary data to serve its own local needs. The central database also can be replicated (b) at all remote locations.

6.3 Using Databases to Improve Business Performance and Decision Making

Businesses use their databases to keep track of basic transactions, such as paying suppliers, processing orders, keeping track of customers, and paying employees. But they also need databases to provide information that will help the company run the business more efficiently and help managers and employees make better decisions. If a company wants to know which product is the most popular or who is its most profitable customer, the answer lies in the data.

For example, by analyzing data from customer credit card purchases, Earl's Restaurants, a Western Canadian restaurant chain, might learn that quality was more important than price for most of its customers, who have some college or university education and like fine wine. Acting on this information, the chain could introduce vegetarian dishes, more seafood selections, and more expensive wines, raising sales significantly.

In a large company with large databases or large systems for separate functions such as manufacturing, sales, and accounting, special capabilities and tools are required for analyzing vast quantities of data and for accessing data from multiple systems. These capabilities include data warehousing, data mining, and tools for accessing internal databases through the Web.

Data Warehouses

Suppose you wanted concise, reliable information about current operations, trends, and changes across the entire company? If you worked in a large company, obtaining this might be difficult because data are often maintained in separate systems, such as sales, manufacturing, or accounting. Some of the data you needed might be found in the sales system, and other pieces in the manufacturing system. Many of these systems are older legacy systems that use outdated data management technologies or file systems where information is difficult for users to access. Hewlett-Packard, described in the chapter-opening case, experienced these problems.

You might have to spend an inordinate amount of time locating and gathering the data you needed, or you would be forced to make your decision based on incomplete knowledge. If you wanted information about trends, you might also have trouble finding data about past events because most firms make only their current data immediately available. Data warehousing addresses these problems.

What Is a Data Warehouse? A **data warehouse** is a database that stores current and historical data of potential interest to decision makers throughout the company. The data originate in many core operational transaction systems, such as systems for sales, customer accounts, and manufacturing, and may include data from Web site transactions. The data warehouse consolidates and standardizes information from different operational databases so that the information can be used across the enterprise for management analysis and decision making.

Figure 6-13 illustrates how a data warehouse works. The data warehouse makes the data available for anyone to access as needed, but it cannot be altered. A data warehouse system also provides a range of ad hoc and standardized query tools, analytical tools, and graphical reporting facilities. Many firms use intranet portals to make the data warehouse information widely available throughout the firm.

The Window on Management illustrates how Canadian Tire's data warehouse can serve as a powerful tool to enhance decision making and operational efficiency. A data warehouse enabled Canadian Tire to integrate and centralize customer data from its three operating "silos" so that it could use business intelligence effectively. As you read this case, try to identify the problem Canadian Tire was facing, what alternative solutions were available to management, and the management, organization, and technology issues that had to be addressed when developing the solution.

Data warehouse

FIGURE 6-13   Components of a data warehouse.

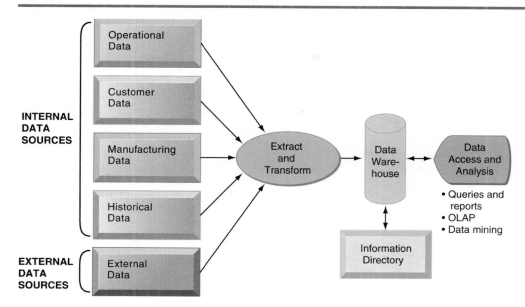

The data warehouse extracts current and historical data from multiple operational systems inside the organization. These data are combined with data from external sources and reorganized into a central database designed for management reporting and analysis. The information directory provides users with information about the data available in the warehouse.

WINDOW ON MANAGEMENT

Canadian Tire Warehouses Business Intelligence for Profitability

In the mid-2000s, Canadian Tire found that it could not leverage its data for decision making across its organizational units. These units include Mark's Work Wearhouse and Partsource. According to Kimi Walker, director of business intelligence at Canadian Tire's enterprise IT division, the company's IT strategy was confined to each business silo; the company did not have an enterprise-wide view of its performance and could not make comparisons between its divisions. For a company with 1180 stores and gas stations scattered across Canada, that was a lot of data to obtain and analyze.

Canadian Tire used Microsoft Office software such as Access and Excel for reporting and analysis but did not have a way to consolidate data or to analyze what would then be massive amounts of data. Not having analytic software that could handle the challenge of business intelligence data mining was an obstacle to the company's decision making. The data warehouse that Canadian Tire did have was on an older, inefficient, and very expensive mainframe.

According to Walker, "We didn't want to remove the access and hands-on capability the business had, but instead give them better capability." A joint proposal from IBM and Cognos, one of the leading purveyors of business intelligence software, was accepted. The fact that the two vendors would work together provided assurance to Canadian Tire that the

data warehouse would work seamlessly with its data-mining software. Other vendors had indicated they would not be willing to work with each other.

Data is now provided when and how Canadian Tire wants it; the company can think in real time and make faster decisions. Customer demands can be met much faster through quicker application development. In addition, the company will be able to exploit new technology and business trends like RFID by leveraging high-quality data.

It took Walker 18 months to hire a data architect since Cognos skills are in great demand. Walker worked with the business units to define the terms of reference and responsibilities for the different units' data groups. This was similar in many ways to the efforts of the Bank of Montreal (BMO).

In 2004, the board of directors of BMO declared information to be a strategic asset. Before that, information at BMO was only casually managed, in information silos, with business intelligence used only as an add-on application. After the board declared that information was a critical asset, it became important, according to Richard Livesley, BMO's head of knowledge management.

The bank then created an enterprise-wide information group that built a data warehouse with data marts. One person within each bank department was assigned responsibility as a data steward to manage the department's data and ensure that the data warehouse was up to date. Still, this venture was viewed not as a technology project, but as a business project. "No one wants to be in the information business; they're in the business of making money," said Livesley.

To Think About

1. Why was it so difficult for Canadian Tire to analyze the data it had collected?

2. What kind of challenges did Canadian Tire encounter when implementing its data warehouse? What management, organization, and technology issues had to be addressed?

3. How did the data warehouse improve decision making and operations at Canadian Tire? Are there benefits to customers?

4. Do you think the issues facing the Bank of Montreal were the same or similar to those faced by Canadian Tire?

MIS in Action

1. Go to **www.cognos.ca** and find information about Cognos' business intelligence products. How much training do you think would be required to learn how to use a Cognos system?

2. How could Canadian Tire managers use their data to help them make decisions related to ordering, inventory, and pricing?

Sources: "The IBM Retail Data Warehouse: Harnessing the Power of Information," http://download.boulder.ibm.com/ibmdl/pub/software/data/sw-library/industry-models/brochure/IBM_Retail_Models.pdf (accessed April 5, 2009); Jeff Jedras, "Mining Gold from Data Silos," *Computer World Canada*, November 10, 2006.

Data Marts Companies often build enterprise-wide data warehouses where a central data warehouse serves the entire organization, or they create smaller, decentralized warehouses called data marts. A **data mart** is a subset of a data warehouse in which a summarized or highly focused portion of the organization's data is placed in a separate database for a specific population of users. For example, a company might develop marketing and sales data marts to deal with customer information. A data mart typically focuses on a single subject area or line of business, so it usually can be constructed more rapidly and at lower cost than an enterprise-wide data warehouse.

Business Intelligence, Multidimensional Data Analysis, and Data Mining

Once data have been captured and organized in data warehouses and data marts, they are available for further analysis. A series of tools enables users to analyze these data to see new patterns, relationships, and insights that are useful for guiding decision making. Consolidating, analyzing, and providing access using these data to help users make better business decisions is referred to as **business intelligence** (BI). Principal tools for business intelligence include software for database querying and reporting, tools for multidimensional data analysis (online analytical processing), and data mining.

When we think of *intelligence* as applied to humans, we typically think of people's ability to combine learned knowledge with new information and change behaviours in such a way that they succeed at their task or adapt to a new situation. Likewise, business intelligence provides firms with the capability to amass information; develop knowledge about customers, competitors, and internal operations; and change decision-making behaviour to achieve higher profitability and other business goals.

For instance, the Best Western Heidelberg Inn, located in Lethbridge, Alberta, is a member of one of the world's largest hotel chains. Using Maximizer, customer-relationship management (CRM) software that is based on a finely tuned database of customer data, Best Western saw its occupancy rate increase by 12 percent in only one year. Wayne Dwornik is responsible for developing long-lasting business relationships with corporate clients to increase hotel occupancy rates. Dwornik can target his contacts with e-mail messages containing information they may find valuable, keeping Best Western in the forefront of his potential clients' thinking. According to Dwornik, "the best way of reaching out and contacting corporate travellers including construction firms, federal employees, oil and gas pipeline operators, is via e-mail." The CRM software tracks details of past stays, telephone conversations, responses to previous e-mails, and special events like birthdays or anniversaries; this helps to further adapt

Data mart
Business intelligence (BI)

FIGURE 6-14   Business intelligence.

Databases   Data Warehouse   Business
                                                               Intelligence

                                    OLAP
                                    Data
                                    Mining

                                  Querying
                                  Reporting

     Keep track of   Find patterns   Decision to respond
      transactions   and insights   to the data and patterns

A series of analytical tools works with data stored in databases to find patterns and insights for helping managers and employees make better decisions to improve organizational performance.

the message that goes to the clients. This type of business intelligence quickly becomes part of a business's strategy.

Figure 6-14 illustrates how business intelligence works. The firm's operational databases keep track of the transactions generated by running the business. These databases feed data to the data warehouse. Managers use business intelligence tools to find patterns and meanings in the data. Managers then act on what they have learned from analyzing the data by making more informed and intelligent business decisions.

This section will introduce you to the most important business intelligence technologies and tools. We will provide more detail about business intelligence applications in Chapter 14.

Online Analytical Processing (OLAP) Suppose your company sells four different products—nuts, bolts, washers, and screws—in the East, West, and Prairie regions. If you wanted to ask a fairly straightforward question, such as how many washers sold during the past quarter, you could easily find the answer by querying your sales database. But what if you wanted to know how many washers sold in each of your sales regions and compare actual results with projected sales?

To obtain the answer, you would need **online analytical processing (OLAP)**. OLAP supports multidimensional data analysis, enabling users to view the same data in different ways using multiple dimensions. Each aspect of information—product, pricing, cost, region, or time period—represents a different dimension. A product manager could use a multidimensional data analysis tool to learn how many washers were sold in the East in June, how that compares with the previous month and the previous June, and how it compares with the sales forecast. OLAP enables users to obtain online answers to ad hoc questions such as these in a fairly rapid amount of time, even when the data are stored in very large databases, such as sales figures for multiple years.

Figure 6-15 shows a multidimensional model that could be created to represent products, regions, actual sales, and projected sales. A matrix of actual sales can be stacked on top of a matrix of projected sales to form a cube with six faces. If you rotate the cube 90 degrees one way, the face showing will be product versus actual and projected sales. If you rotate the cube 90 degrees again, you will see region versus actual and projected sales. If you rotate 180 degrees from the original view, you will see projected sales and product versus region. Cubes can be nested within cubes to build complex views of data. A company would use either a specialized multidimensional database or a tool that creates multidimensional views of data in relational databases.

Online analytical processing (OLAP)

FIGURE 6-15   Multidimensional data model.

The view that is showing is product versus region. If you rotate the cube 90 degrees, the face that will show is product versus actual and projected sales. If you rotate the cube 90 degrees again, you will see region versus actual and projected sales. Other views are possible.

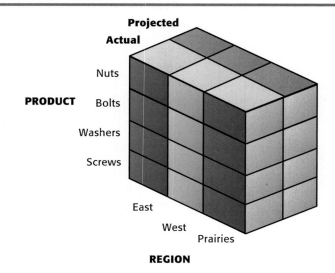

Data Mining Traditional database queries answer questions such as, "How many units of product number 403 were shipped in February 2009?" OLAP, or multidimensional analysis, supports much more complex requests for information, such as "Compare sales of product 403 relative to plan by quarter and sales region for the past two years." With OLAP and query-oriented data analysis, users need to have a good idea about the information for which they are looking.

Data mining is more discovery-driven. Data mining provides insights into corporate data that cannot be obtained with OLAP because it finds hidden patterns and relationships in large databases and infers rules from them to predict future behaviour. The patterns and rules are used to guide decision making and forecast the effect of those decisions. The types of information obtainable from data mining include associations, sequences, classifications, clusters, and forecasts.

- *Associations* are occurrences linked to a single event. For instance, a study of supermarket purchasing patterns might reveal that, when corn chips are purchased, a cola drink is purchased 65 percent of the time, but when there is a promotion, cola is purchased 85 percent of the time. This information helps managers make better decisions because they have learned the profitability of a promotion.

- In *sequences*, events are linked over time. We might find, for example, that if a house is purchased, a new refrigerator will be purchased within two weeks 65 percent of the time, and an oven will be bought within one month of the home purchase 45 percent of the time.

- *Classification* recognizes patterns that describe the group to which an item belongs by examining existing items that have been classified and by inferring a set of rules. For example, businesses such as credit card or telephone companies worry about the loss of steady customers. Classification helps discover the characteristics of customers who are likely to leave and can provide a model to help managers predict who those customers are so that the managers can devise special campaigns to retain such customers.

- *Clustering* works in a manner similar to classification when no groups have yet been defined. A data-mining tool can discover different groupings within data, such as finding affinity groups for bank cards or partitioning a database into groups of customers based on demographics and types of personal investments.

- Although these applications involve predictions, *forecasting* uses predictions in a different way. It uses a series of existing values to forecast what other values will be. For example, forecasting might find patterns in data to help managers estimate the future sales figures.

Data mining

These systems perform high-level analyses of patterns or trends, but they can also drill down to provide more detail when needed. There are data-mining applications for all the functional areas of business, and for government and scientific work. One popular use for data mining is to provide detailed analyses of patterns in customer data for one-to-one marketing campaigns or for identifying profitable customers.

For example, Virgin Mobile Australia uses a data warehouse and data mining to increase customer loyalty and roll out new services. The data warehouse consolidates data from its enterprise system, customer relationship management system, and customer billing systems in a massive database. Data mining has enabled management to determine the demographic profile of new customers and relate it to the handsets they purchased as well as the performance of each store and point-of-sale campaign, consumer reactions to new products and services, customer attrition rates, and the revenue generated by each customer.

Predictive analysis uses data-mining techniques, historical data, and assumptions about future conditions to predict outcomes of events, such as the probability a customer will respond to an offer or purchase a specific product. For example, the Dutch insurance company FBTO Verzekeringen, with about 500 000 customers and more than a million car, health, home, and life insurance policies, needed to reduce its direct-mailing costs while increasing the efficiency of its marketing campaigns and cross-selling existing customers. FBTO used predictive analysis to identify customers and prospects with a better-than-average probability of purchasing one of the company's products. In doing so, FBTO reduced direct mail costs by 35 percent and increased conversion rates (from prospects to customers) by 40 percent. Today FBTO's marketing team can simulate different scenarios and calculate conversion rates and mailing costs in advance.

Text Mining and Web Mining Business intelligence tools deal primarily with data that have been structured in databases and files. However, unstructured data, most in the form of text files, is believed to account for more than 80 percent of an organization's useful information. E-mail, memos, call centre transcripts, survey responses, legal cases, patent descriptions, and service reports are all valuable for finding patterns and trends that will help employees make better business decisions. **Text mining** tools are now available to help businesses analyze these data. These tools are able to extract key elements from large unstructured data sets, discover patterns and relationships, and summarize the information. Businesses might turn to text mining to analyze transcripts of calls to customer service centres to identify major service and repair issues.

Air Products and Chemicals in Allentown, Pennsylvania, is using text mining to help identify documents that require special record retention procedures to comply with the *Sarbanes-Oxley Act*. The company has more than nine terabytes of unstructured data (not including e-mail.). SmartDiscovery software from Inxight Software classifies and organizes these data so that the company can apply business rules to a category of documents rather than individual documents. If a document is found to deal with operations covered by Sarbanes-Oxley, the company will ensure the document meets the law's data retention requirements.

The Web is another rich source of valuable information, some of which can now be mined for patterns, trends, and insights into customer behaviour. The discovery and analysis of useful patterns and information from the World Wide Web is called **Web mining**. Businesses might turn to Web mining to help them understand customer behaviour, evaluate the effectiveness of a particular Web site, or quantify the success of a marketing campaign. For instance, marketers use Google Trends and Google Insights for Search services, which track the popularity of various words and phrases used in Google search queries, to learn what people are interested in and what they are interested in buying.

Web mining looks for patterns in data through content mining, structure mining, and usage mining. *Web content mining* is the process of extracting knowledge from the content of Web pages, which may include text, image, audio, and video data. *Web structure mining* examines data related to the structure of a particular Web site. For example, links pointing to a document indicate the popularity of the document, while links coming out of a document indicate the richness or perhaps the variety of topics covered in the document. *Web usage mining* examines user interaction data recorded by a Web server whenever requests for

Predictive analysis
Text mining
Web mining

FIGURE 6-16   Linking internal databases to the Web.

Users access an organization's internal database through the Web using their desktop PCs and Web browser software.

a Web site's resources are received. The usage data records the user's behaviour when the user browses or makes transactions on the Web site and collects the data in a server log. Analyzing such data can help companies determine the value of particular customers, cross-marketing strategies across products, and the effectiveness of promotional campaigns, etc.

Databases and the Web

Have you ever tried to use the Web to place an order or view a product catalogue? If so, you were probably using a Web site linked to an internal corporate database. Many companies now use the Web to make some of the information in their internal databases available to customers and business partners.

Suppose, for example, a customer with a Web browser wants to search an online retailer's database for pricing information. Figure 6-16 illustrates how that customer might access the retailer's internal database over the Web. The user accesses the retailer's Web site over the Internet using Web browser software on his or her client PC. The user's Web browser software requests data from the organization's database, using HTML commands to communicate with the Web server.

Because many "back-end" databases cannot interpret commands written in HTML, the Web server passes these requests for data to software that translates HTML commands into SQL so that they can be processed by the DBMS working with the database. In a client/server environment, the DBMS resides on a dedicated computer called a **database server**. The DBMS receives the SQL requests and provides the required data. The middleware transfers information from the organization's internal database back to the Web server for delivery in the form of a Web page to the user.

Figure 6-16 shows that the middleware working between the Web server and the DBMS is an application server running on its own dedicated computer (see Chapter 5). The application server software handles all application operations, including transaction processing and data access, between browser-based computers and a company's back-end business applications or databases. The application server takes requests from the Web server, runs the business logic to process transactions based on those requests, and provides connectivity to the organization's back-end systems or databases. Alternatively, the software for handling these operations could be a custom program or a CGI script. A CGI script is a compact program using the *Common Gateway Interface (CGI)* specification for processing data on a Web server.

There are a number of advantages to using the Web to access an organization's internal databases. First, Web browser software is much easier to use than proprietary query tools. Second, the Web interface requires few or no changes to the internal database. It costs much less to add a Web interface in front of a legacy system than to redesign and rebuild the system to improve user access.

Accessing corporate databases through the Web is creating new efficiencies, opportunities, and business models. ThomasNet.com provides an up-to-date online directory of more than 600 000 suppliers of industrial products, such as chemicals, metals, plastics, rubber, and automotive equipment. Formerly called Thomas Register, the company used to send out huge paper catalogues with this information. Now it provides this information to users online via its Web site and has become a smaller, leaner company.

Database server

Other companies have created entirely new businesses based on access to large databases through the Web. One is the social networking site MySpace, which helps users stay connected with each other or meet new people. MySpace features music, comedy, videos, and "profiles" with information supplied by 175 million users about their age, hometown, dating preferences, marital status, and interests. It maintains a massive database to house and manage all of this content. Because the site grew so rapidly, it had to make a series of changes to its underlying database technology. The Window on Technology explores this topic. As you read this case, try to identify the problem MySpace is facing; what alternative solutions are available to management; and the people, organization, and technology issues that have to be addressed when developing the solution.

6.4   Managing Data Resources

Setting up a database is only a start. In order to make sure that the data for your business remain accurate, reliable, and readily available to those who need it, your business will need special policies and procedures for data management.

Establishing an Information Policy

Every business, large and small, needs an information policy. Your firm's data are an important resource, and you do not want people doing whatever they want with them. You need to have rules on how the data are to be organized and maintained and who is allowed to view the data or change them.

An **information policy** specifies the organization's rules for sharing, disseminating, acquiring, standardizing, classifying, and inventorying information. Information policy lays out specific procedures and accountabilities, identifying which users and organizational units can share information, where information can be distributed, and who is responsible for updating and maintaining the information. For example, a typical information policy would specify that only selected members of the payroll and human resources department would have the right to change and view sensitive employee data, such as an employee's salary or social insurance number, and that these departments are responsible for making sure that such employee data are accurate.

Information policy

Technology

WINDOW ON TECHNOLOGY

The Databases behind MySpace

MySpace.com, the popular social networking site, has experienced one of the greatest growth spurts in the history of the Internet. The site launched in November 2003 and by May 2007, it had 175 million member accounts, 6 million of whom were Canadian users. In fact, when MySpace Canada launched in 2007, it was the first time the site had launched a specific country Web site in two languages, choosing to start in both French and English. Throughout its existence, the challenge for MySpace has been to avoid technological letdowns that degrade Web site performance and frustrate its rapidly expanding network of users.

The technical requirements of a site like MySpace are vastly different from other heavily trafficked Web sites. Generally, a small number of people change the content on a news site a few times a day. The site may retrieve thousands of read-only requests from its underlying database without having to update the database. On MySpace, tens of millions of users are constantly updating their content, resulting in an elevated percentage of database interactions that require updates to the underlying database. Each time a user views a profile on MySpace, the resulting page is stitched together from database lookups that organize information from multiple tables stored in multiple databases residing on multiple servers.

In its initial phases, MySpace operated with two Web servers communicating with one database server and a Microsoft SQL

Server database. Such a setup is ideal for small to medium-size sites because of its simplicity. At MySpace, the setup showed signs of stress as more users came aboard. At first, MySpace reduced the load by adding Web servers to handle the increased user requests. But when the number of accounts stretched to 500 000 in 2004, one database server was not sufficient. Deploying additional database servers is more complicated than adding Web servers because the data must be divided among multiple databases without any loss in accessibility or performance. MySpace deployed three SQL Server databases. One served as a master database, which received all new data and copied them to the other two databases. These databases focused on retrieving data for user page requests.

As MySpace approached 2 million accounts, the database servers approached their input/output capacity, which refers to the speed at which they could read and write data. This caused the site to lag behind in content updates. MySpace switched to a vertical partitioning model in which separate databases supported distinct functions of the Web site, such as the log-in screen, user profiles, and blogs.

However, the distinct functions also had occasion to share data, and this became problematic when the site reached 3 million accounts. Furthermore, some functions of the site grew too large to be served by only one database server. After considering a scale-up strategy of investing in more powerful and expensive servers, MySpace instead scaled out by adding many cheaper servers to share the database workload.

The more economical solution of a distributed architecture required a new design in which all of the servers combined to work as one logical computer. Under this design, the workload still needed to be spread out, which was accomplished by dividing the user accounts into groups of 1 million, and putting all the data related to those accounts in a separate instance of SQL Server.

Despite these gains in efficiency, the workload was not distributed evenly, which would sometimes cause an overload in the storage area for a particular database. MySpace tried to correct this issue manually, but the work was demanding and not an effective use of resources. So MySpace switched to a virtualized storage architecture, which ended the practice of attaching disks dedicated to specific applications in favour of a single pool of storage space available to all applications. Under this arrangement, databases could write data to any available disk, thus eliminating the possibility of an application's dedicated disk becoming overloaded.

In 2005, MySpace also fortified its infrastructure by installing a layer of servers between the database servers and the Web servers to store and serve copies of frequently accessed data objects so that the site's Web servers would not have to query the database servers with lookups as frequently.

Despite all these measures, MySpace still overloads more frequently than other major Web sites. Users have expressed frustration at not being able to log in or view certain pages. Log-in errors occur at a rate of 20 to 40 percent some days. Site activity continues to challenge the limitations of the technology. So far, the site's continued growth suggests that users are willing to put up with periodic "Unexpected Error" screens. MySpace developers continue to redesign the Web site's database, software, and storage systems, to keep pace with its exploding growth, but their job is never done.

To Think About

1. What kind of databases and database servers does MySpace use?

2. Why is database technology so important for a business such as MySpace?

3. How effectively does MySpace organize and store the data on its site?

4. What data management problems have arisen? How has MySpace solved, or attempted to solve these problems?

MIS in Action

Explore MySpace.com, examining the features and tools that are not restricted to registered members. Then answer the following questions:

1. Based on what you can view without registering, what are the entities in MySpace's database?

2. Which of these entities have some relationship to individual members?

3. Select one of these entities, and describe the attributes for that entity.

Sources: Joel Martinez, "Deconstructing MySpace.com Part 1—Social Networking Database," www.communitymx.com (accessed June 2, 2008); David F. Carr, "Inside MySpace.com," *Baseline Magazine*, January 16, 2007; Mark Brunelli, "Oracle Database 10g Powers Growing MySpace.com Competitor," SearchOracle.com, January 31, 2007, Pat Hewitt, "MySpace Social Networking Site Launches Canadian Version in English, French," *RedOrbit News*, May 14, 2007.

If you are in a small business, the information policy would be established and implemented by the owners or managers. In a large organization, managing and planning for information as a corporate resource often requires a formal data administration function. **Data administration** is responsible for the specific policies and procedures through which data can be managed as an organizational resource. These responsibilities include developing information policy, planning for data, overseeing logical database design and data dictionary development, and monitoring how information systems specialists and end-user groups use data.

Data administration

You may hear the term **data governance** used to describe many of these activities. Promoted by IBM, data governance deals with the policies and processes for managing the availability, usability, integrity, and security of the data employed in an enterprise, with special emphasis on promoting privacy, security, data quality, and compliance with government regulations.

A large organization will also have a database design and management group within the corporate information systems division that is responsible for defining and organizing the structure and content of the database and maintaining the database. In close cooperation with users, the design group establishes the physical database, the logical relations among elements, and the access rules and security procedures. The functions it performs are called **database administration**.

Ensuring Data Quality

A well-designed database and information policy will go a long way toward ensuring that the business has the information it needs. However, additional steps must be taken to ensure that the data in organizational databases are accurate and remain reliable.

What would happen if a customer's telephone number or account balance were incorrect? What would be the impact if the database had the wrong price for the product you sold or your sales system and inventory system showed different prices for the same product? Data that are inaccurate, untimely, or inconsistent with other sources of information lead to incorrect decisions, product recalls, and financial losses. Inaccurate data in criminal justice and national security databases might even subject you to unnecessary surveillance or detention.

According to Forrester Research, 20 percent of U.S. mail and commercial package deliveries were returned because of incorrect names or addresses. Gartner Inc. reported that more than 25 percent of the critical data in large Fortune 1000 companies' databases is inaccurate or incomplete, including bad product codes and product descriptions, faulty inventory descriptions, erroneous financial data, incorrect supplier information, and incorrect employee data (Gartner, 2007).

Think of all the times you have received several pieces of the same direct-mail advertising on the same day. This is very likely the result of having your name maintained multiple times in a database. Your name may have been misspelled, or you used your middle initial on one occasion and not on another, or the information was initially entered onto a paper form and not scanned properly into the system. Because of these inconsistencies, the database would treat you as different people! Your Canadian author often receives redundant mail addressed to Brabston, Bradston, or Brabstone.

If a database is properly designed and enterprise-wide data standards established, duplicate or inconsistent data elements should be minimal. Most data quality problems, however, such as misspelled names, transposed numbers, or incorrect or missing codes, stem from errors during data input. The incidence of such errors is rising as companies move their businesses to the Web and allow customers and suppliers to enter data into their Web sites that directly update internal systems.

Before a new database is in place, organizations need to identify and correct their faulty data and establish better routines for editing data once their database is in operation. Analysis of data quality often begins with a **data quality audit**, which is a structured survey of the accuracy and level of completeness of the data in an information system. Data quality audits can be performed by surveying entire data files, surveying samples from data files, or surveying end users for their perceptions of data quality.

Data cleansing, also known as *data scrubbing*, consists of activities for detecting and correcting data in a database that are incorrect, incomplete, improperly formatted, or redundant. Data cleansing not only corrects errors but also enforces consistency among different sets of data that originated in separate information systems. Specialized data-cleansing software is available to automatically survey data files, correct errors in the data, and integrate the data in a consistent company-wide format.

Data governance
Database administration
Data quality audit
Data cleansing

SUMMARY

1. **What are the problems of managing data resources in a traditional file environment, and how are they solved by a database management system?**

   Traditional file management techniques make it difficult for organizations to keep track of all of the pieces of data they use in a systematic way and to organize these data so that they can be easily accessed. Different functional areas and groups were allowed to develop their own files independently. Over time, this traditional file management environment creates problems such as data redundancy and inconsistency, program-data dependence, inflexibility, poor security, and lack of data sharing and availability. A database management system (DBMS) solves these problems with software that permits centralization of data and data management so that businesses have a single consistent source for all their data needs. Using a DBMS minimizes redundant and inconsistent files.

2. **What are the major capabilities of data management systems (DBMSs), and why is a relational DBMS so powerful?**

   The principal capabilities of a DBMS includes a data definition capability, a data dictionary capability, and a data manipulation language. The data definition capability specifies the structure and content of the database. The data dictionary is an automated or manual file that stores information about the data in the database, including names, definitions, formats, and descriptions of data elements. A data manipulation language, such as SQL, is a specialized language for accessing and manipulating the data in the database. A relational database is the primary method for organizing and maintaining data today because it is so flexible and accessible. It organizes data in two-dimensional tables with rows and columns called relations. Each table contains data about an entity and its attributes. Each row represents a record, and each column represents an attribute or field. Each table also contains a key field to uniquely identify each record for retrieval or manipulation. Relational database tables can be combined easily to deliver data required by users, provided that any two tables share a common data element.

3. **What are some important principles of database design?**

   Designing a database requires both a logical design and a physical design. The logical design models the database from a business perspective. The organization's data model should reflect its key business processes and decision-making requirements. The process of creating small, stable, flexible, and adaptive data structures from complex groups of data when designing a relational database is termed *normalization*. A well-designed relational database will not have many-to-many relationships, and all attributes for a specific entity will apply only to that entity. It will try to enforce referential integrity rules to ensure that relationships between linked tables remain consistent. An entity-relationship diagram (ERD) graphically depicts the relationship between entities (tables) in a relational database. Database design also considers whether a complete database or portions of the database can be distributed to more than one location to increase responsiveness and reduce vulnerability and costs. There are two major types of distributed databases: replicated databases and partitioned databases.

4. **What are the principal tools and technologies for accessing information from databases to improve business performance and decision making?**

   Powerful tools are available to analyze and access the information in databases. A data warehouse consolidates current and historical data from many different operational systems in a central database designed for reporting and analysis. Data warehouses support multidimensional data analysis, also known as online analytical processing (OLAP). OLAP represents relationships among data as a multidimensional structure, which can be visualized as cubes of data and cubes within cubes of data, enabling more sophisticated data analysis. Data mining analyzes large pools of data, including the contents of data warehouses, to find patterns and rules that can be used to predict future behaviour and guide decision making. Text mining tools help businesses analyze large unstructured data sets consisting of text. Web mining tools focus on analysis of useful patterns and information from the World Wide Web, examining the structure of Web sites and activities of Web site users as well as the contents of Web pages. Conventional databases can be linked via middleware to the Web or a Web interface to facilitate user access to an organization's internal data.

5. **Why are information policy, data administration, and data quality assurance essential for managing the firm's data resources?**

   Developing a database environment requires policies and procedures for managing organizational data as well as a good data model and database technology. A formal information policy governs the maintenance, distribution, and use of information in the organization. In large corporations, a formal data administration function is responsible for information policy, as well as for data planning, data dictionary development, and monitoring data usage in the firm.

   Data that are inaccurate, incomplete, or inconsistent create serious operational and financial problems for businesses because they may create inaccuracies in product pricing, customer accounts, and inventory data, and lead to inaccurate decisions about the actions that should be taken by the firm. Firms must take special steps to make sure they have a high level of data quality. These include using enterprise-wide data standards, databases designed to minimize inconsistent and redundant data, data quality audits, and data cleansing software.

Key Terms

Attribute, 173	Database (rigorous definition), 176	Object-relational DBMS, 179
Business intelligence (BI), 186	Database administration, 193	Online analytical processing
Data administration, 192	Database management system	(OLAP), 187
Data cleansing, 193	(DBMS), 176	Predictive analysis, 189
Data definition, 179	Database server, 190	Primary key, 177
Data dictionary, 179	Distributed database, 183	Program-data dependence, 175
Data governance, 193	Entity, 173	Record, 173
Data inconsistency, 174	Entity-relationship diagram, 182	Referential integrity, 182
Data manipulation language, 179	Field, 173	Relational DBMS, 177
Data mart, 186	File, 173	Repeating data groups, 182
Data mining, 188	Foreign key, 177	Structured Query Language
Data quality audit, 193	Information policy, 191	(SQL), 179
Data redundancy, 174	Key field, 177	Text mining, 189
Data warehouse, 184	Normalization, 181	Tuple, 177
Database, 173	Object-oriented DBMS, 179	Web mining, 189

Review Questions

1. *What are the problems of managing data resources in a traditional file environment, and how are they solved by a database management system?*

   • *List and describe each of the components in the data hierarchy.*

   • *Define and explain the significance of entities, attributes, and key fields.*

   • *List and describe the problems of the traditional file environment.*

   • *Define a database and a database management system and describe how it solves the problems of a traditional file environment.*

2. *What are the major capabilities of DBMS, and why is a relational DBMS so powerful?*

   • *Name and briefly describe the capabilities of a DBMS.*

   • *Define a relational DBMS, and explain how it organizes data.*

   • *List and describe the three operations of a relational DBMS.*

3. *What are some important principles of database design?*

   • *Define and describe normalization and referential integrity, and explain how they contribute to a well-designed relational database.*

   • *Define a distributed database, and describe the two main ways of distributing data.*

4. *What are the principal tools and technologies for accessing information from databases to improve business performance and decision making?*

   • *Define a data warehouse, explaining how it works and how it benefits organizations.*

   • *Define business intelligence, and explain how it is related to database technology.*

   • *Describe the capabilities of online analytical processing (OLAP).*

   • *Define data mining, describing how it differs from OLAP and describing the types of information it provides.*

   • *Explain how text mining and Web mining differ from conventional data mining.*

   • *Describe how users can access information from a company's internal databases through the Web.*

5. *Why are information policy, data administration, and data quality assurance essential for managing a firm's data resources?*

   • *Describe the roles of information policy and data administration in information management.*

   • *Explain why data quality audits and data cleansing are essential.*

Discussion Questions

1. *It has been said that database management software is not needed to create a database environment. Discuss.*

2. *To what extent should end users be involved in the selection of a database management system and database design?*

Collaboration and Teamwork: Identifying Entities and Attributes in an Online Database

With your team of three or four students, select an online database to explore, such as AOL Music, iGo.com, or the Internet Movie Database. Explore one of these Web sites to see what information it provides. Then list the entities and attributes that the company running the Web site must keep track of in its databases. Diagram the relationship between the entities you have identified. If possible, use Google Sites to post links to Web pages, team communication announcements, and work assignments; to brainstorm; and to work collaboratively on project documents. Try to use Google Docs to develop a presentation of your findings for the class.

 Visit the MyMISLab Web site at **www.pearsoned.ca/mymislab**. This online homework and tutorial system puts you in control of your own learning with study and practice tools directly correlated to this chapter's content.

Learning Track Module

The following Learning Tracks provide content relevant to topics covered in this chapter:

1. Database Design, Normalization, and Entity-Relationship Diagramming

2. Introduction to SQL
3. Hierarchical and Network Data Models

HANDS-ON MIS   Projects

The projects in this section give you hands-on experience in analyzing data quality problems, establishing company-wide data standards, creating a database for inventory management, and using the Web to search online databases for overseas business resources.

Management Decision Problems

1. Emerson Process Management, a global supplier of measurement, analytical, and monitoring instruments and services based in Austin, Texas, had a new data warehouse designed for analyzing customer activity to improve service and marketing that was full of inaccurate and redundant data. The data in the warehouse came from numerous transaction processing systems in Europe, Asia, and other locations around the world. The team that designed the warehouse had assumed that sales groups in all these areas would enter customer names and addresses the same way, regardless of their location. In fact, cultural differences combined with complications from absorbing companies that Emerson had acquired led to multiple ways of entering quote, billing, shipping, and other data. Assess the potential business impact of these data quality problems. What decisions have to be made and steps taken to reach a solution?

2. Your industrial supply company wants to create a data warehouse where management can obtain a single corporate-wide view of critical sales information to identify best-selling products in specific geographic areas, key customers, and sales trends. Your sales and product information are stored in two different systems: a divisional sales system running on a Unix server and a corporate sales system running on an IBM mainframe. You would like to create a single standard format that consolidates these data from both systems. The following format has been proposed.

Product_ID	Product_Description	Cost_Per_Unit	Units_Sold	Sales_Region	Division	Customer_ID

The following are sample files from the two systems that would supply the data for the data warehouse:

Corporate Sales System

Product_ID	Product_Description	Unit_Cost	Units_Sold	Sales_Territory	Division
60231	4" steel bearing	5.28	900 245	East	Anderson
85773	SS assembly unit	12.45	992 111	Prairies	Kelly Industries

Mechanical Parts Division Sales System

Prod_No	Product_Description	Cost_Per_Unit	Units_Sold	Sales_Region	Customer_ID
60231	4" Steel bearing	5.28	900 245	East	Anderson
85773	SS assembly unit	12.45	992 111	Prairies	Kelly Industries

1. What business problems are created by not having these data in a single standard format?
2. How easy would it be to create a database with a single standard format that could store the data from both systems? Identify the problems that would have to be addressed.
3. Should the problems be solved by database specialists or by general business managers? Explain.
4. Who should have the authority to finalize a single company-wide format for this information in the data warehouse?

Improving Operational Excellence: Building a Relational Database for Inventory Management

Software skills: Database design, querying, and reporting
Business skills: Inventory management

Businesses today depend on databases to provide reliable information about items in inventory, items that need restocking, and inventory costs. In this exercise, you will use database software to design a database for managing inventory for a small business.

Fictional Sylvester's Bike Shop, located in Hamilton, Ontario, sells road, mountain, hybrid, leisure, and children's bicycles. Currently, Sylvester's purchases bikes from three suppliers but plans to add new suppliers in the near future. This rapidly growing business needs a database system to manage this information.

Initially, the database should house information about suppliers and products. The database will contain two tables: a supplier table and a product table. The reorder level refers to the number of items in inventory that triggers a decision to order more items to prevent a stockout. (In other words, if the number of units of a particular inventory falls below the reorder level, the item should be reordered.) The user should be able to perform several queries and produce several managerial reports based on the data contained in the two tables.

Using the information found in the tables on the MyMISLab for Chapter 6, build a simple relational database for Sylvester's. Once you have built the database, perform the following activities:

1. Prepare a report that identifies the five most expensive bicycles. The report should list the bicycles in descending order from most expensive to least expensive, the quantity on hand for each, and the markup percentage for each.
2. Prepare a report that lists each supplier, the supplier's products, the quantities on hand, and associated reorder levels. The report should be sorted alphabetically by supplier. Within each supplier category, the products should be sorted alphabetically.
3. Prepare a report listing only the bicycles that are low in stock and need to be reordered. The report should provide supplier information for the items identified.
4. Write a brief description of how the database could be enhanced to further improve management of the business. What tables or fields should be added? What additional reports would be useful?

Improving Decision Making: Searching Online Databases for Overseas Business Resources

Software skills: Online databases
Business skills: Researching services for overseas operations

Internet users have access to many thousands of Web-enabled databases with information on services and products in faraway locations. This project develops skills in searching these online databases.

Your company is located in Calgary, Alberta, and manufactures office furniture of various types. You have recently acquired several new customers in Australia, and a study you commissioned indicates that, with a presence there, you could greatly increase your sales. Moreover, your study indicates that you could do even better if you actually manufactured many of your products locally (in Australia). First, you need to set up an office in Melbourne to establish a presence, and then you need to begin importing from Canada. You then can plan to start producing locally.

You will soon be travelling to the area to make plans to actually set up an office, and you want to meet with organizations that can help you with your operation. You will need to engage people or organizations that offer many services necessary for you to open your office, including lawyers,

accountants, import-export experts, telecommunications equipment and support, and even trainers who can help you to prepare your future employees to work for you. Start by searching for Canada Department of Commerce advice and other Canadian agency advice on doing business in Australia. Then try the following online databases to locate companies that you would like to meet with during your coming trip: Australian Business Register (**http://abr.business.gov.au**), Australia Trade Now (**australiatradenow.com**), and the Nationwide Business Directory of Australia (**www.nationwide.com.au**). If necessary, you could also try search engines such as Yahoo! and Google. Then perform the following activities:

- List the companies you would contact to interview on your trip to determine whether they can help you with these and any other functions you think are vital to establishing your office.

- Rate the databases you used for accuracy of name, completeness, ease of use, and general helpfulness.

- What does this exercise tell you about the design of databases?

CASE STUDY

The RCMP and Its Data: More and More and More Data—and What the RCMP Does with Its Data

When we think of crime, we think of law enforcement. With the variety of crime lab shows on television, we assume that all law enforcement agencies should have access to the latest and greatest technologies, not only in laboratory technologies, but also in databases. A quick look at what the Royal Canadian Mounted Police (RCMP) is doing with data certainly supports that view. Let us look at two different data applications the RCMP has implemented and how they work: the DNA database and the crime analysis database.

The national DNA database used by most Canadian law enforcement agencies is called the National DNA Data Bank (NDDB). Also available to foreign law enforcement agencies, the NDDB uses the Sample Tracking and Control System (STaCS) to automate and track processing DNA samples of those convicted of crimes for which DNA was part of the evidence. While criminals can wear gloves to avoid leaving fingerprints at the scenes of their crimes, it is a lot harder to avoid leaving DNA in the form of hairs or epithelial cells. DNA is the newest form of evidence that can be analyzed to identify criminals, and it can be used in court to convict those guilty of a variety of crimes, from sex crimes to murders and robberies.

The NDDB is located in Ottawa and uses the same CODIS (Combined DNA Index System) software that is used by the U.S. FBI and that is so frequently referenced on television shows like *CSI: Crime Scene Investigation*. STaCS software works with the CODIS software to ensure that data can be shared between the two systems and also to ensure privacy for those whose DNA is in the database.

There are a number of scientific, legislative, and ethical issues associated with using DNA in solving crime. Is the DNA actually from a specific person? When was it left at the crime scene? Can DNA be used in court? How close a match must the DNA be to certify that it is a match, presenting both a legal and probability issue? Does collecting DNA violate the privacy of the individual giving the DNA sample? What legal and ethical considerations must be thought through before seeking or granting a search warrant on an individual's DNA? What is an appropriate "margin of error" for processing a DNA sample and linking it to a specific individual?

A number of strategies were developed in order to reduce the margin of error and improve accountability. The STaCS system, developed by the RCMP in conjunction with Anjura Technology, is intended to track, control, and document every step in the process that converts the biological DNA sample into simplified numeric DNA profiles. The process must be transparent so that anyone can see exactly the process the DNA sample went through, ensuring that it is in fact the sample that started the process and has not been tampered with, so there is an audit trail of every activity that takes place in the system. STaCS includes a report portal to permit everyone using the system to see where a DNA sample is in process and what the results are, as well as machine maintenance records and workload on the system.

In developing STaCS, the RCMP gained the licence to the software. The RCMP has since earned revenue from selling the licence to other law enforcement agencies, such as the Florida Department of Law Enforcement. Anjura has the right to market and sell STaCS, but the royalties the RCMP receives are to be used to upgrade the system to maintain the highest level of bioinformatics tools. (Bioinformatics relates to the information about a person's physical characteristics, including DNA, fingerprints, and retinal scans.)

Dr. Ron Fourney, the Officer in Charge of the NDDB, RCMP, states, "The National DNA Data Bank has become the number one tool in the forensic investigative toolbox for good reason. STaCS provides the ability to develop turnkey solutions at half the cost, run by half the staff, at double the efficiency." For example, STaCS' plug-and-play design could be used by a host of other DNA-type applications, from animal husbandry to paternity cases.

In addition to DNA analysis and tracking with the NDDB, the RCMP uses a variety of other data applications to help prevent, solve, track, and report crimes. All law enforcement agencies want to know where crimes are occurring and how often, and what kinds of crime are occurring in specific locations.

Law enforcement officers who want to gather information about the types and frequency of specific criminal activities typically have to do the research manually—sifting through files and then using their handwritten findings to place coloured pins on a map to indicate the number and type of crimes occurring in a particular area. A number of pins in one area would indicate a trend in criminal activity. To automate this process, the RCMP implemented CADVIEW, a data application to track criminal activity. CADVIEW yields better, more timely information, and its data can be mined to provide reports that can indicate where more law enforcement officers may need to be sent in advance of surges in criminal activity in that area.

The data in CADVIEW comes from computer-aided dispatch. Integrating geographic information system data along with tabular data about crimes permits the system to help law enforcement to focus on areas where crime is high—so-called "hot spots." The RCMP dispatch system sends the data to CADVIEW, where a PowerBuilder-based database application developed by xwave, a consulting firm and subdivision of Bell Aliant, stores the data and

permits it to be mined by an intuitive interface. Onscreen reports can show frequency, number of all crimes in an area, types of crimes in an area, or even the sequence of crimes in an area. This visual representation is extremely helpful not only for the RCMP, but also for the community—such as showing what is happening to a Block Watch meeting of concerned citizens. This application has been deployed to the RCMP's 35 communication centres across Canada.

Nancy MacDonald, the xwave developer who developed the CADVIEW program, explains how the CADVIEW map can be used at shift change briefings. "At some detachments, the map is also used as a 'pin map' that is handed out to the officers at the start of their shift. They can see what is happening in their jurisdiction. As the officers go on duty, they know exactly what sort of crimes occurred and what investigations are in progress."

Thinking of data as dry and dense helps us to realize that dry, dense data can be used to better society and to support law enforcement in protecting us from crime. The use of the National DNA Data Bank, STaCS, and CADVIEW systems certainly shows that data can come to life and help protect human life.

A third RCMP data initiative. the National Integrated Interagency Information (N-III) system, is an information-sharing system for police, public safety, and federal agencies across Canada. To begin with, N-III will use two tools: the Police Information Portal (PIP) for law enforcement agencies and the Integrated Query Tool (IQT) for federal government departments and public safety agencies. IQT will provide access to police information filters that will ensure that data-sharing laws are respected and the various agencies access only the data to which they are legally entitled.

Implementation is to begin in the spring of 2009. Almost all of the 192 Canadian police agencies will participate while the remaining agencies should participate after technology-related issues are worked out. Eight federal agencies may also be involved. "There is nothing like it," said Superintendent Charles Richer, N-III project director, RCMP. "As far as records management systems go, there's nothing out there, has never been anything... this is groundbreaking with respect to providing that kind of information to police officers everywhere."

PIP is a searchable index of all police agency Record Management Systems (RMS) across the country. PIP operates as an information broker. "The PIP portal sits among all participants, acting as an information search engine and request broker. Individual agencies decide what information they want to make available to other law enforcement agencies, while retaining ownership of the data. The portal contains only an index of information and not the contents of an electronic record," according to the RCMP Web site. PIP utilizes pre-existing networks. "It's more about having record management systems that can speak to each other," said Richer. "[PIP] is targeted to assist front-line officers and investigators in knowing with whom they are dealing."

While information-sharing initiatives may stir up privacy rights concerns, criminals such as Paul Bernardo, the infamous convicted criminal, have taken the lack of information sharing across jurisdictions to their gross advantage. Mr. Justice Archie Campbell highlighted the need for police information sharing in the 1996 Bernardo Investigation Review. "That's where all this stemmed from, sharing information," said Richer. "You can solve crimes; you can save lives; that's pretty much what we're about."

CASE STUDY QUESTIONS:

1. Evaluate the RCMP's reasons for implementing STaCS and CADVIEW. Compare the need for efficiency with the need for effectiveness. Were both efficiency and effectiveness key factors in these solutions?

2. What management, organization, and technology factors were responsible for the decision to implement these systems?

3. What problems were to be addressed by these systems? How did data management address these problems? How effective are these solutions?

4. What are the privacy issues that arise from the use of these two databases? Are there simple solutions to these issues, or are the privacy issues complex, requiring the courts to adjudicate them?

Sources: Microsoft, "The Royal Canadian Mounted Police: Microsoft Software Helps Solve Crimes," **www.microsoft.com/canada/ casestudies/rcmp.mspx** (accessed April 10, 2007); "2005 Computerworld Honors Case Study: CADVIEW," **www.cwhonors.org/ laureates/government/20055332.pdf** (accessed April 10, 2007); Government Technology, "Case Study: Royal Canadian Mounted Police," **www.govtech.net/digitalcommunities/studies/ sybase_RCMPv2.pdf** (accessed April 10, 2007); Jennifer Kavur, "RCMP Push National Police Data-Sharing Project," *Computer World Canada*, August 18, 2008.

CHAPTER 7

Telecommunications, the Internet, and Wireless Technology

LEARNING OBJECTIVES

After reading this chapter, you will be able to answer the following questions:

1. What are the principal components of telecommunications networks and key networking technologies?

2. What are the main telecommunications transmission media and types of networks?

3. How do the Internet and Internet technology work, and how do they support communication and e-business?

4. What are the principal technologies and standards for wireless networking, communication, and Internet access?

5. Why are radio frequency identification (RFID) and wireless sensor networks valuable for business?

OPENING CASE

Have You Ever Been in a Virgin Megastore?

The first and only Virgin Megastore in Canada opened in Vancouver on Robson Street in 1996 in a building that was previously a public library. The store was located on three levels and totalled 3716 square metres. This store was taken over by HMV in 2005. Although at the time Virgin closed its Vancouver Megastore, it planned to open one of its stores in Toronto, the company chose to exit the Canadian market altogether before doing so.

Inside a Virgin Megastore, you will find racks and racks of CDs, DVDs, books, video games, and clothing, with videos playing on overhead screens. You can use Virgin Vault digital kiosks to preview music, videos, and games. You might also see a DJ sitting in a booth overlooking the sales floor and spinning the latest hits or tracks from undiscovered artists. Virgin Megastores are very media- and technology-intensive.

These stores are a carefully orchestrated response to an intensely competitive environment because the company must compete with stores such as HMV as well as big box discount chains such as Walmart and online music download services. The business must be able to react instantly to sales trends and operate efficiently to keep prices down. A new CD or DVD release might achieve half of its total sales within the first couple of weeks after its release. Too much or too little of a CD in stores at a specific time can translate into large losses. Although Virgin Megastores' inventory data warehouse based on Microsoft SQL Server database software provides up-to-the-minute information on sales and current stock levels, acting on a rapidly changing picture of supply and demand requires human communication.

In the United States, Virgin Megastores USA has 1400 employees in 11 retail locations. Its Los Angeles–based home office shares information with the retail stores via voice mail, e-mail, and audio weekly conference calls, which are used to discuss upcoming promotions and events, product inventory issues, and current market trends. People shied away from conference calling because of its costs, choosing a less expensive but also less immediate way of communicating, such as sending out a mass e-mail message. However, recipients of that message might not respond right away.

To speed up interaction, Virgin Megastores chose unified communications technology that integrated its voice mail, e-mail, conference calling, and instant messaging into a single solution that would be a natural and seamless way of working. In the fall of 2007, it deployed Microsoft's Office Communication Server, Office Communicator, and RoundTable conferencing and collaboration tools. The technology has presence-awareness capabilities that display other people's availability and status (such as whether the person is already using the phone, in a Web conference, or working remotely) within the Microsoft productivity software they use in the course of their work. Users can see the people they work with in one window of Office Communicator and switch from one type of messaging to another as naturally and easily as picking up a telephone.

Calls integrating audio and video are helping employees resolve issues more quickly. The company is saving more than $60 000 annually in conferencing costs and now has in-house video and Web conferencing as well as audio conferencing.

Sources: Marina Strauss, "Virgin's Withdrawal Music to HMV's Ears," *The Globe and Mail*, June 29, 2005; "HMV Group to Open Canada's Largest Dedicated Music, DVD Store," **www.hmvgroup.com/media/view .jsp?id=1007** (accessed April 24, 2009); Lauren McKay, "All Talk," *Customer Relationship Management Magazine*, June 2008; John Edwards, "How to Get the Most from Unified Communications," *CIO*, February 8, 2008; and "Virgin Megastores USA Turns Up the Volume with Unified Communications," **www.microsoft.com** (accessed June 19, 2008).

Virgin Megastores' experience illustrates some of the powerful new capabilities—and opportunities—provided by contemporary networking technology. The company used unified communications technology to provide managers and employees with integrated voice, e-mail, and conferencing capabilities, with the ability to switch seamlessly from one type of messaging to another. Using unified communications accelerated information sharing and decision making, enabling the company to manage its inventory more precisely.

The chapter-opening diagram calls attention to important points raised by this case and this chapter. The retail music industry is exceptionally competitive and time-sensitive. To stay in the game, Virgin Megastores must be able to respond very rapidly to sales trends. The company's outdated networking and voice technology made it difficult to do this. Management decided that new technology could provide a solution and selected a new unified communications technology platform. Switching to unified communications technology saved time and facilitated information sharing between managers and employees and between retail outlets and corporate headquarters. With more up-to-date information, the company is able to respond more rapidly to sales trends and adjust inventory accordingly. These improvements save time and reduce inventory costs. Virgin Megastores had to make some changes in employee job functions and work flow to take advantage of the new technology.

7.1 Telecommunications and Networking in Today's Business World

If you run or work in a business, you cannot do without networks. You need to communicate rapidly with your customers, suppliers, and employees. Until about 1990, you would have used the postal system or telephone system with voice or fax for business communication. Today, however, you and your employees use computers and e-mail, the Internet, cell phones, and mobile computers connected to wireless networks for this purpose. Networking and the Internet are now nearly synonymous with doing business.

Networking and Communication Trends

Firms in the past used two fundamentally different types of networks: telephone networks and computer networks. Telephone networks historically handled voice communication, and computer networks handled data traffic. Telephone networks were built by telephone companies throughout the 20th century using voice transmission technologies (hardware and software), and these companies almost always operated as regulated monopolies throughout the world. Computer networks were originally built by computer companies seeking to transmit data between computers in different locations.

Thanks to continuing telecommunications deregulation and information technology innovation, telephone and computer networks are slowly converging into a single digital network using shared Internet-based standards and equipment. Telecommunications providers, such as Primus and Bell Canada (discussed in Chapter 5), today offer data transmission, Internet access, wireless telephone service, and television programming as well as voice service. Cable companies, such as Shaw and Rogers, now offer voice service and Internet access. Computer networks have expanded to include Internet telephone and limited video services. Increasingly, all of these voice, video, and data communications are based on Internet technology.

Both voice and data communication networks have also become more powerful (faster), more portable (smaller and mobile), and less expensive. For instance, the typical Internet connection speed in 2000 was 56 kilobits per second, but today more than 81 percent of Canadian households have high-speed **broadband** connections provided by telephone and cable TV companies running at 1 million bits per second. The cost for this service has fallen exponentially, from 25 cents per kilobit in 2000 to less than 1 cent today.

Broadband

Increasingly, voice and data communication as well as Internet access are taking place over broadband wireless platforms, such as cell phones, handheld digital devices, and PCs in wireless networks. In fact, mobile wireless broadband Internet access (2.5G and 3G cellular, which we describe in Section 7.4) was the fastest-growing form of Internet access in 2008, growing at a 96 percent compound annual growth rate. Fixed wireless broadband (Wi-Fi) is growing at a 28 percent compound annual growth rate, the second-fastest-growing form of Internet access. Now that cellular phones can use Wi-Fi as well as cellular networks, use of Wi-Fi networks is growing at a faster-than-ever pace.

What Is a Computer Network?

If you had to connect the computers for two or more employees together in the same office, you would need a computer network. Exactly what is a network? In its simplest form, a network consists of two or more connected computers. Figure 7-1 illustrates the major hardware, software, and transmission components used in a simple network: a client computer and a dedicated server computer, network interfaces, a connection medium, network operating system software, and either a hub or a switch.

Each computer on the network contains a network interface device called a **network interface card (NIC).** Most personal computers today have this card built into the motherboard. The connection medium for linking network components can be a telephone wire, coaxial cable, or radio signal in the case of cell phone and wireless localarea networks (Wi-Fi networks).

The **network operating system (NOS)** routes and manages communications on the network and coordinates network resources. It can reside on every computer in the network, or it can reside primarily on a dedicated server computer for all the applications on the network. A server computer is a computer on a network that performs important network functions for client computers, such as serving up Web pages, storing data, and storing the network operating system (and hence controlling the network). Server soft-

Network interface card (NIC)

Network operating system (NOS)

FIGURE 7-1   Components of a simple computer network.

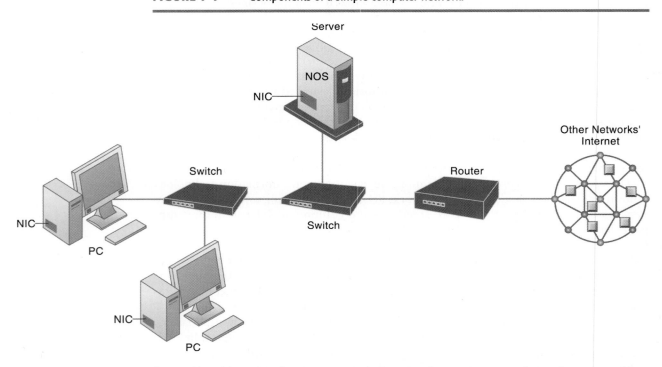

Illustrated here is a very simple computer network, consisting of computers, a network operating system residing on a dedicated server computer, cable (wiring) connecting the devices, network interface cards (NIC), switches, and a router.

ware, such as Microsoft Windows Server, Linux, and Novell NetWare, are the most widely used network operating systems.

Most networks also contain a switch or a hub acting as a connection point between the computers. **Hubs** are very simple devices that connect network components, sending a packet of data to all other connected devices. A **switch** has more intelligence than a hub and can filter and forward data to a specified destination on the network.

What if you want to communicate with another network, such as the Internet? You would need a router. A **router** is a special communications processor used to route packets of data through different networks, ensuring that the data sent gets to the correct address.

Networks in Large Companies The network we have just described might be suitable for a small business. But what about large companies with many different locations and thousands of employees? As a firm grows and collects hundreds of small local area networks (LANs), these networks can be tied together into a corporate-wide networking infrastructure. The network infrastructure for a large corporation consists of a large number of these small local area networks linked to other local area networks and to firm-wide corporate networks. A number of powerful servers support a corporate Web site, a corporate intranet, and perhaps an extranet. Some of these servers link to other large computers supporting back-end systems.

Figure 7-2 provides an illustration of these more complex, larger-scale corporate-wide networks. Here you can see that the corporate network infrastructure supports a mobile sales force using cell phones; mobile employees linking to the company Web site, or internal company networks using mobile wireless local area networks (Wi-Fi networks); and a videoconferencing system to support managers across the world. In addition to these computer networks, the firm's infrastructure usually includes a separate telephone network that handles most voice data. Many firms are dispensing with their traditional telephone networks and using Internet telephones that run on their existing data networks (described later).

As you can see from Figure 7-2, a large corporate network infrastructure uses a wide variety of technologies—everything from ordinary telephone service and corporate data networks to Internet service, wireless Internet, and wireless cell phones. One of the major problems facing corporations today is how to integrate all the different communication networks and channels into a coherent system that enables information to flow from one part of the corporation to another, from one system to another. As more and more communication networks become digital and based on Internet technologies, it will become easier to integrate them.

Key Digital Networking Technologies

Contemporary digital networks and the Internet are based on three key technologies: client/server computing, the use of packet switching, and the development of widely used communications standards (the most important of which is Transmission Control Protocol/Internet Protocol, or TCP/IP) for linking disparate networks and computers.

Client/Server Computing We introduced client/server computing in Chapter 5. Client/server computing is a distributed computing model in which some of the processing power is located within small, inexpensive client computers and resides literally on desktops, laptops, or in handheld devices. These powerful clients are linked to one another through a network that is controlled by a network server computer. The server sets the rules of communication for the network and provides every client with an address so others can find it on the network.

Client/server computing has largely replaced centralized mainframe computing in which nearly all of the processing takes place on a central large mainframe computer. Client/server computing has extended computing to departments, workgroups, factory floors, and other parts of the business that could not be served by a centralized architecture. The Internet is the largest implementation of client/server computing.

Packet Switching **Packet switching** is a method of slicing digital messages into parcels called *packets*, sending the packets along different communication paths as they become

Hubs

Switch

Router

Packet switching

FIGURE 7-2 Corporate network infrastructure.

Today's corporate network infrastructure is a collection of many different networks, from the public switched telephone network, to the Internet, to corporate local area networks linking workgroups, departments, or office floors.

available, and then reassembling the packets once they arrive at their destinations (see Figure 7-3). Prior to the development of packet switching, computer networks used leased, dedicated telephone circuits to communicate with other computers in remote locations. In circuit-switched networks, such as the telephone system, a complete point-to-point circuit is assembled, and then communication can proceed. These dedicated circuit-switching techniques were expensive and wasted available communications capacity—the circuit was maintained whether or not any data were being sent.

Packet switching makes much more efficient use of the communications capacity of a network. In packet-switched networks, messages are first broken down into small, fixed bundles of data; these packets include information for directing each one to the right address and for

FIGURE 7-3 Packed-switched networks and packet communications.

Data are grouped into small packets, which are transmitted independently over various communications channels and reassembled at their final destination.

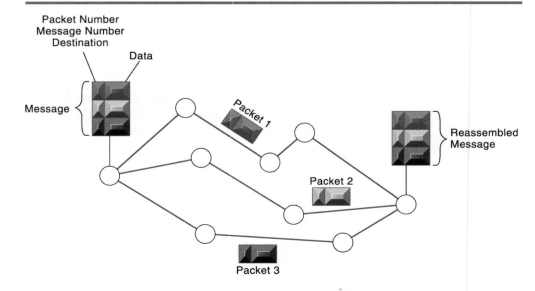

checking transmission errors along with the data. The packets are transmitted over various communications channels using routers, each packet travelling independently. Packets of data originating at one source are routed through many different paths and networks before being reassembled into the original message when they reach their destinations.

TCP/IP and Connectivity In a typical telecommunications network, diverse hardware and software components need to work together to transmit information. Different components in a network communicate with each other only by adhering to a common set of rules called protocols. A **protocol** is a set of rules and procedures governing transmission of information between two points in a network.

In the past, many diverse proprietary and incompatible protocols often forced business firms to purchase computing and communications equipment from a single vendor. But today corporate networks are increasingly using a single, common, worldwide standard called **Transmission Control Protocol/Internet Protocol (TCP/IP)**. TCP/IP was developed during the early 1970s to support U.S. Department of Defense Advanced Research Projects Agency (DARPA) efforts to help scientists transmit data among different types of computers over long distances.

TCP/IP uses a suite of protocols, the main ones being TCP and IP. *TCP* refers to the Transmission Control Protocol (TCP), which handles the movement of data between computers. TCP establishes a connection between the computers, sequences the transfer of packets, and acknowledges the packets sent. *IP* refers to the Internet Protocol (IP), which is responsible for the delivery of packets and includes the disassembling and reassembling of packets during transmission. Figure 7-4 illustrates the four-layered reference model for TCP/IP. Starting from the sending computer, the four layers of the reference model are

1. **Application layer.** The application layer enables client application programs to access the other layers and defines the protocols that applications use to exchange data. One of these application protocols is the Hypertext Transfer Protocol (HTTP), which is used to transfer Web page files.

2. **Transport layer.** The transport layer is responsible for providing the application layer with communication and packet services. This layer includes TCP and other protocols.

3. **Internet layer.** The Internet layer is responsible for addressing, routing, and packaging data packets called IP datagrams. The Internet Protocol is one of the protocols used in this layer.

4. **Network interface layer.** At the bottom of the reference model, the network interface layer is responsible for placing packets on and receiving them from the network medium, which could be any networking technology.

Two computers using TCP/IP are able to communicate even if they are based on different hardware and software platforms. Data sent from one computer to the other passes downward through all four layers, starting with the sending computer's application layer and

Protocol

Transmission Control Protocol/
Internet Protocol (TCP/IP)

FIGURE 7-4 The Transmission Control Protocol/Internet Protocol (TCP/IP) reference model.

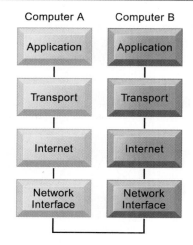

This figure illustrates the four layers of the TCP/IP reference model for communications.

passing through the network interface layer. After the data reach the recipient host computer, they travel up the layers at the receiving computer and are reassembled into a format the receiving computer can use. If the receiving computer finds a damaged packet, it asks the sending computer to retransmit it. This process is repeated when the receiving computer responds.

7.2 Communications Networks and Transmission Media

Let us look more closely at alternative networking technologies available to businesses.

Signals: Digital versus Analog

There are two ways to communicate a message in a network: either an analog signal or a digital signal. An *analog signal* is represented by a continuous waveform that passes through a communications medium; analog signals are used for voice communication. The most common analog devices are the typical wired telephone handset, the speaker on your computer, or your iPod earphone, all of which create analog wave forms that your ear can hear.

A *digital signal* is a discrete, binary waveform, rather than a continuous waveform. Digital signals communicate information as strings of two discrete states: one bit and zero bits, which are represented as on–off electrical pulses.

Computers use digital signals, so if you want to use the analog telephone system to send digital data, you will need a device called a **modem** to translate digital signals into analog form (see Figure 7-5). *Modem* stands for modulator-demodulator. You actually need two modems, one to translate (modulate) from digital to analog, and at the receiving end, one to translate (demodulate) from analog back to digital.

Types of Networks

There are many different kinds of networks and ways of classifying them. One way of looking at networks is in terms of their geographic scope (see Table 7-1).

Local Area Networks If you work in a business that uses networking, you are probably connecting to other employees and groups via a local area network. A **local area network (LAN)** is designed to connect personal computers and other digital devices within a half-mile or 500-metre radius. LANs typically connect a few computers in a small office, all the computers in one building, or all the computers in several buildings in close proximity. LANs can link to long-distance wide area networks (WANs, described later in this section) and other networks around the world using the Internet.

Review Figure 7-1, which could serve as a model for a small LAN that might be used in an office. One computer is a dedicated network file server, providing users with access to shared computing resources in the network, including software programs and data files. The server determines who gets access to what and in which sequence. The router connects the LAN to other networks, which could be the Internet or another corporate network, so that the LAN can exchange information with networks external to it. The most common LAN operating systems are Windows, Linux, and Novell. Each of these network operating systems supports TCP/IP as its default networking protocol.

Modem

Local area network (LAN)

FIGURE 7-5   Functions of the modem.

A modem is a device that translates digital signals from a computer into analog form so that they can be transmitted over analog telephone lines. The modem also translates analog signals back into digital form for the receiving computer.

TABLE 7-1   Types of networks.

TYPE	AREA
Local area network (LAN)	Up to 500 metres (half a mile); an office or floor of a building
Campus area network (CAN)	Up to 1000 metres (a mile); a college campus or corporate facility
Metropolitan area network (MAN)	A city or metropolitan area
Wide area network (WAN)	A transborder or global area

Ethernet is the dominant LAN standard at the physical network level, specifying the physical medium to carry signals between computers, access control rules, and a standardized set of bits used to carry data over the system. Originally, Ethernet supported a data transfer rate of 10 megabits per second (Mbps). Newer versions, such as Fast Ethernet and Gigabit Ethernet, support data transfer rates of 100 Mbps and 1 gigabits per second (Gbps), respectively, and are used in network backbones.

The LAN illustrated in Figure 7-1 uses a client/server architecture where the network operating system resides primarily on a single file server, and the server provides much of the control and resources for the network. Alternatively, LANs may use a **peer-to-peer** architecture. A peer-to-peer network treats all processors equally and is used primarily in small networks with 10 or fewer users. The various computers on the network can exchange data by direct access and can share peripheral devices without going through a separate server.

In LANs using the Windows Server family of operating systems, the peer-to-peer architecture is called the *workgroup network model* in which a small group of computers can share resources, such as files, folders, and printers, over the network without a dedicated server. The Windows *domain network model*, in contrast, uses a dedicated server to manage the computers in the network.

Larger LANs have many clients and multiple servers, with separate servers for specific services, such as storing and managing files and databases (file servers or database servers), managing printers (print servers), storing and managing e-mail (mail servers), or storing and managing Web pages (Web servers).

Sometimes LANs are described in terms of the way their components are connected together, or their **topology.** There are three major LAN topologies: star, bus, and ring (see Figure 7-6).

In a **star topology**, all devices on the network connect to a single hub. Figure 7-6 illustrates a simple star topology in which all network traffic flows through the hub. In an *extended star network*, multiple layers or hubs are organized into a hierarchy.

In a **bus topology,** one station transmits signals, which travel in both directions along a single transmission segment. All of the signals are broadcast in both directions to the entire network. All machines on the network receive the same signals, and software installed on the client's enables each client to listen for messages addressed specifically to it. The bus topology is the most common Ethernet topology.

A **ring topology** connects network components in a closed loop. Messages pass from computer to computer in only one direction around the loop, and only one station at a time may transmit. The ring topology is primarily found in older LANs using Token Ring networking software.

Metropolitan and Wide Area Networks **Wide area networks (WANs)** span broad geographical distances—entire regions, states, continents, or the entire globe. The most universal and powerful WAN is the Internet. Computers connect to a WAN through public networks, such as the telephone system or private cable systems, or through leased lines or satellites. A **metropolitan area network (MAN)** is a network that spans a metropolitan area, usually a city and its major suburbs. Its geographic scope falls between a WAN and a LAN.

Physical Transmission Media

Networks use different kinds of physical transmission media, including twisted wire, coaxial cable, fibre optics, and media for wireless transmission. Each has advantages and limitations.

Peer-to-peer
Topology
Star topology
Bus topology
Ring topology
Wide area networks (WANs)
Metropolitan area network (MAN)

FIGURE 7-6   Network topologies.

The three basic network topologies are the star, bus, and ring.

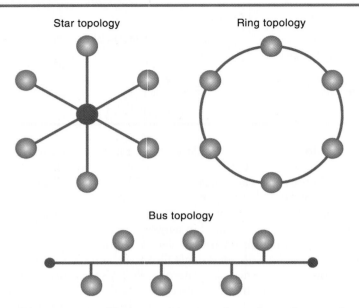

A wide range of speeds is possible for any given medium depending on the software and hardware configuration.

Twisted Wire **Twisted wire** consists of strands of copper wire twisted in pairs and is an older type of transmission medium. Many of the telephone systems in buildings had twisted wires installed for analog communication, but they can be used for digital communication as well. Although an older physical transmission medium, the twisted wires used in today's LANs, such as CAT5, can obtain speeds up to 1 Gbps. Twisted-pair cabling is limited to a maximum recommended run of 100 metres (328 feet).

Coaxial Cable **Coaxial cable,** similar to that used for cable television, consists of thickly insulated copper wire, which can transmit a larger volume of data than twisted wire. Cable was used in early LANs and is still used today for longer (more than 100 metres) runs in large buildings. Coaxial has speeds up to 1 Gbps.

Fibre Optics and Optical Networks **Fibre optic cable** consists of bound strands of clear glass fibre, each the thickness of a human hair. Data are transformed into pulses of light, which are sent through the fibre optic cable by a laser device at rates varying from 500 kilobits to several trillion bits per second in experimental settings. Fibre optic cable is considerably faster, lighter, and more durable than wire media and is well suited to systems requiring transfers of large volumes of data. However, fibre optic cable is more expensive than other physical transmission media and harder to install.

Until recently, fibre optic cable had been used primarily for the high-speed network backbone, which handles the major traffic. Now telecommunications companies are starting to bring fibre lines into homes for new types of services, such as ultra-high-speed Internet access (5 to 50 Mbps) and on-demand video.

Wireless Transmission Media Wireless transmission is based on radio signals of various frequencies. **Microwave** systems, both terrestrial and celestial, transmit high-frequency radio signals through the atmosphere and are widely used for high-volume, long-distance, point-to-point communication. Microwave signals follow a straight line and do not bend with the curvature of the earth. Therefore, long-distance terrestrial transmission systems require that transmission stations be positioned about 60 kilometres apart. Long-distance transmission is also possible by using communication satellites as relay stations for microwave signals transmitted from terrestrial stations.

Communication satellites are typically used for transmission in large, geographically dispersed organizations that would be difficult to network using cabling media or terrestrial

Twisted wire
Coaxial cable
Fibre optic cable
Microwave

FIGURE 7-7   BP's satellite transmission system.

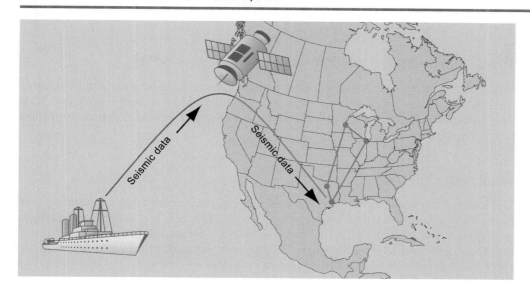

Communication satellites help BP transfer seismic data between oil exploration ships and research centres in the United States.

microwave. For instance, the global energy company BP p.l.c. uses satellites for real-time data transfer of oil field exploration data gathered from searches of the ocean floor. Using geosynchronous satellites, exploration ships transfer these data to central computing centres in the United States for use by researchers in Houston, Tulsa, and suburban Chicago. Figure 7-7 illustrates how this system works.

Cellular systems use radio waves to communicate with radio antennas (towers) placed within adjacent geographic areas called *cells*. Communications transmitted from a **cell phone** to a local cell pass from antenna to antenna—cell to cell—until they reach their final destination.

Wireless networks are supplanting traditional wired networks for many applications and creating new applications, services, and business models. In Section 7.4 we provide a detailed description of the applications and technology standards driving the "wireless revolution."

Transmission Speed The total amount of digital information that can be transmitted through any telecommunications medium is measured in bits per second (bps). One signal change, or cycle, is required to transmit one or several bits; therefore, the transmission capacity of each type of telecommunications medium is a function of its frequency. The number of cycles per second that can be sent through that medium is measured in **hertz**—one hertz is equal to one cycle of the medium.

The range of frequencies that can be accommodated on a particular telecommunications channel is called its **bandwidth.** The bandwidth is the difference between the highest and lowest frequencies that can be accommodated on a single channel. The greater the range of frequencies, the greater the bandwidth and the greater the channel's transmission capacity. Table 7-2 compares the transmission speeds of the major types of media.

Cell phone
Hertz
Bandwidth

TABLE 7-2   Typical speeds and costs of telecommunications transmission media.

MEDIUM	SPEED
Twisted wire	Up to 1 Gbps
Microwave	Up to 600+ Mbps
Satellite	Up to 600+ Mbps
Coaxial cable	Up to 1 Gbps
Fibre optic cable	Up to 6+ Tbps

Mbps = megabits per second
Gbps = gigabits per second
Tbps = terabits per second

7.3 The Internet, Its Technologies, and How They Work

The Global Internet

We all use the Internet, and many of us cannot do without it. It has become an indispensable personal and business tool. But what exactly is the Internet? How does it work, and what does Internet technology have to offer for business? Let us look at the most important Internet features.

What Is the Internet?

The Internet has become the world's most extensive, public communication system that now rivals the global telephone system in reach and range. It is also the world's largest implementation of client/server computing and internetworking, linking millions of individual networks all over the world. This gigantic network of networks began in the early 1970s as a U.S. Department of Defense network to link scientists and university professors around the world.

Most homes and small businesses connect to the Internet by subscribing to an Internet service provider. An **Internet service provider (ISP)** is a commercial organization with a permanent connection to the Internet that sells temporary connections to retail subscribers. Rogers, Shaw, MTS, SaskTel, and Primus are ISPs. Individuals also connect to the Internet through their business firms, universities, or research centres that have designated Internet domains.

There are a variety of services for ISP Internet connections. Connecting via a traditional telephone line and modem, at a speed of 56.6 kilobits per second (Kbps) used to be the most common form of connection worldwide, but it is quickly being replaced by broadband connections. Digital subscriber line (DSL), cable, and satellite Internet connections, and T lines provide these broadband services.

Digital subscriber line (DSL) technologies operate over existing telephone lines to carry voice, data, and video at transmission rates ranging from 385 Kbps all the way up to 9 Mbps. **Cable Internet connections** provided by cable television vendors use digital cable coaxial lines to deliver high-speed Internet access to homes and businesses. They can provide high-speed access to the Internet of up to 10 Mbps. In areas where DSL and cable services are unavailable, it is possible to access the Internet via satellite, although some satellite Internet connections have slower upload speeds than these other broadband services.

T1 and T3 are international telephone standards for digital communication. They are leased, dedicated lines suitable for businesses or government agencies requiring high-speed guaranteed service levels. **T1 lines** offer guaranteed delivery at 1.54 Mbps, and T3 lines offer delivery at 45 Mbps. T3 lines cost approximately three times the monthly charge of T1 lines. An organization can also lease a fractional T1 line.

Internet Addressing and Architecture

The Internet is based on the TCP/IP networking protocol suite described earlier in this chapter. Every computer on the Internet is assigned a unique **Internet Protocol (IP) address,** which currently is a 32-bit number represented by four strings of numbers ranging from 0 to 255 separated by periods. For instance, the IP address of www.microsoft.com is 207.46.250.119.

When a user sends a message to another user on the Internet, the message is first decomposed into packets using the TCP protocol. Each packet contains its destination address. The packets are then sent from the client to the network server and from there on to as many other servers as necessary to arrive at a specific computer with a known address. At the destination address, the packets are reassembled into the original message.

Internet service provider (ISP)
Digital subscriber line (DSL)
Cable Internet connections
T1 lines
Internet Protocol (IP) address

The Domain Name System Because it would be incredibly difficult for Internet users to remember strings of 12 numbers, a **domain name system (DNS)** converts IP addresses to domain names. The **domain name** is the English-like name that corresponds to the unique 32-bit numeric IP address for each computer connected to the Internet. DNS servers maintain a database containing IP addresses mapped to their corresponding domain names. To access a computer on the Internet, users need only specify its domain name.

DNS has a hierarchical structure (see Figure 7-8). At the top of the DNS hierarchy is the root domain. The child domain of the root is called a *top-level domain*, and the child domain of a top-level domain is called is a *second-level domain*. Top-level domains are two- and three-character names you are familiar with from surfing the Web, for example, .com, .edu, .gov, and the various country codes such as .ca for Canada or .it for Italy. Second-level domains have two parts, designating a top-level name and a second-level name—such as aircanada.ca, queensu.ca, or amazon.ca. A host name at the bottom of the hierarchy designates a specific computer on either the Internet or a private network, such as angel.umanitoba.ca.

The most common domain extensions currently available and officially approved are shown in the following list. Countries also have domain names such as .uk, .au, and .fr (United Kingdom, Australia, and France, respectively). In the future, this list will expand to include many more types of organizations and industries.

.com	Commercial organizations/businesses
.edu	Educational institutions
.gov	U.S. government agencies
.mil	U.S. military
.net	Network computers
.org	Nonprofit organizations and foundations
.biz	Business firms
.info	Information providers
.name	Individual named persons
.pro	Professional organization, such as law firms
.coop	For cooperative organizations, such as rural electric cooperatives
.mus	Museums

Internet Architecture and Governance Internet data traffic is carried over transcontinental high-speed backbone networks that generally operate today in the range of 45 Mbps to 2.5 Gbps (see Figure 7-9). These trunk lines are typically owned by long-distance telephone companies (called *network service providers*) or by national governments. Local connection lines are owned by regional telephone and cable television companies that connect retail users in homes and businesses to the Internet. The regional networks lease access to ISPs, private companies, and government institutions.

Each organization pays for its own networks and its own local Internet connection services, a part of which is paid to the long-distance trunk line owners. Individual Internet users pay ISPs for using their service, and they generally pay a flat subscription fee, no matter how much or how little they use the Internet. A debate is now raging on whether this arrangement should continue or whether heavy Internet users who download large video and music files should pay more for the bandwidth they consume. The Window on Organizations section on page 215 explores this topic as it examines the pros and cons of network neutrality.

No one "owns" the Internet, and it has no formal management. However, worldwide Internet policies are established by a number of professional organizations and government bodies, including the Internet Architecture Board (IAB), which helps define the overall structure of the Internet; the Internet Corporation for Assigned Names and Numbers (ICANN), which assigns IP addresses; and the World Wide Web Consortium (W3C), which sets Hypertext Markup Language (HTML) and other programming standards for the Web.

Domain name system (DNS)

Domain name

FIGURE 7-8   The domain name system.

The domain name system is a hierarchical system with a root domain, top-level domains, second-level domains, and host computers at the third level.

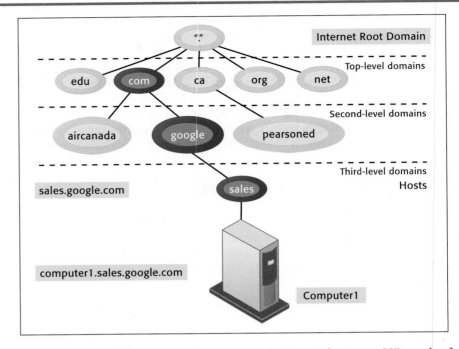

These organizations influence government agencies, network owners, ISPs, and software developers with the goal of keeping the Internet operating as efficiently as possible. The Internet must also conform to the laws of the sovereign nation-states in which it operates, as well as the technical infrastructures that exist within the nation-states. Although in the early years of the Internet and the Web there was very little legislative or executive interference, this situation is changing as the Internet plays a growing role in the distribution of information and knowledge, including content that some find objectionable.

FIGURE 7-9   Internet network architecture.

The Internet backbone connects to regional networks, which in turn provide access to Internet service providers, large firms, and government institutions. Network access points (NAPs) and metropolitan area exchanges (MAEs) are hubs where the backbone intersects regional and local networks and where backbone owners connect with one another.

WINDOW ON ORGANIZATIONS

Should Network Neutrality Continue?

What kind of Internet user are you? Do you primarily use the Net to do a little e-mail and look up phone numbers? Or are you online all day, watching YouTube videos, downloading music files, or playing massively multiplayer online games? If you are the latter, you are consuming a great deal of bandwidth, and hundreds of millions of people like you might start to slow down the Internet. YouTube consumed as much bandwidth in 2007 as the entire Internet did in 2000. That's one of the arguments being made today for charging Internet users based on the amount of transmission capacity they use.

According to one November 2007 report, a research firm projected that user demand for the Internet could outpace network capacity by 2011. If this happens, the Internet might not come to a screeching halt, but users would be faced with sluggish download speeds and slow performance of YouTube, Facebook, and other data-heavy services. Other researchers believe that, as digital traffic on the Internet grows, even at a rate of 50 percent per year, the technology for handling all this traffic is advancing at an equally rapid pace. The increased use of massive data downloading has led to an exaflood, "a surge of data traffic mostly created by video and other forms of new rich media flowing over the Internet," according to Burt Swanson, who coined the term. The prefix *exa* refers to 10 to the 18th power, according to Swanson.

In addition to these technical issues, the debate about metering Internet use centres around the concept of network neutrality. Network neutrality is the idea that Internet service providers must allow customers equal access to content and applications, regardless of the source or nature of the content. Currently, the Internet is indeed neutral: all Internet traffic is treated equally on a first-come, first-served basis by Internet backbone owners. The Internet is neutral because it was built on phone lines, which are subject to common carriage laws. These laws require phone companies to treat all calls and customers equally. They cannot offer extra benefits to customers willing to pay higher premiums for faster or clearer calls, a model known as tiered service.

Now telecommunications and cable companies want to be able to charge differentiated prices based on the amount of bandwidth consumed by content being delivered over the Internet. Today all major ISPs in Canada, as well as several in the United Kingdom, New Zealand, and other countries have moved to usage-based pricing. Other ISPs are also tinkering with alternative pricing models. In June 2008, Time Warner Cable started testing metered pricing for its Internet access service in the city of Beaumont, Texas. Under the pilot program, Time Warner charged customers an additional $1 per month for each gigabyte of content they downloaded or sent over the bandwidth limit of their monthly plan. The company reported that 5 percent of its customers had been using half the capacity on its local lines without paying any more than low-usage customers, and that metered

pricing was "the fairest way" to finance necessary investments in its network infrastructure.

In addition to metered or usage-based pricing, an ISP can slow the flow of data of peer-to-peer traffic during peak demand hours. This is called traffic shaping, and it is targeted at users who have exceeded their ISP's definition of their fair allotment of bandwidth. These users are known as bandwidth hogs. Bell Canada uses this network management policy.

This is not how Internet service has worked traditionally and contradicts the goals of network neutrality. Advocates of net neutrality want the industry to be regulated, requiring network providers to refrain from these types of practices. However, any legislation or even regulation regarding net neutrality is considered unlikely to be passed quickly because of significant resistance by Internet service providers.

Internet service providers point to the upsurge in piracy of copyrighted materials over the Internet. Comcast, the second-largest Internet service provider in the United States, reported that illegal file sharing of copyrighted material was consuming 50 percent of its network capacity. At one point, Comcast slowed down transmission of BitTorrent files, used extensively for piracy and illegal sharing of copyrighted materials, including video. Comcast drew fierce criticism for its handling of BitTorrent packets, and later switched to a "platform-agnostic" approach. It currently slows down the connection of any customer who uses too much bandwidth during congested periods without singling out the specific services the customer is using. In controlling piracy and prioritizing bandwidth usage on the Internet, Comcast claims to be providing better service for its customers who are using the Web legally.

Net neutrality advocates argue that the risk of censorship increases when network operators can selectively block or slow access to certain content. There are already many examples of Internet providers restricting access to sensitive materials (such as anti-Bush comments from an online Pearl Jam concert, a text-messaging program from pro-choice group NARAL, or access to competitors like Vonage). In Canada, Telus restricted access to labour union blogs in 2005. Pakistan's government blocked access to anti-Muslim sites and YouTube as a whole in response to content government officials deemed defamatory to Islam.

Proponents of net neutrality also argue that a neutral Internet encourages everyone to innovate without permission from the phone and cable companies or other authorities, and this level playing field has spawned countless new businesses. Allowing unrestricted information flow becomes essential to free markets and democracy as commerce and society increasingly move online.

Network owners believe regulation like the bills proposed by net neutrality advocates will impede competitiveness by stifling innovation and hurt customers who will benefit from discriminatory network practices. North American Internet service lags behind other many other nations in overall speed, cost, and quality of service, adding credibility to the providers' arguments.

Network neutrality advocates counter that carriers already have too much power due to lack of options for service. Without sufficient competition, the carriers have more freedom to set prices and policies, and customers cannot seek recourse via other options. Carriers can discriminate in favour of their own content. Even broadband users in large metropolitan areas lack many options for service. With enough options for Internet access, net neutrality would not be such a pressing issue. Dissatisfied consumers could simply switch to providers who enforce net neutrality and allow unlimited Internet use.

The issue is a long way from resolution. The Canadian Radio-Television and Telecommunications Commission (CRTC) recently conducted a review of the Internet traffic management practices of ISPs. As this chapter is being written, public hearings on Internet traffic management conducted by the CRTC are under way. Even notable Internet personalities disagree, such as the co-inventors of the Internet Protocol, Vinton Cerf and Bob Kahn. Cerf favours net neutrality, saying that variable access to content would detract from the Internet's continued ability to thrive ("allowing broadband carriers to control what people see and do online would fundamentally undermine the principles that have made the Internet such a success"). Kahn is more cautious, saying that net neutrality removes the incentive for network providers to innovate, provide new capabilities, and upgrade to new technology. Who is right; who is wrong? The debate continues.

To Think About

1. What is network neutrality? Why has the Internet operated under net neutrality up to this point in time?

2. Who is in favour of network neutrality? Who's opposed? Why? Where do you stand on this debate?

3. What would be the impact on individual users, businesses, and government if Internet providers switched to a tiered service model?

4. Are you in favour of legislation enforcing network neutrality? Why or why not?

MIS in Action

1. Visit the Web site of the Open Internet Coalition, and select five member organizations. Then visit the Web site of each of these organizations, or surf the Web to find out more information about each. Write a short essay explaining why each organization is in favour of network neutrality.

2. Calculate how much bandwidth you consume when using the Internet every day. How many e-mails do you send daily, and what is the size of each? (Your e-mail program may have e-mail file size information.) How many music and video clips do you download daily, and what is the size of each? If you view YouTube often, surf the Web to find out the size of a typical YouTube file. Add up the number of e-mail, audio, and video files you transmit or receive on a typical day.

Sources: Josh Stern, "Investigating the Exaflood," *Convergence Magazine*, 2008, http://magazines.humber.ca/convergence2008/exaflood.html (accessed April 26, 2009); Kenneth Corbin, "Time Warner Cable Broadband Pricing Fight Rages," www.internetnews.com/infra/print.php/3815591; Andy Dornan, "Is Your Network Neutral?" *InformationWeek*, May 18, 2008; Rob Preston, "Meter Is Starting to Tick on Internet Access Pricing," *InformationWeek*, June 9, 2008; Damian Kulash, Jr., "Beware of the New New Thing," *The New York Times*, April 5, 2008; Steve Lohr, "Video Road Hogs Stir Fear of Internet Traffic Jam," *The New York Times*, March 13, 2008; Peter Burrows, "The FCC, Comcast, and Net Neutrality," *BusinessWeek*, February 26, 2008; S. Derek Turner, "Give Net Neutrality a Chance," *BusinessWeek*, July 12, 2008; K.C. Jones, "Piracy Becomes Focus of Net Neutrality Debate," *InformationWeek*, May 6, 2008; Jane Spencer, "How a System Error in Pakistan Shut YouTube," *The* Wall Street Journal, February 26, 2008.

The Future Internet: IPv6 and Internet2 The Internet was not originally designed to handle the transmission of massive quantities of data and billions of users. Because many corporations and governments have been given large blocks of millions of IP addresses to accommodate current and future needs, and because of sheer Internet population growth, the world will run out of available IP addresses using the existing addressing convention by 2012 or 2013. Under development is a new version of the IP addressing schema called *Internet Protocol version 6* (*IPv6*), which contains 128-bit addresses (2 to the power of 128), or more than a quadrillion possible unique addresses.

Internet2 and Next-Generation Internet (NGI) are consortia representing 200 universities, private businesses, and government agencies in the United States that are working on a new, robust, high-bandwidth version of the Internet. They have established several new high-performance backbone networks with bandwidths ranging from 2.5 Gbps to 9.6 Gbps. Internet2 research groups are developing and implementing new technologies for more effective routing practices; different levels of service, depending on the type and importance of the data being transmitted; and advanced applications for distributed computation, virtual laboratories, digital libraries, distributed learning, and tele-immersion. CANARIE is the Canadian equivalent of Internet2. CANARIE has deployed the various versions of **CA*net,** the national backbone for Canada with one "drop" per province. CA*net is the foundation

Internet2
CA*net

FIGURE 7-10   CA*net4 infrastructure.

The CA*net4 infrastructure describes how this advanced Internet infrastructure works, not only across Canada but also with links to the United States.

Source: Reprinted with the permission of CANARIE Inc.

for "innovation infrastructure" by interconnecting regional networks, universities, and schools to promote an "innovation culture" through advanced applications, such as tele-learning, grids, and so forth. Today, CA*net has evolved to CA*net4, which is based on optical networking technologies to promote the fastest speeds available over the Internet, primarily for research and education purposes. Figure 7-10 illustrates how this advanced network works. These networks do not replace the public Internet, but they do provide test beds for leading-edge technology that may eventually migrate to the public Internet.

Internet Services and Communication Tools

The Internet is based on client/server technology. Individuals using the Internet control what they do through client applications on their computers, such as Web browser software. The data, including e-mail messages and Web pages, are stored on servers. A client uses the Internet to request information from a particular Web server on a distant computer, and the server sends the requested information back to the client over the Internet. Chapters 5 and 6 describe how Web servers work with application servers and database servers to access information from an organization's internal information systems applications and their associated databases. Client platforms today include not only PCs and other computers but also cell phones, small handheld digital devices, and other information appliances.

Internet Services A client computer connecting to the Internet has access to a variety of services. These services include e-mail, electronic discussion groups, chatting and instant messaging, **Telnet, File Transfer Protocol (FTP),** and the World Wide Web. Table 7-3 provides a brief description of these services.

Each Internet service is implemented by one or more software programs. All of the services may run on a single server computer, or different services may be allocated to different machines. Figure 7-11 illustrates one way that these services might be arranged in a multitiered client/server architecture.

E-mail enables messages to be exchanged from computer to computer. Although some organizations operate their own internal electronic mail systems, most e-mail today is sent

Telnet
File Transfer Protocol (FTP)
E-mail

TABLE 7-3 Major Internet services.

CAPABILITY	FUNCTIONS SUPPORTED
E-mail	Person-to-person messaging; document sharing
Chatting and instant messaging	Interactive conversations
Newsgroups	Discussion groups on electronic bulletin boards
Telnet	Logging on to one computer system and doing work as though the user was working on a distant computer
File Transfer Protocol (FTP)	Transferring files from computer to computer
World Wide Web	Retrieving, formatting, and displaying information (including text, audio, graphics, and video) using hypertext links)

through the Internet. The cost of e-mail is far lower than equivalent voice, postal, or overnight delivery costs. Most e-mail messages arrive anywhere in the world in a matter of seconds.

Nearly 90 percent of North American workplaces have employees communicating interactively using **chat** or instant messaging tools. Chatting enables two or more people who are simultaneously connected to the Internet to hold live, interactive conversations. Chat systems now support voice and video chat as well as written conversations. Many online retail businesses offer chat services on their Web sites to attract visitors, to encourage repeat purchases, and to improve customer service.

Instant messaging is a type of chat service that enables participants to create their own private chat channels. The instant messaging system alerts the user whenever someone on his or her private list is online so that the user can initiate a chat session with other individuals. Companies concerned with security use proprietary instant messaging systems such as Lotus Sametime.

Newsgroups are worldwide discussion groups posted on Internet electronic bulletin boards on which people share information and ideas on a defined topic, such as radiology or rock bands. Anyone can post messages on these bulletin boards for others to read. Many thousands of groups exist that discuss almost every conceivable topic.

Chat
Instant messaging

FIGURE 7-11 Client/server computing on the Internet.

Client computers running Web browser and other software can access an array of services on servers over the Internet. These services may all run on a single server or on multiple specialized servers.

FIGURE 7-12 How Voice over IP works.

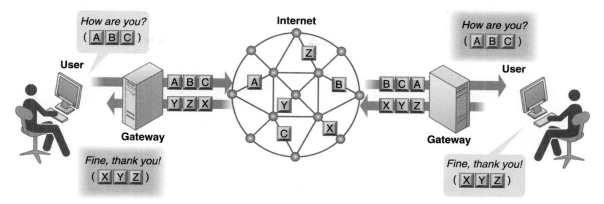

A VoIP phone call digitizes and breaks up a voice message into data packets that may travel along different routes before being reassembled at the final destination. A processor nearest the call's destination, called a gateway, arranges the packets in the proper order and directs them to the telephone number of the receiver or the IP address of the receiving computer.

Employee use of e-mail, instant messaging, and the Internet is supposed to increase worker productivity, but the accompanying Window on Management shows that this may not always be the case. Many company managers now believe they need to monitor and even regulate their employees' online activity. But is this ethical? Although there are some strong business reasons why companies may need to monitor their employees' e-mail and Web activities, what does this mean for employee privacy?

Voice over IP The Internet has also become a popular platform for voice transmission and corporate networking. **Voice over IP (VoIP)** technology delivers voice information in digital form using packet switching, avoiding the tolls charged by local and long-distance telephone networks (see Figure 7-12). Calls that would ordinarily be transmitted over public telephone networks travel over a corporate network based on the Internet Protocol, or the public Internet. Voice calls can be made and received with a desktop computer equipped with a microphone and speakers or with a VoIP-enabled telephone.

Telecommunications service providers (such as Rogers) and cable firms (such as Shaw) provide VoIP services. Skype, acquired by eBay, offers free VoIP worldwide using a peer-to-peer network, and Google has its own free VoIP service.

Although there are upfront investments required for an IP phone system, VoIP can reduce communication and network management costs by 20 to 30 percent. For example, VoIP saves Virgin Entertainment Group $700,000 per year in long-distance bills. In addition to lowering long-distance costs and eliminating monthly fees for private lines, an IP network provides a single voice-data infrastructure for both telecommunications and computing services. Companies no longer have to maintain separate networks or provide support services and personnel for each different type of network.

Voice over IP (VoIP)

Management

WINDOW ON MANAGEMENT

Monitoring Employees on Networks: Unethical or Good Business?

As Internet use has exploded worldwide, so have the use of e-mail and the Web for personal business at the workplace. Several management problems have emerged: First, checking e-mail, responding to instant messages, or sneaking in a brief YouTube or MySpace video create a series of nonstop interruptions that divert employee attention from the job tasks they are supposed to be performing. According to Basex, a business research company, these distractions take up as much as 28 percent of the average worker's day and result in more than $650 billion in lost productivity each year.

Second, these interruptions are not necessarily work-related. A number of studies have concluded that at least

25 percent of employee online time is spent on non-work-related Web surfing, and perhaps as many as 90 percent of employees receive or send personal e-mail at work.

Many companies have begun monitoring their employees' use of e-mail, blogs, and the Internet, sometimes without their knowledge. Although companies have the legal right to monitor employee Internet and e-mail activity while they are at work, is such monitoring unethical, or is it simply good business?

Managers worry about the loss of time and employee productivity when employees are focusing on personal rather than company business. Too much time on personal business, on the Internet or not, can mean lost revenue or overbilled clients because some employees may be charging time they spend trading their personal stocks online or pursuing other personal business to clients.

If personal traffic on company networks is too high, it can also clog the company's network so that legitimate business work cannot be performed. BBBank eG of Germany found that a key business driver was to have an overview of the way its employees used the Internet and for what purposes. According to BBBank's Nelson Gonzales, the bank used monitoring software that has helped to reduce costs and produces all the necessary reporting for accountability purposes. The bank can now properly manage its Internet expenditure, resulting in improved cost controls. "This includes statistical detail reporting by organization, department, and clients. As a consequence, of the reporting information gathered, the bank has deterred seven cases of inappropriate Internet usage and reduced its bandwidth costs by 15 percent," Gonzales says.

When employees use e-mail or the Web at employer facilities or with employer equipment, anything they do, including anything illegal, carries the company's name. Therefore, the employer can be traced and held liable. Management in many firms fear that racist, sexually explicit, hate, or other potentially offensive material accessed or traded by their employees could result in adverse publicity and even lawsuits for the firm. Even if the company is found not to be liable, responding to lawsuits could cost the company tens of thousands of dollars.

Companies also fear leakage of confidential information and trade secrets through e-mail or blogs. Ajax Boiler, based in Santa Ana, California, learned that one of its senior managers was able to access the network of a former employer and read the e-mail of that company's human resources manager. The Ajax employee was trying to gather information for a lawsuit against the former employer.

Companies that allow employees to use personal e-mail accounts at work face legal and regulatory trouble if they do not retain those messages. E-mail today is an important source of evidence for lawsuits, and companies are now required to retain all of their e-mail messages for longer periods than in the past. Courts do not discriminate about whether e-mails involved in lawsuits were sent via personal or business e-mail accounts, and not producing those e-mails could result in a significant fine.

Canadian companies have the legal right to monitor what employees are doing with company equipment during business hours. The question is whether electronic surveillance is an appropriate tool for maintaining an efficient and positive workplace. Some companies try to ban all personal activities on corporate networks—zero tolerance. Others block employee access to specific Web sites or limit personal time on the Web using software that enables IT departments to track the Web sites employees visit, the amount of time employees spend at these sites, and the files they download. Ajax uses software from SpectorSoft Corporation that records all the Web sites employees visit, time spent at each site, and all e-mails sent. BBBank eG uses WebSpy to categorize and filter Web content and block unwanted video.

Some firms have fired employees who have stepped out of bounds. One-third of the companies surveyed in an AMA study had fired workers for misusing the Internet on the job. Among managers who fired employees for Internet misuse, 64 percent did so because the employees' e-mail contained inappropriate or offensive language, and more than 25 percent fired workers for excessive personal use of e-mail.

No solution is problem-free, but many consultants believe companies should write corporate policies on employee e-mail and Internet use. The policies should include explicit ground rules that state, by position or level, under what circumstances employees can use company facilities for e-mail, blogging, or Web surfing. The policies should also inform employees whether these activities are monitored and explain why.

The rules should be tailored to specific business needs and organizational cultures. For example, although some companies may exclude all employees from visiting sites that have explicit sexual material, law firm or hospital employees may require access to these sites. Investment firms will need to allow many of their employees access to other investment sites. A company dependent on widespread information sharing, innovation, and independence could very well find that monitoring creates more problems than it solves.

To Think About

1. Should managers monitor employee e-mail and Internet usage? Why or why not?
2. Describe an effective e-mail and Web use policy for a company.

MIS in Action

Explore the Web site of a company offering online employee monitoring software such as WebSpy, SpectorSoft, or SpyTech NetVizor, and answer the following questions.

1. What employee activities does this software track? What can an employer learn about an employee by using this software?
2. How can businesses benefit from using this software?
3. How would you feel if your employer used this software where you work to monitor what you are doing on the job? Explain your response.

Sources: Nancy Gohring, "Over 50 Percent of Companies Fire Workers for E-mail, Net Abuse," *InfoWorld*, February 28, 2008; "BBBank eG," www.webspy.com/resources/testimonials.aspx (accessed April 26, 2009); Bobby White, "The New Workplace Rules: No Video-Watching," *The Wall Street Journal*, March 4, 2008; Maggie Jackson, "May We Have Your Attention, Please?" *BusinessWeek*, June 23, 2008; Katherine Wegert, "Workers Can Breach Security Knowingly or Not," Dow Jones News Service, June 24, 2007; Andrew Blackman, "Foul Sents," *The Wall Street Journal*, March 26, 2007.

Another advantage of VoIP is its flexibility. Unlike the traditional telephone network, phones can be added or moved to different offices without rewiring or reconfiguring the network. With VoIP, a conference call is arranged by a simple click-and-drag operation on the computer screen to select the names of the conferees. Voice mail and e-mail can be combined into a single directory.

Unified Communications In the past, each of the firm's networks for wired and wireless data, voice communications, and videoconferencing operated independently of each other and had to be managed separately by the information systems department. Now, however, firms are able to merge disparate communications modes into a single universally accessible service using **unified communications** technology. As the chapter-opening case on Virgin Megastores points out, unified communications integrates disparate channels for voice communications, data communications, instant messaging, e-mail, and electronic conferencing into a single experience where users can seamlessly switch back and forth between different communication modes. Presence technology shows whether a person is available to receive a call. Companies will need to examine how work flows and business processes will be altered by this technology in order to gauge its value.

Virtual Private Networks What if you had a marketing group charged with developing new products and services for your firm with members spread across Canada? You would want to be able to e-mail each other and communicate with the home office without any chance that outsiders could intercept the communications. In the past, one answer to this problem was to work with large private networking firms that offered secure, private, dedicated networks to customers. But this was an expensive solution. A much less expensive solution is to create a virtual private network within the public Internet.

A **virtual private network (VPN)** is a secure, encrypted, private network that has been configured within a public network to take advantage of the economies of scale and management facilities of large networks, such as the Internet (see Figure 7-13). A VPN provides your firm with secure, encrypted communications at a much lower cost than the same capabilities offered by traditional non-Internet providers that use their private networks to secure communications. VPNs also provide a network infrastructure for combining voice and data networks.

Several competing protocols are used to protect data transmitted over the public Internet, including *Point-to-Point Tunnelling Protocol (PPTP)*. In a process called tunnelling, packets of data are encrypted and wrapped inside IP packets. By adding this wrapper around a network message to hide its content, business firms create a private connection that travels through the public Internet.

The World Wide Web

You have probably used the World Wide Web to download music, to find information for a term paper, or to obtain news and weather reports. The Web is the most popular Internet service. It is a system with universally accepted standards for storing, retrieving, formatting, and displaying information using a client/server architecture. Web pages are formatted using hypertext with embedded links that connect documents to one another and that also link pages to other objects, such as sound, video, or animation files. When you click a graphic and a video clip plays, you have clicked a hyperlink. A typical **Web site** is a collection of Web pages linked to a home page.

Hypertext Web pages are based on a standard Hypertext Markup Language (HTML), which formats documents and incorporates dynamic links to other documents and pictures stored in the same or remote computers (see Chapter 5). Web pages are accessible through the Internet because Web browser software operating your computer can request Web pages stored on an Internet host server using the **Hypertext Transfer Protocol (HTTP).** HTTP is the communications standard used to transfer pages on the Web. For example, when you type a Web address in your browser, such as www.pearsoned.ca, your browser sends an HTTP request to the pearsoned.ca server requesting the home page of pearsoned.ca.

Unified communications
Virtual private network (VPN)
Web site
Hypertext Transfer Protocol (HTTP)

FIGURE 7-13   A virtual private network using the Internet.

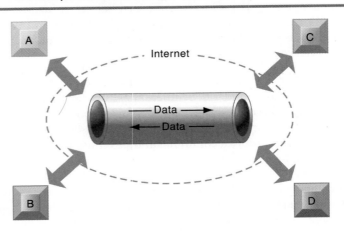

This VPN is a private network of computers linked using a secure "tunnel" connection over the Internet. It protects data transmitted over the public Internet by encoding the data and "wrapping" them within the Internet Protocol (IP). By adding a wrapper around a network message to hide its content, organizations can create a private connection that travels through the public Internet.

HTTP is the first set of letters at the start of every Web address, followed by the domain name, which specifies the organization's server computer that is storing the document. Most companies have a domain name that is the same as or closely related to their official corporate name. The directory path and document name are two more pieces of information within the Web address that help the browser track down the requested page. Together, the address is called a **uniform resource locator (URL).** When typed into a browser, a URL tells the browser software exactly where to look for the information. For example, in the URL www.megacorp.com/content/features/082602.html, *http* names the protocol used to display Web pages, *www.megacorp.com* is the domain name, *content/features* is the directory path that identifies where on the domain Web server the page is stored, and *082602.html* is the document name and the name of the format it is in (it is an HTML page).

Web Servers A Web server is software for locating and managing stored Web pages. It locates the Web pages requested by a user on the computer where they are stored and delivers the Web pages to the user's computer. Server applications usually run on dedicated computers although they can all reside on a single computer in small organizations.

The most common Web server in use today is Apache HTTP Server, which holds 66 percent of the market. Apache is an open source product that is free of charge and can be downloaded from the Web. Microsoft's product Internet Information Services is the second most commonly used Web server, with a 19 percent market share (Netcraft, 2009).

Searching for Information on the Web No one knows for sure how many Web pages there really are. The surface Web is the part of the Web that search engines visit and about which information is recorded. For instance, Google visited about 50 billion pages in 2007 although publicly it acknowledges indexing more than 25 billion. But there is a "deep Web" that contains an estimated 800 billion additional pages, many of them proprietary (such as the pages of *The Wall Street Journal* Online, which cannot be visited without an access code) or that are stored in protected corporate databases.

Obviously, with so many Web pages, finding specific Web pages that can help you or your business, nearly instantly, is an important problem. The question is, how can you find the one or two pages you really want and need out of billions of indexed Web pages? **Search engines** attempt to solve the problem of finding useful information on the Web nearly instantly, and, arguably, they are the "killer app" of the Internet era. Today's search engines can sift through HTML files, files of Microsoft Office applications, and PDF files, with capabilities that are in various stages of development for searching audio, video, and image files. There are hundreds of different search engines in the world, but the vast majority of search results are supplied by three top providers: Google, Yahoo!, and Microsoft.

Web search engines started out in the early 1990s as relatively simple software programs that roamed the nascent Web, visiting pages and gathering information about the content of each page. The first search engines were simple keyword indexes of all the pages they visited, leaving the user with lists of pages that may not have been truly relevant to the search.

Uniform resource locator (URL)
Search engines

In 1994, Stanford University computer science students David Filo and Jerry Yang created a hand-selected list of their favourite Web pages and called it "Yet Another Hierarchical Officious Oracle," or Yahoo!. Yahoo! was not initially a search engine but rather an edited selection of Web sites organized by categories the editors found useful, but it has since developed its own search engine capabilities.

In 1998, Larry Page and Sergey Brin, two other Stanford computer science students, released their first version of Google. This search engine was different: It not only indexed each Web page's words, but it also ranked search results based on the relevance of each page. Page patented the idea of a page ranking system (PageRank System), which essentially measures the popularity of a Web page by calculating the number of sites that link to that page. Brin contributed a unique Web crawler program that indexed not only keywords on a page but also combinations of words (such as authors and the titles of their articles). These two ideas became the foundation for the Google search engine. Figure 7-14 illustrates how Google works.

Web sites for locating information, such as Yahoo!, Google, and MSN, have become so popular and easy to use that they also serve as major portals for the Internet (see Chapter 13). Their search engines have become major shopping tools by offering what is now called **search engine marketing.** When users enter a search term at Google, MSN, Yahoo!, or any of the other sites serviced by these search engines, they receive two types of listings: sponsored links, for which advertisers have paid to be listed (usually at the top of the search results page), and unsponsored "organic" search results. In addition, advertisers can purchase tiny text boxes on the side of the Google and MSN search results page. The paid, sponsored advertisements are the fastest-growing form of Internet advertising and are powerful new marketing tools that precisely match consumer interests with advertising messages at the right moment (see the chapter-ending case study). Search engine marketing monetizes the value of the search process.

Search engine marketing

FIGURE 7-14   How Google works.

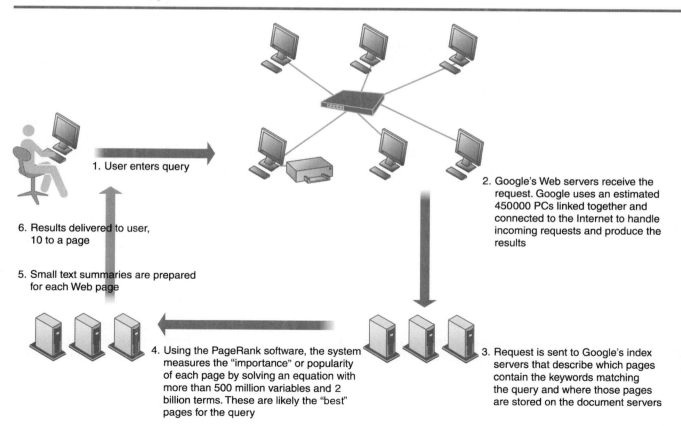

The Google search engine is continuously crawling the Web, indexing the content of each page, calculating its popularity, and storing the pages so that it can respond quickly to user requests to see a page. The entire process takes about one-half second.

Google is the most popular search engine on the Web, handling 60 percent of all Web searches.
Source: Based on data from Nielsen Online and MegaView Search, 2008.

FIGURE 7-15   Top Web search engines.

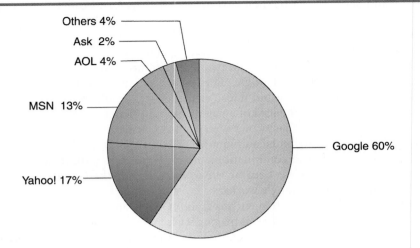

Others 4%
Ask 2%
AOL 4%
MSN 13%
Yahoo! 17%
Google 60%

In 2008, 71 million people each day in the United States alone used a search engine, producing over 10 billion searches a month. There are hundreds of search engines, but the top three (Google, Yahoo!, and MSN) account for 90 percent of all searches (see Figure 7-15).

Although search engines were originally built to search text documents, the explosion in online video and images has created a demand for search engines that can quickly find specific videos. The words "dance," "love," "music," and "girl" are all exceedingly popular in titles of YouTube videos, and searching on these keywords produces a flood of responses even though the actual contents of the video may have nothing to do with the search term. Searching videos is challenging because computers are not very good or quick at recognizing digital images. Some search engines have started indexing movies scripts so it will be possible to search on dialogue to find a movie. One of the most popular video search engines is Blinkx.com, which stores 18 million hours of video and employs a large group of human classifiers who check the contents of uploaded videos against their titles.

Chapter 15 describes the capabilities of software agents with built-in intelligence that can gather or filter information and perform other tasks to assist users. **Shopping bots** use intelligent agent software for searching the Internet for shopping information. Shopping bots such as MySimon or Froogle can help people interested in making a purchase filter and retrieve information about products of interest, evaluate competing products according to criteria the users have established, and negotiate with vendors for price and delivery terms. Many of these shopping agents search the Web for pricing and availability of products specified by the user and return a list of sites that sell the item along with pricing information and a purchase link.

Web 2.0 If you have shared photos over the Internet at Flickr or another photo site, blogged, looked up a word on Wikipedia, or contributed information yourself, you have used services that are part of **Web 2.0.** Today's Web sites do not just contain static content—they also enable people to collaborate, share information, and create new services online. Web 2.0 refers to these second-generation interactive Internet-based services.

The technologies and services that distinguish Web 2.0 include cloud computing, software mashups and widgets, blogs, RSS, and wikis. Mashups and widgets, which we introduced in Chapter 5, are software services that enable users and system developers to mix and match content or software components to create something entirely new. For example, Yahoo's photo storage and sharing site Flickr combines photos with other information about the images provided by users and tools to make the photos and information usable within other programming environments.

These software applications run on the Web itself instead of the desktop and bring the vision of Web-based computing closer to realization. With Web 2.0, the Web is not just a collection of destination sites, but a source of data and services that can be combined to create applications users need. Web 2.0 tools and services have fuelled the creation of

Shopping bots
Web 2.0

social networks and other online communities where people can interact with one another in the manner of their choosing.

These social aspects of Web 2.0 technology are changing the social interactions and culture of the Internet community. While the Web originally permitted individuals to interact with a particular, relatively static Web site, Web 2.0 technologies permit Web users to interact proactively not only with Web sites but also with other individuals who use those Web sites. This is certainly true of sites such as Second Life, MySpace, Facebook, Twitter, and Flickr. As these social and cultural changes impact the use of the Web, they also change the economics of commerce. More and more micro-payments are being generated, and tracking taxes and contractual obligations of these micro-payment-based sales is becoming more and more difficult.

A **blog,** the popular term for a Web log, is an informal yet structured Web site where subscribing individuals can publish stories, opinions, and links to other Web sites of interest. Blogs have become popular personal publishing tools, but they also have business uses (see Chapters 13 and 15). For example, Royal Bank of Canada uses a blog to update those interested in its "Next Great Innovator Challenge," open to more than 20 Canadian colleges and universities.

If you are an avid blog reader, you might use RSS to keep up with your favourite blogs without constantly checking them for updates. **RSS,** which stands for Rich Site Summary or Really Simple Syndication, syndicates Web site content so that it can be used in another setting. RSS technology pulls specified content from Web sites and feeds it automatically to users' computers or handheld devices, where it can be stored for later viewing.

To receive an RSS information feed, you need to install aggregator or news reader software that can be downloaded from the Web. (Microsoft Internet Explorer 7 includes RSS reading capabilities.) Alternatively, you can establish an account with an aggregator Web site. You tell the aggregator to collect all updates from a given Web page, or list of pages, or gather information on a given subject by conducting Web searches at regular intervals. Once subscribed, you automatically receive new content as it is posted to the specified Web site. A number of businesses use RSS internally to distribute updated corporate information. BMO Bank of Montreal uses RSS to deliver news feeds for those interested in corporate information and investor relations as well as other topics offered through its RSS site.

Blogs allow visitors to add comments to the original content, but they do not allow visitors to change the original posted material. **Wikis,** in contrast, are collaborative Web sites where visitors can add, delete, or modify content on the site, including the work of previous authors. Wiki comes from the Hawaiian word for "quick." Probably the best-known wiki site is Wikipedia, the massive online opensource encyclopedia to which anyone can contribute. But wikis are also used for business. For example, as an experiment, CBC used a wiki to let viewers collaborate on a script for the CBC radio show, *Spark*.

Web 3.0: The Future Web Every day, about 75 million Americans enter 330 million queries to search engines. How many of these 330 million queries produce a meaningful result (a useful answer in the first three listings)? Arguably, fewer than half. Google, Yahoo!, Microsoft, and Amazon are all trying to increase the odds of people finding meaningful answers to search engine queries. But with more than 50 billion Web pages indexed, the means available for finding the information you really want are quite primitive, based on the words used on the pages, and the relative popularity of the page among people who use those same search terms. In other words, it is hit or miss.

To a large extent, the future of the Web involves developing techniques to make searching the 50 billion Web pages more productive and meaningful for ordinary people. Web 1.0 solved the problem of obtaining access to information. Web 2.0 solved the problem of sharing that information with others and building new Web experiences. **Web 3.0** is the promise of a future Web where all this digital information, all these contacts, can be woven together into a single meaningful experience.

Sometimes this is referred to as the **Semantic Web.** "Semantic" refers to meaning. Most of the Web's content today is designed for humans to read and for computers to display, not for computer programs to analyze and manipulate. Search engines can discover when a particular term or keyword appears in a Web document, but they do not really understand

Blog
RSS
Wikis
Web 3.0
Semantic Web

its meaning or how it relates to other information on the Web. You can check this out on Google by entering two searches. First, enter "Paris Hilton." Next, enter "Hilton in Paris." Because Google does not understand ordinary English, it has no idea that you are interested in the Hilton Hotel in Paris in the second search. Because it cannot understand the meaning of pages it has indexed, Google's search engine returns the most popular pages for those queries where "Hilton" and "Paris" appear on the pages.

First described in a 2001 *Scientific American* article, the Semantic Web is a collaborative effort led by the World Wide Web Consortium to add a layer of meaning atop the existing Web to reduce the amount of human involvement in searching for and processing Web information (Berners-Lee et al., 2001).

Views on the future of the Web vary, but they generally focus on ways to make the Web more "intelligent," with machine-facilitated understanding of information promoting a more intuitive and effective user experience. For instance, suppose you want to set up a party with your tennis buddies at a local restaurant Friday night after work. One problem is that you had earlier scheduled to go to a movie with another friend. In a Semantic Web 3.0 environment, you would be able to coordinate this change in plans with the schedules of your tennis buddies and the schedule of your movie friend, and make a reservation at the restaurant all with a single set of commands issued as text or voice to your handheld smartphone. Right now, this capability is beyond our grasp.

Work proceeds slowly on making the Web a more intelligent experience, in large part because it is difficult to make machines, including software programs, that are truly intelligent like humans. But there are other views of the future Web. Some see a 3D Web where you can walk through pages in a 3D environment. Others point to the idea of a pervasive Web that controls everything from the lights in your living room, to your car's rear view mirror, not to mention managing your calendar and appointments.

Other complementary trends leading toward a future Web 3.0 include more widespread use of cloud computing and SaaS business models, ubiquitous connectivity among mobile platforms and Internet access devices, and the transformation of the Web from a network of separate siloed applications and content into a more seamless and interoperable whole. These more modest visions of the future Web 3.0 are more likely to be realized in the near term.

Intranets and Extranets

Organizations use Internet networking standards and Web technology to create private networks called *intranets*. We introduced intranets in Chapter 1, explaining that an intranet is an internal organizational network that provides access to data across the enterprise. It uses the existing company network infrastructure along with Internet connectivity standards and software developed for the World Wide Web. Intranets create networked applications that can run on many different kinds of computers throughout the organization, including mobile handheld computers and wireless remote access devices.

While the Web is available to anyone, an intranet is private and is protected from public visits by **firewalls**—security systems with specialized software to prevent outsiders from entering private networks. Intranet software technology is the same as that of the World Wide Web. A simple intranet can be created by linking a client computer with a Web browser to a computer with Web server software using a TCP/IP network and a firewall. We discuss firewalls further in Chapter 8.

Extranets A firm creates an extranet to allow authorized vendors and customers to have limited access to its internal intranet. For example, authorized buyers could link to a portion of a company's intranet from the public Internet to obtain information about the costs and features of the company's products. The company uses firewalls to ensure that access to its internal data is limited and remains secure; firewalls also authenticate users, making sure that only authorized users access the site.

Both intranets and extranets reduce operational costs by providing the connectivity to coordinate disparate business processes within the firm and to link electronically to customers and suppliers. Extranets often are employed for collaborating with other companies for supply chain management, product design and development, and training efforts.

Firewalls

7.4   The Wireless Revolution

If you have a cell phone, do you use it for taking and sending photos, sending text messages, or downloading music clips? Do you take your laptop to class or to the library to link up to the Internet? If so, you are part of the wireless revolution. Cell phones, laptops, and small handheld devices have evolved into portable computing platforms that let you perform some of the computing tasks you used to do at your desk.

Wireless communication helps businesses more easily stay in touch with customers, suppliers, and employees and provides more flexible arrangements for organizing work. Wireless technology has also created new products, services, and sales channels, which we discuss in Chapter 13.

If you require mobile communication and computing power or remote access to corporate systems, you can work with an array of wireless devices: cell phones, personal digital assistants, and smartphones. PCs are also starting to be used in wireless transmission.

Personal digital assistants (PDAs) are small, handheld computers featuring applications such as electronic schedulers, address books, memo pads, and expense trackers. Models with digital cell phone capabilities such as e-mail messaging, wireless access to the Internet, voice communication, and digital cameras are called **smartphones.**

Cellular Systems

Cell phones and smartphones have become all-purpose devices for digital data transmission. In addition to voice communication, mobile phones are now used for transmitting text and e-mail messages, instant messaging, digital photos, and short video clips; for playing music and games; for surfing the Web; and even for transmitting and receiving corporate data. For example, CN equipped its 350 intermodal drivers with BlackBerrys that were loaded with a custom dispatch application that CN had developed. CN has cut down on phone calls from its drivers by 50 percent, and it is easier for CN to track its drivers' progress.

Within a few years, a new generation of mobile processors and faster mobile networks will enable these devices to function as digital computing platforms performing many of the tasks of today's PCs. Smartphones will have the storage and processing power of a PC and be able to run all of your key applications and access all of your digital content.

Cellular Network Standards and Generations Digital cellular service uses several competing standards. In Europe and much of the rest of the world outside North America, the standard is Global System for Mobile Communications (GSM). GSM's strength is its international roaming capability. There are GSM cell phone systems in North America, including Rogers; both Bell Canada and Telus plan to introduce GSM in 2010.

The major standard in North America is Code Division Multiple Access (CDMA), which is the system used by most Canadian cellular service providers. CDMA transmits over several frequencies, occupies the entire spectrum, and randomly assigns users to a range of frequencies over time. In general, CDMA is cheaper to implement, is more efficient in its use of spectrum, and provides higher quality of voice and data than GSM.

Earlier generations of cellular systems were designed primarily for voice and limited data transmission in the form of short text messages. Wireless carriers are now rolling out more powerful cellular networks called **third-generation** or **3G networks,** with transmission speeds ranging from 144 Kbps for mobile users in, for example, a car, to more than 2 Mbps for stationary users. This is sufficient transmission capacity for video, graphics, and other rich media, in addition to voice, making 3G networks suitable for wireless broadband Internet access. Many of the cellular handsets available today are 3G-enabled, including the newest version of Apple's iPhone.

3G networks are widely used in Japan, South Korea, Taiwan, Hong Kong, Singapore, and parts of northern Europe, but these services are not yet available in many North American locations. To compensate, Canadian cellular carriers have upgraded their networks to support higher-speed transmission. These interim **2.5G networks** provide data

Personal digital assistants (PDAs)
Smartphones
Third-generation (3G) networks
2.5G networks

transmission rates ranging from 60 to 354 Kbps, enabling cell phones to be used for Web access, music downloads, and other broadband services. PCs equipped with a special card can use these broadband cellular services for ubiquitous wireless Internet access.

The next complete evolution in wireless communication, termed 4G, will be entirely packet-switched and capable of providing between 1 Mbps and 1 Gbps speeds, with premium quality and high security. Voice, data, and high-quality streaming video will be available to users anywhere, anytime. International telecommunications regulatory and standardization bodies are working for commercial deployment of 4G networks between 2012 and 2015.

Wireless Computer Networks and Internet Access

If you have a laptop computer, you might be able to use it to access the Internet as you move from room to room in your residence hall or table to table in your university library. An array of technologies provide high-speed wireless access to the Internet for PCs and other wireless handheld devices as well as for cell phones. These new high-speed services have extended Internet access to numerous locations that could not be covered by traditional wired Internet services.

Bluetooth **Bluetooth** is the popular name for the 802.15 wireless networking standard, which is useful for creating small **personal area networks (PANs).** It links up to eight devices within a 10-metre area using low-power, radio-based communication and can transmit up to 722 Kbps in the 2.4-GHz band.

Wireless phones, pagers, computers, printers, and computing devices using Bluetooth communicate with each other and even operate each other without direct user intervention (see Figure 7-16). For example, a person could direct a notebook computer to send a document file wirelessly to a printer. Bluetooth connects wireless keyboards and mice to PCs or cell phones to earpieces without wires. Bluetooth has low power requirements, making it appropriate for battery-powered handheld computers, cell phones, or PDAs.

Although Bluetooth lends itself to personal networking, it has uses in large corporations. For example, FedEx drivers use Bluetooth to transmit the delivery data captured by their handheld PowerPad computers to cellular transmitters, which forward the data to corporate computers. Drivers no longer need to spend time docking their handheld units physically in the transmitters, and Bluetooth has saved FedEx $20 million per year.

Bluetooth
Personal-l area networks (PANs)

FIGURE 7-16 A Bluetooth network (PAN).

Bluetooth enables a variety of devices, including cell phones, PDAs, wireless keyboards and mice, PCs, and printers, to interact wirelessly with each other within a small 10 metre area. In addition to the links shown, Bluetooth can be used to network similar devices to send data from one PC to another.

Wi-Fi The 802.11 set of standards for wireless LANs is also known as **Wi-Fi.** There are three standards in this family: 802.11a, 802.11b, and 802.11g. 802.11n is an emerging standard for increasing the speed and capacity of wireless networking.

The 802.11a standard can transmit up to 54 Mbps in the unlicensed 5-GHz frequency range and has an effective distance of 10 to 30 metres. The 802.11b standard can transmit up to 11 Mbps in the unlicensed 2.4-GHz band and has an effective distance of 30 to 50 metres, although this range can be extended outdoors by using tower-mounted antennas. The 802.11g standard can transmit up to 54 Mbps in the 2.4-GHz range. 802.11n will transmit at more than 100 Mbps.

802.11b was the first wireless standard to be widely adopted for wireless LANs and wireless Internet access. 802.11g is increasingly used for this purpose, and dual-band systems capable of handling 802.11b and 802.11g are available.

In most Wi-Fi communications, wireless devices communicate with a wired LAN using access points. An access point is a box consisting of a radio receiver/transmitter and antennas that link to a wired network, router, or hub.

Figure 7-17 illustrates an 802.11 wireless LAN operating in infrastructure mode that connects a small number of mobile devices to a larger wired LAN. Most wireless devices are client machines. The servers that the mobile client stations need to use are on the wired LAN. The access point controls the wireless stations and acts as a bridge between the main wired LAN and the wireless LAN. (A bridge connects two LANs based on different technologies.) The access point also controls the wireless stations.

Laptop PCs now come equipped with chips to receive Wi-Fi signals. Older models may need an add-in wireless network interface card.

Wi-Fi and Wireless Internet Access The 802.11 standard also provides wireless access to the Internet using a broadband connection. In this instance, an access point plugs into an Internet connection, which could come from a cable TV line or DSL telephone service. Computers within range of the access point use it to link wirelessly to the Internet.

Businesses of all sizes are using Wi-Fi networks to provide low-cost wireless LANs and Internet access. Wi-Fi hotspots are springing up in hotels, airport lounges, libraries, cafes, and college campuses to provide mobile access to the Internet. Most colleges and universities now use Wi-Fi for research, course work, and entertainment.

Wi-Fi

FIGURE 7-17   An 802.11 wireless LAN.

Mobile laptop computers equipped with network interface cards link to the wired LAN by communicating with the access point. The access point uses radio waves to transmit network signals from the wired network to the client adapters, which convert them into data that the mobile device can understand. The client adapter then transmits the data from the mobile device back to the access point, which forwards the data to the wired network.

Hotspots typically consist of one or more access points positioned on a ceiling, wall, or other strategic spot in a public place to provide maximum wireless coverage for a specific area. Users in range of a hotspot are able to access the Internet from laptops, handhelds, or cell phones that are Wi-Fi enabled, such as Apple's iPhone. Some hotspots are free or do not require any additional software to use; others may require activation and the establishment of a user account by providing a credit card number over the Web.

Wi-Fi technology poses several challenges, however. Right now, users cannot freely roam from hotspot to hotspot if these hotspots use different Wi-Fi network services. Unless the service is free, users need to log on to separate accounts for each service, each with its own fees.

One major drawback of Wi-Fi is its weak security features, which make these wireless networks vulnerable to intruders. We provide more detail about Wi-Fi security issues in Chapter 8.

Another drawback of Wi-Fi networks is susceptibility to interference from nearby systems operating in the same spectrum, such as wireless phones, microwave ovens, or other wireless LANs. Wireless networks based on the 802.11n specification will solve this problem by using multiple wireless antennas in tandem to transmit and receive data and technology to coordinate multiple simultaneous radio signals. This technology is called *MIMO (multiple input multiple output).*

WiMax A surprisingly large number of areas in Canada and throughout the world do not have access to Wi-Fi or fixed broadband connectivity. The range of Wi-Fi systems is no more than 91 metres from the base station, making it difficult for rural groups that do not have cable or DSL service to find wireless access to the Internet.

The IEEE, formerly known as the Institute of Electrical and Electronics Engineers, is a professional standards developing body and developed a new family of standards known as WiMax to deal with these problems. **WiMax,** which stands for Worldwide Interoperability for Microwave Access, is the popular term for IEEE Standard 802.16, known as the "Air Interface for Fixed Broadband Wireless Access Systems." WiMax has a wireless access range of up to 50 kilometres, compared to 91 metres for Wi-Fi and 10 metres for Bluetooth, and a data transfer rate of up to 75 Mbps. The 802.16 specification has robust security and quality-of-service features to support voice and video.

WiMax antennas are powerful enough to beam high-speed Internet connections to rooftop antennas of homes and businesses miles away. Hydro One, headquartered in Ontario, is about to begin using WiMax so that its smart metres in rural areas can communicate with its base systems.

7.5 Radio Frequency Identification and Wireless Sensor Networks

RFID and Wireless Sensor Networks

Mobile technologies are creating new efficiencies and ways of working throughout the enterprise. In addition to the wireless systems we have just described, radio frequency identification systems and wireless sensor networks are having a major impact.

Radio Frequency Identification (RFID) **Radio frequency identification (RFID)** systems provide a powerful technology for tracking the movement of goods throughout the supply chain. RFID systems use tiny tags with embedded microchips containing data about an item and its location to transmit radio signals over a short distance to special RFID readers. The RFID readers then pass the data over a network to a computer for processing. Unlike bar codes, RFID tags do not need line-of-sight contact to be read.

The RFID tag is electronically programmed with information that can uniquely identify an item plus other information about the item, such as its location, where and when it was made, or its status during production. Embedded in the tag is a microchip for storing the data. The rest of the tag is an antenna that transmits data to the reader.

Hotspots
WiMax
Radio frequency identification (RFID)

FIGURE 7-18   How RFID works.

A microchip holds data including an identification number. The rest of the tag is an antenna that transmits data to a reader.

Has an antenna that constantly transmits. When it senses a tag, it wakes it up, interrogates it, and decodes the data. Then it transmits the data to a host system over wired or wireless connections.

Processes the data from the tag that have been transmitted by the reader.

RFID uses low-powered radio transmitters to read data stored in a tag at distances ranging from a couple of centimetres to 30 metres. The reader captures the data from the tag and sends them over a network to a host computer for processing.

The reader unit consists of an antenna and radio transmitter with a decoding capability attached to a stationary or handheld device. The reader emits radio waves in ranges anywhere from 1 inch to 100 feet, depending on its power output, the radio frequency employed, and surrounding environmental conditions. When an RFID tag comes within the range of the reader, the tag is activated and starts sending data. The reader captures these data, decodes them, and sends them back over a wired or wireless network to a host computer for further processing (see Figure 7-18). Both RFID tags and antennas come in a variety of shapes and sizes.

Active RFID tags are powered by an internal battery and typically enable data to be rewritten and modified. Active tags can transmit for several dozen metres but cost $5 and upward per tag. Automated toll-collection systems such as New York's E-ZPass use active RFID tags.

Passive RFID tags do not have their own power source and obtain their operating power from the radio frequency energy transmitted by the RFID reader. They are smaller, lighter, and less expensive than active tags, but have a range of only a metre or two.

In inventory control and supply chain management, RFID systems capture and manage more detailed information about items in warehouses or in production than bar-coding systems. If a large number of items are shipped together, RFID systems track each pallet, lot, or even unit item in the shipment. This technology may help companies such as Walmart Canada improve receiving and storage operations by improving their ability to "see" exactly what stock is stored in warehouses or on retail store shelves.

Walmart Canada has installed RFID readers at store receiving docks to record the arrival of pallets and cases of goods shipped with RFID tags. The RFID reader reads the tags a second time just as the cases are brought onto the sales floor from backroom storage areas. Software combines sales data from Walmart's point-of-sale systems and the RFID data regarding the number of cases brought out to the sales floor. The program determines which items will soon be depleted and automatically generates a list of items to pick in the warehouse to replenish store shelves before they run out. This information helps Walmart reduce out-of-stock items, increase sales, and further shrink its costs.

The cost of RFID tags used to be too high for widespread use, but now it is approaching 20 cents per passive tag in Canada. As the price decreases, RFID is starting to become cost-effective for some applications.

In addition to installing RFID readers and tagging systems, companies may need to upgrade their hardware and software to process the massive amounts of data produced by RFID systems—transactions that could add up to tens or hundreds of terabytes.

FIGURE 7-19   A wireless sensor network.

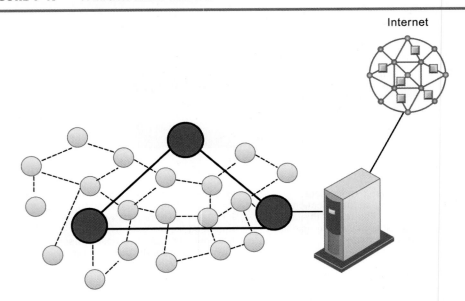

The small circles represent lower-level nodes, and the larger circles represent high-end nodes. Lower-level nodes forward data to each other or to higher-level nodes, which transmit data more rapidly and speed up network performance.

Special software is required to filter, aggregate, and prevent RFID data from overloading business networks and system applications. Applications will need to be redesigned to accept massive volumes of frequently generated RFID data and to share those data with other applications. Major enterprise software vendors, including SAP and Oracle-PeopleSoft, now offer RFID-ready versions of their supply chain management applications.

Wireless Sensor Networks If your company wanted state-of-the-art technology to monitor building security or detect hazardous substances in the air, it might deploy a wireless sensor network. **Wireless sensor networks (WSNs)** are networks of interconnected wireless devices that are embedded into the physical environment to provide measurements of many points over large spaces. These devices have built-in processing, storage, and radio frequency sensors and antennas. They are linked into an interconnected network that routes the data they capture to a computer for analysis.

These networks range from hundreds to thousands of nodes. Because wireless sensor devices are placed in the field for years at a time without any maintenance or human intervention, they must have very low power requirements and batteries capable of lasting for years.

Figure 7-19 illustrates one type of wireless sensor network, with data from individual nodes flowing across the network to a server with greater processing power. The server acts as a gateway to a network based on Internet technology.

Wireless sensor networks are valuable in areas such as monitoring environmental changes; monitoring traffic or military activity; protecting property; efficiently operating and managing machinery and vehicles; establishing security perimeters; monitoring supply chain management; or detecting chemical, biological, or radiological material.

Wireless sensor networks (WSNs)

SUMMARY

1. ***What are the principal components of telecommunications networks and key networking technologies?***

A simple network consists of two or more connected computers. Basic network components include computers, network interfaces, a connection medium, network operating system software, and either a hub or a switch. The networking infrastructure for a large company includes the traditional telephone system, mobile cellular communication, wireless local area networks, videoconferencing systems, a corporate Web site, intranets, extranets, and an array of local and wide area networks, including the Internet. Contemporary networks have been shaped by the rise of client/server computing, the use of packet switching, and the adoption of Transmission Control Protocol/Internet Protocol (TCP/IP) as a universal communications standard for linking disparate networks and computers, including the Internet. Protocols provide a common set of rules that enable communication among diverse components in a telecommunications network.

2. ***What are the main telecommunications transmission media and types of networks?***

The principal physical transmission media are twisted copper telephone wire, coaxial copper cable, fibre optic cable, and wireless transmission. Twisted wire enables companies to use existing wiring for telephone systems for digital communication although it is relatively slow. Fibre optic and coaxial cable are used for high-volume transmission but are expensive to install. Microwave and communications satellites are used for wireless communication over long distances. Local area networks (LANs) connect PCs and other digital devices together within a 500-metre radius and are used today for many corporate computing tasks. Network components may be connected using a star, bus, or ring topology. Wide area networks (WANs) span broad geographical distances, ranging from several kilometres to continents, and are private networks that are independently managed. Metropolitan-area networks (MANs) span a single urban area. Digital subscriber line (DSL) technologies, cable Internet connections, and T1 lines are often used for high-capacity Internet connections. Cable Internet connections provide high-speed access to the Web or corporate intranets at speeds of up to 10 Mbps. A T1 line supports a data transmission rate of 1.544 Mbps.

3. ***How do the Internet and Internet technology work, and how do they support communication and e-business?***

The Internet is a worldwide network of networks that uses the client/server model of computing and the TCP/IP network reference model. Every computer on the Internet is assigned a unique numeric IP address. The domain name system (DNS) converts IP addresses to more user-friendly domain names. Worldwide Internet policies are established by organizations and government bodies, such as the Internet Architecture Board and the World Wide Web Consortium. Major Internet services include e-mail, newsgroups, chatting, instant messaging, Telnet, FTP, and the World Wide Web. Web pages are based on Hypertext Markup Language (HTML) and can display text, graphics, video, and audio. Web site

directories, search engines, and RSS technology help users locate the information they need on the Web. RSS, blogs, and wikis are features of Web 2.0. Web technology and Internet networking standards provide the connectivity and interfaces for internal private intranets and private extranets that be accessed by many different kinds of computers inside and outside the organization. Firms are also starting to realize economies by using Internet VoIP technology for voice transmission and by using virtual private networks (VPNs) as low-cost alternatives to private WANs.

4. ***What are the principal technologies and standards for wireless networking, communication, and Internet access?***

Cellular networks are evolving toward high-speed, high-bandwidth, digital packet-switched transmission. Broadband 3G networks are capable of transmitting data at speeds ranging from 144 Kbps to more than 2 Mbps. However, 3G services are still not available in most Canadian locations, so cellular carriers have upgraded their networks to support higher-speed transmission. These interim 2.5G networks provide data transmission rates ranging from 60 to 354 Kbps, enabling cell phones to be used for Web access, music downloads, and other broadband services.

Major cellular standards include Code Division Multiple Access (CDMA), which is used primarily in North America, and Global System for Mobile Communications (GSM), which is the standard in Europe and most of the rest of the world.

Standards for wireless computer networks include Bluetooth (802.15) for small personal area networks (PANs), Wi-Fi (802.11) for local area networks (LANs), and WiMax (802.16) for metropolitan area networks (MANs).

5. ***Why are radio frequency identification (RFID) and wireless sensor networks valuable for business?***

Radio frequency identification (RFID) systems provide a powerful technology for tracking the movement of goods by using tiny tags with embedded data about an item and its location. RFID readers read the radio signals transmitted by these tags and pass the data over a network to a computer for processing. Wireless sensor networks (WSNs) are networks of interconnected wireless sensing and transmitting devices that are embedded into the physical environment to provide measurements of many points over large spaces.

Key Terms

2.5G networks,   227
3G networks,   227
Bandwidth,   211

Blog,   225
Bluetooth,   228
Broadband,   203

Bus topology,   209
Cable Internet connections,   212
CA*net,   216

Review Questions

1. *What are the principal components of telecommunications networks and key networking technologies?*
   - *Describe the features of a simple network and the network infrastructure for a large company.*
   - *Name and describe the principal technologies and trends that have shaped contemporary telecommunications systems.*

2. *What are the main telecommunications transmission media and types of networks?*
   - *Name the different types of physical transmission media, and compare them in terms of speed and cost.*
   - *Define a LAN, and describe its components and the functions of each component.*
   - *Name and describe the principal network topologies.*

3. *How do the Internet and Internet technology work, and how do they support communication and e-business?*
   - *Define the Internet, describe how it works, and explain how it provides business value.*
   - *Explain how the domain name system (DNS) and IP addressing system work.*
   - *List and describe the principal Internet services.*

   - *Define and describe VoIP and virtual private networks, and explain how they provide value to businesses.*
   - *List and describe alternative ways of locating information on the Web.*
   - *Compare Web 2.0 and Web 3.0.*
   - *Define and explain the difference between intranets and extranets. Explain how they provide value to businesses.*

4. *What are the principal technologies and standards for wireless networking, communications, and Internet access?*
   - *Define Bluetooth, Wi-Fi, WiMax, and 3G networks.*
   - *Describe the capabilities of each of these networks and for which types of applications each is best suited.*

5. *Why are radio frequency identification (RFID) and wireless sensor networks (WSNs) valuable for business?*
   - *Define RFID, and explain how it works and how it provides value to businesses.*
   - *Define WSNs, explain how they work, and describe the kinds of applications that use them.*

Discussion Questions

1. *It has been said that within the next few years, smartphones will become the single most important digital device we own. Discuss the implications of this statement.*

2. *Should all major retailing and manufacturing companies switch to RFID? Why or why not?*

Collaboration and Teamwork: Evaluating Smartphones

Form a group with three or four of your classmates. Compare the capabilities of Apple's iPhone with a smartphone handset from another vendor with similar features. Your analysis should consider the purchase cost of each device, the wireless networks on which each device can operate, service plan and handset costs, and the services available for each device. You should also consider other capabilities of each device, including the ability to integrate with existing corporate or PC applications. Which device would you select? What criteria would you use to guide your selection? If possible, use Google Sites to post links to Web pages, team communication announcements, and work assignments; to brainstorm; and to work collaboratively on project documents. Try to use Google Docs to develop a presentation of your findings for the class.

 Visit the MyMISLab Web site at **www.pearsoned.ca/mymislab.** This online homework and tutorial system puts you in control of your own learning with study and practice tools directly correlated to this chapter's content.

Learning Track Module

The following Learning Tracks provide content relevant to topics covered in this chapter:

1. Computing and Communications Services Provided by Commercial Communications Vendors
2. Broadband Network Services and Technologies
3. Cellular System Generations
4. Wireless Applications for Customer Relationship Management, Supply Chain Management, and Health Care
5. Web 2.0

HANDS-ON MIS   Projects

The projects in this section give you hands-on experience evaluating and selecting communications technology, using spreadsheet software to improve selection of telecommunications services, and using Web search engines for business research.

Management Decision Problems

1. Your company supplies ceramic floor tiles to Rona, Home Depot, and other home improvement stores. You have been asked to start using radio frequency identification tags on each case of the tiles you ship to help your customers improve the management of your products and those of other suppliers in their warehouses. Use the Web to identify the cost of hardware, software, and networking components for an RFID system for your company. What factors should be considered? What are the key decisions that have to be made in determining whether your firm should adopt this technology?

2. Fictional BestMed Medical Supplies Corporation sells medical and surgical products and equipment from over 700 different manufacturers to hospitals, health clinics, and medical offices. The company employs 500 people at seven different locations across Canada, including account managers, customer service and support representatives, and warehouse staff. Employees communicate via traditional telephone voice services, e-mail, instant messaging, and cell phones. Management is inquiring about whether the company should adopt a system for unified communications. What factors should be considered? What are the key decisions that have to be made in determining whether to adopt this technology? Use the Web, if necessary, to find out more about unified communications and its costs.

Improving Decision Making:
Using Spreadsheet Software to Evaluate Wireless Services

Software skills: Spreadsheet formulas, formatting
Business skills: Analyzing telecommunications services and costs

In this project, you will use the Web to research alternative wireless services and use spreadsheet software to calculate wireless service costs for a sales force.

You would like to equip your sales force of 35 based in Windsor, Ontario, with mobile phones that have capabilities for voice transmission, text messaging, and taking and sending photos. Use the Web to select a wireless service provider that provides nationwide service as well as good service in your home area. Examine the features of the mobile handsets offered by each of these vendors. Assume that each of the 35 salespeople will need to spend three hours per day during business hours (8 a.m. to 6 p.m.) on mobile voice communication, send 30 text messages per day, and five photos per week. Use your spreadsheet software to determine the wireless service and handset that will offer the best pricing per user over a two-year period. For the purposes of this exercise, you do not need to consider corporate discounts.

Achieving Operational Excellence:
Using Web Search Engines for Business Research

Software skills: Web search tools
Business skills: Researching new technologies

This project will help develop your Internet skills in using Web search engines for business research.

You want to learn more about ethanol as an alternative fuel for motor vehicles. Use the following search engines to obtain that information: Yahoo!, Google, and MSN. If you wish, try other search engines as well. Compare the volume and quality of information you find with each search tool. Which tool is the easiest to use? Which produced the best results for your research? Why?

CASE STUDY

Google versus Microsoft: Clash of the Technology Titans

Google and Microsoft, two of the most prominent technology companies of the past several decades, are poised to square off for dominance of the workplace, the Internet, and the technological world. In fact, the battle is already well under way. Both companies have already achieved dominance in their areas of expertise. Google has dominated the Internet while Microsoft has dominated the desktop. But both are increasingly seeking to grow into the other's core businesses. The competition between the companies promises to be fierce.

The differences in the strategies and business models of the two companies illustrate why this conflict will shape our technological future. Google began as one search company among many. But the effectiveness of its PageRank search algorithm and online advertising services, along with its ability to attract the best and brightest minds in the industry, have helped Google become one of the most prominent companies in the world. The company's extensive infrastructure allows it to offer the fastest search speeds and a variety of Web-based products.

Microsoft grew to its giant stature on the strength of its Windows operating system and Office desktop productivity applications, which are used by 500 million people worldwide. Sometimes vilified for its anti-competitive practices, the company and its products are nevertheless staples for businesses and consumers looking to improve their productivity with computer-based tasks.

Today, the two companies have very different visions for the future, influenced by the continued development of the Internet and increased availability of broadband Internet connections. Google believes that the maturation of the Internet will allow more and more computing tasks to be performed via the Web, on computers sitting in data centres rather than on your desktop. This idea is known as cloud computing, and it is central to Google's business model going forward. Microsoft, on the other hand, has built its success around the model of desktop computing. Microsoft's goal is to embrace the Internet while persuading consumers to retain the desktop as the focal point for computing tasks.

Only a small handful of companies have the cash flow and human resources to manage and maintain a cloud, and Google and Microsoft are among them. With a vast array of Internet-based products and tools for online search, online advertising, digital mapping, digital photo management, digital radio broadcasting, and online video viewing, Google has pioneered cloud computing. It is obviously betting that Internet-based computing will supplant desktop computing as the way most people work with their computers. Users would use various connectivity devices to access applications from remote servers stored in data centres, as opposed to working locally from their computer.

One advantage to the cloud computing model is that users would not be tied to a particular machine to access information or do work. Another is that Google would be responsible for most of the maintenance of the data centres that house these applications. But the disadvantages of the model are the requirement of an Internet connection to use the applications and the security concerns surrounding Google's handling of your information. Google is banking on the increasing ubiquity of the Internet and availability of broadband and Wi-Fi connections to offset these drawbacks.

Microsoft already has several significant advantages to help remain relevant even if cloud computing is as good as Google advertises. The company has a well-established and popular set of applications that many consumers and businesses feel comfortable using. When Microsoft launches a new product, users of Office products and Windows can be sure that they will know how to use the product and that it will work with their system.

Google itself claims that it is not out to supplant Microsoft but rather wants to provide products and services that will be used in tandem with Microsoft applications. Dave Girouard, president of Google's Enterprise division, says that "people are just using both [Google products and Office] and they use what makes sense for a particular task."

But cloud computing nevertheless represents a threat to Microsoft's core business model, which revolves around the desktop as the centre for all computing tasks. If, rather than buying software from Microsoft, consumers can instead buy access to applications stored on remote servers for a much cheaper cost, the desktop suddenly no longer occupies that central position. In the past, Microsoft used the popularity of its Windows operating system (found on 95 percent of the world's personal computers) and Office to destroy competing products such as Netscape Navigator, Lotus 1-2-3, and WordPerfect. But Google's offerings are Web-based, and thus not reliant on Windows or Office. Google believes that the vast majority of computing tasks, around 90 percent, can be done in the cloud. Microsoft disputes this claim, calling it grossly overstated.

Microsoft clearly wants to bolster its Internet presence in the event that Google is correct. Microsoft's recent attempts to acquire Internet portal Yahoo! indicate this desire. No other company would give Microsoft more Internet search market share than Yahoo!. Google controls over 60 percent of the Internet search market, with Yahoo! a distant second at just over 20 percent, and Microsoft third at under 10 percent. While Microsoft-Yahoo! would still trail Google by a wide margin, the merger would at least increase the possibility of dethroning Google.

However, Microsoft's initial buyout attempts were met with heavy resistance from Yahoo!.

With its attempted acquisition of Yahoo!, Microsoft wanted not only to bolster its Internet presence but also to end the threat of an advertising deal between Google and Yahoo!. In June 2008, those chances diminished further due to a partnership between Google and Yahoo! under which Yahoo! will outsource a portion of its advertising to Google. Google plans to deliver some of its ads alongside some of the less profitable areas of Yahoo!'s search, since Google's technology is far more sophisticated and generates more revenue per search than any competitor. Yahoo! recently introduced a comprehensive severance package that critics dismissed as a "poison pill" intended to make the company less appealing for acquisition to Microsoft. In response to this and other moves he considered to be incompetent, billionaire investor Carl Icahn has built up a large stake in the company and has agitated for change in Yahoo! leadership and reopening of negotiations with Microsoft, but the advertising agreement between Yahoo! and Google casts doubt over whether Microsoft can actually pull off a buyout.

With or without Yahoo!, the company's online presence will need a great deal of improvement. Microsoft's online services division's performance has worsened while Google's has improved. Microsoft lost $732 million in 2007 and was on track for an even worse year in 2008. Google earned $4.2 billion in profits over the same 2007 span.

Microsoft's goals are to "innovate and disrupt in search, win in display ads, and reinvent portal and social media experiences." Its pursuit of Yahoo! suggests skepticism even on Microsoft's own part that the company can do all of this on its own. Developing scale internally is far more difficult than simply buying it outright. In attempting to grow into this new area, Microsoft faces considerable challenges. The industry changes too quickly for one company to be dominant for very long, and Microsoft has had difficulty sustaining its growth rates since the Internet's inception. Even well-managed companies encounter difficulties when faced with disruptive new technologies, and Microsoft may be no exception.

Google faces difficulties of its own in its attempts to encroach on Microsoft's turf. The centrepiece of its efforts is the Google Apps suite. These are a series of Web-based applications that include Gmail, instant messaging, calendar, word processing, presentation, and spreadsheet applications (Google Docs), and tools for creating collaborative Web sites. These applications are simpler versions of Microsoft Office applications, and Google is offering basic versions of them for free, and "Premier"' editions for a fraction of the price. Subscribing to the Premier edition of Google Apps costs $50 per year per person, as opposed to approximately $500 per year per person for Microsoft Office.

Google believes that most Office users do not need the advanced features of Word, Excel, and other Office applications, and have a great deal to gain by switching to Google Apps. Small businesses, for example, might prefer cheaper, simpler versions of word processing, spreadsheet, and electronic presentation applications because they do not require the complex features of Microsoft Office. Microsoft disputes this, saying that Office is the result of many years and dollars of market research about what consumers want and that consumers are very satisfied with Microsoft's products. Many businesses agree, saying that they are reluctant to move away from Office because it is the "safe choice." These firms are often concerned that their data is not stored on-site and that they may be in violation of laws such as the Canadian *Sarbanes-Oxley Sarbanes and Oxley Act*, known more correctly as the Multilateral Instrument 52-109 law or more popularly as Bill C198 (see Chapter 8) as a result, which requires that companies maintain and report their data to the government upon request. Microsoft is also offering more software features and Web-based services to bolster its online presence. These include SharePoint, a Web-based collaboration and document management platform, and Microsoft Office Live, providing Web-based services for e-mail, project management, and organizing information, and online extensions to Office.

The battle between Google and Microsoft is not just being waged in the area of office productivity tools. The two companies are trading blows in a multitude of other fields, including Web browsers, Web maps, online video, cell phone software, and online health record-keeping tools. **Salesforce.com** (see the Window on Organizations in Chapter 5) represents the site of another conflict between the two giants. Microsoft has attempted to move in on the software-as-a-service model popularized by **Salesforce.com**, offering a competing CRM product for a fraction of the cost. Google has gone the opposite route, partnering with Salesforce to integrate that company's CRM applications with Google Apps and creating a new sales channel to market Google Apps to businesses that have already adopted Salesforce CRM software.

Additionally, both companies are attempting to open themselves up as platforms to developers. Google has already launched its Google App Engine, which allows outside programmers to develop and launch their own applications for minimal cost. In a move that represented a drastic change from previous policy, Microsoft announced that it would reveal many key details of its software that were previously kept secret. Programmers will have an easier time building services that work with Microsoft programs.

Microsoft's secrecy once helped the it control the marketplace by forcing other companies to use Windows rather than develop alternatives, but if Microsoft cannot do the same to Google Apps, it makes sense to try a different approach to attract developers.

Time will tell whether or not Microsoft is able to fend off Google's challenge to its dominance in the tech industry. Many other prominent companies have fallen victim to paradigm shifts, such as mainframes to personal computers, traditional print media to Internet distribution, and, if Google has its way, personal computers to cloud computing.

CASE STUDY QUESTIONS:

1. Define and compare the business strategies and business models of Google and Microsoft.

2. Has the Internet taken over the PC desktop as the centre of the action? Why or why not?

3. Why did Microsoft attempt to acquire Yahoo!? How did it affect its business model? Do you believe this was a good move?

4. What is the significance of Google Apps to Google's future success?

5. Would you use Google Apps instead of Microsoft Office applications for computing tasks? Why or why not?

6. Which company and business model do you believe will prevail in this epic struggle? Justify your answer.

Sources: Clint Boulton, "Microsoft Marks the Spot," *eWeek*, May 5, 2008; Andy Kessler, "The War for the Web," *The Wall Street Journal*, May 6, 2008; John Pallatto and Clint Boulton, "An On-Demand Partnership," and Clint Boulton, "Google Apps Go to School," *eWeek*, April 21, 2008; Miguel Helft, "Ad Accord for Yahoo! and Google," *The New York Times*, June 13, 2008, and "Google and Salesforce Join to Fight Microsoft," *The New York Times*, April 14, 2008; Clint Boulton, "Google Tucks Jotspot into Apps," *eWeek*, March 3, 2008; Robert A. Guth, Ben Worthen, and Charles Forelle, "Microsoft to Allow Software Secrets on Internet," *The Wall Street Journal*, February 22, 2008; J. Nicholas Hoover, "Microsoft-Yahoo! Combo Would Involve Overlap—and Choices," *InformationWeek*, February 18, 2008; Steve Lohr, "Yahoo! Offer Is Strategy Shift for Microsoft," *The New York Times*, February 2, 2008; and John Markoff, "Competing as Software Goes to Web," *The New York Times*, June 5, 2007.

CHAPTER 8

Securing Information Systems

LEARNING OBJECTIVES

After reading this chapter, you will be able to answer the following questions:

1. Why are information systems vulnerable to destruction, error, and abuse?

2. What is the business value of security and control?

3. What are the components of an organizational framework for security and control?

4. What are the most important tools and technologies for safeguarding information resources?

OPENING CASE

Canadian Law Firm Wins the Case for E-mail Security

Located in Vancouver, British Columbia, Watson Goepel Maledy LLP is a law firm with a practice that spans many areas of practice. The firm has 37 lawyers on staff along with a number of paralegals and a number of management staff, including an information systems manager, Aaron Zuccolin, and a network systems manager, Fiona Law. The firm was founded in 1984, before e-mail and the World Wide Web were everyday critical issues for almost every organization, including professional practices like law firms.

The firm's philosophy is built on customer service. The firm employs a number of correspondent legal firms across Canada and internationally to ensure that its clients are best served wherever that service needs to be provided. The firm prides itself on having access to state-of-the-art computerized research

and communications technology. The firm also provides multilingual service in nine languages in addition to English. One of its stated values is "Think globally and implement locally."

The firm's practice areas are varied and numerous, including business law, litigation, insurance law, personal services, immigration, and entertainment law. The firm also handles mergers and acquisitions, taxation, and bankruptcy issues. Considering the number of clients the firm represents, the variety of legal issues it addresses, and the number of correspondent legal firms Watson Goepel Maledy works with, the variety and volume of e-mail the firm receives on a daily basis is significant. Due to the varied nature of the practice, these e-mails may come from trusted partners and clients or from unknown parties, including those whose e-mails may

contain viruses, spyware, and other forms of malware (malicious software).

In addition, the firm falls under the *Personal Information Protection and Electronic Documents Act* (PIPEDA, discussed in Chapter 4) and must safeguard its own information and that of its clients from those who might wish to steal or alter the information. After the September 11 attacks, the United States passed the *Patriot Act*, giving American authorities the right to view personal data held by U.S. organizations. Watson Goepel Maledy used e-mail and Web security vendors whose servers were located in the United States. The firm's e-mail and Web-based information could, therefore, have been subject to viewing and access by American authorities, in conflict with PIPEDA and the firm's own policies. The firm needed to negate any risk of violating Canadian law

239

and to safeguard sensitive client information that might arrive by e-mail.

After a search of vendors, Watson Goepel Maledy chose Webroot, a company with offices in the United States, the United Kingdom, and Australia, but with servers in Canada. In addition, Webroot offered a Software as a Service (SaaS, see Chapter 5) application. Webroot's servers, both for primary and "fallover" locations, were located outside the United States. Interestingly, Watson Goepel Maledy was not seeking to reduce its costs, but the new e-mail system results in savings of 50 percent and has better spam-filtering results than the previous system. The new application also provides up-to-date antivirus protection.

Sources: Watson Goepel Maledy, LLP, "About Us," **www.wgmlaw.com** (accessed April 28, 2009); Webroot, "Case Study: Watson Goepel Maledy LLP," **www.webroot.com/shared/pdf/ Webroot_WatsonGoepel_CaseStudy_Email .pdf** (accessed April 28, 2009).

The problems created by e-mail and e-mail vendors for Watson Goepel Maledy illustrate some of the reasons why businesses need to pay special attention to information system security. The potential for violating Canadian privacy legislation and having client information accessible by American authorities meant the firm had to change its e-mail vendor. In doing so, the firm also increased its e-mail security and reduced the volume of spam e-mail it received.

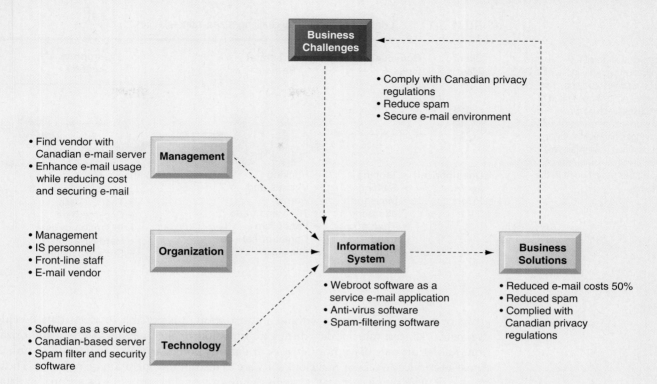

8.1 System Vulnerability and Abuse

Can you imagine what would happen if you tried to link to the Internet without a firewall or antivirus software? Your computer would be disabled in a few seconds, and it might take you many days to recover. If you used the computer to run your business, you might not be able to sell to your customers or place orders with your suppliers while it was down. And you might find that your computer system had been penetrated by outsiders, who perhaps stole or destroyed valuable data, including confidential payment data from your customers. If too much data were destroyed or divulged, your business might never be able to operate.

In short, if you operate a business today, you need to make security and control a top priority. **Security** refers to the policies, procedures, and technical measures used to prevent unauthorized access, alteration, theft, or physical damage to information systems. **Controls** are methods, policies, and organizational procedures that ensure the safety of the organization's assets, the accuracy and reliability of its records, and operational adherence to management standards.

Why Systems Are Vulnerable

When large amounts of data are stored in electronic form, they are vulnerable to many more kinds of threats than when they existed in manual form. Through communications networks, information systems in different locations are interconnected. The potential for unauthorized access, abuse, or fraud is not limited to a single location but can occur at any access point in the network. Figure 8-1 illustrates the most common threats against contemporary information systems. They can stem from technical, organizational, and environmental factors compounded by poor management decisions. In the multitier client/server computing environment illustrated here, vulnerabilities exist at each layer and in the communications between the layers. Users at the client layer can cause harm by introducing

Security
Controls

The architecture of a Web-based application typically includes a Web client, a server, and corporate information systems linked to databases. Each of these components presents security challenges and vulnerabilities. Floods, fires, power failures, and other electrical problems can cause disruptions at any point in the network.

FIGURE 8-1   Contemporary security challenges and vulnerabilities.

errors or by accessing systems without authorization. It is possible to access data flowing over networks, steal valuable data during transmission, or alter messages without authorization. Radiation may disrupt a network at various points as well. Intruders can launch denial-of-service attacks or malicious software to disrupt the operation of Web sites. Those capable of penetrating corporate systems can destroy or alter corporate data stored in databases or files.

Systems malfunction if computer hardware breaks down, is not configured properly, or is damaged by improper use or criminal acts. Errors in programming, improper installation, or unauthorized changes cause computer software to fail. Power failures, floods, fires, or other natural disasters can also disrupt computer systems.

Domestic or offshore partnering with another company adds to system vulnerability if valuable information resides on networks and computers outside the organization's control. Without strong safeguards, valuable data could be lost, destroyed, or fall into the wrong hands, revealing important trade secrets or information that violates personal privacy.

The growing use of mobile devices for business computing adds to these woes. Portability makes cell phones and smartphones easy to lose or steal, and their networks are vulnerable to access by outsiders. Smartphones used by corporate executives may contain sensitive data such as sales figures, customer names, phone numbers, and e-mail addresses. Intruders may be able to access internal corporate networks through these devices. Unauthorized downloads may introduce disabling software.

Internet Vulnerabilities Large public networks, such as the Internet, are more vulnerable than internal networks because they are virtually open to anyone. The Internet is so huge that when abuses do occur, they can have an enormously widespread impact. When the Internet becomes part of the corporate network, the organization's information systems are even more vulnerable to actions from outsiders.

Computers that are constantly connected to the Internet by cable modems or digital subscriber line (DSL) lines are more open to penetration by outsiders because they use fixed Internet addresses where they can be easily identified. (With dial-up service, a temporary Internet address is assigned for each session.) A fixed Internet address creates a fixed target for hackers.

Telephone service based on Internet technology (see Chapter 7) is more vulnerable than the switched voice network if it does not run over a secure private network. Most Voice over IP (VoIP) traffic over the public Internet is not encrypted, so anyone with a network can listen in on conversations. Hackers can intercept conversations or shut down voice service by flooding servers supporting VoIP with bogus traffic.

Vulnerability has also increased from widespread use of e-mail, instant messaging (IM), and peer-to-peer file-sharing programs. E-mail may contain attachments that serve as springboards for malicious software or unauthorized access to internal corporate systems. Employees may use e-mail messages to transmit valuable trade secrets, financial data, or confidential customer information to unauthorized recipients. Popular instant messaging applications for consumers do not use a secure layer for text messages, so they can be intercepted and read by outsiders during transmission over the public Internet. IM activity over the Internet can in some cases be used as a back door to an otherwise secure network. Sharing files over peer-to-peer (P2P) networks, such as those for illegal music sharing, may also transmit malicious software or expose information on either individual or corporate computers to outsiders.

Wireless Security Challenges Is it safe to log onto a wireless network at an airport, library, or other public location? It depends on how vigilant you are. Even the wireless network in your home is vulnerable because radio frequency bands are easy to scan. Both Bluetooth and Wi-Fi networks are susceptible to cracking by eavesdroppers. Although the range of Wi-Fi networks is only several hundred feet, it can be extended up to one-quarter of a mile using external antennae. Local area networks (LANs) using the 802.11 standard can be easily penetrated by outsiders armed with laptops, wireless cards, external antennae, and hacking software. Hackers use these tools to detect unprotected networks, monitor network traffic, and, in some cases, gain access to the Internet or to corporate networks. The Interactive Session on Organizations describes how poor wireless security may have enabled criminals to break into the corporate systems of TJX Companies and other major retailers and steal credit card and personal data on over 41 million people.

Wi-Fi transmission technology was designed to make it easy for stations to find and hear one another. The *service set identifiers (SSIDs)* identifying the access points in a Wi-Fi network are broadcast multiple times and can be picked up fairly easily by intruders' sniffer programs (see Figure 8-2). Wireless networks in many locations do not have basic protections against **war driving,** in which eavesdroppers drive by buildings or park outside and try to intercept wireless network traffic.

War driving

FIGURE 8-2   Wi-Fi security challenges.

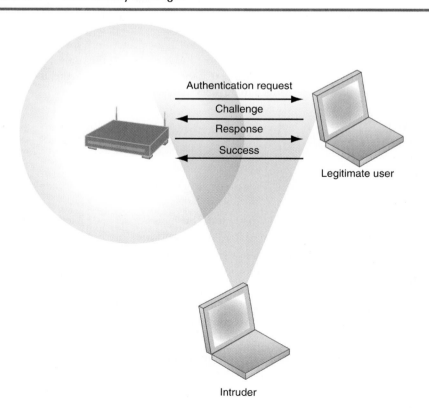

Many Wi-Fi networks can be penetrated easily by intruders using sniffer programs to obtain an address to access the resources of a network without authorization.

WINDOW ON ORGANIZATIONS

Data Theft Hits Canada

In February 2008, a 30-year-old Montreal resident was arrested for stealing data about 3.4 million Ontario and Quebec residents. The man had stolen the data from Bell Canada Enterprises a month earlier, but an anonymous tip to Bell Canada permitted the Montreal police to apprehend the thief.

This is just one of many data thefts occurring in Canada in what appears to be a rising trend of theft of data. While most of us recognize the rising trend in identity theft, theft of corporate data about a company's customers is also increasing. With the increasing use of mobile devices, USB drives, and external hard drives for holding or accessing company data, it is no wonder that data theft is increasing worldwide and not just in Canada.

The Canadian *Personal Information Protection and Electronic Documents Act* we discussed in Chapter 4 mandates companies to provide adequate security for data, including protection from theft of data. This puts the onus on the company to secure its data and raises the potential for monetary fines if a company does not do so. In addition, the public relations consequences of having data stolen can be a nightmare for a company, causing it to lose current as well as future customers.

The Montreal man who stole the Bell data was not a company employee. Experts remind the public that external threats have increased but internal threats from employees still pose a more serious risk for theft than external parties. "Our security and forensic technology teams are combing through the data and determining precisely what's part [of the breach]. . . . It was on a hard drive and on a memory stick and on a CD. It was all electronic; there was no other format," said Mark Langton, a Bell Canada spokesperson. While the data included names, addresses, phone numbers, long-distance calling details, and lists of services received, about 5 percent of the phone numbers in the stolen data were unlisted. According to Langton, the stolen data did not include any financial information, such as credit card numbers or PINs. Oliver Lapoint, a spokesperson for the Montreal Police, said that the police were still looking for other suspects.

Bell corporate security was tipped off when the accused tried to sell the data to the informant. While Langton could not remember Bell ever experiencing a data theft, he did say that the breach could indicate that a review of Bell's data security could be needed. "It's frustrating, but we'll be looking at our entire security system," he said.

Meanwhile, a few months after the Bell data theft, Nick Belmonte, vice president of IT at C-W Group, was accused of stealing a backup tape with data about 3.2 million customers,

likely worth more than $10 million. The tape also contained credit card and banking data about more than 800 000 customers. The data was encrypted, but the tape also contained software that would have permitted a knowledgeable user to decrypt it. According to court records, Belmonte was a "problem employee" with irregular attendance, who would charge lunches with friends to his expense account and who had told colleagues he would soon leave the company.

After the fact, security of data was increased at C-W Group, including changing locks on the computer room and computer access from external computers. According to CEO Gloria Evans, Belmonte had asked a co-worker to bring him three backup tapes, which he then copied. Yet only two tapes were found in Belmonte's office. The missing data contains the company's customer library.

David Senf, director of Canadian security and software research at Toronto-based IDB Canada, says that Canadian companies could increase their efforts to protect confidential data: "Organizations in Canada have a rough idea of what security threats can harm them. But when it comes down to specifics, of which threat is the one they need to focus on, that's where we see trouble." According to Senf, hackers will continue to pose a threat to companies as well as individuals who do not protect themselves. This could happen not only in more traditional ways, but even by using social networking sites. Senf said: "It's no longer hackers having fun. It's someone who wants to make a dollar going after the information." Whether the threat is from inside or outside the company, management must ensure that the company's data is secure. It costs too much to do otherwise.

To Think About

1. List and describe the potential security control weaknesses at Bell Canada and at C-W Group.

2. What management, organization, and technology factors contributed to these weaknesses?

3. What was the business impact of data loss on these companies and their consumers?

4. Can you tell how effectively each company dealt with these problems?

5. Who should be held liable for the potential losses that could be caused by the use of customer credit card information at C-W Group: C-W group or its customers? Justify your answer.

6. What solutions would you suggest to prevent these problems?

MIS in Action

Explore the Web site of the Privacy Commissioner of Canada (**www.priv.gc.ca**) and review the section on Data Breaches and guidelines for responding to breaches of data security.

1. Based on the details in this case study, how well were Bell Canada and C-W Group complying with these guidelines? What guidelines did they fail to meet?

2. Would complying with these guidelines help to prevent the theft customer data in the future?

Sources: Brian Jackson, "Montreal Man Arrested in Bell Canada Data Theft Case," ITBusiness Canada, **www.itbusiness.ca/it/client/en/Home/ DetailNewsPrint.asp?id=47156** (accessed April 30, 2009); Tim Wilson, "Canadian IT Exec Accused of Stealing Customer Database," **www .darkreading.com/shared/printableArticleSrc.jhtml?articleID=212201246**.

A hacker can employ an 802.11 analysis tool to identify the SSID. (Windows XP and Vista have capabilities for detecting the SSID used in a network and automatically configuring the radio NIC within the user's device.) An intruder who has associated with an access point by using the correct SSID is capable of accessing other resources on the network, using the Windows operating system to determine which other users are connected to the network, access their computer hard drives, and open or copy their files.

Intruders also use the information they have gleaned to set up rogue access points on a different radio channel in physical locations close to users to force a user's radio NIC to associate with the rogue access point. Once this association occurs, hackers using the rogue access point can capture the names and passwords of unsuspecting users.

The initial security standard developed for Wi-Fi, called *Wired Equivalent Privacy (WEP)*, is not very effective. WEP is built into all standard 802.11 products, but its use is optional. Many users neglect to use WEP security features, leaving them unprotected. The basic WEP specification calls for an access point and for all of its users to share the same 40-bit encrypted password, which can be easily decrypted by hackers from a small amount of traffic. Stronger encryption and authentication systems are now available, but users must be willing to install them.

Malicious Software: Viruses, Worms, Trojan Horses, and Spyware

Malicious software programs are referred to as **malware** and include a variety of threats, such as computer viruses, worms, and Trojan horses. A **computer virus** is a rogue software program that attaches itself to other software programs or data files in order to be executed, usually without user knowledge or permission. Most computer viruses deliver a "payload." The payload may be relatively benign, such as instructions to display a message or image, or it may be highly destructive—destroying programs or data, clogging computer memory, reformatting a computer's hard drive, or causing programs to run improperly. Viruses typically spread from computer to computer when humans take an action, such as sending an e-mail attachment or copying an infected file.

Most recent attacks have come from **worms,** which are independent computer programs that copy themselves from one computer to other computers over a network. (Unlike viruses, they can operate on their own without attaching to other computer program files and rely less on human behaviour in order to spread from computer to computer. This explains why computer worms spread much more rapidly than computer viruses.) Worms destroy data and programs as well as disrupting or even halting the operation of computer networks.

Worms and viruses are often spread over the Internet from files of downloaded software, from files attached to e-mail transmissions, or from compromised e-mail messages or instant messaging. Viruses have also invaded computerized information systems from "infected" disks or infected machines. E-mail worms are currently the most problematic.

There are now more than 200 viruses and worms targeting mobile phones, such as CABIR, Comwarrior, and Frontal A. Frontal A, for example, installs a corrupted file that causes phone failure and prevents the user from rebooting. Mobile device viruses could

Malware
Computer virus
Worms

TABLE 8-1 Examples of malicious code.

NAME	TYPE	DESCRIPTION
Storm	Worm/Trojan horse	First identified in January 2007. Spreads via e-mail spam with a fake attachment. Infected up to 10 million computers, causing them to join its zombie network of computers engaged in criminal activity.
Sasser.ftp	Worm	First appeared in May 2004. Spread over the Internet by attacking random IP addresses. Causes computers to continually crash and reboot, and infected computers to search for more victims. Affected millions of computers worldwide, disrupting British Airways flight check-ins, operations of British coast guard stations, Hong Kong hospitals, Taiwan post office branches, and Australia's Westpac Bank. Sasser and its variants caused an estimated $18 billion to $22.75 billion in damages worldwide.
MyDoom.A	Worm	First appeared on January 26, 2004. Spreads as an e-mail attachment. Sends e-mail to addresses harvested from infected machines, forging the sender's address. At its peak this worm lowered global Internet performance by 10 percent and Web page loading times by as much as 50 percent. Was programmed to stop spreading after February 12, 2004.
Sobig.F	Worm	First detected on August 19, 2003. Spreads via e-mail attachments and sends massive amounts of mail with forged sender information. Deactivated itself on September 10, 2003, after infecting more than 1 million PCs and doing $6.1 to $12.2 billion in damage.
ILoveYou	Virus	First detected on May 3, 2000. Script virus written in Visual Basic script and transmitted as an attachment to e-mail with the subject line ILOVEYOU. Overwrites music, image, and other files with a copy of itself and did an estimated $12.2 billion to $18.3 billion in damage.
Melissa	Macro virus/worm	First appeared in March 1999. Word macro script mailing infected and sent a Word file to the first 50 entries in user's Microsoft Outlook address book. Infected 15 to 29 percent of all business PCs, causing $366.5 million to $733 million in damage.

pose serious threats to enterprise computing because so many wireless devices are now linked to corporate information systems.

Web 2.0 applications, such as blogs, wikis, and social networking sites such as Facebook and MySpace, have emerged as new conduits for malware or spyware. These applications allow users to post software code as part of the permissible content, and the code can be launched automatically as soon as a Web page is viewed. For example, in August 2008, malicious hackers targeted unsuspecting Facebook users via postings on the site's Wall feature, which is used by members to leave each other messages. Impersonating members' friends, malicious hackers posted messages urging users to click on a link to view a video that transported them to a rogue Web page where they were told to download a new version of Adobe's Flash player in order to view the video. If users authorized the download, the site would install a Trojan horse, Troj/Dloadr-BPL, that funnelled other malicious code to their PCs (Perez, 2008). Table 8-1 describes the characteristics of some of the most harmful worms and viruses that have appeared to date.

Over the past decade, worms and viruses have cause billions of dollars of damage to corporate networks, e-mail systems, and data. According to Consumer Reports' State of the Net 2008 survey, U.S. consumers lost $8.5 billion because of malware and online scams, and the majority of these losses came from malware (Consumer Reports, 2008).

A **Trojan horse** is a software program that appears to be benign but then does something other than expected. The Trojan horse is not itself a virus because it does not replicate but is often a way for viruses or other malicious code to be introduced into a computer system. The term *Trojan horse* is based on the huge wooden horse used by the Greeks to trick the Trojans into opening the gates to their fortified city during the Trojan War. Once inside the city walls, Greek soldiers hidden in the horse revealed themselves and captured the city.

An example of a modern-day Trojan horse is Pushdo Trojan, which uses electronic greeting-card lures in e-mail to trick Windows users into launching an executable program. Once the Trojan horse is executed, it pretends to be an Apache Web server and tries to deliver executable malware programs to the infected Windows machines.

Trojan horse

Some types of **spyware** also act as malicious software. These small programs install themselves surreptitiously on computers to monitor user Web surfing activity and serve up advertising. Thousands of forms of spyware have been documented. Harris Interactive found that 92 percent of the companies surveyed in its Web@Work study reported detecting spyware on their networks (Mitchell, 2006).

Many users find such spyware annoying and some critics worry about its infringement on computer users' privacy. Some forms of spyware are especially nefarious. **Keyloggers** record every keystroke made on a computer to steal serial numbers for software, to launch Internet attacks, to gain access to e-mail accounts, to obtain passwords to protected computer systems, or to pick up personal information such as credit card numbers. Other spyware programs reset Web browser home pages, redirect search requests, or slow computer performance by taking up too much memory.

Hackers and Computer Crime

A **hacker** is an individual who intends to gain unauthorized access to a computer system. Within the hacking community, the term *cracker* is typically used to denote a hacker with criminal intent although in the public press, the terms *hacker* and *cracker* are used interchangeably. Hackers and crackers gain unauthorized access by finding weaknesses in the security protections employed by Web sites and computer systems, often taking advantage of various features of the Internet that make it an open system that is easy to use.

Hacker activities have broadened beyond mere system intrusion to include theft of goods and information, as well as system damage and **cybervandalism,** the intentional disruption, defacement, or even destruction of a Web site or corporate information system. For example, cybervandals have turned many of the MySpace "group" sites, which are dedicated to interests such as home beer brewing or animal welfare, into cyber-graffiti walls, filled with offensive comments and photographs (Kirk, 2008).

Spoofing and Sniffing Hackers attempting to hide their true identities often spoof, or misrepresent, themselves by using fake e-mail addresses or masquerading as someone else. **Spoofing** also may involve redirecting a Web link to an address different from the intended one, with the site masquerading as the intended destination. For example, if hackers redirect customers to a fake Web site that looks almost exactly like the true site, they can then collect and process orders, effectively stealing business as well as sensitive customer information from the true site. We provide more detail on other forms of spoofing in our discussion of computer crime.

A **sniffer** is a type of eavesdropping program that monitors information travelling over a network. When used legitimately, sniffers help identify potential network trouble spots or criminal activity on networks, but when used for criminal purposes, they can be damaging and very difficult to detect. Sniffers enable hackers to steal proprietary information from anywhere on a network, including e-mail messages, company files, and confidential reports.

Denial-of-Service Attacks In a **denial-of-service (DoS) attack,** hackers flood a network server or Web server with many thousands of false communications or requests for services to crash the network. The network receives so many queries that it cannot keep up with them and is thus unavailable to service legitimate requests. A **distributed denial-of-service (DDoS)** attack uses numerous computers to inundate and overwhelm the network from numerous launch points. For example, in 2000, Michael Calce, a high school student from Montreal, launched a DDoS attack against the Web sites of Amazon, HMV, Yahoo!, eBay, Dell, and E*Trade.

Although DoS attacks do not destroy information or access restricted areas of a company's information systems, they often cause a Web site to shut down, making it impossible for legitimate users to access the site. For busy e-commerce sites, these attacks are costly; while the site is shut down, customers cannot make purchases. Especially vulnerable are small and midsize businesses whose networks tend to be less protected than those of large corporations.

Spyware
Keyloggers
Hacker
Cybervandalism
Spoofing
Sniffer
Denial-of-service (DoS) attack
Distributed denial-of-service (DDoS)

TABLE 8-2   Examples of computer crime.

COMPUTERS AS TARGETS OF CRIME	COMPUTERS AS INSTRUMENTS OF CRIME
Breaching the confidentiality of protected computerized data	Theft of trade secrets Unauthorized copying of software or copyrighted intellectual property, such as articles, books, music, and video
Accessing a computer system without authority	Schemes to defraud
Knowingly accessing a protected computer to commit fraud	Using e-mail for threats or harassment
Intentionally accessing a protected computer and causing damage, negligently or deliberately	Intentionally attempting to intercept electronic communication
Knowingly transmitting a program, program code, or command that intentionally causes damage to a protected computer	Illegally accessing stored electronic communications, including e-mail and voice mail
Threatening to cause damage to a protected computer	Transmitting or possessing child pornography using a computer

Perpetrators of DoS attacks often use thousands of "zombie" PCs infected with malicious software without their owners' knowledge that are organized into a **botnet.** Hackers create these botnets by infecting other people's computers with bot malware that opens a back door through which an attacker can give instructions. The infected computer then becomes a slave, or zombie, serving a master computer belonging to someone else. Once a hacker infects enough computers, her or she can use the amassed resources of the botnet to launch DDoS attacks, phishing campaigns, or unsolicited "spam" e-mail.

In the first six months of 2007, security product provider Symantec observed more than 5 million distinct bot-infected computers. Bots and botnets are an extremely serious threat because they can be used to launch very large attacks using many different techniques. For example, the Storm worm, which was responsible for one of the largest e-mail attacks in the past few years, was propagated via a massive botnet of nearly 2 million computers. Botnet attacks thought to have originated in Russia were responsible for crippling the Web sites of the Estonian government in April 2007 and the Georgian government in July 2008.

Computer Crime Most hacker activities are criminal offences, and the vulnerabilities of systems we have just described make them targets for other types of computer crime as well. **Computer crime** is defined by the Investigative Bureau of the Ontario Provincial Police as "any criminal activity involving the copy of, use of, removal of, interference with, access to, manipulation of computer systems, and/or their related functions, data or programs" (Stinnesen, p. 3). Table 8-2 provides examples of the computer as a target of crime and as an instrument of crime.

No one knows the magnitude of the computer crime problem—how many systems are invaded, how many people engage in the practice, or the total economic damage. According to the 2007 CSI Computer Crime and Security Survey of nearly 500 companies, participants' average annual loss from computer crime and security attacks was $428 000 (Richardson, 2007). Many companies are reluctant to report computer crimes because the crimes may involve employees, or the company fears that publicizing its vulnerability will hurt its reputation. The most economically damaging kinds of computer crime are DoS attacks, introducing viruses, theft of services, and disruption of computer systems.

Identity Theft With the growth of the Internet and electronic commerce, identity theft has become especially troubling. **Identity theft** is a crime in which an impostor obtains key pieces of personal information, such as social insurance numbers, driver's licence numbers, or credit card numbers, to impersonate someone else. The information may be used to obtain credit, merchandise, or services in the name of the victim or to provide the thief with false credentials. In Canada in 2005, Equifax and TransUnion (the two largest Canadian credit bureaus), received approximately 1400 to 1800 complaints of identity theft per month. PhoneBusters, an organization that studies and reports on identity theft,

Botnet
Computer crime
Identity theft

collects data, educates the public, and assists both Canadian and U.S. law enforcement agencies, reported about 11 000 complaints in 2005 (compared to approximately 8000 in 2002), at a cost of $8.6 million (compared to $11.7 million in 2002). About one-third related to credit cards, including false applications, and 10 to 12 percent related to cell phones (Canadian Internet Policy and Public Interest Clinic, 2007).

Identify theft has flourished on the Internet, with credit card files a major target of Web site hackers. Moreover, e-commerce sites are wonderful sources of customer personal information—name, address, and phone number. Armed with this information, criminals are able to assume new identities and establish new credit for their own purposes.

One increasingly popular tactic is a form of spoofing called **phishing.** Phishing involves setting up fake Web sites or sending e-mail messages that look like those of legitimate businesses to ask users for confidential personal data. The e-mail message instructs recipients to update or confirm records by providing social insurance numbers, bank and credit card information, and other confidential data either by responding to the e-mail message, by entering the information at a bogus Web site, or by calling a telephone number. EBay, PayPal, Amazon.com, Walmart, and a variety of banks are among the top spoofed companies.

New phishing techniques called *evil twins* and *pharming* are harder to detect. **Evil twins** are wireless networks that pretend to offer trustworthy Wi-Fi connections to the Internet, such as those in airport lounges, hotels, or coffee shops. The bogus network looks identical to a legitimate public network. These criminals try to capture passwords or credit card numbers of unwitting users who log on to the network.

Pharming redirects users to a bogus Web page, even when the individual types the correct Web page address into his or her browser. This is possible if pharming perpetrators gain access to the Internet address information stored by Internet service providers to speed up Web browsing and the ISP companies have flawed software on their servers that allows the criminals to hack in and change those addresses.

Parliament addressed the threat of computer crime in 1985 with the *Criminal Law Amendment Act.* This act makes it illegal to access a computer system without authorization. The United States and nations in Europe have comparable legislation although this type of legislation is either not present or ineffective in some areas of the world. Other parliamentary acts and criminal legislation around Canada make virus distribution a crime, enforce privacy, address e-mail threats and harassment, and address the issue of online transmission and possession of child pornography.

Click Fraud   When you click on an ad displayed by a search engine, the advertiser typically pays a fee for each click, which is supposed to direct potential buyers to its products. **Click fraud** occurs when an individual or computer program fraudulently clicks on an online ad without any intention of learning more about the advertiser or making a purchase. Click fraud has become a serious problem at Google and other Web sites that feature pay-per-click online advertising.

Some companies hire third parties (typically from low-wage countries) to fraudulently click on a competitor's ads to weaken them by driving up their marketing costs. Click fraud can also be perpetrated with software programs doing the clicking, and botnets are often used for this purpose. Search engines such as Google attempt to monitor click fraud but have been reluctant to publicize their efforts to deal with the problem.

Global Threats: Cyberterrorism and Cyberwarfare   The cybercriminal activities we have described—launching malware, denial-of-service attacks, and phishing probes—are borderless. Computer security firm Sophos reported that 37 percent of the malware it identified in early 2008 originated in the United States, while 27 percent came from China, and 9 percent from Russia (Sophos, 2009). The global nature of the Internet makes it possible for cybercriminals to operate—and to do harm—anywhere in the world (see Figure 8-3).

Concern is mounting that the vulnerabilities of the Internet or other networks make digital networks easy targets for digital attacks by terrorists, foreign intelligence services, or other groups seeking to create widespread disruption and harm. Those cyberattacks might target the software that runs electrical power grids, air traffic control systems, or

Phishing
Evil twins
Pharming
Click fraud

FIGURE 8-3   Regional breakdown of malware.

Malware is active throughout the globe. These three charts show the regional distribution of worms and computer viruses worldwide reported by online security provider Trend Micro over periods of 24 hours, 7 days, and 30 days. The virus count represents the number of infected files, and the percentage shows the relative prevalence in each region compared to worldwide statistics for each measuring period.

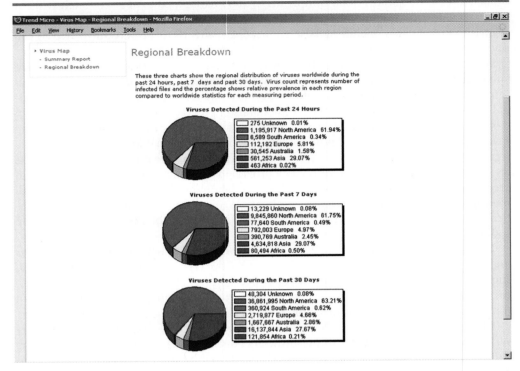

networks of major banks and financial institutions. At least 20 countries, including China, are believed to be developing offensive and defensive cyberwarfare capabilities. In 2007, there were 12 986 reported attacks on U.S. government agencies, with incursions on U.S. military networks up 55 percent from a year earlier. U.S. defence department contractors have also come under siege (Grow et al., 2008).

Internal Threats: Employees

We tend to think the security threats to a business originate outside the organization. In fact, company insiders pose serious security problems. Employees have access to privileged information, and in the presence of sloppy internal security procedures, they are often able to roam throughout an organization's systems without leaving a trace.

Studies have found that user lack of knowledge is the single greatest cause of network security breaches. Many employees forget their passwords to access computer systems or allow co-workers to use them, which compromises the system. Malicious intruders seeking system access sometimes trick employees into revealing their passwords by pretending to be legitimate members of the company in need of information. This practice is called **social engineering.**

Both end users and information systems specialists are also a major source of errors introduced into information systems. End users introduce errors by entering faulty data or by not following the proper instructions for processing data and using computer equipment. Information systems specialists may create software errors as they design and develop new software or maintain existing programs.

Software Vulnerability

Software errors pose a constant threat to information systems, causing untold losses in productivity. Growing complexity and size of software programs, coupled with demands for timely delivery to markets, have contributed to an increase in software flaws or vulnerabilities For example, a flawed software upgrade shut down the BlackBerry e-mail service

Social engineering

throughout North America for about 12 hours between April 17 and April 18, 2007. Millions of business users who depended on BlackBerry were unable to work, and BlackBerry's reputation for reliability was tarnished (Martin, 2007).

A major problem with software is the presence of hidden **bugs** or program code defects. Studies have shown that it is virtually impossible to eliminate all bugs from large programs. The main source of bugs is the complexity of decision-making code. A relatively small program of several hundred lines will contain tens of decisions leading to hundreds or even thousands of different paths. Important programs within most corporations are usually much larger, containing tens of thousands or even millions of lines of code, each with many times the choices and paths of the smaller programs.

Zero defects cannot be achieved in larger programs. Complete testing simply is not possible. Fully testing programs that contain thousands of choices and millions of paths would require thousands of years. Even with rigorous testing, you would not know for sure that a piece of software was dependable until the product proved itself after much operational use.

Flaws in commercial software not only impede performance but also create security vulnerabilities that open networks to intruders. Each year security firms identify about 5000 software vulnerabilities in Internet and PC software. For instance, in 2007 Symantec identified 39 vulnerabilities in Microsoft Internet Explorer, 34 in Mozilla browsers, 25 in Apple Safari, and 7 in Opera. Some of these vulnerabilities are critical (Symantec, 2007).

To correct software flaws once they are identified, the software vendor creates small pieces of software called **patches** to repair the flaws without disturbing the proper operation of the software. An example is Microsoft's Windows Vista Service Pack 1, released in February 2008, which includes some security enhancements to counter malware and hackers. It is up to users of the software to track these vulnerabilities, test, and apply all patches. This process is called *patch management*.

Because a company's IT infrastructure is typically laden with multiple business applications, operating system installations, and other system services, maintaining patches on all devices and services used by a company is often time consuming and costly. Malware is being created so rapidly that companies have very little time to respond between the time a vulnerability and a patch are announced and the time malicious software appears to exploit the vulnerability.

8.2 Business Value of Security and Control

Many firms are reluctant to spend heavily on security because it is not directly related to sales revenue. However, protecting information systems is so critical to the operation of the business that it deserves a second look.

Companies have very valuable information assets to protect. Systems often house confidential information about individuals' taxes, financial assets, medical records, and job performance reviews. They also can contain information on corporate operations, including trade secrets, new product development plans, and marketing strategies. Government systems may store information on weapons systems, intelligence operations, and military targets. These information assets have tremendous value, and the repercussions can be devastating if they are lost, destroyed, or placed in the wrong hands. One study estimated that when the security of a large firm is compromised, the company loses approximately 2.1 percent of its market value within two days of the security breach, which translates into an average loss of $1.65 billion in stock market value per incident (Cavusoglu, Mishra, and Raghunathan, 2004).

Inadequate security and control may result in serious legal liability. Businesses must protect not only their own information assets but also those of customers, employees, and business partners. Failure to do so may open the firm to costly litigation for data exposure or theft. An organization can be held liable for needless risk and harm created if the organization fails to take appropriate protective action to prevent loss of confidential information, data corruption, or breach of privacy (see the Window on Organizations

Bugs

Patches

on page 244 for a glimpse of these issues). A sound security and control framework that protects business information assets can thus produce a high return on investment.

Strong security and control also increase employee productivity and lower operational costs. For example, Axia NextMedia Corp., a Calgary, Alberta, firm that builds and manages open-access broadband networks, saw employee productivity go up and costs go down after it installed an information systems configuration and control system in 2004. Before then, Axia had lost valuable employee work time because of security or other network incidents that caused system outages. Between 2004 and 2007, the new configuration and control system saved the company $704 000 by minimizing system outages (Bartholomew, 2007).

Legal and Regulatory Requirements for Electronic Records Management

Recent Canadian government regulations are forcing companies to take security and control more seriously by mandating the protection of data from abuse, exposure, and unauthorized access. Firms face new legal obligations for the retention and storage of electronic records as well as for privacy protection.

If you work in the health care industry, your firm will need to comply with the provincial health information privacy legislation mandated in several provinces or with the original *Canada Privacy Act* or the newer *Personal Information Protection and Electronic Documents Act* (PIPEDA). These acts specify privacy, security, and electronic transaction standards for health care providers handling patient information, providing penalties for breaches of medical privacy or disclosure of patient records.

Almost all organizations, specifically those that conduct transaction, must conform to the *Personal Information Protection and Electronic Documents Act* (see Chapter 4 for more detail on PIPEDA). In 2002, the Ontario Legislature passed Bill 198, known as Canadian SOX, or **C-SOX,** in response to the U.S. *Sarbanes-Oxley Act.* Both acts were designed to protect investors after the financial scandals at Enron, WorldCom, and other public companies. It imposes responsibility on companies and their management to safeguard the accuracy and integrity of financial information that is used internally and released externally. One of the Learning Tracks for this chapter discusses C-SOX in detail.

C-SOX is fundamentally about ensuring that internal controls are in place to govern the creation and documentation of information in financial statements. Because information systems are used to generate, store, and transport such data, the legislation requires firms to consider information systems security and other controls required to ensure the integrity, confidentiality, and accuracy of their data. Each system application that deals with critical financial reporting data requires controls to make sure the data are accurate. Controls to secure the corporate network, prevent unauthorized access to systems and data, and ensure data integrity and availability in the event of disaster or other disruption of service are essential as well.

Electronic Evidence and Computer Forensics

Security, control, and electronic records management have become essential for responding to legal actions. Much of the evidence today for stock fraud, embezzlement, theft of company trade secrets, computer crime, and many civil cases is in digital form. In addition to information from printed or typewritten pages, legal cases today increasingly rely on evidence represented as digital data stored on portable floppy disks, CDs, and computer hard disk drives, as well as in e-mail, instant messages, and e-commerce transactions over the Internet. E-mail is currently the most common type of electronic evidence.

In a legal action, a firm is obligated to respond to a discovery request for access to information that may be used as evidence, and the company is required by law to produce those data. The cost of responding to a discovery request can be enormous if the company has trouble assembling the required data or if the data have been corrupted or destroyed. Courts now impose severe financial and even criminal penalties for improper destruction of electronic documents.

An effective electronic document retention policy ensures that electronic documents, e-mail, and other records are well organized, accessible, and neither retained too long nor discarded too soon. It also reflects an awareness of how to preserve potential evidence for computer forensics. **Computer forensics** is the scientific collection, examination, authentication, preservation, and analysis of data held on or retrieved from computer storage media in such a way that the information can be used as evidence in a court of law. It deals with the following problems:

- Recovering data from computers while preserving evidential integrity
- Securely storing and handling recovered electronic data
- Finding significant information in a large volume of electronic data
- Presenting the information to a court of law

Electronic evidence may reside on computer storage media in the form of computer files and as *ambient data,* which are not visible to the average user. An example might be a file that has been deleted on a PC hard drive. Data that a computer user may have deleted on computer storage media can be recovered through various techniques. Computer forensics experts try to recover such hidden data for presentation as evidence.

An awareness of computer forensics should be incorporated into a firm's contingency planning process. The CIO, security specialists, information systems staff, and corporate legal counsel should all work together to have a plan in place that can be executed if a legal need arises. You can find out more about computer forensics in the Learning Tracks for this chapter.

8.3 Establishing a Framework for Security and Control

Even with the best security tools, your information systems will not be reliable and secure unless you know how and where to deploy them. You will need to know where your company is at risk and what controls you must have in place to protect your information systems. You will also need to develop a security policy and plans for keeping your business running if your information systems are not operational.

Information Systems Controls

Information systems controls are both manual and automated and consist of both general controls and application controls. **General controls** govern the design, security, and use of computer programs and the security of data files throughout the organization's IT infrastructure. On the whole, general controls apply to all computerized applications and consist of a combination of hardware, software, and manual procedures that create an overall control environment.

General controls include software controls, physical hardware controls, computer operations controls, data security controls, controls over implementation of system processes, and administrative controls. Table 8-3 describes the functions of each of these controls.

Application controls are specific controls unique to each computerized application, such as payroll or order processing. They include both automated and manual procedures that ensure that only authorized data are completely and accurately processed by that application. Application controls can be classified as (1) input controls, (2) processing controls, and (3) output controls.

Input controls check data for accuracy and completeness when they enter the system. There are specific input controls for input authorization, data conversion, data editing, and error handling. *Processing controls* establish that data are complete and accurate during

Computer forensics
General controls
Application controls

TABLE 8-3 General controls.

TYPE OF GENERAL CONTROL	DESCRIPTION
Software controls	Monitor the use of system software and prevent unauthorized access of software programs, system software, and computer programs.
Hardware controls	Ensure that computer hardware is physically secure and check for equipment malfunction. Organizations that are critically dependent on their computers also must make provisions for backup or continued operation to maintain constant service.
Computer operations controls	Oversee the work of the computer department to ensure that programmed procedures are consistently and correctly applied to the storage and processing of data. They include controls over the setup of computer processing jobs and backup and recovery procedures for processing that ends abnormally.
Data security controls	Ensure that valuable business data files on either disk or tape are not subject to unauthorized access, change, or destruction while they are in use or in storage.
Implementation controls	Audit the systems development process at various points to ensure that the process is properly controlled and managed.
Administrative controls	Formalize standards, rules, procedures, and control disciplines to ensure that the organization's general and application controls are properly executed and enforced.

updating. *Output controls* ensure that the results of computer processing are accurate, complete, and properly distributed. You can find more detail about application and general controls in our Learning Tracks.

Risk Assessment

Before your company commits resources to security and information systems controls, it must know which assets require protection and the extent to which these assets are vulnerable. A risk assessment helps answer these questions and determine the most cost-effective set of controls for protecting assets.

A **risk assessment** determines the level of risk to the firm if a specific activity or process is not properly controlled. Not all risks can be anticipated and measured, but most businesses will be able to acquire some understanding of the risks they face. Business managers working with information systems specialists should try to determine the value of information assets, points of vulnerability, the likely frequency of a problem, and the potential for damage. For example, if an event is likely to occur no more than once a year, with a maximum of a $1000 loss to the organization, it is not feasible to spend $20 000 on the design and maintenance of a control to protect against that event. However, if that same event could occur at least once a day, with a potential loss of more than $300 000 a year, $100 000 spent on a control might be entirely appropriate.

Risk assessment

Table 8-4 illustrates sample results of a risk assessment for an online order processing system that processes 30 000 orders per day. The likelihood of each exposure occurring

TABLE 8-4 Online order processing risk assessment.

EXPOSURE	PROBABILITY OF OCCURRENCE (%)	LOSS RANGE/AVERAGE ($)	EXPECTED ANNUAL LOSS ($)
Power failure	30%	$5000–$200,000 ($102 500)	$30 750
Embezzlement	5%	$1000–$50 000 ($25 500)	$1275
User error	98%	$200–$40 000 ($20 100)	$19 698

over a one-year period is expressed as a percentage. The next column shows the highest and lowest possible loss that could be expected each time the exposure occurred and an average loss calculated by adding the highest and lowest figures together and dividing by two. The expected annual loss for each exposure can be determined by multiplying the average loss by its probability of occurrence.

This risk assessment shows that the probability of a power failure occurring in a one-year period is 30 percent. Loss of order transactions while power is down could range from $5000 to $200 000 (averaging $102 500) for each occurrence, depending on how long processing is halted. The probability of embezzlement occurring over a yearly period is about 5 percent, with potential losses ranging from $1000 to $50 000 (and averaging $25 500) for each occurrence. User errors have a 98 percent chance of occurring over a yearly period, with losses ranging from $200 to $40 000 (and averaging $20 100) for each occurrence.

Once the risks have been assessed, system developers will concentrate on the control points with the greatest vulnerability and potential for loss. In this case, controls should focus on ways to minimize the risk of power failures and user errors because anticipated annual losses are highest for these areas.

Security Policy

Once you have identified the main risks to your systems, your company will need to develop a security policy for protecting the company's assets. A **security policy** includes statements ranking information risks, identifying acceptable security goals, and identifying the mechanisms for achieving these goals. What are the firm's most important information assets? Who generates and controls this information in the firm? What existing security policies are in place to protect the information? What level of risk is management willing to accept for each of these assets? Is it willing, for instance, to lose customer credit data once every 10 years? Or will it install a security system for credit card data that can withstand the once-in-100-years disaster? Management must estimate how much it will cost to achieve this level of acceptable risk.

The security policy drives policies determining acceptable use of the firm's information resources and which members of the company have access to its information assets. An **acceptable-use policy (AUP)** defines acceptable uses of the firm's information resources and computing equipment, including desktop and laptop computers, wireless devices, telephones, and the Internet. The policy should clarify company policy regarding privacy, user responsibility, and personal use of company equipment and networks. A good AUP defines unacceptable and acceptable actions for every user and specifies consequences for noncompliance.

Authorization policies determine differing levels of access to information assets for different levels of users. **Authorization management systems** establish where and when a user is permitted to access certain parts of a Web site or a corporate database. Such systems allow each user access only to those portions of a system that person is permitted to enter, based on information established by a set of access rules.

The authorization management system knows exactly what information each user is permitted to access as shown in Figure 8-4. This figure illustrates the security allowed for two sets of users of an online personnel database containing sensitive information, such as employees' salaries, benefits, and medical histories. One set of users consists of all employees who perform clerical functions, such as inputting employee data into the system. All individuals with this type of profile can update the system but can neither read nor update sensitive fields, such as salary, medical history, or earnings data. Another profile applies to a divisional manager, who cannot update the system but who can read all employee data fields for his or her division, including medical history and salary. These profiles are based on access rules supplied by business groups. The system illustrated in Figure 8-4 provides very fine-grained security restrictions, such as allowing authorized personnel users to inquire about all employee information except that in confidential fields, such as salary or medical history.

Security policy
Acceptable-use policy (AUP)
Authorization policies
Authorization management systems

FIGURE 8-4   Security profiles for a personnel system.

These two examples represent two security profiles or data security patterns that might be found in a personnel system. Depending on the security profile, a user would have certain restrictions on access to various systems, locations, or data in an organization.

SECURITY PROFILE 1

User: Personnel Dept. Clerk

Location: Division 1

Employee Identification
Codes with This Profile: 00753, 27834, 37665, 44116

Data Field Restrictions	Type of Access
All employee data for Division 1 only	Read and Update
• Medical history data	None
• Salary	None
• Pensionable earnings	None

SECURITY PROFILE 2

User: Divisional Personnel Manager

Location: Division 1

Employee Identification
Codes with This Profile: 27321

Data Field Restrictions	Type of Access
All employee data for Division 1 only	Read Only

Disaster Recovery Planning and Business Continuity Planning

If you run a business, you need to plan for events, such as power outages, floods, earthquakes, and terrorist attacks, that will prevent your information systems and your business from operating. **Disaster recovery planning** devises plans for the restoration of computing and communications services after they have been disrupted. Disaster recovery plans focus primarily on the technical issues involved in keeping systems up and running, such as which files to back up and the maintenance of backup computer systems or disaster recovery services.

For example, disaster recovery firms provide hot sites housing spare computers at locations far away from the "home" location where subscribing firms can run their critical applications in an emergency. Goodman and Carr, LLP, a large law firm in Toronto, contracted with Fusepoint Managed Services to provide site replication on a minute-by-minute basis.

Business continuity planning focuses on how the company can restore business operations after a disaster strikes. The business continuity plan identifies critical business processes and determines action plans for handling mission-critical functions if systems go down. For example, Deutsche Bank, which provides investment banking and asset management services in 74 different countries, has a well-developed business continuity plan that it continually updates and refines. It maintains full-time teams in Singapore, Hong Kong, Japan, India, and Australia to coordinate plans addressing loss of facilities, personnel, or critical systems so that the company can continue to operate when a catastrophic event occurs. Deutsche Bank's plan distinguishes between processes critical for business survival and those critical to crisis support and is coordinated with the company's disaster recovery planning for its computer centres.

Business managers and information technology specialists need to work together on both types of plans to determine which systems and business processes are most critical to the company. They must conduct a business impact analysis to identify the firm's most critical systems and the impact a systems outage would have on the business.

Disaster recovery planning
Business continuity planning

Management must determine the maximum amount of time the business can survive with its systems down and which parts of the business must be restored first.

Having a disaster recovery plan and a business continuity plan is not enough; the plans must be tested to ensure that they will work if and when the time comes to implement them. On August 14, 2003, shortly after 4 p.m., Ontario and much of the northeastern United States experienced the largest blackout ever in North America. Fifty million people were without power—as were all businesses. Power remained out for a large portion of the affected area until August 16, but Toronto's subway remained out of service until August 18 (CBC News, August 18, 2003; CBC News, August 20, 2003). Businesses without appropriate disaster recovery and business continuity plans experienced serious impacts from the outage. Those with sufficient, tested plans managed to recover quickly, with little impact on sales or profits.

The Role of Auditing

How does management know that information systems security and controls are effective? To answer this question, organizations must conduct comprehensive and systematic audits. An **MIS audit** examines the firm's overall security environment as well as controls governing individual information systems. The auditor should trace the flow of sample transactions through the system and perform tests, using, if appropriate, automated audit software. The MIS audit may also examine data quality, as described in Chapter 6.

Security audits review technologies, procedures, documentation, training, and personnel. A thorough audit will even simulate an attack or disaster to test the response of the technology, information systems staff, and business employees.

The audit lists and ranks all control weaknesses and estimates the probability of their occurrence. It then assesses the financial and organizational impact of each threat. Figure 8-5 is a sample auditor's listing of control weaknesses for a loan system. It includes a section for notifying management of these weaknesses and for management's response. Management is expected to devise a plan for countering significant weaknesses in controls.

MIS audit

FIGURE 8-5 Sample auditor's list of control weaknesses.

Function: Loans Location: Lethbridge, AB	Prepared by: J. Ericson Date: June 16, 2009		Received by: T. Benson Review date: June 28, 2009	
Nature of Weakness and Impact	Chance for Error/Abuse		Notification to Management	
	Yes/No	Justification	Report date	Management response
User accounts with missing passwords	Yes	Leaves system open to unauthorized outsiders or attackers	5/10/09	Eliminate accounts without passwords
Network configured to allow some sharing of system files	Yes	Exposes critical system files to hostile parties connected to the network	5/10/09	Ensure only required directories are shared and that they are protected with strong passwords
Software patches can update production programs without final approval from Standards and Controls group	No	All production programs require management approval; Standards and Controls group assigns such cases to a temporary production status		

This chart is a sample page from a list of control weaknesses that an auditor might find in a loan system in a local commercial bank. This form helps auditors record and evaluate control weaknesses and shows the results of discussing those weaknesses with management, as well as any corrective actions taken by management.

8.4 Technologies and Tools for Safeguarding Information Resources

Businesses have an array of tools and technologies for protecting their information resources. These include tools and technologies for securing systems and data, ensuring system availability, and ensuring software quality.

Access Control

Access control consists of all the policies and procedures a company uses to prevent improper access to systems by unauthorized insiders and outsiders. To gain access, a user must be authorized and authenticated. **Authentication** refers to the ability to know that a person is who he or she claims to be. Access control software is designed to allow only authorized users to use systems or to access data using some method for authentication.

Authentication is often established by using passwords known only to authorized users. An end user uses a password to log on to a computer system and may also use passwords for accessing specific systems and files. However, users often forget passwords, share them, or choose poor passwords that are easy to guess, which compromises security. However, password systems that are too rigorous hinder employee productivity. When employees must change complex passwords frequently, they often take shortcuts, such as choosing passwords that are easy to guess or writing down their passwords at their workstations in plain view. Passwords can also be "sniffed" if transmitted over a network or stolen through social engineering.

New authentication technologies, such as tokens, smart cards, and biometric authentication, overcome some of these problems. A **token** is a physical device, similar to an identification card, that is designed to prove the identity of a single user. Tokens are small gadgets that typically fit on key rings and display passcodes that change frequently. A **smart card** is a device about the size of a credit card that contains a chip formatted with access permission and other data. (Smart cards are also used in electronic payment systems.) A reader device interprets the data on the smart card and allows or denies access.

Biometric authentication uses systems that read and interpret individual human traits, such as fingerprints, irises, and voices, in order to grant or deny access. Biometric

Access control
Authentication
Token
Smart card
Biometric authentication

This NEC PC has a biometric fingerprint reader for fast yet secure access to files and networks. New models of PCs are starting to use biometric identification to authenticate users.

authentication is based on the measurement of a physical or behavioural trait that makes each individual unique. It compares a person's unique characteristics, such as the fingerprints, face, or retinal image, against a stored profile of these characteristics to determine whether there are any differences between these characteristics and the stored profile. If the two profiles match, access is granted. Fingerprint and facial recognition technologies are just beginning to be used for security applications. PC laptops are starting to be equipped with fingerprint identification devices.

Firewalls, Intrusion Detection Systems, and Antivirus Software

Without protection against malware and intruders, connecting to the Internet would be very dangerous. Firewalls, intrusion detection systems, and antivirus software have become essential business tools.

Firewalls Chapter 7 describes the use of *firewalls* to prevent unauthorized users from accessing private networks. A firewall is a combination of hardware and software that controls the flow of incoming and outgoing network traffic. It is generally placed between the organization's private internal networks and distrusted external networks, such as the Internet, although firewalls can also be used to protect one part of a company's network from the rest of the network (see Figure 8-6).

The firewall acts like a gatekeeper that examines each user's credentials before access is granted to a network. The firewall identifies names, IP addresses, applications, and other characteristics of incoming traffic. It checks this information against the access rules that have been programmed into the system by the network administrator. The firewall prevents unauthorized communication into and out of the network.

In large organizations, the firewall often resides on a specially designated computer separate from the rest of the network, so no incoming request directly accesses private

FIGURE 8-6   A corporate firewall.

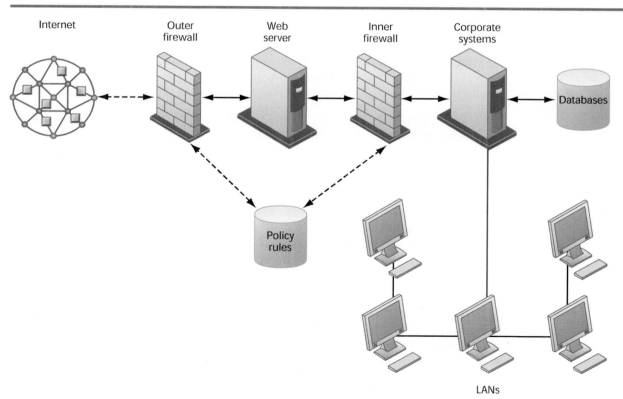

The firewall is placed between the firm's private network and the public Internet or another distrusted network to protect against unauthorized traffic.

network resources. There are a number of firewall screening technologies, including static packet filtering, stateful inspection, Network Address Translation, and application proxy filtering. They are frequently used in combination to provide firewall protection.

Packet filtering examines selected fields in the headers of data packets flowing back and forth between the trusted network and the Internet, examining individual packets in isolation. This filtering technology can miss many types of attacks. *Stateful inspection* provides additional security by determining whether packets are part of an ongoing dialogue between a sender and a receiver. It sets up state tables to track information over multiple packets. Packets are accepted or rejected based on whether they are part of an approved conversation or whether they are attempting to establish a legitimate connection.

Network Address Translation (NAT) can provide another layer of protection when static packet filtering and stateful inspection are employed. NAT conceals the IP addresses of the organization's internal host computer(s) to prevent sniffer programs outside the firewall from ascertaining them and using that information to penetrate internal systems.

Application proxy filtering examines the application content of packets. A proxy server stops data packets originating outside the organization, inspects them, and passes a proxy to the other side of the firewall. If a user outside the company wants to communicate with a user inside the organization, the outside user first "talks" to the proxy application, and the proxy application communicates with the firm's internal computer. Likewise, a computer user inside the organization goes through the proxy to talk with computers on the outside.

To create a good firewall, an administrator must maintain detailed internal rules identifying the people, applications, or addresses that are allowed or rejected. Firewalls can deter, but not completely prevent, network penetration by outsiders and should be viewed as one element in an overall security plan.

Intrusion Detection Systems In addition to firewalls, commercial security vendors now provide intrusion detection tools and services to protect against suspicious network traffic and attempts to access files and databases. **Intrusion detection systems** feature full-time monitoring tools placed at the most vulnerable points or "hotspots" of corporate networks to detect and deter intruders continually. The system generates an alarm if it finds a suspicious or unusual event. Scanning software looks for patterns indicative of known methods of computer attacks, such as bad passwords, checks to see if important files have been removed or modified, and sends warnings of vandalism or system administration errors. Monitoring software examines events as they are happening to discover security attacks in progress. The intrusion detection tool can also be customized to shut down a particularly sensitive part of a network if it receives unauthorized traffic.

Antivirus and Antispyware Software Defensive technology plans for both individuals and businesses must include antivirus protection for every computer. **Antivirus software** is designed to check computer systems and drives for the presence of computer viruses. Often the software eliminates the virus from the infected area. However, most antivirus software is effective only against viruses already known when the software was written. To remain effective, the antivirus software must be continually updated. Antivirus products are available for many different types of mobile and handheld devices in addition to servers, workstations, and desktop PCs.

Leading antivirus software vendors, such as McAfee, Symantec, and Trend Micro, have enhanced their products to include protection against spyware. Antispyware software tools such as Ad-Aware, Spybot S&D, and Spyware Doctor are also very helpful.

Unified Threat Management Systems To help businesses reduce costs and improve manageability, security vendors have combined into a single appliance various security tools, including firewalls, virtual private networks, intrusion detection systems, and Web content filtering and anti-spam software. These comprehensive security management products are called **unified threat management (UTM)** systems. Although initially aimed at small and medium-sized businesses, UTM products are available for all sizes of networks. Leading UTM vendors include Crossbeam, Fortinet, and Secure Computing, and networking vendors such as Cisco Systems and Juniper Networks provide some UTM capabilities in their equipment.

Intrusion detection systems
Antivirus software
Unified threat management (UTM)

Securing Wireless Networks

Despite its flaws, WEP provides some margin of security if Wi-Fi users remember to activate it. A simple first step to thwart hackers is to assign a unique name to your network's SSID and instruct your router not to broadcast it. Corporations can further improve Wi-Fi security by using it in conjunction with virtual private network (VPN) technology when accessing internal corporate data.

In June 2004, the Wi-Fi Alliance industry trade group finalized the 802.11i specification (also referred to as Wi-Fi Protected Access 2 or WPA2) that replaces WEP with stronger security standards. Instead of the static encryption keys used in WEP, the new standard uses much longer keys that continually change, making them harder to crack. It also employs an encrypted authentication system with a central authentication server to ensure that only authorized users access the network.

Encryption and Public Key Infrastructure

Many businesses use encryption to protect digital information that they store, physically transfer, or send over the Internet. **Encryption** is the process of transforming plain text or data into cipher text that cannot be read by anyone other than the sender and the intended receiver. Data are encrypted by using a secret numerical code, called an *encryption key*, that transforms plain data into cipher text. The message must be decrypted by the receiver.

Two methods for encrypting network traffic on the Web are SSL and S-HTTP. **Secure Sockets Layer (SSL)** and its successor Transport Layer Security (TLS) enable client and server computers to manage encryption and decryption activities as they communicate with each other during a secure Web session. **Secure Hypertext Transfer Protocol (S-HTTP)** is another protocol used for encrypting data flowing over the Internet, but it is limited to individual messages while SSL and TLS are designed to establish a secure connection between two computers.

The capability to generate secure sessions is built into Internet client browser software and servers. The client and the server negotiate what key and what level of security to use. Once a secure session is established between the client and the server, all messages in that session are encrypted.

There are two alternative methods of encryption: symmetric key encryption and public key encryption. In symmetric key encryption, the sender and receiver establish a secure Internet session by creating a single encryption key and sending it to the receiver so both the sender and receiver share the same key. The strength of the encryption key is measured by its bit length. Today, a typical key will be 128 bits long (a string of 128 binary digits).

The problem with all symmetric encryption schemes is that the key itself must be shared somehow among the senders and receivers, which exposes the key to outsiders who might just be able to intercept and decrypt the key. A more secure form of encryption called **public key encryption** uses two keys: one shared (or public) and one totally private as shown in Figure 8-7. The keys are mathematically related so that data encrypted

Encryption
Secure Sockets Layer (SSL)
Secure Hypertext Transfer Protocol (S-HTTP)
Public key encryption

FIGURE 8-7   Public key encryption.

A public key encryption system can be viewed as a series of public and private keys that lock data when they are transmitted and unlock the data when they are received. The sender locates the recipient's public key in a directory and uses it to encrypt a message. The message is sent in encrypted form over the Internet or a private network. When the encrypted message arrives, the recipient uses his or her private key to decrypt the data and read the message.

FIGURE 8-8 Digital certificates.

Digital certificates help establish the identity of people or electronic assets. They protect online transactions by providing secure, encrypted, online communication.

with one key can be decrypted using only the other key. To send and receive messages, communicators first create separate pairs of private and public keys. The public key is kept in a directory and the private key must be kept secret. The sender encrypts a message with the recipient's public key. On receiving the message, the recipient uses his or her private key to decrypt it.

Digital certificates are data files used to establish the identity of users and electronic assets for protection of online transactions (see Figure 8-8). A digital certificate system uses a trusted third party, known as a certificate authority (CA), to validate a user's identity. There are many CAs in Canada and around the world, including Grid Canada and EW-Canada, VeriSign and IdenTrust in the U.S., and Australia's KeyPost.

The CA verifies a digital certificate user's identity offline. This information is put into a CA server, which generates an encrypted digital certificate containing owner identification information and a copy of the owner's public key. The certificate authenticates that the public key belongs to the designated owner. The CA makes its own public key available publicly either in print or perhaps on the Internet. The recipient of an encrypted message uses the CA's public key to decode the digital certificate attached to the message, verifies it was issued by the CA, and then obtains the sender's public key and identification information contained in the certificate. Using this information, the recipient can send an encrypted reply. The digital certificate system would enable, for example, a credit card user and a merchant to validate that their digital certificates were issued by an authorized and trusted third party before they exchange data. **Public key infrastructure (PKI),** the use of public key cryptography working with a certificate authority, is now widely used in e-commerce.

Ensuring System Availability

As companies increasingly rely on digital networks for revenue and operations, they need to take additional steps to ensure that their systems and applications are always available. Firms such as those in the airline and financial services industries with critical applications requiring online transaction processing have traditionally used fault-tolerant computer systems to ensure 100-percent availability. In **online transaction processing,** transactions entered online are immediately processed by the computer. Many changes to databases, reporting, and requests for information occur each instant.

Digital certificates
Public key infrastructure (PKI)
Online transaction processing

Fault-tolerant computer systems contain redundant hardware, software, and power supply components that create an environment that provides continuous, uninterrupted service. Fault-tolerant computers use special software routines or self-checking logic built into their circuitry to detect hardware failures and automatically switch to a backup device. Parts from these computers can be removed and repaired without disruption to the computer system.

Fault tolerance should be distinguished from **high-availability computing.** Both fault tolerance and high-availability computing try to minimize downtime. **Downtime** refers to periods of time in which a system is not operational. However, high-availability computing helps firms recover quickly from a system crash while fault tolerance promises continuous availability and the elimination of recovery time altogether.

High-availability computing environments are a minimum requirement for firms with heavy e-commerce processing or for firms that depend on digital networks for their internal operations. High-availability computing requires backup servers, distribution of processing across multiple servers, high-capacity storage, and good disaster recovery and business continuity plans. The firm's computing platform must be extremely robust with scalable processing power, storage, and bandwidth.

Researchers are exploring ways to make computing systems recover even more rapidly when mishaps occur, an approach called **recovery-oriented computing.** This work includes designing systems that recover quickly and implementing capabilities and tools to help operators pinpoint the sources of faults in multi-component systems and easily correct their mistakes.

The Window on Technology section on the next page describes the efforts of Salesforce.com to make sure its systems are always available to subscribers. Salesforce.com is a Web-based on-demand customer relationship management (CRM) and business services provider. Companies subscribing to its service use Salesforce.com's software programs running on its servers. If Salesforce.com's services fail, they cannot run their CRM applications. That is exactly what happened when Salesforce.com was hit by a series of service outages in late 2005 and early 2006. As you read this case, try to identify the problem Salesforce.com encountered; what alternative solutions were available to management; and the management, organization, and technology issues that had to be addressed when developing the solution.

Controlling Network Traffic: Deep Packet Inspection Have you ever tried to use your campus network and found it was very slow? It may be because your fellow students are using the network to download music or watch YouTube. Bandwidth-consuming applications such as file-sharing programs, Internet phone service, and online video are able to clog and slow down corporate networks, degrading performance. As mentioned in Chapter 7, many ISPs in Canada, the United States, and elsewhere are prioritizing Internet traffic, permitting files with faster download times to have priority over online video, music, and other such programs.

A technology called **deep packet inspection (DPI)** helps solve this problem. DPI examines data files and sorts out low-priority online material while assigning higher priority to business-critical files. Based on the priorities established by a network's operators, it decides whether a specific data packet can continue to its destination or should be blocked or delayed while more important traffic proceeds. Using a DPI system from Allot Communications, Ball State University in Indiana was able to cap the amount of file-sharing traffic and assign it a much lower priority. Ball State's preferred network traffic speeded up (White, 2007).

Security Outsourcing Many companies, especially small businesses, lack the resources or expertise to provide a secure high-availability computing environment on their own so they outsource many security functions to **managed security service providers (MSSPs)** that monitor network activity and perform vulnerability testing and intrusion detection. Toronto's Sentry Metrics, Guardent (acquired by VeriSign), BT Counterpane, VeriSign, and Symantec are leading providers of MSSP services.

Fault-tolerant computer systems
High-availability computing
Downtime
Recovery-oriented computing
Deep packet inspection (DPI)
Managed security service providers (MSSPs)

WINDOW ON TECHNOLOGY

Can Salesforce.com On-Demand Remain in Demand?

In Chapter 5, you learned about Salesforce.com, a leader in cloud computing specializing in on-demand customer relationship management (CRM) services. As of April 2009, Salesforce.com served more than 1 million subscribers in more than 55 000 companies around the world, including Canadian companies such as Greyhound Canada. More businesses use Salesforce.com than any other on-demand CRM company in the world.

Imagine, then, the impact if Salesforce.com's services are not available. That is exactly what happened during a six-week period in late 2005 and early 2006. Starting on December 20, 2005, Salesforce.com clients could not access the company's servers and obtain their customer records for more than three hours. A rare database software bug was the source of the problem. Oracle Database 10g and Oracle Grid Computing are key technologies for Salesforce.com's service and internal operations, and these tools are considered among the best in the business. Salesforce.com was careful not to blame Oracle for the outage and instead focused on working with Oracle to eradicate the bug. It has not resurfaced since the initial occurrence. But with no access to customers' records, some businesses came to a standstill for the duration of the outage.

Salesforce.com experienced two more outages in January and several in early February attributed to "system performance issues." A January 30 performance problem was traced to a shortcoming in the company's database cluster or collection of databases. Salesforce.com had to restart each database instance in the cluster, interrupting service to do so. Its service was down for about four hours. Even when the service was brought back up, its application programming interface (API) was disabled for a few more hours.

On February 9, 2006, a primary hardware server failed, and one of the company's four North American servers did not automatically recover. Salesforce.com had to restart the database running on this server manually. The outage lasted slightly more than one hour.

These service outages could not have occurred at a worse time. Salesforce.com was growing rapidly and seeking to attract more large customers with new software and services in addition to CRM. In January 2006, it launched AppExchange, an online marketplace for applications and Web services from other vendors and developers that can be customized and integrated with Salesforce.com's CRM service. Salesforce.com would not be able to convince enterprise customers to let it run their applications if it could not guarantee that that its services were 100 percent reliable.

The outages caused some clients and analysts to ask whether Salesforce.com had run into capacity or scalability problems. At the time of the first incident, analysts agreed that a one-time outage would not cause a crisis of confidence on the part of clients. Many clients admitted that Salesforce.com had a better record of maintaining uptime than the clients' own companies did. What was of more concern to some clients was the failure of Salesforce.com to communicate adequately with its clients about the outage. They were left in the dark as to what exactly was happening with the on-demand service. At least one client dropped Salesforce.com in favour of an internal system.

In the weeks that followed that outage, it became apparent that the problems at Salesforce.com were not limited to a software bug. The recurring outages raised doubts about the fidelity of the service's infrastructure as a whole. These outages coincided with the end of the month and, for some companies, the end of the fiscal year. It was an extraordinarily inconvenient time to lose access to customer data.

The complaints from clients grew louder. They focused not only on the failure of the on-demand service, but on poor customer service and a tepid response from Salesforce.com management. Salesforce.com's CEO, Mark Benioff, was roundly criticized for downplaying the interruptions as minor. Having the company's CEO minimize an outage that brings customer businesses to a halt as a "minor issue" is not acceptable. Of course, there were plenty of clients that found the increasing downtime unacceptable as well.

Salesforce.com moved quickly to improve its client communication. The company used direct communications and customer support outlets to update clients on efforts to resolve service problems. By the end of February 2006, Salesforce.com had launched Trust. Salesforce.com, a Web site that displayed both real-time and historical data related to the performance of all key system components for its services. The site provided a measure of transparency into the level of database and service performance that clients were receiving, which they valued. Trust. Salesforce.com logs specific metrics, such as API transactions and page views. The site also gives general conditions using a colour scheme to indicate service status for network nodes: green for OK, yellow for a performance issue, and red for an outage.

Even prior to the outages, Salesforce.com had been building up and redesigning its infrastructure to ensure better service. The company invested $50 million in Mirrorforce technology, a mirroring system that creates a duplicate database in a separate location and synchronizes the data instantaneously. If one database is disabled, the other takes over. Salesforce.com added two data centres in addition to its Silicon Valley facility and built an additional facility to support new product development. The company distributed processing for its larger customers among these centres to balance its database load. The investment in Mirrorforce necessitated a complete overhaul of Salesforce.com's hardware and software.

Also helpful are Salesforce's PC applications that tie into its services so users can work offline. These applications were designed for on-the-go and disconnected users, and they lack some the features of Salesforce's online software. However, they do provide stopgap measures during a service outage. Market research firm Harris Interactive recommends that its users download Salesforce's offline applications, which contain a copy of contacts and accounts. When they are able to access Salesforce online again, they can synchronize their data.

Salesforce.com's accelerated growth and switch to the new data centres had contributed to the outages. But by March 2006, the infrastructure had been stabilized, and no more outages occurred until February 11, 2008. Salesforce.com had just migrated a subset of its overall user base to a new updated version of its software. In the process, the company experienced an outage to its NA5 server that lasted intermittently for about seven hours but affected only a small set of customers.

On the public relations front, spokesman Bruce Francis has said, "There's no such thing as a minor outage because we know that even one moment of degraded availability is a moment our customers can't do what they need to do." Salesforce.com continues striving to achieve 99.999 percent availability.

To Think About

1. How did the problems experienced by Salesforce.com impact its business?

2. How did the problems impact its customers?

3. What steps did Salesforce.com take to solve the problems? Were these steps sufficient?

4. List and describe other vulnerabilities discussed in this chapter that might create outages at Salesforce.com and measures to safeguard against them.

MIS in Action

Go to www.trust.salesforce.com, explore the site, and answer the following questions:

1. How does this site help Salesforce.com promote security among its users?

2. If you ran a business, would you feel confident about using Salesforce.com's on-demand service? Why or why not?

Sources: J. Nicholas Hoover, "Service Outages Force Cloud Adopters to Rethink Tactics," *InformationWeek*, August 18, 2008; Renee Boucher Ferguson, "Outages Hit Online Apps," *eWeek*, February 18, 2008; Laton McCartney, "**Salesforce.com:** When On-Demand Goes Off," *Baseline Magazine*, January 7, 2007; John Pallatto, "Rare Database Bug Causes **Salesforce.com** Outage," eWeek.com, December 22, 2005 and "**Salesforce.com** Confirms 'Minor' CRM Outage," **eWeek.com,** January 6, 2006; Alorie Gilbert, "**Salesforce.com** Users Lament Ongoing Outages," cnet **News.com,** February 1, 2006; and Bill Snyder, "**Salesforce.com** Outage Strikes Again," **TheStreet.com,** January 6, 2006.

Ensuring Software Quality

In addition to implementing effective security and controls, organizations can improve system quality and reliability by employing software metrics and rigorous software testing. Software metrics are objective assessments of the system in the form of quantified measurements. Ongoing use of metrics allows the information systems department and end users to jointly measure the performance of the system and identify problems as they occur. Examples of software metrics include the number of transactions that can be processed in a specified unit of time, online response time, the number of payroll cheques printed per hour, and the number of known bugs per hundred lines of program code. For metrics to be successful, they must be carefully designed, formal, objective, and used consistently.

Early, regular, and thorough testing will contribute significantly to system quality. Many view testing as a way to prove the correctness of work they have done. In fact, we know that all sizable software is riddled with errors, and we must test to uncover these errors.

Good testing begins before a software program is even written by using a *walkthrough*—a review of a specification or design document by a small group of people carefully selected based on the skills needed for the particular objectives being tested. Once developers start writing software programs, coding walkthroughs also can be used to review program code. However, code must be tested by computer runs. When errors are discovered, the source is found and eliminated through a process called *debugging*. You can find out more about the various stages of testing required to put an information system into operation in Chapter 9. Our Learning Tracks also contain descriptions of methodologies for developing software programs that also contribute to software quality.

SUMMARY

1. **Why are information systems vulnerable to destruction, error, and abuse?**

   Digital data are vulnerable to destruction, misuse, error, fraud, and hardware or software failures. The Internet is designed to be an open system and makes internal corporate systems more vulnerable to actions from outsiders. Hackers can unleash denial-of-service (DoS) attacks or penetrate corporate networks, causing serious system disruptions. Wi-Fi networks can easily be penetrated by intruders using sniffer programs to obtain an address to access the resources of the network. Computer viruses and worms can disable systems and Web sites. Software presents problems because software bugs may be impossible to eliminate and because software vulnerabilities can be exploited by hackers and malicious software. End users often introduce errors.

2. **What is the business value of security and control?**

   Lack of sound security and control can cause firms relying on computer systems for their core business functions to lose sales and productivity. Information assets, such as confidential employee records, trade secrets, or business plans, lose much of their value if they are revealed to outsiders or if they expose the firm to legal liability. New laws, such as the *Personal Information Protection and Electronic Documents Act*, require companies to practise stringent electronic records management and adhere to strict standards for security, privacy, and control. Legal actions requiring electronic evidence and computer forensics also require firms to pay more attention to security and electronic records management.

3. **What are the components of an organizational framework for security and control?**

   Firms need to establish a good set of both general and application controls for their information systems. A risk assessment evaluates information assets, identifies control points and control weaknesses, and determines the most cost-effective set of controls. Firms must also develop a coherent corporate security policy and plans for continuing business operations in the event of disaster or disruption. The security policy includes policies for acceptable use and authorization. Comprehensive and systematic MIS auditing helps organizations determine the effectiveness of security and controls for their information systems.

4. **What are the most important tools and technologies for safeguarding information resources?**

   Firewalls prevent unauthorized users from accessing a private network when it is linked to the Internet. Intrusion detection systems monitor and protect private networks from suspicious network traffic and attempts to access corporate systems. Passwords, tokens, smart cards, and biometric authentication are used to authenticate system users. Antivirus software checks computer systems for infections by viruses and worms and often eliminates the malicious software while antispyware software combats intrusive and harmful spyware programs. Encryption, the coding and scrambling of messages, is a widely used technology for securing electronic transmissions over unprotected networks. Digital certificates combined with public key encryption provide further protection of electronic transactions by authenticating a user's identity. Companies can use fault-tolerant computer systems or create high-availability computing environments to make sure that their information systems are always available. Use of software metrics and rigorous software testing help improve software quality and reliability.

Key Terms

Acceptable-use policy (AUP), 255
Access control, 258
Antivirus software, 260
Application controls, 253
Authentication, 258
Authorization management systems, 255
Authorization policies, 255
Biometric authentication, 258
Botnet, 248
Bugs, 251
Business continuity planning, 256
C-SOX, 252
Click fraud, 249
Computer crime, 248
Computer forensics, 253
Computer virus, 245

Controls, 241
Cybervandalism, 247
Deep packet inspection (DPI), 263
Denial-of-service (DoS) attack, 247
Digital certificates, 262
Disaster recovery planning, 256
Distributed denial-of-service (DDoS), 247
Downtime, 263
Encryption, 261
Evil twins, 249
Fault-tolerant computer systems, 263
General controls, 253
Hacker, 247
High-availability computing, 263
Identity theft, 248
Intrusion detection systems, 260

Keyloggers, 247
Malware, 245
Managed security service providers (MSSPs), 263
MIS audit, 257
Online transaction processing, 262
Patches, 251
Pharming, 249
Phishing, 249
Public key encryption, 261
Public key infrastructure (PKI), 262
Recovery-oriented computing, 263
Risk assessment, 254
Secure Hypertext Transfer Protocol (S-HTTP), 261
Secure Sockets Layer (SSL), 261

Review Questions

1. *Why are information systems vulnerable to destruction, error, and abuse?*
   - *List and describe the most common threats against contemporary information systems.*
   - *Define malware and distinguish among a virus, a worm, and a Trojan horse.*
   - *Define the term hacker, and explain how hackers create security problems and damage systems.*
   - *Define computer crime. Provide two examples of crime in which computers are targets and two examples in which computers are used as instruments of crime.*
   - *Define identity theft and phishing, and explain why identity theft is such a big problem today.*
   - *Describe the security and system reliability problems created by employees.*
   - *Explain how software defects affect system reliability and security.*

2. *What is the business value of security and control?*
   - *Explain how security and control provide value for businesses.*
   - *Describe the relationship between security and control and recent government regulatory requirements and computer forensics.*

3. *What are the components of an organizational framework for security and control?*
   - *Define general controls, and describe each type of general control.*
   - *Define application controls, and describe each type of application control.*
   - *Describe the function of risk assessment, and explain how it is conducted for information systems.*
   - *Define and describe the following: security policy, acceptable-use policy, authorization policy.*
   - *Explain how MIS auditing promotes security and control.*

4. *What are the most important tools and technologies for safeguarding information resources?*
   - *Name and describe three authentication methods.*
   - *Describe the roles of firewalls, intrusion detection systems, and antivirus software in promoting security.*
   - *Explain how encryption protects information.*
   - *Describe the role of encryption and digital certificates in a public key infrastructure.*
   - *Distinguish between fault-tolerant and high-availability computing, and between disaster recovery planning and business continuity planning.*
   - *Describe measures for improving software quality and reliability*

Discussion Questions

1. *Security isn't simply a technology issue, it is a business issue. Discuss your opinion.*

2. *If you were developing a business continuity plan for your company, where would you start? What aspects of the business would the plan address?*

Collaboration and Teamwork: Evaluating Security Software Tools

With a group of three or four students, use the Web to research and evaluate security products from two competing vendors, such as antivirus software, firewalls, or antispyware software. For each product, describe its capabilities, for what types of businesses it is best suited, and its cost to purchase and install.

Which is the best product? Why? If possible, use Google Sites to post links to Web pages, team communication announcements, and work assignments; to brainstorm; and to work collaboratively on project documents. Try to use Google Docs to develop a presentation of your findings for the class.

Visit the MyMISLab Web site at **www.pearsoned.ca/mymislab.** This online homework and tutorial system puts you in control of your own learning with study and practice tools directly correlated to this chapter's content.

Learning Track Module

The following Learning Tracks provide content relevant to topics covered in this chapter:

1. The Booming Job Market in IT Security
2. *The C-SOX Act*

3. Computer Forensics
4. General and Application Controls for Information Systems
5. Software Vulnerability and Reliability
6. Management Challenges of Security and Control

HANDS-ON MIS Projects

The projects in this section give you hands-on experience analyzing security vulnerabilities, using spreadsheet software for risk analysis, and using Web tools to research security outsourcing services.

Management Decision Problems

1. K2 Network operates online game sites used by about 16 million people in more than 100 countries. Players are allowed to enter a game for free but must buy digital "assets" from K2, such as swords to fight dragons, if they want to be deeply involved. The games can accommodate millions of players at once and are played simultaneously by people all over the world. Prepare a security analysis for this Internet-based business. What kinds of threats should it anticipate? What would be their impact on the business? What steps can it take to prevent damage to its Web sites and continuing operations?

2. A survey of your firm's information technology infrastructure has produced the following security analysis statistics:

SECURITY VULNERABILITIES BY TYPE OF COMPUTING PLATFORM

Platform	Number of Computers	High Risk	Medium Risk	Low Risk	Total Vulnerabilities
Windows Server (corporate applications)	1	11	37	19	
Windows Vista Ultimate (high-level administrators)	3	56	242	87	
Linux (e-mail and printing services)	1	3	154	98	
Sun Solaris (UNIX) (E-commerce and Web servers)	2	12	299	78	
Windows Vista Ultimate (user desktops and laptops with office productivity tools that can also be linked to the corporate network running corporate applications and intranet)	195	14	16	1237	

High-risk vulnerabilities include nonauthorized users accessing applications, guessable passwords, user names matching the password, active user accounts with missing passwords, and the existence of unauthorized programs in application systems.

Medium-risk vulnerabilities include the ability of users to shut down the system without being logged on, passwords and screen saver settings that were not established for PCs, and outdated versions of software still being stored on hard drives.

Low-risk vulnerabilities include the inability of users to change their passwords, user passwords that have not been changed periodically, and passwords that were smaller than the minimum size specified by the company.

1. Calculate the total number of vulnerabilities for each platform. What is the potential impact of the security problems for each computing platform on the organization?

2. If you only have one information systems specialist in charge of security, which platforms should you address

first in trying to eliminate these vulnerabilities? Second? Third? Last? Why?

3. Identify the types of control problems illustrated by these vulnerabilities and explain the measures that should be taken to solve them.

4. What does your firm risk by ignoring the security vulnerabilities identified?

Improving Decision Making: Using Spreadsheet Software to Perform a Security Risk Assessment

Software skills: Spreadsheet formulas and charts
Business skills: Risk assessment

This project uses spreadsheet software to calculate anticipated annual losses from various security threats identified for a small company.

Fictional Mercer Paints is a small but highly regarded paint manufacturing company located in Saskatchewan. The company has a network in place linking many of its business operations. Although the firm believes that its security is adequate, the recent addition of a Web site has become an open invitation to hackers. Management requested a risk assessment, which identified a number of potential exposures. These exposures, their associated probabilities, and average losses are summarized in the following table.

- In addition to the potential exposures listed, you should identify at least three other potential threats to Mercer Paints, assign probabilities, and estimate a loss range.
- Use spreadsheet software and the risk assessment data to calculate the expected annual loss for each exposure.

MERCER PAINTS RISK ASSESSMENT

Exposure	Probability of Occurrence (%)	Average Loss ($)
Malware attack	60%	$75 000
Data loss	12%	$70 000
Embezzlement	3%	$30 000
User errors	95%	$25 000
Threats from hackers	95%	$90 000
Improper use by employees	5%	$5 000
Power failure	15%	$300 000

- Present your findings in the form of a chart. Which control points have the greatest vulnerability? What recommendations would you make to Mercer Paints? Prepare a written report that summarizes your findings and recommendations.

Improving Decision Making: Evaluating Security Outsourcing Services

Software skills: Web browser and presentation software
Business skills: Evaluating business outsourcing services

Businesses today have a choice of whether to outsource the security function or maintain their own internal staff for this purpose. This project will help develop your Internet skills in using the Web to research and evaluate security outsourcing services.

As an information systems expert in your firm, you have been asked to help management decide whether to outsource security or keep the security function within the firm. Search the Web to find information to help you decide whether to outsource security. and to locate security outsourcing services.

- Present a brief summary of the arguments for and against outsourcing computer security for your company.
- Select two firms that offer computer security outsourcing services, and compare them and their services.
- Prepare an electronic presentation for management summarizing your findings. Your presentation should make the case on whether or not your company should outsource computer security. If you believe your company should outsource, the presentation should identify which security outsourcing service should be selected and justify your selection.

A Rogue Trader at Société Générale Roils the World Financial System

Société Générale is one of the world's most respected corporate and investment banks and one of France's oldest and most highly regarded financial institutions. Founded in 1864 by Napoleon III, the company has more than 130 000 employees and 22.5 million customers worldwide. The three core businesses of the company include corporate and investment banking, retail banking and financial services, and global investment management services. Known within the financial services industry as SocGen, the company's reputation was badly tarnished in early 2008 by the revelation that a rogue trader was responsible for losses totalling approximately 5 billion euros ($11.3 billion).

In January 2008, SocGen discovered that one of its traders, 31-year-old Jerome Kerviel, had been making unauthorized trades over the course of the previous year that somehow went unnoticed by the bank's security and risk management systems. The losses represented the largest fraud in investment banking history at a time when world markets were already under pressure due to the subprime mortgage crisis. Kerviel was so successful in evading SocGen's internal controls that he was able to amass more than $86.8 billion in uncovered positions, well over the bank's total market capitalization of approximately $63 billion, en route to the $11.3 billion loss.

Kerviel himself was a quiet and unassuming trader with an unimpressive pedigree compared to many of his SocGen co-workers. He earned an advanced degree in trading from the University of Lyon before joining the company in 2000. By contrast, many of the bank's top officials and traders attended top French universities such as Polytechnique and École Nationale d'Administration. He initially worked in the company's risk management office, which was scornfully nicknamed "the mine" by the higher-level trading units. There, he gained familiarity with many of the company's security procedures and back-office systems. He was eventually promoted to a lower-level trading desk known as Delta One. Kerviel's desire to impress his fellow traders, who generally had more prestigious educational backgrounds, may have motivated him to abuse his knowledge of the company's trading transaction systems in his new role.

Kerviel's task at the Delta One desk was to trade index futures. He was entrusted to purchase one portfolio of European stock index futures and at the same time sell a similar mixture of index futures of different value as a hedge. The goal was to produce a small, low-risk profit stream as a result of performing a large volume of these transactions over time. Kerviel was able to bypass nearly every control for the company's information systems to accomplish something quite different—amassing uncovered and unauthorized positions with the potential to either make or lose billions based on the market activity of that day. He accomplished this by performing legitimate transactions in one direction, but falsifying the hedges that were supposed to "offset" the legitimate ones. Kerviel made his first fictitious transactions in late 2005 but took increasingly larger positions in 2006 and 2007 en route to his eventual $86.8 billion in accumulated positions. How could Kerviel have possibly gotten away with this?

Kerviel's first task was to enter fictitious trades so that they would be undetectable against his real trades. To do this, he entered the false transactions in a separate portfolio, distinct from the one containing his real trades, and did so in such a way that no actual cash was required to exchange hands. When his books were checked together, the real portfolio and fake portfolio offset one another and appeared to be well within Kerviel's limit for acceptable risk. These actions made it possible for Kerviel's supervisors to see a balanced book when in fact he was exposing the bank to substantial risk. The limit for the entire Delta One desk where Kerviel worked was 125 million euros; using this method, Kerviel was able to place single positions worth more than 600 million euros.

Kerviel still had to evade SocGen's more thorough internal checks on each trader's books, which would have revealed his fictitious portfolio. Because he knew the schedule of SocGen's internal controls, he was able to eliminate his fake trades from the system just minutes prior to the scheduled checks and re-enter them soon after. The temporary imbalance did not trigger an alert. He also used this tactic to cancel and enter new trades before confirmations of the trades were ever sent to other banks. Kerviel allegedly used other employees' access codes and user information to accomplish this, leading to reports that Kerviel had "hacked" SocGen's systems to commit fraud. But it is not yet clear whether or not Kerviel performed any complicated computer operations to get around SocGen's controls.

Finally, Kerviel had to somehow keep his schemes from co-workers and supervisors. A common practice among investment bankers is to take scheduled vacation days so that their portfolios can be scrutinized by other bankers while they are away. This increases the chances of uncovering the kinds of fraud Kerviel committed. Kerviel reportedly worked late into the night long after other traders had gone home and took only four vacation days over the course of 2007 to prevent this from occurring. And while his supervisors did spot mistakes in his books, Kerviel was able to cover his tracks enough to quickly "fix" errors and then continue his fraudulent activities.

The extent to which Kerviel's co-workers and superiors had knowledge of his fraudulent activities while he was committing them is still unclear. SocGen maintains that Kerviel was acting alone, but Kerviel has expressed skepticism that his superiors could have been unaware of his actions. Some reports claim that Kerviel used the computer of his manager, Eric Cordelle, to execute several of his fraudulent trades with Cordelle looking on. Several other brokers supposedly responsible for entering some of Kerviel's authentic trades in full knowledge of his schemes have undergone questioning by police. Kerviel's defence lawyers argue that he acted with the tacit approval of his superiors during his more successful initial period of fraudulent activity, when he accumulated more than $2.4 billion in gains for SocGen that were never realized. Also, the bank ignored many warning signs that Kerviel was capable of this level of fraud. In 2005, Kerviel was reprimanded for exceeding his trading limits with bets on Allianz SE securities and was told he would be fired for doing so in the future. The bank also reportedly failed to follow up on 75 warnings on Kerviel's positions over the course of the past several years. SocGen dismissed the warnings, claiming that all traders amass similar numbers of warnings over time.

Two striking aspects of Kerviel's fraudulent activity are how simplistic his methods were and how little Kerviel stood to gain personally from his trades. SocGen's controls were capable of detecting more complicated errors and fraudulent transactions than those committed by Kerviel, but in the end, Kerviel's simple strategies were more than sufficient to bypass them. The manager of SocGen's investment banking division said of the fraud that "Société Générale got caught just like someone who would have installed a highly sophisticated alarm . . . and gets robbed because he forgot to shut the window." And while Kerviel may have been hoping to secure a larger bonus for himself through his fraudulent trading activity, it does appear that he was motivated primarily by "earning money for my bank."

If SocGen had performed random checks on the trading history of its traders, Kerviel would likely have been caught well before his losses spiralled out of control. Likewise, if SocGen had a system to track deleted or altered trades, Kerviel's methods would have been uncovered quickly and without incident. And if Kerviel's supervisors had bothered to investigate how a trader whose job was supposed to amass modest profits based on careful bets could have racked up billions in gains and eventually in losses, they could perhaps have lessened the damage done to a large degree. Kerviel himself has stated that his supervisors must have known that he was resorting to unusual tactics to earn such large sums of money, but that "as long as you earn money and it isn't too obvious, and it's convenient, nobody says anything."

Instead, SocGen was left with a mess on its hands and may have made things much worse with its handling of it. SocGen decided to unload Kerviel's positions soon after discovering the fraud, despite the fact that the market conditions at the time were decidedly unfavourable. When SocGen dumped Kerviel's positions into the weak world markets, it hastened an even larger plunge in late January 2008. On the Monday after the fraud was revealed, the DAX, FTSE, and CAC-40 indexes fell 7.2, 5.5, and 6.8 percent, respectively, with the DAX continuing to fall in the ensuing days. Their abrupt drop was believed to be a major reason for the Federal Reserve's cutting interest rates in the United States soon afterward. Then the SEC launched an investigation into whether or not SocGen violated U.S. securities laws by unwinding Kerviel's positions covertly after the fraud was revealed as well as whether or not insider information played a role in the selling of SocGen stock prior to the

announcement of the scandal. Some estimates indicate that the losses incurred by Kerviel amounted to closer to 2 billion euros, and the bank's handling of Kerviel's positions resulted in the remainder of the 4.9 billion euro loss.

The incident was the most glaring example among many of the failures of risk management controls at a prominent international financial institution. Together, these failures contributed heavily to the subprime mortgage crisis and resulting credit crunch that victimized other investment banks.

So what does SocGen plan to do to prevent future fraudulent trades? The answer remains to be seen. Even if Kerviel is the malevolent genius that SocGen claims, his ability to accumulate positions larger than the bank's net worth indicates severe failings in the company's control systems. One former SocGen risk auditor, Maxime Legrand, called the control procedures used to monitor the activity of its traders a sham and stated that management "pretend[s] to have an inspection to please the banking commission." In the wake of SocGen's fraud and other investment banking failures like the collapse of Bear Stearns, financial institutions will be under a great deal of pressure to improve their risk management systems and internal controls.

CASE STUDY QUESTIONS:

1. What concepts in this chapter are illustrated in this case?

2. Describe the control weaknesses at SocGen. What management, organization, and technology factors contributed to those weaknesses?

3. Who should be held responsible for Kerviel's trading losses? What role did SocGen's systems play? What role did management play?

4. What are some ways SocGen could have prevented Kerviel's fraud?

5. If you were responsible for redesigning SocGen's systems, what would you do to address its control problems?

Sources: Natasha de Teran, "Market Targets Loopholes in Equity Derivatives," **Financialnews-US.com,** March 28, 2008; Brian Cleary, "Employee Role Changes and SocGen: Good Lessons from a Bad Example," **SCMagazineUS.com,** April 1, 2008; Nicola Clark and David Jolly, "French Bank Says Rogue Trader Lost $7 Billion," *The New York Times,* January 25, 2008; Nicolas Parasie, "SocGen Discloses More Detail, Chronology of Alleged Fraud," **MarketWatch.com,** January 27, 2008; Andrew Hurst and Thierry Leveque, "SocGen under Pressure as Rogue Trader Released," Yahoo! News, January 28, 2008; David Gauthier-Villars and Carrick Mollenkamp, "The Loss Where No One Looked," *The Wall Street Journal,* January 28, 2008; Randall Smith and Kate Kelly, "Once Again, the Risk Protection Fails," *The Wall Street Journal,* January 25, 2008; Adam Sage, "Ex-SocGen Risk Auditor Calls Systems a Sham," *The Times,* February 7, 2008; "Trader Says SocGen Bosses Had to Know," *The New York Times,* January 29, 2008; David Gauthier-Villars, Carrick Mollenkamp, and Alistair Macdonald, "French Bank Rocked by Rogue Trader," *The Wall Street Journal,* January 25, 2008; David Gauthier-Villars and Stacy Meichtry, "Kerviel Felt out of His League," *The Wall Street Journal,* January 31, 2008; Heather Smith and Gregory Viscusi, "SocGen Threatened to Fire Kerviel in 2005, Court Document Says," **Bloomberg.com,** March 25, 2008.

Part II CANADIAN CASE STUDY:
Wi-Fi in Canada: The Good, the Bad, and the Ugly

More than two-thirds of Canadians are connected to the Internet today. About 15 percent of Canadians, or 23 percent of those Canadians connected to the Internet, use wireless fidelity, one of the newer standards for telecommunication.

As detailed in Chapter 8, IEEE standard 802.11 governs wireless networking, with three sub-standards, a, b, and g. 802.11a is not compatible with either 802.11b or 802.11g, but the latter two are compatible with each other. The 802.11b standard has been the most widely used standard for creating wireless LANs and providing wireless Internet access. However, 802.11g may become more popular in the next few years, and dual-band systems capable of handling 802.11b and 802.11g are expected to proliferate. Today most computers are sold with 802.11b or 802.11g networking capability built in, either through a wireless networking card or more recently, with a wireless chip on the motherboard that holds the processing and RAM chips.

How are Canadian businesses and individuals using Wi-Fi? What are the challenges of implementing and using Wi-Fi?

THE GOOD

Baycrest Centre for Geriatric Care, headquartered in Toronto, uses Wi-Fi to support its voice for nurse call system, supporting hundreds of concurrent users. Voice for nurse systems permit nurses to communicate from wherever they are in the hospital through a device that they wear. Services such as bedside charting, monitoring, and order entry are carried out using 50 wireless-enabled computers-on-wheels (COWs) to access Baycrest's Meditech System. The doctors, nurses, and administrators needed a single wireless network over which they could transmit voice and data, simply and cost-effectively. IT staff were paid $100 per hour, so keeping costs to a minimum, even after implementation, was critical. Security, of course, was also a paramount concern. The system would need to support a wide variety of wireless devices, from VoIP telephones to laptop computers, handheld personal digital assistants, and voice communication badges, the device worn by the nurses.

Baycrest implemented a wireless LAN switching system that included a suite of wireless applications. The system was relatively self-configuring, resulting in ease of use and easy addition or movement of the various nodes on the network. It was also simple to add capacity as demand increased. The new wireless network also made it easy to transmit very large files, such as those used in medical imaging. Baycrest implemented data encryption to meet the requirements of the federal *Personal Information Protection and Electronic Documents Act*. In addition, virtual private networks are hosted on the wireless network, permitting staff to log in from home to leave patient orders or check on their patients' conditions.

Baycrest is one of many companies in the health care field that are adopting wireless technologies.

The Royal Ottawa Hospital opened to patients in late 2006, using a wireless mesh network for telemedicine to serve all of the hospital's facilities and grounds. Doctors, researchers, and hospital staff, numbering over a thousand, use the Nortel Mobility mesh network to deliver the highest quality of care. "Hospitals tend to be large facilities," says Brian McFadden, chief research officer of Nortel Networks. The mesh network "allows connectivity to a network with broadband capabilities, wirelessly. It allows clinical staff to stay online throughout the facility regardless of the task being undertaken." According to Bruce Swan, CEO, Royal Ottawa Health Care Group, "It builds in flexibility for clinicians." Wireless connectivity, he adds, "makes better use of people's time. It allows information to be recorded at the time of the procedure, rather than having clinicians go back to a workstation to input it."

According to Swan, the design of the Royal Ottawa Hospital building incorporated the ability to install a mesh network. "Positioning of the nodes required to transmit information where they will be the most practical is easier than retrofitting a hospital because you don't have to work around existing infrastructure." Wireless-enabled laptops and other handheld devices can help clinical teams to access the hospital's internal network, patient records, the Internet, e-mail, shared files, and other applications. "It is going to drastically reduce the potential for errors," according to McFadden.

Wi-Fi is also coming to consumers at their favourite places of business through Wi-Fi "hotspots." A Wi-Fi hotspot is an area where consumers can log on to the Internet wirelessly, typically for a charge. Via Rail Canada offers Wi-Fi connectivity on most trains with routes in southern Ontario and Quebec for Via 1 (Via's first class) passengers. Already, Via Rail offers Wi-Fi connectivity to Via 1 and sleeper-class passengers in its Panorama Lounges in many stations. Wireless service does not come cheaply for passengers. Via 1 passengers can select from three different payment plans. They can select the pay-per-use plan, for which the first 15 minutes cost $3.99, and each additional minute cost $0.30, the daily access plan with a flat rate of $8.95 for a 24-hour period, or the monthly access plan, which costs $46.

Guy Faulkner, product manager for corridor service at Via, believes Wi-Fi access gives the company a potential advantage over its competition. Faulkner anticipates a growing interest among Via's passengers in onboard Internet service. Bell Canada, a division of BCE, Inc. in Montreal, is working with Via to provide this service. The satellite signals are fed into an onboard server and then to a wireless access point in the first-class car that users can then access from their laptops or handhelds. The return signal from user devices is fed from the access point in the car to the server and then over Bell's terrestrial CDMA network, with an average data rate of about 70 Kbs.

But you don't have to ride the rails or fly the skies to have mobile access to wireless Internet service. Hotspots are appearing in any number of retail outlets, primarily coffee shops and restaurants. Many Second Cup locations in Canada offer Wi-Fi access through Rogers Wireless, Inc.; Second Cup customers can read their e-mail or surf the Web while drinking their cup of coffee. Rogers is rolling out its brand new Wi-Fi service through Second Cup, starting in Second Cup shops in Toronto. In the United States, the Schlotzsky's Deli chain offers Wi-Fi free access to its customers in 30 of its 600 locations. According to Schlotzsky's CEO John Wooley, the free Wi-Fi access results in an additional 15 000 visits per restaurant per year by customers who spend an average of $7 per visit. That means Wi-Fi service brings in more than CDN $117 000 per year per outlet in return for an investment of under CDN $10 000. Experts speculate that once free Wi-Fi access is universal, the return on investment for that type of service will decrease.

Starbucks was one of the first retail companies to incorporate Wi-Fi hotspots into its outlets, finally partnering with Bell Canada in late 2005 to offer hotspots throughout Canada. Along with its competitors Bell Mobility and Telus Mobility, Rogers is creating a national standard to make roaming between competing hotspot locations possible. With the Rogers Connect plan, subscribers who have cellular phone service with Rogers can use the Wi-Fi service and charge the cost to their cell phone bill.

Many hotels are offering Wi-Fi access in their meeting rooms or conference areas, where conference attendees can connect during conference breaks. Some hotels are even offering Wi-Fi service—for a fee—from hotel rooms.

After the outbreaks of SARS and West Nile virus and a 30 percent drop in business, Toronto's Forest Hills' Business Improvement Area created a two-block-long stretch of wireless Internet access to try to lure customers. Wireless Internet access is available from any store or even outside on Spadina Road. The "village" uses an outdoor Wi-Fi access point with 20 times the regular range with a single business DSL connection. Before customers can actually surf the Web, though, they must sit through one minute of ads—a small price to pay for free access.

Air Canada announced in 2008 that it would begin offering in-flight broadband Internet to passengers on trans-border flights to the United States in 2009. The service will cost $12.95 per flight per passenger. In an arrangement with Aircell LLC, an American company, Air Canada plans to expand Wi-Fi coverage to domestic flights later in 2009. Aircell does not have cell tower coverage in Canada and will license a Canadian network to handle the domestic flights.

Canadian municipalities have rolled out Wi-Fi networks to make themselves more attractive to businesses and technology-savvy citizens. In Ontario, hydro companies are looking at Wi-Fi as a potential backhaul system for the smart meters mandated by the provincial government. With WiMax, a new standard for wireless telecommunication, and its promise of high-speed links over longer distances than Wi-Fi, wireless access may be possible from almost anywhere. One of the key barriers to these advances is the billing dilemma: How do you bill customers for Wi-Fi or WiMax access that is carried through cellular phone carriers? There is little incentive for cellular carriers to permit their customers to make calls over Wi-Fi since they do not bill for those calls. Somehow, a compromise must be reached in the area of billing to converge cellular and wireless broadband technologies.

Web sites are available that list hotspots around the world, such as **www.wi-fihotspotlist.com**. Users can simply enter the address where they wish to access a hotspot, and the Web site returns a list of hotspots that are available, with the address of the hotspot, and a further link detailing a little more about the type of store (if the hotspot is hosted by a store), the type of link, and other potentially useful information.

The dual advantages of the fast data-transfer rate of Wi-Fi type technology and the broad range of a cellular phone network are brought together by WiMax, also known as IEEE standard 802.16. The first WiMax-enabled commercial products are planned to be released soon; development of WiMax product standards has stalled development for some time. WiMax, an Internet Protocol (IP)-based technology, makes it possible to move all types of communication, from voice to data to video, as packets over the same network. According to experts, WiMax will offer potential rates of 75 megabits per second over a distance of more than 50 kilometres. However, as the range of WiMax is extended, the speed of transmission is reduced.

But sometimes the technology is ready—even before the applications are ready. A Windows Pocket PC device turned into a dual-mode phone with capabilities to send and receive both cellular and Wi-Fi calls through the same dialler has been created by Cicero Softphone. With Wi-Fi service, the Softphone routes calls across the Internet, or it defaults to the cellular connection. Skype, the free VoIP provider, now offers a mobile version, permitting smartphones, including the iPhone, with Wi-Fi access to make phone calls for free or for very low charges (e.g., CDN $0.03 per minute to almost anywhere in the world).

THE BAD

In addition to the billing dilemma, most experts believe that security of wireless networks is difficult to establish and manage. It has become so simple to install wireless routers that almost anyone can do it. In fact, many people installing their own home wireless networks never even refer to the user's manual for their wireless routers. They use the default setups found in the installation wizards and feel that they are connected throughout their homes. That's the problem. As the CBC video that accompanies this case study shows, wireless access is accessible over a specific geographic area, meaning that war-walkers, war-bikers, and war-drivers can steal your wireless signal to log on to the Internet.

Many computer aficionados feel that all wireless service should be free. If you have paid to have wireless access in your home, where's the harm if someone else also uses it since it's already there? But accessing your wireless signal means that these interlopers can hack into your home network, perhaps stealing your files and your data or just logging on to the Internet as you and downloading pornography or other objectionable material.

Toronto police stopped a man for a traffic violation and realized the man, who was naked from the waist down, was using his laptop to access a pornographic video that he had downloaded and was watching over a residential wireless hotspot. He was eventually charged, not only with the traffic violation, but also with theft of telecommunications, a first in Canada. The owners of the hotspot he used were not charged, but it may be only a matter of time until Internet service providers and owners of unsecured wireless networks in their own homes could be liable for permitting unlawful access to their networks. Lawyers feel that homeowners could be held liable for being negligent in securing their wireless networks.

Security on wireless networks is not that hard to establish: network installers simply need to read the installation manual and follow the instructions to restrict access to your wireless network, including using logon IDs and passwords that are unique to your network.

As the video that accompanies this case shows, tracking down Wi-Fi ports while in a car (war-driving), on a bike (war-biking), or simply walking (war-chalking) is easy to do with the proper, inexpensive equipment. Chalked symbols on streets and sidewalks show others where they can access open wireless networks. According to research by WorldWide WarDrive, more than two-thirds of the approximately 88100 access points found by war drivers around the world did not have basic security enabled.

Whether someone is gaining illegal wireless access while walking, biking, or driving, they are stealing a valuable service. According to **Wartalking.com,** a person was arrested for hacking into a court's wireless network just to prove that the court's network could be hacked.

A new wireless security standard called 801.11i was finalized in 2004 but has been slow to be implemented over the more popular, but less secure, WEP and WPA. Standard 802.11i requires firmware or driver support for both the wireless host and the wireless client. Another solution would be to make setting up wireless security easier and make it easier to turn security on. Even simpler would be to have security enabled out of the box. But experts feel that ease of setup is most important for Wi-Fi "newbies." Experts also think that if security were enabled to default settings, soon everyone would be using the default password, and that would make hacking on a large scale even more possible and even more dangerous.

THE UGLY

Vancouver police detective Mark Fenton told his superiors that his city's plans for a city-wide wireless Internet system, housing transit systems, traffic signals, and electric utility systems puts the city at risk of a terrorist attack during the 2010 Winter Olympic games. The city wants to make a free or low-cost wireless network available even before the Olympics starts. The plan calls for much of the city's infrastructure to use the platform for wireless communications and remote operations. "If you have an open wireless system across the city, as a bad guy, I could sit on a bus with a laptop and do global crime," Fenton stated. "It would be virtually impossible to find me."

There is another "ugly" problem, that of evil twin hotspots. In England, in London's financial district, many Wi-Fi networks lack basic security. NTA Monitor, a security testing company, recently used passive monitoring to determine that internal resources, such as printer queues, could easily be found, and many even used no encryption whatsoever.

What is the future of Wi-Fi? Perhaps it will eventually give way to newer, faster technologies with a broader geographical reach, such as WiMax. But for now, Wi-Fi will be here for several years as the newer technologies mature and applications become available to make use of them.

CASE STUDY QUESTIONS

1. What are the implications of having competing wireless standards, such as three 802.11 standards and WiMax? Do you see convergence of these standards, one standard winning the battle for users, or a newer standard coming forward in the next three to five years?

2. Do you think that the advent of wireless hotspots will change the way people compute? If people change the way they use their computers (e.g., the place, the time), do you think that the hardware (e.g., the type of computers people use) will change? If so, how will they change?

3. Looking at the health care industry, what are some of the ways, in addition to those mentioned above, that you think health care professionals can make use of wireless technology? Are there any uses of information technology for which wireless is not an appropriate telecommunications method?

4. What are some of the privacy and security considerations in examining wireless technologies? How can these concerns be addressed?

Sources: Brian Eaton, "Ottawa—A Hospital Built for Mesh," *IT World Canada*, August 2, 2005, **www.techworld.com/features/index .cfm?featureID=1607** (accessed September 23, 2009); "Secure Voice and Data over Wi-Fi Moves Baycrest to Switch to Aruba," April 2004, **www.arubanetworks.com/pdf/baycrest_cs.pdf** (accessed September 24, 2005); "Wireless Internet in Via 1 Class," **www.viarail.ca/ wirelessinternet/en_index.html** (accessed September 24, 2005); Bob Brewin, "All Aboard with Wi-Fi on Via Rail Canada," *Computerworld Canada*, July 10, 2003, **www.computerworld.com/printthis/2003/ 0,4814,82940,00.html** (accessed September 23, 2009); "Computerworld: Free Hot Spots Pay Dividends," October 22, 2003, **www.bmannconsulting.com/node/614** (accessed September 23, 2009; Tyler Hamilton, "Wi-Fi 'Hotspots' Coming to a Coffee Shop

Near You," *Toronto Star*, February 18, 2005, **www.thestar.com/ NASApp/cs/ContentServer?pagename=thestar/Layout/ Article_Type1&c=Article&cid=1108680612792&call_pageid=96835 0072197&col=Columnist971715454851&DPL=lvsNDS%2f7ChAX& tacodalogin=yes** (accessed September 24, 2005); Michael Martin, "The Wi-Fi/Cell Conundrum," September 16, 2005, **www .itworldcanada.com//Pages/Docbase/ViewArticle.aspx?ID=idgml-b2e4cb03-ddff-4c06-9aec-ad8679abf822** (accessed September 23, 2009); Peter Judge, "Converged Softphone Cuts Bill," September 8, 2005, **www.itworldcanada.com/a/search/e10c3e79-22ad-4c3d-a8d4-47e0c1dc6123.html** (accessed September 24, 2005); Dan McLean, "Bluetooth and WiFi, Meet WiMax Technology," August 4, 2005, **www.itworldcanada.com/a/search/6fa973d9-511a-4d6c-a3e3-c9209578f0df.html** (accessed September 24, 2005); Rosie Lombardi, "Canadian Researchers Uncover New 'Wireless' Possibilities," July 29, 2005, **www.itworldcanada.com/a/search/a8dd82dc-62b6-46d1-846f-6a50e74b24bf.html** (accessed September 24, 2005);

Sean Carruthers, "Forest Hills Cuts the Cords," November 6, 2003, - **www.hubacanada.com/story_10783_4** (accessed September 26, 2005); "Wi-Fi Arrest Highlights Security Dangers," **http://news.zdnet. com/2102-1009_22=5112000.html** (accessed July 16, 2007); Randy Shore, "WiFi Could Pose Threat during Vancouver Olympics," **http:// www.canada.com/topics/news/national/story.html?id=207f6d54-68fc-40da-8ae3-dc9f057c2f54&k=25065** (accessed September 23, 2009); and John E. Dunn, "Wi-Fi Networks Still Insecure in London's City," Techworld,com, **www.itworldcanada.com/a/Enterprise-Infrastructure/4de93aab-8968-47ce-9611-05566a5ad095.html** (accessed July 16, 2007); "Air Canada to Offer In-Flight WiFi," United Press International, **www.upi.com/Business_News/2008/09/09/ Air-Canada-to-offer-in-flight-WiFi/UPI-26991221016927/print** (accessed September 23, 2009).

Video Resource: "Wireless Internet (WI-FI)," Venture 883 (June 8, 2003).

Part III

Developing and Managing Information Systems

PART III

CANADIAN CASE STUDY

In Tech We Trust: The Story of SAP in Canada

CHAPTER 9

Developing Information Systems

LEARNING OBJECTIVES

After reading this chapter, you will be able to answer the following questions:

1. How does developing new information systems produce organizational change

2. What are the core activities in the information systems development process?

3. What are the principal methodologies for modelling and designing information systems?

4. What are the alternative methods for developing information systems?

5. What are new approaches for information systems development in the digital firm era?

OPENING CASE

Protecting Patients by Tracking Instruments

If you were to go to a hospital for a medical procedure, whether in the emergency room, or for elective or major surgery, could you envision that you might get an infection from one of the instruments used in your procedure? Or could you envision that the instrument that was needed for your procedure could not be found? That is a scary thought, but one that could happen without the benefit of a hospital instrument tracking system.

For many hospitals, managing and tracking instruments through storage, use, and sterilization (and back to storage) is a manual, paper-based process that is rife with errors and could lead to cross-contamination and infection. Like most hospitals, The Ottawa Hospital (TOH) relied on a paper-based system to track instrument inventory, using sheets and binders. Inaccuracies were linked to hospital staff, whose primary job was not instrument inventory, but who were required to update the instrument inven-

tory records. When the operating room department requested certain instruments, there was a lot of time expended on finding the correct entry in the paper trail and then locating the correct instrument. Sterilization technicians assemble sets of instruments on a tray based on the type of procedure. In the sterilization area, technicians also had a hard time maintaining these paper records and noting where in the sterilization process each instrument was: cleaning, sterilizing, reassembly, or storage.

TOH decided to implement a computer-based instrument tracking program that was already established, called Alex Gold (perhaps one of the systems developers was a fan of the musician) produced by TGX Medical, a medical software company. Lynne Trott, director of logistical services at TOH, made the decision to implement Alex Gold and to do so across all three hospital campuses. For her, lack of integrated information was a primary issue. "We

couldn't guarantee we had accurate information on which tray was used for a specific patient. With Alex, we can now tie that to patient information."

Alex Gold coordinates better management of every facet of instrument and equipment use within the health care facility, allowing doctors to have properly sterilized instrument sets at the right time and at the right location. The system uses Web-based technology to allow easy, effective communication across all levels of users. Gold tracks instruments from the operating room through sterilization to storage, ensuring that they have been properly cleaned, assembled, and maintained.

Before implementation of Alex Gold, the paper data had to be converted to electronic data, completing an inventory of all the hospital's instruments. The data were then placed in a database that included cleaning and sterilization instructions. These instructions differ, not only based on type of instrument, but even based on manufacturer of the instrument. Training was then given to sterilization technicians in how to use the new system.

The implementation took more than a year. The instruments had to be barcoded, with special strips that could withstand the heat and chemicals involved in sterilization, so the instruments could be scanned and recorded at every step of the instrument cycle.

According to Michael Good, CEO of TGX Medical Systems, "We did a lot of custom work at TOH beyond what's in the packaged product." According to Kay Lee, manager of instrument systems for the Johnson and Johnson, the Canadian distributor of Alex Gold, sterilization technicians, who are gloved and masked and have a hard time looking at paper records, "need extensive training [on paper-based systems], but that requirement drops dramatically with Alex."

Using Alex Gold, TOH can even budget and track maintenance costs for the instruments. The new system flags instruments that need to be sent out for maintenance and lets the hospital monitor how many instruments are being processed to allow TOH to determine proper staffing levels of sterilization technicians. TOH has also seen a dramatic decrease in errors in instrument processing; the system can even quantify that for TOH. Even with recent pandemic planning at TOH, the hospital's documentation shows its confidence in the instrument tracking system.

Sources: "The Ottawa Hospital Launches an Instrument Tracking System," **www.summitc onnects.com/In_the_News/ARCHIVE/ 2005_10.htm** (accessed September 24, 2009); Rosie Lombardi, "From Paper Trail to Patient Care,"**www.itworldcanada.com/a/ E-Government/78a168dc-e318-4702-ada5- 0c93c482afca.html** (accessed April 17, 2007); TGX Medical Systems, **www.tgxmedical.com/products_and_ services/alex_gold.asp** (accessed April 17, 2007); "The Ottawa Hospital Pandemic Influenza Plan Rough Draft #2, June 29, 2007, **www.champlainhealthworkers.ca/doc .aspx?id=61** (accessed May 27, 2009).

The experience of TOH illustrates some of the steps required to design and develop new information systems. Developing the new system entailed analyzing the organization's problems with existing information systems, assessing people's information requirements, selecting appropriate technology, and redesigning business processes and jobs. Management had to monitor the systems development effort and evaluate its benefits and costs. The new information system represented a process of planned organizational change.

The chapter-opening Business Challenges diagram calls attention to important points raised by this case and this chapter. The TOH instrument tracking system was heavily manual and could not support the large number of instruments and processes

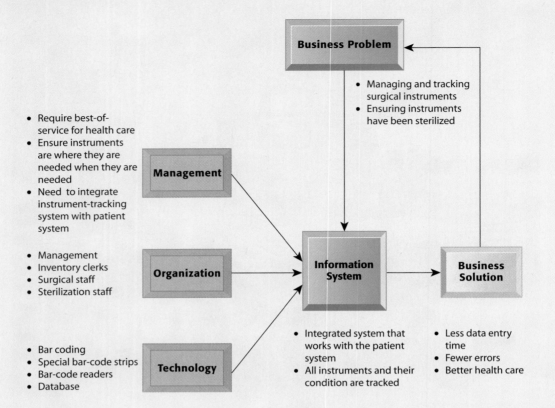

- Require best-of-service for health care
- Ensure instruments are where they are needed when they are needed
- Need to integrate instrument-tracking system with patient system

- Management
- Inventory clerks
- Surgical staff
- Sterilization staff

- Bar coding
- Special bar-code strips
- Bar-code readers
- Database

Business Problem
- Managing and tracking surgical instruments
- Ensuring instruments have been sterilized

Management

Organization

Technology

Information System
- Integrated system that works with the patient system
- All instruments and their condition are tracked

Business Solution
- Less data entry time
- Fewer errors
- Better health care

that needed to be coordinated. Consequently, instrument processes, such as cleaning, sterilizing, and storing, had higher error rates than were desirable. The TOH instrument tracking process required many steps and coordination of multiple groups and campuses. Given the constraints of the problem, the best solution was to rapidly create a system using a vendor's application software package, with customization by both the hospital and the vendor. The new system reduces the amount of time, effort, and errors in the instrument tracking process. The Ottawa Hospital logistics leadership had to design a new instrument tracking process and manage the transition from the old manual instrument tracking processes to the new system.

9.1   Systems as Planned Organizational Change

Developing a new information system is one kind of planned organizational change. The introduction of a new information system involves much more than new hardware and software. It also includes changes in jobs, skills, management, and organization. When we design a new information system, we are redesigning the organization. System developers must understand how a system will affect specific business processes and the organization as a whole.

Systems Development and Organizational Change

Information technology can promote various degrees of organizational change, ranging from incremental to far-reaching. Figure 9-1 shows four kinds of structural organizational change that are enabled by information technology: (1) automation, (2) rationalization, (3) re-engineering, and (4) paradigm shifts. Each carries different rewards and risks.

The most common form of IT-enabled organizational change is **automation.** The first applications of information technology involved assisting employees with performing their tasks more efficiently and effectively. Calculating paycheques and payroll registers,

Automation

FIGURE 9-1   Organizational change carries risks and rewards.

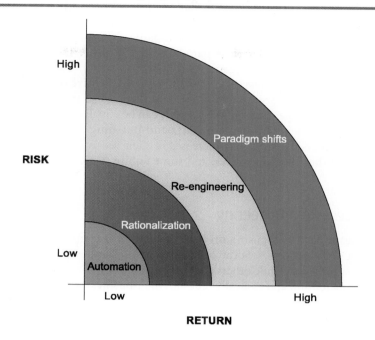

RISK

High

Low

Paradigm shifts

Re-engineering

Rationalization

Automation

Low   High

RETURN

The most common forms of organizational change are automation and rationalization. These relatively slow-moving and slow-changing strategies present modest returns but little risk. Faster and more comprehensive change—such as re-engineering and paradigm shifts—carries high rewards but offers substantial chances of failure.

giving bank tellers instant access to customer deposit records, and developing a nationwide network of airline reservation terminals for airline reservation agents are all examples of early automation.

A deeper form of organizational change—one that follows quickly from early automation—is **rationalization of procedures.** Automation frequently reveals new bottlenecks in production and makes the existing arrangement of procedures and structures painfully cumbersome. Rationalization of procedures is the streamlining of standard operating procedures. For example, The Ottawa Hospital's new instrument tracking system described in the chapter-opening case is effective not only because it uses computer technology but also because its design enables the organization to operate more efficiently. The hospital had to have standard identification codes for each type of instrument and each location, and standard rules for entering tracking information online. Without a certain amount of rationalization in The Ottawa Hospital's organization, its computer technology would have been useless.

A more powerful type of organizational change is **business process re-engineering (BPR),** in which business processes are analyzed, simplified, and redesigned. Using information technology, organizations can rethink and streamline their business processes to improve speed, service, and quality. Business re-engineering reorganizes work flows, combining steps to cut waste and eliminating repetitive, paper-intensive tasks. (Often the new design eliminates jobs as well.) It is much more ambitious than rationalization of procedures, requiring a new vision of how the process is to be organized.

A widely cited example of business re-engineering is Ford Motor Company's invoiceless processing, which reduced head count in Ford's North American accounts payable organization of 500 people by 75 percent. Accounts payable clerks used to spend most of their time resolving discrepancies between purchase orders, receiving documents, and invoices. Ford re-engineered its accounts payable process so that the purchasing department enters a purchase order into an online database that can be checked by the receiving department when the ordered items arrive. If the received goods match the purchase order, the system automatically generates a cheque for accounts payable to send to the vendor. There is no need for vendors to send invoices.

Rationalizing procedures and redesigning business processes are limited to specific parts of a business. New information systems can ultimately affect the design of the entire

Rationalization of procedures

Business process re-engineering (BPR)

organization by transforming how the organization carries out its business or even the nature of the business. For instance, the Canadian trucking and transportation firm Trans-X used new information systems to change its business model. Trans-X created a new business managing the logistics for other companies. This more radical form of business change is called a **paradigm shift.** A paradigm shift involves rethinking the nature of the business and the nature of the organization.

Paradigm shifts and re-engineering often fail because extensive organizational change is so difficult to orchestrate (see Chapter 10). Why, then, do so many corporations contemplate such radical change? Because the rewards can be equally high (see Figure 9-1). In many instances, firms seeking paradigm shifts and pursuing re-engineering strategies achieve stunning, order-of-magnitude increases in their returns on investment (or productivity). Some of these success stories, and some failure stories, are included throughout this book.

Business Process Re-engineering

Many companies today are focusing on developing new information systems that will improve their business processes. Some of these system projects represent radical restructuring of business processes while others entail more incremental process change.

If organizations rethink and radically redesign their business processes before applying computing power, they can potentially obtain very large payoffs from their investments in information technology. Let us look at how the home mortgage industry in Canada accomplished this.

The application process for a home mortgage used to take about six to eight weeks. Leading banks, such as Scotiabank and ING Direct, have redesigned the mortgage application process to reduce the cost and time to obtain a mortgage to less than one week.

In the past, a mortgage applicant filled out a paper loan application. A bank entered the application into its computer system. Specialists, such as credit analysts and underwriters from various departments, accessed and evaluated the application individually. If the loan application was approved, the closing was scheduled. After the closing, bank specialists dealing with insurance or funds in escrow serviced the loan. This "desk-to-desk" assembly-line approach might take weeks.

Today loan originators in the field, in "online offices," or in bank branches enter the mortgage application directly into their desktop or laptop computers. Software checks the application transaction to make sure that all of the information is correct and complete.

At ING Direct, the Mortgage Application Processing Solution (MAPS) accepts mortgages from ING Direct's Web site or mortgage brokers and integrates with ING Direct's customer-relationship management software. The MAPS software automatically integrates with other external entities to allow ING's mortgage underwriters to quickly assess applications. Meanwhile, mortgage applicants and clients can check online on the status of their applications, and any ING staff member can be in immediate contact with the client without leaving their computer. Once the application is approved, MAPS produces the commitment letter with the specifics of the mortgage and automatically images and associates the signed documents (which have been faxed back to ING by the customer) with the correct account and mortgage. Introducing MAPS to its outdated mortgage processing process increased ING's conversion rates to 50 percent in 6 months and cut the time required to underwrite a mortgage by more than 200 percent. The time to process a mortgage has dropped from one week to a maximum of two days.

Like ING Direct, Scotiabank also felt pressured to meet the demands of its clients for faster mortgage processing. Prior to automating the mortgage work flow process, Scotiabank personnel filled out mortgage applications and faxed them to a central mortgage processing unit, where the data from the application were manually keyed into a centralized database. If the data were incomplete, the entire process had to be repeated. Today, using work flow software, branch personnel or mortgage originators input, edit, and confirm mortgage data, after which it is transmitted electronically to the central mortgage processing unit. Before, bank personnel who wanted to check on their clients' mortgage applications had to e-mail the central mortgage processing unit, where the request was printed out and manually distributed to an underwriter to respond to the request. Today, such requests are automatically transferred to an underwriter, who can respond quickly.

By rethinking their approaches to mortgage processing, mortgage banks have achieved remarkable efficiencies. They have not focused on redesigning a single business process, but instead they have re-examined the entire set of logically connected processes required to obtain a mortgage.

To support the new mortgage application process, the banks have implemented work flow and document management software. **Work flow management** is the process of streamlining business procedures so that documents can be moved easily and efficiently. Work flow and document management software automates processes such as routing documents to different locations, securing approvals, scheduling, and generating reports. Two or more people can work simultaneously on the same document, allowing much quicker completion time. Work need not be delayed because a file is out or a document is in transit. And with a properly designed indexing system, users will be able to retrieve files in many different ways, based on the content of the document.

Steps in Effective Re-engineering One of the most important strategic decisions that a firm can make is not deciding how to use information systems to improve business processes but rather understanding what business processes need improvement. Businesses are composed of hundreds, sometimes thousands, of business processes. How can you decide which need to be changed and which could really benefit from information systems? When systems are used to strengthen the wrong business model or business processes, the business can become more efficient at doing what it should not do (Hammer, 2002). As a result, the firm becomes vulnerable to competitors that may have discovered the right business model. Considerable time and cost can also be spent improving business processes that have little impact on overall firm performance and revenue. You will need to determine what business processes are the most important to focus on when applying new information technology and how improving these processes will help the firm execute its strategy.

You will also need to understand and measure the performance of existing processes as a baseline. If, for example, the objective of process redesign is to reduce time and cost in developing a new product or filling an order, you will need to measure the time and cost consumed by the unchanged process. For example, before re-engineering, Cemex, the international provider of cement and ready-mix concrete, required an average time of three hours to make a delivery. After Cemex's processes were re-engineered, average delivery time dropped to 20 minutes. Without measuring the baseline original process, you will have no way to judge improvements.

Following these steps does not automatically guarantee that re-engineering will always be successful. The majority of re-engineering projects do not achieve breakthrough gains in business performance because the organizational changes are often very difficult to manage. Managing change is neither simple nor intuitive, and companies committed to re-engineering need a good change management strategy (see Chapter 10).

Interorganizational processes, such as those for supply chain management, not only need to be streamlined but also coordinated and integrated with those of customers and suppliers. In these cases, re-engineering will involve multiple companies working together to jointly redesign their shared processes. A Learning Track for this chapter explains business process redesign in greater detail.

Process Improvement: Business Process Management, Total Quality Management, and Six Sigma

Business process re-engineering is primarily a one-time effort, focusing on identifying one or two strategic business processes that need radical change. BPR projects tend to be expensive and organizationally disruptive. But organizations have many business processes and support processes that must be constantly revised to keep the business competitive. Business

Work flow management

process management and quality improvement programs provide opportunities for more incremental and ongoing types of business process change.

Business Process Management Mergers and acquisitions, changes in business models, new industry requirements, and changing customer expectations all pose multiple process-related problems that continually confront organizations. **Business process management (BPM)** enables organizations to manage incremental process changes that are required simultaneously in many areas of the business. It provides a methodology and tools for dealing with the organization's ongoing need to revise—and ideally optimize— its numerous internal business processes and processes shared with other organizations. It enables organizations to make continual improvements to many business processes simultaneously and to use processes as the fundamental building blocks of corporate information systems.

BPM includes work flow management, business process modelling, quality management, change management, and tools for recasting the firm's business processes into a standardized form where they can be continually manipulated. Companies practising business process management use process-mapping tools to identify and document existing processes and to create models of improved processes that can then be translated into information systems. The process models might require entirely new systems or could be based on existing systems and data. BPM software tools automatically manage processes across the business, extract data from various sources and databases, and generate transactions in multiple related systems.

BPM also includes process monitoring and analytics. Organizations must be able to verify that process performance has been improved and measure the impact of process changes on key business performance indicators. A number of commercial software vendors, including IBM, Oracle-BEA Systems, Vitria, and TIBCO, supply business process management products.

Total Quality Management and Six Sigma Quality management is another area of continuous process improvement. In addition to increasing organizational efficiency, companies must fine-tune their business processes to improve the quality in their products, services, and operations. Many are using the concept of **total quality management (TQM)** to make quality the responsibility of all people and functions within an organization. TQM holds that the achievement of quality control is an end in itself. Everyone is expected to contribute to the overall improvement of quality—the engineer who avoids design errors, the production worker who spots defects, the sales representative who presents the product properly to potential customers, and the secretary who avoids keyboarding mistakes. TQM derives from quality management concepts developed by American quality experts such as W. Edwards Deming and Joseph Juran, but it was popularized by the Japanese after World War II.

Another quality concept that is being widely implemented today is six sigma. **Six sigma** is a specific measure of quality, representing 3.4 defects per million opportunities. Most companies cannot achieve this level of quality but use six sigma as a goal to implement a set of methodologies and techniques for improving quality and reducing costs. Studies have repeatedly shown that the earlier in the business cycle a problem is eliminated, the less it costs the company. Thus, quality improvements not only raise the level of product and service quality, but can also lower costs.

How Information Systems Support Quality Improvements TQM and six sigma are considered to be more incremental than business process re-engineering. TQM typically focuses on making a series of continuous improvements rather than dramatic bursts of change. Six sigma uses statistical analysis tools to detect flaws in the execution of an existing process and make minor adjustments. Sometimes, however, processes may have to be fully re-engineered to achieve a specified level of quality. Information systems can help firms achieve their quality goals by helping them simplify products or processes, make improvements based on customer demands, reduce cycle time, improve the quality and precision of design and production, and meet benchmarking standards.

Business process
  management (BPM)
Total quality management (TQM)
Six sigma

Benchmarking consists of setting strict standards for products, services, and other activities and then measuring performance against those standards. Companies may use external industry standards, standards set by other companies, internally developed high standards, or some combination of the three. L.L. Bean, the Freeport, Maine, outdoor clothing company, used benchmarking to achieve an order-shipping accuracy of 99.9 percent. Its old batch order fulfillment system could not handle the surging volume and variety of items to be shipped. After studying German and Scandinavian companies with leading-edge order fulfillment operations, L.L. Bean carefully redesigned its order fulfillment process and information systems so that orders could be processed as soon as they were received and shipped within 24 hours. You can find other examples of systems promoting quality improvements throughout this text. The Ottawa Hospital had benchmarked its instrument tracking errors; we know this because management could tell that there had been a dramatic decrease in such errors after the implementation of the Alex Gold instrument tracking system.

9.2   Overview of Systems Development

New information systems are an outgrowth of a process of organizational problem solving. A new information system is developed as a solution to some type of problem or set of problems the organization perceives it is facing. The problem may be one in which managers and employees realize that the organization is not performing as well as expected, or that the organization should take advantage of new opportunities to perform more successfully.

The activities that go into producing an information system solution to an organizational problem or opportunity are called **systems development.** Systems development is a structured kind of problem solving with distinct activities. These activities consist of systems analysis, systems design, programming, testing, conversion, and production and maintenance.

Figure 9-2 illustrates the systems development process. The systems development activities depicted here usually take place in sequential order. But some of the activities may need to be repeated, and some may take place simultaneously, depending on the approach to systems development that is being employed (see Section 9.4).

Systems Analysis

Systems analysis is the analysis of the problem that the organization will try to solve with an information system. It consists of defining the problem, identifying its causes, specifying the solution, and identifying the information requirements that must be met by a system solution.

Benchmarking
Systems development
Systems analysis

FIGURE 9-2   The systems development process.

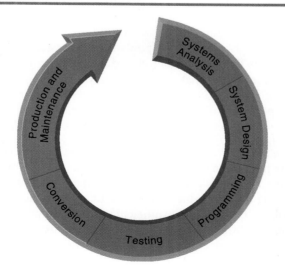

Developing a system can be broken down into six core activities.

The systems analyst creates a road map of the existing organization and systems, identifying the primary owners and users of data along with existing hardware and software. The systems analyst then details the problems of existing systems. By examining documents, work papers, and procedures; observing system operations; and interviewing key users of the systems, the analyst can identify the problem areas and objectives a solution would achieve. Often the solution requires developing a new information system or improving an existing one.

The systems analysis would include a **feasibility study** to determine whether that solution was feasible or achievable from a financial, technical, and organizational standpoint. The feasibility study would determine whether the proposed system was a good investment, whether the technology needed for the system was available and could be handled by the firm's information systems specialists, and whether the organization could handle the changes introduced by the system.

Normally, the systems analysis process identifies several alternative solutions that the organization can pursue. The process then assesses the feasibility of each. A written systems proposal report describes the costs and benefits, advantages and disadvantages of each alternative. It is up to management to determine which mix of costs, benefits, technical features, and organizational impacts represents the most desirable alternative.

Establishing Information Requirements Perhaps the most challenging task of the systems analyst is to define the specific information requirements that must be met by the system solution selected. At the most basic level, the **information requirements** of a new system involve identifying who needs what information, where, when, and how. Requirements analysis carefully defines the objectives of the new or modified system and develops a detailed description of the functions that the new system must perform. Faulty requirements analysis is a leading cause of systems failure and high systems development costs (see Chapter 10). A system designed around the wrong set of requirements either will have to be discarded because of poor performance or will need to undergo major modifications. Section 9.3 describes alternative approaches to eliciting requirements that help minimize this problem.

Some problems do not require an information system solution but instead need an adjustment in management, additional training, or refinement of existing organizational procedures. If the problem is information related, systems analysis still may be required to diagnose the problem and arrive at the proper solution.

Systems Design

Systems analysis describes what a system should do to meet information requirements, and **systems design** shows how the system will fulfill this objective. The design of an information system is the overall plan or model for that system. Like the blueprint of a building or house, it consists of all the specifications that give the system its form and structure.

The systems designer details the system specifications that will deliver the functions identified during systems analysis. These specifications should address all of the managerial, organizational, and technological components of the system solution. Table 9-1 lists the types of specifications that would be produced during systems design.

Like houses or buildings, information systems may have many possible designs. Each design represents a unique blend of all technical and organizational components. What makes one design superior to others is the ease and efficiency with which it fulfills user requirements within a specific set of technical, organizational, financial, and time constraints.

The Role of End Users User information requirements drive the entire systems development effort. Users must have sufficient control over the design process to ensure that the system reflects their business priorities and information needs, not the biases of the technical staff. Working on design increases users' understanding and acceptance of the system. As we describe in Chapter 10, insufficient user involvement in the design effort is a major cause of system failure. However, some systems require more user participation in design than others, and Section 9.3 shows how alternative systems development methods address the user participation issue.

Feasibility study
Information requirements
Systems design

TABLE 9-1 Design specifications.

OUTPUT	CONTROLS
Medium	Input controls (characters, limit, reasonableness)
Content	Processing controls (consistency, record counts)
Timing	Output controls (totals, samples of output)
INPUT	Procedural controls (passwords, special forms)
Origins	**SECURITY**
Flow	Access controls
Data entry	Catastrophe plans
USER INTERFACE	Audit trails
Simplicity	**DOCUMENTATION**
Efficiency	Operations documentation
Logic	Systems documents
Feedback	User documentation
Errors	**CONVERSION**
DATABASE DESIGN	Transfer files
Logical data model	Initiate new procedures
Volume and speed requirements	Select testing method
File organization and design	Cut over to new system
Record specifications	**TRAINING**
PROCESSING	Select training techniques
Computations	Develop training modules
Program modules	Identify training facilities
Required reports	**ORGANIZATIONAL CHANGES**
Timing of outputs	Task redesign
MANUAL PROCEDURES	Job design
What activities	Process design
Who performs them	Organization structure design
When	Reporting relationships
How	
Where	

The Window on Organizations section on the next page demonstrates the importance of user involvement in designing and developing a successful solution. Dorfman Pacific, a U.S. manufacturer of headwear and handbags, could not effectively expand its business because it was hampered by an outdated warehouse system and heavily manual processes. It decided to implement a new wireless warehouse that changed the way it worked. As you read this case, try to identify the problem this organization was facing, what alternative solutions were available to management, and how well the chosen solution worked.

Completing the Systems Development Process

The remaining steps in the systems development process translate the solution specifications established during systems analysis and design into a fully operational information system. These concluding steps consist of programming, testing, conversion, production, and maintenance.

Programming During the **programming** stage, system specifications that were prepared during the design stage are translated into software program code. Today, many organizations no longer do their own programming for new systems. Instead, they purchase the software that meets the requirements for a new system from external sources such as software packages from a commercial software vendor, software services from an application service provider, or outsourcing firms that develop custom application software for their clients (see Section 9.3).

Testing Exhaustive and thorough **testing** must be conducted to ascertain whether the system produces the right results. Testing answers the question, "Will the system produce the desired results under known conditions?"

The amount of time needed to answer this question has been traditionally underrated in systems project planning (see Chapter 10). Testing is time consuming: test data must be carefully prepared, results reviewed, and corrections made in the system. In some instances, parts of the system may have to be redesigned. The risks resulting from glossing over this step are enormous.

Testing an information system can be broken down into three types of activities: unit testing, system testing, and acceptance testing. **Unit testing,** or program testing, consists of testing each program separately in the system. It is widely believed that the purpose of unit testing is to guarantee that programs are error-free, but this goal is realistically impossible. Testing should be viewed instead as a means of locating errors in programs, focusing on finding all the ways to make a program fail. Once they are pinpointed, problems can be corrected.

System testing tests the functioning of the information system as a whole. It tries to determine whether discrete modules will function together as planned and whether discrepancies exist between the way the system actually works and the way it was conceived. Among the areas examined are performance time, capacity for file storage and handling peak loads, recovery and restart capabilities, and manual procedures.

Acceptance testing provides the final certification that the system is ready to be used in a production setting. System tests are evaluated by users and reviewed by management. When all parties are satisfied that the new system meets their standards, the system is formally accepted for installation.

Programming
Testing
Unit testing
System testing
Acceptance testing

WINDOW ON ORGANIZATIONS

Dorfman Pacific Rolls Out a New Wireless Warehouse

You may not have heard of Dorfman Pacific, but you have probably seen its hats on celebrities featured in *People* and *InStyle* magazines. Dorfman Pacific, based in Stockton, California, has been manufacturing and distributing headwear and handbags for more than 85 years. The company's philosophy has been to keep up with fashion trends while offering quality products with strong customer service, on-time deliveries, and competitive prices.

Traditionally, Dorfman served the mom-and-pop sector of the retail market. The company's warehouse processes reflected this. Warehouse activities relied on paper-based processes and tacit knowledge of the facility and Dorfman Pacific's customers.

In the 1980s and 1990s, Dorfman Pacific started adding big-box stores like Walmart and JC Penney to its roster of customers. These stores quickly came to represent half of Dorfman's business. More significantly, the large retailers had a much greater appetite for thousands of different items and box types.

Serving retailers like Walmart with a paper-based order-picking process in a 9300-square-metre warehouse was stressful and an ineffective means of doing business. During seasonal peaks in demand, Dorfman had to hire extra workers and pay hefty overtime wages to satisfy the demand. The extra wages amounted to more than $300 000 every year. The company's IT systems were spread out over various functional areas and did little to support a transparent inventory.

Dorfman eventually increased its warehouse space to 25 600 square metres, but the space alone was not enough to overcome flawed business processes. Top management at Dorfman realized that major changes were necessary if the company was going to expand its operations successfully. CEO Douglas Highsmith committed to a complete overhaul of the technology in the warehouse. He wanted to eliminate the paper systems and replace them with wireless technology.

The traditional order-fulfilment process at Dorfman began with a warehouse worker, called a picker, receiving a paper pick ticket from a supervisor. The picker then drove a forklift to the area of the warehouse where he or she expected to find the bin that stored the product on the ticket. The worker manually picked boxes off the shelf and then brought them to a packing area to be boxed, labelled, and loaded onto a truck. The warehouse was really set up only for picking, which left the remaining order-fulfillment processes as afterthoughts.

Confusing the process were bins that were labelled manually, making them difficult to read, and boxes that sometimes held more than one product. Additionally, each picker had his or her own preferred path to performing picking duties.

The inefficiencies of these practices were magnified by special orders. The company's ERP system offered little help because it did not integrate well with other systems. Mark Dulle, Dorfman's IT Services director, recognized that picking by order would not work in an era of expansion.

Dorfman approached the change as a business project rather than an IT project. A cross-functional team consisting of an outside consultant as project manager and managers from distribution, purchasing, customer service, and sales worked on the transformation. The IT department took responsibility for choosing hardware, installing the hardware and software for the wireless warehouse, and appointing an administrator for the new warehouse management system.

Highsmith's goals were to reduce labour costs and create the most efficient way for a streamlined warehouse staff to pick products with the smallest error rate. A successful implementation required a number of steps. First, the project team sought to learn everything it could about how Dorfman's 25 000 products were received, replenished, picked, packed, and shipped. This study included measuring the dimension and weight of each product, as well as the size of every bin and storage shelf, and determining whether products were stored in the correct places.

Next, Dorfman brought in Texas Bar Code Systems to test the feasibility of a wireless system in the warehouse. The project would have been fruitless if wireless signals did not function properly amidst the warehouse's concrete walls, steel doors, and metal storage shelves. The testing also helped to determine where the best wireless access points were located. Dorfman's warehouse required an unusually high number of access points, 15, because the floor space expansions over the years created an irregular layout, which was dense with inventory.

Dulle led the effort to revamp Dorfman's IT infrastructure, including replacing all of the old networking cables and switches with the most advanced networking technology available. He also reconfigured the ERP system and installed a new warehouse management system from HighJump Software complete with wireless capabilities and the ability to sort through warehouse and shipping data. To this system, which was based on a wireless LAN, Dulle added bar-coding equipment from Zebra Technologies, integration software, durable mobile computers, and additional computers mounted on forklifts.

With these components in place, paper was no longer necessary. The new ERP system and the warehouse management system used software to manage the picking, packing, and shipping processes. Pickers carrying mobile devices receive data telling them where to go, what to pick, and where to bring the merchandise using the most efficient route.

Dorfman employees had to change the way they worked. The new warehouse management system required a different warehouse floor configuration as well as new ways to pick, pack, and ship products. Dorfman took the job of selling the new systems to its workers very seriously, convincing them that the wireless warehouse would improve their lives and their job performance.

Once the new warehouse system was deployed, pickers armed with wireless scanning devices could be assured that the bar-code-labelled bins to which they were directed contained only one product type each. Tracking inventory became seamless. According to Dulle, Dorfman can now handle twice the number of orders during peak seasons, and labour costs are down almost 30 percent. Eliminating the need for temporary workers and overtime has saved the company more than $300 000 and counting.

To Think About

1. Compare Dorfman Pacific's old and new order-picking processes. Diagram the processes.

2. What role did end users play in developing Dorfman's wireless warehouse system? What would have happened to the project if users had not been so involved? Explain your answer.

3. What types of systems development methods and tools did Dorfman use for developing its wireless warehouse system?

4. How did the new system change the way Dorfman ran its business?

5. What problems did the new system solve? Was it successful?

MIS in Action

Use your Web-searching capabilities to answer the following questions:

1. What are some of the components of a wireless warehouse system?

2. What companies manufacture these components?

3. What other businesses or organizations have implemented wireless warehouses?

4. If you were implementing a wireless warehouse, what potential problems would worry you most?

Sources: Thomas Wailgum, "How to Take Your Warehouse Wireless," and "Wireless—Five Steps to a Successful Wireless Rollout," *CIO Magazine*, February 1, 2007; Jim Fulcher, "Rise of User-Friendly Devices Propels Strategic Use of Wireless Technology," *Manufacturing Business Technology*, February 18, 2007; Lisa M. Kempfer, "Hats Off to Wireless," *Material Handling Management*, January 2007; and "Hats-Off: Dorfman Pacific Implements Symbol Enterprise Mobility Solution for Paperless Warehouse Operations," www.symbol.com, September 13, 2006.

FIGURE 9-3 A sample test plan to test a record change.

When developing a test plan, it is imperative to include the various conditions to be tested, the requirements for each condition tested, and the expected results. Test plans require input from both end users and information systems specialists.

Procedure	Address and Maintenance "Record Change Series"		Test Series 2		
	Prepared By:	Date:	Version:		
Test Ref.	Condition Tested	Special Requirements	Expected Results	Output On	Next Screen
2.0	Change records				
2.1	Change existing record	Key field	Not allowed		
2.2	Change nonexistent record	Other fields	"Invalid key" message		
2.3	Change deleted record	Deleted record must be available	"Deleted" message		
2.4	Make second record	Change 2.1 above	OK if valid	Transaction file	V45
2.5	Insert record		OK if valid	Transaction file	V45
2.6	Abort during change	Abort 2.5	No change	Transaction file	V45

The systems development team works with users to devise a systematic test plan. The **test plan** includes all of the preparations for the series of tests we have just described.

Figure 9-3 shows an example of a test plan. The general condition being tested is a record change. The documentation consists of a series of test-plan screens maintained on a database (perhaps a PC database) that is ideally suited to this kind of application.

Conversion is the process of changing from the old system to the new system. Four main conversion strategies can be employed: the parallel strategy, the direct cutover strategy, the pilot study strategy, and the phased approach strategy.

In a **parallel strategy,** both the old system and its potential replacement are run together for a time until everyone is assured that the new one functions correctly. This is the safest conversion approach because, in the event of errors or processing disruptions, the old system can still be used as a backup. However, this approach is very expensive, and additional staff or resources may be required to run the extra system.

The **direct cutover strategy** replaces the old system entirely with the new system on an appointed day. It is a very risky approach that can potentially be more costly than running two systems in parallel if serious problems with the new system are found. There is no other system to fall back on. Dislocations, disruptions, and the cost of corrections may be enormous.

The **pilot study strategy** introduces the new system to only a limited area of the organization, such as a single department or operating unit. When this pilot version is complete and working smoothly, it is installed throughout the rest of the organization, either simultaneously or in stages.

The **phased approach strategy** introduces the new system in stages, either by functions or by organizational units. If, for example, the system is introduced by functions, a new payroll system might begin with hourly workers who are paid weekly, followed six months later by adding salaried employees (who are paid monthly) to the system. If the system is introduced by organizational units, corporate headquarters might be converted first, followed by outlying operating units four months later.

Moving from an old system to a new one requires that end users be trained to use the new system. Detailed **documentation** showing how the system works from both technical and end-user standpoints is finalized during conversion time for use in training and everyday operations. Lack of proper training and documentation contributes to system failure, so this portion of the systems development process is very important.

Production and Maintenance After the new system is installed and conversion is complete, the system is said to be in **production.** During this stage, the system will be reviewed by both users and technical specialists to determine how well it has met its original objectives

Test plan
Conversion
Parallel strategy
Direct cutover strategy
Pilot study strategy
Phased approach strategy
Documentation
Production

TABLE 9-2   Systems development.

CORE ACTIVITY	DESCRIPTION
Systems analysis	Identify problem(s)
	Specify solutions
	Establish information requirements
Systems design	Create design specifications
Programming	Translate design specifications into program code
Testing	Unit test
	Systems test
	Acceptance test
Conversion	Plan conversion
	Prepare documentation
	Train users and technical staff
Production and maintenance	Operate the system
	Evaluate the system
	Modify the system

and to decide whether any revisions or modifications are in order. In some instances, a formal **post-implementation audit** document is prepared. After the system has been fine-tuned, it must be maintained while it is in production to correct errors, meet requirements, or improve processing efficiency. Changes in hardware, software, documentation, or procedures to a production system to correct errors, meet new requirements, or improve processing efficiency are termed **maintenance.**

Approximately 20 percent of the time devoted to maintenance is used for debugging or correcting emergency production problems. Another 20 percent is concerned with changes in data, files, reports, hardware, or system software. But 60 percent of all maintenance work consists of making user enhancements, improving documentation, and recoding system components for greater processing efficiency. The amount of work in the third category of maintenance problems could be reduced significantly through better systems analysis and design practices. Table 9-2 summarizes the systems development activities.

Modelling and Designing Systems: Structured and Object-Oriented Methodologies

There are alternative methodologies for modelling and designing systems. Structured methodologies and object-oriented development are the most prominent.

Structured Methodologies Structured methodologies have been used to document, analyze, and design information systems since the 1970s. **Structured** refers to the fact that the techniques are step by step, with each step building on the previous one. Structured methodologies are top-down, progressing from the highest, most abstract level to the lowest level of detail—from the general to the specific.

Structured development methods are process-oriented, focusing primarily on modelling the processes or actions that capture, store, manipulate, and distribute data as the data flow through a system. These methods separate data from processes. A separate programming procedure must be written every time someone wants to take an action on a particular piece of data. The procedures act on data that the program passes to them.

The primary tool for representing a system's component processes and the flow of data between them is the **data flow diagram (DFD).** The data flow diagram offers a logical graphical model of information flow, partitioning a system into modules that show manageable levels of detail. It rigorously specifies the processes or transformations that occur within each module and the interfaces that exist between them.

Post-implementation audit
Maintenance
Structured
Data flow diagram (DFD)

The system has three processes: Verify availability (1.0), Enrol student (2.0), and Confirm registration (3.0). The name and content of each of the data flows appear adjacent to each arrow. There is one external entity in this system: the student. There are two data stores: the student master file and the course file.

FIGURE 9-4 Data flow diagram for mail-in university registration system.

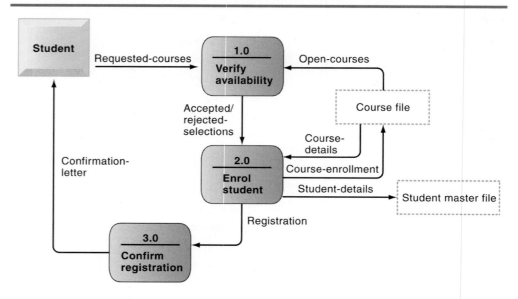

Figure 9-4 shows a simple data flow diagram for a mail-in university course registration system. The rounded boxes represent processes, which portray the transformation of data. The square box represents an external entity, which is an originator or receiver of information located outside the boundaries of the system being modelled. The open rectangles represent data stores, which are either manual or automated inventories of data. The arrows represent data flows, which show the movement between processes, external entities, and data stores. They contain packets of data with the name or content of each data flow listed beside the arrow.

This data flow diagram shows that students submit registration forms with their name, identification number, and the numbers of the courses they wish to take. In process 1.0, the system verifies that each course selected is still open by referencing the university's course file. The file distinguishes courses that are open from those that have been cancelled or filled. Process 1.0 then determines which of the student's selections can be accepted or rejected. Process 2.0 enrols the student in the courses for which he or she has been accepted.

It updates the university's course file with the student's name and identification number and recalculates the class size. If maximum enrolment has been reached, the course number is flagged as closed. Process 2.0 also updates the university's student master file with information about new students or changes in address. Process 3.0 then sends each student applicant a confirmation-of-registration letter listing the courses for which he or she is registered and noting the course selections that could not be fulfilled.

The diagrams can be used to depict higher-level processes as well as lower-level details. Through levelled data flow diagrams, a complex process can be broken down into successive levels of detail. An entire system can be divided into subsystems with a high-level data flow diagram. Each subsystem, in turn, can be divided into additional subsystems with second-level data flow diagrams, and the lower-level subsystems can be broken down again until the lowest level of detail has been reached.

Another tool for structured analysis is a data dictionary, which contains information about individual pieces of data and data groupings within a system (see Chapter 6). The data dictionary defines the contents of data flows and data stores so that systems developers understand exactly what pieces of data they contain. **Process specifications** describe the transformation occurring within the lowest level of the data flow diagrams. They express the logic for each process.

In structured methodology, software design is modelled using hierarchical structure charts. The **structure chart** is a top-down chart, showing each level of design, its relationship to other levels, and its place in the overall design structure. The design first considers the main function of a program or system, then breaks this function into subfunctions, and

Process specifications

Structure chart

FIGURE 9-5   High-level structure chart for a payroll system.

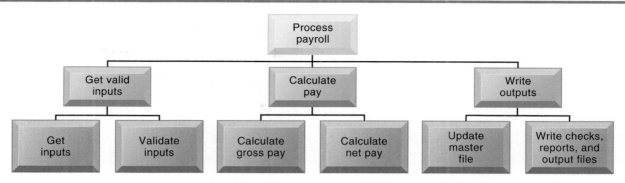

This structure chart shows the highest or most abstract level of design for a payroll system, providing an overview of the entire system.

decomposes each subfunction until the lowest level of detail has been reached. Figure 9-5 shows a high-level structure chart for a payroll system. If a design has too many levels to fit onto one structure chart, it can be broken down further on more detailed structure charts. A structure chart may document one program, one system (a set of programs), or part of one program.

Object-Oriented Development Structured methods are useful for modelling processes, but do not handle the modelling of data well. They also treat data and processes as logically separate entities while in the real world this separation seems unnatural. Different modelling conventions are used for analysis (the data flow diagram) and for design (the structure chart).

Object-oriented development addresses these issues. Object-oriented development uses the **object** as the basic unit of systems analysis and design. An object combines data and the specific processes that operate on those data. Data encapsulated in an object can be accessed and modified only by the operations or methods associated with that object. Instead of passing data to procedures, programs send a message for an object to perform an operation that is already embedded in it. The system is modelled as a collection of objects and the relationships among them. Because processing logic resides within objects rather than in separate software programs, objects must collaborate with each other to make the system work.

Object-oriented modelling is based on the concepts of *class* and *inheritance*. Objects belonging to a certain class or general categories of similar objects have the features of that class. Classes of objects in turn can inherit all the structure and behaviours of a more general class and then add variables and behaviours unique to each object. New classes of objects are created by choosing an existing class and specifying how the new class differs from the existing class, instead of starting from scratch each time.

We can see how class and inheritance work in Figure 9-6, which illustrates the relationships among classes concerning employees and how they are paid. Employee is the common ancestor, or superclass, for the other three classes. Salaried, Hourly, and Temporary are subclasses of Employee. The class name is in the top compartment, the attributes for each class are in the middle portion of each box, and the list of operations is in the bottom portion of each box.

The features that are shared by all employees (ID, name, address, date hired, position, and pay) are stored in the Employee superclass while each subclass stores features that are specific to that particular type of employee. Specific to Hourly employees, for example, are their hourly rates and overtime rates. A solid line from the subclass to the superclass is a generalization path showing that the subclasses Salaried, Hourly, and Temporary have common features that can be generalized into the superclass Employee.

Object-oriented development is more iterative and incremental than traditional structured development. During analysis, systems developers document the functional requirements of the system, specifying its most important properties and what the proposed system must do. Interactions between the system and its users are analyzed to identify

Object-oriented development

Object

FIGURE 9-6   Class and inheritance.

This figure illustrates how classes inherit the common features of their superclass.

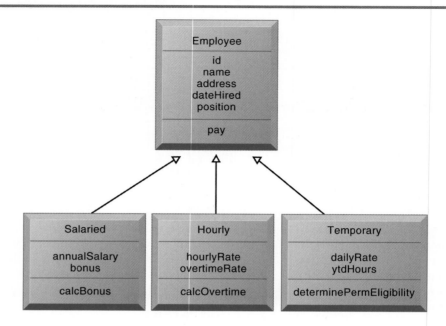

objects, which include both data and processes. The object-oriented design phase describes how the objects will behave and how they will interact with one other. Similar objects are grouped together to form a class, and classes are grouped into hierarchies in which a subclass inherits the attributes and methods from its superclass.

The information system is implemented by translating the design into program code, reusing classes that are already available in a library of tested reusable software objects and adding new ones created during the object-oriented design phase. Implementation may also involve the creation of an object-oriented database. The resulting system must be thoroughly tested and evaluated.

Because objects are already tested and reusable, object-oriented development could potentially reduce the time and cost of writing software because organizations can reuse software objects that have already been created as building blocks for other applications. New systems can be created by using some existing objects, changing others, and adding a few new objects. Object-oriented frameworks have been developed to provide reusable, semicomplete applications that the organization can further customize into finished applications.

Computer-Aided Software Engineering   **Computer-aided software engineering (CASE)**—sometimes called *computer-aided systems engineering*—provides software tools to automate the methodologies we have just described to reduce the amount of repetitive work the developer needs to do. CASE tools also facilitate the creation of clear documentation and the coordination of team development efforts. Team members can share their work easily by accessing each other's files to review or modify what has been done. Modest productivity benefits can also be achieved if the tools are used properly.

CASE tools provide automated graphics facilities for producing charts and diagrams, screen and report generators, data dictionaries, extensive reporting facilities, analysis and checking tools, code generators, and documentation generators. In general, CASE tools try to increase productivity and quality by doing the following:

- Enforce a standard development methodology and design discipline
- Improve communication between users and technical specialists
- Organize and correlate design components and provide rapid access to them using a design repository
- Automate tedious and error-prone portions of analysis and design
- Automate code generation and testing and control rollout

Computer-aided software engineering (CASE)

CASE tools contain features for validating design diagrams and specifications. CASE tools thus support iterative design by automating revisions and changes and providing prototyping facilities. A CASE information repository stores all the information defined by the analysts during the project. The repository includes data flow diagrams, structure charts, entity-relationship diagrams, data definitions (see Chapter 6), process specifications, screen and report formats, notes and comments, and test results.

To be used effectively, CASE tools require organizational discipline. Every member of a development project must adhere to a common set of naming conventions and standards as well as to a development methodology. The best CASE tools enforce common methods and standards, which may discourage their use in situations where organizational discipline is lacking.

9.3 Alternative Systems-Development Approaches

Systems differ in terms of their size and technological complexity and in terms of the organizational problems they are meant to solve. A number of systems-development approaches have been developed to deal with these differences.

This section describes these alternative methods: the traditional systems life cycle, prototyping, end-user development, and application software packages and outsourcing.

Traditional Systems Life Cycle

The **systems life cycle** is the oldest method for developing information systems. The life cycle methodology is a phased approach to developing a system, dividing systems development into formal stages. Systems development specialists have different opinions on how to partition the systems-development stages, but they roughly correspond to the stages of systems development that we have just described.

The systems life cycle methodology maintains a very formal division of labour between end users and information systems specialists. Technical specialists, such as system analysts and programmers, are responsible for much of the systems analysis, design, and implementation work; end users are limited to providing information requirements and reviewing the technical staff's work. The life cycle also emphasizes formal specifications and paperwork, so many documents are generated during the course of a systems project.

The systems life cycle is still used for developing large complex systems that require a rigorous and formal requirements analysis, predefined specifications, and tight controls over the systems-development process. However, the systems life cycle approach can be costly, time consuming, and inflexible. Although systems developers can go back and forth among stages in the life cycle, the systems life cycle is predominantly a "waterfall" approach (see Figure 9-7) in which tasks in one stage are completed before work for the next stage begins. Activities can be repeated, but volumes of new documents must be generated and steps retraced if requirements and specifications need to be revised. This encourages freezing of specifications relatively early in the development process. The life cycle approach is also not suitable for many small desktop systems, which tend to be less structured and more individualized.

Prototyping

Prototyping consists of developing an experimental system rapidly and inexpensively for end users to evaluate. By interacting with the prototype, users can get a better idea of their information requirements. The prototype endorsed by the users can be used as a template to create the final system.

The **prototype** is a working version of an information system or part of the system, but it is meant to be only a preliminary model. Once operational, the prototype will be further refined until it conforms precisely to users' requirements. Once the design has been finalized, the prototype can be converted to a polished production system.

Systems life cycle

Prototyping

Prototype

FIGURE 9-7 The waterfall model illustrates the traditional systems development life cycle.

The waterfall model of systems development consists of a formal division between the stages of systems development, with each stage completed before starting the next one.

Source: Trung Hung VO, Waterfall Process, http://cnx.org/content/m14619/latest/graphics1.png.

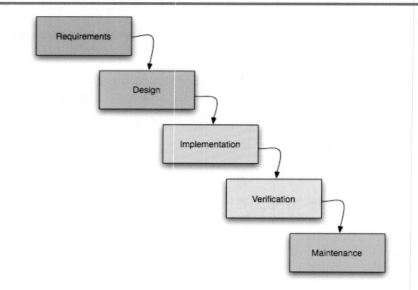

The process of developing a preliminary design, trying it out, refining it, and trying again has been called an **iterative** process of systems development because the steps required to develop a system can be repeated over and over again. Prototyping is more explicitly iterative than the conventional life cycle, and it actively promotes system design changes. It has been said that prototyping replaces unplanned rework with planned iteration, with each version more accurately reflecting users' requirements.

Steps in Prototyping Figure 9-8 shows a four-step model of the prototyping process, which consists of the following:

Step 1: *Identify the users' basic requirements.* The system designer (usually an information systems specialist) works with the users only long enough to capture the users' basic information needs.

Step 2: *Develop an initial prototype.* The system designer creates a working prototype quickly, using tools for rapidly generating software.

Step 3: *Use the prototype.* The users are encouraged to work with the system to determine how well the prototype meets their needs and to make suggestions for improving the prototype.

Step 4: *Revise and enhance the prototype.* The system developer notes all changes the users request and refines the prototype accordingly. After the prototype has been revised, the cycle returns to step 3. Steps 3 and 4 are repeated until the users are satisfied.

When no more iterations are required, the approved prototype then becomes an operational prototype that furnishes the final specifications for the application. Sometimes the prototype is adopted as the production version of the system although typically the prototype does not handle the volume of transactions or level of security required of the finished system.

Advantages and Disadvantages of Prototyping Prototyping is most useful when there is some uncertainty about requirements or design solutions and for designing an information system's **end-user interface** (the part of the system with which end users interact, such as online display and data-entry screens, reports, or Web pages). Because prototyping encourages intense end-user involvement throughout the systems development life cycle, it is more likely to produce systems that fulfill user requirements.

Iterative

End-user interface

FIGURE 9-8   The prototyping process.

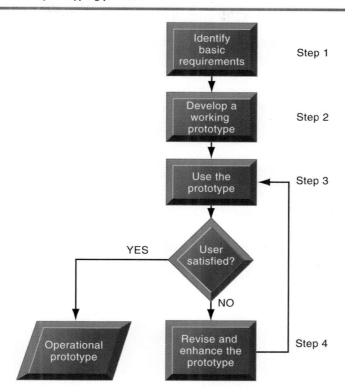

The process of developing a prototype can be broken down into four steps. Because a prototype can be developed quickly and inexpensively, systems developers can go through several iterations, repeating steps 3 and 4, to refine and enhance the prototype before arriving at the final operational one.

However, rapid prototyping can gloss over essential steps in systems development. If the completed prototype works reasonably well, management may not see the need for reprogramming, redesign, or full documentation and testing to develop a polished production system. Some of these hastily constructed systems may not easily accommodate large quantities of data or a large number of users in a production environment.

End-User Development

Some types of information systems can be developed by end users with little or no formal assistance from technical specialists. This phenomenon is called **end-user development.** A series of software tools categorized as fourth-generation languages makes this possible. **Fourth-generation languages** are software tools that enable end users to create reports or develop software applications with minimal or no technical assistance. Some of these fourth-generation tools also enhance professional programmers' productivity.

Fourth-generation languages tend to be nonprocedural, or less procedural, than conventional programming languages. Procedural languages require specification of the sequence of steps, or procedures, that tell the computer what to do and how to do it. Nonprocedural languages need only specify what has to be accomplished rather than provide details about how to carry out the task.

Table 9-3 shows that there are seven categories of fourth-generation languages: PC software tools, query languages, report generators, graphics languages, application generators, application software packages, and very high-level programming languages. The table shows the tools ordered in terms of ease of use by nonprogramming end users. End users are most likely to work with PC software tools and query languages. **Query languages** are software tools that provide immediate online answers to requests for information that are not predefined, such as "Who are the highest-performing sales representatives?" Query languages are often tied to data management software and to database management systems (see Chapter 6).

On the whole, end-user-developed systems can be completed more rapidly than those developed through the conventional systems life cycle. Allowing users to specify their own

End-user development
Fourth-generation languages
Query languages

TABLE 9-3 Categories of fourth-generation languages.

FOURTH-GENERATION TOOL	DESCRIPTION	EXAMPLE	
PC software tools	General-purpose application software packages for PCs.	WordPerfect Microsoft Access	**Oriented toward end users**
Query languages	Languages for retrieving data stored in databases or files. Capable of supporting requests for information that are not predefined.	SQL	↑
Report generators	Extract data from files or databases to create customized reports in a wide range of formats not routinely produced by an information system. Generally provide more control over the way data are formatted, organized, and displayed than query languages.	Crystal Reports	
Graphics languages	Retrieve data from files or databases and display them in graphic format. Some graphics software can perform arithmetic or logical operations on data as well.	SAS Graph Systat	
Application generators	Contain preprogrammed modules that can generate entire applications, including Web sites, greatly speeding development. A user can specify what needs to be done, and the application generator will create the appropriate program code for input, validation, update, processing, and reporting.	WebFOCUS QuickBase	
Application software packages	Software programs sold or leased by commercial vendors that eliminate the need for custom-written, in-house software.	Oracle PeopleSoft HCM mySAP ERP	↓
Very high-level programming languages	Generate program code with fewer instructions than conventional languages, such as COBOL or FORTRAN. Designed primarily as productivity tools for professional programmers.	APL Nomad2	**Oriented toward IS professionals**

business needs improves requirements gathering and often leads to a higher level of user involvement and satisfaction with the system. However, fourth-generation tools still cannot replace conventional tools for some business applications because they cannot easily handle the processing of large numbers of transactions or applications with extensive procedural logic and updating requirements, and they cannot typically provide needed security and control.

End-user computing also poses organizational risks because it occurs outside traditional mechanisms for information systems management and control. When systems are created rapidly, without a formal development methodology, testing and documentation may be inadequate. Control over data can be lost in systems outside the traditional information systems department. To help organizations maximize the benefits of end-user applications development, management should control the development of end-user applications by requiring cost justification of end-user information system projects and by establishing hardware, software, and quality standards for user-developed applications.

Application Software Packages and Outsourcing

Chapter 5 points out that the software for most systems today is not developed in-house but is purchased from external sources. Firms can rent the software from a software service provider, they can purchase a software package from a commercial vendor, or they can have a custom application developed by an outside outsourcing firm.

Application Software Packages During the past several decades, many systems have been developed on an application software package foundation. Many applications are common to all business organizations—for example, payroll, accounts receivable, general ledger, or inventory control. For such universal functions with standard processes that do not change a great deal over time, a generalized system will fulfill the requirements of many organizations.

If a software package can fulfill most of an organization's requirements, the company does not have to write its own software. The company can save time and money by using the prewritten, predesigned, pretested software programs from the package. Package vendors supply much of the ongoing maintenance and support for the system, including enhancements to keep the system in line with ongoing technical and business developments.

If an organization has unique requirements that the package does not address, many packages include capabilities for customization. **Customization** allows a software package to be modified to meet an organization's unique requirements without destroying the integrity of the package software. If a great deal of customization is required, additional programming and customization work may become so expensive and time consuming that they negate many of the advantages of software packages.

When a system is developed using an application software package, systems analysis will include a package evaluation effort. The most important evaluation criteria are the functions provided by the package, flexibility, user-friendliness, hardware and software resources, database requirements, installation and maintenance efforts, documentation, vendor quality, and cost. The package evaluation process often is based on a **Request for Proposal (RFP),** which is a detailed list of questions submitted to packaged-software vendors.

When a software package solution is selected, the organization no longer has total control over the system design process. Instead of tailoring the system design specifications directly to user requirements, the design effort will consist of trying to mould user requirements to conform to the features of the package. If the organization's requirements conflict with the way the package works and the package cannot be customized, the organization will have to adapt to the package and change its procedures.

Outsourcing If a firm does not want to use its internal resources to develop or operate information systems, it can outsource the work to an external organization that specializes in providing these services. Cloud computing and SaaS providers, which we describe in Chapter 5, are one form of outsourcing. Subscribing companies would use the software and computer hardware provided by the service as the technical platform for their systems. In another form of outsourcing, a company could hire an external vendor to design and create the software for its system, and that company might even operate the system on its own computers. The outsourcing vendor might be domestic or in another country.

Domestic outsourcing is driven primarily by the fact that outsourcing firms possess skills, resources, and assets that their clients do not have. Installing a new supply chain management system in a very large company might require hiring an additional 30 to 50 people with specific expertise in supply chain management software licensed, say, from i2 or another vendor. Rather than hire permanent new employees, most of whom would need extensive training in the software package, and then release them after the new system is developed, it makes more sense, and is often less expensive, to outsource this work for a 12-month period.

In the case of **offshore outsourcing,** the decision tends to be much more cost-driven. A skilled programmer in India or Russia earns about $11 000 per year, compared to

Customization
Request for Proposal (RFP)
Offshore outsourcing

$65 000 per year for a comparable programmer in Canada. The Internet and low-cost communications technology have drastically reduced the expense and difficulty of coordinating the work of global teams in faraway locations. In addition to cost savings, many offshore outsourcing firms offer world-class technology assets and skills. Wage inflation outside North America has recently eroded some of these advantages, and some jobs have moved back home to North America.

Nevertheless, there is a very strong chance that at some point in your career, you will be working with offshore outsourcers or global teams. Your firm is most likely to benefit from outsourcing if it takes the time to evaluate all the risks and to make sure outsourcing is appropriate for its particular needs. Any company that outsources its applications must thoroughly understand the project, including its requirements, method of implementation, anticipated benefits, cost components, and metrics for measuring performance.

Many firms underestimate costs for identifying and evaluating vendors of information technology services, for transitioning to a new vendor, for improving internal software development methods to match those of outsourcing vendors, and for monitoring vendors to make sure they are fulfilling their contractual obligations. Companies will need to allocate resources for documenting requirements, sending out requests for proposal (RFPs), travel expenses, negotiating contracts, and project management. Experts claim it takes from three months to a full year to fully transfer work to an offshore partner and make sure the vendor thoroughly understands your business.

Outsourcing offshore incurs additional costs for coping with cultural differences that drain productivity and dealing with human resources issues, such as terminating or relocating domestic employees. All of these hidden costs undercut some of the anticipated benefits from outsourcing. Firms should be especially cautious when using an outsourcer to develop or to operate applications that could give it some type of competitive advantage.

Figure 9-9 shows best- and worst-case scenarios for the total cost of an offshore outsourcing project. It shows how much hidden costs affect the total project cost. The best case reflects the lowest estimates for additional costs, and the worst case reflects the highest estimates for these costs. As you can see, hidden costs increase the total cost of an offshore outsourcing project by an extra 15 to 57 percent. Even with these extra costs, many firms will benefit from offshore outsourcing if they manage the work well. Under the worst-case scenario, a firm would still save about 15 percent.

The Window on Management describes a recent outsourcing arrangement between Chrysler LLC and Tata Consultancy Services (TCS), a global provider of information technology and business services based in India. As you read this case, try to apply what you have just read. Was outsourcing to TCS the right decision?

FIGURE 9-9   Total cost of offshore outsourcing.

If a firm spends $10 million on offshore outsourcing contracts, that company will actually spend 15.2 percent in extra costs even under the best-case scenario. In the worst-case scenario, where there is a dramatic drop in productivity along with exceptionally high transition and layoff costs, a firm can expect to pay up to 57 percent in extra costs on top of the $10 million outlay for an offshore contract.

TOTAL COST OF OFFSHORE OUTSOURCING				
Cost of outsourcing contract			$10 000 000	
Hidden Costs	Best Case	Additional Cost ($)	Worst Case	Additional Cost ($)
1. Vendor selection	0%	20 000	2%	200 000
2. Transition costs	2%	200 000	3%	300 000
3. Layoffs & retention	3%	300 000	5%	500 000
4. Lost productivity/cultural issues	3%	300 000	27%	2 700 000
5. Improving development processes	1%	100 000	10%	1 000 000
6. Managing the contract	6%	600 000	10%	1 000 000
Total additional costs		1 520 000		5 700 000
	Outstanding Contract ($)	Additional Cost ($)	Total Cost ($)	Additional Cost
Total cost of outsourcing (TCO) best case	10 000 000	1 520 000	11 520 000	15.2%
Total cost of outsourcing (TCO) worst case	10 000 000	5 700 000	15 700 000	57.0%

9.4 Application Development for the Digital Firm

In the digital firm environment, organizations need to be able to add, change, and retire their technology capabilities very rapidly to respond to new opportunities. Companies are starting to use shorter, more informal development processes that provide fast solutions. In addition to using software packages and external service providers, businesses are relying more heavily on fast-cycle techniques such as rapid application development (RAD), joint application design (JAD), agile development, and reusable standardized software components that can be assembled into a complete set of services for e-commerce and e-business.

Rapid Application Development (RAD), Joint Application Design (JAD), and Agile Development

Object-oriented software tools, reusable software, prototyping, and fourth-generation language tools are helping systems developers create working systems much more rapidly than they could using traditional systems-development methods and software tools. The term **rapid application development (RAD)** is used to describe this process of creating workable systems in a very short period of time. RAD can include the use of visual programming and other tools for developing graphical user interfaces, iterative prototyping of key system elements, the automation of program code generation, and close teamwork among end users and information systems specialists. Simple systems often can be assembled from predeveloped components. The process does not have to be sequential, and key parts of development can occur simultaneously.

Rapid application development (RAD)

WINDOW ON MANAGEMENT

How to Get Outsourcing Right: Avoid Getting It Wrong

Among large corporations in the last decade, there has been a stampede to turn technology management, system ownership, customer service, and back-office functions over to third parties. The leading motivation for outsourcing is the belief that it will save money for the company, but there are other reasons as well: to gain access to technology expertise, to avoid capital expenditures on infrastructure the firm uses sporadically, to free up internal staff, to keep head count down, and so on. Outsourcing vendor firms are in business to make money. They claim they can do the job better, faster, and cheaper than your internal staff and still make a profit. They claim to have the economies of scale to do the basic computing cheaper, and to have the complementary assets in the form of people and expertise that your firm needs.

So it would seem we have a marriage of interests where both parties see advantage and where both parties should benefit. But the reality of outsourcing is not so simple. A staggering 50 percent of all outsourcing deals fall apart, many ending in court proceedings. In a recent survey of 420 business IT professionals, only a third are neutral on outsourcing deals, and 17 percent called them complete disasters. Some recent bad outcomes include Sprint Nextel taking IBM (the outsourcing vendor) to court, claiming IBM failed to achieve productivity gains and owes Sprint 119 000 hours of work.

It was a US $400 million deal. After IBM failed to increase productivity by 6.4 percent, Sprint took 4500 outsourced call centre employees back. When IBM valued those services and sent a bill to Sprint management for the workers who had been "reclaimed," Sprint had sticker shock. In another case, Sears Kmart tore up its US $1.6 billion outsourcing contract with Computer Sciences Corporation (CSC) "for cause." CSC is suing Sears Kmart.

What's going on here? Why is it so difficult for large firms to get along with their outsourcing partners and cut a deal that makes sense for both parties? There are many sources of the problem, but chief among them are the failure of firms to adequately value their internal staffs and failure to understand their own cost structure. And when an outsourcer comes along and says "We can do it cheaper, faster, and better," management of many firms really have no data to evaluate these claims. Once they sign the contract, they quickly learn that the vendors will charge for every hour of work, and they often find out it was cheaper to do the work in-house rather than pay market rates charged by vendors, plus a healthy profit margin.

But there are also lessons here from the successful outsourcing deals. Ontario Power Generation (OPG) has had a long-term $1 billion relationship with consulting firm Capgemini, which provides 80 percent of the power company's IT services. In this case, the firms did something quite unique: They set up a joint venture company to perform the work and share the risks and the rewards. In this way, both firms had an incentive to save OPG money and to do the work properly. Campbell Soup has had a successful outsourcing relationship with IBM since 1995 although the relationship has gone through periods of strain.

In both Campbell Soup's and OPG's cases, the firms have developed long-term strategic alliances with their vendors. Both parties have been able to take the other partner's interests into account as the relationship has evolved. Flexibility, trust, performance, and even self-sacrifice seem to be the key factors here. In these cases, it is not just about money, it is also about continuing a mutually beneficial relationship even if, sometimes, in some cases, you pay a financial price. These deals are so big and so long term, it is impossible to write iron-clad contracts. However, successful strategic alliances have a high failure rate. When they work, it is wonderful, and when they do not, it is awful.

Researchers at MIT Center for Information Systems Research (CISR) have identified two other outsourcing models: transaction relationships and co-sourcing alliances. In transaction relationships, the firm precisely understands its costs and has a well-defined understanding of the functions it wants to outsource. In these cases, writing contracts for relatively small chunks of IT services is more straightforward and less given to later surprises and misinterpretations. In co-sourcing alliances, both the vendor and the firm co-manage and co-own the outsourcing project. Here too there tends to be a more precise understanding of costs and benefits, and a greater transparency because both partners "own" the outcome. Over two-thirds of transaction relationships and co-sourcing alliances work out successfully.

1. What is the basis for vendor firms claiming they can provide IT services more economically than a firm's own IT staff?
2. Why is it difficult to write iron-clad legal contracts specifying in detail strategic alliance outsourcing relationships?
3. Why do joint ventures and co-sourcing outsourcing relationships have a better chance of success?

1. Capgemini is one of the largest IT service firms. Visit its Web site (**www.capgemini.com**). Identify and describe the company's outsourcing services. What are the benefits it promises to deliver?
2. At the Capgemini Web site, read one of the company's success stories of collaboration with a Canadian firm for providing IT services. Describe what is being outsourced and identify what type of outsourcing relationship is being used (strategic, transaction, or co-sourcing). Do you think this is the right model for the work being performed?
3. Review the article "In Depth: Customers Analyze Outsourcing Vendors and Strategies," by Paul McDougall, *InformationWeek*, June 19, 2006. This article is available at **www.informationweek.com**. What are the motivations for using outsourcing? Is outsourcing expected to grow, and why?

Sources: Stephanie Overby, "Big Deals, Big Savings, Big Problems," *CIO Magazine*, February 1, 2006 and "Simple Successful Outsourcing," *CIO Magazine*, October 1, 2005; and Paul McDougall, "In Depth: When Outsourcing Goes Bad," *InformationWeek*, June 19, 2006.

Sometimes a technique called **joint application design** (**JAD**) is used to accelerate the generation of information requirements and to develop the initial systems design. JAD brings end users and information systems specialists together in an interactive session to discuss the system's design. Properly prepared and facilitated, JAD sessions can significantly speed up the design phase and involve users at an intense level.

Agile development focuses on rapid delivery of working software by breaking a large project into a series of small sub-projects that are completed in short periods of time using iteration and continuous feedback. Each mini-project is worked on by a team as if it were a complete project, including planning, requirements analysis, design, coding, testing, and documentation. Improvement or addition of new functionality takes place within the next iteration as developers clarify requirements. This helps to minimize the overall risk, and allows the project to adapt to changes more quickly. Agile methods emphasize face-to-face communication over written documents, encouraging people to collaborate and make decisions quickly and effectively.

Component-Based Development and Web Services

We have already described some of the benefits of object-oriented development for developing systems that can respond to rapidly changing business environments, including Web applications. To further expedite software creation, groups of objects have been assembled to provide software components for common functions such as a graphical user interface or online ordering capability that can be combined to create large-scale business applications. This approach to software development is called **component-based development**, and it

Joint application design (JAD)
Agile development
Component-based development

enables a system to be developed by assembling and integrating existing software components. Businesses are using component-based development to create their e-commerce applications by combining commercially available components for shopping carts, user authentication, search engines, and catalogues with pieces of software for their own unique business requirements.

Web Services and Service-Oriented Computing Chapter 5 introduced *Web services* as loosely coupled, reusable software components deliverable using Extensible Markup Language (XML) and other open protocols and standards that enable one application to communicate with another with no custom programming required to share data and services.

In addition to supporting internal and external integration of systems, Web services can be used as tools for developing new information system applications or enhancing existing systems. Because these software services use a universal set of standards, they promise to be less expensive and less difficult to weave together than proprietary components.

Web services can perform certain functions on their own, and they can also engage other Web services to complete more complex transactions, such as checking credit, procurement, or ordering products. By creating software components that can communicate and share data regardless of the operating system, programming language, or client device, Web services can provide significant cost savings in systems development while opening up new opportunities for collaboration with other companies.

The Capability Maturity Model The Capability Maturity Model (CMM) was originally developed as a tool for objectively assessing the ability of government contractors' processes to perform a contracted software project. Today, many organizations use it to assess the level at which their information systems support their business processes. The model identifies five levels of process maturity for an organization:

1. Initial (chaotic, ad hoc, heroic)—the starting point for use of a new process
2. Repeatable (project management, process discipline)—the process is used repeatedly
3. Defined (institutionalized)—the process is defined/confirmed as a standard business process
4. Managed (quantified)—process management and measurement takes place
5. Optimizing (process improvement)—process management includes deliberate process optimization/improvement

Obviously, the higher level indicates more maturity in the organization's business processes. This finding can be used as a benchmark either within the organization or in comparison to other organizations.

SUMMARY

1. *How does developing new information systems produce organizational change?*

   Developing a new information system is a form of planned organizational change. Four kinds of technology-enabled change are (a) automation, (b) rationalization of procedures, (c) business re-engineering, and (d) paradigm shift, with far-reaching changes carrying the greatest risks and rewards. Many organizations are attempting business re-engineering to redesign work flows and business processes in the hope of achieving dramatic productivity breakthroughs. Information systems can also be used to support business process management, total quality management (TQM), six sigma, and other initiatives for incremental process improvement.

2. *What are the core activities in the information systems development process?*

   The core activities in information systems development are systems analysis, systems design, programming, testing, conversion, production, and maintenance. Systems analysis is the study and analysis of problems of existing systems and the identification of requirements for their solutions. Systems design provides the specifications for an information system solution, showing how its technical and organizational components fit together. The next four activities are typically done in order.

3. *What are the principal methodologies for modelling and designing information systems?*

The two principal methodologies for modelling and designing information systems are structured methodologies and object-oriented development. Structured methodologies focus on modelling processes and data separately. The data flow diagram is the principal tool for structured analysis, and the structure chart is the principal tool for representing structured software design. Object-oriented development models a system as a collection of objects that combine processes and data. Object-oriented modelling is based on the concepts of class and inheritance.

4. *What are the alternative methods for developing information systems?*

The oldest method for developing systems is the systems life cycle, which requires that information systems be developed in formal stages. The stages must proceed sequentially and have defined outputs; each requires formal approval before the next stage can commence. The systems life cycle is useful for large projects that need formal specifications and tight management control over each stage of systems development, but it is very rigid and costly.

Prototyping consists of developing an experimental system rapidly and inexpensively for end users to interact with and evaluate. Prototyping encourages end-user involvement in systems development and iteration of design until specifications are captured accurately. The rapid creation of prototypes can result in systems that have not been completely tested or documented or that are technically inadequate for a production environment.

Using a software package reduces the amount of design, programming, testing, installation, and maintenance work required to develop a system. Application software packages are helpful if a firm does not have the internal information systems staff or financial resources to custom develop a system. To meet an organization's unique requirements, packages may require extensive modifications that can substantially raise development costs.

End-user development is the development of information systems by end users, either alone or with minimal assistance from information systems specialists. End-user-developed systems can be created rapidly and informally using fourth-generation software tools. However, end-user development may create information systems that do not necessarily meet quality assurance standards and that are not easily controlled by traditional means.

Outsourcing consists of using an external vendor to develop (or operate) a firm's information systems instead of the organization's internal information systems staff. Outsourcing can save application development costs or enable firms to develop applications without an internal information systems staff. However, firms risk losing control over their information systems and becoming too dependent on external vendors. Outsourcing also entails "hidden" costs, especially when the work is sent offshore.

5. *What are new approaches for systems development in the digital firm era?*

Companies are turning to rapid application design, joint application design (JAD), agile development, and reusable software components to accelerate the systems development process. Rapid application development (RAD) uses object-oriented software, visual programming, prototyping, and fourth-generation tools for very rapid creation of systems. Agile development breaks a large project into a series of small sub-projects that are completed in short periods of time using iteration and continuous feedback. Component-based development expedites application development by grouping objects into suites of software components that can be combined to create large-scale business applications. Web services provide a common set of standards that enable organizations to link their systems regardless of their technology platform through standard plug- and-play architecture.

Key Terms

Review Questions

1. *How does developing new information systems produce organizational change?*

- *Describe each of the four kinds of organizational change that can be promoted with information technology.*

- *Define business process re-engineering, and explain how it differs from business process management. Describe the steps required for effective re-engineering.*

- *Explain how information systems support process changes that promote quality in an organization.*

2. *What are the core activities in the information systems development process?*

- *Distinguish between systems analysis and systems design. Describe the activities for each.*

- *Define information requirements, and explain why they are difficult to determine correctly.*

- *Explain why the testing stage of systems development is so important. Name and describe the three stages of testing for an information system.*

- *Describe the role of programming, conversion, production, and maintenance in systems development.*

3. *What are the principal methodologies for modelling and designing information systems?*

- *Compare object-oriented and traditional structured approaches for modelling and designing systems.*

4. *What are the alternative methods for developing information systems?*

- *Define the traditional systems life cycle. Describe each of its steps and its advantages and disadvantages for systems development.*

- *Define information systems prototyping. Describe its benefits and limitations. List and describe the steps in the prototyping process.*

- *Define an application software package. Explain the advantages and disadvantages of developing information systems based on software packages.*

- *Define end-user development, and describe its advantages and disadvantages. Name some policies and procedures for managing end-user development.*

- *Describe the advantages and disadvantages of using outsourcing for developing information systems.*

5. *What are new approaches for information systems development in the digital firm era?*

- *Define rapid application development (RAD) and agile development, and explain how they can speed up system development.*

- *Explain how component-based development and Web services help firms develop and enhance their information systems.*

Discussion Questions

1. *Why is selecting a systems development approach an important business decision? Who should participate in the selection process?*

2. *Some have said that the best way to reduce systems development costs is to use application software packages or fourth-generation tools. Do you agree? Why or why not?*

Collaboration and Teamwork: Preparing Web Site Design Specifications

With three or four of your classmates, select a system described in this text that uses the Web. Review the Web site for the system you select. Use what you have learned from the Web site and the description in this book to prepare a report describing some of the design specifications for the system you select. If possible, use Google Sites to post links to Web pages, team communication announcements, and work assignments; to brainstorm; and to work collaboratively on project documents. Try to use Google Docs to develop a presentation of your findings for the class.

Visit the MyMISLab Web site at **www.pearsoned.ca/mymislab.** This online homework and tutorial system puts you in control of your own learning with study and practice tools directly correlated to this chapter's content.

Learning Track Module

The following Learning Tracks provide content relevant to topics covered in this chapter:

1. Unified Modelling Language (UML)

2. A Primer on Business Process Design and Documentation

HANDS-ON MIS   Projects

The projects in this section give you hands-on experience analyzing business process problems, designing and developing a customer system for auto sales, and redesigning business processes for a company that wants to purchase goods over the Web.

Management Decision Problems

1. For an additional fee, a customer purchasing a Sears appliance, such as a washing machine, can purchase a three-year service contract. The contract provides free repair service and parts for the specified appliance using an authorized Sears service provider. When a person with a Sears service contract needs to repair an appliance, such as a washing machine, he calls the Sears Repairs & Parts department to schedule an appointment. The department makes the appointment and gives the caller the date and approximate time of the appointment. The repair technician arrives during the designated time frame and diagnoses the problem. If the problem is caused by a faulty part, the technician either replaces the part if he is carrying the part with him or orders the replacement part from Sears. If the part is not in stock at Sears, Sears orders the part and gives the customer an approximate time when the part will arrive. The part is shipped directly to the customer. After the part has arrived, the customer must call Sears to schedule a second appointment for a repair technician to replace the ordered part. This process is very lengthy. It may take two weeks to schedule the first repair visit, another two weeks to order and receive the required part, and another week to schedule a second repair visit after the ordered part has been received.

   - Diagram the existing process.
   - What is the impact of the existing process on Sears's operational efficiency and customer relationships?
   - What changes could be made to make this process more efficient? How could information systems support these changes? Diagram the new improved process.

2. Management at your agricultural chemicals corporation has been dissatisfied with production planning. Production plans are created using best guesses of demand for each product, which are based on how much of each product has been ordered in the past. If a customer places an unexpected order or requests a change to an existing order after it has been placed, there is no way to adjust production plans. The company may have to tell customers it cannot fill their orders, or it may run up extra costs maintaining additional inventory to prevent stockouts.

   At the end of each month, orders are totalled and manually keyed into the company's production planning system. Data from the past month's production and inventory systems are manually entered into the firm's order management system. Analysts from the sales department and from the production department analyze the data from their respective systems to determine what the sales targets and production targets should be for the next month. These estimates are usually different. The analysts then get together at a high-level planning meeting to revise the production and sales targets to take into account senior management's goals for market share, revenues, and profits. The outcome of the meeting is a finalized production master schedule.

   The entire production planning process takes 17 business days to complete. Nine of these days are required to enter and validate the data. The remaining days are spent developing and reconciling the production and sales targets and finalizing the production master schedule.

   - Draw a diagram of the existing production planning process.
   - Analyze the problems this process creates for the company.
   - How could an enterprise system solve these problems? In what ways could it lower costs? Diagram what the production planning process might look like if the company implemented enterprise software.

Improving Decision Making: Using Database Software to Design a Customer System for Auto Sales

Software skills: Database design, querying, reporting, and forms
Business skills: Sales lead and customer analysis

This project requires you to perform a systems analysis and then design a system solution using database software.

Fictional Ace Auto Dealers specializes in selling new vehicles from Subaru. The company advertises in local newspapers and also is listed as an authorized dealer on the Subaru Web site and other major Web sites for auto buyers. The company benefits from a good local word-of-mouth reputation and name recognition and is a leading source of information for Subaru vehicles in the Halifax, Nova Scotia, area.

Upon entering the showroom, a customer is greeted by an Ace sales representative. The sales representative manually fills out a form with information such as the prospective customer's name, address, telephone number, date of visit, and make and model of the vehicle in which the customer is interested. The representative also asks where the prospect heard about Ace—whether it was from a newspaper ad, the Web, or word of mouth—and this information is also noted on the form. If the customer decides to purchase a vehicle, the dealer fills out a bill of sale form.

Ace does not believe it has enough information about its customers. It cannot easily determine which prospects have made auto purchases, and it cannot identify which customer touch points have produced the greatest number of sales leads or actual sales so it can focus advertising and marketing more on the channels that generate the most revenue. Are purchasers discovering Ace from newspaper ads, from word of mouth, or from the Web?

Prepare a systems analysis report detailing Ace's problem and a system solution that can be implemented using PC database management software. Then use database software to develop a simple system solution. Your systems analysis report should include the following:

- Description of the problem and its organizational and business impact
- Proposed solution, solution objectives, and solution feasibility
- Costs and benefits of the solution you have selected; the company has a PC with Internet access and the full suite of Microsoft Office desktop productivity tools
- Information requirements to be addressed by the solution
- Management, organization, and technology issues to be addressed by the solution, including changes in business processes

On the basis of the requirements you have identified, design the database and populate it with at least 10 records per table. Consider whether you can use or modify Ace's existing customer database in your design. You can find this database on the MyMISLab for Chapter 9. Print out the database design. Then use the system you have created to generate queries and reports that would be of most interest to management. Create several prototype data input forms for the system and review them with your instructor. Then revise the prototypes.

Achieving Operational Excellence: Redesigning Business Processes for Web Procurement

Software skills: Web browser software
Business skills: Procurement

This project requires you to rethink how a business should be redesigned when it moves to the Web.

You are in charge of purchasing for your firm and would like to use the Acklands-Grainger.com (**www.acklandsgrainger.com**) B2B e-commerce site for this purpose. Find out how to place an order for painting supplies by exploring the capabilities of this site. Do not register at the site. Describe all the steps your firm would need to take to use this system to place orders online for 30 litres of paint stripper. Include a diagram of what you think your firm's business process for purchasing should be and the information required by this process.

In a traditional purchase process, whoever is responsible for making the purchase fills out a requisition form and submits it for approval based on the company's business rules. When the requisition is approved, a purchase order with a unique purchase order identification number is sent to the supplier. The purchaser might want to browse supplier catalogues to compare prices and features before placing the order. The purchaser might also want to determine whether the items to be purchased are available. If the purchasing firm were an approved customer, that company would be granted credit to make the purchase and would be billed for the total cost of the items purchased and shipped after the order was shipped. Alternatively, the purchasing company might have to pay for the order in advance or pay for the order using a credit card. Multiple payment options might be possible. How might this process have to change to make purchases electronically from the Acklands-Grainger site?

CASE STUDY   Lemontonic and .NET: A Match Made on the Web

Lemontonic is not just another Canadian Web site developed within the Microsoft .NET environment. It is a Canadian online dating site that is active in Quebec, Ontario, and British Columbia, as well as around the world.

Based in Toronto, Lemontonic identified four challenges in the online dating industry for which the company felt instant messaging (IM) was the answer. These challenges were connectivity (eliminating blind dates), control (selecting who can communicate with you), comfort (sharing and involvement), and convenience (instant connection). Unlike other online dating services that use e-mail, Lemontonic decided that its Web presence would revolve around instant messaging.

Scott Rogers, vice president of marketing at Lemontonic, says, "The reason I was so keen on starting this business was that I saw from my time at another online dating service that a number of consumer needs weren't being satisfied. We wanted to make the online dating experience more lifelike and realized we needed to create a dating application that had both a Web component and an instant messaging component." Rogers felt this would provide a more realistic and enjoyable way through which individuals could meet online.

To do this, Lemontonic engaged Eidenai Innovations (EI), a Canadian "software solutions firm," that is, an outsourcing consulting firm. EI was founded in 1999 by two IT professionals, Sunil Abraham and Orren Johnson, with experience working in larger firms. EI has experience with some of Canada's leading financial firms, such as CIBC and Bank of Montreal, telecommunications firms (Vonage and Nortel), and others, such as Labatt Breweries. EI is a Microsoft Gold Certified and Managed Partner, and in 2003, EI became Microsoft's number-two subcontracted development partner in terms of revenue and contracts awarded in Canada. Lemontonic decided that EI provided the right skill set to develop the Web site and customer service site for the online dating service. In less than a year from awarding the contract to EI, Lemontonic's Web presence and customer service site were online. This rapid application development cost Lemontonic about $6 million over a two-year period.

Because of the speed needed to get the Web site up and running, EI used the .NET environment. According to David Benoliel, executive vice president of EI, "We built a case for using .NET because we needed the ability to quickly deploy solutions." We had a very short time-to-market schedule and had two large projects to finish: the Web site and the instant messaging application." The .NET platform also could enable these two applications to integrate with other .NET-compatible technologies.

The "Lemontonic Solution Platform" includes a Microsoft .NET-based rich-client IM application that is available for free download. The IM application integrates with the Web-based interface to give the user an enhanced interaction with the ability to have direct, real-time communication with prospective dates. There are also corporate functions including content validation and account management as well as direct marketing and campaigning and business reporting. The site should support 10 million registered users with 100 000 simultaneous active users.

EI used many Microsoft products to develop these applications, including ASP.NET and Visual C#® development tool in Visual Studio® .NET. EI also used Commerce Server 2002, enabling the company to quickly develop functionality, such as billing, subscription, and promotions into the application. SQL Server 2000 provides the scalability needed for the rapid growth Lemontonic envisioned. Interestingly, EI also incorporated Microsoft Passport, used by many worldwide for logging into Hotmail and similar Microsoft-related sites, to authenticate users. By integrating Microsoft CRM, Microsoft's

customer relationship management application, Lemontonic was also able to route user requests to the company's customer service representatives.

The result: In its first three months, Lemontonic signed up 60 000 members. In addition, the system was developed for high-availability computing, with fault tolerance built in throughout the IT infrastructure.

Three months after the Web site was first launched, the instant messaging application was launched. The IM application includes chat, video, and audio functionality, and even permits two users to jointly explore the Web in a shared browser. Rogers wanted this exploration capability to give the users an activity to do together after the first moments of saying hello, when awkward silences can occur in an online relationship just starting out.

It is interesting that the most traditional activity—finding and getting to know people to date—has been translated almost intact to the Web. Instead of asking a potential date if he or she wants to "hang out" or "go to the movies," individuals can ask potential dates if they want to "look at my favourite Web site with me" or "meet up in a chat room" or "watch a video online together." Rogers's vision for Lemontonic recognized this and incorporated the familiarity of starting out dating into Lemontonic's Web presence, producing a site that has grown rapidly to more than 5 million users worldwide. In 2006, Lemontonic was acquired by Pioneering Technology, Inc. in a reverse merger acquisition. By October 2008, Lemontonic had become a partner in the Badoo social networking site that has more than 27 million members.

CASE STUDY QUESTIONS:

1. Write a systems analysis report about the Lemontonic instant messaging system. What do you think may have been the problems with previous similar systems? What management, organization, and technology factors do you think caused the problems? What do you think was the impact of these problems? What are the objectives and information requirements of a new systems solution?

2. As part of your report, diagram the new member subscription process for joining Lemontonic. How could this process be improved?

3. Describe what you think the role of end users and technical specialists should have been in analyzing the Lemontonic situation and developing a solution.

Sources: "Online Daters Get Up Close and Personal at Microsoft .NET-based Lemontonic.com," **www.microsoft.com/canada/casestudies/ lemontonic.mspx** (accessed September 24, 2009); "Lemontonic Appoints Kaleil Isaza Tuzman to Board," **www.newswire.ca/releases/ archive/February2005/24/c7770.html?view=print** (accessed April 19, 2007); "EI Case Studies: Lemontonic," **www.eidenai.ca/EI/ SiteContent/CaseStudies/Pages/LemontonicCaseStudy.html** (accessed April 19, 2007); "About EI: Vision," **www.eidenai.ca/EI/ SiteContent/About/Vision** (accessed April 19, 2007); "About EI: Clients," **www.eidenai.ca/EI/SiteContent/About/Clients** (accessed April 19, 2007); "Lemontonic: The Revolution of Life Online," **www.lemontonic.com** (accessed April 19, 2007).

CHAPTER 10

Information Resource Management and Project Management

OPENING CASE

Cargo Portal Services Brings Competitors Together

We have seen how UPS, Federal Express, and several other companies have taken advantage of the World Wide Web and the Internet to improve customer service and lower customer costs. By permitting customers to book online—and even be billed online—these companies have offered smaller shipping customers greatly improved service while lowering their own and their customers' costs.

Another company that is using the Web and Internet to its advantage is Cargo Portal Services (CPS), owned and run by Unisys, the computer manufacturer and consulting firm. CPS is an electronic booking and shipment management service for the air cargo industry. It was designed in cooperation with major carriers and forwarders. Access to CPS is free for forwarders through the Internet and through secure system-to-system connections. CPS serves more than 5000 branch offices of 2000 forwarding companies in 120 countries. CPS is the first full-service Internet portal for the air cargo industry. CPS opened for business in 2003 with only three carriers (Air Canada, United Airlines, and Northwest Airlines) and today offers transportation services from 580 cities in over 100 countries through the global cargo networks of Air Canada, Austrian Airlines, KLM, Delta Airlines, United Airlines, Continental Airlines, American Airlines, Air France, and SAS.

CPS provides neutral multi-carrier booking facilities with agreed rates and allotments; proactive shipment event management and tracking in-line with industry best practice; and computer system-to-system communications for better integration between forwarders and carriers.

Air cargo has struggled to enter the Internet age. Web-based solutions for booking space and managing shipments have either failed due to unrealistic visions or have been slowed down by complex IT integration issues. A major problem is the wide range of different legacy systems in use by airlines and their freight forwarder customers. Booking procedures also vary from airline to airline. Personal relationships remain important, preventing new technology take-up.

Three airlines—Northwest Airlines, United Airlines, and Air Canada—decided to break through that barrier. Putting aside their commercial rivalry, they agreed on an approach for a Web-based booking and shipment management system. In May 2002, they asked Unisys to make that vision a reality. Working closely with the original three carriers and their customers, Unisys used XML interfaces and a modular approach to deliver a system that was so flexible and easy to use that it quickly gained market acceptance.

Unisys offered in-depth experience in the realities of the cargo business combined with a will to help make it more successful. Its air cargo system was used by two of the carriers, and it also had valuable Web development and integration expertise from other projects.

Cost and speed were also key factors. With a rival platform already up and running, the three carriers were keen to bring their solution to market very quickly. After September 11, 2001, investments had also been slashed in the airline industry. Unisys could draw on its existing air cargo solutions and bring world-class expertise from other parts of its business to provide a faster and more cost-effective solution. The solution was able to go live just six months after Unisys was appointed.

The big challenge was to devise a system that could work not just with a wide range of legacy IT systems but also with the different procedures among airlines. These included not only divergent booking procedures but also different attitudes to pricing. Recognizing that most shipments are sold at negotiated rates, the group decided not to waste time developing a price quotation system. As a result, the group avoided one of the pitfalls of failed dot-com solutions that had tried to use auction models of selling capacity.

It was also important to create a solution that would be acceptable not just to the forwarder customers, but also other carriers. "Forwarders don't want to go to a large number of carrier sites; they want one portal they can use to book across airlines," said Mark Haeussler, director of cargo strategic planning and business development at United Airlines. That meant the site had to not only meet the needs of the three launch carriers but also had to make adoption easy for other carriers that would join after the portal went live.

The technology decisions made by CPS were not unduly complex. For flexibility of interfaces, XML was the obvious choice. XML was the best way to connect the portal with the diverse systems in the air cargo industry and allowed for future customization. "There is now recognition among carriers that XML is the way forward, even if they are progressing at different speeds," said Steve Schuppenhauer, Unisys technical architect. "We are taking advantage of that trend and driving it forward."

Most important of all in the swift and successful development of the system, however, was the way the airlines and Unisys worked together. The three carriers remained closely involved in the project, taking on project roles and holding weekly development meetings with Unisys. Forwarders, the users of the system and the key to its success or failure, were also involved at all stages. "A key factor for success is that early on we focused on a clear set of requirements," said Jim Friedel, president of Northwest Airlines Cargo. "We hammered down our different wish lists to something achievable. That is a key reason why the project was able to succeed."

The result, however, was that before a line of code was written, the exact functionality of the portal had been clearly defined. "This was the most challenging aspect of the project," said Unisys project manager Dave Fischer. "But I have to hand it to the carriers. They really came together, and we merged three perspectives into a common approach so the objectives were very clear."

Involvement of forwarders also dated back to the early days of the project. A group of nine forwarders of varying sizes and scope had been consulted by the three carriers when drawing up their original plans. They continued to participate fully in the specification and development phases through a series of meetings and test sessions. This involvement was important to minimize the amount of reworking needed during the test phase. Glitches were ironed out at an early stage, and customer views were reflected in the final design.

The real importance of forwarder participation came when the system went live in January 2003. The biggest barrier CPS had to overcome in the industry at large was a resistance to new technology: Front-line staff in forwarder offices remained fond of traditional booking methods such as the phone and fax. The solution was to undertake exhaustive testing of CPS's functionality with an advisory group of ten forwarders throughout

the development process. Too often the real users are ignored when systems are being developed. CPS ensured that the portal was offering what booking staff needed and in the way that they needed it. To save costs and speed up adoption, it was also important to minimize the need to train forwarder staff. "If you put the system in front of them, they should be able to use it straightaway," said Air Canada's manager of cargo marketing, sales planning and support, Gerald Simpson, who took charge of training for the portal. Early tests were successful. "After demonstration sessions in October and November 2002, we asked forwarders what training they needed," recalls Simpson. "They said that they were comfortable, after one viewing, that they could tell the rest of their staff how it worked."

For Friedel, CPS represents a case study in successful project management. "Success was all about the people on the project team and the way they took decisions. We avoided transformational technology. We did not try and rebuild institutions—just to substitute technology for what is currently done by phone. Most of all, we kept the design simple for users. With a vision that simple and the team approach to the technical aspects, the odds of success were 100 percent." Since opening the portal in 2003, CPS continues to increase functionality. In 2004, CPS added waybill (a receipt for shipped goods) processing and a reusable template for recurring bookings

to its services. CPS introduced house waybill services in response to the new United States Customs and Border Patrol four-hour ruling. The ruling requires that airlines and forwarders provide the house waybill details of shipments no less than four hours in advance of flights arriving into the United States. If this information is not provided to U.S. Customs, shipments will be delayed, often creating a domino effect because more than one flight segment may be required before a shipment arrives at its final destination. CPS now offers three ways in which carriers and forwarders can use the new house waybill service: via the Web; through an XML system-to-system interface with forwarder systems; or through an EDI-Internet interface with forwarder systems using the FHL message. CPS also launched "recycle booking," which gives users an easy way to submit their permanent or recurring bookings. CPS continues to add airline partners and freight forwarder clients to its portal. As can be seen by the recent introduction of additional service, CPS is attempting to be the "go-to" air cargo portal.

Sources: "Cargo Portal Services Launches Two New Services," *Enterprise Networks and Servers*, October 2004; "Multi-carrier Web-Based Booking for Air Cargo," available **www.unisys.com/transportation/clients/featured__case__studies/northwest__airlines_c0__united__airlines__and__air__canada__case__study.htm** (accessed May 22, 2005); "American Airlines Cargo to Join Unisys-Operated Cargo Portal Services," *Logistics Management*, May 2, 2005.

One of the principal challenges posed by information systems is ensuring they can deliver genuine business benefits. There is a very high failure rate among information systems projects because organizations have incorrectly assessed their business value or because firms have failed to manage the organizational change surrounding the introduction of new technology.

CPS's management realized this when it authorized its electronic booking and shipment management project. The project was massive and ambitious, but CPS succeeded because it practised sound project management.

The chapter-opening diagram calls attention to important points raised by this case and this chapter. CPS is in a competitive industry; there are low profit margins. The company was able to

improve booking and shipping management by implementing a project that met both customers' and users' needs. Although the project was large and complex, management carefully defined the project goals, scope, requirements, and implementation team responsibilities. Strong management leadership and communication between information systems specialists and end users were essential.

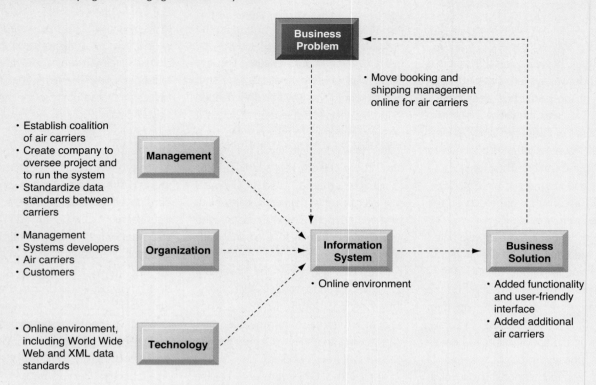

10.1   Information Resource Management

Information resource management (IRM) is the process of managing information systems—including hardware, software, data and databases, telecommunications, people, and the facilities that house these IS components—as an asset or resource that is critical to the organization. As recently as 30 years ago, the information systems department was thought of as an "ivory tower" peopled by "pointy-headed geeks" who spoke "technobabble." Running the IS department as though it were any other business function was considered impossible by non-IS managers. What a difference 30 years makes!

Today IS departments are well managed, with personnel regulations and budgets, just like every other department. Like all departments, appropriate, well-thought-out management principles should be used to maximize the value of the IS department. That is the heart of IRM. In the following subsections, we review the basic components of IRM. While we assume that IS managers need to know these components, we also feel strongly that all managers should understand IRM in order to interact effectively and efficiently with the IS department. The IS department is a service provider to other departments and should be held accountable for the level of service provided. Managers who understand the components of IRM can accurately evaluate the level of service their department is provided by the IS department.

The Information Systems Department

Almost every organization today has a computer. Whether there is only one computer and only one individual who uses it or whether there are thousands of computers located around the world, the duties and functions of the information systems department are vested in one or more individuals. Whether these duties are explicit, as they are in middle- to large-sized organizations, or implicit, as in a "mom-and-pop" shop, these duties must be handled. The IS department has the following duties and functions:

- Manage computer operations
- Manage systems development and systems development projects
- Manage IS personnel
- Budget for the department and others in the organization who use computers
- Plan for strategic, tactical, and operational level systems and for the IS department's operations
- Justify financial investment in information systems

IS departments are structured like other departments; they have managers at all levels and frequently division of duties and reporting responsibilities. A typical IS department will have divided its duties into several divisions, such as systems development, telecommunications, e-commerce/Web, database management, user relations/support, and operations. Each of these divisions might have subdivisions; for example, systems development might have two subdivisions, such as new development and maintenance. Each of the divisions would have a manager to whom those IS staff members assigned to that division would report. Division managers would report to the IS department manager. Figure 10-1 shows a typical IS department structure.

The IS department manager may or may not be the **chief information officer (CIO).** The CIO is the strategic level manager for information systems. As a member of senior management, the CIO is responsible for strategic level IS planning and for ensuring that all IS plans, systems, and operations support the organization's overall strategy. Some organizations have begun calling the CIO a chief technology officer (CTO) or chief knowledge officer (CKO).

In addition to the CIO at the strategic level, the organization may also make use of a management information systems (MIS) steering committee. The **MIS steering committee** sets policy and priorities for the IS department, including approving budgets for major projects and hearing progress reports on those major projects. The MIS steering committee is usually composed of the CIO and other members of senior management. In the best case scenario, the organization's CEO is also a member of the MIS steering committee. It is the responsibility of the CIO to represent the IS department on the MIS steering committee and to communicate effectively with the committee's membership, "selling" them and other top managers on the IS department's plans and projects.

Chief information officer (CIO)
MIS steering committee

FIGURE 10-1 A typical information systems department structure.

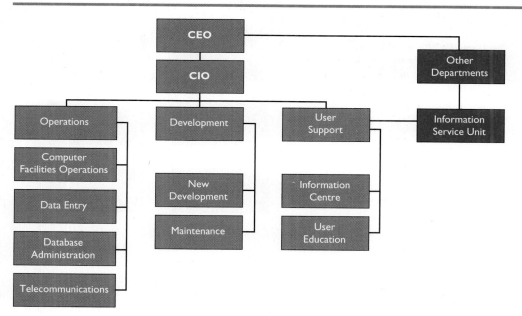

Each division has subdivisions to manage the overall departmental responsibilities.

Managing Planning, Strategy, and External Relations

Again, like every other department, the IS department should conduct periodic planning at all levels. Strategic IS plans describe, from a broad perspective, the major strategic information systems that support or will support the organization's strategy. These are long-range plans that have a huge impact on the organization and on the IS department. Tactical IS plans have a shorter focus and concentrate on breaking down the strategic IS plan into more detailed plans that middle-level managers can focus on implementing. Finally, operational level IS plans detail how the strategic IS plan will be implemented during the coming short term, usually one year. Specific goals and objectives permit measurement of how the IS department is performing in supporting the organization's strategy. Each of these sets of IS plans—strategic, tactical, and operational—should be *aligned* with the organization's strategy and with the organization's strategic-, tactical-, and operational-level plans (see Figure 10-2).

The CIO is responsible for ensuring that these plans are developed and aligned with the organization's plans. The CIO is also the major link to external parties, such as senior-level managers at vendor organizations and strategic partners' CIOs. While many CIOs have been promoted from the ranks of the IS department, because of the communication-intensive nature of the position, many CIOs come from other areas of the organization, such as finance or human resources.

Managing Systems Development

Systems development has many facets or perspectives. In Chapter 9, we looked at the systems development life cycle and at systems development as organizational change. In this chapter, we look at systems development in terms of managing the implemented system, personnel assignments to develop systems, and project management.

FIGURE 10-2 How information systems strategy and planning are aligned with organizational strategy and planning.

Figure 10-2A represents the organization's strategy and planning steps and levels while Figure 10-2B represents the IS department's strategy and planning steps and levels. The dashed lines represent alignment between the organizational and IS strategies and plans at all steps and levels.

Source: Mary Brabston, Robert Zmud, and John Carlson, "Strategic Vision for Information Technology," in *Strategic Information Technology: Opportunities for Competitive Advantage*, edited by Raymond Papp, Idea Group Publishing, 2000

In Chapter 8, we discussed information systems quality, security, and control in detail. These topics are also part of information resource management. Once a system has been implemented, it is the IS department's responsibility to ensure that policies, guidelines, and decisions about the implemented systems are followed. These responsibilities include ensuring that backups are made, that IS audits are conducted when and where appropriate, that appropriate security processes and appropriate controls, such as passwords and locked doors, are maintained and followed. Included in this are network, database, and Web management, which ensure that organizational and department policies are followed in each of these areas and that these parts of the organization's information systems are secure, reliable, available, and accessible as needed.

In previous chapters, we briefly discussed the role of systems analysts and programmers. IS departments also employ **systems operators** who run the hardware, including loading tape and disk drives, starting and stopping computer "jobs," and ensuring that backups are carried out as dictated by policy. **Data entry operators** enter data in computer-readable format and are managed by database managers. **Network managers** supervise networks while **Web masters** handle the organization's Web-based presence. Every organization organizes its IS department and information system components differently. Every organization also calls people who hold these generic positions by different names. A network manager in one organization may be a LAN coordinator in another, but the employee's function is the same.

Many organizations centralize their information systems so that most of the information systems components (hardware, software, etc.) are located centrally and managed by a central IS department. In centralized IS departments, most decisions about information systems are made in the IS department. Other organizations choose to decentralize their information systems, permitting organizational departments or divisions to make their own decisions about what information systems to develop or purchase, frequently housing their own networks, hardware, and software. Many of these decentralized organizations also employ extra IS staff who report to the decentralized unit.

Today, the trend is toward information service units and information centres. Figure 10-1 depicts this modern type of IS department structure. An information service unit is an IS group located within a non-IS department, such as marketing. The information service unit is employed by and reports to the IS department; the IS unit handles requests for systems development, training, or assistance from its assigned department, serving as an interface to the IS department. An information centre, also known as user support, is housed in the IS department but handles requests for support, training, assistance, and guidance from other departments. If the marketing department needs to determine whether to upgrade the operating system its desktop computers use, staff could call the information centre for advice.

Assigning Personnel to Develop Systems How does an IS manager decide who will be assigned to a particular systems development project? Should an experienced person be assigned to new projects or to maintaining those projects on which he or she has already worked? Should less experienced personnel be assigned to maintenance projects so that they may gain experience?

New systems development is considered to be creative and more desirable than maintenance, which is viewed similarly to semiannual checkups with your dentist: it has to be done, but you would rather not have to do it. Every organization handles the assignment of programmers and analysts to individual projects differently. Frequently, rotation is used, so that personnel may be assigned to new development for a project and, when that project is completed, move on to a maintenance project. Just as frequently, less experienced IS staff are partnered with more experienced staff on projects, who act as mentors and help them to gain higher levels of expertise.

Finally, the IS department is a service department, providing systems development and other services to other departments. Many businesses have implemented *service-level agreements*, in which the IS department signs an agreement with a department for which it is developing a system. The service-level agreement specifies milestones and deadlines,

Systems operators
Data entry operators
Network managers
Web masters

the budget, the level of service to be achieved, and other requested benchmarks. The IS department agrees to these terms and is held accountable by corporate management for meeting these benchmarks.

Managing Personnel

We mentioned above that IS staff were formerly viewed as "pointy-headed geeks." Previous generations of hardware and software required a high level of technical knowledge and expertise. Today's systems permit lower levels of technical knowledge, enabling those with a middle level of technical expertise to succeed as programmers and analysts. This trend has opened IS career tracks to non–computer science majors.

While computer science focuses more on the technical side of information systems, the management information system (MIS) field focuses on the needs of business that can be met by computer-based information systems. Today's IS departments hire both computer science and MIS staff to fulfill their personnel requirements. In addition, yesterday's pointy-headed geeks receive education and training in business applications and how to communicate effectively without using technobabble. More and more, the language of the IS department is "business-ese" instead of technobabble.

Regardless of whether IS staff members were hired with a computer science or MIS background, like all other organizational employees they must be evaluated periodically. Determining metrics on which to base IS staff evaluation is a difficult task. Should a programmer be evaluated on number of lines of code generated? The code could be inefficient and time consuming to run. Should function points be used instead? Function points define where an actual function has been performed, but some functions are complex while others are not. Do you evaluate an analyst on how well the assigned user area is satisfied with their analyst? Or how well the analyst works with his or her programming teams? Determining what criteria should be used in evaluating IS staff is a difficult task because each staff member's job presents a different mix of the technical and behavioural elements; the variation within the technical or behavioural elements and the mixing of the two, depending on the specific job, makes it difficult to develop and use evaluation criteria over a long period of time. A detailed discussion of this topic is beyond the scope of this text, but IS personnel must be evaluated and counselled on their performance on a periodic basis.

The last ten years have seen the salaries of IS staff increase rapidly and then level off. How does an organization recruit and retain IS staff when it cannot afford to give periodic raises that are as high as the local rate of increase for their classification? Some organizations have taken to giving bonuses based on work done, projects completed, or tenure in the organization. For example, in the late 1990s, The North West Company on occasion gave a "signing bonus" to new employees, accompanied by a retention bonus after one year on the job. Other organizations, such as the City of Winnipeg, have given their IS staff a year-end bonus, up to several thousand dollars, to those employees who have been there for several years. These loyalty bonuses serve to defuse the natural desire of IS staff to "follow the money." How does that fit the company's salary policy?

We sometimes hear in Canada about a "brain drain" to the South, in which skilled Canadians are being hired by U.S. companies at inflated salaries. Interestingly, there are experts on each side of the brain-drain issue—those who feel Canada is losing its best and brightest to the U.S. and those who disagree, arguing that the "brain drain" is based on almost mythical anecdotal evidence. Regardless of which opinion is correct, the bottom line for IRM is that IS managers must attempt to keep their employees happy. In a time when IS jobs are going unfilled, this makes sense. The depressed economy, particularly in the United States, should reduce the number of new IS jobs available. At least in this regard, perhaps the brain drain—if there ever was one—will subside. Today the number of IS jobs available has returned to pre–dot-com-bubble-bursting levels; in fact, a shortfall in the number of qualified applicants for entry-level and mid-level IS jobs is predicted for the short and even longer term, particularly in Canada.

With technology advancing so rapidly, how do IS staff keep their skills up to date? IS departments need to develop policies for staff to receive training and to upgrade their skills. Issues to be addressed by IS training policies are funding and time off to attend seminars, workshops, and courses; eligibility for funding and time off; the number of courses that can be taken in a given period; and the locus of the decision about continuing education (who decides which courses employees will take).

In addition to keeping employees' skills up to date, providing training opportunities is an excellent way to motivate employees and to retain them. The flip side of the coin is, of course, that the employees will now have advanced skills with which to seek other jobs. Maintaining a challenging, positive environment with a few "perks" such as casual day (now more of a norm than an exception) or an on-site day-care service also helps to retain employees.

Managing Budgets

How can an IS manager know what the budget for the IS department should be for the coming year? A detailed analysis of projects that are ongoing and projects that may come forward during the next year is required, along with determining the need to upgrade technologies. The IS department must also examine the potential for extraordinary raises or bonuses for exceptional performance to retain key IS staff in light of the trend in IS salaries. These are not easy calculations. IS projects are notorious for running over budget (see the discussion on change management later in this chapter.).

How do you know when you should upgrade hardware or software? What do you do when your most productive and effective analyst comes to you with a job offer in hand for a 10 percent raise and requests only a 5 percent raise to stay in your organization? How does that fit within the budget? Every IS organization handles its budgeting issues differently.

Many IS departments receive revenue from other departments in the form of *charge-backs*, or internal transfers of funds to reflect payment for services rendered. Chargebacks for a department can be calculated based on the department's computer usage, the number of nodes the department maintains on the LAN, IS department overhead charges based on the department's size in terms of number of employees or revenues generated, or myriad other ways. It is important that the method of chargeback is well communicated to department heads so that they understand the process and the charges.

Taken together, the topics discussed above comprise the major components of IRM. Being able to justify financial investments in information systems is also part of planning at all levels. The IS department must be able to explain and demonstrate that its budget and systems are worth the organization's financial commitment.

10.2   The Importance of Project Management

There is a very high failure rate among information systems projects. In nearly every organization, information systems projects take much more time and money to implement than originally anticipated, or the completed system does not work properly. When an information system fails to work properly or costs too much to develop, companies may not realize any benefit from their information system investment, and the system may not be able to solve the problems for which it was intended.

The development of a new system must be carefully managed and orchestrated, and the way a project is executed is likely to be the most important factor influencing its outcome. That is why it is essential to have some knowledge about managing information systems projects and the reasons that they succeed or fail.

Runaway Projects and System Failure

How badly are projects managed? On average, private-sector projects are underestimated by one-half in terms of budget and time required to deliver the complete system promised in

FIGURE 10-3   Consequences of poor project management.

the system plan. A very large number of projects are delivered with missing functionality (promised for delivery in later versions). The Standish Group consultancy, which monitors IT project success rates, found that only 29 percent of all technology investments were completed on time, on budget, and with all features and functions originally specified (Levinson, 2009). Between 30 and 40 percent of all software projects are "runaway" projects that far exceed the original schedule and budget projections and fail to perform as originally specified.

As illustrated in Figure 10-3, a systems development project without proper management will most likely suffer these consequences:

- Costs that vastly exceed budgets
- Unexpected time slippage
- Technical performance that is less than expected
- Failure to obtain anticipated benefits

The systems produced by failed information projects are often not used in the way they were intended, or they are not used at all. Users often have to develop parallel manual systems to make these systems work.

The actual design of the system may fail to capture essential business requirements or improve organizational performance. Information may not be provided quickly enough to be helpful; it may be in a format that is impossible to digest and use; or it may represent the wrong pieces of data.

The way in which nontechnical business users must interact with the system may be excessively complicated and discouraging. A system may be designed with a poor user interface. The **user interface** is the part of the system with which end users interact. For example, an online input form or data entry screen may be so poorly arranged that no one wants to submit data or request information. System outputs may be displayed in a format that is too difficult to comprehend (Spier and Morris, 2003).

Web sites may discourage visitors from exploring further if the Web pages are cluttered and poorly arranged, if users cannot easily find the information they are seeking, or if it takes too long to access and display the Web page on the user's computer.

Additionally, the data in the system may have a high level of inaccuracy or inconsistency. The information in certain fields may be erroneous or ambiguous, or it may not be organized properly for business purposes. Information required for a specific business function may be inaccessible because the data are incomplete.

The chapter-ending case provides an example of a failed project. To this day, the Canadian gun registry is the target of negative politics. A major factor in this failure was poor project management.

Project Management Objectives

A **project** is a planned series of related activities for achieving a specific business objective. Information systems projects include the development of new information systems, enhancement of existing systems, or upgrade or replacement of the firm's information technology (IT) infrastructure.

Project management refers to the application of knowledge, skills, tools, and techniques to achieve specific targets within specified budget and time constraints. Project management activities include planning the work, assessing risk, estimating resources required to accomplish the work, organizing the work, acquiring human and material

---

Without proper management, a systems development project takes longer to complete and most often exceeds the allocated budget. The resulting information system most likely is technically inferior and may not be able to demonstrate any benefits to the organization.

User interface
Project
Project management

resources, assigning tasks, directing activities, controlling project execution, reporting progress, and analyzing the results. As in other areas of business, project management for information systems must deal with five major variables: scope, time, cost, quality, and risk.

Scope defines what work is or is not included in a project. For example, the scope of a project for a new order processing system might be to include new modules for inputting orders and transmitting them to production and accounting but not any changes to related accounts receivable, manufacturing, distribution, or inventory control systems. Project management defines all the work required to complete a project successfully and should ensure that the scope of a project not expand beyond what was originally intended.

Time is the amount of time required to complete the project. Project management typically establishes the amount of time required to complete major components of a project. Each of these components is further broken down into activities and tasks. Project management tries to determine the time required to complete each task and establish a schedule for completing the work.

Cost is based on the time to complete a project multiplied by the cost of human resources required to complete the project. Information systems project costs also include the cost of hardware, software, and work space. Project management develops a budget for the project and monitors ongoing project expenses.

One of the types of projects that clearly has large scope is that of integrating systems between companies that have merged or been acquired. The Window on Management discusses how to handle this type of large, complex project.

Scope

Management

WINDOW ON MANAGEMENT

Managing IT in the Merger and Acquisition Game

Mergers and acquisitions (M&As) are on the rise in Canada. In the first three months of 2007, Ed Giacomellie of Crosbie & Co. counted 13 bids valued at more than $1 billion each. According to Giacomellie, "For the past seven quarters, we've been reporting activity of between 400 and 550 deals per quarter in Canada." "Due diligence" is the concept used to describe what acquirers should perform before they make an acquisition. Technically, for public firms, due diligence is a legal requirement of senior management to ensure the financial and business statements of firms they are acquiring are accurate and complete.

In the past, acquiring firms have lost a great deal of money by ignoring a very important element of the acquired firm's business, namely, its information systems. Because M&As are typically entered into for financial reasons (greater market share, elimination of competitors, greater efficiency and profitability) and are led by financial managers, it is understandable that sizing up the target company's IT infrastructure is last on the list of due diligence activities.

But there is a price to pay for ignoring the IT/IS element in mergers. There are a number of systems-related risks in M&As. The target company may have stopped spending on maintenance years ago to decrease costs and increase profits. It may have fallen behind competitors in new applications. Its software licences may not be transferable to the new company without significant new fees. The infrastructure may be outdated. The target company's systems may be totally incompatible with the acquirer's systems. For example, one important reason Logicalis, a U.K.–based IT integration and consulting company, backed off acquiring a value-added reseller was that the company's CRM system was incompatible with its own.

So how do companies perform due diligence in the information systems area? What are some management tactics for dealing with the merger of two or more very different IT infrastructures? The first step is to classify the assets your firm is about to acquire, create an inventory of these assets, and establish the value of these systems to the newly merged firm. For instance, you could divide the target firm's IT assets into four categories: transactional systems that perform the basic transactions of the firm; informational systems that inform management about the state of operations; strategic systems that differentiate the firm in the marketplace; and basic infrastructure that includes both the hardware and software installed as well as the services provided by the IS group to the business.

Once you have created an inventory of the target firm's IT assets, you will need to value their potential contribution to the new firm. There are four options: keep the target company systems if they are better than your own; keep your own systems and retire the target company systems if yours are better; choose the best of both companies' systems; or use the M&A to develop an entirely new infrastructure.

In general, firms rarely decide to develop a new infrastructure completely. Most commonly, the acquiring firms shut down systems of the acquired company and extend the reach of their own systems. Target firms are usually smaller and less capitalized than acquiring firms and have systems that lag behind those of the acquiring firm. Moreover, the financial rationale for many mergers is scale economies. The argument is that the existing IT/IS infrastructure of the acquiring firm can be expanded with minimal cost while the merged companies' revenues will increase manyfold. The same fixed costs in infrastructure will be able to support a much larger and more profitable business.

But the evidence that managers at acquiring firms really understand the risks of mergers and acquisitions is not encouraging. Studies of M&A activity over the past 75 years show that about 60 percent actually destroy shareholder value and result in falling stock prices for the acquiring company. The reasons are that the acquiring firm overvalues the assets of the target firm and systematically underestimates the risks of the acquisition, especially the costs of merging the operational activities and information system infrastructures of two firms.

To Think About

1. What are some of the risks involved when one firm acquires another firm's IT infrastructure?

2. Why do firms often fail to take the target firm's information systems and IT infrastructure into account when purchasing other firms?

3. How would you go about assessing the value of another firm's IT infrastructure and operational capabilities? What questions would you ask?

MIS in Action

1. Bain and Company is one of the premiere international business consulting firms specializing in advice about mergers and acquisitions. Visit **www.bain.ca,** to learn about the company's Canadian operations, and explore the advice on the company's main Web site, **www.bain.com,** on how to conduct a successful merger by clicking on the Consulting Expertise tab, then selecting Consulting Capabilities, and finally selecting Mergers & Acquisitions. Read this page, then click on Client Successes and choose the Mergers and Acquisitions capability. Why does Bain advise managers to stay close to its "core business?" Why might this advice ease the change in information systems infrastructure when mergers take place? What does Bain recommend about "integration" of the business and how would this affect IS/IT decisions?

2. On the Web, explore the IT/IS integration issues raised by one of these mega mergers of the past few years: Great West Life, Canada Life; Clarica/Sun Life; Toronto Dominion Bank, Canada Trust Bank; UJF/Mitsubishi Tokyo Financial; HEXAL/Novartis; or Kellogg/Keebler. You can explore these mergers using Google searches such as "Kellogg Keebler merger."

Sources: Eric Chabrow, "IT Plays Linchpin Role in High-Stakes M&As," *InformationWeek,* June 26, 2006; Spencer McIlmurray,]"M&A Survival Kit: Relearning Enterprise Addition and Subtraction," *CIO Magazine,* October 24, 2006; Nick Moore, "The New Role of the CIO in M&A Due Diligence," *Software Mag.com,* July, 2006; Dale Jackson, "You Can't Beat Barbarians, So Why Not Join the Invasion? A Money Manager Assesses Valuations to Predict Targets," CTV, **http://ctv2.theglobeandmail.com/servlet/story/LAC.20070410.RPRIVATE10/business/Business/Business/&id=LAC_20070410_ RPRIVATE10** (accessed April 20, 2007); CBC News, "Canadian Corporate Takeovers That Made News," **www.cbc.ca/news/background/mergers** (accessed April 20, 2007).

Quality is an indicator of how well the end result of a project satisfies the objectives specified by management. The quality of information systems projects usually boils down to improved organizational performance and decision making. Quality also considers the accuracy and timeliness of information produced by the new system and ease of use.

Risk refers to potential problems that would threaten the success of a project. These potential problems might prevent a project from achieving its objectives by increasing time and cost, lowering the quality of project outputs, or preventing the project from being completed altogether. Section 10.5 describes the most important risk factors for information systems.

10.3 Selecting Projects

Companies typically are presented with many different projects for solving problems and improving performance. There are far more ideas for systems projects than there are resources. Firms will need to select from this group the projects that promise the greatest benefit to the business. Obviously, the firm's overall business strategy should drive project selection.

FIGURE 10-4   Management control of systems projects.

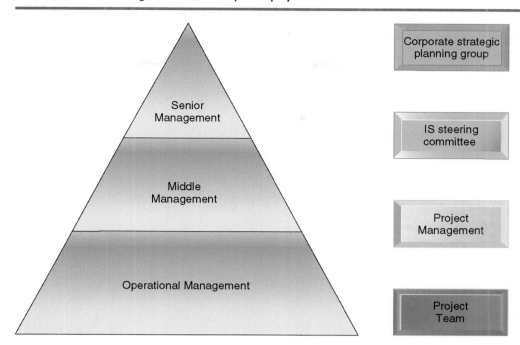

Each level of management in the hierarchy is responsible for specific aspects of systems projects, and this structure helps give priority to the most important systems projects for the organization.

Management Structure for Information Systems Projects

Figure 10-4 shows the elements of a management structure for information systems projects in a large corporation. It helps ensure that the most important systems projects are given priority.

At the apex of this structure is the corporate strategic planning group and the information system steering committee. The corporate strategic planning group is responsible for developing the firm's strategic plan, which may require the development of new systems.

The information systems steering committee is the senior management group with responsibility for systems development and operation. It is composed of department heads from both end-user and information systems areas. The steering committee reviews and approves plans for systems in all divisions, seeks to coordinate and integrate systems, and occasionally becomes involved in selecting specific information systems projects.

The project team is supervised by a project management group composed of information systems managers and end-user managers responsible for overseeing several specific information systems projects. The project team is directly responsible for the individual systems project. It consists of systems analysts, specialists from the relevant end-user business areas, application programmers, and perhaps database specialists. The mix of skills and the size of the project team depend on the specific nature of the system solution.

Linking Systems Projects to the Business Plan

In order to identify the information systems projects that will deliver the most business value, organizations need to develop an **information systems plan** that supports their overall business plan and in which strategic systems are incorporated into top-level planning. The plan serves as a road map indicating the direction of systems development (the purpose of the plan), the rationale, the current systems/situation, new developments to consider, the management strategy, the implementation plan, and the budget (see Table 10-1).

The plan contains a statement of corporate goals and specifies how information technology will support the attainment of those goals. The report shows how general goals will be achieved by specific systems projects. It identifies specific target dates and milestones that can be used later to evaluate the plan's progress in terms of how many objectives were

Information systems plan

TABLE 10-1 Information systems plan.

1. **PURPOSE OF THE PLAN**
   Overview of plan contents
   Current business organization and future organization
   Key business processes
   Management strategy

2. **STRATEGIC BUSINESS PLAN RATIONALE**
   Current situation
   Current business organization
   Changing environments
   Major goals of the business plan
   Firm's strategic plan

3. **CURRENT SYSTEMS**
   Major systems supporting business functions and processes
   Current infrastructure capabilities:
       Hardware
       Software
       Database
       Telecommunications and the Internet
   Difficulties meeting business requirements
   Anticipated future demands

4. **NEW DEVELOPMENTS**
   New system projects:
       Project descriptions
       Business rationale
       The role of applications in strategy
   New infrastructure capabilities required:
       Hardware
       Software
       Database
       Telecommunications and Internet

5. **MANAGEMENT STRATEGY**
   Acquisition plans
   Milestones and timing
   Organizational realignment
   Internal reorganization
   Management controls
   Major training initiatives
   Personnel strategy

6. **IMPLEMENTATION PLAN**
   Anticipated difficulties in implementation
   Progress reports

7. **BUDGET REQUIREMENTS**
   Requirements
   Potential savings
   Financing
   Acquisition cycle

actually attained in the time frame specified in the plan. The plan indicates the key management decisions concerning hardware acquisition; telecommunications; centralization/decentralization of authority, data, and hardware; and required organizational change. Organizational changes are also usually described, including management and employee training requirements; recruiting efforts; changes in business processes; and changes in authority, structure, or management practice.

In order to plan effectively, firms will need to inventory and document all of their information system applications and IT infrastructure components. For projects in which benefits involve improved decision making, managers should try to identify the decision improvements that would provide the greatest additional value to the firm. They should then develop a set of metrics to quantify the value of more timely and precise information on the outcome of the decision (see Chapter 14 for more detail on this topic).

Critical Success Factors

To develop an effective information systems plan, the organization must have a clear understanding of both its long- and short-term information requirements. The **critical success factors (CSFs)** approach argues that an organization's information requirements are determined by a small number of critical success factors of managers. If these goals can be attained, success of the firm or organization is assured (Rockart, 1979; Rockart and Treacy, 1982). CSFs are shaped by the industry, the firm, the manager, and the broader environment. For example, CSFs for the automobile industry might include styling, quality, and cost to meet the goals of increasing market share and raising profits. New information systems should focus on providing information that helps the firm meet these goals.

The principal method used in CSF analysis is personal interviews—three or four—with a number of top managers identifying their goals and the resulting CSFs. These personal CSFs are aggregated to develop a picture of the firm's CSFs. Then systems are developed to deliver information on these CSFs. (For the method of developing CSFs in an organization, see Figure 10-5.)

Only top managers are interviewed, and the questions focus on a small number of CSFs rather than requiring a broad inquiry into what information is used in the organization. It is especially suitable for top management and for the development of decision-support

Critical success factors (CSFs)

FIGURE 10-5   Using CSFs to develop systems.

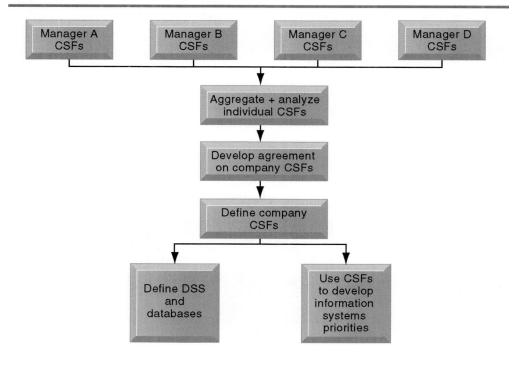

The CSF approach relies on interviews with key managers to identify their CSFs. Individual CSFs are aggregated to develop CSFs for the entire firm. Systems can then be developed to deliver information on these CSFs.

systems (DSS) and executive support systems (ESS). The CSF method focuses organizational attention on how information should be handled.

The method's primary weakness is that there is no particularly rigorous way in which individual CSFs can be aggregated into a clear company pattern. In addition, interviewees (and interviewers) often become confused when distinguishing between individual and organizational CSFs. These types of CSFs are not necessarily the same. What may be considered critical to a manager may not be important for the organization as a whole. This method is clearly biased toward top managers although it could be extended to elicit ideas for promising new systems from lower-level members of the organization (Peffers and Gengler, 2003).

Portfolio Analysis

Once strategic analyses have determined the overall direction of systems development, portfolio analysis can be used to evaluate alternative system projects. **Portfolio analysis** inventories all of the organization's information systems projects and assets, including infrastructure, outsourcing contracts, and licences. This portfolio of information systems investments can be described as having a certain profile of risk and benefit to the firm (see Figure 10-6) similar to a financial portfolio.

Each information systems project carries its own set of risks and benefits. (Section 10.5 describes the factors that increase the risks of systems projects.) Firms try to improve the return on their portfolios of IT assets by balancing the risk and return from their systems investments. Although there is no ideal profile for all firms, information-intensive industries (e.g., finance) should have a few high-risk, high-benefit projects to ensure that they stay current with technology. Firms in non-information-intensive industries generally should focus on high-benefit, low-risk projects.

Most desirable, of course, are systems with high benefit and low risk. These promise early returns and low risks. Second, high-benefit, high-risk systems should be examined; low-benefit, high-risk systems should be avoided; and low-benefit, low-risk systems should be re-examined for the possibility of rebuilding and replacing them with more desirable systems having higher benefits. By using portfolio analysis, management can determine the optimal mix of investment risk and reward for their firms, balancing riskier high-reward projects with safer lower-reward ones. Firms where portfolio analysis is aligned with business strategy have been found to have a superior return on their IT assets, better alignment of information technology investments with business objectives, and better organization-wide coordination of IT investments (Jeffrey and Leliveld, 2004).

Scoring Models

A **scoring model** is useful for selecting projects where many criteria must be considered. It assigns weights to various features of a system and then calculates the weighted totals. Using Table 10-2, the firm must decide among two alternative enterprise resource planning (ERP) systems. The first column lists the criteria that decision makers will use to evaluate the

Portfolio analysis
Scoring model

FIGURE 10-6   A system portfolio.

Companies should examine their portfolio of projects in terms of potential benefits and likely risks. Certain kinds of projects should be avoided altogether and others developed rapidly. There is no ideal mix. Companies in different industries have different profiles.

TABLE 10-2 Example of a scoring model for an ERP system.

CRITERIA	WEIGHT	ERP SYSTEM A %	ERP SYSTEM A SCORE	ERP SYSTEM B %	ERP SYSTEM B SCORE
1.0 Order Processing					
1.1 Online order entry	4	67	268	73	292
1.2 Online pricing	4	81	324	87	348
1.3 Inventory check	4	72	288	81	324
1.4 Customer credit check	3	66	198	59	177
1.5 Invoicing	4	73	292	82	328
Total Order Processing			1370		1469
2.0 Inventory Management					
2.1 Production forecasting	3	72	216	76	228
2.2 Production planning	4	79	316	81	324
2.3 Inventory control	4	68	272	80	320
2.4 Reports	3	71	213	69	207
Total Inventory Management			1017		1079
3.0 Warehousing					
3.1 Receiving	2	71	142	75	150
3.2 Picking/packing	3	77	231	82	246
3.3 Shipping	4	92	368	89	356
Total Warehousing			741		752
Grand Total			3128		3300

systems. These criteria are usually the result of lengthy discussions among the decision-making group. Often the most important outcome of a scoring model is not the score but agreement on the criteria used to judge a system.

Table 10-2 shows that this particular company attaches the most importance to capabilities for sales order processing, inventory management, and warehousing. The second column in Table 10-2 lists the weights that decision makers attached to the decision criteria. Columns 3 and 5 show the percentage of requirements for each function that each alternative ERP system can provide. Each vendor's score can be calculated by multiplying the percentage of requirements met for each function by the weight attached to that function. ERP System B has the highest total score.

As with all "objective" techniques, there are many qualitative judgments involved in using the scoring model. This model requires experts who understand the issues and the technology. It is appropriate to cycle through the scoring model several times, changing the criteria and weights, to see how sensitive the outcome is to reasonable changes in criteria. Scoring models are used most commonly to confirm, to rationalize, and to support decisions, rather than as the final arbiters of system selection.

10.4 Establishing the Business Value of Information Systems

Even if a system project supports a firm's strategic goals and meets user information requirements, it needs to be a good investment for the firm. The value of systems from a financial perspective essentially revolves around the issue of return on invested capital. Does a particular information system investment produce sufficient returns to justify its costs?

Information System Costs and Benefits

Table 10-3 lists some of the more common costs and benefits of systems. **Tangible benefits** can be quantified and assigned a monetary value. **Intangible benefits,** such as more efficient customer service or enhanced decision making, cannot be immediately quantified but may lead to quantifiable gains in the long run. Transaction and clerical systems that displace labour and save space always produce more measurable, tangible benefits than management information systems, decision-support systems, and computer-supported collaborative work systems (see Chapters 2 and 15).

Chapter 5 introduced the concept of total cost of ownership (TCO), which is designed to identify and measure the components of information technology expenditures beyond the initial cost of purchasing and installing hardware and software. However, TCO analysis provides only part of the information needed to evaluate an information technology investment because it does not typically deal with benefits, cost categories such as complexity costs, and "soft" and strategic factors discussed later in this section.

Tangible benefits
Intangible benefits

TABLE 10-3   Costs and benefits of information systems.

Costs
Hardware
Telecommunications
Software
Services
Personnel
Tangible Benefits (Cost Savings)
Increased productivity
Lower operational costs
Reduced workforce
Lower computer expenses
Lower outside vendor costs
Lower clerical and professional costs
Reduced rate of growth in expenses
Reduced facility costs
Intangible Benefits
Improved asset utilization
Improved resource control
Improved organizational planning
Increased organizational flexibility
More timely information
More information
Increased organizational learning
Legal requirements attained
Enhanced employee goodwill
Increased job satisfaction
Improved decision making
Improved operations
Higher client satisfaction
Better corporate image

Capital Budgeting for Information Systems

To determine the benefits of a particular project, you will need to calculate all of its costs and all of its benefits. Obviously, a project where costs exceed benefits should be rejected. But even if the benefits outweigh the costs, additional financial analysis is required to determine whether the project represents a good return on the firm's invested capital. Capital budgeting models are one of several techniques used to measure the value of investing in long-term capital investment projects.

Capital budgeting methods rely on measures of cash flows into and out of the firm; capital projects generate those cash flows. The investment cost for information systems projects is an immediate cash outflow caused by expenditures for hardware, software, and labour. In subsequent years, the investment may cause additional cash outflows that will be balanced by cash inflows resulting from the investment. Cash inflows take the form of increased sales of more products (for reasons such as new products, higher quality, or increasing market share) or reduced costs in production and operations. The difference between cash outflows and cash inflows is used for calculating the financial worth of an investment. Once the cash flows have been established, several alternative methods are available for comparing different projects and deciding about the investment.

The principal capital budgeting models for evaluating IT projects are the payback method, the accounting rate of return on investment (ROI), net present value, and the internal rate of return (IRR). You can find out more about how these capital budgeting models are used to justify information system investments in the Learning Tracks for this chapter.

Real Options Pricing Models

Some information systems projects are highly uncertain, especially investments in IT infrastructure. Their future revenue streams are unclear, and their upfront costs are high. Suppose, for instance, that a firm is considering a $20 million investment to upgrade its IT infrastructure—its hardware, software, data management tools, and networking technology. If this upgraded infrastructure were available, the organization would have the technology capabilities to respond more easily to future problems and opportunities. Although the costs of this investment can be calculated, not all of the benefits of making this investment can be established in advance. But if the firm waits a few years until the revenue potential becomes more obvious, it might be too late to make the infrastructure investment. In such cases, managers might benefit from using real options pricing models to evaluate information technology investments.

Real options pricing models (ROPMs) use the concept of options valuation borrowed from the financial industry. An option is essentially the right, but not the obligation, to act at some future date. A typical call option, for instance, is a financial option in which a person buys the right (but not the obligation) to purchase an underlying asset (usually a stock) at a fixed price (strike price) on or before a given date.

For instance, on October 4, 2009, for $21.90, you could purchase the right (a call option) maturing in January 2010 to buy a share of Royal Bank of Canada (RY) common stock for $30 per share. If, by the end of January 2010, the price of RY stock did not rise above $30 per share, you would not exercise the option, and the value of the option would fall to zero on the strike date. If, however, the price of RY common stock rose to, say, $100 per share, you could purchase the stock for the strike price of $30 and retain the profit of $70 per share minus the cost of the option. (Because the option is sold as a 100-share contract, the cost of the contract would be $100 \times \$21.90$ before commissions, or $2190, and you would be purchasing and obtaining a profit from 100 shares of RY.) The stock option enables the owner to benefit from the upside potential of an opportunity while limiting the downside risk.

ROPMs value information systems projects similarly to stock options where an initial expenditure on technology creates the right, but not the obligation, to obtain the benefits associated with further development and deployment of the technology as long as management has the freedom to cancel, defer, restart, or expand the project. ROPMs give managers the flexibility to stage their IT investment or to test the waters with small pilot projects or prototypes to gain more knowledge about the risks of a project before investing

Capital budgeting
Real options pricing models (ROPMs)

in the entire implementation. The disadvantages of this model are primarily in estimating all the key variables affecting option value, including anticipated cash flows from the underlying asset and changes in the cost of implementation. Models for determining option value of information technology platforms are being developed (Fichman, 2004; McGrath and MacMillan, 2000).

Limitations of Financial Models

The traditional focus on the financial and technical aspects of an information system tends to overlook the social and organizational dimensions of information systems that may affect the true costs and benefits of the investment. Many companies' information systems investment decisions do not adequately consider costs from organizational disruptions created by a new system, such as the cost to train end users, the impact that users' learning curves for a new system have on productivity, or the time managers need to spend overseeing new system-related changes. Benefits, such as more timely decisions from a new system or enhanced employee learning and expertise, may also be overlooked in a traditional financial analysis (Ryan, Harrison, and Schkade, 2002).

10.5   Managing Project Risk

We have already introduced the topic of information system risks and risk assessment in Chapter 8. In this chapter, we describe the specific risks to information systems projects and show what can be done to manage them effectively.

Dimensions of Project Risk

Systems differ dramatically in their size, scope, level of complexity, and organizational and technical components. Some systems development projects are more likely to create the problems we have described earlier or to suffer delays because they carry a much higher level of risk than others. The level of project risk is influenced by project size, project structure, and the level of technical expertise of the information systems staff and project team.

- Project size. The larger the project—as indicated by the dollars spent, the size of the implementation staff, the time allocated for implementation, and the number of organizational units affected—the greater the risk. Very large-scale systems projects have a failure rate that is 50 to 75 percent higher than that for other projects because such projects are complex and difficult to control. The organizational complexity of the system—how many units and groups use it and how much it influences business processes—contribute to the complexity of large-scale systems projects just as much as technical characteristics, such as the number of lines of program code, length of project, and budget (Xia and Lee, 2004; Concours Group, 2000; Laudon, 1989). In addition, there are few reliable techniques for estimating the time and cost to develop large-scale information systems.

- Project structure. Some projects are more highly structured than others. Their requirements are clear and straightforward so outputs and processes can be easily defined. Users know exactly what they want and what the system should do; there is almost no possibility of the users changing their minds. Such projects run a much lower risk than those with relatively undefined, fluid, and constantly changing requirements; with outputs that cannot be fixed easily because they are subject to users' changing ideas; or with users who cannot agree on what they want.

- Experience with technology. The project risk rises if the project team and the information system staff lack the required technical expertise. If the team is unfamiliar with the hardware, system software, application software, or database management system proposed for the project, it is highly likely that the project will experience technical problems or take more time to complete because of the need to master new skills.

Although the difficulty or complexity of the technology is one risk factor in information systems projects, the other factors are primarily organizational, dealing with the complexity of information requirements, the scope of the project, and how many parts of the organization will be affected by a new information system.

Change Management and the Concept of Implementation

The introduction or alteration of an information system has a powerful behavioural and organizational impact. Changes in the way that information is defined, accessed, and used to manage the organization's resources often lead to new distributions of authority and power. This internal organizational change breeds resistance and opposition and can lead to the demise of an otherwise good system.

A very large percentage of information systems projects stumble because the process of organizational change surrounding systems development was not properly addressed. Successful systems development requires careful change management.

The Concept of Implementation   To manage the organizational change surrounding the introduction of a new information system effectively, you must examine the process of implementation. Implementation refers to all organizational activities working toward the adoption, management, and routinization of an innovation, such as a new information system. In the implementation process, the systems analyst is a **change agent.** The analyst not only develops technical solutions but also redefines the configurations, interactions, job activities, and power relationships of various organizational groups. The analyst is the catalyst for the entire change process and is responsible for ensuring that all parties involved accept the changes created by a new system. The change agent communicates with users, mediates between competing interest groups, and ensures that the organizational adjustment to such changes is complete.

The Role of End Users   System implementation generally benefits from high levels of user involvement and management support. User participation in the design and operation of information systems has several positive results. First, if users are heavily involved in systems design, they have more opportunities to mould the system according to their priorities and business requirements and more opportunities to control the outcome. Second, they are more likely to react positively to the completed system because they have been active participants in the change process. Incorporating user knowledge and expertise leads to better solutions.

The relationship between users and information systems specialists has traditionally been a problem area for information systems implementation efforts. Users and information systems specialists tend to have different backgrounds, interests, and priorities. This is referred to as the **user–designer communications gap.** These differences lead to divergent organizational loyalties, approaches to problem solving, and vocabularies.

Information systems specialists, for example, often have a highly technical, or machine, orientation to problem solving. They look for elegant and sophisticated technical solutions in which hardware and software efficiency is optimized at the expense of ease of use or organizational effectiveness. Users prefer systems that are oriented toward solving business problems or facilitating organizational tasks. Often the orientations of both groups are so at odds that they appear to speak in different languages.

These differences are illustrated in Table 10-4, which depicts the typical concerns of end users and technical specialists (information systems designers) regarding the development of a new information system. Communication problems between end users and designers are a major reason user requirements are not properly incorporated into information systems and why users are driven out of the implementation process.

Systems development projects run a very high risk of failure when there is a pronounced gap between users and technical specialists and when these groups continue to pursue different goals. Under such conditions, users are often driven away from the project. Because they cannot comprehend what the technicians are saying, users conclude that the entire project is best left in the hands of the information specialists alone.

Change agent
User–designer communications gap

TABLE 10-4 The user–designer communications gap.

User Concerns	Designer Concerns
Will the system deliver the information I need for my work?	How much disk storage space will the master file consume?
How quickly can I access the data?	How many lines of program code will it take to perform this function?
How easily can I retrieve the data?	How can we cut down on CPU time when we run the system?
How much clerical support will I need to enter data into the system?	What is the most efficient way of storing these data?
How will the operation of the system fit into my daily business schedule?	What database management system should we use?

Management Support and Commitment If an information systems project has the backing and commitment of management at various levels, it is more likely to be perceived positively by both users and the technical information services staff. Both groups will believe that their participation in the development process will receive higher-level attention and priority. They will be recognized and rewarded for the time and effort they devote to implementation. Management backing also ensures that a systems project receives sufficient funding and resources to be successful. Furthermore, to be enforced effectively, all the changes in work habits and procedures and any organizational realignments associated with a new system depend on management backing. If a manager considers a new system a priority, the system will more likely be treated that way by his or her subordinates.

Change Management Challenges for Business Process Re-engineering, Enterprise Applications, and Mergers and Acquisitions Given the challenges of innovation and implementation, it is not surprising to find a very high failure rate among enterprise application and business process re-engineering (BPR) projects, which typically require extensive organizational change and which may require replacing old technologies and legacy systems that are deeply rooted in many interrelated business processes. A number of studies have indicated that 70 percent of all business process re-engineering projects fail to deliver promised benefits. Likewise, a high percentage of enterprise applications fail to be fully implemented or to meet the goals of their users even after three years of work.

Many enterprise application and re-engineering projects have been undermined by poor implementation and **change management** practices that failed to address employees' concerns about change. Dealing with fear and anxiety throughout the organization; overcoming resistance by key managers; changing job functions, career paths, and recruitment practices; and training have posed greater threats to re-engineering than the difficulties companies faced visualizing and designing breakthrough changes to business processes. All of the enterprise applications require tighter coordination among different functional groups as well as extensive business process change (see Chapter 12).

Projects related to mergers and acquisitions have a similar failure rate. Mergers and acquisitions are deeply affected by the organizational characteristics of the merging companies as well as by their IT infrastructures. Combining the information systems of two different companies usually requires considerable organizational change and complex systems projects to manage. If the integration is not properly managed, firms can emerge with a tangled hodgepodge of inherited legacy systems developed by aggregating the systems of one firm after another. Without a successful systems integration, the benefits anticipated from the merger cannot be realized, or, worse, the merged entity cannot execute its business processes effectively.

Change management

Controlling Risk Factors

Various project management, requirements gathering, and planning methodologies have been developed for specific categories of implementation problems. Strategies have also been devised for ensuring that users play appropriate roles throughout the implementation period and for managing the organizational change process. Not all aspects of the implementation process can be easily controlled or planned. However, anticipating potential implementation problems and applying appropriate corrective strategies can increase the chances for system success.

The first step in managing project risk involves identifying the nature and level of risk confronting the project (Schmidt et al., 2001). Implementers can then handle each project with the tools and risk management approaches geared to its level of risk (Iversen, Mathiassen, and Nielsen, 2004; Barki, Rivard, and Talbot, 2001; McFarlan, 1981).

Managing Technical Complexity   Projects with challenging and complex technology for users to master benefit from **internal integration tools.** The success of these projects depends on how well their technical complexity can be managed. Project leaders need both heavy technical and administrative experience. They must be able to anticipate problems and develop smooth working relationships among a predominantly technical team. The team should be under the leadership of a manager with a strong technical and project management background, and team members should be highly experienced. Team meetings should take place frequently. Essential technical skills or expertise not available internally should be secured from outside the organization.

Formal Planning and Control Tools   Large projects benefit from appropriate use of **formal planning tools** and **formal control tools** for documenting and monitoring project plans. The two most commonly used methods for documenting project plans are Gantt charts and PERT charts. A **Gantt chart** lists project activities and their corresponding start and completion dates. The Gantt chart visually represents the timing and duration of different tasks in a development project as well as their human resource requirements (see Figure 10-7). It shows each task as a horizontal bar whose length is proportional to the time required to complete it.

Although Gantt charts show when project activities begin and end, they do not depict task dependencies, how one task is affected if another is behind schedule, or how tasks should be ordered. That is where PERT charts are useful. PERT stands for Program Evaluation and Review Technique, a methodology developed by the U.S. Navy. A **PERT chart** graphically depicts project tasks and their interrelationships. The PERT chart lists the specific activities that make up a project and the activities that must be completed before a specific activity can start, as illustrated in Figure 10-8 on page 333.

The PERT chart portrays a project as a network diagram consisting of numbered nodes (either circles or rectangles) representing project tasks. Each node is numbered and shows the task, its duration, the starting date, and the completion date. The direction of the arrows on the lines indicates the sequence of tasks and shows which activities must be completed before the commencement of another activity. In Figure 10-8, the tasks in nodes 2, 3, and 4 are not dependent on each other and can be undertaken simultaneously, but each is dependent on completion of the first task. PERT charts for complex projects can be difficult to interpret, and project managers often use both techniques.

These project management techniques can help managers identify bottlenecks and determine the impact that problems will have on project completion times. They can also help systems developers partition projects into smaller, more manageable segments with defined, measurable business results. Standard control techniques can successfully chart the progress of the project against budgets and target dates, so deviations from the plan can be spotted.

Project Management Software Tools

Commercial software tools that automate many aspects of project management facilitate the project management process. Project management software typically features capabilities

Internal integration tools
Formal planning tools
Formal control tools
Gantt chart
PERT chart

FIGURE 10-7   A Gantt chart.

HRIS COMBINED PLAN–HR — Gantt chart

Task list

HRIS COMBINED PLAN–HR	Da	Who
DATA ADMINISTRATION SECURITY		
QMF security review/setup	20	EF TP
Security orientation	2	EF JA
QMF security maintenance	35	TP GL
Data entry sec. profiles	4	EF TP
Data entry sec. views est.	12	EF TP
Data entry security profiles	65	EF TP
DATA DICTIONARY		
Orientation sessions	1	EF
Data dictionary design	32	EFWV
DD prod. coordn-query	20	GL
DD prod. coordn-live	40	EF GL
Data dictionary cleanup	35	EF GL
Data dictionary maint.	35	EF GL
PROCEDURES REVISION		
DESIGN PREP		
Work flows (old)	10	PK JL
Payroll data flows	31	JL PK
HRIS P/R model	11	PK JL
P/R interface orient. mtg.	6	PK JL
P/R interface coordn. 1	15	PK
P/R interface coordn. 2	8	PK
Benefits interfaces (old)	5	JL
Benefits interfaces (new flow)	8	JL
Benefits communication strategy	3	PK JL
New work flow model	15	PK JL
Posn. data entry flows	14	WV JL

RESOURCE SUMMARY

Name	Rate	Who	2008 Oct	Nov	Dec	2009 Jan	Feb	Mar	Apr	May	Jun	Jul	Aug	Sep	Oct	Nov	Dec	2010 Jan	Feb	Mar
Edith Farrell	5.0	EF	2	21	24	24	23	22	22	27	34	34	29	26	28	19	14			
Woody Vinton	5.0	WV	5	17	20	19	12	10	14	10	2							4	3	
Charles Pierce	5.0	CP			5	11	20	13	9	10	7	6	8	4	4	4	4			
Ted Leurs	5.0	TL		12	17	17	19	17	14	12	15	16	2	1	1	1	1			
Toni Cox	5.0	TC	1	11	10	11	11	12	19	19	21	21	21	17	17	12	9			
Patricia Knopp	5.0	PC	7	23	30	34	27	25	15	24	25	16	11	13	17	10	3	3	2	
Jane Lawton	5.0	JL	1	9	16	21	19	21	21	20	17	15	14	12	14	8	5			
David Holloway	5.0	DH	4	4	5	5	5	2	7	5	4	16	2							
Diane O'Neill	5.0	DO	6	14	17	16	13	11	9	4										
Joan Albert	5.0	JA	5	6				7	6	2	1			5	5	1				
Marie Marcus	5.0	MM	15	7	2	1	1													
Don Stevens	5.0	DS	4	4	5	4	5	1												
Casual	5.0	CASL		3	4	3			4	7	9	5	3	2						
Kathy Mendez	5.0	KM			1	5	16	20	19	22	19	20	18	20	11	2				
Anna Borden	5.0	AB						9	10	16	15	11	12	19	10	7	1			
Gail Loring	5.0	GL			3	6	5	9	10	17	18	17	10	13	10	10	7	17		
UNASSIGNED	0.0	X												9	236	225	230	14	13	
Co-op	5.0	CO		6	4				2	3	4	4	2	4	16			216	178	
Casual	5.0	CAUL									3	3	3							
TOTAL DAYS			49	147	176	196	194	174	193	195	190	181	140	125	358	288	284	237	196	12

The Gantt chart in this figure shows the task, person-days, and initials of each responsible person, as well as the start and finish dates for each task. The resource summary provides a good manager with the total person-days for each month and for each person working on the project to manage the project successfully. The project described here is a data administration project.

FIGURE 10-8   A PERT chart.

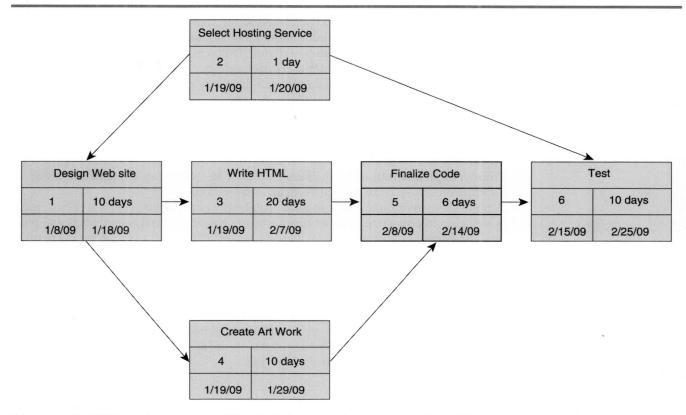

This is a simplified PERT chart for creating a small Web site. It shows the ordering of project tasks and the relationship of a task with preceding and succeeding tasks.

for defining and ordering tasks, assigning resources to tasks, establishing starting and ending dates to tasks, tracking progress, and facilitating modifications to tasks and resources. Many automate the creation of Gantt and PERT charts.

Some of these tools are large, sophisticated programs for managing very large projects, dispersed work groups, and enterprise functions. These high-end tools can manage very large numbers of tasks and activities and complex relationships.

Microsoft Office Project 2007 has become the most widely used project management software today. It is PC-based, with capabilities for producing PERT and Gantt charts and for supporting critical path analysis (which shows the shortest route to finishing a project, with the least amount of slack time built in), resource allocation, project tracking, and status reporting. Project also tracks the way changes in one aspect of a project affect others. MS Project Professional 2007 provides collaborative project management capabilities when used with Microsoft Office Project Server 2007. MS Project Server stores project data in a central SQL Server database, enabling authorized users to access and update the data over the Internet. MS Project Server 2007 is tightly integrated with the Microsoft Windows SharePoint Services collaborative workspace platform. These features help large enterprises manage projects in many different locations. Products such as EasyProjects.NET and Vertabase are also useful for firms that want Web-based project management tools.

Increasing User Involvement and Overcoming User Resistance Projects with relatively little structure and many undefined requirements must involve users fully at all stages. Users must be mobilized to support one of many possible design options and to remain committed to a single design. **External integration tools** consist of ways to link the work of the implementation team to users at all organizational levels. For instance, users can become active members of the project team, take on leadership roles, and take

External integration tools

charge of installation and training. The implementation team can demonstrate its responsiveness to users, promptly answering questions, incorporating user feedback, and showing their willingness to help (Gefen and Ridings, 2002).

Participation in implementation activities may not be enough to overcome the problem of user resistance to organizational change. Different users may be affected by the system in different ways. While some users may welcome a new system because it brings changes they perceive as beneficial to them, others may resist these changes because they believe the shifts are detrimental to their interests.

If the use of a system is voluntary, users may choose to avoid it; if use is mandatory, resistance will take the form of increased error rates, disruptions, turnover, and even sabotage. Therefore, the implementation strategy must not only encourage user participation and involvement but also address the issue of counterimplementation (Keen, 1981). **Counterimplementation** is a deliberate strategy to thwart the implementation of an information system or an innovation in an organization.

Strategies to overcome user resistance include user participation (to elicit commitment as well as to improve design), user education and training, management edicts and policies, and better incentives for users who cooperate. The new system can be made more user-friendly by improving the end-user interface. Users will be more cooperative if organizational problems are solved prior to introducing the new system.

The Window on Organizations provides an example of a large-scale project where many of these issues are at work. The U.S. Centers for Disease Control and Prevention (CDC) have had trouble implementing a nationwide system to alert health care providers and agencies to potential health crises such as flu pandemics or bioterrorist attacks. As you read this case, try to identify the risks of this project and whether the appropriate strategies were used for dealing with these risks.

Designing for the Organization

Because the purpose of a new system is to improve the organization's performance, information systems projects must explicitly address the ways in which the organization will change when the new system is installed, including installation of intranets, extranets, and Web applications. In addition to procedural changes, transformations in job functions, organizational structure, power relationships, and the work environment should be carefully planned.

Areas where users interface with the system require special attention, with sensitivity to ergonomics issues. **Ergonomics** refers to the interaction of people and machines in the work environment. It considers the design of jobs, health issues, and the end-user interface of information systems. Table 10-5 lists the organizational dimensions that must be addressed when planning and implementing information systems.

Although systems analysis and design activities are supposed to include an organizational impact analysis, this area has traditionally been neglected. An **organizational impact analysis** explains how a proposed system will affect organizational structure, attitudes, decision making, and operations. To integrate information systems successfully with the organization, thorough and fully documented organizational impact assessments must be given more attention in the development effort.

Counterimplementation
Ergonomics
Organizational impact analysis

TABLE 10-5   Organizational factors in systems planning and implementation.

Employee participation and involvement
Job design
Standards and performance monitoring
Ergonomics (including equipment, user interfaces, and the work environment)
Employee grievance resolution procedures
Health and safety
Government regulatory compliance

WINDOW ON ORGANIZATIONS

Why Can't BioSense Take Off?

If you turn on the television, read a newspaper, or surf the Web, you are bound to find many dire predictions about large-scale loss of life from biological or chemical attacks or an avian or swine influenza pandemic. Computer models estimate that between 2 and 100 million people could die in the event of a flu pandemic.

On May 3, 2006, the United States government issued an Implementation Plan for its National Strategy for Pandemic Influenza to improve coordination among federal, state, and local authorities and the private sector for pandemics and other public health emergencies. The implementation plan called for improving mechanisms for "real-time" clinical surveillance of hospital emergency rooms, intensive care units, and laboratories to inform local, state, and federal public health officials about rapidly spreading illness.

The centrepiece of this plan is the BioSense Real-Time Clinical Connections Program developed by the U.S. CDC. BioSense sits atop a hospital's existing information systems, continually gathering and analyzing data as the data are generated. Custom software developed by CDC monitors the facility's network traffic and captures relevant patient records, diagnoses, and prescription information. The data include patient age, sex, zip code of residence, zip code of the medical facility handling the patient, the principal medical complaint, symptoms, onset of illness, diagnoses, medical procedures, medications prescribed, and laboratory results. The software converts these data to the HL7 data messaging format, which is the standard for the health care industry, encrypts the data, and transmits them every 15 minutes over the Web to the CDC where they are maintained in a large data repository.

The system summarizes and presents analytical results by source, day, and syndrome for each zip code, state, and metropolitan area using maps, graphs, and tables. Registered state and local public health agencies as well as hospitals and health care providers are allowed to access data that pertain to their jurisdiction using a Web-based application over a secure data network. Information from BioSense could show early signs of a pandemic or biologic attack and alert local hospitals, health workers, and federal and state agencies to take preventive measures.

The traditional process for public health surveillance is manual and much slower. Hospitals, physicians, and laboratories would mail or fax paper reports to public health agencies, which would then call health care providers for more detailed information. This slow chain of person-to-person communication is not well suited to a major public health emergency.

BioSense first became operational in 2004 when it began gathering daily data from U.S. Defense Department and Veterans Affairs (VA) hospitals and Laboratory Corporation of America (LabCorp) orders for medical tests. (LabCorp operates a large nationwide network of testing locations and service centres and is one of the largest clinical lab service providers in the United States.) Approximately 700 Defense Department and 1110 VA facilities report data to BioSense. In late 2005, CDC started to expand the BioSense network to civilian hospitals in major metropolitan areas.

However, in 2006 and 2007, BioSense encountered significant resistance from hospital administrators and physicians around the country. As of May, 2008, only 563 hospitals and state health organizations were participating. To transmit data to BioSense, each hospital must standardize its patient and other medical data. Most hospitals use their own coding systems for symptoms, diseases, and medications. CDC's contractors would have to work with each hospital to translate its data codes into the standards used by CDC's software. This is a massive task, given hospitals' limited IT staffs and resources.

Some in the medical community question whether the BioSense network is worth the effort. According to Dr. John Rosenberg, director of the Infectious Disease Laboratory at the State of California's Department of Health Services in Richmond, California, if an epidemic broke out, "You'd know it before the data rolled in. When your emergency rooms fill up, you make a phone call; this is probably a better measure."

Although participation in BioSense is voluntary, physicians and health officials might resent the system because it enables the federal government to encroach on what has traditionally been the domain of local health care providers and organizations. They note that they and not the CDC have the responsibility for responding to and managing a pandemic. Additionally, hospitals are reluctant to sign up because of concerns about maintaining privacy and security of patient information. BioSense would let the CDC "listen in" on their treatment of patients on a real-time basis although the CDC does not use any data that would identify individual patients.

After investing an estimated $100 million on hospital recruitment and technology for BioSense in 2005 and 2006, the CDC decided in 2007 to work with state and local public health care systems instead of competing with them. It will continue to use BioSense in its limited form while simultaneously pursuing information-sharing measures with state health departments. CDC will not require states to move their detailed data into a national repository but instead will encourage them to link their databases with that of BioSense into some sort of nationwide bio-surveillance system. The final design of the system is still unclear. CDC is piloting different strategies to determine the best approach. One effort, for example, focuses on building an alert system to notify state and regional public health care officials electronically about pandemic outbreaks instead of relying on e-mail or the telephone.

To Think About

1. Identify the risks in the BioSense project.

2. What management, organization, and technology factors explain why this project has been difficult to implement?

3. Is the CDC's new approach to improving pandemic warnings a viable solution? Why or why not?

4. Is a system like BioSense a good idea for Canadian health care? What can Canadian public health officials learn from the BioSense project to help them implement a system like BioSense?

MIS in Action

Explore the BioSense Web site (**www.cdc.gov/biosense**) and then answer the following question:

1. What information technologies do you see mentioned in the description of BioSense? Why would they be especially useful for this type of application?

2. On the BioSense Web site, click on Application Access and Support. How can an organization gain approval to access BioSense? What does the section on Building the Power of Technology tell you about the guiding philosophy behind BioSense?

Sources: Doug Bartholomew and Chris Gonsalves, "CDC Issues Pandemic Systems Plan," *Baseline Magazine*, April 2008; Doug Bartholomew, "Second Opinions," *Baseline Magazine*, March 2006; and Wilson P. Dizard III, "CDC Weaving National Information Web," *Government Computer News*, April 3, 2006.

Sociotechnical Design One way of addressing human and organizational issues is to incorporate **sociotechnical design** practices into information systems projects. Designers set forth separate sets of technical and social design solutions. The social design plans explore different workgroup structures, allocation of tasks, and the design of individual jobs. The proposed technical solutions are compared with the proposed social solutions. The solution that best meets both social and technical objectives is selected for the final design. The resulting sociotechnical design is expected to produce an information system that blends technical efficiency with sensitivity to organizational and human needs, leading to higher job satisfaction and productivity.

Sociotechnical design

SUMMARY

1. **What are the various components of information resource management and the issues involved in each component?**

The IS department may be structured in any of several ways: centralized as its own department, decentralized within other departments, or with personnel located both centrally and in various information service units and information centres. The CIO and MIS steering committee set IS policies and prioritize and review major projects. IS planning takes place at the strategic, tactical, and operational levels and should be aligned with organizational strategy at each level.

Systems development actually involves a number of IS personnel roles and includes the staff assignments to various projects as well as ensuring that security issues are addressed. IS personnel must be recruited, hired, retained, and evaluated and must be permitted to keep their skill sets up to date. Like every other department in an organization, the IS department must set a budget, which is difficult at best given the trend toward rapidly changing technology and escalating IS personnel salaries.

2. **What are the objectives of project management, and why is it so essential in developing information systems?**

Good project management is essential for ensuring that systems are delivered on time and on budget, and provide genuine business benefits. Project management activities include planning the work, assessing the risk, estimating and acquiring resources required to accomplish the work, organizing the work, directing execution, and analyzing the results. Project management must deal with five major variables: scope, time, cost, quality, and risk.

3. **What methods can be used for selecting and evaluating information systems projects and aligning them with the firm's business goals?**

Organizations need an information systems plan that describes how information technology supports the attainment of their business goals and documents all their system applications and IT infrastructure components. Large corporations will have a management structure to ensure the most important systems projects receive priority. Critical success factors, portfolio analysis, and scoring models can be used to identify and evaluate alternative information systems projects.

4. How can firms assess the business value of information systems projects?

To determine whether an information systems project is a good investment, one must calculate its costs and benefits. Tangible benefits are quantifiable, and intangible benefits that cannot be immediately quantified may provide quantifiable benefits in the future. Benefits that exceed costs should be analyzed using capital budgeting methods to make sure a project represents a good return on the firm's invested capital. Real options pricing models, which apply the same techniques for valuing financial options to systems investments, can be useful when considering highly uncertain IT investments.

5. What are the principal risk factors in information systems projects?

The level of risk in a systems development project is determined by (1) project size, (2) project structure, and (3) experience with technology. IS projects are more likely to fail when there is insufficient or improper user participation in the systems development process, lack of management support, and poor management of the implementation process. There is a very high failure rate among projects involving business process re-engineering, enterprise applications, and mergers and acquisitions because they require extensive organizational change.

6. What strategies are useful for managing project risk and system implementation?

Implementation refers to the entire process of organizational change surrounding the introduction of a new information system. User support and involvement and management support and control of the implementation process are essential, as are mechanisms for dealing with the level of risk in each new systems project. Project risk factors can be brought under some control by a contingency approach to project management. The risk level of each project determines the appropriate mix of external integration tools, internal integration tools, formal planning tools, and formal control tools to be applied.

Key Terms

Capital budgeting,   327
Change agent,   329
Change management,   330
Chief information officer (CIO)   313
Counterimplementation,   334
Critical success factors (CSFs),   323
Data entry operators,   315
Ergonomics,   334
External integration tools,   333
Formal control tools,   331
Formal planning tools,   331

Gantt chart,   331
Information systems plan,   321
Intangible benefits,   326
Internal integration tools,   331
MIS steering committee,   313
Network managers,   315
Organizational impact analysis,   334
PERT chart,   331
Portfolio analysis,   324
Project,   318
Project management,   318

Real options pricing models
    (ROPMs),   327
Scope,   319
Scoring model,   324
Sociotechnical design,   336
Systems operators,   315
Tangible benefits,   326
User–designer communications
    gap,   329
User interface,   318
Web masters,   315

Review Questions

1. What are the various components of information resource management and the issues involved in each component?

- Name and describe the components involved in information resource management.
- Compare the role of the CIO with that of the MIS steering committee.
- Name and describe the types or levels of IS planning.
- Name and describe the various roles IS personnel have in the IS department.

2. What are the objectives of project management, and why is it so essential in developing information systems?

- Describe information system problems resulting from poor project management.
- Define project management. List and describe the project management activities and variables addressed by project management.

3. What methods can be used for selecting and evaluating information systems projects and aligning them with the firm's business goals?

- Name and describe the groups responsible for the management of information systems projects.
- Describe the purpose of an information systems plan and list the major categories in the plan.
- Explain how critical success factors, portfolio analysis, and scoring models can be used to select information systems projects.

4. How can firms assess the business value of information systems projects?

- List and describe the major costs and benefits of information systems.
- Distinguish between tangible and intangible benefits.
- Explain how real options pricing models can help managers evaluate information technology investments.

5. *What are the principal risk factors in information systems projects?*
   - *Identify and describe each of the principal risk factors in information systems projects.*
   - *Explain why builders of new information systems need to address implementation and change management.*
   - *Explain why eliciting support of management and end users is so essential for successful implementation of information systems projects.*
   - *Explain why is there such a high failure rate for implementations involving enterprise applications,* *business process re-engineering, and mergers and acquisitions.*

6. *What strategies are useful for managing project risk and system implementation?*
   - *Identify and describe the strategies for controlling project risk.*
   - *Identify the organizational considerations that should be addressed by project planning and implementation.*
   - *Explain how project management software tools contribute to successful project management.*

Discussion Questions

1. *How much does project management impact the success of a new information system?*

2. *It has been said that most systems fail because systems developers ignore organizational behaviour problems. Why might this be so?*

Collaboration and Teamwork: Identifying Implementation Problems

Form a group with two or three other students. Write a description of the implementation problems you might expect to encounter in one of the systems described in the Window on sections or chapter-ending cases in this text. Write an analysis of the steps you would take to solve or prevent these problems. If possible, use Google Sites to post links to Web pages, team communication announcements, and work assignments; to brainstorm; and to work collaboratively on project documents. Try to use Google Docs to develop a presentation of your findings for the class.

 Visit the MyMISLab Web site at **www.pearsoned.ca/mymislab.** This online homework and tutorial system puts you in control of your own learning with study and practice tools directly correlated to this chapter's content.

Learning Track Modules

The following Learning Tracks provide content relevant to topics covered in this chapter:

1. Capital Budgeting Methods for Information System Investments

2. Information Technology Investments and Productivity

3. Enterprise Analysis (Business Systems Planning)

HANDS-ON MIS   Projects

The projects in this section give you hands-on experience evaluating information systems projects, using spreadsheet software to perform capital budgeting analyses for new information systems investments, and using Web tools to analyze the financing for a new home.

Management Decision Problems

1. In 2001, McDonald's Restaurants undertook a project called Innovate to create an intranet connecting headquarters with its 30 000 restaurants in 120 countries to provide detailed operational information in real time. The new system would, for instance, inform a manager at the company's Illinois headquarters immediately if sales were slowing at a franchise in London, Ontario, or if the grill temperature in a Thunder Bay restaurant was not hot enough. The idea was to create a global ERP application touching the workings of every McDonald's restaurant. Some of these restaurants were in countries that lacked network infrastructures. After spending more than $1 billion over several years, including $170 million on consultants and initial implementation planning, McDonald's terminated the project. What should management have known or done at the outset to prevent this outcome?

2. Caterpillar is the world's leading maker of earthmoving machinery and supplier of agricultural equipment, operating in many Canadian cities as Toromont CAT. Caterpillar wants to end its support for its Dealer Business System (DBS), which it licenses to its dealers to help them run their businesses. The software in this system is becoming out of date, and senior management wants to transfer support for the hosted version of the software to Accenture so it can concentrate on its core business. Caterpillar never required its dealers to use DBS, but the system had become a de facto standard for doing business with the company. The majority of the 50 Cat dealers in North America use some version of DBS, as do about half of the 200 or so Cat dealers in the rest of the world. Before Caterpillar turns the product over to Accenture, what factors and issues should it consider? What questions should it ask? What questions should its dealers ask?

Improving Decision Making:
Using Spreadsheet Software for Capital Budgeting for a New CAD System

Software skills: Spreadsheet formulas and functions
Business skills: Capital budgeting

This project provides you with an opportunity to use spreadsheet software to use the capital budgeting models discussed in this chapter to analyze the return on an investment for a new CAD system.

Your company would like to invest in a new CAD system that requires purchasing hardware, software, and networking technology, as well as expenditures for installation, training, and support. The MyMISLab for Chapter 10 contains tables showing each cost component for the new system as well as annual maintenance costs over a five-year period. It also

features a Learning Track on capital budgeting models. You believe the new system will produce annual savings by reducing the amount of labour required to generate designs and design specifications, thus increasing your firm's annual cash flow.

1. Using the data provided in these tables, create a worksheet that calculates the costs and benefits of the investment over a five-year period and analyzes the investment using the four capital budgeting models presented in this chapter's Learning Track.

2. Is this investment worthwhile? Why or why not?

Improving Decision Making:
Using Web Tools for Buying and Financing a Home

Software skills: Internet-based software
Business skills: Financial planning

This project will develop your skills using Web-based software for searching for a home and calculating mortgage financing for that home.

You have found a new job in Calgary, Alberta, and would like to purchase a home in that area. Ideally, you would like to find a single-family house with at least three

bedrooms and one bathroom that costs between $150 000 and $225 000 and finance it with a 30-year fixed-rate mortgage. You can afford a down payment that is 20 percent of the value of the house. Before you purchase a house, you would like to find out what homes are available in your price range, find a mortgage, and determine the amount of your monthly payment. You would also like to see how much of your mortgage payment represents principal and how much represents interest. Use Yahoo!'s Real Estate site to help you with the following tasks:

1. Locate homes in your price range in Calgary, Alberta. Find out as much information as you can about the houses, including the real estate listing agent, condition of the house, number of rooms, and school district.

2. Find a mortgage for 80 percent of the list price of the home. Compare rates from at least three sites (use search engines to find sites other than Yahoo!).

3. After selecting a mortgage, calculate your closing costs.

4. Calculate the monthly payment for the mortgage you select.

5. Calculate how much of your monthly mortgage payment represents principal and how much represents interest, assuming you do not plan to make any extra payments on the mortgage.

When you are finished, evaluate the whole process. For example, assess the ease of use of the site and your ability to find information about houses and mortgages; the accuracy of the information you found; the breadth of choice of homes and mortgages; and how helpful the whole process would have been for you if you were actually in the situation described in this project.

CASE STUDY

Canadian Gun Registry: A Boondoggle or Simply a Complex Project?

How can anyone—let alone a government—have a project estimated to cost about $2 million and then have the project costs be closer to $2 billion? That is the question. It begs another question: Who was minding the shop on this one?

After 14 women were gunned down on the campus of L'École Polytechnique in Montreal in 1989, Canadians urged their government to put into place some form of gun registry to control and track firearms in Canada. The legislation put forward would mandate that all gun owners comply with the gun registry by a specified date; if an unregistered gun was owned after that date, the owner would be in violation of the law. Bill C-68, as the gun control legislation was known, was passed in 1995. The government budgeted $2 million (after calculating revenue from registration fees) to develop the national gun registry information system to house registry data and to provide access to the data to law enforcement officials across Canada.

As early as 2000, the Canadian Firearms Program (CFP) issued a report stating that the costs to develop the gun registry were rising, due to backlogs in registration, fee waivers for early applications, and high error rates on applications being submitted by firearms owners. By 2001, it was estimated that costs had risen to $527 million. The CFP blamed the computer system that it used to process the applications for the difficulty in tracking licence fees that had been collected.

As early as 2004, the press was claiming that the cost of the registry system would rise to $2 billion. The Auditor General's office investigated the CFP and observed that "information on the program was so impenetrable she was forced to end her audit early"; she also charged the Justice Department, which supervises the CFP, with hiding the rising costs from Parliament.

The actual custom database software had considerable technical problems. The decision by project managers to acquire custom software as opposed to customizing existing software was at best questionable. The government

has expertise in large, complex database implementations and could have used technology with which developers already had expertise but chose not to do so. Project managers also did not work closely enough with those who would be affected most by the registry—firearms owners—to understand the reluctance of many Canadian firearms owners to register their firearms, resulting in an onslaught of late registration applications, creating a massive backlog. Police have suggested that up to 25 percent of the data entries are unreliable, rendering the database relatively useless.

Costs for the gun registry system were listed as $629 million in 2002. The costs were allocated as $2 million to help police enforce the gun control legislation; a minimum of $60 million for public relations to publicize the gun registry so that firearms owners would know to register their firearms; $227 million in direct computer costs, largely due the complexity of the applications forms driving up the costs and slowing processing times; and $332 million for other programming costs, including paying staff to process the applications.

The stakeholders that would be affected by the registry program—firearms owners and local law enforcement—do not seem to have had the opportunity for much input into the process of developing and implementing the registry. That is bad project management in and of itself, but project managers also do not appear to have reported the cost overruns on a timely basis to their superiors, yet another example of bad project management.

By 2004, Ottawa had finally had enough of the rising costs of the registry system. The government limited annual expenditures on the registry to $25 million per year in response to learning that annual spending on the registry had run between $33 million and $48 million. The Report of the Commissioner of Firearms estimated that 2004 costs for the registry were less than $100 million for 2004 and indicated that costs would be reduced to about $85 million for the next year.

To make matters worse, it appears that the system can easily be hacked. According to John Hicks, a former Web master for the system, random-number-generating software could be used to generate a valid PIN code, enabling a criminal to hack the system. Hicks claimed he had hacked the Web site just a few days prior to his interview with *The Edmonton Sun.* A registry spokesperson denied that the system had been hacked to date.

The registry is only one of many high-profile boondoggle projects, running either massive cost overruns or being scrapped completed, or both. Sobey's initial implementation of SAP (it has since successfully implemented SAP), the U.S. Internal Revenue Service's massive database system upgrade, and the Denver, Colorado, airport baggage logistics system are just three that come to mind. Poor project management in each case meant that problems in systems development went undetected or unreported for too long a period of time, making reversing the poor quality of project management almost impossible.

This chapter is being written in mid-2009. To this date, there is still a lot of bad press about the Canadian gun registry project. While most of the press emphasizes the political consequences, the economic and crime-fighting consequences have not been ignored. The situation would not seem as bad if Canadians could believe that the government and its project managers would learn lessons from this instance of poor project management. The question remains: Will they learn?

CASE STUDY QUESTIONS:

1. How important is the Canadian gun registry project for Canadian law enforcement? How does it impact decision making and operational activities?

2. Evaluate the risks of the registry project and its key risk factors.

3. Classify and describe the problems the CFP faced in implementing its new registry system. What management, organization, and technology factors caused these problems?

4. Describe the steps you would have taken to control the risk in this project.

5. If you were in charge of managing this project, what else would you have done differently to increase chances for success?

Sources: Doug Beazley, "Gun Files Easy to Hack,: *The Edmonton Sun,* March 10, 2006; CBC News, "Gun Registry Cost Soars to $2 Billion," February 13, 2004; CBC News, "Implementing the *Firearms Act*—the Rising Cost," June 19, 2006; "Case Study: A Billion Dollar Boondoggle," **www.maxwideman.com/papers/boondoggle/intro.htm.**

CHAPTER 11

Managing Global Systems

LEARNING OBJECTIVES

After reading this chapter, you will be able to answer the following questions:

1. What major factors are driving the internationalization of business?

2. What are the alternative strategies for developing global businesses?

3. How can information systems support different global business strategies?

4. What are the challenges posed by global information systems, and management solutions for these challenges?

5. What are the issues and technical alternatives to be considered when developing international information systems?

OPENING CASE

SeverStal Creates an IT Infrastructure for Global Steelmaking

SeverStal ("Northern Steel") is one of Russia's largest steelmakers. It operates primarily in Russia but maintains facilities in Italy, the United Kingdom, France, and the United States. With more than 100 000 employees worldwide and more than $18 billion in revenue in 2007, it is on its way to redefining global steel making.

Some North American firms have left the steel production market because it is very capital-intensive. SeverStal is not worried about that. This company's managers are convinced that they are at the helm of a global profitability leader in the steel and mining industry.

SeverStal's corporate strategy calls for providing high-margin value-added products in attractive niche markets worldwide while keeping costs low. The company is developing a global platform for best-practice sharing and competencies development. SeverStal wants to leverage best practices and

technologies across its global operations and improve efficiencies by locating mills closer to key automotive customers. In 2004, for example, SeverStal North America (SNA) purchased Rouge Industries in Dearborn, Michigan, originally part of Henry Ford's massive River Rouge manufacturing complex, to gain access to the North American market for automotive steel. SNA is now the fourth-largest integrated steelmaker in North America.

Most of SeverStal's customers have operations throughout the world, and they want to be supplied with the same-quality steel, no matter their location. SeverStal's strategy "is to create a global production platform that can supply high-quality steel to customers, wherever they are located," says Sergei Kuznetsov, SeverStal North America's chief financial officer.

All these plans call for a flexible IT infrastructure that is agile enough to meet changing global business

requirements and support efficient growth. SNA's IT infrastructure was a hodgepodge of different systems, including Oracle PeopleSoft Enterprise for financials, Indus Enterprise PAC for purchasing and maintenance, and a variety of custom systems. Information was unable to flow freely across different functional areas.

Instead of upgrading its existing applications, SNA standardized on Oracle E-Business Suite 12, an enterprise applications suite that includes modules for financials, purchasing, enterprise asset management, manufacturing, and order management. The applications in Oracle E-Business Suite are integrated, making it easier to access data from different functional areas for decision making while creating more efficient work flows and enhancing productivity. Instead of optimizing individual business processes, the company is able to optimize end-to-end processes. For example, SNA's procure-to-pay

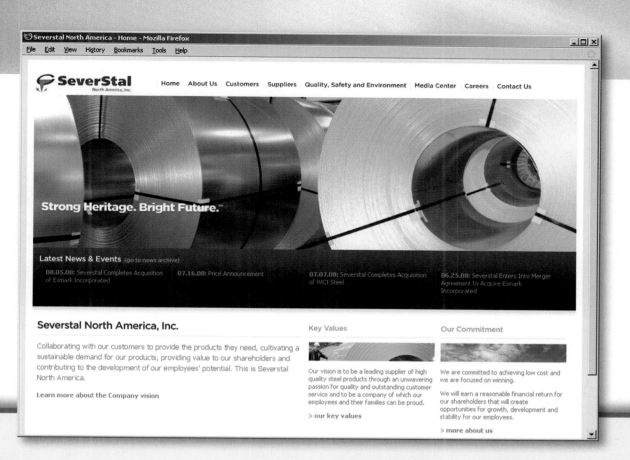

processes are integrated with its purchasing system.

The new system also reduced the time required to close the company's books from 10 days to 5 days or less, providing more timely and higher-quality information to the SeverStal parent company in Russia. Oracle iSupplier Portal, Oracle iProcurement, and Oracle Sourcing include capabilities for electronic

quoting and self-service applications, facilitating communication and collaboration with SNA's suppliers and business partners. In 2008, SeverStal bought a controlling interest in Canada's High River Gold Ltd. Interestingly, all of High River's assets, that is, the company's gold mines, are in Russia and Africa. SeverStal has been in the gold mining business since 2007. As SeverStal

grows organically or through acquisitions, the Oracle software will help it integrate new units on the same platform.

Sources: David A. Kelly, "Managing in a Global Economy: SeverStal," *Profit Magazine*, February 2008, **www.severstal.com/eng** (accessed June 28, 2008); and "SeverStal Boosts Stake in Canada's High River Gold Ltd., **www.tradingmarkets.com/print.site/news/Stock%20News/2039414** (accessed September 25, 2009).

SeverStal's efforts to create a global IT infrastructure identify some of the issues that organizations need to consider if they want to operate across the globe. In order to operate as a global business, the company had to have the right set of business processes and information systems in place.

The chapter-opening diagram calls attention to important points raised by this case and this chapter. SeverStal is trying to eke profits in a competitive and capital-intensive industry by providing products that can command higher prices in niche markets, but it still needs to keep its operating costs low. It adopted

a global production model to meet this challenge. SeverStal's legacy information systems did not support global business processes and information flows, so the company replaced them with a set of enterprise applications. The company is now able to respond flexibly to opportunities all over the world.

11.1 The Growth of International Information Systems

In other chapters, we describe the emergence of a global economic system and global world order driven by advanced networks and information systems. The new world order is sweeping away many national corporations, national industries, and national economies controlled by domestic politicians. Many localized firms will be replaced by fast-moving networked corporations that transcend national boundaries. The growth of international trade has radically altered domestic economies around the globe.

Today, the production and design of many electronic products are parcelled out to a number of different countries. Consider the path to market for a Hewlett-Packard (HP) laptop computer, which is illustrated in Figure 11-1.

The idea for the product and initial design came from HP's Laptop Design Team in the United States. HP headquarters in Houston approved the concept. Graphics processors were designed in Canada and manufactured in Taiwan. Taiwan and South Korea provided the liquid-crystal display screens and many of the memory chips. The laptop's hard disk drive came from Japan. Sources in China, Japan, Singapore, South Korea, and the United States supplied other components. Laptop assembly took place in China. Contractors in Taiwan did the machine's engineering design and collaborated with the Chinese manufacturers.

Developing an International Information Systems Architecture

This chapter describes how to go about building an international information systems architecture suitable for your international strategy. An **international information systems architecture** consists of the basic information systems required by organizations to coordinate worldwide trade and other activities. Figure 11-2 illustrates the reasoning we follow throughout the chapter and depicts the major dimensions of an international information systems architecture.

The basic strategy to follow when building an international system is to understand the global environment in which your firm is operating. This means understanding the overall market forces or business drivers that are pushing your industry toward global competition. A **business driver** is a force in the environment to which businesses must respond and that influences the direction of the business. Likewise, examine carefully the inhibitors or negative factors that create *management challenges*—factors that could scuttle the development of a global business. Once you have examined the global environment, you will need to consider a corporate strategy for competing in that environment.

International information systems
architecture

Business driver

FIGURE 11-1   An HP laptop's path to market.

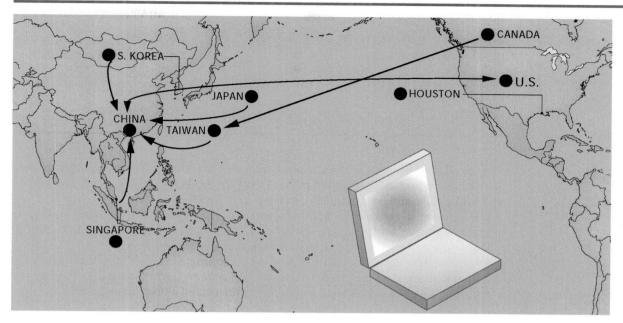

Hewlett-Packard and other electronics companies assign distribution and production of their products to a number of different countries.

How will your firm respond? You could ignore the global market and focus on domestic competition only, sell to the globe from a domestic base, or organize production and distribution around the globe. There are many in-between choices.

After you have developed a strategy, it is time to consider how to structure your organization so it can pursue the strategy. How will you accomplish a division of labour across a global environment? Where will production, administration, accounting, marketing, and human resource functions be located? Who will handle the systems function?

Next, you must consider the management issues in implementing your strategy and making the organization design come alive. Key here will be the design of business

FIGURE 11-2   International information systems architecture.

The major dimensions for developing an international information systems architecture are the global environment, the corporate global strategies, the structure of the organization, the management and business processes, and the technology platform.

TABLE 11-1   The global environment: Business drivers and challenges.

GENERAL CULTURAL FACTORS	SPECIFIC BUSINESS FACTORS
Global communication and transportation technologies	Global markets
Development of global culture	Global production and operations
Emergence of global social norms	Global coordination
Political stability	Global workforce
Global knowledge base	Global economies of scale

processes. How can you discover and manage user requirements? How can you induce change in local units to conform to international requirements? How can you re-engineer on a global scale, and how can you coordinate systems development?

The last issue to consider is the technology platform. Although changing technology is a key driving factor leading toward global markets, you need to have a corporate strategy and structure before you can rationally choose the right technology.

After you have completed this process of reasoning, you will be well on your way toward an appropriate international information systems portfolio capable of achieving your corporate goals. Let us begin by looking at the overall global environment.

The Global Environment: Business Drivers and Challenges

Table 11-1 lists the business drivers in the global environment that are leading all industries toward global markets and competition.

The global business drivers can be divided into two groups: general cultural factors and specific business factors. Easily recognized general cultural factors have driven internationalization since World War II. Information, communication, and transportation technologies have created a *global village* in which communication (by telephone, television, radio, or computer network) around the globe is no more difficult and not much more expensive than communication down the block. The cost of moving goods and services to and from geographically dispersed locations has fallen dramatically.

The development of global communications has created a global village in a second sense: A **global culture** created by television, the Internet, and other globally shared media such as movies now permits different cultures and peoples to develop common expectations about right and wrong, desirable and undesirable, heroic and cowardly. The collapse of the Eastern bloc has speeded the growth of a world culture enormously, increased support for capitalism and business, and reduced the level of cultural conflict considerably.

A last factor to consider is the growth of a global knowledge base. At the end of World War II, knowledge, education, science, and industrial skills were highly concentrated in North America, western Europe, and Japan, with the rest of the world euphemistically called the *Third World*. This is no longer true. Latin America, China, India, southern Asia, and eastern Europe have developed powerful educational, industrial, and scientific centres, resulting in a much more democratically and widely dispersed knowledge base.

These general cultural factors leading toward internationalization result in specific business globalization factors that affect most industries. The growth of powerful communications technologies and the emergence of world cultures create the condition for *global markets*—global consumers interested in consuming similar products that are culturally approved. Coca-Cola, American runners (made in Korea but designed in Los Angeles), and Cable News Network (CNN) programming can now be sold in Latin America, Africa, and Asia. Roots clothing is sold in North America and in Asia while Nygård has offices in Canada, the United States, and Asia with sales across North America.

Responding to this demand, global production and operations have emerged with precise online coordination between far-flung production facilities and central headquarters thousands of miles away. The new global markets and pressure toward global production and operation have called forth whole new capabilities for global coordination.

Global culture

Production, accounting, marketing and sales, human resources, and systems development (all the major business functions) can be coordinated on a global scale. In Canada, two Ontario doctors used telerobotic surgery on a North Bay General Hospital patient hundreds of miles away. The pilot was deemed a success by the surgical teams who performed this first-time procedure. A U.S. surgeon has already operated on a patient in France using telerobotics; it is only a matter of time before this is commonplace.

In marketing, Frito Lay can develop a sales force automation system in the United States and may try the same techniques and technologies in Spain. Micromarketing—marketing to very small geographic and social units—no longer means marketing to neighbourhoods in the U.S., but to neighbourhoods throughout the world. These new levels of global coordination permit for the first time the location of business activity according to comparative advantage. Design should be located where it is best accomplished, as should marketing, production, and finance.

Finally, global markets, production, and administration create the conditions for powerful, sustained global economies of scale. Production driven by worldwide global demand can be concentrated where it can best be accomplished, fixed resources can be allocated over larger production runs, and production runs in larger plants can be scheduled more efficiently and can be more precisely estimated. Lower cost factors of production can be exploited wherever they emerge. The result is a powerful strategic advantage to firms that can organize globally. These general and specific business drivers have greatly enlarged world trade and commerce.

Not all industries are similarly affected by these trends. Clearly, manufacturing has been much more affected than services that still tend to be domestic and highly inefficient. However, the localism of services is breaking down in telecommunications, entertainment, transportation, financial services, and general business services including law. Clearly, those firms within an industry that can understand the internationalization of the industry and respond appropriately will reap enormous gains in productivity and stability.

In fact, not all countries are similarly affected by these trends. While some may be affected over a longer period of time, four countries are developing rapidly enough that have been labelled the BRIC countries. These are Brazil, Russia, India, and China. These four countries, combined, currently account for more than a quarter of the world's land area and more than 40 percent of the world's population. While BRIC countries have not yet formed a strategic alliance, they have instituted a BRIC Summit and made informal arrangements. This type of alliance should be monitored as these countries and other alliances can significantly influence our information systems, markets, and other business dynamics.

Business Challenges Although the possibilities of globalization for business success are significant, fundamental forces are operating to inhibit a global economy and to disrupt international business. Table 11-2 lists the most common and powerful challenges to the development of global systems.

At a cultural level, **particularism,** making judgments and taking action on the basis of narrow or personal characteristics, in all its forms (religious, nationalistic, ethnic, regionalism, geopolitical position) rejects the very concept of a shared global culture and rejects the penetration of domestic markets by foreign goods and services. Differences among

Particularism

TABLE 11-2 Challenges and obstacles to global business systems.

GLOBAL	SPECIFIC
Cultural particularism: Regionalism, nationalism, language differences	Standards: Different Electronic Data Interchange (EDI), e-mail, telecommunications standards
Social expectations: Brand-name expectations, work hours	Reliability: Phone networks not uniformly reliable
Political laws: Transborder data and privacy laws, commercial regulations	Speed: Different data transfer speeds, many slower than Canada
	Personnel: Shortages of skilled consultants

cultures produce differences in social expectations, politics, and ultimately legal rules. In certain countries, such as Canada, consumers expect domestic name-brand products to be built domestically and are disappointed to learn that much of what they thought of as domestically produced is in fact foreign-made.

Different cultures produce different political regimes. Among the many different countries of the world are different laws governing the movement of information, information privacy of their citizens, origins of software and hardware in systems, and radio and satellite telecommunications. Even the hours of business and the terms of business trade vary greatly across political cultures. These different legal regimes complicate global business and must be considered when developing global systems.

For instance, European countries have very strict laws concerning transborder data flow and privacy. **Transborder data flow** is defined as the movement of information across international boundaries in any form. Some European countries prohibit the processing of financial information outside their boundaries or the movement of personal information to foreign countries. The *European Union Data Protection Directive*, which went into effect in October 1998, restricts the flow of any information to countries (such as Canada; see Chapter 4 for more on this topic) that do not meet strict European information laws on personal information. Financial services, travel, and health care companies could be directly affected. In response, most multinational firms develop information systems within each European country to avoid the cost and uncertainty of moving information across national boundaries.

Cultural and political differences profoundly affect organizations' business processes and applications of information technology. A host of specific barriers arises from the general cultural differences, everything from differing reliability of phone networks to the shortage of skilled consultants.

National laws and traditions have created disparate accounting practices in various countries, which impact the ways profits and losses are analyzed. German companies generally do not recognize the profit from a venture until the project is completely finished and they have been paid. Conversely, British firms begin posting profits before a project is completed, when they are reasonably certain they will get the money.

These accounting practices are tightly intertwined with each country's legal system, business philosophy, and tax code. Canadian, British, U.S., and Dutch firms share a predominantly Anglo-Saxon outlook that separates tax calculations from reports to shareholders to focus on showing shareholders how fast profits are growing. Continental European accounting practices are less oriented toward impressing investors, focusing rather on demonstrating compliance with strict rules and minimizing tax liabilities. These diverging accounting practices make it difficult for large international companies with units in different countries to evaluate their performance.

Language remains a significant barrier. Although English has become a kind of standard business language, this is truer at higher levels of companies and not throughout the middle and lower ranks. Software may have to be developed with local language interfaces before a new information system can be successfully implemented.

Currency fluctuations can play havoc with planning models and projections. A product that appears profitable in Mexico or Japan may actually produce a loss because of changes in foreign exchange rates.

These inhibiting factors must be taken into account when you are designing and developing international systems for your business. For example, companies trying to implement "lean production" systems spanning national boundaries typically underestimate the time, expense, and logistical difficulties of making goods and information flow freely across different countries.

State of the Art

Given the opportunities for achieving competitive advantages as outlined previously and the interest in future applications, one might think that most international companies have rationally developed marvellous international systems architectures. Nothing could be further from the truth. Most companies have inherited patchwork international systems from

Transborder data flow

the distant past, often based on concepts of information processing developed in the 1960s—batch-oriented reporting from independent foreign divisions to corporate headquarters, manual entry of data from one legacy system to another, with little online control and communication. Corporations in this situation increasingly face powerful competitive challenges in the marketplace from firms that have rationally designed truly international systems. Still other companies have recently developed technology platforms for international systems but have nowhere to go because they lack global strategy.

As it turns out, there are significant difficulties in developing appropriate international architectures. The difficulties involve planning a system appropriate to the firm's global strategy, structuring the organization of systems and business units, solving implementation issues, and choosing the right technical platform. Let us examine these problems in greater detail.

11.2   Organizing International Information Systems

Three organizational issues face corporations seeking a global position: choosing a strategy, organizing the business, and organizing the information systems management area. The first two are closely connected, so we discuss them together.

Global Strategies and Business Organization

Four main global strategies form the basis for global firms' organizational structure. These are domestic exporter, multinational, franchiser, and transnational. Each of these strategies is pursued with a specific business organizational structure (see Table 11-3). For simplicity's sake, we describe three kinds of organizational structure or governance: centralized (in the home country), decentralized (to local foreign units), and coordinated (all units participate as equals). Other types of governance patterns can be observed in specific companies (e.g., authoritarian dominance by one unit, a confederacy of equals, a federal structure balancing power among strategic units, and so forth).

The **domestic exporter** strategy is characterized by heavy centralization of corporate activities in the home country of origin. Nearly all international companies begin this way, and some move on to other forms. Production, finance/accounting, sales/marketing, human resources, and strategic management are organized to optimize resources in the home country. International sales are sometimes dispersed using agency agreements or subsidiaries, but, even here, foreign marketing is totally reliant on the domestic home base for marketing themes and strategies. Caterpillar Corporation and other heavy capital-equipment manufacturers, as well as Roots and Nygård, fall into this category of firm.

The **multinational** strategy concentrates financial management and control out of a central home base while decentralizing production, sales, and marketing operations to units in other countries. The products and services on sale in different countries are adapted to suit local market conditions. The organization becomes a far-flung confederation of production and marketing facilities in different countries. Many financial service firms, such as TD Canada Trust, along with a host of manufacturers, such as Bombardier, Chrysler, and Intel, fit this pattern.

Domestic exporter
Multinational

TABLE 11-3   Global business strategy and structure.

BUSINESS FUNCTION	DOMESTIC EXPORTER	MULTINATIONAL	FRANCHISER	TRANSNATIONAL
Production	Centralized	Dispersed	Coordinated	Coordinated
Finance/Accounting	Centralized	Centralized	Centralized	Coordinated
Sales/Marketing	Mixed	Dispersed	Coordinated	Coordinated
Human Resources	Centralized	Centralized	Coordinated	Coordinated
Strategic Management	Centralized	Centralized	Centralized	Coordinated

Franchisers are an interesting mix of old and new. On the one hand, the product is created, designed, financed, and initially produced in the home country, but for product-specific reasons, must rely heavily on foreign personnel for further production, marketing, and human resources. Food franchisers such as McDonald's, Mrs. Fields Cookies, and KFC fit this pattern. McDonald's created a new form of fast-food chain in the United States and continues to rely largely on the United States for inspiration of new products, strategic management, and financing. Nevertheless, because the product must be produced locally—it is perishable—extensive coordination and dispersal of production, local marketing, and local recruitment of personnel are required.

Generally, foreign franchisees are clones of the mother-country units, but fully coordinated worldwide production that could optimize factors of production is not possible. For instance, potatoes and beef can generally not be bought where they are cheapest on world markets but must be produced and purchased reasonably close to the area of consumption.

Transnational firms are the stateless, truly globally managed firms that may represent a larger part of international business in the future. Transnational firms have no single national headquarters but instead have many regional headquarters and perhaps a world headquarters. In a **transnational** strategy, nearly all the value-adding activities are managed from a global perspective without reference to national borders, optimizing sources of supply and demand wherever they appear, and taking advantage of any local competitive advantages. Transnational firms take the globe, not the home country, as their management frame of reference. The governance of these firms has been likened to a federal structure in which there is a strong central management core of decision making, but considerable dispersal of power and financial muscle throughout the global divisions. Few companies have actually attained transnational status, but Nestlé, Citicorp, Sony, Ford Motor Company, and others are attempting this transition.

Information technology and improvements in global telecommunications are giving international firms more flexibility to shape their global strategies. Protectionism and a need to serve local markets better encourage companies to disperse production facilities and at least become multinational. At the same time, the drive to achieve economies of scale and take advantage of short-term local advantage moves transnationals toward a global management perspective and a concentration of power and authority. Hence, there are forces of decentralization and dispersion as well as forces of centralization and global coordination.

Global Systems to Fit the Strategy

Information technology and improvements in global telecommunications are giving international firms more flexibility to shape their global strategies. The configuration, management, and development of systems tend to follow the global strategy chosen. Figure 11-3 depicts the typical arrangements. By *systems*, we mean the full range of activities involved in building and operating information systems: conception and alignment with the strategic business plan, systems development, and ongoing operation and maintenance. For the sake of simplicity, we consider four types of systems configuration. *Centralized systems* are those

Franchisers
Transnational

FIGURE 11-3 Global strategy and systems configurations.

The large Xs show the dominant patterns, and the small Xs show the emerging patterns. For instance, domestic exporters rely predominantly on centralized systems, but there is continual pressure and some development of decentralized systems in local marketing regions.

SYSTEM CONFIGURATION	Strategy			
	Domestic Exporter	Multinational	Franchiser	Transnational
Centralized	X			
Duplicated			X	
Decentralized	x	X	x	
Networked		x		X

in which systems development and operation occur totally at the domestic home base. *Duplicated systems* are those in which development occurs at the home base but operations are handed over to autonomous units in foreign locations. *Decentralized systems* are those in which each foreign unit designs its own unique solutions and systems. *Networked systems* are those in which systems development and operations occur in an integrated and coordinated fashion across all units.

As can be seen in Figure 11-3, domestic exporters tend to have highly centralized systems in which a single domestic systems development staff develops worldwide applications. Multinationals offer a direct and striking contrast: Here, foreign units devise their own systems solutions based on local needs with few if any applications in common with headquarters (the exceptions being financial reporting and some telecommunications applications). Franchisers have the simplest systems structure: Like the products they sell, franchisers develop a single system usually at the home base and then replicate it around the world. Each unit, no matter where it is located, has identical applications. Last, the most ambitious form of systems development is found in the transnational: Networked systems are those in which there is a solid, singular global environment for developing and operating systems. This usually presupposes a powerful telecommunications backbone, a culture of shared applications development, and a shared management culture that crosses cultural barriers. The networked systems structure is the most visible in financial services where the homogeneity of the product—money and money instruments—seems to overcome cultural barriers.

Reorganizing the Business

How should a firm organize itself for doing business on an international scale? To develop a global company and information systems support structure, a firm needs to follow these principles:

1. Organize value-adding activities along lines of comparative advantage. For instance, marketing/sales functions should be located where they can best be performed, for least cost and maximum impact; likewise with production, finance, human resources, and information systems.

2. Develop and operate systems units at each level of corporate activity—regional, national, and international. To serve local needs, there should be host-country systems units of some magnitude. Regional systems units should handle telecommunications and systems development across national boundaries that take place within major geographic regions (European, Asian, North American, South American, etc.). Transnational systems units should be established to create the linkages across major regional areas and coordinate the development and operation of international telecommunications and systems development (Roche, 1992).

3. Establish at world headquarters a single office responsible for development of international systems—a global chief information officer (CIO) position.

Many successful companies have devised organizational systems structures along these principles. The success of these companies relies not only on the proper organization of activities, but also on a key ingredient—a management team that can understand the risks and benefits of international systems and that can devise strategies for overcoming the risks. We turn to these management topics next.

11.3 Managing Global Systems

Table 11-4 lists the principal management problems posed by developing international systems. It is interesting to note that these problems are the chief difficulties managers experience in developing ordinary domestic systems as well. But these are enormously complicated in the international environment.

TABLE 11-4   Management challenges in developing global systems.

Agreeing on common user requirements
Introducing changes in business processes
Coordinating applications development
Coordinating software releases
Encouraging local users to support global systems.

A Typical Scenario: Disorganization on a Global Scale

Let us look at a common scenario. A traditional multinational consumer-goods company based in Canada and operating in Europe would like to expand into Asian markets and knows that it must develop a transnational strategy and a supportive information systems structure. Like most multinationals, it has dispersed production and marketing to regional and national centres while maintaining a world headquarters and strategic management in Canada. Historically, it has allowed each of the subsidiary foreign divisions to develop its own systems. The only centrally coordinated system is financial controls and reporting. The central systems group in Canada focuses only on domestic functions and production.

The result is a hodgepodge of hardware, software, and telecommunications. The e-mail systems between Europe and Canada are incompatible. Each production facility uses a different manufacturing resources planning system (or a different version of the same ERP system), and different marketing, sales, and human resource systems. Hardware and database platforms are wildly different. Communications between different sites are poor, given the high cost of European intercountry communications. The central systems group at headquarters in Canada recently was decimated and dispersed to Canadian local sites in the hope of serving local needs better and reducing costs.

What do you recommend to the senior management leaders of this company, who now want to pursue a transnational strategy and develop an information systems architecture to support a highly coordinated global systems environment? Consider the problems you face by re-examining Table 11-4. The foreign divisions will resist efforts to agree on common user requirements; they have never thought about much other than their own units' needs. The systems groups in Canadian local sites, which have been enlarged recently and told to focus on local needs, will not easily accept guidance from anyone recommending a transnational strategy. It will be difficult to convince local managers anywhere in the world that they should change their business procedures to align with other units in the world, especially if this might interfere with their local performance. After all, local managers are rewarded in this company for meeting local objectives of their division or plant. Finally, it will be difficult to coordinate development of projects around the world in the absence of a powerful telecommunications network and, therefore, difficult to encourage local users to take on ownership in the systems to be developed.

Global Systems Strategy

Figure 11-4 lays out the main dimensions of a solution. First, consider that not all systems should be coordinated on a transnational basis; only some core systems are truly worth sharing from a cost and feasibility point of view. **Core systems** are systems that support functions that are absolutely critical to the organization. Other systems should be partially coordinated because they share key elements, but they do not have to be totally common across national boundaries. For such systems, a good deal of local variation is possible and desirable. A final group of systems is peripheral, truly provincial, and needed to suit local requirements only.

Define the Core Business Processes   How do you identify core systems? The first step is to define a short list of critical core business processes. Business processes are defined and described in Chapter 2, which you should review. Briefly, business processes are sets

Core systems

FIGURE 11-4   Local, regional, and global systems.

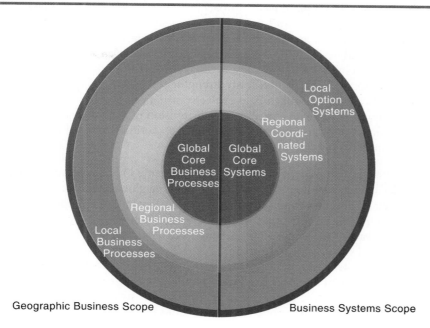

Geographic Business Scope   Business Systems Scope

Agency and other coordination costs increase as the firm moves from local option systems toward regional and global systems. However, transaction costs of participating in global markets probably decrease as firms develop global systems. A sensible strategy is to reduce agency costs by developing only a few core global systems that are vital for global operations, leaving other systems in the hands of regional and local units.

Source: From *Managing Information Technology in Multinational Corporations* by Edward M. Roche, © 1993. Adapted by permission of Prentice Hall, Inc., Upper Saddle River, N.J.

of logically related tasks to produce specific business results, such as shipping out correct orders to customers or delivering innovative products to the market. Each business process typically involves many functional areas, communicating and coordinating work, information, and knowledge.

The way to identify these core business processes is to conduct a business process analysis. How are customer orders taken, what happens to them once they are taken, who fills the orders, and how are they shipped to the customers? What about suppliers? Do they have access to manufacturing resource planning systems so that supply is automatic? You should be able to identify and set priorities in a short list of 10 business processes that are absolutely critical for the firm.

Next, can you identify centres of excellence for these processes? Is the customer order fulfillment superior in Canada, manufacturing process control superior in Germany, and human resources superior in Asia? You should be able to identify some areas of the company, for some lines of business, where a division or unit stands out in the performance of one or several business functions.

When you understand the business processes of a firm, you can rank-order them. You then can decide which processes should be core applications—centrally coordinated, designed, and implemented around the globe—and which should be regional and local. At the same time, by identifying the critical business processes, the really important ones, you have gone a long way toward defining a vision of the future that you should be working toward.

Identify the Core Systems to Coordinate Centrally By identifying the critical core business processes, you begin to see opportunities for transnational systems. The second strategic step is to conquer the core systems and define these systems as truly transnational. The financial and political costs of defining and implementing transnational systems are extremely high. Therefore, keep the list to an absolute minimum, letting experience be the guide and erring on the side of minimalism. By dividing off a small group of systems as absolutely critical, you divide opposition to a transnational strategy. At the same time, you can appease those who oppose the central worldwide coordination implied by transnational systems by permitting peripheral systems development to progress unabated, with the exception of some technical platform requirements.

Choose an Approach: Incremental, Grand Design, Evolutionary A third step is to choose an approach. Avoid piecemeal approaches. These surely will fail for lack of visibility, opposition from all who stand to lose from transnational development, and lack of power to convince senior management that the transnational systems are worth it. Likewise, avoid grand design approaches that try to do everything at once. These also tend to fail because of an inability to focus resources. Nothing gets done properly, and opposition to organizational change is needlessly strengthened because the effort requires huge resources. An alternative approach is to evolve transnational applications incrementally from existing applications with a precise and clear vision of the transnational capabilities the organization should have in five years. This is sometimes referred to as the "salami strategy," or "one slice at a time."

Make the Benefits Clear What is in it for the company? One of the worst situations to avoid is building global systems for the sake of building global systems. From the beginning, it is crucial that senior management at headquarters and foreign division managers clearly understand the benefits that will come to the company as well as to individual units. Although each system offers unique benefits to a particular budget, the overall contribution of global systems lies in four areas.

Global systems—truly integrated, distributed, and transnational systems—contribute to superior management and coordination. A simple price tag cannot be put on the value of this contribution, and the benefit will not show up in any capital budgeting model. It includes the ability to switch suppliers on a moment's notice from one region to another in a crisis, the ability to move production in response to natural disasters, and the ability to use excess capacity in one region to meet raging demand in another.

A second major contribution is vast improvement in production, operation, and supply and distribution. Imagine a global value chain, with global suppliers and a global distribution network. For the first time, senior managers can locate value-adding activities in regions where they are most economically performed.

Third, global systems mean global customers and global marketing. Fixed costs around the world can be amortized over a much larger customer base. This will unleash new economies of scale at production facilities.

Last, global systems mean the ability to optimize the use of corporate funds over a much larger capital base. This means, for instance, that capital in a surplus region can be moved efficiently to expand the production of capital-starved regions and that cash can be managed more effectively within the company and put to use more effectively.

These strategies will not by themselves create global systems. You will have to implement what you strategize.

The Management Solution

We now can reconsider how to handle the most vexing problems facing managers developing the global information systems architectures that were described in Table 11-4.

Agreeing on Common User Requirements Establishing a short list of the core business processes and core support systems will begin a process of rational comparison across the many divisions of the company, develop a common language for discussing the business, and naturally lead to an understanding of common elements (as well as the unique qualities that must remain local).

Introducing Changes in Business Processes Your success as a change agent will depend on your legitimacy, your authority, and your ability to involve users in the change design process. **Legitimacy** is defined as the extent to which your authority is accepted on grounds of competence, vision, or other qualities. The selection of a viable change strategy, which we have defined as evolutionary but with a vision, should assist you in convincing others that change is feasible and desirable. Involving people in change, assuring them that change is in the best interests of the company and their local units, is a key tactic.

Legitimacy

Coordinating Applications Development Choice of change strategy is critical for this problem. At the global level, there is far too much complexity to attempt a grand design strategy of change. It is far easier to coordinate change by making small, incremental steps toward a larger vision. Imagine a five-year plan of action rather than a two-year plan of action, and reduce the set of transnational systems to a bare minimum to reduce coordination costs.

The Window on Management describes how Colgate-Palmolive Company developed a strategy for coordinating information systems projects on a global basis. SAP's Resource and Portfolio Management software helped Colgate take a global perspective in selecting, staffing, and tracking projects.

Management

WINDOW ON MANAGEMENT

Colgate-Palmolive Keeps the World Smiling

Colgate-Palmolive Company is the second-largest consumer products company in the world, whose products are marketed in over 200 countries and territories. The company has 36 000 employees worldwide and $17 billion annual revenue. Colgate has been keeping people smiling and clean around the world, with more than three-quarters of its sales in recent years coming from outside the United States. Colgate's brands in oral products, soap, and pet food are recognized around the world, including Colgate, Palmolive, Mennen, Softsoap, Irish Spring, Protex, Sorriso, Kolynos, Elmex, Tom's of Maine, Ajax, Axion, Fabuloso, Soupline, and Suavitel, as well as Hill's Science Diet and Hill's Prescription Diet.

The secret to continued growth and stability since 1990 has been Colgate's ability to move its brands off-shore to Latin America, Europe, and Asia. Managing IT projects in a company operating in 200 countries poses unique challenges, not least of which is keeping track of who in the company is working on what IT projects and how much money is being spent on all these projects. In the past, Colgate divided the world into geographic regions: Latin America, Europe, Asia, and North America. Each region planned its own IT projects and deployed available resources to build those systems. Within regions, IT resources (which included human and financial capital) were coordinated with spreadsheets being e-mailed among the operating companies and offices within each region. At the global corporate level, spreadsheets were also used to roll up the numbers to central planners in the United States.

In other words, a state of global system disorganization existed at Colgate typical of firms that grew rapidly into multinational giants.

As long as the regions did not need to share resources or information and projects were localized, this patchwork system worked, more or less. Still, central executives in the United States had no idea who was working on which project, and had lost control over IT resources to the regions. This all

changed as global operations became more integrated. A U.S.-based team was building a factory in Poland, and Asian teams were working with their European counterparts on sharing IT systems. There was no mechanism for coordinating the company's global IT operation. Senior management realized that Colgate needed a coordinated, global approach to IT resources and that the regional system was terribly inefficient and ineffective.

In order to establish some control over IT projects worldwide, Colgate adopted SAP's Resource and Portfolio Management (RPM) software. SAP RPM is an integrated or "composite" application that uses the functions from SAP NetWeaver Business Intelligence (SAP NetWeaver BI) to report data. This application enables companies to inventory and track resources, skills, and budgets related to planning and managing of projects. It uses user-friendly dashboards with traffic-light indicators to relay the status of budgets, schedules, and key performance indicators (KPIs). Because it is a composite application, it integrates with SAP ERP Human Capital Management (SAP ERP HCM) and other SAP systems. SAP claims that its RPM application will enable a company to achieve a "real-time" view of its IT project portfolio and better synchronize those projects with corporate strategy and priorities.

This is how it works. Every year, Colgate's corporate IT department reviews a slate of projects submitted by various corporate groups, establishes priorities, and approves or disapproves projects. Monthly, IT personnel from around the world submit "Actuals Reports" that identify the actual use of IT people and funds in that month. These data are rolled up into a comprehensive resource report for the entire company. One result is a listing of available people to work on new approved projects and who can be shared across the organization, as well as a comprehensive overview of who is working on maintenance programs, and who is developing new applications. One objective of the new application is to outsource as much maintenance work as possible to less-expensive off-shore firms while promoting more development work for internal IT staff in the regions that are closer to the customer.

The monitoring and reporting capabilities of SAP RPM enable the Colgate IT team to better align its priorities to business objectives. The measurement of actual time spent working on IT initiatives has enabled a clear understanding of the percentage of time spent on application development and support. Over a two-year period, CIO Tom Greene believes he has discovered a hidden 20 percent resource pool in the IT organization as it became apparent many people were not being used efficiently. Outsourcing of maintenance work has increased by 40 percent, allowing internal IT staff to focus on developing systems to serve customer needs.

To Think About

1. Why was the traditional method of allocating IT resources to profits no longer effective?

2. Why is it important for central management to understand the global disposition of IT personnel and funds?

3. Which of the four global business strategies described in this chapter is Colgate pursuing, and how has this affected its selection of an IT resource management system?

4. What elements of "The Management Solution," described in this chapter, are mentioned in the Colgate case study? What elements are missing?

MIS in Action

Explore the Colgate Web (**www.colgate.com**), site and then answer the following questions:

1. Go to the SAP Web site (be sure to use **sap.com**, not **spa.ca**) and search on "RPM." Read SAP's description of the product and identify (a) other firms that use the product, and (b) how RPM integrates into ("snaps" into) larger SAP resource management applications.

2. Visit SAP's largest competitor, Oracle.com, and identify similar applications provided by Oracle. What do you think are the most important management and business considerations in deciding between Oracle and SAP solutions for global projects?

3. Visit HP.com and search on "Business Technology Optimization." BTO is a suite of products provided by HP to optimize the use of IT resources. Describe this suite of offerings, and identify one global firm that uses this technology. Describe the global strategy of this firm, how it has changed in recent years, and the reasons for adopting this HP software.

Sources: Evan Albright, "Colgate-Palmolive Takes Control of Global IT with SAP RPM," *SAPNetWeaver Magazine*, October 2008; Thomson, Inc., "SAP xApp Resource and Portfolio Management and SAP Consulting Enable Enterprise Wide Strategic and Operational R&D Portfolio Management," SAP White Paper, **www.sap.com** (accessed October 15, 2008); Colgate-Palmolive, Inc. Form 10K, filed with the Securities and Exchange Commission for the fiscal year ending December 31, 2007, filed February 28, 2008; ZDNet Australia, "Effective Management of Multiple Projects with SAP xApp Resource and Portfolio Management," August 28, 2007; and Bloomberg News, "New Products and Demand in Emerging Markets Fatten Profits at P&G and Colgate," *The New York Times*, January 31, 2007.

Coordinating Software Releases Firms can institute procedures to ensure that all operating units convert to new software updates at the same time so that everyone's software is compatible.

Encouraging Local Users to Support Global Systems The key to this problem is to involve users in the creation of the design without giving up control over the development of the project to parochial interests. The overall tactic for dealing with resistant local units in a transnational company is cooptation. **Cooptation** is defined as bringing the opposition into the process of designing and implementing the solution without giving up control over the direction and nature of the change. As much as possible, raw power should be avoided. Minimally, however, local units must agree on a short list of transnational systems, and raw power may be required to solidify the idea that transnational systems of some sort are truly required.

How should cooptation proceed? Several alternatives are possible. One alternative is to permit each country unit the opportunity to develop one transnational application first in its home territory, and then throughout the world. In this manner, each major country systems group is given a piece of the action in developing a transnational system, and local units feel a sense of ownership in the transnational effort. On the downside, this assumes that the ability to develop high-quality systems is widely distributed, and that, a German team, for example, can successfully implement systems in France and Italy. This will not always be the case.

A second tactic is to develop new transnational centres of excellence, or a single centre of excellence. There may be several centres around the globe that focus on specific business processes. These centres draw heavily from local national units, are based on multinational teams, and must report to worldwide management. Centres of excellence perform the initial

Cooptation

identification and specification of business processes, define the information requirements, perform the business and systems analysis, and accomplish all design and testing. Implementation, however, and pilot testing are rolled out to other parts of the globe. Recruiting a wide range of local groups to transnational centres of excellence helps send the message that all significant groups are involved in the design and will have an influence.

Even with the proper organizational structure and appropriate management choices, it is still possible to stumble over technology issues. Choices of technology platforms, networks, hardware, and software are the final element in building transnational information system architectures.

11.4 Technology Issues and Opportunities for Global Value Chains

Once firms have defined a global business model and systems strategy, they must select hardware, software, and networking standards along with key system applications to support global business processes. Hardware, software, and networking pose special technical challenges in an international setting.

One major challenge is finding some way to standardize on a global computing platform when there is so much variation from operating unit to operating unit and from country to country. Another major challenge is finding specific software applications that are user-friendly and that truly enhance the productivity of international work teams. The universal acceptance of the Internet around the globe has greatly reduced networking problems. But the mere presence of the Internet does not guarantee that information will flow seamlessly throughout the global organization because not all business units use the same applications, and the quality of Internet service can be highly variable (just as with the telephone service). For instance, German business units may use an open source collaboration tool to share documents and communicate, which is incompatible with American headquarters teams, which use Lotus Notes. Overcoming these challenges requires systems integration and connectivity on a global basis.

Computing Platforms and Systems Integration

The development of a transnational information systems architecture based on the concept of core systems raises questions about how the new core systems will fit in with the existing suite of applications developed around the globe by different divisions, by different people, and for different kinds of computing hardware. The goal is to develop global, distributed, and integrated systems to support digital business processes spanning national boundaries. Briefly, these are the same problems faced by any large domestic systems development effort. However, the problems are magnified in an international environment. Just imagine the challenge of integrating systems based on the Windows, Linux, Unix, or proprietary operating systems running on IBM, Sun, Hewlett-Packard, and other hardware in many different operating units in many different countries.

Moreover, having all sites use the same hardware and operating system does not guarantee integration. Some central authority in the firm must establish data and other technical standards, with which sites are to comply. For instance, technical accounting terms such as the beginning and end of the fiscal year must be standardized (review the earlier discussion of the cultural challenges to building global businesses) and the acceptable interfaces between systems, communication speeds and architectures, and network software. (The global move to accept the International Financial Reporting Standards put forth by the International Accounting Board will help to reconcile accounting differences.)

Connectivity

Truly integrated global systems must have connectivity—the ability to link together the systems and people of a global firm into a single integrated network just like the phone system

TABLE 11-5   Problems of international networks.

Quality/reliability of service
Security
Costs and tariffs
Network management
Installation delays
Poor quality of international service
Regulatory constraints
Network capacity

but capable of voice, data, and image transmissions. The Internet has provided an enormously powerful foundation for providing connectivity among the dispersed units of global firms. However, many issues remain. The public Internet does not guarantee any level of service (even in Canada). Few global corporations trust the security of the Internet and generally use private networks to communicate sensitive data, and Internet virtual private networks (VPN) for communications that require less security. Not all countries support even basic Internet service that requires obtaining reliable circuits, coordinating among different carriers and the regional telecommunications authority, obtaining bills in a common currency standard, and obtaining standard agreements for the level of telecommunications service provided. Table 11-5 lists the major challenges posed by international networks.

An increasingly attractive alternative is to create global networks based on the Internet and Internet technology. Companies can create global intranets for internal communication or extranets to exchange information more rapidly with business partners in their supply chains. They can use the public Internet to create global networks using VPNs from Internet service providers, which provide many features of a private network using the public Internet (see Chapter 7). However, VPNs may not provide the same level of quick and predictable response as private networks, especially during times of the day when Internet traffic is very congested, and they may not be able to support large numbers of remote users.

The high cost of PCs, along with low incomes, limit access to Internet service in many developing countries (see Figure 11-5). Where an Internet infrastructure exists in

FIGURE 11-5   Internet penetration by region.

The percentage of the total population using the Internet in developing countries is much smaller than in North America and Europe.

Source: Internetworldstats.com, 2008.

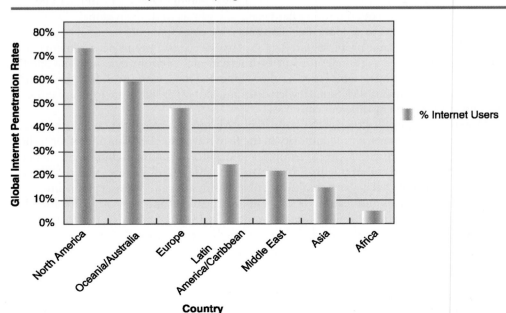

less-developed countries, it often lacks bandwidth capacity and is unreliable in part due to power grid issues. The purchasing power of most people in developing countries makes access to Internet services very expensive in local currencies. In addition, many countries monitor transmissions. Governments in China, Singapore, Iran, and Saudi Arabia monitor Internet traffic and block access to Web sites considered morally or politically offensive. On the other hand, the rate of growth in the Internet population is far faster in Asia, Africa, and the Middle East than in North America and Europe, where the Internet population is growing slowly, if at all. In 2009, China, for instance, has more than 200 million Internet users compared to Canada with about 28 million, even though Canada is a larger country in terms of geographic size. Therefore, in the future, Internet connectivity will be much more widely available and reliable in less-developed regions of the world, and it will play a significant role in integrating these economies with the world economy.

The Window on Organizations describes how cell phones provide a partial solution to this problem. Their use is mushrooming in developing countries and they are starting to become engines for economic development.

Software Localization

The development of core systems poses unique challenges for application software: How will the old systems interface with the new? Entirely new interfaces must be built and tested if old systems are kept in local areas (which is common). These interfaces can be costly and messy to build. If new software must be created, another challenge is to develop software that can be realistically used by multiple business units from different countries given that these business units are accustomed to their unique business processes and definitions of data.

 # WINDOW ON ORGANIZATIONS

Can Cell Phones Close the Global Digital Divide?

As cell phones, the Internet, high-speed Internet connections, and other information and communication technologies become increasingly widespread, more and more people are experiencing the benefits each technology has to offer. Many of these technologies have not yet closed the "digital divide" separating the world's well-developed and underdeveloped nations. Some countries, like Canada, have access to most new technologies, but most residents of poorer countries still struggle with challenges like abject poverty and obtaining reliable electricity. Recent trends in cell phone design and consumer research indicate that cellular phones are poised to cross the digital divide and become a truly ubiquitous technology, enhancing the quality of life for millions of people while also increasing the strength of the global economy.

Sixty-eight percent of the world's mobile phone subscriptions are in developing countries, compared with 20 percent of the world's Internet users. Because cell phones combine features of watches, alarm clocks, cameras and video cameras, stereos, televisions, and perhaps even wallets soon due to the growing popularity of mobile banking, they are growing in usefulness even as they decrease in price. Most importantly, cell phones are increasingly becoming the most convenient and affordable way to connect to the Internet and perform other tasks traditionally associated with computers.

The possession of a cell phone greatly increases efficiency and quality of life, so the global economy would stand to benefit on a proportionally large scale. Many economists believe that widespread cell phone usage in developing countries would have a profound and revolutionary effect on their economic well-being in a way that traditional methods of foreign aid have failed to achieve.

Cellular phone companies such as Nokia are sending what they call "human-behaviour researchers" or "user anthropologists" to gather as much useful information as they can about consumer habits and the lives of potential cell phone buyers. They pass on that information to cell phone designers and technology architects. This process represents a new approach to designing phones known as "human-centred design." Human-centred design is important to high-tech companies trying to build products that people find appealing and easy to use and are thus more likely to be bought.

Nokia and other companies face significant challenges in marketing their phones to the poorest segment of Africa's and Asia's populations. Barriers include lack of electricity in many areas, incomes too low to afford a cell phone, and potential lack of service in non-urban areas. India currently leads the way in affordable cell phone subscriptions, with 226 million

(19 percent of its total population), but many other countries lag far behind both in cell phone usage and rates of Internet access. For example, Morocco, one of Africa's leaders in cell phone and Internet usage, boasts 6.1 million Internet users, or 18.1 percent of its total population. By comparison, Canada has more than 28 million Internet users, or 84 percent of its total population.

Despite this, the outlook for cell phone companies and the residents of Africa's and Asia's poorest countries remains bright. Cell phones are spreading at a breakneck pace that shows little signs of slowing. It took 20 years for the first billion phones to sell, four years for the second billion, and only two years for the third billion. Eighty percent of the world's population lives within range of a cellular network, double the level in 2000.

The World Resources Institute published a report detailing how the poor in developing countries allocate their money. Even the poorest families dedicated significant portions of their small budgets to communication technologies such as cell phones. Cell phones are a tremendous advantage for members of populations that are constantly on the move due to war, drought, natural disasters, or extreme poverty, primarily because they allow people to remain reachable under practically any circumstances. Cell phones also have implications for medicine in these countries: patients can more easily reach doctors, and doctors can more easily acquire information pertaining to diseases and ailments they may need to treat.

In addition to the benefit of being able to stay in touch with others, cell phones are also useful as a business tool. Evidence suggests that possession of a cell phone increases profits on an individual level, allowing people to more easily identify and take advantage of business opportunities. A recent study by the Centre for Economic Policy Research also showed that for every additional 10 cellular phones per 100 people a country acquires, that country's gross domestic product (GDP) rises 0.5 percent.

Creative use of cell phones in developing countries includes "phone ladies" in Bangladesh who charge small commissions for their fellow villagers to make and receive calls, and Ugandans using prepaid air time as an intermediary to transfer currency. Tradenet.biz in Ghana enables people in several West African countries to trade a variety of products using cell phone text messaging to communicate. Harvard University economics professor Robert Jensen found that when fishermen off the coast of Kerala in southern India started using cell phones to contact prospective buyers, their profits rose by an average of 8 percent while consumer prices in the local marketplace dropped 4 percent.

Many proponents of encouraging the growth of underdeveloped countries through commerce, as opposed to simply providing them with international aid money without changing their underlying economies, support the proliferation of cell phones because of this. Access to the Internet via cell phones also promises to bring about societal and political change in developing countries in which repressive governments exert control over all forms of media.

To Think About

1. What strategies are cell phone companies using to "close the digital divide" and market phones to the poorest segment of the world's population?

2. Why do economists predict that widespread cell phone usage in developing countries would have an unprecedented effect on the growth of those countries?

3. What are some examples of how cell phones might increase quality of life for residents of developing countries?

4. Do you believe that cell phones will proliferate widely through Africa and Asia? Why or why not?

MIS in Action

Explore the Web site for One Laptop per Child (**www.laptop.org**), and then answer the following questions:

1. What are the capabilities of the XO laptop? How well suited is this machine for developing countries?

2. How would use of the XO laptop narrow the global digital divide? Compare the potential impact of this machine to that of cell phones in developing nations.

Sources: Nicole Ferraro, "Africa's Portal to the Internet," *InformationWeek*, February 4, 2008 and Sara Corbett, "Can the Cellphone Help End Global Poverty?" *The New York Times Magazine*, April 13, 2008; "Top 20 Countries—Internet Usage," **Internetworldstats.com**, May 2008; and "Canada: Internet Usage, Broadband, and Telecommunication Reports," **Internetworldstats.com**, June 2009.

Aside from integrating new with old systems, there are problems of human interface design and functionality of systems. For instance, to be truly useful for enhancing productivity of a global workforce, software interfaces must be easily understood and mastered quickly. Graphical user interfaces are ideal for this but presuppose a common language—often English. When international systems involve knowledge workers only, English may be the assumed international standard. But as international systems penetrate deeper into management and clerical groups, a common language may not be assumed, and human interfaces must be developed to accommodate different languages

FIGURE 11-6   Pearson Education Web page translated into Japanese by Babel Fish.

This page from the Pearson Education Canada Web site was translated into Japanese. Web sites and software interfaces for global systems may have to be translated into multiple languages to accommodate users in other parts of the world.

and even conventions. The entire process of converting software to operate in a second language is called **software localization** (see Figure 11-6).

What are the most important software applications? Many international systems focus on basic transaction and management reporting systems. Increasingly, firms are turning to supply chain management and enterprise systems to standardize their business processes on a global basis and to create coordinated global supply chains. However, these cross-functional systems are not always compatible with differences in languages, cultural heritages, and business processes in other countries (Martinons, 2004; Liang et al., 2004; Davison, 2002). Company units in countries that are not technically sophisticated may also encounter problems trying to manage the technical complexities of enterprise applications.

Electronic data interchange (EDI) systems and supply chain management systems are widely used by manufacturing and distribution firms to connect to suppliers on a global basis. Collaboration systems, e-mail, and videoconferencing are especially important worldwide collaboration tools for knowledge- and data-based firms, such as advertising firms, research-based firms in medicine and engineering, and graphics and publishing firms. Internet-based tools will be increasingly employed for such purposes.

Software localization

SUMMARY

1. **What major factors are driving the internationalization of business?**

   The growth of cheap international communication and transportation has created a world culture with stable expectations or norms. Political stability and a growing global knowledge base that is widely shared contribute also to the world culture. These general factors create the conditions for global markets, global production, coordination, distribution, and global economies of scale.

2. **What are the alternative strategies for developing global businesses?**

   There are four basic international strategies: domestic exporter, multinational, franchiser, and transnational. In a transnational strategy, all factors of production are coordinated on a global scale. However, the choice of strategy is a function of the type of business and product.

3. **How can information systems support different global business strategies?**

   There is a connection between firm strategy and information systems design. Transnational firms must develop networked system configurations and permit considerable decentralization of development and operations. Franchisers almost always duplicate systems across many countries and use centralized financial controls. Multinationals typically rely on decentralized independence among foreign units with some movement toward development of networks. Domestic exporters typically are centralized in domestic headquarters with some decentralized operations permitted.

4. **What are the challenges posed by global information systems, and management solutions for these challenges?**

   Global information systems pose challenges because cultural, political, and language diversity magnifies differences in organizational culture and business processes and encourages proliferation of disparate local information systems that are difficult to integrate. Typically, international systems have evolved without a conscious plan. The remedy is to define a small subset of core business processes and focus on building systems to support these processes. Tactically, managers will have to co-opt widely dispersed foreign units to participate in the development and operation of these systems, being careful to maintain overall control.

5. **What are the issues and technical alternatives to be considered when developing international information systems?**

   Implementing a global system requires an implementation strategy that considers both business design and technology platforms. The main hardware and telecommunications issues are systems integration and connectivity. The choices for integration are to go either with a proprietary architecture or with open systems technology. Global networks are extremely difficult to develop and operate. Firms can build their own global networks or they can create global networks based on the Internet (intranets or virtual private networks). The main software issues concern building interfaces to existing systems and selecting applications that can work with multiple cultural, language, and organizational frameworks.

Key Terms

Business driver, 344
Cooptation, 356
Core systems, 352
Domestic exporter, 349
Franchisers, 350

Global culture, 346
International information systems
   architecture, 344
Legitimacy, 354
Multinational, 349

Particularism, 347
Software localization, 361
Transborder data
   flow, 348
Transnational, 350

Review Questions

1. *What major factors are driving the internationalization of business?*
   - *List and describe the five major dimensions for developing an international information systems architecture.*
   - *Describe the five general cultural factors and the four specific business factors leading toward growth in global business. Describe the interconnection among these factors.*
   - *List and describe the major challenges to the development of global systems.*

   - *Explain why some firms have not planned for the development of international systems.*

2. *What are the alternative strategies for developing global businesses?*
   - *Describe the four main strategies for global business and organizational structure.*

3. *How can information systems support different global business strategies?*
   - *Describe the four different system configurations that can be used to support different global strategies.*

4. What are the challenges posed by global information systems, and management solutions for these challenges?

- List and describe the major management issues in developing international systems.
- Identify and describe three principles to follow when organizing the firm for global business.
- Identify and describe three steps of a management strategy for developing and implementing global systems.

- Define cooptation, and explain how can it be used in developing global systems.

5. What are the issues and technical alternatives to be considered when developing international information systems?

- Describe the main technical issues facing global systems.
- Identify some technologies that will help firms develop global systems.

Discussion Questions

1. If you were a manager in a company that operates in many countries, what criteria would you use to determine whether an application should be developed as a global application or as a local application?

2. Describe ways the Internet can be used in international information systems.

Collaboration and Teamwork: Identifying Technologies for Global Business Strategies

With a group of students, identify an area of information technology, and explore how this technology might be useful for supporting global business strategies. For instance, you might choose an area such as digital telecommunications (e.g., e-mail, wireless communications, virtual private networks), enterprise systems, collaboration software, or the Web. It will be necessary to choose a business scenario to discuss the technology. You might choose an automobile parts franchise or a clothing franchise, such as Express, as example businesses. Which applications would you make global, which core business processes would you choose, and how would the technology be helpful? If possible, use Google Sites to post links to Web pages, team communication announcements, and work assignments; to brainstorm; and to work collaboratively on project documents. Try to use Google Docs to develop a presentation of your findings for the class.

Visit the MyMISLab Web site at **www.pearsoned.ca/mymislab**. This online homework and tutorial system puts you in control of your own learning with study and practice tools directly correlated to this chapter's content.

HANDS-ON MIS   Projects

The projects in this section give you hands-on experience conducting international market research, analyzing international systems issues for an expanding business, and building a job-posting database and Web page for an international company.

Management Decision Problems

1. United Parcel Service (UPS) has been expanding its package delivery and logistics services in China, serving both multinational companies and local businesses. UPS drivers in China need to use UPS systems and tools such as its handheld Driver Information Acquisition Device (DIAD) for capturing package delivery data. UPS wants to make its WorldShip, CampusShip, and other shipping management services accessible to Chinese and multinational customers via the Web. What are some of the international systems issues UPS must consider in order to operate successfully in China?

2. Your company manufactures and sells tennis rackets and would like to start selling outside Canada. You are in charge of developing a global Web strategy, and the first countries you are thinking of targeting are Brazil, China, Germany, Italy, and Japan. Using the statistics in the *CIA World Factbook* (**www.cia.gov/library/publications/the-world-factbook**), which of these countries would you target first? What criteria would you use? What other considerations should you address in your Web strategy? What features would you put on your Web site to attract buyers from the countries you target?

Achieving Operational Excellence: Building a Job Database and Web Page for an International Consulting Firm

Software skills: Database and Web page design
Business skills: Human resources internal job postings

Companies with many overseas locations need a way to inform employees about available job openings in these locations. In this project, you will use database software to design a database for posting internal job openings and a Web page for displaying this information.

Fictional KTP Consulting operates in various locations around the world. KTP specializes in designing, developing, and implementing enterprise systems for medium- to large-size companies. KTP offers its employees opportunities to travel, live, and work in various locations throughout Canada, the United States, Europe, and Asia. The firm's human resources department has a simple database that enables its staff to track job vacancies. When an employee is interested in relocating, he or she contacts the human resources department for a list of KTP job vacancies. KTP also posts its employment opportunities on the company Web site.

What type of data should be included in the KTP job vacancies database? What information should not be included in this database? Based on your answers to these questions, build a job vacancies database for KTP. Populate the database with at least 20 records. You should also build a simple Web page that incorporates job vacancy data from your newly created database. Send a copy of the KTP database and Web page to your professor.

Improving Decision Making: Conducting International Marketing and Pricing Research

Software skills: Internet-based software
Business skills: International pricing and marketing

When companies sell overseas, it is important to determine whether their products are priced properly for nondomestic markets. In this project, you will use the Web to conduct research on overseas distributors and customs regulations, and use Internet-based software to calculate prices in foreign currencies.

You are in charge of marketing for a Canadian manufacturer of office furniture that has decided to enter the international market. You have been given the name of (fictional) Sorin SRL, a major Italian office furniture retailer, but your source had no other information. You want to test the market by contacting this firm to offer it a specific desk chair that you have to sell at about $125. Using the Web, locate the information needed to contact this firm and to find out how many European euros you would need to get for the chair in the current market. One source for locating European companies is the Europages Business Directory (**www.europages.com**). In addition, consider using the Universal Currency Converter Web site (**www.xe.net/ucc**), which determines the value of one currency expressed in other currencies. Obtain both the information needed to contact the firm and the price of your chair in their local currency. Then locate and obtain customs and legal restrictions on the products you will export from Canada and import into Italy. Finally, locate a company that will represent you as a customs agent and gather information on shipping costs.

CASE STUDY   Nestlé Tries for an All-for-One Global Strategy

Nestlé is the largest food and beverage company in the world. Headquartered in Vevey, Switzerland, the company has annual revenues in excess of $112 billion and 283 000 employees at 500 facilities in 200 countries. Best known for its chocolate, coffee (it invented instant coffee), and milk products, Nestlé sells hundreds of thousands of other items, most of which are adapted to fit local markets and cultures.

Traditionally, this huge firm allowed each local organization to conduct business as it saw fit, taking into account the local conditions and business cultures. To support this decentralized strategy, it had 80 different information technology units that ran nearly 900 IBM AS/400 midrange computers, 15 mainframes, and 200 Unix systems, quite a hodgepodge of hardware and operating systems.

However, Nestlé's management found that allowing these local differences created inefficiencies and extra costs that could prevent the company from competing effectively in electronic commerce. The lack of standard business processes prevented Nestlé from, for example, leveraging its worldwide buying power to obtain lower prices for its raw materials. Even though each factory used the same global suppliers, each negotiated its own deals and prices.

Several years ago, Nestlé embarked on a program to standardize and coordinate its information systems and business processes. The company initially installed SAP's R/3 enterprise resource planning (ERP) software to integrate material, distribution, and accounting applications in Canada, the United States, and Europe.

Nestlé then extended its enterprise systems strategy to all of its facilities to make them act as a single-minded e-business. Once this project is completed, Nestlé will be able to use sales information from retailers on a global basis to measure the effectiveness of its promotional activities and reduce overstocking and spoilage caused by having products sit around too long on grocery shelves.

Achieving global standardization of operational processes has been a complex task. None of Nestlé's products is considered a truly global brand, with perhaps the exception of Nescafé, of which 100 million cups are served around the world each year. But even Nescafé is rebranded, repackaged, and reformulated to create more than 200 product versions for different regional preferences. This is just a small representation of the complexity that CEO Peter Brabeck wanted to address when he decided to bring a sense of order to the company's business operations.

In 1995, Nestlé facilities in 14 countries were running their businesses on SAP R/2, an older version of its ERP software. They all ran the software differently and used different schemes for formatting data and managing forms. The system disparity resulted in increasing maintenance costs. Compiling financial reports to gain a company-wide view of performance became more laborious.

Between 1994 and 1999, Nestlé increased its spending on information systems from $575 million to $750 million. Brabeck arrived in 1997, and while the technology budget was growing, he was actually decreasing the size of the company by selling off Nestlé brands. The cost of tracking the sales chain, as a percentage of total sales, rose from 1.2 percent in 1994 to 1.6 percent in 1999.

By April 2000, Brabeck had had enough of a corporate philosophy that allowed for thousands of differently configured supply chains, multiple methods of forecasting demand, and innumerable practices for invoicing customers and collecting payments. The inconsistencies and inefficiencies across the enterprise were chipping away at Nestlé's profits. Brabeck, chief financial officer Mario Corti, and the entire executive board launched a $2.8 billion initiative to compel the company's market heads around the world to adopt a single set of business processes and systems for procurement, distribution, and sales management.

Chris Johnson, who was in charge of Nestlé's Taiwan market, was asked to lead the initiative that would come to be known as GLOBE (Global Business Excellence). Johnson was instructed to find a way to harmonize processes, standardize data, and standardize systems. All of Nestlé's worldwide business units were to use the same processes for making sales commitments, establishing factory production schedules, billing customers, compiling management reports, and reporting financial results. The units would no longer be permitted to adhere to local customs for conducting business except in cases where the laws of a particular country required that they do so. Every Nestlé facility would

format and store data identically, using the same set of information systems. Johnson would have to oversee the confluence of divergent processes into a "single source of truth." Johnson would have three and a half years to deploy the GLOBE strategy in 70 percent of the company's global markets.

Such an undertaking was unusual for Nestlé. Large projects, such as the construction of a coffee factory, generally cost the company in the range of $35 million to $46 million. Putting up billions of dollars to fund a project was risky, but for Brabeck, the potential benefits were too important. He could significantly curb IT spending, which was growing dangerously. In addition, he could gain an advantage over competitors like Unilever and Kraft Foods in improving operational efficiency while continuing to grow with new markets and new products. Nestlé would also be able to reduce its number of suppliers from 600 000 to 167 000, and save hundreds of millions of dollars in the process. The savings would be reinvested in innovation, pleasing its largest customers like Walmart, Tesco, and further strengthening Nestlé's position among the other global food suppliers. It would be the first global enterprise to conduct business as though it were operating in a single country.

The goal was lofty, and previous attempts at cooperative standards had mixed results. Technology experts from headquarters had emphasized standards and best practices to the 14 countries that deployed SAP in the past. Their pleas for a unified corporate culture had been largely ignored. On the other hand, market managers in Asia had come together to develop a common system for managing their supply chains using software from SSA Global. The Business Excellence Common Application flourished in Indonesia, Malaysia, the Philippines, and Thailand, and even spread to South Africa. The American division of Nestlé also standardized its practices using SAP software in a project known as BEST (Business Excellence through Systems Technology). However, it was the Asian effort that would serve as the model due to its success in crossing cultures and satisfying multiple market managers.

GLOBE, under the leadership of Johnson, launched on July 4, 2000. Johnson had support from Olivier Gouin, chief information officer for Nestlé in France, and a panel of 12 senior executives with various backgrounds who had been chosen specifically for the project. Even before beginning the likely difficult task of convincing market managers worldwide to adopt a centralized culture, the GLOBE team had a more pressing challenge to confront: Was it actually possible to convert 70 percent of the business to a common set of best practices and systems by the December 2003 deadline?

There were to be no shortcuts. Everything had to be standardized on the new mySAP Internet-based software. Moreover, the deadline had already appeared in a company newsletter, so changing the date could have damaged confidence in the project.

Johnson's team studied the experiences of competitors, and received feedback from consultants at Pricewaterhouse-Coopers and deployment experts at SAP. Johnson and Gouin were not surprised to determine that the parameters of the project would have to be adjusted. GLOBE required a larger staff, more funding, and a larger window of time than the executive board had allotted. The GLOBE team predicted that its staff would need to grow to a maximum of 3500 workers.

The team's projections also gave rise to the $2.4 billion budget. Gouin softened the blow of the cost by pointing out that the status quo, individual markets managing their own systems, was projected to cost $3.7 billion over five years. In the end, considering the scope of the project, Johnson's team also concluded that the schedule was too ambitious.

The schedule was revised so that a "majority of the company's key markets," rather than 70 percent, would be GLOBE-enabled by the end of 2005, instead of 2003.

Instead of technology managers, Johnson tried to build his team from a diverse group of business managers who had experience in a variety of business sectors including manufacturing, finance, marketing, and human resources. He recruited from Nestlé offices all over the world. He went after the best of the best—managers who were considered "untouchables" because they were too valuable in their current capacities to be let go for new projects.

Johnson put his first team together in the fall of 2000. By the following winter, the team had added 400 executives with diverse career backgrounds at Nestlé covering 40 different countries. In February 2001, this core group began the critical process of compiling the GLOBE Best Practices Library. The 400 were knowledgeable in how the company actually conducted business. They would need to know the processes for everything from calculating product demand and managing the supply chain to generating an invoice and ordering office equipment. Many of these processes had never been documented and were simply passed down by word of mouth. Johnson described the task as converting Nestlé's oral history into decoding "the DNA of how Nestlé does business."

The 400 executives documented the best ways of performing each process. Then the GLOBE team brought in experts in each area to challenge the processes, find their weaknesses, and pare the list down to the best practice for each process. In this way, the Best Practices Library evolved into an online database of step-by-step guides for 1000 processes, divided into 45 solution sets that focused on disciplines such as demand planning or financial reporting.

Some best practices, such as getting a product to market, were afforded a degree of flexibility to account for the wide variety of Nestlé products and the breadth of markets in which they were sold. Other practices, such as financial reporting, were given no wiggle room. Salespeople were to enter orders with precision in a standard format and by a specific date every month. Financial terms and recording dates were standardized across the enterprise. Johnson later described the accounting software as being "kind of like handcuffs in a way to make you do the right thing."

It became apparent to Johnson that the greatest challenge of GLOBE might not be technical, but personal. Despite clear support for the project from the highest-ranking executives, including Brabeck, managers resisted the idea of giving up control over their business processes to participate in a centralized solution. They feared the loss of decision-making power. Many thought that making back-office operations identical in so many different countries was impractical. They might agree to standardization, but only if it was their particular practices that were made the GLOBE standard. The resistance was fortified by the fact that each country's operations would have to spend its own money to pay for the project.

In the fall of 2001, Johnson was on the defensive. He was given a full day of a three-day meeting to convince market managers that falling in step with GLOBE was in their best interest and in the best interest of the company. The managers peppered him with questions that were intended to demonstrate how GLOBE would make their jobs more difficult and degrade the performance of their units. Johnson did the best he could to satisfy them and then took a frank approach. The project was going to proceed. If they did not get behind GLOBE, he would be fired, and Brabeck would select one of them to head the massive undertaking. The other managers were not interested in that outcome.

Johnson did receive support that day from Jose Lopez, the head of the Malaysia and Singapore markets, which were being used to test GLOBE's back-office systems. It was too early to measure the benefits of the project, but Lopez expressed his belief in the premise and his willingness to cooperate.

A year and a half later in the spring of 2003, the market heads had another opportunity to question Johnson. While there were still plenty of questions, a number of them described the operational efficiencies they had achieved since implementing GLOBE standards. For example, their financial reports and demand forecasts were better and faster.

By a third meeting in May 2005, 20 market heads were able to endorse the benefits of GLOBE. In the interim, however, an unwelcome financial problem arose. GLOBE was not controlling information technology costs as expected. As a percentage of sales, costs were approaching 2 percent. Brabeck instituted a cap on information technology expenses at 1.9 percent. In order to meet the cap, Johnson and Gouin revised the schedule of the project again. They set a goal of 80 percent of Nestlé being on the GLOBE system by the end of 2006. The extended schedule allowed the GLOBE team to maintain Brabeck's spending cap and protect the company's profits.

In the fall of 2005, the percentage of Nestlé units running GLOBE reached 25 percent, and costs were within the limit.

To help the rollouts along, Johnson asked each country to name a GLOBE manager who would facilitate the adoption of the system. These managers also provided value to each other by exchanging their experiences with the system and the solutions they employed for specific challenges. Johnson also established a steering committee at company headquarters to schedule and manage the rollouts. The steering committee oversaw the reduction of company data centres from 100 to four, including the centre in Vevey, which stored the GLOBE templates, Best Practices Library, and central functions.

One of Brabeck's biggest concerns was that the rollouts occur with no effect on customers. A rollout could be a true success only if no one outside the company noticed it. The initial test markets found this daunting because they would have to fix bugs and confront unanticipated problems during the deployment. Nestlé also had to implement the new business processes concurrently with the new systems. There was no opportunity to perfect the processes. And, finally, the managers and their workers had no time to train on the new systems before they deployed them and began using them. Despite these challenges, the test markets experienced few problems, and rollouts proceeded around the world. After the test-markets, market managers had at least nine months to document their processes and perfect them until they conformed with the GLOBE templates.

Along the way, Nestlé did encounter some technical issues. For example, Canadian market managers used special promotions liberally to attract business from local and regional grocery chains. The mySAP software was not designed to accommodate the extra data points generated by so many promotions. Nestlé worked with SAP to develop a "multiple angles approach" to allow for such a difference. The approach enabled Nestlé to separate the storage of data by market. This way, a country like Canada could have the extra storage space in the central system that it needed for its promotion data.

By the end of 2005, Nestlé had converted 30 percent of its business to GLOBE and had the capacity for one major rollout every month. The 80 percent number by the end of 2006 was still looming, but the company had learned how to operate as a single unit on a global scale. Johnson was not entirely satisfied with the results, citing delayed and flawed summary reports compromising the work of factory and country managers. He was also eager to see reports made available instantly on a 24/7 basis rather than having to wait for them to be completed overnight each day.

To make sure that the data entering GLOBE's streamlined data centres are accurate and complete, each country has a data manager. Johnson believes that the system will never achieve perfection as long as time constraints remain a factor. However, Nestlé is much closer to achieving its goal of standardizing all processes, data, and systems. The closer the company comes to developing the perfect system, the better the company can serve its customers.

CASE STUDY QUESTIONS:

1. Analyze Nestlé using the competitive forces and value chain models. What challenges did Nestlé face?

2. What type of global business and systems strategy did Nestlé adopt? Was this strategy appropriate for Nestlé's business model?

3. What management, organization, and technology challenges did Nestlé have to deal with to standardize its business processes and systems?

4. What strategies did Nestlé management use to deal with these challenges? How successful were these strategies? Explain your answer.

Sources: Tom Steinert-Threlkeld, "Nestlé Pieces Together Its Global Supply Chain," *Baseline Magazine*, January 20, 2006; "Nestlé Group in 2005: Record Sales and Profits—Higher Dividend Proposed," - **www.nestle.com**, February 23, 2006; and The Associated Press, "Nestle Reports 14 Percent Rise in Sales," MSNBC.com, April 25, 2006.

Part III CANADIAN CASE STUDY:
In Tech We Trust: The Story of SAP in Canada

The road to ERP success is littered with the corpses of many a company and many a CIO who tried and failed at this complex and demanding undertaking. Why do ERP implementations go wrong? Is it IRM practices or change management? What steps can be taken to help put them on the right track?

Are there certain factors about an organization—for example, its type (e.g., retail, utility, manufacturing), size, or geographical dispersion—that make it harder or easier to implement an enterprise resource planning system, and specifically to implement SAP or other enterprise systems? Let's look at some Canadian and other companies that have experienced problems—and successes—with SAP implementations.

NOVA Chemicals, a Calgary-based commodity chemical firm, has reached a level of ERP maturity. NOVA produces styrenics and olefins/polyolefins at 18 locations in Canada, the United States, France, the Netherlands, and the United Kingdom.

By the mid-1990s, NOVA had made a number of acquisitions and had gone through several reorganizations, resulting in a host of outdated legacy systems and a variety of systems running different parts of its business. The company was ripe for significant business process re-engineering. Seeing some of its competitors already going the ERP route, NOVA decided to head in that direction as well.

In retrospect, some of NOVA's initial reasons for embarking on its ERP journey may not have been the right ones. As Senior Vice President and CIO John Wheeler observed, "NOVA is a commodity chemical company. We're not as big or as diverse as some of our competitors. But because of the commonality of our business, one of the things we can do is focus on best practices. So over time, it became apparent that ERP was not about technology. It wasn't even about information systems. It was really about building a company that could leverage best practices. It was about business process." But when NOVA first embarked on ERP, that realization was still years away. Whether developing, purchasing, or outsourcing systems, the first step in the systems development life cycle should be to properly identify the needs of the company and what type of system solution should be planned to meet those needs. NOVA failed to do that at first.

NOVA'S INITIAL IMPLEMENTATION

NOVA first took the ERP plunge in 1995 when it decided to implement SAP's new distributed R3 Version 2.2. SAP is the third-largest software company in the world and specializes in client/server enterprise application software modules (see Chapter 12 for a more complete description). That first plunge into ERP can be like taking a dip in a northern lake on a windy January day. NOVA attempted to do a pilot installation in a small U.S.-based styrenics business, but the project faltered and was abandoned, causing the company to step back and regroup.

During that first installation, NOVA did not have a CIO. But after that initial setback, it was decided that a CIO was necessary, and the company's vice president and controller, Larry MacDonald, was given that responsibility.

Reflecting on the company's early experiences with ERP, MacDonald pointed to the newness of the SAP/R3 product and its integrated nature as two early stumbling blocks. "The distributed R3 version was brand new, and people weren't used to the complexity of SAP implementations," he said. "Having something that was so broad and touched on the business from beginning to end—the total supply chain—was something that we did not understand well. We didn't understand the complexities that integration brought to an implementation." Again, proper IRM practices would have elicited that understanding and helped NOVA better prepare for implementation of its ERP.

As a result, NOVA underestimated the scope of the business process improvement and the need to get key people from across the business involved. It also underestimated what it would take to deliver the project, train employees to use the software, and persuade employees to use it as well.

Complicating matters was the reluctance by many people on the business side to embrace SAP. NOVA was implementing all modules, so SAP was being installed virtually "wall to wall" throughout the business. First, the company had to learn how to do the implementation, and then it had to learn how to bring it into the culture of the organization. A lot of people resisted the early implementations, because they weren't receiving much value from them in those days.

"The change that this was bringing to how people did their work was tremendous," noted MacDonald. "We really had to work on the cultural piece, the education piece, and then the technical piece of it." An adequate change management program might have shown the value to both management and line employees and helped to change the culture.

In the end, consulting firm Deloitte and Touche was NOVA's main implementation partner, bringing a strong change-management capability, as well as strong project- and IT-management methodologies and good knowledge of SAP. According to Wheeler, NOVA's strong operations and change-management capability today can be attributed to practices introduced by its consulting partner.

THE TURNAROUND

Rallying line management was crucial to the success of the implementation. Recalled MacDonald, "Once providing resources to support the implementation became part of line management's job expectations and was clearly embedded in their performance requirements, we started to see a lot of progress. In the initial stages, it wasn't high on the priority list. It had to come from the president that this was important—we had to pay attention to it, and we had to dedicate resources to making this successful."

When newly appointed CIO Wheeler arrived, business support for ERP was still an issue. His goal was to strengthen support by moving ownership for the system toward the business. A significant measure of management's commitment to the success of NOVA's IT program was current CEO Jeff Lipton's appointment of Wheeler to the company's executive leadership team. Says Wheeler, "Being part of the senior team provides a clear understanding of the expectations of business leaders and an important forum to ensure that we work together to achieve the company's strategic goals."

"In the early days, the criticism is usually that ERP is an IT implementation. You need to move that ownership toward the business and make IT the enabler. To the extent you can do that earlier rather than later, you'll be more successful," he said. "The truly mature IT program is the one in which the business owns the process, the system, the costs, and the value. IT's role is to be in partnership with the business, using technology to enable business needs."

Wheeler believes that ERP projects require full-time commitment from business people. And those full-time people should be quality people. "Sometimes the people you get turn out to be the people who are available, rather than the best people. And that's a mistake," he cautioned. "When you're changing your business process in a fundamental way, you cannot afford not to have your best people—and to have them relatively full time."

SAP: THE COMPANY

Founded in 1972 by four former IBM employees, SAP (Systems, Applications, and Products in Data Processing—pronounced S-A-P) is a dynamic, German-based company that creates client/server enterprise application software modules. Today more than 12 million users and 41 200 companies in more than 120 countries run more than 121 000 installations of SAP software. The company has subsidiaries in more than 50 countries.

SAP's former CEO and current chair of its supervisory board, Hasso Plattner, is the company's "visioneer," who sees all departments becoming one, not only across an organization, but across its environment as well. He calls this the "City of E."

SAP Canada Inc. was established in 1989 and is the fourth-largest company subsidiary of the parent SAP with offices in Toronto, Montreal, Ottawa, Calgary, and Vancouver. SAP Canada and its Business Objects subsidiary employ more than 2300 employees to service their 1200 Canadian customers. The Canadian SAP subsidiary is not only interested in making sales. State-of-the-art software products are created by SAP Labs Canada for the mySAP Business Suite family of solutions. The research centre in Montreal is an integral part of SAP's global development network. Developers in SAP Labs Canada software developers are constantly engaged in designing applications for SAP's CRM, Retail and Manufacturing, and Mobile Business solutions. In 2009, SAP Canada was named one of Canada's Top Fifty Employers by Hewitt Associates, a global provider of human resources outsourcing and consulting services.

The two main versions of SAP are SAP ERP and mySAP, the latest Web-enabled version. Companies can buy entire ERP packages for their particular industry, such as SAP Retail, SAP Mining, or SAP Banking, or they can buy individual modules, such as human resources or financial applications. Implementation of SAP can run into the tens of millions of dollars, including hardware, software, networking, personnel, and consulting components. SAP will not permit a company to adopt its software unless there are SAP-certified programmers and consultants on board for the project. SAP's latest version is called Accelerated SAP and is targeted at companies with less than $250 million in sales. Accelerated Solutions are pre-configured, scaled-down versions of SAP ERP. Accelerated SAP claims to have a four-month implementation schedule and is offered at a fixed cost, rather than a per-user cost.

SAP's ERP software can translate foreign currencies and languages and handle taxes that vary worldwide, making it a truly global application. It is a birth-to-grave application that can cover the life of a product from financing the production plant to payment from the customer after the product has arrived. But SAP does so in its own individual fashion.

SAP software implements "best practices" of companies it has studied, including its customers. Any organization—for profit, not-for-profit, governmental agency—that implements SAP must change its business processes to reflect those found in the way SAP's applications operate. Failure to do so is asking for implementation failure.

Just look at Sobeys, Canada's second-largest supermarket chain, which in early 2001 pulled the plug on its SAP implementation after writing off an after-tax loss of about $50 million. Bill McEwan, president and CEO of Nova Scotia–based Sobeys Inc., said that the two-year-old project had "systemic problems of a much more serious nature" than the growing pains they had been led to expect. SAP implementation—after two years—resulted in "unprecedented" stockouts in December 2000 throughout eastern Canada according to McEwan. He continued, "The SAP Retail software couldn't effectively deal with the extreme, high number of transactions in our retail operating environment." Business operations were affected for four to five weeks while problems were reconciled.

Related to the story of Sobeys, though, is the story of chapters.indigo.ca. When the retailer was considering adopting SAP to improve its merchandise assortment planning, Indigo chief technical officer (CTO) Doug Caldwell called an old friend of his—who worked as an executive at Sobeys—to get his opinion on the problems Sobeys had experienced with SAP. The Sobeys executive admitted that many of the problems had been Sobeys problems, rather than problems with SAP. After talking with his friend, Caldwell decided to implement SAP at Indigo. SAP even sponsors a users' conference annually, partly to let SAP customers talk with each other.

Enterprises need to look to software vendors for support, says Michael Moreia, senior technical consultant, IS architecture, at ATI Technologies Inc., a graphics equipment manufacturer based in Markham, Ontario. ATI did precisely that to overcome the obstacles in its SAP implementation. Moreia, however, criticized SAP and its experts: for failing to bring more support people to Canada. The SAP advisors did help ATI, but the calls they made to Germany happened rather late by Eastern Standard Time. If they had utilized local help, it would have afforded more reasonable work hours for the ATI staff.

City of Ottawa staffers channelled their anger toward Deidre Stirling, the City of Ottawa's manager of business application management, and the SAP software her team was trying to install across the city's IT infrastructure. What added fuel to the fire was the municipal amalgamation process that was being undertaken in the national capital region at the same time. The implementation was a lengthy and difficult process, but Stirling said, "I survived." Her project did, too. Ottawa spent $40 million on SAP software, but it has already saved $2 million in operational costs. It is expected that the new financial, HR, and property applications will save the city $8 million a year.

For employees of companies that have implemented SAP, one of the major changes is that they work mostly with data and software, rather than with people, according to Barry Hasler of Sony Canada. Another change is that they cannot get the exact reports and information they were used to getting; SAP reports are standard and do the job, but staff must change the information they need as well as what they do with it in the SAP environment.

But for those who are willing to exercise appropriate change management initiatives, including changes to their policies and procedures, reporting relationships, and training, SAP does its job well. In other words, it's "The SAP Way, or No Way." Organizations that successfully implement SAP spend about one-third of their SAP budget on change management initiatives—training, communicating, consulting, and selling.

CASE STUDY QUESTIONS

1. What sort of businesses should invest in SAP's ERP applications? Should a company adopt all of the SAP modules? How does a company decide that it needs an ERP solution?

2. What specific change management actions might a company adopting SAP take to ensure implementation success?

3. Why does SAP consider it necessary for SAP-certified programmers and consultants to work with companies implementing SAP?

4. It has been said that SAP is a change management program or philosophy. Do you agree or disagree? Why? What might happen to implementation if a company chose to try to adapt SAP to its own processes rather than adapting its processes to SAP?

Sources: David Carey, "Surviving the ERP Journey," *CIO Canada*, May 1, 2001; Rebecca Maxwell, "Rayovac Gets a Charge from Accelerated SAP," *ComputerWorld Canada*, September 10, 2000; Curtis Cook and Michelle Schoffro, "SAP Not Just for Big Companies," *Canada Computes*, October 9, 1999; Lucas Mearlan, "Sobeys Says Goodbye to SAP," *ComputerWorld Online*, February 2, 2001; "mySAP.com to Power Canada's National Newspaper, *The Globe and Mail*," SAP press release, **www.sap.com** (accessed August 13, 2001); SAP Web site, **www.sap .com** (accessed October 1, 2005); SAP Canada Web site, **www.sap .com/Canada/company** (accessed October 1, 2005); Chris Conrath, "SAP Is Sold on the Internet," *Network World Canada*, July 28, 2000; Stefan Dubowski, "Book Retailer Spins Its Tale of SAP Tips," *ComputerWorld Canada*, June 10, 2005, **www.itworldcanada.com/a/ search/6edebed9-0d6c-4909-b41a-204441899dcc.html** (accessed October 1, 2005).

Video Resource: "In Tech We Trust," *CBC UNDERcurrents* 113 (October 31, 1999).

Part IV

How Digital Businesses Use Information and Systems

PART IV

CANADIAN CASE STUDY

Second Life: A New Generation of Online Application

CHAPTER 12

Enterprise Applications to Manage Supply Chains and Respond to Customers

LEARNING OBJECTIVES

After reading this chapter, you will be able to answer the following questions:

1. How do enterprise systems help businesses achieve operational excellence?

2. How do supply chain management systems coordinate planning, production, and logistics with suppliers?

3. How do customer relationship management systems help firms achieve customer intimacy?

4. What are the challenges posed by enterprise applications?

5. How are enterprise applications used in platforms for new cross-functional services?

OPENING CASE

Allan Candy: How Sweet Independence Is!

The Allan Candy Company Limited was founded in 1931, when Allan Vertlieb opened a retail store in his own home. Over the next 60 years, the company grew and was sold in 1945, although Vertlieb continued to work at the company. In 1995, its owners sold Allan Candy to Cadbury Chocolate Canada, part of the global Cadbury Schweppes PLC group. In 2006, as part of its global strategy, Cadbury decided to focus on a smaller range of the larger and more profitable core brands and it put the Allan Candy division up for sale.

In 2007, the Allan division was purchased by a private-equity firm, which renamed the acquired company The Allan Candy Company Limited. Known for recognizable brand names like BIG FOOT, HOT LIPS, LACES, and DOPS, the company today is a mid-market regional confectioner with revenue in excess of $100 million derived from sales of gummies, jujubes, gum drops, toffees, mints, and candy canes, together with a wide

range of chocolate novelty items. Allan Candy serves a variety of markets and trade channels including drug, grocery, mass, club and other stores in both Canada and the U.S., using distributor and broker distribution as well as direct sales. According to Management, "With Allan now operating as an independent company once again, we believe that significant benefits will be created for customers through faster and nimbler processes, more aggressive product and process innovation, and better overall speed to market."

Ah, but there's the rub! How to get there? When Allan Candy separated from Cadbury, it left behind all of its information systems. As a much smaller company, Allan Candy's managers needed a 'right-sized' enterprise resource planning and IT infrastructure, but did not have the expertise to develop systems in-house nor the appetite to spend against deploying big ERP solutions.

First, Allan Candy contracted with Metafore for hardware and software installation. Metafore designed and implemented a new LAN/WAN infrastructure for Allan Candy, provisioned all necessary hardware & software, then provided a full complement of services that would enable it to function as the client's "virtual IT department." The entire Allan Candy's infrastructure is hosted and managed at Metafore, another Mississauga-based company. Both Metafore and Allan Candy, with only two IT specialists, knew that the company needed a relatively simple, "out-of-the-box" enterprise solution for its IT applications. Allan Candy contracted with Markham-based TGO Consulting to implement Microsoft Dynamic GP software.

Steve Diakowsky, Allan Candy's new President and CEO, spent eight years doing system implementation work, before taking on the CEO role at Allan Candy. He wanted to improve and streamline its IT and manufacturing processes and to receive information on key performance indicators quickly. For example, staff needed a quicker means to process purchase orders and access financial information in real time. Diakowsky said, "We're firm believers that technology innovation is key to our growth."

Using Microsoft Dynamics GP, there was no customization required, and the interface was similar to other software the company had implemented. The new ERP system lets staff customize reporting and workflow features to improve inventory and distribution processes. TGO provides staff training and ongoing IT support as Allan Candy expands the CRM component of the ERP.

Today, employees can update information in real time and monitor inventory data to ensure that it is accurate and up-to-date. Managers are automatically notified of business-critical activity, such as customer shipments, purchasing, and invoicing. Project status reports that were previously produced by managers over a period of several days can now be produced in real time.

Today, the two IT specialists do not deal with hardware, thanks to Metafore. They concentrate on high-level tasks such as overseeing IT projects, reporting and analytics. Analytics are critical to the company, for example, to produce the master production schedule. Using analytics, the company can ensure that it has enough inventory on hand to

meet its production schedule without holding excessive amounts of inventory. For the future, Allan Candy's Diakowsky says he has a "wish list" that includes RFID and a more seamlessly integrated supply chain.

Sources: Kathleen Lau, "The Sweet Business of Making Candy," *Computerworld Canada*, May 22, 2009; "Allan Candy Sweetens Sales, Streamlines IT using Microsoft Dynamics GP," available at **www.microsoft.com/canada/ casestudies/allan_candy.mspx,** accessed June 3, 2009; "The Allan Candy Company Limited," *BusinessWeek*, available at investing .businessweek.com/businessweek/research/ stocks/private/snapshot.asp?privcapid=34720 9007, accessed June 3, 2009; "Allan," available at **www.rhcapitalpartners.com/ news_06_07allan.html**, accessed June 3, 2009; "Our History," Allan Candy Company, available at **www.allancandy.com/node/20**, accessed June 3, 2009.

Allan Candy needed to manage both its upstream and downstream production and distribution processes and have real-time access to inventory, production, and distribution (e.g., customer, invoicing) data. The company's managers also needed easy access to real-time financial data. These needs are met by enterprise applications.

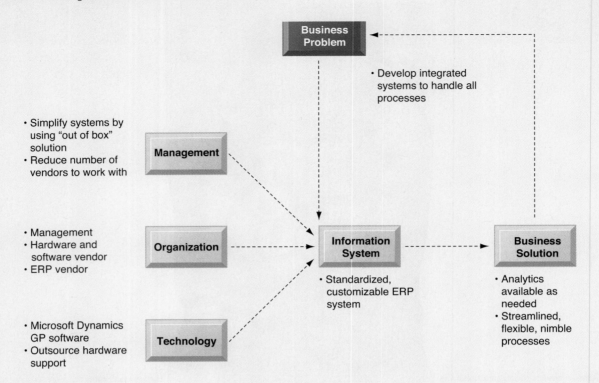

- Simplify systems by using "out of box" solution
- Reduce number of vendors to work with

Management

- Develop integrated systems to handle all processes

Business Problem

- Management
- Hardware and software vendor
- ERP vendor

Organization

Information System

- Standardized, customizable ERP system

Business Solution

- Analytics available as needed
- Streamlined, flexible, nimble processes

- Microsoft Dynamics GP software
- Outsource hardware support

Technology

The chapter-opening diagram calls attention to important points raised by this case and this chapter. Starting basically from scratch, Allan Candy had several choices open to it. Management could have chosen to add more employees or lease piecemeal applications that would have been difficult to integrate. Instead, it decided to implement an enterprise-wide system. The enterprise system integrated financial, order entry, scheduling, and manufacturing information and made it more widely available throughout the company. Data on manufacturing output and warehouse shipments are captured as soon as they are created. Instant availability of more timely and accurate information helps employees work more efficiently and helps managers make better decisions.

12.1 Enterprise Systems

Around the globe, companies are increasingly becoming more connected, both internally and with other companies. If you run a business, you will want to be able to react instantaneously when a customer places a large order or when a shipment from a supplier is delayed. You may also want to know the impact of these events on every part of the business and how the business is performing at any point in time, especially if you are running a large company. Enterprise systems provide the integration to make this possible. Let us look at how they work and what they can do for the firm.

What Are Enterprise Systems?

Imagine that you had to run a business based on information from tens or even hundreds of different databases and systems, none of which could speak to one another. Imagine your company had 10 different major product lines, each produced in separate factories, and

FIGURE 12-1 How enterprise systems work.

Enterprise systems feature a set of integrated software modules and a central database that enables data to be shared by many different business processes and functional areas throughout the enterprise.

each with separate and incompatible sets of systems controlling production, warehousing, and distribution.

Chapter 2 introduced enterprise systems, also known as enterprise resource planning (ERP) systems, which are based on a suite of integrated software modules and a common central database. The database collects data from many different divisions and departments in a firm and from a large number of key business processes in manufacturing and production, finance and accounting, sales and marketing, and human resources, making the data available for applications that support nearly all of an organization's internal business activities. When new information is entered by one process, the information is made immediately available to other business processes (see Figure 12-1).

If a sales representative places an order for tire rims, for example, the system verifies the customer's credit limit, schedules the shipment, identifies the best shipping route, and reserves the necessary items from inventory. If inventory stock were insufficient to fill the order, the system schedules the manufacture of more rims, ordering the needed materials and components from suppliers. Sales and production forecasts are immediately updated. General ledger and corporate cash levels are automatically updated with the revenue and cost information from the order. Users could tap into the system and find out where that particular order was at any minute. Management could obtain information at any point in time about how the business was operating. The system could also generate enterprise-wide data for management analyses of product cost and profitability.

Enterprise Software

Enterprise software is built around thousands of predefined business processes that reflect best practices. Table 12-1 describes some of the major business processes supported by enterprise software.

Companies implementing this software would have to first select the functions of the system they wished to use and then map their business processes to the predefined

Enterprise software

TABLE 12-1   Business processes supported by enterprise systems.

Financial and accounting processes, including general ledger, accounts payable, accounts receivable, fixed assets, cash management and forecasting, product-cost accounting, cost-centre accounting, asset accounting, tax accounting, credit management, and financial reporting

Human resources processes, including personnel administration, time accounting, payroll, personnel planning and development, benefits accounting, applicant tracking, time management, compensation, workforce planning, performance management, and travel expense reporting

Manufacturing and production processes, including procurement, inventory management, purchasing, shipping, production planning, production scheduling, material requirements planning, quality control, distribution, transportation execution, and plant and equipment maintenance

Sales and marketing processes, including order processing, quotations, contracts, product configuration, pricing, billing, credit checking, incentive and commission management, and sales planning

business processes in the software. (One of our Learning Tracks shows how SAP enterprise software handles the procurement process for a new piece of equipment.) Cadbury's Canadian business, described briefly in the chapter-opening case, identified its existing business processes and then translated them into the business processes built into the SAP ERP software it had selected. A firm would use configuration tables provided by the software to tailor a particular aspect of the system to the way it does business. For example, the firm could use these tables to select whether it wants to track revenue by product line, geographical unit, or distribution channel.

If the enterprise software does not support the way the organization does business, companies can rewrite some of the software to support the way their business processes work. However, enterprise software is unusually complex, and extensive customization may degrade system performance, compromising the information and process integration that are the main benefits of the system. If companies want to reap the maximum benefits from enterprise software, they must change the way they work to conform to the business processes in the software. Major enterprise software vendors include SAP, Oracle (with its acquisition of PeopleSoft), Microsoft Dynamics Great Plains, and SSA Global. There are versions of enterprise software packages designed for small businesses and versions obtained through software service providers over the Web. Although initially designed to automate the firm's internal "back-office" business processes, enterprise systems have become more externally oriented and capable of communicating with customers, suppliers, and other organizations.

Business Value of Enterprise Systems

Enterprise systems provide value both by increasing operational efficiency and by providing firm-wide information to help managers make better decisions. Large companies with many operating units in different locations have used enterprise systems to enforce standard practices and data so that everyone does business the same way worldwide.

Coca Cola, for instance, implemented a SAP enterprise system to standardize and coordinate important business processes in 200 countries. Lack of standard, company-wide business processes prevented the company from leveraging its worldwide buying power to obtain lower prices for raw materials and from reacting rapidly to market changes. Nestlé SA installed a SAP enterprise system to standardize business processes in 500 facilities in 80 countries for the same reason.

Enterprise systems help firms respond rapidly to customer requests for information or products. Because the system integrates order, manufacturing, and delivery data, manufacturing is better informed about producing only what customers have ordered, procuring exactly the right amount of components or raw materials to fill actual orders, staging production, and minimizing the time that components or finished products are in inventory.

After implementing enterprise software from Oracle, Alcoa eliminated many redundant processes and systems. The enterprise system helped Alcoa reduce requisition-to-pay cycle time (the total elapsed time from when a purchase requisition is generated to the time the payment for the purchase is made) by verifying receipt of goods and automatically generating receipts for payment. Alcoa's accounts payable transaction processing time dropped by 89 percent. Alcoa was able to centralize financial and procurement activities, which helped the company reduce nearly 20 percent of its worldwide costs.

Enterprise systems provide much valuable information for improving management decision making. Corporate headquarters has access to up-to-the-minute data on sales, inventory, and production and uses this information to create more accurate sales and production forecasts. Enterprise software includes analytical tools for using data captured by the system to evaluate overall organizational performance. Enterprise system data have common standardized definitions and formats that are accepted by the entire organization. Performance figures mean the same thing across the company. Enterprise systems allow senior management to easily find out at any moment how a particular organizational unit is performing, determine which products are most or least profitable, or calculate costs for the company as a whole.

For example, Alcoa's enterprise system includes functionality for global human resources management that shows correlations between investment in employee training and quality; measures the company-wide costs of delivering services to employees; and measures the effectiveness of employee recruitment, compensation, and training.

12.2   Supply Chain Management Systems

If you manage a small firm that makes a few products or sells a few services, chances are you will have a small number of suppliers. You could coordinate your supplier orders and deliveries using a telephone and fax machine. But if you manage a firm that produces more complex products and services, then you will have hundreds of suppliers, and your suppliers will each have their own set of suppliers. Suddenly, you are in a situation where you will need to coordinate the activities of hundreds or even thousands of other firms in order to produce your products and services. Supply chain management systems, which we introduced in Chapter 2, are an answer to these problems of supply chain complexity and scale.

The Supply Chain

A firm's **supply chain** is a network of organizations and business processes for procuring raw materials, transforming these materials into intermediate and finished products, and distributing the finished products to customers. It links suppliers, manufacturing plants, distribution centres, retail outlets, and customers to supply goods and services from source through consumption. Materials, information, and payments flow through the supply chain in both directions.

Goods start out as raw materials and, as they move through the supply chain, are transformed into intermediate products (also referred to as components or parts), and finally, into finished products. The finished products are shipped to distribution centres and from there to retailers and customers. Returned items flow in the reverse direction from the buyer back to the seller.

Let us look at the supply chain for Nike runners as an example. Nike designs, markets, and sells runners, socks, athletic clothing, and accessories throughout the world. Its primary

Supply chain

FIGURE 12-2   Nike's supply chain.

This figure illustrates the major entities in Nike's supply chain and the flow of information upstream and downstream to coordinate the activities involved in buying, making, and moving a product. Shown here is a simplified supply chain, with the upstream portion focusing only on the suppliers for runners and runners soles.

suppliers are contract manufacturers with factories in China, Thailand, Indonesia, Brazil, and other countries. These companies fashion Nike's finished products.

Nike's contract suppliers do not manufacture runners from scratch. They obtain components for the runners—the laces, eyelets, uppers, and soles—from other suppliers and then assemble them into finished runners. These suppliers in turn have their own suppliers. For example, the suppliers of soles have suppliers for synthetic rubber, suppliers for chemicals used to melt the rubber for moulding, and suppliers for the moulds into which to pour the rubber. Suppliers of laces would have suppliers for their thread, for dyes, and for the plastic lace tips.

Figure 12-2 provides a simplified illustration of Nike's supply chain for runners; it shows the flow of information and materials among suppliers, Nike, Nike's distributors, retailers, and customers. Nike's contract manufacturers are its primary suppliers. The suppliers of soles, eyelets, uppers, and laces are the secondary (Tier 2) suppliers. Suppliers to these suppliers are the tertiary (Tier 3) suppliers.

The *upstream* portion of the supply chain includes the company's suppliers, the suppliers' suppliers, and the processes for managing relationships with them. The *downstream* portion consists of the organizations and processes for distributing and delivering products to the final customers. Companies doing manufacturing, such as Nike's contract suppliers of runners, also manage their own *internal supply chain* processes for transforming materials, components, and services furnished by their suppliers into finished products or intermediate products (components or parts) for their customers and for managing materials and inventory.

The supply chain illustrated in Figure 12-2 has been simplified. It shows only two contract manufacturers for runners and only the upstream supply chain for runners soles. Nike has hundreds of contract manufacturers turning out finished runners, socks, and athletic clothing, each with its own set of suppliers. The upstream portion of Nike's supply chain would actually comprise thousands of entities. Nike also has numerous distributors and many thousands of retail stores where its shoes are sold, so the downstream portion of its supply chain is also large and complex.

Information Systems and Supply Chain Management

Inefficiencies in the supply chain, such as parts shortages, underutilized plant capacity, excessive finished goods inventory, or high transportation costs, are caused by inaccurate or untimely information. For example, manufacturers may keep too many parts in inventory because they do not know exactly when they will receive their next shipments from their suppliers. Suppliers may order too few raw materials because they do not have precise information on demand. These supply chain inefficiencies waste as much as 25 percent of a company's operating costs.

If a manufacturer had perfect information about exactly how many units of product customers wanted, when they wanted them, and when they could be produced, it would be possible to implement a highly efficient **just-in-time strategy.** Components would arrive exactly at the moment they were needed, and finished goods would be shipped as they left the assembly line.

In a supply chain, however, uncertainties arise because many events cannot be foreseen—uncertain product demand, late shipments from suppliers, defective parts or raw materials, or production process breakdowns. To satisfy customers, manufacturers often deal with such uncertainties and unforeseen events by keeping more material or products in inventory than they think they may actually need. The *safety stock* acts as a buffer for the lack of flexibility in the supply chain. Although excess inventory is expensive, low fill rates are also costly because business may be lost from cancelled orders.

One recurring problem in supply chain management is the **bullwhip effect,** in which information about the demand for a product gets distorted as it passes from one entity to the next across the supply chain. A slight rise in demand for an item might cause different members in the supply chain—distributors, manufacturers, suppliers, secondary suppliers (suppliers' suppliers), and tertiary suppliers (suppliers' suppliers' suppliers)—to stockpile inventory so each has enough "just in case." These changes ripple throughout the supply chain, magnifying what started out as a small change from planned orders, creating excess inventory, production, warehousing, and shipping costs (see Figure 12-3).

For example, Procter & Gamble (P&G) found it had excessively high inventories of its Pampers disposable diapers at various points along its supply chain because of such distorted information. Although customer purchases in stores were fairly stable, orders from distributors would spike when P&G offered aggressive price promotions. Pampers and Pampers' components accumulated in warehouses along the supply chain to meet demand that did not actually exist. To eliminate this problem, P&G revised its marketing, sales, and supply chain processes and used more accurate demand forecasting (Lee, Padmanabhan, and Wang, 1997).

The bullwhip is tamed by reducing uncertainties about demand and supply when all members of the supply chain have accurate and up-to-date information. If all supply chain members share dynamic information about inventory levels, schedules, forecasts, and shipments, they have more precise knowledge about how to adjust their sourcing, manufacturing, and distribution plans. Supply chain management systems provide the kind of information that helps members of the supply chain make better purchasing and scheduling decisions. Table 12-2 describes how firms benefit from these systems.

Supply Chain Management Software

Supply chain software is classified as either software to help businesses plan their supply chains (supply chain planning) or software to help them execute the supply chain steps (supply chain execution). **Supply chain planning systems** enable the firm to model its existing supply chain, generate demand forecasts for products, and develop optimal sourcing and manufacturing plans. These systems help companies make better decisions such as determining how much of a specific product to manufacture in a given time period; establishing inventory levels for raw materials, intermediate products, and finished goods; determining where to store finished goods; and identifying the transportation mode to use for product delivery.

Just-in-time strategy
Bullwhip effect
Supply chain planning systems

FIGURE 12-3 The bullwhip effect.

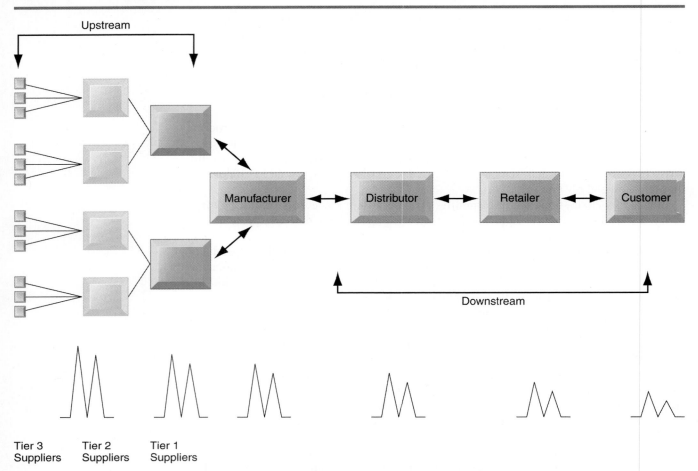

Inaccurate information can cause minor fluctuations in demand for a product to be amplified as one moves further back in the supply chain. Minor fluctuations in retail sales for a product can create excess inventory for distributors, manufacturers, and suppliers.

For example, if a large customer places a larger order than usual or changes that order on short notice, it can have a widespread impact throughout the supply chain. Additional raw materials or a different mix of raw materials may need to be ordered from suppliers. Manufacturing may have to change job scheduling. A transportation carrier may have to reschedule deliveries. Supply chain planning software makes the necessary adjustments to production and distribution plans. Information about

TABLE 12-2 How information systems facilitate supply chain management.

INFORMATION FROM SUPPLY CHAIN MANAGEMENT SYSTEMS HELPS FIRMS:
Decide when and what to produce, store, and move
Rapidly communicate orders
Track the status of orders
Check inventory availability and monitor inventory levels
Reduce inventory, transportation, and warehousing costs
Track shipments
Plan production based on actual customer demand
Rapidly communicate changes in product design

changes is shared among the relevant supply chain members so that their work can be coordinated. One of the most important—and complex—supply chain planning functions is **demand planning,** which determines how much product a business needs to make to satisfy all of its customers' demands.

Whirlpool Corporation, which produces washing machines, dryers, refrigerators, ovens, and other home appliances, uses supply chain planning systems to make sure what it produces matches customer demand. The company uses supply chain planning software from i2 Technologies that includes modules for Master Scheduling, Deployment Planning, and Inventory Planning. Whirlpool also installed i2's Web-based tool for Collaborative Planning, Forecasting, and Replenishment (CPFR) for sharing and combining its sales forecasts with those of its major sales partners. Improvements in supply chain planning helped Whirlpool increase availability of products in stock when customers needed them to 97 percent, while reducing the number of excess finished goods in inventory by 20 percent and forecasting errors by 50 percent (i2, 2007).

Supply chain execution systems manage the flow of products through distribution centres and warehouses to ensure that products are delivered to the right locations in the most efficient manner. They track the physical status of goods, the management of materials, warehouse and transportation operations, and financial information involving all parties. Manugistics and i2 Technologies (both acquired by JDA Software) are major supply chain management software vendors, and enterprise software vendors SAP and Oracle-PeopleSoft offer supply chain management modules.

The Window on Technology describes how supply chain management software improves operational performance and decision making at Procter & Gamble. This multinational giant manages global supply chains for more than 300 brands, each of which has many different configurations. The company's supply chains are numerous and complex, and P&G has many supply chain management applications. The one described here is for inventory optimization.

Demand planning
Supply chain execution systems

WINDOW ON TECHNOLOGY

Procter & Gamble Tries to Optimize Inventory

The shampoo and lipstick aisles at Zellers and Walmart hardly seem like battlegrounds, but they are actually sites for an unending struggle among consumer products companies for retail shelf space. No company knows this better than Procter & Gamble (P&G), one of the world's largest consumer goods companies, with annual revenue surpassing $93 billion and 138 000 employees in 80 countries.

The company sells more than 300 brands worldwide, including Cover Girl cosmetics, Olay skin care, Crest, Charmin, Tide, Pringles, and Pampers. Demand variability for P&G's products from its Beauty division is very high. A popular eye shadow or lipstick colour may quickly fall out of favour, while fashion trends call for new products continually to come on-stream. Major retail outlets such as Zellers and Walmart compete by offering brand-name products at the lowest price possible.

In response to these pressures, P&G is constantly searching for ways to reduce supply chain costs and improve efficiency throughout its entire manufacturing and distribu-

tion network. It recently implemented a multi-echelon inventory optimization system to manage its supply chain more efficiently.

The supply chains of a company as large as P&G are extremely complicated, featuring thousands of suppliers, manufacturing facilities, and markets. Even the slightest of changes at any part of the supply chain has significant effects on all of the other participants. Because P&G's supply chains are so extensive, the chance for any errors or inefficiencies to occur are greater than with smaller, more compact supply chains. Inventory optimization for a company as large as P&G is therefore critical to cutting costs and increasing revenues. P&G was already renowned for its supply chain management, successfully reducing its surplus inventory with sales and operations planning, better forecasting, just-in-time delivery strategies, and vendor-managed inventory activity. But multi-echelon inventory optimization has provided the company with a new means to achieve even higher levels of efficiency.

Multi-echelon networks are networks in which products are located in a variety of locations along their path to distribution, some of which are in different "echelons," or tiers, of the enterprise's distribution network. For example, large retailers' distribution networks often consist of a regional distribution centre and a larger number of forward distribution centres. The presence of multiple echelons in a distribution network makes inventory management more difficult because each echelon is isolated from other echelons, so changes in inventory made by one echelon may have unpredictable consequences on the others.

Multi-echelon inventory optimization seeks to minimize the total inventory in all of the echelons of a company's supply chain. This is more complicated than traditional inventory optimization because of the additional lead times between each echelon, the bullwhip effect, and the need to synchronize orders and control costs between echelons. Companies with this level of complexity in their supply chains must replenish and divide their inventories at each distribution point along the supply chain, as opposed to just one distribution point or even just the inventory of the initial supplier. Each point in the supply chain is also unaware of the inventory levels of points beyond those with which it has immediate contact, which creates a lack of visibility up and down the supply chain.

The multi-echelon approach to inventory management consists of the following factors: multiple independent forecast updates in each echelon; accounting for all lead times and variations in lead times; management of the bullwhip effect; creation of visibility up and down the demand chain; synchronized order strategies; and appropriate modelling of the effects of different echelons' replenishment strategies on one another.

P&G prefers to develop its own analytical tools, but in this case turned to Optiant for its PowerChain Suite multi-echelon inventory optimization solution. Gillette, which P&G was preparing to acquire at the time, had already begun using Optiant software with strong results.

PowerChain Suite determines appropriate inventory configurations that can adapt smoothly to quickly changing demand. The solution uses mathematical models, based on award-winning research from MIT, which balance costs, resources, and customer service to arrive at these configurations. PowerChain tools pool inventory to minimize risk across products, components, and customers and also coordinate inventory policy across different items. PowerChain enables companies to design new supply chains and to model their end-to-end supply chain. They can then quickly evaluate the cost and performance of alternate supply chain structures and sourcing options to make better decisions. Optiant has provided supply chain management for other leading manufacturers such as Canadian Tire, Black & Decker, Hewlett-Packard, IKEA, Imation, Intel, Kraft, and Microsoft.

P&G's beauty division served as the pilot project for the adoption of the Optiant software. Beauty is one of the company's largest, most complicated, and most profitable divisions. P&G believed that if multi-echelon inventory strategies could increase profitability at this division, they would work at any unit of the company.

The Optiant software first configured P&G's existing cosmetics supply chain, pulling in the previous 18 months of demand data and using the previous three months' demand variability. It then optimized the inventory strategy within that supply chain, aiming for target service levels above 99 percent. A third step identified alternate supply chain designs, and the final step created an optimal redesign of the supply network.

Results have been impressive. P&G's beauty division trimmed its total inventory by 3 to 7 percent and maintained service levels above 99 percent. In the first fiscal year after implementation of the new software, the division's earnings rose 13 percent, and sales rose 7 percent. Inventory days on hand were down by eight days compared to the previous fiscal year. The results were so successful that P&G began rolling out multi-echelon inventory strategies across all of its various manufacturing branches.

To Think About

1. Why are larger supply chains more difficult to manage? List several reasons.

2. Why is supply chain management so important at a company such as P&G?

3. How did inventory optimization impact operations and decision making at P&G?

4. Why might a small company not derive as much benefit from multi-echelon inventory optimization as a large company? Explain your answer.

MIS in Action

1. Surf the Web for the ingredients of a Procter & Gamble product such as Crest toothpaste or Cover Girl lipstick, or look for the list of ingredients on the packaging for some of these products in a retail store. Make a list of the ingredients for the product you selected.

2. Use the Web to find the major suppliers for each of these ingredients and their locations.

3. What did you learn from your investigation about P&G's supply chains for these products? What factors would determine price and availability of these products?

Sources: John Kerr, "Procter & Gamble Takes Inventory Up a Notch," *Supply Chain Management Review*, February 13, 2008; Optiant, "Optiant Announces Multi-Echelon Inventory Optimization Enterprise Agreement with P&G," October 17, 2007; and www.optiant.com (accessed July 17, 2008).

FIGURE 12-4   Intranets and extranets for supply chain management.

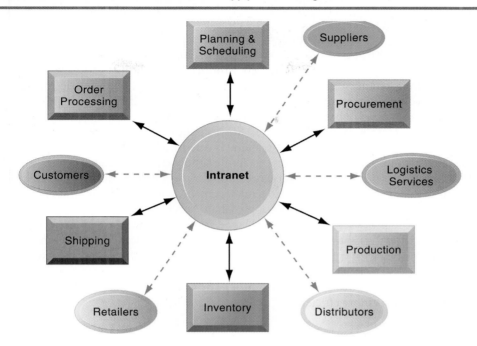

Intranets integrate information from isolated business processes within the firm to help manage its internal supply chain. Access to these private intranets can also be extended to authorized suppliers, distributors, logistics services, and, sometimes, to retail customers to improve coordination of external supply chain processes.

Global Supply Chains and the Internet

Before the Internet, supply chain coordination was hampered by the difficulties of making information flow smoothly among disparate internal supply chain systems for purchasing, materials management, manufacturing, and distribution. It was also difficult to share information with external supply chain partners because the systems of suppliers, distributors, or logistics providers were based on incompatible technology platforms and standards. Enterprise systems supply some integration of internal supply chain processes but they are not designed to deal with external supply chain processes.

Some supply chain integration is supplied inexpensively using Internet technology. Firms use intranets to improve coordination among their internal supply chain processes, and they use extranets to coordinate supply chain processes shared with their business partners (see Figure 12-4).

Using intranets and extranets, all members of the supply chain are instantly able to communicate with each other, using up-to-date information to adjust purchasing, logistics, manufacturing, packaging, and schedules. A manager will use a Web interface to tap into suppliers' systems to determine whether inventory and production capabilities match demand for the firm's products. Business partners will use Web-based supply chain management tools to collaborate online on forecasts. Sales representatives will access suppliers' production schedules and logistics information to monitor customers' order status.

Global Supply Chain Issues More and more companies are entering international markets, outsourcing manufacturing operations, and obtaining supplies from other countries as well as selling abroad. Their supply chains extend across multiple countries and regions. There are additional complexities and challenges to managing a global supply chain.

Global supply chains typically span greater geographic distances and time differences than domestic supply chains and have participants from a number of different countries. Although the purchase price of many goods might be lower abroad, there are often additional costs for transportation, inventory (the need for a larger buffer of safety stock), and local taxes or fees. Performance standards may vary from region to region or from nation to nation. Supply chain management may need to reflect foreign government regulations and cultural differences. All of these factors impact how a company takes orders, plans distribution, sizes warehousing, and manages inbound and outbound logistics throughout the global markets it services.

The Internet helps companies manage many aspects of their global supply chains, including sourcing, transportation, communications, and international finance. Today's apparel industry, for example, relies heavily on outsourcing to contract manufacturers in China and other low-wage countries. Apparel companies, such as Canada's Nygård International, are starting to use the Web to manage their global supply chain and production issues. As goods are being sourced, produced, and shipped, communication is required among retailers, manufacturers, contractors, agents, and logistics providers. Many, especially smaller companies, still share product information over the phone, via e-mail, or through faxes. These methods slow down the supply chain and also increase errors and uncertainty. With a Web-based SCM application, all supply chain members communicate through a Web-based system. If one of a company's vendors makes a change in the status of a product, everyone in the supply chain sees the change.

In addition to contract manufacturing, globalization has encouraged outsourcing warehouse management, transportation management, and related operations to third-party logistics providers, such as UPS Supply Chain Services, TransX, and American Port Services. These logistics services offer Web-based software to give their customers a better view of their global supply chains. American Port Services invested in software to synchronize processes with freight forwarders, logistics hubs, and warehouses around the world that it uses for managing its clients' shipments and inventory. Customers are able to check a secure Web site to monitor inventory and shipments, helping them run their global supply chains more efficiently.

Demand-Driven Supply Chains: From Push to Pull Manufacturing and Efficient Customer Response In addition to reducing costs, supply chain management systems facilitate efficient customer response, enabling the workings of the business to be driven more by customer demand. (We introduced efficient customer response systems in Chapter 3.)

Earlier supply chain management systems were driven by a push-based model (also known as build-to-stock). In a **push-based model**, production master schedules are based on forecasts or best guesses of demand for products, and products are "pushed" to customers. With new flows of information made possible by Web-based tools, supply chain management more easily follows a **pull-based model.** In a pull-based model, also known as a demand-driven model or build-to-order, actual customer orders or purchases trigger events in the supply chain. Transactions to produce and deliver only what customers have ordered move up the supply chain from retailers to distributors to manufacturers and eventually to suppliers. Only products to fulfill these orders move back down the supply chain to the retailer. Manufacturers use only actual order demand information to drive their production schedules and the procurement of components or raw materials, as illustrated in Figure 12-5. Walmart's continuous replenishment system and Dell Inc.'s build-to-order system, both described in Chapter 3, are examples of the pull-based model.

Push-based model
Pull-based model

FIGURE 12-5 Push- versus pull-based supply chain models.

The difference between push- and pull-based models is summarized by the slogan "Make what we sell, not sell what we make."

FIGURE 12-6   The future Internet-driven supply chain.

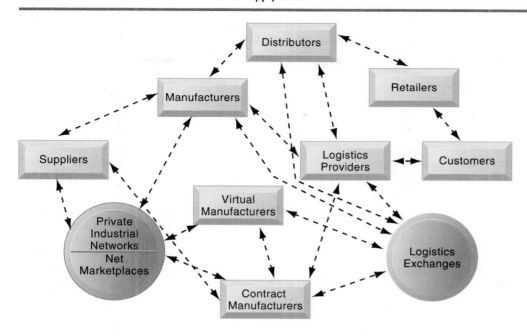

The future Internet-driven supply chain operates like a digital logistics nervous system. It provides multidirectional communication among firms, networks of firms, and e-marketplaces so that entire networks of supply chain partners can immediately adjust inventories, orders, and capacities.

The Internet and Internet technology make it possible to move from sequential supply chains, where information and materials flow sequentially from company to company, to concurrent supply chains, where information flows in many directions simultaneously among members of a supply chain network. Members of the network immediately adjust to changes in schedules or orders. Ultimately, the Internet could create a "digital logistics nervous system" throughout the supply chain (see Figure 12-6).

Business Value of Supply Chain Management Systems

You have just seen how supply chain management systems enable firms to streamline both their internal and external supply chain processes and provide management with more accurate information about what to produce, store, and move. By implementing a networked and integrated supply chain management system, companies match supply to demand, reduce inventory levels, improve delivery service, speed product time to market, and use assets more effectively (see Figure 12-6).

Total supply chain costs represent the majority of operating expenses for many businesses and in some industries approach 75 percent of the total operating budget. Reducing supply chain costs may have a major impact on firm profitability.

In addition to reducing costs, supply chain management systems help increase sales. If a product is not available when a customer wants it, customers often try to purchase it from someone else. More precise control of the supply chain enhances the firm's ability to have the right product available for customer purchases at the right time.

12.3   Customer Relationship Management Systems

You have probably heard phrases such as "The customer is always right" or "The customer comes first." Today these words ring truer than ever. Because competitive advantage based on an innovative new product or service is often very short-lived, companies are realizing that their only enduring competitive strength may be their relationships with their customers. Some say that the basis of competition has switched from who sells the most products and services to who "owns" the customer and that customer relationships represent a firm's most valuable asset.

What Is Customer Relationship Management?

What kinds of information would you need to build and nurture strong, long-lasting relationships with customers? You would want to know exactly who your customers are, how to contact them, whether they are costly to service and sell to, what kinds of products and services they are interested in, and how much money they spend on your company. If you could, you would want to make sure you knew each of your customers well, as if you were running a small-town store. And you would want to make your good customers feel special.

In a small business operating in a neighbourhood, it is possible for business owners and managers to really know their customers on a personal, face-to-face basis. But in a large business operating on a metropolitan, regional, national, or even global basis, it is impossible to "know your customer" in this intimate way. In these kinds of businesses there are too many customers and too many different ways that customers interact with the firm (over the Web, by phone, by fax, and face to face). It becomes especially difficult to integrate information from all these sources and to deal with large numbers of customers.

A large business's processes for sales, service, and marketing tend to be highly compartmentalized, and these departments do not share much essential customer information. Some information on a specific customer might be stored and organized in terms of that person's account with the company. Other pieces of information about the same customer might be organized by products that were purchased. There is no way to consolidate all of this information to provide a unified view of a customer across the company.

This is where customer relationship management systems help. Customer relationship management (CRM) systems, which we introduced in Chapter 2, capture and integrate customer data from all over the organization, consolidate the data, analyze the data, and then distribute the results to various systems and customer touch points across the enterprise. A **touch point** (also known as a contact point) is a method of interaction with the customer, such as telephone, e-mail, customer service desk, conventional mail, Web site, wireless device, or retail store.

Well-designed CRM systems provide a single enterprise view of customers that is useful for improving both sales and customer service. These systems likewise provide customers with a single view of the company regardless of what touch point the customer uses (see Figure 12-7).

Good CRM systems provide data and analytical tools for answering questions such as these: "What is the value of a particular customer to the firm over his or her lifetime?" "Who are our most loyal customers?" (It can cost six times more to sell to a new customer than to an existing customer.) "Who are our most profitable customers?" and "What do

Touch point

FIGURE 12-7   Customer relationship management (CRM) systems.

CRM systems examine customers from a multifaceted perspective. These systems use a set of integrated applications to address all aspects of the customer relationship, including customer service, sales, and marketing.

Sales
• Telephone sales
• Web sales
• Retail store sales
• Field sales

Customer

Marketing
• Campaign data
• Content
• Data analysis

Service
• Call centre data
• Web self-service data
• Wireless data

these profitable customers want to buy?" Firms use the answers to these questions to acquire new customers, provide better service and support to existing customers, customize their offerings more precisely to customer preferences, and provide ongoing value to retain profitable customers.

CRM Software

Commercial CRM software packages range from niche tools that perform limited functions, such as personalizing Web sites for specific customers, to large-scale enterprise applications that capture myriad interactions with customers, analyze them with sophisticated reporting tools, and link to other major enterprise applications, such as supply chain management and enterprise systems. The more comprehensive CRM packages contain modules for **partner relationship management (PRM)** and **employee relationship management (ERM)**.

PRM uses many of the same data, tools, and systems as customer relationship management to enhance collaboration between a company and its selling partners. If a company does not sell directly to customers but rather works through distributors or retailers, PRM helps these channels sell to customers directly. It provides a company and its selling partners with the ability to trade information and distribute leads and data about customers, integrating lead generation, pricing, promotions, order configurations, and availability. It also provides a firm with tools to assess its partners' performances so it can make sure its best partners receive the support they need to close more business.

ERM software deals with employee issues that are closely related to CRM, such as setting objectives, employee performance management, performance-based compensation, and employee training. Major CRM application software vendors include Oracle-owned Siebel Systems and PeopleSoft, SAP, Salesforce.com, and Microsoft Dynamics CRM.

Customer relationship management systems typically provide software and online tools for sales, customer service, and marketing. We briefly describe some of these capabilities.

Sales Force Automation (SFA) Sales force automation modules in CRM systems help sales staff increase their productivity by focusing sales efforts on the most profitable customers, those who are good candidates for sales and services. CRM systems provide sales prospect and contact information, product information, product configuration capabilities, and sales quote generation capabilities. SFA software can assemble information about a particular customer's past purchases to help the salesperson make personalized recommendations. CRM software enables sales, marketing, and delivery departments to easily share customer and prospect information. It increases each salesperson's efficiency in reducing the cost per sale as well as the cost of acquiring new customers and retaining old ones. CRM software also has capabilities for sales forecasting, territory management, and team selling.

Customer Service Customer service modules in CRM systems provide information and tools to increase the efficiency of call centres, help desks, and customer support staff. They have capabilities for assigning and managing customer service requests.

One such capability is an appointment or advice telephone line: When a customer calls a standard phone number, the system routes the call to the correct service person, who inputs information about that customer into the system only once. Once the customer's data are in the system, any service representative can handle the customer relationship. Improved access to consistent and accurate customer information helps call centres handle more calls per day and decrease the duration of each call. Thus, call centres and customer service groups achieve greater productivity, reduced transaction time, and higher quality of service at lower cost. The customer is happier because he or she spends less time on the phone restating the problem to customer service representatives.

CRM systems may also include Web-based self-service capabilities: The company Web site can be set up to provide inquiring customers personalized support information as well as the option to contact customer service staff by phone for additional assistance.

Marketing CRM systems support direct-marketing campaigns by providing capabilities for capturing prospect and customer data, for providing product and service information,

Partner relationship management (PRM)

Employee relationship management (ERM)

FIGURE 12-8   How CRM systems support marketing.

Customer relationship management software provides a single point for users to manage and evaluate marketing campaigns across multiple channels, including e-mail, direct mail, telephone, the Web, and wireless messages.

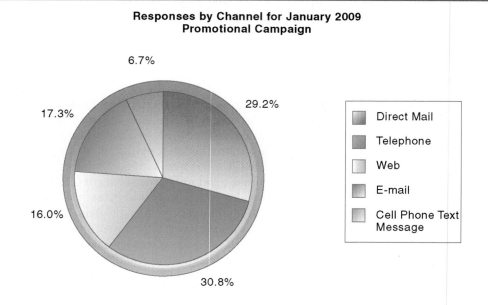

Responses by Channel for January 2009 Promotional Campaign

6.7%

29.2%

17.3%

16.0%

30.8%

- Direct Mail
- Telephone
- Web
- E-mail
- Cell Phone Text Message

for qualifying leads for targeted marketing, and for scheduling and tracking direct-marketing mailings or e-mail (see Figure 12-8). Marketing modules also include tools for analyzing marketing and customer data, identifying profitable and unprofitable customers, designing products and services to satisfy specific customer needs and interests, and identifying opportunities for cross-selling.

Cross-selling is the marketing of complementary products to customers. (For example, in financial services, a customer with a chequing account might be sold a money market account or a home improvement loan.) CRM tools also help firms manage and execute marketing campaigns at all stages, from planning to determining the rate of success for each campaign.

Cross-selling

WINDOW ON ORGANIZATIONS

Organizations

Why Novartis Backed Off from Enterprise Software

Novartis A.G. is a leading global pharmaceutical and health care company headquartered in Basel, Switzerland. It operates in more than 140 countries around the world, employing about 77 200 people and producing nearly $29 billion in revenue in 2003.

Novartis is replacing legacy systems at Novartis offices in more than 50 countries with SAP enterprise software for human resources, supplier relationship management, and supply chain management. Management believes the SAP software will help the company cut down system integration costs as well as standardize and streamline administrative processes, work flow, and reporting in its worldwide operations. The SAP software would also help the company comply with U.S. Food and Drug Administration regulations on electronic records and signatures for the pharmaceutical industry.

A research survey conducted by Frost & Sullivan, a global consulting company specializing in emerging high-technology and industrial markets, recognized SAP as the dominant enterprise resource planning and supply chain management vendor for the global pharmaceuticals industry. Pharmaceutical companies seeking a single system that could tie together their operations in various countries were impressed by SAP's ability to address their industry-specific business requirements as well as the vendor's superior global service and support network.

Novartis had already adopted SAP's R/3 enterprise resource planning and financial modules for many of its operating units. Given the company's enthusiasm for enterprise systems and SAP, it was surprising to learn that the accounts payable department at Novartis Pharmaceuticals, the U.S. arm of the company, was having problems with its SAP enterprise system.

Somewhere in the process of paying invoices, payments were being held, and a backlog of overdue bills was building. A few vendors even withheld credit from the company.

The accounts payable and strategic sourcing departments fingered a recent upgrade to the SAP R/3 financial modules as the source of their financial crisis. Novartis had insisted that SAP be its global standard, and the software just was not working for them. In frustration, these groups began meeting to figure out a way to redesign their requisition-to-pay process, even if it meant scrapping SAP modules that did not meet their needs. They did not want to work with the Novartis information systems department.

Novartis' information systems staff, on the other hand, believed the unpaid invoices were not entirely caused by the SAP software. The company's existing process for invoicing was inefficient, requiring manual approvals from many different managers. It was not a true integrated requisition-to-pay process. Work was still structured into silos and no one knew what was going on.

The information systems staff thought a recent implementation of the SAP R/3 software would solve the problem. It believed that if it let the SAP software handle as many business processes as possible, it would not have to deal with so many interfaces between different information systems. The information systems department had assigned special staff members to serve as business information managers (BIMs) who could work more closely with end-user departments to clarify and support business goals. Nevertheless, because of tight deadlines and limited budget, information systems specialists scrimped on training and did not pay sufficient attention to the new system's impact on business processes.

Something had to be done to get user and information systems groups to cooperate. Ray Pawlicki, Novartis's vice president for information and chief information officer, invited accounts payable and information systems groups to a six-month program to foster joint leadership. The groups met many times. Eventually, both groups started listening to each other and committed to two outcomes.

One was to create a new way for the information systems, accounts payable, and strategic sourcing departments to work together to facilitate rapid business transformation. The other outcome was a proposal to improve the purchasing process for Novartis departments so that they would no longer make independent purchases. Instead, all requisitions would be channelled through the strategic sourcing department. By centralizing purchases, the company would be able to obtain larger discounts from suppliers because it was buying in larger quantities. About $4.6 million to $5.8 million could be saved annually this way.

BIMs from the information systems department emerged with a deeper appreciation of business requirements and how these matched up with SAP and other software providers. In the end, the information systems group agreed to what accounts payable and strategic sourcing had originally requested: a solution that was the "best of breed," irrespective of the software vendor, that would best support the company's redesigned purchasing process.

In May 2003, the information systems department agreed to update an old system from Ariba that would reduce late payments by automatically reconciling sourcing and accounts payable. The Ariba upgrade improved Novartis's purchasing process so much that $4.6 to $5.8 million in savings were achieved within six months.

To Think About

1. Why was Novartis having trouble with its requisition-to-pay process?

2. What management, organization, and technology factors were involved?

3. Was the solution to this problem a good one? Why or why not?

MIS in Action

Visit the Web sites of Ariba (**www.ariba.com**) and SAP (**www.sap.com/canada/index.epx**), and explore their "solutions" sections. Then answer the following questions:

1. List and describe the capabilities of the purchasing or sourcing solutions/modules.

2. How would these modules benefit a company such as Novartis (**www.novartis.com**)? Describe how Novartis could use these capabilities. What other modules do each of these companies have that could benefit Novartis?

Sources: Stephanie Overby, "Can't We All Just Get Along?" *CIO Australia*, March 10, 2004 and "SAP Chosen by Novartis as a Major Building Block," *EETimes*, June 16, 2003.

Figure 12-9 illustrates the most important capabilities for sales, service, and marketing processes that would be found in major CRM software products. Like enterprise software, this software is business-process driven, incorporating hundreds of business processes thought to represent best practices in each of these areas. To achieve maximum benefit, companies need to revise and model their business processes to conform to the best-practice business processes in the CRM software.

Figure 12-10 illustrates how a best practice for increasing customer loyalty through customer service might be modelled by CRM software. Directly servicing customers provides firms with opportunities to increase customer retention by singling out profitable long-term customers for preferential treatment. CRM software can assign each customer a score

FIGURE 12-9 CRM software capabilities.

The major CRM software products support business processes in sales, service, and marketing, integrating customer information from many different sources. Included are support for both the operational and analytical aspects of CRM.

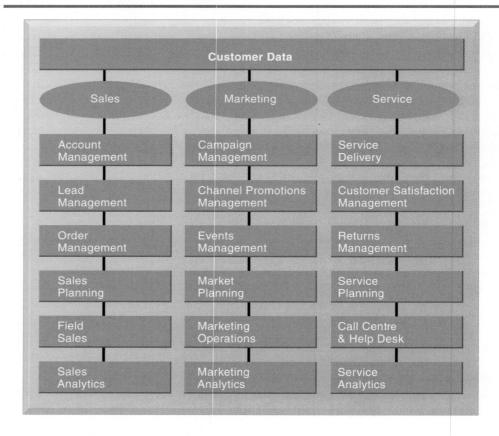

based on that person's value and loyalty to the company and provide that information to help call centres route each customer's service request to agents who can best handle that customer's needs. The system would automatically provide the service agent with a detailed profile of that customer that included the customer's score for value and loyalty. The service agent would use this information to present special offers or additional service to the customer to encourage the customer to keep transacting business with the company. You will

FIGURE 12-10 Customer loyalty management process map.

This process map shows how a best practice for promoting customer loyalty through customer service would be modelled by customer relationship management software. The CRM software helps firms identify high-value customers for preferential treatment.

FIGURE 12-11 Analytical CRM data warehouse.

Analytical CRM uses a customer data warehouse and tools to analyze customer data collected from the firm's customer touch points and from other sources.

find more information on other best-practice business processes in CRM systems in this chapter's Learning Tracks.

Operational and Analytical CRM

All of the applications we have just described support either the operational or analytical aspects of customer relationship management. **Operational CRM** includes customer-facing applications, such as tools for sales force automation, call centre and customer service support, and marketing automation. **Analytical CRM** includes applications that analyze customer data generated by operational CRM applications to provide information for improving business performance.

Analytical CRM applications are based on data warehouses that consolidate the data from operational CRM systems and customer touch points for use with online analytical processing (OLAP), data mining, and other data analysis techniques (see Chapter 6). Customer data collected by the organization might be combined with data from other sources, such as customer lists for direct-marketing campaigns purchased from other companies or demographic data. Such data are analyzed to identify buying patterns, to create segments for targeted marketing, and to pinpoint profitable and unprofitable customers (see Figure 12-11).

Another important output of analytical CRM is the customer's lifetime value to the firm. **Customer lifetime value (CLTV)** is based on the relationship between the revenue produced by a specific customer, the expenses incurred in acquiring and servicing that customer, and the expected life of the relationship between the customer and the company.

Business Value of Customer Relationship Management Systems

Companies with effective customer relationship management systems realize many benefits, including increased customer satisfaction, reduced direct-marketing costs, more effective marketing, and lower costs for customer acquisition and retention. Information from CRM systems increases sales revenue by identifying the most profitable customers and segments for focused marketing and cross-selling.

Customer churn is reduced as sales, service, and marketing better respond to customer needs. The **churn rate** measures the number of customers who stop using or purchasing products or services from a company. It is an important indicator of the growth or decline of a firm's customer base.

Operational CRM
Analytical CRM
Customer lifetime value (CLTV)
Churn rate

12.4 Enterprise Applications: New Opportunities and Challenges

Many firms have implemented enterprise systems and systems for supply chain management and customer relationship management because they are such powerful instruments for achieving operational excellence and enhancing decision making. But precisely because they are so powerful in changing the way the organization works, they are challenging to implement. Let us briefly examine some of these challenges as well as new ways of obtaining value from these systems.

Enterprise Application Challenges

Promises of dramatic reductions in inventory costs, order-to-delivery time, more efficient customer response, and higher product and customer profitability make enterprise systems and systems for supply chain management and customer relationship management very alluring. But to obtain this value, you must clearly understand how your business has to change to use these systems effectively.

Enterprise applications involve complex pieces of software that are very expensive to purchase and implement. It might take a large company several years to complete a large-scale implementation of an enterprise system or a system for supply chain management or customer relationship management. The total implementation cost of a large system, including software, database tools, consulting fees, personnel costs, training, and perhaps hardware costs, might amount to four to five times the initial purchase price for the software.

Enterprise applications require not only deep-seated technological changes but also fundamental changes in the way the business operates. Companies must make sweeping changes to their business processes to work with the software. Employees must accept new job functions and responsibilities. They must learn how to perform a new set of work activities and understand how the information they enter into the system can affect other parts of the company. This requires new organizational learning.

Supply chain management systems require multiple organizations to share information and business processes. Each participant in the system may have to change some of its processes and the way it uses information to create a system that best serves the supply chain as a whole.

Some firms experienced enormous operating problems and losses when they first implemented enterprise applications because they did not understand how much organizational change was required.

- Sobeys grocery store chain dropped SAP when the system caused a five-week backlog in transactions processing. Sobeys claimed that implementing SAP's supply chain management applications had put it behind its timeline; a Sobeys spokesperson also indicated there were "a number of other issues." Interestingly, four years later, Sobeys did in fact implement SAP's supply chain management application successfully.

- Hershey Foods' profitability dropped when it tried to implement SAP enterprise software, Manugistics SCM software, and Siebel Systems CRM software on a crash schedule in 1999 without thorough testing and employee training. Shipments ran two weeks late and many customers did not receive enough candy to stock shelves during the busy Halloween selling period. Hershey lost sales and customers during that period although the new systems eventually improved operational efficiency.

Enterprise applications also introduce "switching costs." Once you adopt an enterprise application from a single vendor, such as SAP, Oracle, or others, it is very costly to switch vendors, and your firm becomes dependent on the vendor to upgrade its product and maintain your installation.

Enterprise applications are based on organization-wide definitions of data. You will need to understand exactly how your business uses its data and how the data would be organized in a customer relationship management, supply chain management, or enterprise system. CRM systems typically require some data cleansing work.

The Window on Organizations on pages 388–389 described another company's struggle to implement enterprise software. Novartis, a leading international pharmaceutical house, had trouble making some of the modules supplied by SAP perform properly. Its experience illustrates some of the problems that occur when a company tries to make enterprise software work with its unique business processes.

In a nutshell, it takes a lot of work to get enterprise applications to work properly. Everyone in the organization must be involved. Of course, for those companies that have successfully implemented CRM, SCM, and enterprise systems, the results have justified the effort.

Next-Generation Enterprise Applications

Today, enterprise application vendors are delivering more value by becoming more flexible, Web-enabled, and capable of integration with other systems. Standalone enterprise systems, customer relationship systems, and supply chain management systems are becoming a thing of the past.

The major enterprise software vendors have created what they call *enterprise solutions*, *enterprise suites*, or *e-business suites* to make their customer relationship management, supply chain management, and enterprise systems work closely with each other, and link to systems of customers and suppliers. SAP Business Suite, Oracle's e-Business Suite, and Microsoft's Dynamics suite (aimed at midsized companies) are examples, and they now utilize Web services and service-oriented architecture (SOA, see Chapter 5).

SAP's next-generation enterprise applications are based on its enterprise service-oriented architecture. It incorporates SOA standards and uses its NetWeaver tool as an integration platform linking SAP's own applications and also Web services developed by independent software vendors. The goal is to make enterprise applications easier to implement and manage.

For example, the current version of SAP enterprise software combines key applications in finance, logistics and procurement, and human resources administration into a core ERP component. Businesses then extend these applications by linking to function-specific Web services such as employee recruiting or collections management provided by SAP and other vendors. SAP provides more than 500 Web services through its Web site.

Oracle also has included SOA and business process management capabilities into its Fusion middleware products. Businesses can use Oracle tools to customize Oracle's applications without breaking the entire application.

Next-generation enterprise applications also include open source and on-demand solutions. Compared to commercial enterprise application software, open-source products such as Compiere, Open for Business, and Openbravo are not as mature, nor do they include as much support. However, companies such as small manufacturers are choosing this option because there are no software licensing fees. (Support and customization for open source products cost extra.)

The most explosive growth in SaaS (software as a service) offerings has been for customer relationship management. Salesforce.com (see Chapters 5 and 8) and Oracle's Siebel Systems have been the leaders in hosted CRM solutions, and Microsoft Dynamics CRM has an online on-demand version. SaaS versions of enterprise systems are much less popular and not yet available from the major enterprise vendors.

Salesforce.com and Oracle now include some Web 2.0 capabilities that enable organizations to identify new ideas more rapidly, improve team productivity, and deepen interactions with customers. For example, Salesforce Ideas allows employees, customers, and business partners to suggest and then vote on new ideas. Dell Inc. deployed this technology as Dell IdeaStorm (www.dellideastorm.com) to enable customers to suggest and vote on new concepts and feature changes in Dell products. Ideas contributed on the service encouraged Dell to add higher-resolution screens to the Dell 1530 laptop (Greenfield, 2008).

Service Platforms Another way of extending enterprise applications is to use them to create service platforms for new or improved business processes that integrate information from multiple functional areas. These enterprise-wide service platforms provide a greater degree of cross-functional integration than the traditional enterprise applications. A **service platform** integrates multiple applications from multiple business functions, business units, or business partners to deliver a seamless experience for the customer, employee, manager, or business partner.

For instance, the order-to-cash process involves receiving an order and seeing it all the way through obtaining payment for the order. This process begins with lead generation, marketing campaigns, and order entry, which are typically supported by CRM systems. Once the order is received, manufacturing is scheduled and parts availability is verified—processes that are usually supported by enterprise software. The order then is handled by processes for distribution planning, warehousing, order fulfillment, and shipping, which are usually supported by supply chain management systems. Finally, the order is billed to the customer, which is handled by either enterprise financial applications or accounts receivable. If the purchase at some point required customer service, customer relationship management systems would again be invoked.

A service such as order-to-cash requires data from enterprise applications and financial systems to be further integrated into an enterprise-wide composite process. To accomplish this, firms need software tools that use existing applications as building blocks for new cross-enterprise processes (see Figure 12-12). Enterprise application vendors provide middleware and tools that use XML and Web services for integrating enterprise applications with older legacy applications and systems from other vendors.

Increasingly, these new services will be delivered through portals. Portal software can integrate information from enterprise applications and disparate in-house legacy systems, presenting it to users through a Web interface so that the information appears to be coming from a single source. For example, Société de transport de Montréal STM—Montreal, Quebec's public transportation company—used SAP NetWeaver Portal to track vehicle repairs and maintenance and turn this information into work orders.

Service platform

FIGURE 12-12 Order-to-cash service.

Order-to-cash is a composite process that integrates data from individual enterprise systems and legacy financial applications. The process must be modelled and translated into a software system using application integration tools.

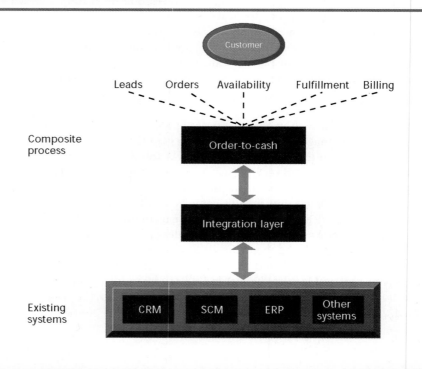

SUMMARY

1. *How do enterprise systems help businesses achieve operational excellence?*

Enterprise software is based on a suite of integrated software modules and a common central database. The database collects data from and feeds the data into numerous applications that can support nearly all of an organization's internal business activities. When new information is entered by one process, the information is made available immediately to other business processes.

Enterprise systems support organizational centralization by enforcing uniform data standards and business processes throughout the company and a single unified technology platform. The firm-wide data generated by enterprise systems helps managers evaluate organizational performance.

2. *How do supply chain management systems coordinate planning, production, and logistics with suppliers?*

Supply chain management systems automate the flow of information among members of the supply chain so they can use it to make better decisions about when and how much to purchase, produce, or ship. More accurate information from supply chain management systems reduces uncertainty and the impact of the bullwhip effect.

Supply chain management software includes software for supply chain planning and for supply chain execution. Internet technology facilitates the management of global supply chains by providing the connectivity for organizations in different countries to share supply chain information. Improved communication among supply chain members also facilitates efficient customer response and movement toward a demand-driven model.

3. *How do customer relationship management systems help firms achieve customer intimacy?*

Customer relationship management (CRM) systems integrate and automate customer-facing processes in sales, marketing, and customer service, providing an enterprise-wide view of customers. Companies can use this customer knowledge when they interact with customers to provide them with better service or to sell new products and services. These systems also identify profitable or unprofitable customers or opportunities to reduce the churn rate.

The major customer relationship management software packages provide capabilities for both operational CRM and analytical CRM. They often include modules for managing relationships with selling partners (partner relationship management) and for employee relationship management.

4. *What are the challenges posed by enterprise applications?*

Enterprise applications are difficult to implement. They require extensive organizational change, large new software investments, and careful assessment of how these systems will enhance organizational performance. Enterprise applications cannot provide value if they are implemented atop flawed processes or if firms do not know how to use these systems to measure performance improvements. Employees require training to prepare for new procedures and roles. Attention to data management is essential.

5. *How are enterprise applications used in platforms for new cross-functional services?*

Service platforms integrate data and processes from the various enterprise applications (customer relationship management, supply chain management, and enterprise systems), as well as from disparate legacy applications to create new composite business processes. Web services tie various systems together. The new services are delivered through enterprise portals, which can integrate disparate applications so that information appears to be coming from a single source.

Key Terms

Analytical CRM, 391	Employee relationship management (ERM), 387	Push-based model, 384
Bullwhip effect, 379	Enterprise software, 375	Service platform, 394
Churn rate, 391	Just-in-time strategy, 379	Supply chain, 377
Cross-selling, 388	Operational CRM, 391	Supply chain execution systems, 381
Customer lifetime value (CLTV), 391	Partner relationship management (PRM), 387	Supply chain planning systems, 379
Demand planning, 381	Pull-based model, 384	Touch point, 386

Review Questions

1. *How do enterprise systems help businesses achieve operational excellence?*

- *Define an enterprise system, and explain how enterprise software works.*
- *Describe how enterprise systems provide value for a business.*

2. *How do supply chain management systems coordinate planning, production, and logistics with suppliers?*

- *Define supply chain, and identify each of its components.*
- *Explain how supply chain management systems help reduce the bullwhip effect and how they provide value for a business.*

- Define and compare supply chain planning systems and supply chain execution systems.
- Describe the challenges of global supply chains and how Internet technology can help companies manage them better.
- Distinguish between a push-based and pull-based model of supply chain management, and explain how contemporary supply chain management systems facilitate a pull-based model.

3. How do customer relationship management systems help firms achieve customer intimacy?
- Define customer relationship management, and explain why customer relationships are so important today.
- Describe how partner relationship management (PRM) and employee relationship management (ERM) are related to customer relationship management (CRM).

- Describe the tools and capabilities of customer relationship management software for sales, marketing, and customer service.
- Distinguish between operational and analytical CRM.

4. What are the challenges posed by enterprise applications?
- List and describe the challenges posed by enterprise applications.
- Explain how these challenges can be addressed.

5. How are enterprise applications used in platforms for new cross-functional services?
- Define a service platform and describe the tools for integrating data from enterprise applications.

Discussion Questions

1. Supply chain management is less about managing the physical movement of goods and more about managing information. Discuss the implications of this statement.

2. If a company wants to implement an enterprise application, it had better do its homework. Discuss the implications of this statement.

Collaboration and Teamwork: Analyzing Enterprise Application Vendors

With a group of three or four students, use the Web to research and evaluate the products of two vendors of enterprise application software. You could compare, for example, the SAP and Oracle enterprise systems, the supply chain management systems from i2 and SAP, or the customer relationship management systems of Oracle's Siebel Systems and Salesforce.com. Use what you have learned from these companies' Web sites to compare the software packages you have selected in terms of business functions supported, technology platforms, cost, and ease of use. Which vendor would you select? Why? Would you select the same vendor for a small business as well as a large one? If possible, use Google Sites to post links to Web pages, team communication announcements, and work assignments; to brainstorm; and to work collaboratively on project documents. Try to use Google Docs to develop a presentation of your findings for the class.

 Visit the MyMISLab Web site at **www.pearsoned.ca/mymislab**. This online homework and tutorial system puts you in control of your own learning with study and practice tools directly correlated to this chapter's content.

Learning Track Modules

The following Learning Tracks provide content relevant to topics covered in this chapter:

1. SAP Business Process Map

2. Business Processes in Supply Chain Management and Supply Chain Metrics

3. Best-Practice Business Processes in CRM Software

HANDS-ON MIS Projects

The projects in this section give you hands-on experience analyzing business process integration, suggesting supply chain management and customer relationship management applications, using database software to manage customer service requests, and evaluating supply chain management business services.

Management Decision Problems

1. Toronto-based Mercedes-Benz Canada, with a network of 55 dealers, did not know enough about its customers. Dealers provided customer data to the company on an ad hoc basis. Mercedes did not force dealers to report this information, and its process for tracking dealers that failed to report was cumbersome. There was no real incentive for dealers to share information with the company. How could customer relationship management (CRM) and partner relationship management (PRM) systems help solve this problem?

2. Office Depot sells a wide range of office products and services in North America and internationally, including general office supplies, computer supplies, business machines (and related supplies), and office furniture. The company tries to offer a wider range of office supplies at lower cost than other retailers by using just-in-time replenishment and tight inventory control systems. It uses information from a demand forecasting system and point-of-sale data to replenish its inventory in its 1600 retail stores. Explain how these systems help Office Depot minimize costs and any other benefits they provide. Identify and describe other supply chain management applications that would be especially helpful to Office Depot.

Improving Decision Making: Using Database Software to Manage Customer Service Requests

Software skills: Database design; querying and reporting
Business skills: Customer service analysis

In this exercise, you will use database software to develop an application that tracks customer service requests and analyzes customer data to identify customers meriting priority treatment.

Prime Service is a fictional large service company that provides maintenance and repair services for close to 1200 commercial businesses in Ontario and Quebec. Its customers include businesses of all sizes. Customers with service needs call into its customer service department with requests for repairing heating ducts, broken windows, leaky roofs, broken water pipes, and other problems. The company assigns each request a number and writes down the service request number, identification number of the customer account, the date of the request, the type of equipment requiring repair, and a brief description of the problem. The service requests are handled on a first-come, first-served basis. After the service work has been completed, Prime calculates the cost of the work, enters the price on the service request form, and bills the client.

Management is not happy with this arrangement because the most important and profitable clients—those with accounts of more than $70 000—are treated no differently from its clients with small accounts. It would like to find a way to provide its best customers with better service.

Management would also like to know which types of service problems occur the most frequently so that it can make sure it has adequate resources to address them.

Prime Service has a small database with client account information, which can be found on the MyMISLab for Chapter 12. A sample is shown on the next page, but the Web site may have a more recent version of this database for this exercise. The database table includes fields for the account ID, company (account) name, street address, city, province, postal code, account size (in dollars), contact last name, contact first name, and contact telephone number.

The contact is the name of the person in each company who is responsible for contacting Prime about maintenance and repair work. Use your database software to design a solution that would enable Prime's customer service representatives to identify the most important customers so that they could receive priority service. Your solution will require more than one table. Populate your database with at least 15 service requests. Create several reports that would be of interest to management, such as a list of the highest- and lowest-priority accounts or a report showing the most frequently occurring service problems. Create a report showing customer service representatives which service calls they should respond to first on a specific date.

Achieving Operational Excellence: Evaluating Supply Chain Management Services

Software skills: Web browser and presentation software
Business skills: Evaluating supply chain management services

Trucking companies no longer merely carry goods from one place to another. Some also provide supply chain management services to their customers and help them manage their information. In this project, you will use the Web to research and evaluate two of these business services.

Investigate the Web sites of two companies, TransX and Schneider Logistics, to see how these companies' services can be used for supply chain management. Then respond to the following questions:

1. What supply chain processes can each of these companies support for their clients?

2. How can customers use the Web sites of each company to help them with supply chain management?

3. Compare the supply chain management services provided by these companies. Which company would you select to help your firm manage its supply chain? Why?

CASE STUDY   Symantec's ERP Turmoil

Symantec Corporation is a leading software vendor specializing in security and information management. The company is well known for its Norton brand of security products in addition to a variety of other security and storage software. Symantec has operations in more than 40 countries and more than 17 500 employees. A major source of Symantec's growth since the company's creation in the 1980s has been the acquisition of other companies, including Norton, Brightmail, Altiris, and many smaller software developers. In 2005, the company made its largest acquisi-

tion to date, acquiring Veritas Software for approximately $16.5 billion in what was the largest software industry merger ever at that time.

While Symantec's focus was security and information management for consumers, Veritas specialized in storage management software geared toward large-scale licensing. Because the two companies were of similar size and specialized in different types of software, many industry pundits questioned whether they were ideal candidates for a merger. Today, those questions appear to have been well founded, in large part because of the difficulties incurred by Symantec's attempts to complete an overhaul of its enterprise resource planning systems.

Shortly after acquiring Veritas in late 2005, Symantec began an ERP rollout, referred to internally as "Project Oasis," intended to standardize and unify the Symantec and Veritas information systems. The goal of the rollout was to create a single ERP system, within which all of the company's extensive network of resellers, integrators, distributors, and customers could place orders for more than 250 000 different products Symantec offered in the same way. The two companies had each used Oracle E-Business Suite 11d prior to the merger, but both used highly customized versions of the systems that made integration a daunting task.

An overhaul of the combined company's enterprise systems was needed to combine Symantec and Veritas's data from key business processes. A common enterprise system would also reduce the costs of maintaining Symantec's IT infrastructure and licensing fees for the enterprise software.

For its new system, Symantec opted to upgrade to Oracle's E-Business Suite 11i, running it on Sun Solaris servers. The system used an Oracle Fusion middleware portal on the front end, providing a single contact point for all of Symantec's partners and customers. Both Symantec's security applications and Veritas's backup and storage applications are available via the same portal. On the front end, the new Oracle system was linked to Salesforce.com's on-demand customer relationship management system and on the back end, the system linked to Symantec's Oracle PeopleSoft Enterprise human resources applications.

The initial reaction to the launch of the new system was decidedly negative. While the system itself was technically sound and working exactly as intended, users struggled to process the large amount of information provided to them and were overwhelmed by the increased number of steps, all of them new, required to place orders. Unhappy with the new system, customers began calling Symantec's support team in record numbers, but the company was unprepared to meet the increased demand for customer support. Wait times ballooned from an average of 2 minutes to an average of 25 minutes for a typical customer support call. Once customers reached a Symantec employee, they could spend up to 20 more minutes troubleshooting the problems and were often told that nothing could be done.

Symantec also neglected to coordinate the development of its new ERP system with the launch of other products from different divisions within the company, compounding the issues with customer support and response times. For example, the new system's launch coincided with the launch of the newest version of Symantec Backup Exec 10d, one of the company's flagship products. There was simply too much change occurring all at once for typical customers to handle. Even longtime partners expressed displeasure at the steep drop in the quality of Symantec's customer service.

Customers were also unhappy with Symantec's changes to its stock-keeping unit product system, or SKU system. Symantec improved the system by creating a single set of codes for all of its applications. Although reducing the num-

ber of codes made ordering products simpler and easier, it also caught many smaller partners of Symantec off-guard. Some smaller distributors and partners did not update their systems to handle the new SKUs and were unable to submit purchase orders electronically, forcing Symantec to process orders manually. Although Symantec extended the deadline for its partners to switch to the new purchasing system to accommodate these customers, the overhaul still represented an annoyance for many who had been satisfied with the previous system.

Symantec's changes to the software licensing process were another irritant to customers. Prior to the ERP rollout, the software licensing program worked well. Customers could put in an order and receive a licence certificate promptly, usually within a couple of days. After the rollout, licensing became much more difficult for Symantec's customers and partners, forcing them to wait weeks before receiving their licenses. When licences did not show up, unhappy customers called Symantec for support, further burdening its already-overworked customer service department. The changes to the licensing system were also not coordinated with the rest of Project Oasis, creating unnecessary confusion.

Symantec had designed the new enterprise system to show customers their existing licences. However, one company could have multiple accounts with variations in corporate names when divisions and branch offices purchased their own licences separately from the central office.

Channel partners reported that buying Symantec products through distribution via companies like Ingram Micro became unusually difficult. One Symantec channel partner commented that "the multiplication of cryptically described part numbers has rendered it impossible to purchase Symantec licenses from Ingram Micro without assistance from the licensing help desk. This makes the process much more time-consuming." For its part, Ingram Micro said it was working with Symantec to fix these issues, but many partners were unhappy with Symantec's slow response.

As a result of these many missteps, Symantec was in danger of losing many loyal customers. Most of the issues were due to the company's shortsightedness in implementing Project Oasis. Although the ERP rollout cost 7.75 percent less than budgeted, Symantec reported lower-than-expected earnings in the third quarter of 2007 and blamed these results on its ERP woes. Management said the company would need to cut $244 million in annual costs through layoffs or restructuring activities. Symantec CEO John Thompson said of the botched upgrade, "Systems changes such as these certainly don't come without issues. And we may have had more than our fair share of them with this set of changes, where we incurred higher expenses than planned and lost some revenue opportunities during the quarter."

Almost immediately, the company set about undoing mistakes with a follow-up project, named Project Nero. The goal of Project Nero was to recapture the loyalty of customers who were disenchanted by the changes brought about by Oasis, both by reaching out to those customers and by fixing the problems with their information systems to improve response times and streamline operations. Symantec had overlooked the needs of many customers while designing a technically sound but user-unfriendly ERP system. Project Nero's purpose was to assure those customers that Symantec still had their best interests in mind.

The company began by adding more than 150 new customer representatives to handle the increased volume of calls, reducing wait times and increasing customer satisfaction. Symantec's executives travelled the country in order to improve relations with angered customers and partners. To correct the issue of product updates being released at the same time as the ERP overhaul, the company introduced a master list of product releases readily available and standardized its communication methods between departments regarding new projects and change management.

Symantec also used Net Promoter methodology to measure and increase customer loyalty. Developed shortly before the acquisition of Veritas, Net Promoter was an initiative in which the company periodically surveyed customers to gauge their satisfaction with Symantec. The results from Net Promoter identified specific criticisms and problems of customers and dramatically aided Symantec in correcting those problems. One such example is the master list of product releases, which was a direct result of customer suggestions received via Net Promoter.

Symantec's customer satisfaction levels were at all-time lows after the launch of Project Oasis, but Project Nero has helped the company to weather the worst of the crisis. Symantec reports that it now enjoys satisfaction levels on par with the rest of its industry and averted a potential disaster. However, the company does not release the results of its Net Promoter surveys to the public, so the extent to which it has

repaired its reputation is unclear. Smaller value-added resellers and distributors report that they are receiving more attention from their regional representatives at Symantec than ever before, with some reporting that CEO Thompson routinely calls to check up on the quality of customer service. Although Symantec has done well to recover from the fallout after its initial ERP implementation, Project Oasis serves as a cautionary tale for businesses undertaking ERP overhauls. Even the most careful planning and well-designed systems can quickly go awry if customers are unable to make use of the new system.

CASE STUDY QUESTIONS:

1. What concepts in this chapter are illustrated in this case?

2. What management, organization, and technology factors were responsible for Symantec's difficulties in overhauling its ERP systems?

3. Was Symantec's response to the problem adequate? Explain your reasoning.

4. What would you have done differently to prevent the implementation problems that arose at Symantec?

5. If you were a partner or customer of Symantec, would you have switched vendors in response to the ERP overhaul issues? Why or why not?

Sources: Lawrence Walsh, "Symantec's Midnight at the Oasis," *Baseline Magazine*, March 31, 2008; Kevin McLaughlin, "Partners Still Hung Over from Symantec ERP Upgrade," ChannelWeb, March 2, 2007; Marc L. Songini, "ERP Rollout Whacks Symantec's Bottom Line," *Computerworld*, January 31, 2007, "ERP Rollout Continues to Weigh Down Symantec," *Computerworld*, February 5, 2007, and "ERP Rollout Weighs Symantec Down," *Computerworld*, February 12, 2007.

CHAPTER 13

E-Commerce: Digital Markets and Digital Goods

LEARNING OBJECTIVES

After reading this chapter, you will be able to answer the following questions:

1. What are the unique features of e-commerce, digital markets, and digital goods?

2. How has Internet technology changed business models?

3. What are the various types of e-commerce, and how has e-commerce changed consumer retailing and business-to-business transactions?

4. What is the role of m-commerce in business, and what are the most important m-commerce applications?

5. What are the principal payment systems for electronic commerce?

OPENING CASE

Nexon Games: E-Commerce Goes Social

If you like to play online games, you may already be familiar with MapleStory. It is an online role-playing game in which players assume the identities of warriors, magicians, and thieves to collectively fight monsters. You can play the game for free, but if you want your avatar to have a new outfit, wacky hairstyle, or funny pet, you will need to pay for these extras. And if you want your MapleStory characters to marry each other in an elaborate Las Vegas ceremony attended by other in-game buddies, it will cost $20 to $30.

MapleStory is a recent creation of Nexon Holdings Inc., the world leader in massively multiplayer online role-playing games. Nexon is headquartered in South Korea, with branch offices in China, Japan, and the United States. For several years, Nexon had a Canadian subsidiary, Humanature Studios, operating as NPNA (Nexon Publishing North America), located in Vancouver. Nexon closed its Vancouver office in January 2009.

Nexon pioneered in the "item" (microtransactions) business model,

where users can access the full game for free but later opt to pay for game enhancements (items). Nexon charges players anywhere from 30 cents to $30 each for virtual "items" to enhance their game experiences. MapleStory has 85 million users globally, with 6 million registered in North America. In 2007, players worldwide purchased more than 1.3 million articles of clothing and more than 1 million hair makeovers for their MapleStory characters.

One source of Nexon's popularity is the ability to socialize with other users. According to Min Kim, vice president of marketing at Nexon's U.S. division, "we sell social experiences, not packaged product." During much of the last decade, most games were played alone. As the Internet and PCs developed more capabilities for rich media experiences, solitary gaming gave way to social gaming. Whether it is integrated instant messaging, Voice over IP, or text messaging, there are now multiple mechanisms for players to communicate with their friends. Video games now

attract a whole new type of consumer—people who want to have a social experience.

Other popular Nexon games include Sugar Rush, Mabinogi, and Kart Rider. Kart Rider is an anime-style (meaning in the style of Japanese animation) online racing game that allows players to customize their vehicles and chat with friends. Sugar Rush players are able to fight each other while collecting virtual coins. Inspired by Celtic mythology, Mabinogi allows players to participate in mundane tasks such as farming, writing music, and marrying as well as fighting. The game continuously evolves through the release of patches (termed "Generations" and "Chapters") that introduce new areas to explore and advance the story line. All Nexon games feature forums where players are invited to socialize with friends, share hints, or just "hang out."

Nexon looks like it has a winning formula for success online. In the United States alone, 2007 revenue tripled to $35.8 million from $10.4 million the

401

previous year. Prepaid cards used to purchase Nexon game items are now the second-best-selling entertainment gift card (after Apple's iTunes Store) at Target Stores. In Canada, cards are available at Future Shop, Sobeys, Shoppers Drug Mart, 7-11, and other stores that carry gift cards from other merchants. In fact, there are quite a few blog and chat entries that ask other community members to report on where to find Nexon cards.

Sources: Nick Wingfield, "Korea's Nexon Bets on Sales of Virtual Gear for Free Online Games," *The Wall Street Journal*, May 23, 2008; Kara Swisher, "Playing with Others," *The Wall Street Journal*, June 9, 2008; "Nexon Vancouver Shutters Office," available **www.techvibes.com/ blog/nexon-vancouver-shutters-office** (accessed October 4, 2009); and **www.nexon .com** (accessed June 4, 2009).

Nexon's online games exemplify the new face of e-commerce. Selling physical goods on the Internet is still important, but much of the excitement and interest now centres around services and social experiences—social networking, photo sharing, sharing music, sharing ideas, and multiplayer online games where users communicate and interact with other users. The ability to link with other users and with other Web sites has spawned a huge wave of new businesses built around linking and sharing.

The chapter-opening diagram calls attention to important points raised by this case and this chapter. Nexon's business is a response to these questions: How do we make money on the Web today? How can we take advantage of more widespread broadband access to the Internet and to new Web 2.0 technologies? Nexon pioneered the micro- transactions business model and became a leading provider of massively multi- player online games. The company pro- vides games replete with action and interactivity where players can socialize with friends or other players. By playing up social features of online games and providing the ability to make online micro- payments for small purchases, Nexon's games have huge numbers of users and a continuing stream of revenue.

13.1 Electronic Commerce and the Internet

Have you ever purchased music over the Web? Have you ever used the Web to search for information about your sneakers before you bought them in a retail store? If so, you have participated in e-commerce. So have hundreds of millions of people around the globe. And although most purchases still take place through traditional channels, e-commerce continues to grow rapidly and to transform the way many companies do business.

E-Commerce Today

E-commerce refers to the use of the Internet and the Web to transact business. More formally, e-commerce is about digitally enabled commercial transactions between and among organizations and individuals. For the most part, this means transactions that occur over the Internet and the Web. Commercial transactions involve the exchange of value (e.g., money) across organizational or individual boundaries in return for products and services.

E-commerce began in 1995 when one of the first Internet portals, Netscape.com, accepted the first ads from major corporations and popularized the idea that the Web could be used as a new medium for advertising and sales. No one envisioned at the time what would turn out to be an exponential growth curve for e-commerce retail sales, which tripled and doubled in the early years. Only since 2006 has consumer e-commerce "slowed" to a still solid 16 percent annual growth rate in 2008 (see Figure 13-1).

Mirroring the history of many technological innovations, such as the telephone, radio, and television, the very rapid growth in e-commerce in the early years created a market bubble in e-commerce stocks. Like all bubbles, the dot-com bubble burst in March 2001. A large number of e-commerce companies failed during this process. Yet for many others, such as Amazon, e-Bay, Expedia, and Google, the results have been more positive: soaring revenues, fine-tuned business models that produce profits, and rising stock prices. By 2004, e-commerce revenues returned to solid growth again and have continued to be the fastest-growing form of retail trade in North America, Europe, and Asia.

- Online consumer sales increased by more than 61 percent between 2005 and 2007 to an estimated $12.8 billion (including travel services), with 8.4 million Canadians purchasing online (Statistics Canada, 2008).

- The number of individuals online in Canada expanded to 28 million in 2008, up from 12.7 million in 2000. In the world, more than 1.4 billion people are now connected to

FIGURE 13-1   The growth of e-commerce.

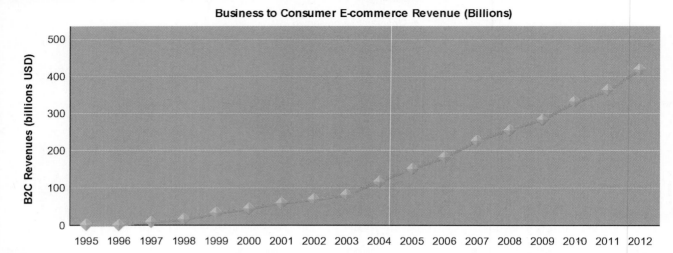

Business to Consumer E-commerce Revenue (Billions)

Retail e-commerce revenues have grown exponentially since 1995 and have only recently "slowed" to a very rapid 16 percent annual increase in 2008, which is projected to remain at this growth rate through 2010.

the Internet (Internet World Stats). Growth in the overall Internet population has spurred growth in e-commerce.

• B2B e-commerce—use of the Internet for business-to-business commerce and collaboration among business partners is driving the e-commerce marketplace, with as much as 75 percent of online sales volume.

The e-commerce revolution is still unfolding. Individuals and businesses will increasingly use the Internet to conduct commerce as more products and services come online and households switch to broadband telecommunications. More industries will be transformed by e-commerce, including travel reservations, music and entertainment, news, software, education, and finance. Table 13-1 highlights these new e-commerce developments.

Why E-Commerce Is Different

Why has e-commerce grown so rapidly? The answer lies in the unique nature of the Internet and the Web. Simply put, the Internet and e-commerce technologies are much more rich and powerful than previous technology revolutions like radio, television, and the telephone. Table 13-2 describes the unique features of the Internet and Web as a commercial medium. Let us explore each of these unique features in more detail.

Ubiquity In traditional commerce, a marketplace is a physical place, such as a retail store, that you visit to transact business. E-commerce is ubiquitous, meaning that is it available just about everywhere, at all times. It makes it possible to shop from your desktop, at home, at work, or even from your car, using mobile commerce. The result is called a **marketspace**—a marketplace extended beyond traditional boundaries and removed from a temporal and geographic location.

From a consumer point of view, ubiquity reduces **transaction costs**—the costs of participating in a market. To transact business, it is no longer necessary that you spend time or money travelling to a market, and much less mental effort is required to make a purchase.

Global Reach E-commerce technology permits commercial transactions to cross cultural and national boundaries far more conveniently and cost-effectively than is true in traditional commerce. As a result, the potential market size for e-commerce merchants is roughly equal to the size of the world's online population (more than 1 billion, and growing rapidly).

In contrast, most traditional commerce is local or regional—it involves local merchants or national merchants with local outlets. Television and radio stations and newspapers, for instance, are primarily local and regional institutions with limited, but

Marketspace

Transaction costs

TABLE 13-1   The growth of e-commerce.

BUSINESS TRANSFORMATION

- E-commerce remains the fastest-growing form of commerce when compared to physical retail stores, services, and entertainment.

- The first wave of e-commerce transformed the business world of books, music, and air travel. In the second wave, nine new industries are facing a similar transformation scenario: advertising, telephones, movies, television, jewellery, real estate, hotels, bill payments, and software.

- The breadth of e-commerce offerings grows, especially in the services economy of social networking, travel, information clearinghouses, entertainment, retail apparel, appliances, and home furnishings.

- The online demographics of shoppers broaden to match that of ordinary shoppers.

- Pure e-commerce business models are refined further to achieve higher levels of profitability while traditional retail brands, such as Sears, Canadian Tire, Chapters, and Walmart, use e-commerce to retain their dominant retail positions.

- Small businesses and entrepreneurs continue to flood the e-commerce marketplace, often riding on the infrastructures created by industry giants, such as Amazon and eBay.

TECHNOLOGY FOUNDATIONS

- Wireless Internet connections (Wi-Fi, Wi-Max, and 3G smart mobile phones) grow rapidly.

- Powerful handheld mobile devices support music, Web surfing, and entertainment as well as voice communication. Podcasting takes off as a medium for distribution of video, radio, and user-generated content.

- The Internet broadband foundation becomes stronger in households and businesses as transmission prices fall. More than 81 percent of Canadian households had broadband access to the Internet in 2007 (Statistics Canada, 2008).

- RSS grows to become a major new form of user-controlled information distribution that rivals e-mail in some applications.

- New Internet-based models of computing, such as .NET and Web services, expand B2B opportunities.

NEW BUSINESS MODELS EMERGE

- More than half the Internet user population join an online social network, contribute to social bookmarking sites, create blogs, and share photos. Together these sites create a massive online audience as large as television that is attractive to marketers.

- The traditional advertising business model is severely disrupted as Google and other technology players such as Microsoft and Yahoo! seek to dominate online advertising and expand into offline ad brokerage for television and newspapers.

- Newspapers and other traditional media adopt online, interactive models but are losing advertising revenues to the online players despite gaining online readers.

---

powerful, national networks that can attract a national audience but not easily cross national boundaries to a global audience.

Universal Standards   One strikingly unusual feature of e-commerce technologies is that the technical standards of the Internet and, therefore, the technical standards for conducting e-commerce are universal standards. They are shared by all nations around the world and enable any computer to link with any other computer regardless of the technology platform each is using. In contrast, most traditional commerce technologies differ from one nation to the next. For instance, television and radio standards differ around the world, as does cell telephone technology.

Universal Technical Standards   The universal technical standards of the Internet and e-commerce greatly lower **market entry costs**—the cost merchants must pay simply to bring their goods to market. At the same time, for consumers, universal standards reduce **search costs**—the effort required to find suitable products.

Market entry costs
Search costs

TABLE 13-2 Eight unique features of e-commerce technology.

E-COMMERCE TECHNOLOGY DIMENSION	BUSINESS SIGNIFICANCE
Ubiquity. Internet/Web technology is available everywhere: at work, at home, and elsewhere via mobile devices, anytime.	The marketplace is extended beyond traditional boundaries and is removed from a temporal and geographic location. "Marketspace" is created; shopping can take place anywhere. Customer convenience is enhanced, and shopping costs are reduced.
Global reach. The technology reaches across national boundaries, around the earth.	Commerce is enabled across cultural and national boundaries seamlessly and without modification. The marketspace includes, potentially, billions of consumers and millions of businesses worldwide.
Universal standards. There is one set of technology standards, namely Internet standards.	With one set of technical standards across the globe, disparate computer systems can easily communicate with each other.
Richness. Video, audio, and text messages are possible.	Video, audio, and text marketing messages are integrated into a single marketing message and consumer experience.
Interactivity. The technology works through interaction with the user.	Consumers are engaged in a dialogue that dynamically adjusts the experience to the individual and makes the consumer a co-participant in the process of delivering goods to the market.
Information density. The technology reduces information costs and raises quality.	Information processing, storage, and communication costs drop dramatically while currency, accuracy, and timeliness greatly improve. Information becomes plentiful, cheap, and more accurate.
Personalization/customization. The technology allows personalized messages to be delivered to individuals as well as groups.	Personalization of marketing messages and customization of products and services are based on individual characteristics.
Social technology. User content generation and social networking.	New Internet social and business models enable user content creation and distribution, and support social networks.

Richness Information **richness** refers to the complexity and content of a message. Traditional markets, national sales forces, and small retail stores have great richness: They are able to provide personal, face-to-face service using aural and visual cues when making a sale. The richness of traditional markets makes them powerful selling or commercial environments. Prior to the development of the Web, there was a trade-off between richness and reach: The larger the audience reached, the less rich the message. The Web makes it possible to deliver rich messages with text, audio, and video simultaneously to large numbers of people.

Interactivity Unlike any of the commercial technologies of the 20th century, with the possible exception of the telephone, e-commerce technologies are interactive, meaning they allow for two-way communication between merchant and consumer. Television, for instance, cannot ask viewers any questions or enter into conversations with them, and it cannot request that customer information be entered into a form. In contrast, all of these activities are possible on an e-commerce Web site. Interactivity allows an online merchant to engage a consumer in ways similar to a face-to-face experience but on a massive, global scale.

Information Density The Internet and the Web vastly increase **information density**— the total amount and quality of information available to all market participants, consumers, and merchants alike. E-commerce technologies reduce information collection, storage, processing, and communication costs while greatly increasing the currency, accuracy, and timeliness of information.

Information density in e-commerce markets makes prices and costs more transparent. **Price transparency** refers to the ease with which consumers can find out the variety of prices in a market; **cost transparency** refers to the ability of consumers to discover the actual costs merchants pay for products.

There are advantages for merchants as well. Online merchants can discover much more about consumers than in the past. This allows merchants to segment the market into groups who are willing to pay different prices and permits merchants to engage in

Richness
Information density
Price transparency
Cost transparency

price discrimination—selling the same goods, or nearly the same goods, to different targeted groups at different prices. For instance, an online merchant can discover a consumer's avid interest in expensive, exotic vacations and then pitch high-end vacation plans to that consumer at a premium price, knowing this person is willing to pay extra for such a vacation. At the same time, the online merchant can pitch the same vacation plan at a lower price to a more price-sensitive consumer. Information density also helps merchants differentiate their products in terms of cost, brand, and quality.

Personalization/Customization E-commerce technologies permit **personalization.** Merchants can target their marketing messages to specific individuals by adjusting the message to a person's name, interests, and past purchases. The technology also permits **customization**—changing the delivered product or service based on a user's preferences or prior behaviour. Given the interactive nature of e-commerce technology, much information about the consumer can be gathered in the marketplace at the moment of purchase. With the increase in information density, a great deal of information about the consumer's past purchases and behaviour can be stored and used by online merchants.

The result is a level of personalization and customization unthinkable with traditional commerce technologies. For instance, you may be able to shape what you see on television by selecting a channel, but you cannot change the content of the channel you have chosen. In contrast, the *Globe and Mail Online* allows you to select the type of news stories you want to see first and gives you the opportunity to be alerted when certain events happen.

Social Technology: User Content Generation and Social Networking In contrast to previous technologies, the Internet and e-commerce technologies have evolved to be much more social by allowing users to create and share with their personal friends (and a larger worldwide community) content in the form of text, videos, music, or photos. Using these forms of communication, users are able to create new social networks and strengthen existing ones.

All previous mass media in modern history, including the printing press, use a broadcast model (one-to-many) where content is created in a central location by experts (professional writers, editors, directors, and producers), and audiences are concentrated in huge numbers to consume a standardized product. The new Internet and e-commerce empower users to create and distribute content on a large scale and permit users to program their own content consumption. The Internet provides a many-to-many model of mass communications, which is unique.

Key Concepts in E-Commerce: Digital Markets and Digital Goods in a Global Marketplace

The location, timing, and revenue models of business are based in some part on the cost and distribution of information. The Internet has created a digital marketplace where millions of people all over the world are able to exchange massive amounts of information directly, instantly, and for free. As a result, the Internet has changed the way companies conduct business and increased their global reach.

The Internet shrinks information asymmetry. An **information asymmetry** exists when one party in a transaction has more information that is important for the transaction than the other party. That information helps determine their relative bargaining power. In digital markets, consumers and suppliers can "see" the prices being charged for goods, and in that sense digital markets are said to be more "transparent" than traditional markets.

For example, until car retailing sites appeared on the Web, there was a pronounced information asymmetry between car dealers and customers. Only the car dealers knew the manufacturers' prices, and it was difficult for consumers to shop around for the best price. Car dealers' profit margins depended on this asymmetry of information. Today's consumers have access to a legion of Web sites providing competitive pricing information, and most car buyers use the Internet to shop around for the best deal. Thus, the Web has reduced the information asymmetry surrounding a car purchase. The Internet has

Price discrimination

Personalization

Customization

Information asymmetry

FIGURE 13-2   The benefits of disintermediation to the consumer.

The typical distribution channel has several intermediary layers, each of which adds to the final cost of a product, such as a sweater. Removing layers lowers the final cost to the consumer.

also helped businesses seeking to purchase from other businesses reduce information asymmetries and locate better prices and terms.

Digital markets are very flexible and efficient because they operate with reduced search and transaction costs, lower **menu costs** (merchants' costs of changing prices), price discrimination, and the ability to change prices dynamically based on market conditions. In **dynamic pricing,** the price of a product varies depending on the demand characteristics of the customer or the supply situation of the seller.

These markets may either reduce or increase switching costs, depending on the nature of the product or service being sold, and they may cause some extra delay in gratification. Unlike a physical market, you cannot immediately consume a product such as clothing purchased over the Web (although immediate consumption is possible with digital music downloads and other digital products).

Digital markets provide many opportunities to sell directly to the consumer, bypassing intermediaries, such as distributors or retail outlets. Eliminating intermediaries in the distribution channel can significantly lower purchase transaction costs. To pay for all the steps in a traditional distribution channel, a product may have to be priced as high as 135 percent of its original cost to manufacture.

Figure 13-2 illustrates the savings that result from eliminating each of these layers in the distribution process. By selling directly to consumers or reducing the number of intermediaries, companies are able to raise profits while charging lower prices. The removal of organizations or business process layers responsible for intermediary steps in a value chain is called **disintermediation.**

Disintermediation is affecting the market for services. Airlines and hotels operating their own reservation sites online earn more per ticket because they have eliminated travel agents as intermediaries. Table 13-3 summarizes the differences between digital markets and traditional markets.

Digital Goods The Internet digital marketplace has greatly expanded sales of digital goods. **Digital goods** are goods that can be delivered over a digital network. Music tracks, video, software, newspapers, magazines, and books can all be expressed, stored, delivered, and sold as purely digital products. Currently, most of these products are sold as physical goods, for example, CDs, DVDs, and hard-copy books. But the Internet offers the possibility of delivering all these products on demand as digital products.

In general, for digital goods, the marginal cost of producing another unit is about zero (it costs nothing to make a copy of a music file). However, the cost of producing the original first unit is relatively high—in fact it is nearly the total cost of the product because there are few other costs of inventory and distribution. Costs of delivery over the Internet are very low, marketing costs remain the same, and pricing can be highly variable. (On the Internet, the merchant can change prices as often as desired because of low menu costs.)

Menu costs
Dynamic pricing
Disintermediation
Digital goods

TABLE 13-3 Digital markets compared to traditional markets.

	DIGITAL MARKETS	**TRADITIONAL MARKETS**
Information asymmetry	Asymmetry reduced	Asymmetry high
Search costs	Low	High
Transaction costs	Low (sometimes virtually nothing)	High (time, travel)
Delayed gratification	High (or lower in the case of a digital good)	Lower (purchase now)
Menu costs	Low	High
Dynamic pricing	Low cost, instant	High cost, delayed
Price discrimination	Low cost, instant	High cost, delayed
Market segmentation	Low cost, moderate precision	High cost, less precision
Switching costs	Higher/lower (depending on product characteristics)	High
Network effects	Strong	Weaker
Disintermediation	More possible/likely	Less possible/unlikely

The impact of the Internet on the market for these kinds of digital goods is nothing short of revolutionary, and we see the results around us every day. Businesses dependent on the physical products for sales—such as bookstores, book publishers, music labels, and film studios—face the possibility of declining sales and even destruction of their businesses. Newspapers and magazines are losing readers to the Internet and losing advertisers. Record label companies are losing sales to Internet piracy, and record stores are going out of business. Video rental firms, such as Blockbuster, based on a physical DVD market and physical stores have lost sales to NetFlix using an Internet model. Hollywood studios also face the prospect that Internet pirates will distribute their product as a digital stream, bypassing Hollywood's monopoly on DVD rentals and sales, which now accounts for more than half of industry film revenues (see the Chapter 3 ending case). Table 13-4 describes digital goods and how they differ from traditional physical goods.

Internet Business Models

The bottom line result of these changes in the economics of information is nearly a revolution in commerce, with many new business models appearing and many old business models no longer tenable. Table 13-5 describes some of the most important Internet business models that have emerged. All, in one way or another, use the Internet to add extra value to existing products and services or to provide the foundation for new products and services.

TABLE 13-4 How the Internet changes the markets for digital goods.

	DIGITAL GOODS	**TRADITIONAL GOODS**
Marginal cost/unit	Zero	Greater than zero, high
Cost of production	High (most of the cost)	Variable
Copying cost	Approximately 0	Greater than zero, high
Distributed delivery cost	Low	High
Inventory cost	Low	High
Marketing cost	Variable	Variable
Pricing	More variable (bundling, random pricing games)	Fixed, based on unit costs

TABLE 13-5 Internet business models.

CATEGORY	DESCRIPTION	EXAMPLES
Virtual storefront	Sells physical products directly to consumers or to individual businesses.	Amazon.com RedEnvelope.com
Information broker	Provides product, pricing, and availability information to individuals and businesses. Generates revenue from advertising or from directing buyers to sellers.	Edmunds.com Kbb.com Insweb.com, Realtor.com
Transaction broker	Saves users money and time by processing online sales transactions and generating a fee each time a transaction occurs. Also provides information on rates and terms.	Baystreet.ca Expedia.ca TDAmeritrade.com
Online marketplace	Provides a digital environment where buyers and sellers can meet, search for products, display products, and establish prices for those products. Can provide online auctions or reverse auctions in which buyers submit bids to multiple sellers to purchase at a buyer-specified price as well as negotiated or fixed pricing. Can serve consumers or B2B e-commerce, generating revenue from transaction fees.	eBay.com Priceline.com ChemConnect.com
Content provider	Creates revenue by providing digital content, such as digital news, music, photos, or video, over the Web. The customer may pay to access the content, or revenue may be generated by selling advertising space.	GlobeandMail.com iTunes.ca Canada.com
Social network	Provides an online meeting place where people with similar interests can communicate and find useful information. Creates revenue through advertising.	LinkedIn.com Facebook.com iVillage.com
Portal	Provides initial point of entry to the Web along with specialized content and other services. Revenue derives from advertising.	Yahoo.ca MSN.ca, Canoe.ca
Service provider	Provides Web 2.0 applications such as photo sharing, video sharing, and user-generated content (in blogs and social networking sites) as services. Provide other services such as online data storage and backup. Uses either a subscription or advertising revenue model.	Google Maps Flickr.com YouTube.com Xdrive.com

Communication and Social Networking

Some of these new business models take advantage of the Internet's rich communication capabilities. EBay is an online auction forum that uses e-mail and other interactive features of the Web, which we described in the Chapter 3 opening case. The system accepts bids entered on the Internet, evaluates the bids, and notifies the highest bidder. EBay collects a small commission on each listing and sale. EBay has become so popular that its site serves as a huge trading platform for other companies, hosting hundreds of thousands of "virtual storefronts."

Business-to-business auctions have also emerged. GoIndustry, for instance, features Web-based auction services for business-to-business sales of industrial equipment and machinery.

The Internet has created online communities where people with similar interests are able to communicate with each other from many different locations. A major source of revenue for these communities involves providing ways for corporate clients to target customers, including the placement of banner ads and pop-up ads on their Web sites. A **banner ad** is a graphic display on a Web page used for advertising. The banner is linked to the advertiser's Web site so that a person clicking the banner is transported to a Web page with more information about the advertiser. **Pop-up ads** work in the opposite manner. They automatically open up when a user accesses a specific Web site, and the user must click the ad to make it disappear.

Banner ad
Pop-up ads

Social networking sites are a type of online community that has become extremely popular. Social networking is the practice of expanding the number of one's business or social contacts by making connections through individuals. Social networking sites link people through their mutual business or personal connections, enabling them to mine their friends (and their friends' friends) for sales leads, job-hunting tips, or new friends. MySpace, Facebook, and Friendster appeal to people who are primarily interested in extending their friendships while LinkedIn.com focuses on job and professional networking.

Members of social networking sites spend hours surfing pages, checking out other members, and exchanging messages, revealing a great deal of information about themselves. Businesses harvest this information to create carefully targeted promotions that far surpass the typical text and display ads found on the Web. They also use the sites to interact with potential customers. For example, Procter & Gamble set up a Facebook profile page for Crest toothpaste.

The most popular of these sites attract so many visitors and are so "sticky" that they have become very powerful marketing tools. The chapter-ending case study discusses Facebook as a business model.

Social networking is so appealing that it has inspired a new type of e-commerce experience called **social shopping.** Social shopping sites such as Kaboodle, ThisNext, and Stylehive.com provide online meeting places for people to swap shopping ideas. These sites provide tools for users to create their own Web pages with information and images about items they like to help other shoppers.

Digital Content, Entertainment, and Services In 2008, perhaps no industry experienced more Internet-driven change than the entertainment industry, roughly defined as television, movies, music, radio, and text content. The ability to deliver digital goods and digital content over the Web has created new alternatives to traditional print and broadcast media. There are Web sites for digital versions of print publications, such as the *Globe and Mail* or the *National Post*, and for new online journals such as Salon.com.

Some of the most popular Web sites deliver entertainment in digital form. Online games attract huge numbers of players. Nexon's games, described in the chapter-opening case, have millions of users.

You can listen to some of your favourite radio channels, such as Classic Rock or the BBC, on the Web as well as many independent channels. Because the radio signal is relayed over the Internet, it is possible to access stations from anywhere in the world, even on a mobile device. Services such as Yahoo!'s Launchcast even put together individualized radio channels for listeners.

Broadband connections now make it possible for Web sites to display full-length films and television shows. Apple, Amazon, Movielink, and CinemaNow have downloading services for full-length movies. MLB.com, the Web site for Major League Baseball, delivers live streaming video of MLB baseball games to paid subscribers. Some online television and video services, such as iVillage Live, provide instant messaging capabilities allowing viewers to discuss the show as it is being broadcast.

Many of you use the Web to preview and download music. Although some of this Internet music is free of charge, Apple's iTunes and other sites are generating revenue by charging for each song or album downloaded from their Web sites. The phenomenal popularity of Apple's iTunes music service and Apple's iPod portable music player have inspired a new form of digital content delivery called *podcasting*. **Podcasting** is a method of publishing audio broadcasts via the Internet, allowing subscribing users to download audio files onto their personal computers or portable music players. Video clips designed to be downloaded and viewed on a portable device are called *vcasts*.

Podcasting enables independent producers to self-publish their own audio content and gives broadcast media a new distribution method. Podcasts also have internal uses for businesses that want to distribute information in audio form to their employees. Internet security firm SonicWALL uses podcasts to demonstrate its expertise to customers and to provide new product information to its resellers.

Social networking

Social shopping

Podcasting

The Web's information resources are so vast and rich that portals have emerged as an Internet business model to help individuals and organizations locate information more efficiently. In Chapter 2, we defined a portal as a Web interface for presenting integrated, personalized information from a variety of sources. As an e-commerce business model, a portal is a "super site" that provides a comprehensive entry point for a huge array of resources and services on the Internet.

Yahoo! is an example. It provides capabilities for locating information on the Internet along with news, sports, weather, telephone directories, maps, games, shopping, e-mail, chat, discussion boards, and links to other sites. Also, specialized portals help users with specific interests. For example, StarMedia is a portal customized for Hispanic Internet users.

Yahoo! and other portals and Web content sites often combine content and applications from many different sources and service providers. Other Internet business models use syndication providing additional value. For example, E*TRADE, the discount Web trading site, purchases most of its content from outsider sources such as Reuters (news) and BigCharts.com (charts). Online **syndicators,** which aggregate content or applications from multiple sources, package them for distribution, and resell them to third-party Web sites, have emerged as another variant of the online content provider business model. The Web makes it much easier for companies to aggregate, repackage, and distribute information and information-based services.

Flickr is an online photo-sharing service that works with other Web 2.0 applications and services. Other online service providers offer services such as remote storage of data (Xdrive.com). Online service providers generate revenue from subscription fees or from advertising.

Most of the business models described in Table 13-5 are called **pure-play** business models because they are based purely on the Internet. These firms did not have an existing bricks-and-mortar business when they designed their Internet business. However, many existing retail firms, such as Canadian Tire, Office Depot, The Bay, and the *National Post* have developed Web sites as extensions of their traditional bricks-and-mortar businesses. These businesses represent a hybrid **clicks-and-mortar** business model.

The Window on Technology describes another clicks-and-mortar business. J&R Electronics sells music, office equipment, cameras, computers, movies, and games through multiple channels: a massive retail store in New York City, a print catalogue, and a Web site. As you read this case, try to determine the role of the Web in this company's business model and business strategy.

13.2 Electronic Commerce

Although most commercial transactions still take place through traditional retail channels, rising numbers of consumers and businesses are using the Internet for electronic commerce. Today, e-commerce revenue represents about 5 percent of all retail sales in North America, and there is tremendous upside potential for growth.

Types of Electronic Commerce

There are many ways to classify electronic commerce transactions. One is by looking at the nature of the participants in the electronic commerce transaction. The three major electronic commerce categories are business-to-consumer (B2C) e-commerce, business-to-business (B2B) e-commerce, and consumer-to-consumer (C2C) e-commerce.

- **Business-to-consumer (B2C) electronic commerce** involves retailing products and services to individual shoppers. Chapters.Indigo.ca, which sells books, DVDs, and music to individual consumers, is an example of B2C e-commerce.

- **Business-to-business (B2B) electronic commerce** involves sales of goods and services among businesses. ChemConnect's Web site for buying and selling natural gas liquids, refined and intermediate fuels, chemicals, and plastics is an example of B2B e-commerce.

Syndicators

Pure-play

Clicks-and-mortar

Business-to-consumer (B2C) electronic commerce

Business-to-business (B2B) electronic commerce

- **Consumer-to-consumer (C2C) electronic commerce** involves consumers selling directly to consumers. For example, eBay, the giant Web auction site, enables individuals to sell their goods to other consumers by auctioning the merchandise to the highest bidder.

Another way of classifying electronic commerce transactions is in terms of the participants' physical connection to the Web. Until recently, almost all e-commerce transactions took place over wired networks. Now mobile phones and other wireless handheld digital appliances are Internet-enabled to send text messages and e-mail, access Web sites, and make purchases. Companies are offering new types of Web-based products and services that can be accessed by these wireless devices. The use of handheld wireless devices for purchasing goods and services from any location has been termed **mobile commerce** or **m-commerce**. Both business-to-business and business-to-consumer e-commerce transactions can take place using m-commerce technology, which we discuss in detail in Section 13.3.

Consumer-to-consumer (C2C)
electronic commerce

Mobile commerce

M-commerce

WINDOW ON TECHNOLOGY

Technology

Can J&R Electronics Grow with E-Commerce?

J&R Electronics is a mom-and-pop shop for the modern age. Joe and Rachelle Friedman started the business as an audio equipment store in 1971. Today, J&R Electronics encompasses a lucrative catalogue business and 10 specialty electronics stores covering 28 000 square feet of retail space on Park Row in New York City. Among the stores are the famed J&R Music World and J&R Computer World.

The J&R empire sells nearly every type of electronic device imaginable. However, the Friedmans have resisted the advice of suppliers, such as record companies, which have told them the only way to compete with big box stores was to become a chain. Rachelle Friedman explained that "by staying on the block... we maintain control, which the chain stores lose."

How does J&R continue to survive with only one location in an industry dominated by Walmart, Best Buy, and Circuit City? One reason is that the company found ways to make its Web site as popular a destination online as its bricks-and-mortar store.

J&R went online in 1998 using InterWorld's Commerce Exchange e-commerce software. InterWorld did not survive the dot-com bust in 2000, and J&R then had to support its online presence on its own. The company's information systems staff managed to piece together a customized e-commerce application that could handle the 400 000 products that J&R sold. However, the solution did not support some of the features that online retail competitors offered, such as the ability to collect and display customer reviews and provide information on inventory statistics and shipping time.

By that time, 30 percent of J&R's $488 million in revenue came from JR.com, and the company needed to inject new life into its Web site. For the new site, J&R chose an e-commerce platform from Blue Martini and a CRM package made by

Loyalty Lab. In addition, management wanted to populate the site with videos and customer reviews. Those features were valuable tools that customers could use to educate themselves about products and comparison-shop before they committed to buying.

In May 2006, J&R unveiled an online loyalty program to encourage shoppers to visit JR.com directly rather than connect from a link on another site, such as a price comparison search engine. The strategy intends to raise the number of unique visitors to the site and, as Jason Friedman, J&R's vice president of e-commerce, put it, relieve J&R from "fighting over pennies with our competitors." For participating in the program, customers receive gift cards equalling 2 percent of their purchases. If successful, the loyalty program will keep past customers from giving their business to other stores, as well as entice new customers to join the J&R community. Catalogue shoppers are also eligible for loyalty rewards.

Mark H. Goldstein, CEO of Loyalty Lab, noted that J&R already had a loyal customer base as a result of its top-notch customer service and focus on building relationships. All that the company lacked was a program that recognized customer loyalty. Loyalty Lab's CRM package helped fill that void by hosting the modules that enabled J&R customers to register for accounts, manage their accounts, and redeem the incentives they have earned. The Loyalty Lab program also reduces the "Google tax." This is the 20 to 30 percent charge that J&R pays to search sites when visitors are directed to J&R from another site, a fee that J&R avoids when shoppers visit JR.com directly.

J&R selected Blue Martini as its new e-commerce platform because Blue Martini functions well with J&R's ERP software from a technical perspective. The two systems are able to exchange data easily. Blue Martini provides a better opportunity to share the strengths of J&R's bricks-and-mortar channels online.

J&R has plenty of advantages, or differentiators, to showcase. Its prices are very competitive, yet it maintains a vast inventory that rarely leaves customers disappointed. J&R also has a reputation for being at the leading edge of new technology.

The company has a penchant for being the first retailer to sell new products or the latest versions of already popular products. J&R often caters to those trends before other stores are prepared to do so. Aside from good prices, perhaps the element of J&R that appeals to customers most is its sales staff. Customers who enter J&R stores know that the workers they encounter will be well informed and adept at explaining the features and specifications of even the newest and most high-tech products.

With Blue Martini, J&R will try to emulate the expertise of its sales staff online. The platform provides a Guided Selling application, which collects input from the shopper and produces a narrowed-down view of the product catalogue that is tailored for the requirements and preferences of a particular customer. Customers are able to view products by brand, price, popularity, size, and availability of special offers. By providing interactive recommendations, J&R can put more information about products in the hands of the customers, which makes them more comfortable in their purchases.

Comprehensive product descriptions, product reviews from customers and other sources, and comparison grids will also make it easier for shoppers to understand and select products. Going a step further, Blue Martini enables J&R to deepen its Web content with videos, including hundreds of clips that feature staff members giving tutorials on specific products. The videos bring a personalization to the online shopping experience that normally would be available only in a bricks-and-mortar store. J&R even films the videos in its stores.

The new JR.com launched in March 2007 with a host of new customer conveniences. If a customer selects a product that is out of stock, the site is prepared with a list of similar products. The site also has real-time integration with store inventory, so onsite purchases are reflected in the availability of products online. J&R has also made the checkout process more efficient so shoppers arrive at final price more quickly. The shipping section has been restructured to improve the accuracy of delivery dates and shipping fees.

Jason Friedman recognizes that despite the increased functionality provided by Blue Martini, his company is still limited by having physical stores located solely in New York City. He notes that where chain stores can offer customers the option of ordering merchandise online and picking it up that day in person at the nearest store, J&R can make that option available only to customers in the New York City area. However, he feels that emphasizing e-commerce carries great potential for the business and represents the company's future.

In August 2008, J&R contracted with the Toy advertising agency to coordinate its TV, print, radio, events, digital, and in-store promotions. Although J&R spends millions of dollars each year on advertising through various channels, this is the first time it has worked with an advertising agency. Toy will further shape J&R's brand image of quality, customer service, and leading-edge technology offerings among new audiences in a rapidly changing retail environment.

To Think About

1. Analyze J&R Electronics using the competitive forces and value chain models. What is its business model and business strategy? How does it provide value?

2. What is the role of the Internet in J&R's business strategy? Is it providing a solution to J&R's problems? Why or why not?

3. Can J&R keep up with the competition since it is more or less a local brand competing with nationwide chains? How would you measure its success in keeping up with the competition?

MIS in Action

Visit J&R's online store at JR.com, then answer the following questions:

1. What features described in this case are you able to find on the site?

2. How effective is the implementation of these features? Do they seem to be achieving the goals that J&R set for them?

3. Compare JR.com to the Web sites of Visions or Best Buy. Evaluate them in terms of product selection and availability, tools for providing product information and customer service, and ease of use. Which site would you use to purchase a computer or MP3 player? Why?

Sources: "J&R Music Turns to Toy," *Adweek*, August 19, 2008; **www.jr.com** (accessed August 28, 2008); Laton McCartney, "Mid-Market Case: J&R Electronics Pumps Up the Volume," *Baseline Magazine*, March 13, 2007; "J&R Electronics Taps Loyalty Lab's On-Demand Suite for First Shopper Loyalty Program," *Rtmilestones.com* (accessed May 1, 2007); and "J&R Electronics Migrating to Blue Martini E-Commerce Platform," *InternetRetailer.com*, November 8, 2006.

Achieving Customer Intimacy: Interactive Marketing, Personalization, and Self-Service

The unique dimensions of e-commerce technologies that we have just described offer many new possibilities for marketing and selling. The Internet provides companies with additional channels of communication and interaction for closer yet more cost-effective relationships with customers in sales, marketing, and customer support.

Interactive Marketing and Personalization The Internet and e-commerce have helped some merchants achieve the holy grail of marketing: making products for millions of consumers that are personal, an impossible task in traditional markets. Web sites, such as that for Lands' End (shirts and pants), Nike (athletic shoes), and VistaPrint (business cards, note cards, and labels), feature online tools that allow consumers to purchase products tailored to their individual specifications. Even M&Ms candy will let you personalize the colour and message on their candies. Sites such as these encourage customers to participate in designing products they want.

Web sites have become a bountiful source of detailed information about customer behaviour, preferences, needs, and buying patterns that companies can use to tailor promotions, products, services, and pricing. Some customer information may be obtained by asking visitors to "register" online and provide information about themselves, but many companies also collect customer information using software tools that track the activities of Web site visitors.

Clickstream tracking tools collect data on customer activities at Web sites and store them in a log. The tools record the site that users visited prior to coming to a particular Web site and where these users go when they leave that site. They also record the specific pages visited on the site, the time spent on each page, the types of pages visited, and what the visitors purchased (see Figure 13-3). Firms analyze this information about customer interests and behaviour to develop precise profiles of existing and potential customers.

This type of information enables firms to create unique personalized Web pages that display content or ads for products or services of special interest to each user, improving the customer's experience and creating additional value (see Figure 13-4). By using personalization technology to modify the Web pages presented to each customer, marketers achieve the benefits of using individual salespeople at dramatically lower costs.

One technique for Web personalization is **collaborative filtering,** which compares information gathered about a specific user's behaviour at a Web site to data about other customers with similar interests to predict what the user would like to see next. The software then makes recommendations to users based on their assumed interests. For example, Amazon.com and Chapters.Indigo.ca use collaborative filtering software to prepare

Clickstream tracking
Collaborative filtering

FIGURE 13-3   Web site visitor tracking.

Click 1

The shopper clicks on the home page. The store can tell that the shopper arrived from the Yahoo! portal at 2:30 PM (which might help determine staffing for customer service centers) and how long she lingered on the home page (which might indicate trouble navigating the site).

Click 2

Click 3

Click 4

The shopper clicks on blouses, clicks to select a woman's white blouse, then clicks to view the same item in pink. The shopper clicks to select this item in a size 10 in pink and clicks to place it in her shopping cart. This information can help the store determine which sizes and colors are most popular.

Click 5

Click 6

From the shopping cart page, the shopper clicks to close the browser to leave the Web site without purchasing the blouse. This action could indicate the shopper changed her mind or that she had a problem with the Web site's checkout and payment process. Such behavior might signal that the Web site was not well designed.

E-commerce Web sites have tools to track a shopper's every step through an online store. Close examination of customer behaviour at a Web site selling women's clothing shows what the store might learn at each step and what actions it could take to increase sales.

FIGURE 13-4   Web site personalization.

Firms can create unique personalized Web pages that display content or ads for products or services of special interest to individual users, improving the customer experience and creating additional value.

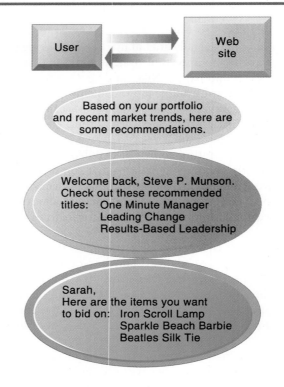

personalized book recommendations: "Customers who bought this book also bought. . ." These recommendations are made just at the point of purchase, an ideal time to prompt a consumer into purchasing a related product.

Blogs and Wikis Blogs, which we introduced in Chapter 7, have emerged as another promising Web-based tool for marketing. A blog, the popular term for a Web log, is a personal Web page that typically contains a series of chronological entries (newest to oldest) by its author and links to related Web pages.

The blog may include a blogroll (a collection of links to other blogs) and trackbacks (a list of entries in other blogs that refer to a post on the first blog). Most blogs allow readers to post comments on the blog entries as well. Blogs are either hosted by a third-party site such as Blogger.com, LiveJournal.com, Typepad.com, and Xanga.com, or prospective bloggers can download software such as Movable Type to create a blog that is housed by the user's ISP. Blogger and Twitter have added features to allow users to post short notes and photos to their blogs from cell phones.

Blog pages are usually variations on templates provided by the blogging service or software. Therefore, millions of people without HTML skills of any kind can post their own Web pages and share content with others. The totality of blog-related Web sites is often referred to as the **blogosphere.**

The content of blogs range from individual musings to corporate communications. Blogs have a significant impact on political affairs and have gained increasing notice for their role in breaking and shaping the news. Blogs have become hugely popular. There are at least 70 million blogs on the Web and nearly 100 000 new ones added daily.

Companies that maintain public blogs use them as a new channel for reaching customers. These corporate blogs provide a personal and conversational way for businesses to present information to the public and prospective customers about new products and services. Readers are often invited to post comments. For example, the Window on Organizations describes how Stonyfield Farm Inc., the world's third-largest organic food company, maintains blogs on childrearing (see Figure 13-5) and organic dairy farms to create a more personal relationship with consumers than the traditional selling relationship.

Blogosphere

WINDOW ON ORGANIZATIONS

Stonyfield Farm and Others Blog for Communication

The story of Stonyfield Farm is something of a legend. In 1983, friends and social activists Gary Hirschberg and Samuel Kaymen started out with a great yogurt recipe, seven cows, and a dream. They set up an organic yogurt company in Wilton, New Hampshire, to capitalize on baby boomers' growing concerns with pure foods and health, and to revitalize the New England dairy industry. Stonyfield Farms has grown to become the third-largest organic company in the world, with more than $91 million in annual sales in 50 states. It produces more than 18 million cups of yogurt each month.

Stonyfield Farm's phenomenal growth is in part attributable to its ability to provide a product for a special niche market—people who treasure healthy foods and want to protect the environment. These values have become embedded in the company's "personality." Stonyfield pledges to use in its products only natural ingredients and milk that have not been produced with antibiotics, synthetic growth hormones, or toxic pesticides and fertilizers. The company donates 10 percent of its profits each year to efforts that help protect or restore the Earth.

As the company expanded, management feared it would lose touch with its loyal and committed customer base. Traditional media-based advertising was expensive and would not really help the company "connect" with the kinds of people it was trying to reach. This company prefers word-of-mouth approaches that get its message to customers in ways that are more compatible with its grassroots, organic, activist people-friendly image. Stonyfield has several active e-mail newsletters with more than 500 000 subscribers, and it regularly places messages promoting causes it supports on the lids of its yogurt cups. Now it is turning to blogs to further personalize its relationship with customers and reach even more people.

Inspired by Howard Dean's presidential campaign and tutorials from Dean's bloggers, CEO Hirschberg became convinced that Stonyfield could use blogs to create a more personal relationship with consumers that is different from the traditional selling relationship. "The blogs give us what we call a handshake with consumers" and "a little more access to us as a people with a mission," he says.

Stonyfield now publishes two different blogs on its Web site—Baby Babble and the Bovine Bugle. At one time, Stonyfield was managing five blogs but decided to retire three of them because they were not attracting enough readers.

Baby Babble provides a forum for Stonyfield employees and other parents of young children to meet and talk about child development and balancing work with family. Stonyfield started that blog because baby yogurts are one of its most popular product lines, and blogs about parenting seem to draw large numbers of readers.

The Bovine Bugle provides reports from Jonathan Gates's organic dairy farm in Franklin, Vermont, a member of the

organic cooperative that supplies the milk for Stonyfield products. This blog elicits a large number of nostalgic comments from readers remembering their childhood on a farm. As organic foods go mainstream, these blogs help the company show how its brand differs from others and invite customers to help them in that effort.

Stonyfield continually posts new content to each of the blogs. Readers can subscribe to any of these blogs and automatically receive updates when they become available. And of course, they can respond to the postings.

At this point, the benefits of Stonyfield's blogs have not yet been quantified, but management has faith that there are real benefits. The blogs have created a positive response to the Stonyfield brand by providing readers with something that inspires them or piques their interest. If the blogs give readers new information, inspire them to take environmental actions, or ask for opinions, management believes they will remember the brand when they stand in front of the yogurt case at the supermarket or grocery store and that they will reach for Stonyfield rather than a competing product when given the choice.

Stonyfield has a very large Web site. The blogs provide a way to highlight some of the Web content that might otherwise get lost. This, too, helps steer some blog readers to buy Stonyfield products.

Speaking of milk products and animals that give milk, how about a Canadian company named for those animals?

Toronto-based Tucows is an Internet services company that provides back-office solutions and wholesale Internet services to a global network of more than 6000 Web-hosting companies, Internet service providers (ISPs), and other service providers worldwide. The original software download site, Tucows.com, earned its reputation early on for being the first to provide software on a "freeware" or "shareware" basis. Tucows currently hosts more than 40 000 software titles (all tested virus- and spyware-free) through its international network of partners (i.e., mirror sites). These sites provide users with fast, local, and safe virus- and spyware-free downloads.

Most of Tucows' business rests on domain registration and downloading of freeware and shareware around the world. Second only to CNet in shareware downloading, Tucows President and CEO Elliot Noss wanted a way to let Tucows users know more about what was happening at the company, particularly in the area of downloads and acquisitions, and to find out from users what the impact of the company's growth, acquisitions, and service was on its customers. Tucows' blog consists of newsy articles about conferences Tucows' senior and technical staff have attended, tips and clues on how to work with the various software available from Tucows, and what is going at the company, particularly in terms of acquisition of new software packages for download. Users can—and do—respond, providing even more tips or more user-friendly ways to handle the software and commenting on the more editorial pieces, such as the appropriateness of sponsored blogs.

To Think About

1. What are Stonyfield Farm's business model and business strategy? What challenges and problems does the company face? What challenges face Tucows?

2. How do blogs help these companies solve these problems and compete in their industries?

3. What are the advantages and disadvantages of using blogs for companies such as Stonyfield Farm and Tucows?

MIS in Action

Visit Stonyfield Farm's Web site (**www.stonyfield.com**), and explore each of its blogs. Read some of the postings and related material. Then answer these questions:

1. Describe the kind of topics discussed on Stonyfield Farm's blogs. Are they closely related to Stonyfield's products? What kinds of people would they attract?

2. Is there any other content on the blog pages to promote Stonyfield products? Describe what you see and how it might help the company.

3. What types of content does Tucows have on its blog? Does Tucows need more than one blog? What additional blogs would you recommend for Tucows?

4. Should all companies use blogs to reach their customers? Why or why not?

Sources: "Stonyfield Farm's Chief Blogger Leaves," *Backbone Corporate Blogging Survey*, March 24, 2006; "Online Extra: Stonyfield Farm's Blog Culture," *BusinessWeek*, May 2, 2005; Sarah Needleman, "Blogging Becomes a Corporate Job: Digital 'Handshake'?" *The Wall Street Journal*, May 31, 2005; **www.stonyfieldfarms.com**, (accessed September 12, 2006); Tucows Blog Site, **http://blog.tucows.com/blog** (accessed May 6, 2007).

Marketers are analyzing blogs as well as chat groups and message boards to see what is being said online about new products, old brands, and ad campaigns. Blog-watching services that monitor popular blogs claim that "blog watching" can be cheaper and faster for analyzing consumer interests and sentiment than traditional focus groups and surveys. For example, Polaroid learned from blogs that consumers online frequently discuss photo longevity and archiving, prompting it to pay more attention to long-lasting photos in its product development. Companies are also posting ads on some of the most popular blogs published by individuals or by other organizations.

FIGURE 13-5 Stonyfield Farms' Baby Babble blog.

Stonyfield Farms' Baby Babble blog provides a channel for the company to talk to customers with young children directly and hear back from them.

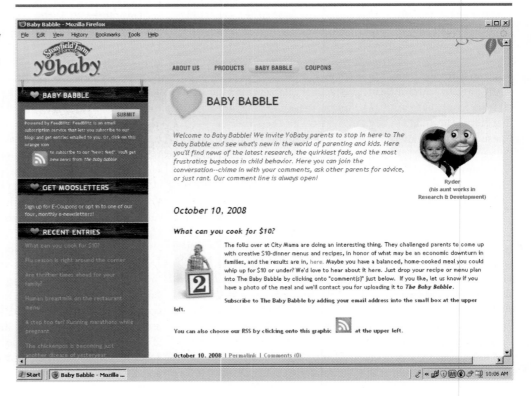

Customer Self-Service Many companies use their Web sites and e-mail to answer customer questions or to provide customers with product information, reducing the need for human customer-support expert. For instance, Air Canada and other major airlines have created Web sites where customers can review flight departure and arrival times, seating charts, and airport logistics; check frequent-flyer miles; and purchase tickets online. Chapter 1 describes how customers of UPS use its Web site to track shipments, calculate shipping costs, determine time in transit, and arrange for a package pickup. DHL, FedEx, and other package delivery firms provide similar Web-based services. Automated self-service or other Web-based responses to customer questions cost only a fraction of what a live customer service representative on the telephone would cost.

New software products are even integrating the Web with customer call centres, where customer service problems have been traditionally handled over the telephone. A **call centre** is an organizational department responsible for handling customer service issues by telephone and other channels. For example, visitors to Apple's Web site can request a phone call from customer service by entering their telephone numbers. A call-centre system directs a customer service representative to place a voice telephone call to the user's phone.

Business-to-Business E-Commerce: New Efficiencies and Relationships

About 80 percent of B2B e-commerce is still based on proprietary systems for electronic data interchange (EDI). **Electronic data interchange (EDI)** enables the computer-to-computer exchange between two organizations of standard transactions such as invoices, bills of lading, shipment schedules, or purchase orders. Transactions are automatically transmitted from one information system to another through a network, eliminating the printing and handling of paper at one end and the inputting of data at the other. Each major industry has EDI standards that define the structure and information fields of electronic documents for that industry.

EDI originally automated the exchange of documents such as purchase orders, invoices, and shipping notices. Although some companies still use EDI for document automation, firms engaged in just-in-time inventory replenishment and continuous production use EDI as a system for continuous replenishment. Suppliers have online access to selected parts of the purchasing firm's production and delivery schedules and automatically ship materials and goods to meet prespecified targets without intervention by firm purchasing agents (see Figure 13-6).

Although many organizations still use private networks for EDI, they are increasingly Web-enabled because Internet technology provides a much more flexible and low-cost platform for linking to other firms. Businesses are able to extend digital technology to a wider range of activities and broaden their circle of trading partners.

Take procurement, for example. **Procurement** involves not only purchasing goods and materials but also sourcing, negotiating with suppliers, paying for goods, and making delivery arrangements. Businesses can now use the Internet to locate the lowest-cost supplier, search online catalogues of supplier products, negotiate with suppliers, place orders,

Call centre
Electronic data interchange (EDI)
Procurement

FIGURE 13-6 Electronic data interchange (EDI).

Companies use EDI to automate transactions for B2B e-commerce and continuous inventory replenishment. Suppliers can automatically send data about shipments to purchasing firms. The purchasing firms can use EDI to provide production and inventory requirements and payment data to suppliers.

FIGURE 13-7   A private industrial network.

A private industrial network, also known as a private exchange, links a firm to its suppliers, distributors, and other key business partners for efficient supply chain management and other collaborative commerce activities.

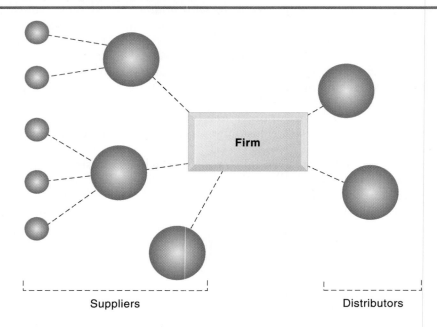

make payments, and arrange transportation. They are not limited to partners linked by traditional EDI networks.

The Internet and Web technology enable businesses to create new electronic storefronts for selling to other businesses with multimedia graphic displays and interactive features similar to those for B2C commerce. Alternatively, businesses can use Internet technology to create extranets or electronic marketplaces for linking to other businesses for purchase and sale transactions.

Private industrial networks typically consist of a large firm using an extranet to link to its suppliers and other key business partners (see Figure 13-7). The network is owned by the buyer, and it permits the firm and designated suppliers, distributors, and other business partners to share product design and development, marketing, production scheduling, inventory management, and unstructured communication, including graphics and e-mail. Another term for a private industrial network is a **private exchange.**

An example is VW Group Supply, which links the Volkswagen Group and its suppliers. VW Group Supply handles 90 percent of all global purchasing for Volkswagen, including all automotive and parts components.

Net marketplaces, which are sometimes called *e-hubs*, provide a single, digital marketplace based on Internet technology for many different buyers and sellers (see Figure 13-8). They are industry owned or operate as independent intermediaries between buyers and sellers. Net marketplaces generate revenue from purchase and sale transactions and other services provided to clients. Participants in Net marketplaces can establish prices through online negotiations, auctions, or requests for quotations, or they can use fixed prices.

There are many different types of Net marketplaces and ways of classifying them. Some Net marketplaces sell *direct goods* and some sell *indirect goods*. *Direct goods* are goods used in a production process, such as sheet steel for auto body production. Indirect goods are all other goods not directly involved in the production process, such as office supplies or products for maintenance and repair. Some Net marketplaces support contractual purchasing based on long-term relationships with designated suppliers, and others support short-term spot purchasing, where goods are purchased based on immediate needs, often from many different suppliers.

Some Net marketplaces serve vertical markets for specific industries, such as automobiles, telecommunications, or machine tools while others serve horizontal markets for goods and services that can be found in many different industries, such as office equipment or transportation.

Private industrial networks
Private exchange
Net marketplaces

FIGURE 13-8   A Net marketplace.

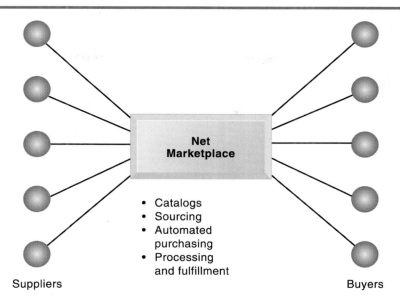

Net marketplaces are online marketplaces where multiple buyers can purchase from multiple sellers.

Net Marketplace

- Catalogs
- Sourcing
- Automated purchasing
- Processing and fulfillment

Suppliers   Buyers

Exostar is an example of an industry-owned Net marketplace, focusing on long-term contract purchasing relationships and on providing common networks and computing platforms for reducing supply chain inefficiencies. This aerospace and defence industry-sponsored Net marketplace was founded jointly by BAE Systems, Boeing, Lockheed Martin, Raytheon, and Rolls-Royce plc to connect these companies to their suppliers and facilitate collaboration. More than 16 000 trading partners in the commercial, military, and government sectors use Exostar's sourcing, e-procurement, and collaboration tools for both direct and indirect goods.

Exchanges are independently owned third-party Net marketplaces that connect thousands of suppliers and buyers for spot purchasing. Many exchanges provide vertical markets for a single industry, such as food, electronics, or industrial equipment, and they primarily deal with direct inputs. For example, FoodTrader.com automates spot purchases among buyers and sellers from more than 180 countries in the food and agriculture industry.

Exchanges proliferated during the early years of e-commerce, but many have failed. Suppliers were reluctant to participate because the exchanges encouraged competitive bidding that drove prices down and did not offer any long-term relationships with buyers or services to make lowering prices worthwhile. Many essential direct purchases are not conducted on a spot basis because they require contracts and consideration of issues such as delivery timing, customization, and quality of products.

13.3   M-Commerce

Wireless mobile devices are starting to be used for purchasing goods and services as well as for transmitting messages. In the United States, m-commerce is still in its infancy but is starting to grow as 3G cell phones become more common. In Asia and Europe, mobile commerce is much more widely adopted. Although m-commerce represents a small fraction of total e-commerce transactions, revenue has been steadily growing (see Figure 13-9). In 2008, there were an estimated 3 billion cell phone subscribers worldwide, with over 500 million in China alone. In the United States, there are about 255 million cell phone subscribers.

M-Commerce Services and Applications

M-commerce applications have taken off for services that are time-critical, that appeal to people on the move, or that accomplish a task more efficiently than other methods. They are

Exchanges

FIGURE 13-9   Global m-commerce revenue, 2000–2012.

M-commerce sales represent a small fraction of total e-commerce sales, but that percentage is steadily growing.
Source: eMarketer, 2008; Gartner, 2008; author estimates.

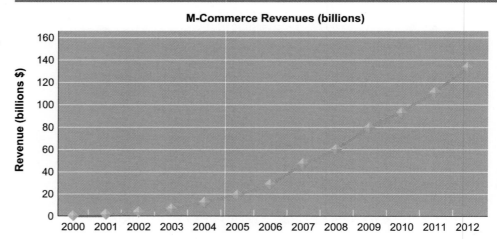

especially popular in Europe, Japan, South Korea, and other countries where fees for conventional Internet usage are very expensive. Here are some examples.

Location-Based Services Many mobile device providers or suppliers of applications for mobile devices offer services that enable users to locate nearby restaurants, ATMs, and gasoline stations, and find local entertainment, providing maps showing how to reach the locations. MeetMoi provides a dating service that helps users identify people who are nearby and looking for dates. Smarter Agent is an application out of the United States that enables users of cell phones with global positioning systems (GPS) to find nearby vacant apartments.

Banking and Financial Services Banks are rolling out services that let customers manage their bank accounts from their cell phones or other mobile devices. Customers of most modern banks can use their cell phones to check account balances, transfer funds, and pay bills.

Wireless Advertising Cell phone service providers have information valuable to advertisers about where subscribers live, their location the moment they view ads, their age, and the games, music, and other services they use on their phones. Advertisers must find a way to deal with privacy issues and consumer reactions to ads on their phones. But when done right, mobile campaigns yield high response rates and increased consumer engagement.

Yahoo! displays ads on its mobile home page for companies such as Pepsi, Procter & Gamble, Hilton, Nissan, and Intel. Google is displaying ads linked to cell phone searches by users of the mobile version of its search engine while Microsoft offers banner and text advertising on its MSN Mobile portal in the United States. Ads are starting to be embedded in downloadable applications such as games and videos. Less than $1 billion was spent on mobile advertising in 2007, but spending on mobile ads could surge to $12 billion to $25 billion over the next five years (Bellman and Engineer, 2008).

Games and Entertainment Cell phones are quickly turning into portable entertainment platforms. Mobile phone services offer downloadable digital games, music, and ringtones (digitized snippets of music that play on mobile phones when a user receives or places a call). More and more handset models combine the features of a cell phone and a portable music player.

Users of broadband services from the major wireless vendors can download ondemand video clips, news clips, and weather reports. Toronto's QuickPlay Media offers a service through Bell and Rogers to deliver mobile TV, video, and radio services. Film companies are starting to produce short films explicitly designed to play on mobile phones. News Corporation, which owns the Fox Network, coined the trademark "mobisodes" for short cell phone videos.

User-generated content is also appearing in mobile form. Users can access YouTube and social networking sites such as Facebook and MySpace from their mobile devices.

Accessing Information from the Wireless Web

Although cell phones, PDAs, and other handheld mobile devices are able to access the Web at any time and from any place, the amount of information that they can actually handle at one time is very limited. Until 3G broadband service comes into widespread use, these devices will not be able to transmit or receive large amounts of data. The information must fit onto small display screens.

Major search providers Google, Yahoo!, and Microsoft have introduced search services for mobile phones that provide useful information with minimal typing. Their **wireless portals** (also known as *mobile portals*) feature content and services optimized for mobile devices to steer users to the information they are most likely to need. Google's mobile service remembers recent place names in searches, so that when users initiate a search for "movies," it returns a list of movies playing locally and makes it easy to find show times and purchase tickets. Microsoft's Tellme service allows users to speak into their phones to search movie listings, stock quotes, news, and other information and then see the results on their phone screens.

13.4 Electronic Commerce Payment Systems

Several electronic payment systems have been developed to pay for goods electronically on the Internet. Electronic payment systems for the Internet include systems for digital credit card payments, digital wallets, accumulated balance digital payment systems, online stored value payment systems, digital chequing, and electronic billing presentment and payment systems.

Types of Electronic Payment Systems

Nearly all online payments use credit cards or rely on the credit card system. Businesses can also contract with services that extend the functionality of existing credit card payment systems. **Digital wallets** make paying for purchases over the Web more efficient by eliminating the need for shoppers to enter their address and credit card information repeatedly each time they buy something. The digital wallet securely stores credit card and owner identification information and enters the shopper's name, credit card number, and shipping information automatically when invoked to complete a purchase. Google Checkout is an example.

Micropayment systems have been developed for purchases of less than $10, such as downloads of individual articles or music clips, which would be too small for conventional credit card payments. **Accumulated balance digital payment systems** enable users to make micropayments and purchases on the Web, accumulating a debit balance that they must pay periodically on their credit card or telephone bills. Examples are Valista's PaymentsPlus used by AOL, Vodafone, and NTT DoCoMo, and Clickshare, which is widely used by the online newspaper and publishing industry.

Online stored value payment systems enable consumers to make instant online payments to merchants and other individuals based on value stored in an online digital account. Some online stored value payment systems such as Valista are merchant platforms. Others are focused on peer-to-peer payments, such as PayPal. PayPal is owned by eBay and makes it possible for people to send money to vendors or individuals who are not set up to accept credit card payments.

Digital chequing systems such as PayByCheck extend the functionality of existing chequing accounts so they can be used for online shopping payments. Digital cheques are processed much faster than traditional paper-based chequing.

Electronic billing presentment and payment systems are used for paying routine monthly bills. They enable users to view their bills electronically and pay them through electronic fund transfers from bank or credit card accounts. These services notify purchasers about bills that are due, present the bills, and process the payments. Some of these services, such as CheckFree, consolidate subscribers' bills from various sources so that

Wireless portals
Digital wallets
Micropayment
Accumulated balance digital payment systems
Online stored value payment systems
Digital chequing systems
Electronic billing presentment and payment systems

TABLE 13-6 Examples of electronic payment systems for e-commerce.

PAYMENT SYSTEM	DESCRIPTION	COMMERCIAL EXAMPLE
Credit card payment systems	Protect information transmitted among users, merchant sites, and processing banks	Visa, MasterCard American Express
Digital wallet	Software that stores credit card and other information to facilitate form completion and payment for goods on the Web	Google Checkout
Accumulated balance digital payment systems	Accumulate micropayment purchases as a debit balance that must be paid periodically on credit card or telephone bills	Valista PaymentsPlus Clickshare
Stored value payment systems	Enable consumers to make instant payments to merchants or individuals based on value stored in a digital account	PayPal, Valista
Digital chequing	Provides electronic cheques with a secure digital signature	PayByCheck
Electronic billing presentment and payment systems	Support electronic payments for online and physical store purchases of goods or services after the purchase have taken place	Yahoo! Bill Pay, CheckFree, ePost

they can all be paid at one time. Table 13-6 summarizes the features of some of these e-commerce payment systems.

Digital Payment Systems for M-Commerce

Use of mobile handsets as payment devices is already well established in Europe, Japan, and South Korea. Three kinds of mobile payment systems are used in Japan, and these provide a glimpse of the future of mobile payment in North America. Japanese cell phones support stored value systems charged by credit cards or bank accounts, mobile debit cards (tied to personal bank accounts), and mobile credit cards. Japanese cell phones act like mobile wallets, containing a variety of payment mechanisms. Consumers can pay merchants by simply waving the cell phone at a merchant payment device that can accept payments. Japan's largest phone company NTT DoCoMo introduced wireless RFID cell phones and a related payment system (FeliCa) in 2004. Currently 10 million wallet phones are in use in Japan.

In North America, the cell phone has not yet evolved into a fully capable mobile commerce and payment system. The cell phone in North America is not connected to a wide network of financial institutions, but instead resides behind the wall of the telephone providers although Canadian banks have extended access to customers' accounts to their customers' mobile devices. In Europe and Asia, cell phone users can pay for a very wide variety of real goods and services, and there, phones are integrated into a large array of financial institutions.

A significant issue in e-commerce deals with contractual law. In Canada, most contract law is governed provincially. A further significant issue is that of taxation. Retail sales made in stores are easy to track and ensure that taxes on sales are being properly assessed, collected, reported, and submitted to governmental agencies. Retail sales are made in one geographic location to a buyer who is at that location; therefore, it is easy to determine which government agencies are due the taxes. But what if a buyer is in Ontario and makes an online purchase from a company in Alberta? What if a buyer in PEI makes an online purchase of digital material from a company in France? To which provinces and countries are taxes payable and at what rates? And what about customs duties?

In terms of taxes on online sales, it appears that organizations are responsible for collecting and remitting:

- HST (which includes GST) for Nova Scotia, New Brunswick, Newfoundland/Labrador
- GST for B.C., Alberta, Saskatchewan, Manitoba, Ontario, Quebec, P.E.I., Northwest Territories, Nunavut, Yukon
- PST/RST for orders shipped to customers in your own province (unless your "home" province or territory is Alberta, the Northwest Territories, Nunavut, or Yukon, which have no PST/RST)

SUMMARY

1. **What are the unique features of e-commerce, digital markets, and digital goods?**

   E-commerce involves digitally enabled commercial transactions between and among organizations and individuals. Unique features of e-commerce technology include ubiquity, global reach, universal technology standards, richness, interactivity, information density, capabilities for personalization and customization, and social technology.

   Digital markets are said to be more "transparent" than traditional markets, with reduced information asymmetry, search costs, transaction costs, and menu costs, along with the ability to change prices dynamically based on market conditions. Digital goods, such as music, video, software, and books, can be delivered over a digital network. Once a digital product has been produced, the cost of delivering that product digitally is extremely low.

2. **How has Internet technology changed business models?**

   The Internet can help companies add extra value to existing products and services or create new products and services. Many different business models for electronic commerce on the Internet have emerged, including virtual storefronts, information brokers, transaction brokers, online marketplaces, content providers, social networks, service providers, and portals. Business models that take advantage of the Internet's capabilities for communication, community building, and digital goods distribution have become especially prominent.

3. **What are the various types of e-commerce, and how has e-commerce changed consumer retailing and business-to-business transactions?**

   The three major types of electronic commerce are business-to-consumer (B2C), business-to-business (B2B), and consumer-to-consumer (C2C). Mobile commerce, or m-commerce, is the purchase of goods and services using handheld wireless devices.

   The Internet creates new channels for marketing, sales, and customer support and to eliminate intermediaries in buy-and-sell transactions. Interactive capabilities on the Web can be used to build closer relationships with customers in marketing and customer support. Web personalization technologies deliver Web pages with content geared to the specific interests of each user. Web sites and e-mail reduce transaction costs for placing orders and customer service.

   B2B e-commerce generates efficiencies by enabling companies to locate suppliers, solicit bids, place orders, and track shipments in transit electronically. Net marketplaces provide a single, digital marketplace for many buyers and sellers. Private industrial networks link a firm with its suppliers and other strategic business partners to develop highly efficient and responsive supply chains.

4. **What is the role of m-commerce in business, and what are the most important m-commerce applications?**

   M-commerce is especially well suited for location-based applications, such as finding local hotels and restaurants, monitoring local traffic and weather, and providing personalized location-based marketing. Mobile phones and handhelds are being used for mobile bill payment; banking; securities trading; transportation schedule updates; and downloads of digital content, such as music, games, and video clips. M-commerce requires wireless portals and special digital payment systems that can handle micropayments.

5. **What are the principal payment systems for electronic commerce?**

   The principal e-commerce payment systems are digital credit card payment systems, digital wallets, accumulated balance digital payment systems, stored value payment systems, digital chequing, and electronic billing presentment and payment systems.

Key Terms

Accumulated balance digital payment systems, 423
Banner ad, 410
Blogosphere, 416
Business-to-business (B2B) electronic commerce, 412
Business-to-consumer (B2C) electronic commerce, 412
Call centre, 419
Clicks-and-mortar, 412
Clickstream tracking, 415
Collaborative filtering, 415

Consumer-to-consumer (C2C) electronic commerce, 413
Cost transparency, 406
Customization, 407
Digital chequing systems, 423
Digital goods, 408
Digital wallets, 423
Disintermediation, 408
Dynamic pricing, 408
Electronic billing presentment and payment systems, 423
Electronic data interchange (EDI), 419

Exchanges, 421
Information asymmetry, 407
Information density, 406
Market entry costs, 405
Marketspace, 404
Menu costs, 408
Micropayment, 423
Mobile commerce (m-commerce), 413
Net marketplaces, 420
Online stored value payment systems, 423
Personalization, 407

Review Questions

1. *What are the unique features of e-commerce, digital markets, and digital goods?*
   - *Name and describe four business trends and three technology trends shaping e-commerce today.*
   - *List and describe the seven unique features of e-commerce.*
   - *Define a digital market and digital goods, and describe their distinguishing features.*

2. *How has Internet technology changed business models?*
   - *Explain how the Internet is changing the economics of information and business models.*
   - *Name and describe six Internet business models for electronic commerce. Distinguish between a pure-play Internet business model and a clicks-and-mortar business model.*

3. *What are the various types of e-commerce, and how has e-commerce changed consumer retailing and business-to-business transactions?*
   - *Name and describe the various categories of electronic commerce.*
   - *Explain how the Internet facilitates sales and marketing for individual customers, and describe the role played by Web personalization.*

   - *Explain how the Internet can enhance customer service.*
   - *Explain how Internet technology supports business-to-business electronic commerce.*
   - *Define and describe Net marketplaces, and explain how they differ from private industrial networks (private exchanges).*

4. *What is the role of m-commerce in business and what are the most important m-commerce applications?*
   - *List and describe important types of m-commerce services and applications.*
   - *Explain how wireless portals help users access information on the wireless Web.*
   - *Describe some of the barriers to m-commerce.*

5. *What are the principal payment systems for electronic commerce?*
   - *Name and describe the principal electronic payment systems used on the Internet.*
   - *Describe the types of payment systems used in m-commerce.*

Discussion Questions

1. *How does the Internet change consumer and supplier relationships?*

2. *The Internet may not make corporations obsolete, but the corporations will have to change their business models. Do you agree? Why or why not?*

Collaboration and Teamwork: Performing a Competitive Analysis of E-Commerce Sites

Form a group with three or four of your classmates. Select two businesses that are competitors in the same industry and that use their Web sites for electronic commerce. Visit these Web sites. You might compare, for example, the Web sites for iTunes and Napster, Amazon.ca and Chapters.Indigo.ca, or TDAmeritrade and Scottrade. Prepare an evaluation of each business's Web site in terms of its functions, user-friendliness, and ability to support the company's business strategy. Which Web site does a better job? Why? Can you make some recommendations to improve these Web sites? If possible, use Google Sites to post links to Web pages, team communication announcements, and work assignments; to brainstorm; and to work collaboratively on project documents. Try to use Google Docs to develop a presentation of your findings for the class.

 Visit the MyMISLab Web site at **www.pearsoned.ca/mymislab**. This online homework and tutorial system puts you in control of your own learning with study and practice tools directly correlated to this chapter's content.

Learning Track Modules

The following Learning Tracks provide content relevant to topics covered in this chapter:

1. E-Commerce Challenges: The Story of Online Groceries

2. Build an E-Commerce Business Plan

3. Hot New Careers in E-Commerce

HANDS-ON MIS   Projects

The projects in this section give you hands-on experience developing e-commerce strategies for businesses, using spreadsheet software to research the profitability of an e-commerce company, and using Web tools to research and evaluate e-commerce hosting services.

Management Decision Problems

1. Columbiana is a small, independent island in the Caribbean. It wants to develop its tourist industry and attract more visitors. The island has many historical buildings, forts, and other sites, along with rain forests and striking mountains. A few first-class hotels and several dozen less-expensive accommodations can be found along its beautiful white sand beaches. The major airlines have regular flights to Columbiana, as do several small airlines. Columbiana's government wants to increase tourism and develop new markets for the country's tropical agricultural products. How can a Web presence help? What Internet business model would be appropriate? What functions should the Web site perform?

2. Explore the Web sites of the following companies: Nygård, Canadian Tire, Tim Horton's, and Air Canada. Determine which of these Web sites would benefit most from adding a company-sponsored blog to the Web site. List the business benefits of the blog. Specify the intended audience for the blog. Decide who in the company should author the blog, and select some topics for the blog.

Improving Decision Making: Using Spreadsheet Software to Analyze a Dot-Com Business

Software skills: Spreadsheet downloading, formatting, and formulas
Business skills: Financial statement analysis

Publicly traded companies, including those specializing in e-commerce, are required to file financial data with the System for Electronic Document Analysis and Retrieval (SEDAR) operated for the Canadian Securities Administrators (CSA). By analyzing this information, you can determine the profitability of an e-commerce company and the viability of its business model.

Pick one Canadian company that conducts e-commerce on the Internet, for example, Hudson's Bay Company. Study the Web pages that describe the company, and explain its purpose and structure. Use the Web to find articles that comment on the company. Then visit the SEDAR Web site at **www.sedar.com,** select your company, and select View This Public Company's Documents to access the company's news releases and financial reports showing income statements

and balance sheets. Select only the sections of the financial reports containing the desired portions of financial statements that you need to examine, and print them out and enter the data into your spreadsheet. Create simplified spreadsheets of the company's balance sheets and income statements for the past three years.

1. Is the company a dot-com success, borderline business, or failure? What information forms the basis of your decision? Why? When answering these questions, pay special attention to the company's three-year trends in revenues, cost of sales, gross margins, operating expenses, and net margins. See MyMISLab for Chapter 13 for definitions of these terms and how they are calculated.

2. Prepare an overhead presentation (with a minimum of five slides), including appropriate spreadsheets or charts, and present your work to your professor and classmates.

Achieving Operational Excellence: Evaluating E-Commerce Hosting Services

Software skills: Web browser software
Business skills: Evaluating e-commerce hosting services

This project will help develop your Internet skills in commercial services for hosting an e-commerce site for a small startup company.

You would like to set up a Web site to sell towels, linens, pottery, and tableware from Portugal and are examining services for hosting small business Internet storefronts. Your Web site should be able to take secure credit card payments and to calculate shipping costs and taxes. Initially, you would like to display photos and descriptions of 40 different products. Visit Yahoo! Small Business, GoDaddy, and Volusion and compare the range of e-commerce hosting services they offer to small business, their capabilities, and costs. Also examine the tools they provide for creating an e-commerce site. Compare these services and decide which you would use if you were actually establishing a Web store. Write a brief report indicating your choice and explaining the strengths and weaknesses of each.

CASE STUDY   Facebook's Dilemma

Facebook is one of the largest social networking sites in the world, currently surpassed in North America only by MySpace. Founded in 2004 by Mark Zuckerberg, the site had 118 million worldwide users as of June 2008. Facebook allows users to create a profile and join various types of self-contained networks, including college-wide, workplace, and regional networks. The site includes a wide array of tools that allow users to connect and interact with other users, including messaging, groups, photo-sharing, and user-created applications.

The site was originally open only to a small handful of colleges, but the site has grown explosively since it opened its doors to all college students and eventually the general public. Facebook is now one of the most recognizable sites on the Web. Compared to its rival, MySpace, Facebook's interface is simplistic and clean and tends to attract those looking for a more structured social networking environment.

Facebook represents a unique opportunity for advertisers to reach highly targeted audiences based on their demographic information, hobbies and personal preferences, geographical regions, and other narrowly specified criteria in a comfortable and engaging environment. Businesses can place advertisements that are fully integrated into primary features of the site, such as the News Feed, a continually updating list of news stories about members' friends' activities on Facebook. Firms also can create Facebook pages where users can learn more about and interact with their companies. For example, a restaurant can advertise by having Facebook place items in the News Feeds of its customers indicating that those people ate there recently. Blockbuster has recent rentals and reviews of its movies appearing in similar fashion. Many companies, including eBay, Central Mountain Air, the Canadian Cancer Society, and *The Globe and Mail* maintain Facebook pages where users can learn more about the company and its products.

For advertisers, Facebook presents unique and exciting opportunities. It represents a gold mine of opportunity because of the information the site has gathered and because of the richness of the social networking environment. The site has also benefited from its status as a first-mover in the social networking marketplace, amassing a large audience whose users are reluctant to leave for fear of leaving the rest of their friends behind.

Despite these advantages, Facebook's path to profitability has not been smooth. The company has encountered more than its fair share of controversy, mostly concerning its handling and usage of the extensive information it collects from its users. Though users contribute most of their information to Facebook willingly, the privacy and user controls over the information granted to Facebook are the biggest concerns most users have with the site.

Facebook's dilemma is finding a way to turn a profit and to continue to increase revenues using the information its users voluntarily provide without violating the privacy of these users. Thus far, its attempts to do so have not been successful. Facebook's traffic continues to rise at a healthy rate, and the company's sales reached $183 million in 2007, but the company continues to spend more money than it earns. To truly capitalize on the massive audience and immersive environment of the site, Facebook needs to innovate and find new ways to grow revenue that do not alienate the very users that the company is depending on to spur its growth. The personal information collected on the site represents a motherlode to advertisers, but one that will remain largely untapped if Facebook users do not feel comfortable enough or have sufficient incentive to share it.

The launch of the company's Beacon advertising service was an example of Facebook grossly miscalculating the privacy demands of its users. Beacon was intended to inform users when their friends made purchases and engaged in other activities outside Facebook. The trouble with the service is that it shared information about users that they had not explicitly intended or agreed to share. The service was opt-out, meaning users had to actively turn off Beacon or the service would share private personal information under the assumption that Facebook had the consent of the user to do so. As Facebook soon found out, this assumption was often mistaken. Not only that, Beacon was continuing to send information to Facebook even once the user had elected to opt out, regardless of whether or not the user was logged into Facebook at the time.

The civic action group MoveOn.org created a Facebook group to protest Beacon and grew to more than 50 000 members in 10 days. In response to the media firestorm, Facebook changed Beacon to be an opt-in service and gave users the ability to disable it completely. Beacon represented Facebook's hopes to expand its sources of revenue by offering advertisers access to its users' information, but the company utterly failed to grasp the extent to which the service violated its users' privacy as well as the uproar such a service was likely to cause. Companies such as Coca-Cola and Overstock.com pulled out of the program when they learned about the privacy concerns it raised. The launch and subsequent embarrassment of Beacon damaged Facebook's reputation as a provider of a safe, secure environment for its users. Facebook has subsequently changed the privacy controls for the service, as well as for the rest of its site, to be more transparent.

The inception and handling of the News Feed feature of the site is another example of the company incorrectly anticipating its users' stance on the privacy of their personal information. News Feed is a feature that provides updates to your friends when you perform actions via Facebook, such as updating your profile, adding new friends, or adding new applications. When this feature was introduced, it met with significant resistance from Facebook users, who considered the feature to be overly invasive. As with Beacon, users protested the feature through the Groups feature of the site, forming more than 500 groups to protest it, with one group, Students Against Facebook News Feed, reaching well over 700 000 members at its peak.

In an open letter to Facebook members, Zuckerberg apologized for the abrupt introduction of the feature but defended the feature itself as a positive thing, noting that users could control which types of items appeared on the News Feed and who could view those items. Also, the News Feed does not provide any additional details about users that are not already available—it simply collects profile updates and displays them in such a way that checking all of your friends' individual profiles isn't necessary to keep track of the updates they have made. In his letter, Zuckerberg said of News Feed: "This is information people used to dig for on a daily basis, nicely reorganized and summarized so people can learn about the people they care about." Now, the News Feed is one of the most popular features on the site and has been imitated by MySpace and other competing social networking sites.

Facebook has also come under fire for its handling of the personal information of people who attempt to remove their profiles from the site. Facebook offers users the ability to deactivate their accounts, but the company's servers maintain copies of the information contained in those accounts indefinitely. The company's reasoning for this is that reactivating accounts is far easier if Facebook retains copies of

profile content and other personal information. Users who attempted to delete their accounts met with resistance and often required outside assistance from watchdog groups. One user, Nipon Das, a business consultant in Manhattan, spent two months attempting to delete his profile unsuccessfully while still receiving updates and messages through the site. Now, Facebook has joined MySpace, Friendster, and other social networking sites in offering a simpler process to permanently delete your account and the personal information it contains.

Currently, Facebook's most promising prospects to become more profitable involve the development of applications for use via Facebook Platform. In May 2007, Facebook announced the launch of Facebook Platform, which was an effort by the company to open up its site to third-party developers to become a platform for their applications. These applications, sometimes also referred to as widgets, consist of games, plug-in features for user profiles, and other programs that are fully integrated with the Facebook site. They are independently developed. As of mid-2008, more than 24 000 applications had been created.

Facebook Platform has been beneficial for both Facebook and the developers who are creating applications for it: Facebook's environment has become even more engaging and self-sufficient, and developers gain unparalleled exposure for their applications. A small percentage of these applications have turned into viable businesses. Companies attracting large numbers of users to their applications on Facebook are able to sell goods, services, or advertising. For example, more than 2 million people use FunSpace daily to post messages, videos, or cards on their friends' profile pages, and 1.6 million use Top Friends to highlight their closest friends in a box on their own Facebook pages. With more than 400 000 daily users, Scrabulous allows Facebook users to play an adaptation of Scrabble. All of these applications earn advertising revenue.

Others are using the exposure on Facebook to raise their business visibility. Flixter, an online community for movie fans, has a Facebook application called Movies that allows people to tell their Facebook friends about the movies they've seen and share reviews. Flixter's management reports that this application, with about 482 000 daily users, has hugely expanded its customer base and business opportunities.

It is currently unclear as to whether there is significant revenue to be made through the development of these applications. Some believe that Facebook applications are "the next big thing," and that traditional advertisers will gravitate toward Facebook to reach highly targeted audiences with their applications. On the flip side, others believe Facebook's own popularity will injure its chances to attract advertisers to its site, claiming that the engaging and immersive environment that draws visitors to the site makes users less likely to click on ads. Skeptics also believe that the current application system, where applications tend to support one another via advertising through other applications without the aid of extensive outside advertising, is an unsustainable model over the long term. So far, only 200 Facebook applications have attracted more than 10000 users per day, and 60 percent failed to attract even 100 daily users.

There is little doubt that Facebook applications will make Facebook a "stickier" destination for its users as they will be able to do more of the things they like to do on the Web without having to leave Facebook. However, that may not necessarily translate to increased profitability.

In 2007, Microsoft purchased a small stake in Facebook, buying 1.6 percent of the company for $300 million. That investment put Facebook's valuation at approximately $18 billion. It remains to be seen whether or not the company can turn its heavy site traffic and trove of personal information into new revenue streams. The initial furor and subsequent acceptance of the News Feed feature shows that Facebook users' stances on their privacy may be subject to change or persuasion, and many users may not even be aware or care about the dissemination of their personal information. Even if they did, the benefits of being a part of Facebook, thanks to its large audience and wealth of features and content, may outweigh the reservations its users have regarding their privacy. But it appears that enough Facebook users are concerned and aware of their privacy to prevent services as invasive as Beacon's initial incarnation from becoming realities.

In March 2008, Facebook launched a new series of privacy controls, including a feature that allows users to sort friends into groups and grant access to photo albums or parts of their profiles only to specific groups of friends. For example, users can post pictures of their family vacation and share them with just their family members on Facebook, or users can disable co-workers from seeing those embarrassing party pictures from a night out.

This is a step in the right direction, but the toughest task for Facebook will be to continue to preserve the privacy of its members while monetizing the user data it has collected. Shortly after the launch of these new features, a Canadian computer technician uncovered a flaw in Facebook's security that allowed some photo albums and information, including

party photos of Paris Hilton and a personal album of Zuckerberg's, to be accessed by any Facebook member. Although Facebook promptly corrected the flaw, the incident continued to damage the site's already shaky reputation regarding its user privacy controls.

Only time will tell whether Facebook is able to make good on its tremendous potential for revenue growth, but one thing is for sure: the privacy concerns of its users will play a central role in its efforts to become profitable.

CASE STUDY QUESTIONS:

1. What concepts in this chapter are illustrated in this case?

2. What is the role of e-commerce and Web 2.0 technologies in Facebook's widespread popularity?

3. Describe the weaknesses of Facebook's privacy policies and features. What management, organization, and technology factors have contributed to those weaknesses?

4. Does Facebook have a viable business model? Explain your answer

5. If you were responsible for coordinating Facebook's advertising, how would you balance the desire to become increasingly profitable with the need to protect the privacy of your users?

Sources: Riva Richmond, "Some Facebook Applications Thrive, Others Flop," *The Wall Street Journal*, June 16, 2008; Jim Carr, "Facebook Privacy Flap Should Spark Concern for Business," SCMagazineUS.com, March 26, 2008; Thomas Claburn, "Social Networks Find Ways to Monetize User Data," *InformationWeek*, November 10, 2007; Vauhini Vara, "Facebook CEO Seeks Help as Site Grows Up," *The Wall Street Journal*, March 5, 2008; Adam Cohen, "One Friend Facebook Hasn't Made Yet: Privacy Rights," *The New* York Times, February 18, 2008; Alan Krauss, "Piggybacking on Facebook," *The New York Times*, February 20, 2008; Maria Aspan, "How Sticky Is Membership on Facebook? Just Try Breaking Free," *The New York Times*, February 11, 2008; Maria Aspan, "Quitting Facebook Gets Easier," *The New York Times*, February 13, 2008; Brad Stone, "In Facebook, Investing in a Theory," *The New York Times*, October 4, 2007; and Randall Rothenberg, "Facebook's Flop," *The Wall Street Journal*, December 14, 2007.

CHAPTER 14

Enhancing Decision Making

LEARNING OBJECTIVES

After reading this chapter, you will be able to answer the following questions:

1. What are the different types of decisions, and how does the decision-making process work?

2. How do information systems support the activities of managers and management decision making?

3. How do decision-support systems (DSS) differ from management information systems (MIS), and how do they provide value to the business?

4. How do executive support systems (ESS) help senior managers make better decisions?

5. What is the role of information systems in helping people working in a group make decisions more efficiently?

OPENING CASE

Libro Financial Group's Dashboard Provides Better Lending Processes

For nearly 60 years, Libro Financial Group has grown by "helping our owners to be successful," says Frank Kennes, vice president Credit. Libro delivers a full range of chequing, savings, investment, RRSP, insurance, and loan products along with financial coaching and advice for consumers, and farm and business owners. Libro has grown each year by 10 percent to become a $1.6 billion–plus financial institution in southwestern Ontario, serving more than 52 000 customers. The company's customer focus is so strong that Libro refers to its customers as "owners." Trying to make its owners successful has involved many innovative projects.

In its quest to be southwestern Ontario's "preferred choice for financial services" Libro is known for innovation. For example, it offered ATMs and promoted weekly mortgage payments before other financial institutions. Maintaining a culture of innovation,

Libro recently implemented an automated system for margin-based lending. The company wanted to improve this process to provide better service to its primary customers, small- and medium-size businesses. Libro partnered with Covarity, a provider of commercial loan management solutions. Since implementation, Libro has been able to automate the underwriting and ongoing monitoring of commercial loans, achieve greater consistency in risk management, improve efficiency, and offer its borrowers a broader range of services.

For organizations offering margin-based loans, the manual process by which these loans are set up, monitored, and adjusted presents many challenges. Borrowers may fail to meet reporting requirements, and lenders waste valuable time chasing the required information. This can result in adjustments to credit availability not being timely, and when these adjust-

ments are made, the rationale is not always apparent to the borrower. The process is subject to error, delinquency, higher risk, and inconsistency of analysis.

The entire industry experiences these challenges, with more than 200 credit unions in Canada offering more than 5000 margin-based loans. In 2003, Credit Union Central of Canada (CUCC), the national trade association and central finance facility for Canadian credit unions, realized it needed to take action to resolve these issues. Working with the National Lenders Policy Committee, CUCC focused on these issues and determined that the Covarity Dashboard could work to automate the commercial loan process.

Libro Financial Group was an early adopter of the Covarity Dashboard, implementing the Dashboard in all 15 of its branches. Now account managers' focus on growth and making new loans is supplemented with the ability to monitor the loan and track collateral security. The streamlined and automated process prohibits managers from ignoring needed steps in the process; instead "the solution provides visibility to problems with security months in advance," says Ken Filson, senior account manager, Agriculture and Commercial.

The Covarity Dashboard has two main components, the Lender Dashboard and the Borrower Dashboard. When Libro extends a loan, it uses the Lender Dashboard to capture the margin-based rules for credit availability and customer reporting requirements. Customers are automatically sent a reminder e-mail; after receiving the e-mail, customers upload whatever data is requested through their Borrower Dashboard. Uploads take place over the Internet directly from most leading accounting packages, customized Excel templates, or various other file formats.

The Dashboard expedites credit evaluation and adjustment, making transparent the rationale for any adjustments, based on individual accounts receivable, accounts payable, and inventory position. Users of the Lender Dashboard benefit from being able to access timely information that lets them more effectively manage their risk. Users of the Borrower Dashboard benefit from being able to see their credit availability and access a number of reports that capture trends in financial data.

For many financial institutions, the margin-based lending processes are not well defined, leading to poor audits, loans going bad, high-risk exposure, time-consuming analysis, and labour-intensive paper-based systems. As a result, account managers may be constrained in building and maintaining high-quality portfolios of loans.

With the transparency created by the Covarity Dashboard, problems are elevated and addressed earlier. Libro's account managers can access a daily picture of their portfolios regarding which client is late in reporting and which is in breach of the loan's covenants. Account managers spend less time monitoring clients and their loans, so they can place more emphasis on growing the business. According to Greg McQueen, regional manager, "Covarity helps us to focus on elements of the business building role."

Credit analysts using the Dashboard say the solution helps them to see a true picture every month, providing them with needed information in a single screen. "The Covarity process instills a discipline where loan losses on margin can be more effectively avoided," according to Owen Smelski, account manager.

Borrowers using the Dashboard appreciate both the online support and the direct line back to technical specialists. System features like the standard e-mail reminder and statement upload help users to meet their reporting requirements. And the Dashboards' reporting capabilities have been identified by borrowers as practical and convenient tools for internal presentment of financial trends and comparisons.

"The number one benefit of the Covarity Dashboard is a better quality loan portfolio derived from greater productivity and better quality risk management. It is good for Libro Financial Group, and it is good for our owners," said Frank Kennes, vice president Credit.

Sources: "Case Study: Libro Financial Group Uses Covarity to Deliver Superior Customer

Service While Driving Process Efficiencies and Improving Risk Management Controls," **www.covarity.com/content/pressrelease/ case-study-libro-financial-group-uses- covarity-deliver-superior-customer-servic** (accessed October 6, 2009); and **www.libro.ca**.

Libro Financial Group's dashboards are a powerful illustration of how information systems improve decision making. Management was unable to make good decisions about how and when to notify loan clients of their loan status because the required data were difficult to access. Like many other financial institutions, Libro could have continued to use its outdated processes. Instead, it opted for a business intelligence solution that could extract, consolidate, and analyze data and present the data in a user-friendly format as needed. It chose a platform from Covarity because the credit union's professional association had already evaluated the dashboard.

The chosen solution provides two dashboards visible to authorized users, including the borrowers, throughout the organization. Decision makers are able to quickly access a unified high-level view of needed data. Increased availability of this information has helped account managers make better decisions about loans and to monitor the loans they do make and track collateral.

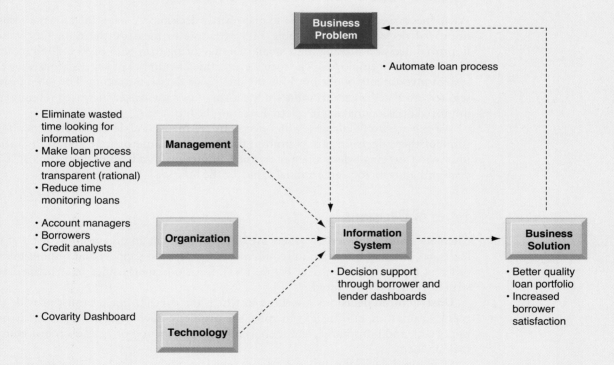

14.1 Decision Making and Information Systems

Decision making in businesses used to be limited to management. Today, lower-level employees are responsible for some of these decisions as information systems make information available to lower levels of the business. But what do we mean by better decision

TABLE 14-1   Business value of enhanced decision making.

EXAMPLE DECISION	DECISION MAKER	NUMBER OF ANNUAL DECISIONS	ESTIMATED VALUE TO FIRM OF A SINGLE IMPROVED DECISION	ANNUAL VALUE
Allocate support to most valuable customers	Accounts manager	12	$ 100 000	$1 200 000
Predict call centre daily demand	Call centre management	4	150 000	600 000
Decide parts inventory levels daily	Inventory manager	365	5000	1 825 000
Identify competitive bids from major suppliers	Senior management	1	2 000 000	2 000 000
Schedule production to fill orders	Manufacturing manager	150	10 000	1 500 000
Allocate labour to complete a job	Production floor manager	100	4000	400 000

making? How does decision making take place in businesses and other organizations? Let us take a closer look.

Business Value of Improved Decision Making

What does it mean to the business to make better decisions? What is the monetary value of improved decision making? Table 14-1 attempts to measure the monetary value of improved decision making for a small manufacturing firm with $280 million in annual revenue and 140 employees. The firm has identified a number of key decisions where new system investments might improve the quality of decision making. The table provides selected estimates of annual value (in the form of cost savings or increased revenue) from improved decision making in selected areas of the business.

We can see from Table 14-1 that decisions are made at all levels of the firm and that some of these decisions are common, routine, and numerous. Although the value of improving any single decision may be small, improving hundreds of thousands of "small" decisions adds up to a large annual value for the business.

Types of Decisions

Chapters 1 and 2 showed that there are different levels in an organization. Each of these levels has different information requirements for decision support and responsibility for different types of decisions (see Figure 14-1). Decisions are classified as structured, semi-structured, and unstructured.

Unstructured decisions are those in which the decision maker must provide judgment, evaluation, and insight to solve the problem. Each of these decisions is novel, important, and nonroutine, and there is no well-understood or agreed-on procedure for making them.

Structured decisions, by contrast, are repetitive and routine, and they involve a definite procedure for handling them so that they do not have to be treated each time as if they were new. Many decisions have elements of both types of decisions and are **semistructured,** where only part of the problem has a clear-cut answer provided by an accepted procedure. In general, structured decisions are more prevalent at lower organizational levels while unstructured problems are more common at higher levels of the firm.

Senior executives face many unstructured decision situations, such as establishing the firm's five- or ten-year goals or deciding new markets to enter. Answering the question "Should we enter a new market?" would require access to news, government reports, and industry views as well as high-level summaries of firm performance. However, the answer would also require senior managers to use their own best judgment and poll other managers for their opinions.

Unstructured decisions

Structured decisions

Semistructured

FIGURE 14-1   Information requirements of key decision-making groups in a firm.

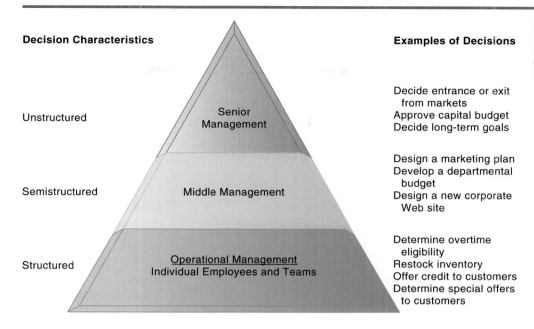

Senior managers, middle managers, operational managers, and employees have different types of decisions and information requirements.

Middle management faces more structured decision scenarios but their decisions may include unstructured components. A typical middle-level management decision might be "Why is the reported order fulfillment report showing a decline over the past six months at a distribution centre in Windsor?" This middle manager will obtain a report from the firm's enterprise system or distribution management system on order activity and operational efficiency at the Windsor distribution centre. This is the structured part of the decision. But before arriving at an answer, this middle manager will have to interview employees and gather more unstructured information from external sources about local economic conditions or sales trends.

Operational management and rank-and-file employees tend to make more structured decisions. For example, a supervisor on an assembly line has to decide whether an hourly paid worker is entitled to overtime pay. If the employee worked more than eight hours on a particular day, the supervisor would routinely grant overtime pay for any time beyond eight hours that was clocked on that day.

A sales account representative often has to make decisions about extending credit to customers by consulting the firm's customer database that contains credit information. If the customer met the firm's pre-specified criteria for granting credit, the account representative would grant that customer credit to make a purchase. In both instances, the decisions are highly structured and are routinely made thousands of times each day in most large firms. The answer has been pre-programmed into the firm's payroll and accounts receivable systems.

The Decision-Making Process

Making a decision is a multistep process. Simon (1960) described four different stages in decision making: intelligence, design, choice, and implementation (see Figure 14-2).

Intelligence consists of discovering, identifying, and understanding the problems occurring in the organization—why a problem exists, where, and what effects it is having on the firm.

Design involves identifying and exploring various solutions to the problem.

Choice consists of choosing among solution alternatives.

Implementation involves making the chosen alternative work and continuing to monitor how well the solution is working.

What happens if the solution you have chosen doesn't work? Figure 14-2 shows that you can return to an earlier stage in the decision-making process and repeat it if necessary.

Intelligence
Design
Choice
Implementation

FIGURE 14-2   Stages in decision making.

The decision-making process is broken down into four stages.

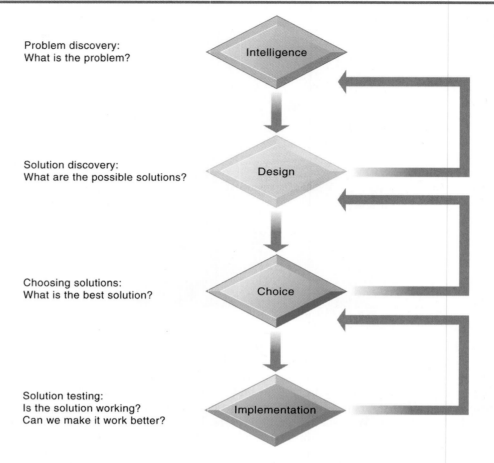

Problem discovery:
What is the problem?

Intelligence

Solution discovery:
What are the possible solutions?

Design

Choosing solutions:
What is the best solution?

Choice

Solution testing:
Is the solution working?
Can we make it work better?

Implementation

For instance, in the face of declining sales, a sales management team may decide to pay the sales force a higher commission for making more sales to spur on the sales effort. If this does not produce sales increases, managers would need to investigate whether the problem stems from poor product design, inadequate customer support, or a host of other causes that call for a different solution.

Managers and Decision Making in the Real World

The premise of this book and this chapter is that systems to support decision making produce better decision making by managers and employees, above-average returns on investment for the firm, and ultimately higher profitability. However, information systems cannot improve all the different kinds of decisions taking place in an organization. Let us examine the role of managers and decision making in organizations to see why this is so.

Managerial Roles Managers play key roles in organizations. Their responsibilities range from making decisions, to writing reports, to attending meetings, to arranging birthday parties. We are able to better understand managerial functions and roles by examining classical and contemporary models of managerial behaviour.

The **classical model of management,** which describes what managers do, was largely unquestioned for the more than 70 years since the 1920s. Henri Fayol and other early writers first described the five classical functions of managers as planning, organizing, coordinating, deciding, and controlling. This description of management activities dominated management thought for a long time, and it is still popular today.

The classical model describes formal managerial functions but does not address what exactly managers do when they plan, decide things, and control the work of others. For this, we must turn to the work of contemporary behavioural scientists who have studied managers in daily action. **Behavioural models** state that the actual behaviour of managers

Classical model of management
Behavioural models

appears to be less systematic, more informal, less reflective, more reactive, and less well organized than the classical model would have us believe.

Observers find that managerial behaviour actually has five attributes that differ greatly from the classical description. First, managers perform a great deal of work at an unrelenting pace—studies have found that managers engage in more than 600 different activities each day, with no break in their pace. Second, managerial activities are fragmented; most activities last for less than nine minutes, and only 10 percent of the activities exceed one hour in duration. Third, managers prefer current, specific, and ad hoc information (printed information often will be too old). Fourth, they prefer oral forms of communication to written forms because oral media provide greater flexibility, require less effort, and bring a faster response. Fifth, managers give high priority to maintaining a diverse and complex web of contacts that acts as an informal information system and helps them execute their personal agendas and short- and long-term goals.

Analyzing managers' day-to-day behaviour, Mintzberg found that it could be classified into 10 managerial roles. **Managerial roles** are expectations of the activities that managers should perform in an organization. Mintzberg found that these managerial roles fell into three categories: interpersonal, informational, and decisional.

Interpersonal Roles   Managers act as figureheads for the organization when they represent their companies to the outside world and perform symbolic duties, such as giving out employee awards. Managers act as leaders, attempting to motivate, counsel, and support subordinates. Managers also act as liaisons between various organizational levels; within each of these levels, they serve as liaisons among the members of the management team. Managers provide time and favours, which they expect to be returned. With all of these activities managers fulfill their **interpersonal role.**

Informational Roles   In their **informational role,** managers act as the nerve centres of their organizations, receiving the most concrete, up-to-date information and redistributing it to those who need to be aware of it. Managers are therefore information disseminators and spokespersons for their organizations.

Decisional Roles   Managers make decisions. In their **decisional role,** they act as entrepreneurs by initiating new kinds of activities; they handle disturbances arising in the organization; they allocate resources to staff members who need them; and they negotiate conflicts and mediate between conflicting groups.

Table 14-2, based on Mintzberg's role classifications, is one look at where systems can and cannot help managers. The table shows that information systems do not yet contribute

Managerial roles
Interpersonal role
Informational role
Decisional role

TABLE 14-2   Managerial roles and supporting information systems.

Role	Behaviour	Support Systems
Interpersonal Roles		
Figurehead		None exist
Leader	Interpersonal	None exist
Liaison		Electronic communication systems
Informational Roles		
Nerve centre		Management information systems, ESS
Disseminator	Information	Mail, office systems
Spokesperson	processing	Office and professional systems, workstations
Decisional Roles		
Entrepreneur	Decision	None exist
Disturbance handler	making	None exist
Resource allocator		DSS systems
Negotiator		None exist

Sources: Kenneth C. Laudon and Jane P. Laudon; and Mintzberg, 1971.

TABLE 14-3 Information quality dimensions.

QUALITY DIMENSION	DESCRIPTION
Accuracy	Do the data represent reality?
Integrity	Are the structure of data and relationships among the entities and attributes consistent?
Consistency	Are data elements consistently defined?
Completeness	Are all the necessary data present?
Validity	Do data values fall within defined ranges?
Timeliness	Are data available when needed?
Accessibility	Are the data accessible, comprehensible, and usable?

to some important areas of management life although generally e-mail can help with all 10 of Mintzberg's roles.

Real-World Decision Making We now see that information systems are not helpful for all managerial roles. And in those managerial roles where information systems might improve decisions, investments in information technology do not always produce positive results. There are three main reasons: information quality, management filters, and organizational culture (see Chapter 3).

Information Quality High-quality decisions require high-quality information. Table 14-3 describes information quality dimensions that affect the quality of decisions. If the output of information systems does not meet these quality criteria, decision making will suffer. Chapter 6 has shown that corporate databases and files have varying levels of inaccuracy and incompleteness, which in turn will degrade the quality of decision making.

Management Filters Even with timely, accurate information, some managers make bad decisions. Managers (like all human beings) absorb information through a series of filters to make sense of the world around them. Managers have selective attention, focus on certain kinds of problems and solutions, and have a variety of biases that reject information that does not conform to their prior conceptions.

For instance, Wall Street firms such as Bear Stearns and Lehman Brothers imploded in 2008 because they underestimated the risk of their investments in complex mortgage securities, many of which were based on subprime loans that were more likely to default. The computer models they and other financial institutions used to manage risk were based on overly optimistic assumptions and overly simplistic data about what might go wrong. Management wanted to make sure that their firms' capital was not all tied up as a cushion against defaults from risky investments, preventing them from investing it to generate profits. So the designers of these risk management systems were encouraged to measure risks in a way that did not pick them all up. Some trading desks also oversimplified the information maintained about the mortgage securities to make them appear as simple bonds with higher ratings than were warranted by their underlying components (Hansell, 2008).

Organizational Culture Organizations are bureaucracies with limited capabilities and competencies for acting decisively. When environments change and businesses need to adopt new business models to survive, strong forces within organizations resist making decisions calling for major change. Decisions taken by a firm often represent a balancing of the firm's various interest groups rather than the best solution to the problem.

Studies of business restructuring find that firms tend to ignore poor performance until threatened by outside takeovers, and they systematically blame poor performance on external forces beyond their control such as economic conditions (the economy), foreign competition, and rising prices, rather than blaming senior or middle management for poor business judgment (John, Lang, Netter, et al., 1992).

14.2   Systems for Decision Support

There are four kinds of systems for supporting the different levels and types of decisions we have just described. We introduced some of these systems in Chapter 2. *Management information systems (MIS)* provide routine reports and summaries of transaction-level data to middle- and operational-level managers to provide answers to structured and semistructured decision problems. *Decision-support systems (DSS)* provide analytical models or tools for analyzing large quantities of data for middle managers who face semistructured decision situations. *Executive support systems (ESS)* are systems that provide senior management, making primarily unstructured decisions, with external information (news, stock analyses, and industry trends) and high-level summaries of firm performance.

In this chapter, you will also learn about systems for supporting decision-makers working as a group. **Group decision-support systems (GDSS)** are specialized systems that provide a group electronic environment in which managers and teams are able to collectively make decisions and design solutions for unstructured and semistructured problems.

Management Information Systems (MIS)

MIS, which we introduced in Chapter 2, help managers monitor and control the business by providing information on the firm's performance. They typically produce fixed, regularly scheduled reports based on data extracted and summarized from the firm's underlying transaction processing systems (TPS). Sometimes, MIS reports are exception reports, highlighting only exceptional conditions, such as when the sales quotas for a specific territory fall below an anticipated level or employees have exceeded their spending limits in a dental care plan. Today, many of these reports are available online through an intranet, and more MIS reports are generated on demand. Table 14-4 provides some examples of MIS applications.

Decision-Support Systems (DSS)

While MIS primarily address structured problems, DSS support semistructured and unstructured problem analysis. The earliest DSS were heavily model-driven, using some type of model to perform "what-if" and other kinds of analyses. Their analysis capabilities were based on a strong theory or model combined with a good user interface that made the system easy to use. The voyage-estimating DSS and Air Canada maintenance system described in Chapter 2 are examples of model-driven DSS.

The Window on Management describes another model-driven DSS. In this particular case, the system did not perform as well as expected because of the assumptions driving the model and user efforts to circumvent the system. As you read this case, try to identify the problem airlines face, what alternative solutions might be available to management, and how well the chosen solution worked for this one airline.

Some contemporary DSS are **data-driven,** using online analytical processing (OLAP), and data mining to analyze large pools of data. The business intelligence applications

Group decision-support systems (GDSS)

Data-driven

TABLE 14-4   Examples of MIS applications.

COMPANY	MIS APPLICATION
Cartier Kitchens	Brampton, Ontario firm that uses an MIS system to generate a report every morning on sales until they are completed, flagging any service issues or other reasons for incomplete installations.
Shoppers Drug Mart	Healthwatch MIS contains the pharmaceutical profiles of all the patients and informs the pharmacist who carries out the ordinance of any allergic reaction or possible interaction.
Environment Canada	National Enforcement Management Information System and Intelligence System allows tracking and management of pollution and wildlife enforcement activities and actions relating to legislation enforced by Environment Canada.
Taco Bel	Total Automation of Company Operations (TACO) system provides information on food, labour, and period-to-date costs for each restaurant.

FIGURE 14-3   Overview of a decision-support system.

The main components of the DSS are the DSS database, the user interface, and the DSS software system. The DSS database may be a small database residing on a PC or a large data warehouse.

described in Chapter 6 are examples of these data-driven DSS, as are the spreadsheet pivot table applications we describe in this section. Data-driven DSS support decision making by enabling users to extract useful information that was previously buried in large quantities of data. The Window on Technology on page 442 provides an example.

Components of DSS Figure 14-3 illustrates the components of a DSS. They include a database of data used for query and analysis; a software system with models, data mining, and other analytical tools; and a user interface.

The **DSS database** is a collection of current or historical data from a number of applications or groups. It may be a small database residing on a PC that contains a subset of corporate data that has been downloaded and possibly combined with external data. Alternatively, the DSS database may be a massive data warehouse that is continuously updated by major corporate TPS (including enterprise applications) and data generated by Web site transactions. The data in DSS databases are generally extracts or copies of production databases so that using the DSS does not interfere with critical operational systems.

DSS database

Too Many Bumped Fliers: Why?

In a seemingly simpler and less hectic time, overbooked flights presented an opportunity. Frequent travellers regularly and eagerly chose to give up their seats and delay their departures by a few hours in exchange for rewards such as a voucher for a free ticket.

Today, fewer people are volunteering to give up their seats for a flight because there are fewer and fewer seats to be bumped to. Airlines are struggling to stay in business and look to save costs wherever possible. They are scheduling fewer flights and those flights are more crowded. Instead of delaying his or her trip by a few hours, a passenger who accepts a voucher for being bumped may have to wait several days before a seat becomes available on another flight. And passengers are being bumped from flights involuntarily more often.

Airlines routinely overbook flights to compensate for the millions of no-shows who cut into expected revenue. The purpose of overbooking is not to leave passengers without a seat, but to come as close as possible to filling every seat on every flight. The revenue lost from an empty seat is much greater than the costs of compensating a bumped passenger. Airlines are much closer today to filling every seat on flights than at any point in their history. The problem is, the most popular routes often sell out, so bumped passengers may be stranded for days.

The airlines do not approach overbooking haphazardly. They employ young, sharp minds with backgrounds in math and economics as analysts. The analysts use computer modelling to predict how many passengers will fail to show up for a flight. They recommend overbooking based on the numbers generated by the software.

The software used by US Airways, for example, analyzes the historical record of no-shows on flights and looks at the rate at every fare level available. The lowest-priced fares are generally nonrefundable, and passengers at those fare levels tend to carry their reservations through. Business travellers with the high-priced fares no-show more often. The software examines the fares people are booking on each upcoming flight and takes other data into account, such as the rate of no-shows on flights originating from certain geographic regions. Analysts then predict the number of no-shows on a particular flight, based on which fares passengers have booked, and overbook the flight accordingly.

Of course, the analysts do not always guess correctly. And their efforts may be hampered by a number of factors. Ticket agents report that faulty computer algorithms result in miscalculations. Changes in weather can introduce unanticipated weight restrictions. Sometimes a smaller plane is substituted for the scheduled plane. All of these circumstances result in fewer seats being available for the same number of passengers, which might have been set too high already.

Regardless of how much support the analysts have from airline management, gate attendants complain because they are the ones who receive the brunt of overbooked passengers' wrath. Attendants have been known to call in sick to avoid dealing with the havoc caused by overbooked flights.

Some gate attendants have gone as far as creating phony reservations, sometimes in the names of airline executives or cartoon characters, such as Mickey Mouse, in an effort to stop analysts from overbooking. This tactic may save the attendants some grief in the short term, but their actions often come back to haunt them. The modelling software counts the phony reservations as no-shows, which leads the analysts to overbook the flight even more the next time. Thomas Trenga, vice president for revenue management at US Airways, refers to this game of chicken as "the death spiral." US Airways discourages the practice of entering phony reservations.

With fewer passengers volunteering to accept vouchers, tensions often escalate. The number of passengers bumped involuntarily in 2006 rose 23 percent from the previous year and has continued to rise. The encouraging statistic is that only 676 408 of the 555 million people who flew in 2006 were bumped, voluntarily or involuntarily.

W. Douglas Parker, CEO of US Airways, said that airlines have to overbook their flights as long as they allow passengers to no-show without penalty. US Airways has a no-show rate of between 7 and 8 percent and claimed that overbooking contributed to at least $1.2 billion of its 2006 revenue of $14 billion. With a profit of only $371 million, that extra revenue was critical to the survival of the business. Some airlines, such as JetBlue, have avoided the overbooking controversy by offering only nonrefundable tickets. No-shows cannot reclaim the price of their tickets. Business travellers often buy the most expensive seats, but also want the flexibility of refundable tickets, so JetBlue is considering a change in its policy. WestJet, on the other hand, claims that it does not overbook, while Air Canada does in fact bump passengers when necessary, offering passengers not only eventual travel to their destination but also rewards from Aeroplan miles to discounts on future tickets.

The airlines are supposed to hold their analysts accountable for their work, but they are rarely subject to critical review. Some analysts make an effort to accommodate the wishes of the airport workers by finding a compromise in the overbooking rate. Unfortunately, analysts often leave their jobs for new challenges once they become proficient at overbooking.

To Think About

1. Is the decision support system being used by airlines to overbook flights working well? Answer from the perspective of the airlines and from the perspective of customers.

2. What is the impact on the airlines if they are bumping too many passengers?

3. What are the inputs, processes, and outputs of this DSS?

4. What people, organization, and technology factors are responsible for excessive bumping problems?

5. How much of this is a "people" problem? Explain your answer.

MIS in Action

Visit the Web sites for US Airways, JetBlue, and Air Canada. Search the sites to answer the following questions:

1. What is the policy of each of these airlines for dealing with involuntary refunds (overbookings)? (*Hint:* These matters are often covered in the Contract of Carriage.)

2. In your opinion, which airline has the best policy? What makes this policy better than the others?

3. How are each of these policies intended to benefit customers? How do they benefit the airlines?

Sources: Dean Foust and Justin Bachman, "You Think Flying Is Bad Now . . . ," *BusinessWeek*, May 28, 2008; "The Unfriendly Skies," *USA Today*, June 4, 2008; Jeff Bailey, "Bumped Fliers and Plan B," *The New York Times*, May 30, 2007; and Alice LaPlante, "Travel Problems? Blame Technology," *InformationWeek.com*, June 11, 2007; Chris Sorenson, "Air Canada Warned Against Bumping Passengers," *The Toronto Star*, December 20, 2007.

The DSS user interface permits easy interaction between users of the system and the DSS software tools. Many DSS today have Web interfaces to take advantage of graphical displays, interactivity, and ease of use.

The **DSS software system** contains the software tools that are used for data analysis. It may contain various OLAP tools, data mining tools, or a collection of mathematical and analytical models that are accessible to the DSS user. A **model** is an abstract representation that illustrates the components or relationships of a phenomenon. A model may be a physical model (such as a model airplane), a mathematical model (such as an equation), or a verbal model (such as a description of a procedure for writing an order).

DSS software system
Model

WINDOW ON TECHNOLOGY

Hospital Credits Business Intelligence with Improving Patient Care

Since 1985, Credit Valley Hospital (CVH) has given patients access to leading-edge medical research, programs, and treatment in Mississauga, Ontario. CVH delivers community health care services to more than 24 000 inpatients, 407 000 outpatients and 70 000 emergency room visitors annually. CVH employs more than 2100 including almost 250 doctors who have privileges to practise there.

Ontario's health care system is under increasing pressure to show value for money. The provincial government recently introduced a new Healthcare Accountability Agreement to ensure that mutual expectations are clear and accountable to the taxpaying public; since the government furnishes most hospital funding within Ontario, showing accountability, that is, value for funding, is critical. All publicly funded hospitals like CVH are mandated to maintain rigorous financial, quality, and performance measurements concerning service levels.

CVH wanted to exceed the new provincial requirements. According to Dan Germain, chief financial and information officer at CVH, to promote greater transparency and accountability, CVH needed a more cost-effective method to track and monitor medical information.

"We're faced with a health care system that is under intense pressure to meet regulatory requirements and patient needs. We want to track information accurately while ensuring that our resources are being utilized effectively. Our goal is to use performance management tools to access information quickly and, ultimately, to deliver patient service better," says Germain.

For example, the hospital wanted to move from the use of white boards and manual lists and more effectively manage its clinical and financial databases. The challenge was that tracking metrics and measuring performance management indicators involved e-mailing numerous standalone documents and spreadsheets across the organization—a cumbersome and potentially error-prone process that was creating concerns about data accuracy and consistency.

"We've recently committed to a series of performance measurement and business intelligence metrics and needed a solution that enabled us to monitor the metrics on an ongoing basis," says Germain. "The new tool has to meet our analytical

needs on both the regulatory and accountability side, and increase our operational efficiency as well."

CVH worked with a Microsoft Gold Certified Partner, Systemgroup Inc., to implement a new business intelligence (BI) solution. After reviewing several options, including tools from Cognos and SAS, Credit Valley decided on Microsoft Office PerformancePoint Server 2007.

PerformancePoint Server 2007 is an integrated performance management application that permits decision makers to monitor, analyze, and plan their operations and to drive accountability and insight into organizational data. The tool, which is helping CVH improve both its processes and its financial performance, is attractive because it provides a user experience similar to the familiar Microsoft Office system.

"The Credit Valley Hospital is one of the most cost-efficient hospitals in the Greater Toronto Area. We have adopted a strategy to focus on a single vendor stack as much as possible to economize our efficiency and cost structure," says Jamie Bowie, director of Information Systems & Telecommunications at CVH. "We had already concentrated on Microsoft and saw an opportunity to continue that strategy and bring in PerformancePoint Server 2007 to ensure consistent measurement of targets and results throughout the hospital."

The solution also integrates with CVH's data warehouse, which is also based on a Microsoft product, Microsoft SQL Server® 2005 Enterprise Edition, and houses both financial and clinical data. Using a single integrated executive dashboard in PerformancePoint, the hospital can now track and monitor KPIs of approximately 100 operational measurements within the hospital and can also have additional drill-down capabilities.

"The ability to drill down and access data in the system to get information on an ad hoc basis for reporting purposes is extremely critical for Credit Valley. Healthcare providers can now conduct more proactive planning based on clinical data that they're getting on a daily basis. As well, they now have access to trending analysis and analytics that tells them who is getting sick with what, and breaks down data by demographics. This is crucial in delivering enhanced and cost-effective patient care," says Tim Yeomans, Director of Client Services at Systemgroup Inc.

With the help of PerformancePoint Server 2007, CVH is now equipped with a Business Intelligence (BI) platform that provides a better way to access and manage performance data. By using scorecards and KPIs to drive accountability across the organization, CVH has transformed into a dynamic, metrics-based organization—improving its ability to efficiently manage resources and track patient flow across the organization.

Credit Valley is now better positioned to ensure consistent measurement of targets and results throughout the organization by setting targets at the enterprise level. The ability to track and understand patient flow has dramatically improved, allowing the hospital to boost overall accountability by more effectively managing resources.

The organization has also been able to improve corporate governance and drive deeper accountability throughout the various levels of the organization. As a result, the hospital now has more confidence in the quality of its data and in its ability to analyze it in real time.

Health care professionals can easily track and monitor medical and patient data and make better sense of what the data analysis is telling them. They can also take advantage of advanced visualization capabilities to help spot trends and opportunities, allowing for better business planning.

"In health care, despite having sources of disparate and duplicate information, we have to have the right information at the right time. The white board and manual lists are gone – patient information is now quickly and easily accessible from anywhere in the department. The new Microsoft-based BI solution is really helping us deliver a higher standard for the patients we serve," says Germain.

To Think About

1. What problems did CVH face with its data tracking and reporting? How did they affect decision making and business performance?

2. What did the hospital do to remedy those problems?

3. Was the business intelligence tool an appropriate selection for CVH? Why or why not?

4. Has improved reporting permitted the hospital to be more accountable to the provincial government? Explain your answer.

MIS in Action

Explore the PerformancePoint Server Web site, and then answer the following questions:

1. Describe the capabilities of PerformancePoint software. List the capabilities that would be most useful for supporting decisions for CVH. Explain how the software would help CVH's employees with these decisions.

2. Interestingly, since this was written, PerformancePoint Server 2007 will no longer be available for purchase. When the next version of Microsoft Office is released, the Monitoring and Analytics capabilities will be included with SharePoint Server Enterprise. Microsoft will, however, continue to support PerformancePoint. What do you think the response to Microsoft's discontinuation of this package will be from its customers?

Sources: "Credit Valley Hospital: Hospital Delivers Better Business Insight with PerformancePoint Server 2007," **www.microsoft.com/canada/casestudies/cvh052008.mspx** (accessed October 7, 2009); and **http://office.microsoft.com/en-us/performancepoint/FX101680481033.aspx** (accessed October 7, 2009).

Statistical modelling helps establish relationships, such as relating product sales to differences in age, income, or other factors between communities. Optimization models determine optimal resource allocation to maximize or minimize specified variables, such as cost or time. A classic use of optimization models is to determine the proper mix of products within a given market to maximize profits.

Forecasting models are often used to forecast sales. The user of this type of model might supply a range of historical data to project future conditions and the sales that might result from those conditions. The decision maker could vary those future conditions (entering, for example, a rise in raw materials costs or the entry of a new, low-priced competitor in the market) to determine how new conditions might affect sales.

Sensitivity analysis models ask "what-if" questions repeatedly to determine the impact on outcomes of changes in one or more factors. *What-if analysis*—working forward from known or assumed conditions—allows the user to vary certain values to test results to better predict outcomes if changes occur in those values. What happens if we raise product price by 5 percent or increase the advertising budget by $100 000? What happens if we keep the price and advertising budgets the same? Desktop spreadsheet software, such as Microsoft Excel, is often used for this purpose (see Figure 14-4). Backward-sensitivity analysis software helps decision makers with goal seeking. If I want to sell 1 million product units next year, how much must I reduce the price of the product?

Sensitivity analysis

FIGURE 14-4 Sensitivity analysis.

Total fixed costs	19000					
Variable cost per unit	3					
Average sales price	17					
Contribution margin	14					
Break-even point	1357					
			Variable Cost per Unit			
Sales	1357	2	3	4	5	6
Price	14	1583	1727	1900	2111	2375
	15	1462	1583	1727	1900	2111
	16	1357	1462	1583	1727	1900
	17	1267	1357	1462	1583	1727
	18	1188	1267	1357	1462	1583

This table displays the results of a sensitivity analysis of the effect of changing the sales price of a necktie and the cost per unit on the product's break-even point. It answers the question, "What happens to the break-even point if the sales price and the cost to make each unit increase or decrease?"

Using Spreadsheet Pivot Tables to Support Decision Making

Managers also use spreadsheets to identify and understand patterns in business information. For instance, let us a take a look at one day's worth of transactions at an online firm Online Management Training Associations Inc. (OMTA Inc.), which sells online management training videos and books to corporations and individuals who want to improve their management techniques. On a single day, the firm experienced 517 order transactions. Figure 14-5 shows the first 25 records of transactions produced at the firm's Web site on that day. The names of customers and other identifiers have been removed from this list.

You might think of this list as a database composed of transaction records (the rows). The fields (column headings) for each customer record are customer ID, region of purchase, payment method, source of contact (e-mail versus Web banner ad), amount of purchase, the product purchased (either online training or a book), and time of day (in 24-hour time).

FIGURE 14-5 Sample list of transactions for Online Management Training Associations Inc.

This list shows a portion of the order transactions for Online Management Training Associations Inc. (OMTA Inc.) on October 28, 2008.

There is a great deal of valuable information in this transaction list that might help managers answer important questions and make important decisions:

- Where do most of our customers come from? The answer might tell managers where to spend more marketing resources or to initiate new marketing efforts.

- Are there regional differences in the sources of our customers? Perhaps in some regions, e-mail is the most effective marketing tool, while in other regions, Web banner ads are more effective. The answer to this more complicated question might help managers develop a regional marketing strategy.

- Where are the average purchases higher? The answer might tell managers where to focus marketing and sales resources, or pitch different messages to different regions.

- What form of payment is the most common? The answer might be used to emphasize in advertising the most preferred means of payment.

- Are there any times of day when purchases are most common? Do people buy products while at work (likely during the day) or at home (likely in the evening)?

- Are there regional differences in the average purchase? If one region is much more lucrative, managers could focus their marketing and advertising resources on that region.

Notice that these questions often involve multiple dimensions: region and average purchase; time of day and average purchase; payment type and average purchase; and region, source of customer, and purchase. Also, some of the dimensions are categorical, such as payment type, region, and source. If the list were small, you might simply inspect the list and find patterns in the data. But this is impossible when you have a list of more than 500 transactions.

Fortunately, the spreadsheet pivot table provides a powerful tool for answering such questions using large data sets. A **pivot table** is a table that displays two or more dimensions of data in a convenient format. Microsoft Excel's PivotTable capability makes it easy to analyze lists and databases by automatically extracting, organizing, and summarizing the data.

For instance, let us take the first question, "Where do our customers come from?" We'll start with region and ask the question, "How many customers come from each region?" To find the answer using Excel 2007, you would create a pivot table by selecting the range of data, the fields you want to analyze, and a location for the PivotTable report, as illustrated in Figure 14-6. The PivotTable report shows most of our customers come from the western region.

Pivot table

FIGURE 14-6   A pivot table that determines the regional distribution of customers.

This pivot table report was created using Excel 2007 to quickly produce a table showing the relationship between region and number of customers.

FIGURE 14-7   A pivot table that examines customer regional distribution and advertising source.

In this pivot table, we are able to examine where customers come from in terms of region and advertising source. It appears nearly 30 percent of the customers respond to e-mail campaigns, and there are some regional variations.

Does the source of the customer make a difference in addition to region? We have two sources of customers: e-mail campaigns and online banner advertising. In a few seconds, you will find the answer shown in Figure 14-7. The pivot table shows that Web banner advertising produces most of the customers, and this is true of all the regions.

You can use pivot tables to answer all the questions we have posed about the Online Management Training data. The complete Excel file for these examples is available on the MyMISLab for this chapter. One of the Hands-On MIS Projects for this chapter asks you to find answers to a number of other questions regarding this data file.

Data Visualization and Geographic Information Systems

Data from information systems are made easier for users to digest and act on by using graphics, charts, tables, maps, digital images, three-dimensional presentations, animations, and other data visualization technologies. By presenting data in graphical form, **data visualization** tools help users see patterns and relationships in large amounts of data that would be difficult to discern if the data were presented as traditional lists of text. Some data visualization tools are interactive, enabling users to manipulate data and see the graphical displays change in response to the changes they make.

Geographic information systems (GIS) are a special category of DSS that use data visualization technology to analyze and display data for planning and decision making in the form of digitized maps. The software assembles, stores, manipulates, and displays geographically referenced information, tying data to points, lines, and areas on a map (see Figure 14-8). GIS have modelling capabilities, enabling managers to change data and automatically revise business scenarios to find better solutions.

GIS support decisions that require knowledge about the geographic distribution of people or other resources. For example, GIS might be used to help provincial and municipal governments calculate emergency response times to natural disasters, to help retail chains identify profitable new store locations, or to help banks identify the best locations for installing new branches or ATMs.

Data visualization
Geographic information systems (GIS)

FIGURE 14-8   A GIS can help track the movement of bird and other animal populations.

Canadian Wildlife Service biologist Jim Hawkings uses GIS to make sense of decades of data related to the movements of birds and animals in the Yukon and their use of habitat. This GIS-generated map shows where bands were recovered from ducks banded in the Yukon. Some were recovered in Alaska, and others on the major flyways heading south through the heart of North America.

Source: "Your Yukon," www.taiga.net/yourYukon/index.html.

Web-Based Customer Decision-Support Systems

The growth of electronic commerce has encouraged many companies to develop DSS for customers that use Web information resources and capabilities for interactivity and personalization to help users select products and services. People are now using more information from multiple sources to make purchasing decisions (such as purchasing a car or computer) before they interact with the product or sales staff. For instance, nearly all automobile companies use customer decision-support systems that allow Web site visitors to configure their desired car. **Customer decision-support systems (CDSS)** support the decision-making process of an existing or potential customer.

People interested in purchasing a product or service are able to use Internet search engines, intelligent agents, online catalogues, Web directories, newsgroup discussions, e-mail, and other tools to help them locate the information they need to help with their decisions. Companies have developed specific customer Web sites where all the information, models, or other analytical tools for evaluating alternatives are concentrated in one location.

Customer decision-support systems (CDSS)

Web-based DSS have become especially popular in financial services because so many people are trying to manage their own assets and retirement savings. For example, RiskGrades.com, a Web site run by RiskMetrics Group, lets users input all their stock, bond, and mutual fund holdings to determine how much their portfolios might decline under various conditions. Users see how the addition or subtraction of a holding might affect overall portfolio volatility and risk.

Group Decision-Support Systems (GDSS)

The DSS we have just described focus primarily on individual decision making. However, so much work is accomplished in groups within firms that a special category of systems called group decision-support systems (GDSS) has been developed to support group and organizational decision making.

A GDSS is an interactive computer-based system for facilitating the solution of unstructured problems by a set of decision makers working together as a group in the same location or in different locations. Groupware and Web-based tools for videoconferencing and electronic meetings described earlier in this text support some group decision processes, but their focus is primarily on communication. GDSS, however, provide tools and technologies geared explicitly toward group decision making.

GDSS-guided meetings take place in conference rooms with special hardware and software tools to facilitate group decision making. The hardware includes computer and networking equipment, overhead projectors, and display screens. Special electronic meeting software collects, documents, ranks, edits, and stores the ideas offered in a decision-making meeting. The more elaborate GDSS use a professional facilitator and support staff. The facilitator selects the software tools and helps organize and run the meeting.

A sophisticated GDSS provides each attendee with a dedicated desktop computer under that person's individual control. No one will be able to see what the participants do on their computers until those participants are ready to share information. Their input is transmitted over a network to a central server that stores information generated by the meeting and makes it available to all on the meeting network. Data can also be projected on a large screen in the meeting room.

GDSS make it possible to increase meeting size while at the same time increasing productivity because individuals contribute simultaneously rather than one at a time. A GDSS promotes a collaborative atmosphere by guaranteeing contributors' anonymity so that attendees focus on evaluating the ideas themselves without fear of personally being criticized or of having their ideas rejected based on who the contributor is. GDSS software tools follow structured methods for organizing and evaluating ideas and for preserving the results of meetings, enabling non-attendees to locate needed information after the meeting. GDSS effectiveness depends on the nature of the problem and the group and on how well a meeting is planned and conducted.

14.3   Executive Support Systems (ESS) and the Balanced Scorecard Framework

The purpose of *executive support systems (ESS)*, introduced in Chapter 2, is to help managers focus on the really important performance information that affect the overall profitability and success of the firm. There are two parts to developing ESS. First, you will need a methodology for understanding exactly what is "the really important performance information" for a specific firm, and second, you will need to develop systems capable of delivering this information to the right people in a timely fashion.

Currently, the leading methodology for understanding the really important information needed by a firm's executives is called the **balanced scorecard method** (Kaplan and Norton, 1992). The balanced scorecard is a framework for operationalizing a firm's strategic plan by focusing on measurable outcomes on four dimensions of firm performance: financial,

Balanced scorecard method

FIGURE 14-9   The balanced scorecard framework.

In the balanced scorecard framework, the firm's strategic objectives are operationalized along four dimensions: financial, business process, customer, and learning and growth. Each dimension is measured using several key performance indicators (KPIs).

business process, customer, and learning and growth (Figure 14-9). Performance on each dimension is measured using **key performance indicators (KPIs),** which are the measures proposed by senior management for understanding how well the firm is performing along any given dimension. For instance, one key indicator of how well an online retail firm is meeting its customer performance objectives is the average length of time required to deliver a package to a consumer. If your firm is a bank, one KPI of business process performance is the length of time required to perform a basic function like creating a new customer account.

The balanced scorecard framework is thought to be "balanced" because it causes managers to focus on more than just financial performance. In this view, financial performance is past history—the result of past actions—and managers should focus on the things they are able to influence today, such as business process efficiency, customer satisfaction, and employee training.

Once a scorecard is developed by consultants and senior executives, the next step is automating a flow of information to executives and other managers for each of the key performance indicators. There are literally hundreds of consulting and software firms that offer these capabilities, which are described below. Once these systems are implemented, they are typically referred to as "executive support systems."

The Role of Executive Support Systems in the Firm

Use of ESS has migrated down several organizational levels so that the executive and subordinates are able to look at the same data in the same way. Today's systems try to avoid the problem of data overload by filtering data and presenting it in graphical or dashboard format. ESS have the ability to **drill down**, moving from a piece of summary data to lower and lower levels of detail. The ability to drill down is useful not only to senior executives but also to employees at lower levels of the firm who need to analyze data. OLAP tools for analyzing large databases provide this capability.

A major challenge of executive support systems has been to integrate data from systems designed for very different purposes so that senior executives are able to review organizational performance from an enterprise-wide perspective. Most ESS now rely on data provided by the firm's existing enterprise applications (enterprise resource planning, supply chain management, and customer relationship management) rather than entirely new information flows and systems.

Key performance indicators (KPIs)
Drill down

While the balanced scorecard framework focuses on internal measures of performance, executives also need a wide range of external data, from current stock market news to competitor information, industry trends, and even projected legislative action. Through their ESS, many managers have access to news services, financial market databases, economic information, and whatever other external data they may require.

Contemporary ESS include tools for modelling and analysis. With only a minimum of experience, most managers are able to use these tools to create graphic comparisons of data by time, region, product, price range, and so on. (While DSS use such tools primarily for modelling and analysis in a fairly narrow range of decision situations, ESS use them primarily to provide status information about organizational performance.)

Business Value of Executive Support Systems

Much of the value of ESS is found in their flexibility and their ability to analyze, compare, and highlight trends. The easy use of graphics enables the user to look at more data in less time with greater clarity and insight than paper-based systems provide. Executives are using ESS to monitor key performance indicators for the entire firm and to measure firm performance against changes in the external environment. The timeliness and availability of the data result in needed actions being identified and carried out earlier than previously possible. Problems will be handled before they become too damaging, and opportunities will be identified earlier. These systems thus help businesses move toward a "sense-and-respond" strategy.

Well-designed ESS dramatically improve management performance and increase upper management's span of control. Immediate access to so much data increases executives' ability to monitor activities of lower units reporting to them. That very monitoring ability enables decision making to be decentralized and to take place at lower operating levels. Executives are often willing to push decision making further down into the organization as long as they are assured that all is going well. Alternatively, executive support systems based on enterprise-wide data potentially increase management centralization, enabling senior executives to monitor the performance of subordinates across the company and to take appropriate action when conditions change.

To illustrate the different ways in which ESS enhance decision making, we now describe important types of ESS applications for gathering business intelligence and monitoring corporate performance.

National Life: ESS for Business Intelligence Headquartered in Toronto, Canada, National Life markets life insurance, health insurance, and retirement/investment products to individuals and groups. The company has more than 370 employees in Toronto and its regional offices. National Life uses an executive information system based on Information Builders' WebFOCUS, which allows senior managers to access information from corporate databases through a Web interface. The system provides statistical reporting and the ability to drill down into current sales information, which is organized to show premium dollars by salesperson. Authorized users are able to drill down into these data to see the product, agent, and client for each sale. They can examine the data many different ways—by region, by product, and by broker, accessing data for monthly, quarterly, and annual time periods (Information Builders, 2005).

Rohm and Haas and Pharmacia Corporation: Monitoring Corporate Performance with Digital Dashboards and Balanced Scorecard Systems ESS are increasingly configured to summarize and report on key performance indicators for senior management in the form of a digital dashboard or "executive dashboard." The dashboard displays on a single screen all of the critical measurements for piloting a company, similar to the cockpit of an airplane or an automobile dashboard. The dashboard presents key performance indicators as graphs and charts in a Web browser format, providing a one-page overview of all the critical measurements necessary to make key executive decisions.

Rohm and Haas, a chemical and specialty materials firm headquartered in Philadelphia, has 13 different business units, each operating independently and using more than 300 disparate information systems. To obtain a company-wide overview of performance, it implemented a series of Web-based dashboards developed with SAP tools atop an enterprise system and enterprise data warehouse.

Management defined a handful of key performance indicators to provide high-level measurements of the business and had the information delivered on dashboards. The KPIs may be broken down into their components. For example, a gross profit KPI can be broken down into figures for sales and cost of sales. A manager is able to drill down further to see that the cost of sales figures are based on manufacturing and raw materials costs. If raw materials costs appear to be problematic, the system allows the manager to drill down further to identify the costs of individual raw materials.

The dashboards are customized for multiple layers of management. An Executive Dashboard is geared toward the CEO, CFO, and other senior managers and consists of Business Financials, which include all of the major KPIs. The Pulse is aimed at a wider range of users and displays only three KPIs: sales, standard gross profit, and volume. The Reporting and Analysis Toolkit provides a set of analysis tools that allow managers and business analysts to drill down into specifics to answer questions such as "Why are raw materials costs higher than expected?" The Analysis Accelerator focuses on standard sales and gross-profit analyses, allowing users to drill down to the individual customer level. The most popular dashboard is the daily sales report against Plan.

Rohm and Haas claims that the dashboards have made its management decision making more proactive. Managers are able to quickly anticipate problems before they erupt and take corrective action. For example, even though the cost of raw materials based on petrochemicals has escalated in recent years, the company has been able to maintain a high level of profitability by working out pricing changes and modifying its sales techniques (Maxcer, 2007).

Pharmacia Corporation, a global pharmaceutical firm based in Peapack, New Jersey, uses Oracle's Balanced Scorecard software and a data warehouse to ensure the entire organization is operating in a coordinated manner. Pharmacia spends about $2.5 billion annually on research and development, and the company wanted to make more effective use of the funds allocated for research. The balanced scorecard reports show, for example, how Pharmacia's U.S. or European clinical operations are performing in relation to corporate objectives and other parts of the company. Pharmacia uses the scorecard system to track the attrition rate of new compounds under study, to monitor the number of patents in clinical trials, and to see how funds allocated for research are being spent (Oracle, 2003).

SUMMARY

1. **What are the different types of decisions, and how does the decision-making process work?**

   The different levels in an organization (strategic, management, operational) have different decision-making requirements. Decisions can be structured, semistructured, or unstructured, with structured decisions clustering at the operational level of the organization and unstructured decisions at the strategic level. Decision making can be performed by individuals or groups and includes employees as well as operational, middle, and senior managers. There are four stages in decision making: intelligence, design, choice, and implementation. Systems to support decision making do not always produce better manager and employee decisions that improve firm performance because of problems with information quality, management filters, and organizational culture.

2. **How do information systems support the activities of managers and management decision making?**

   Early classical models of managerial activities stress the functions of planning, organizing, coordinating, deciding, and controlling. Contemporary research looking at the actual behaviour of managers has found that managers' real activities are highly fragmented, variegated, and brief in duration and that managers shy away from making grand, sweeping policy decisions.

   Information technology provides new tools for managers to carry out both their traditional and newer roles, enabling them to monitor, plan, and forecast with more precision and speed than ever before and to respond more rapidly to the changing business environment. Information systems have been most helpful to managers by providing support for their roles in disseminating information, providing liaisons between organizational levels, and allocating resources. However, information systems are less successful at supporting unstructured decisions. Where information systems are useful, information quality, management filters, and organizational culture can degrade decision making.

3. How do decision-support systems (DSS) differ from management information systems (MIS), and how do they provide value to the business?

Management information systems (MIS) provide information on firm performance to help managers monitor and control the business, often in the form of fixed regularly scheduled reports based on data summarized from the firm's transaction processing systems. MIS support structured decisions and some semistructured decisions.

DSS combine data, sophisticated analytical models and tools, and user-friendly software into a single powerful system that can support semistructured or unstructured decision making. The components of a DSS are the DSS database, the user interface, and the DSS software system. There are two kinds of DSS: model-driven DSS and data-driven DSS. DSS can help support decisions for pricing, supply chain management, and customer relationship management as well as modelling alternative business scenarios. DSS targeted toward customers as well as managers are becoming available on the Web. A special category of DSS called geographic information systems (GIS) uses data visualization technology to analyze and display data for planning and decision making with digitized maps.

4. How do executive support systems (ESS) help senior managers make better decisions?

ESS help senior managers with unstructured problems that occur at the strategic level of the firm, providing data from both internal and external sources. ESS help senior executives monitor firm performance, spot problems, identify opportunities, and forecast trends. These systems can filter out extraneous details for high-level overviews, or they can drill down to provide senior managers with detailed transaction data if required. The balanced scorecard is the leading methodology for understanding the most important information needed by a firm's executives.

ESS help senior managers analyze, compare, and highlight trends so that the managers may more easily monitor organizational performance or identify strategic problems and opportunities. They are very useful for environmental scanning, providing business intelligence to help management detect strategic threats or opportunities from the organization's environment. ESS can increase the span of control of senior management, allowing them to oversee more people with fewer resources.

5. What is the role of information systems in helping people working in a group make decisions more efficiently?

Group decision-support systems (GDSS) help people working together in a group arrive at decisions more efficiently. GDSS feature special conference room facilities where participants contribute their ideas using networked computers and software tools for organizing ideas, gathering information, making and setting priorities, and documenting meeting sessions.

Key Terms

Review Questions

1. *What are the different types of decisions, and how does the decision-making process work?*

   • *List and describe the different levels of decision making and decision-making constituencies in organizations. Explain how their decision-making requirements differ.*

   • *Distinguish between an unstructured, semistructured, and structured decision.*

   • *List and describe the stages in decision making.*

2. *How do information systems support the activities of managers and management decision making?*

   • *Compare the descriptions of managerial behaviour in the classical and behavioural models.*

   • *Identify the specific managerial roles that can be supported by information systems.*

3. *How do decision-support systems (DSS) differ from management information systems (MIS), and how do they provide value to the business?*

   • *Distinguish between DSS and MIS.*

   • *Compare a data-driven DSS to a model-driven DSS. Give examples.*

- *Identify and describe the three basic components of a DSS.*
- *Define geographic information system (GIS), and explain how it supports decision making.*
- *Define customer decision-support system, and explain how the Internet can be used for this purpose.*

4. *How do executive support systems (ESS) help senior managers make better decisions?*
   - *Define and describe the capabilities of an ESS.*
   - *Describe how the balanced scorecard helps managers identify important information requirements.*

- *Explain how ESS enhance managerial decision making and provide value for a business.*

5. *What is the role of information systems in helping people working in a group make decisions more efficiently?*
   - *Define group decision-support system (GDSS), and explain how it differs from a DSS.*
   - *Explain how a GDSS works and how it provides value for a business.*

Discussion Questions

1. *As a manager or user of information systems, what would you need to know to participate in the design and use of a DSS or an ESS? Why?*

2. *If businesses used DSS, GDSS, and ESS more widely, would managers and employees make better decisions? Why or why not?*

Collaboration and Teamwork: Designing a University GDSS

With three or four of your classmates, identify several groups in your university that might benefit from a GDSS. Design a GDSS for one of those groups, describing its hardware, software, and people elements. If possible, use Google Sites to post links to Web pages, team communication announcements, and work assignments; to brainstorm; and to work collaboratively on project documents. Try to use Google Docs to develop a presentation of your findings for the class.

 Visit the MyMISLab Web site at **www.pearsoned.ca/mymislab**. This online homework and tutorial system puts you in control of your own learning with study and practice tools directly correlated to this chapter's content.

Learning Track Module

The following Learning Track provides content relevant to topics covered in this chapter:

1. Building and Using Pivot Tables

HANDS-ON MIS Projects

The projects in this section give you hands-on experience analyzing opportunities for DSS, using a spreadsheet pivot table to analyze sales data, and using online retirement planning tools for financial planning.

Management Decision Problems

1. During the 1990s, the Canadian Pacific Railway used a tonnage-based operating model in which freight trains ran only when there was sufficient traffic to justify the expense. This model focused on minimizing the total number of freight trains in service and maximizing the size of each train. However, it did not necessarily use crews, locomotives, and equipment efficiently, and it resulted in inconsistent transit times and delivery schedules. Canadian Pacific

and other railroads were losing business to trucking firms, which offered more flexible deliveries that could be scheduled at the times most convenient for customers. How could a DSS help Canadian Pacific and other railroads compete with trucking firms more effectively?

2. Applebee's is the largest casual dining chain in the world, with 1970 locations throughout North America and nearly 20 other countries worldwide. The menu features beef, chicken, and pork items, as well as burgers, pasta, and seafood. The Applebee's CEO wants to make the restaurants more profitable by developing menus that are tastier and contain more items that customers want and are willing to pay for despite rising costs for gasoline and agricultural products. How might information systems help management implement this strategy? What pieces of data would Applebee's need to collect? What kinds of reports would be useful to help management make decisions on how to improve menus and profitability?

Improving Decision Making: Using Pivot Tables to Analyze Sales Data

Software skills: Pivot tables
Business skills: Analyzing sales data

This project gives you an opportunity to learn how to use Excel's PivotTable functionality to analyze a database or data list. Use the data list for Online Management Training Associations Inc. described earlier in the chapter. This is a list of the sales transactions at OMTA for one day. You can find this spreadsheet file on the MyMISLab for this chapter.

Use Excel's PivotTable to help you answer the following questions:

1. Where are the average purchases higher? The answer might tell managers where to focus marketing and sales resources or pitch different messages to different regions.

2. What form of payment is the most common? The answer might be used to emphasize in advertising the most preferred means of payment.

3. Are there any times of day when purchases are most common? Do people buy products while at work (likely during the day) or at home (likely in the evening)?

4. What is the relationship between region, type of product purchased, and average sales price?

Improving Decision Making: Using a Web-Based DSS for Retirement Planning

Software skills: Internet-based software
Business skills: Financial planning

This project will help develop your skills in using Web-based DSS for financial planning. The Web site for TD Waterhouse (www.tdcanadatrust.com/planning/yrs.jsp) provides Web-based DSS for financial planning and decision making. Use this site to determine how much you need to save to have enough income for your retirement. Assume that you are 50 years old and plan to retire in 16 years. You have one dependant and $100 000 in savings. Your current annual income is $85 000. Your goal is to be able to generate an annual retirement income of $60 000, including all pension benefit payments. Use the Web site to determine how much money you need to save to help you achieve your retirement goal. Then critique the site—its ease of use, its clarity, the value of any conclusions reached, and the extent to which the site helps investors understand their financial needs and the financial markets.

CASE STUDY | Can Decision Support Systems Make Your Health Care Better?

Imagine that you have just been admitted to the hospital with a blood clot in your leg. You are already taking Tagamet for treating ulcers. The hospital prescribes Coumadin to dissolve the clot. You refuse to take the medicine until someone double-checks the prescription to make sure there will be no adverse interaction with your other medication. In the end, you learn that you were correct. The Tagamet interacts adversely with the Coumadin, leading to excess blood thinning and bleeding, and you must stop taking the Tagamet until your blood clot has dissolved.

Or suppose you report to the emergency room of your local hospital because you feel very unwell. At the ER, a nurse or doctor (typically a nurse) assesses you to prioritize where in the roster of patients to place you. How does the nurse know what questions to ask you and which questions to ask as follow-up? What if the nurse is having a bad day and assesses your condition incorrectly? You could be in the middle of a heart attack, or your ulcer could have just perforated, and you might wait hours in Canada's over-strapped medical system to be seen by a physician.

Once I waited in an emergency room for seven-and-a-half hours to be seen for acute abdominal pain; meanwhile, a patient came by ambulance who had only broken a finger (but was immobile otherwise due to having had a stroke several years before, hence the ambulance). Because the other patient came in by ambulance, he went ahead of me in the queue. The doctor who finally saw me told me that I had not been properly "triaged," the term for evaluating and ranking patients in order of severity of medical problem.

Shouldn't there be a system to assist triage nurses in evaluating patients and assigning them their places in the ER queue? It turns out there are such systems in Canada.

It turns out there are several systems available. Even more interesting, in Ottawa, potential ER patients are urged to call a nurse on call for the purpose and describe their symptoms; the "telenurse" then advises the patient on care, such as going to the ER or calling their own physician, or reporting to a clinic the next day (if the call is at night as many are).

Just last year, a computerized cardiac teletriage decision support system was developed and tested at the University of Ottawa Heart Institute. There, nurse coordinators receive more than 1500 calls annually from patients requesting advice for cardiology and cardiac surgery concerns. Until last year, there was no standardized protocol to guide the nurse coordinators, nor did they receive any formal training.

Last year, as part of a masters thesis, a teletriage decision support system was developed and tested at the Heart Institute. Cardiac best-practice algorithms, or "rules of thumb," were programmed into a handheld device to be used by the telenurses. Before the DSS was introduced, the nurses used only a pen and pad of paper while on the phone with the patient. Using the DSS in the test experimental phase, the quality of assessment for each type of cardiac-related scenario improved significantly. It is hoped that a successful triage decision support system can be developed soon to help in Canada's real emergency rooms. The worry of health care professionals is that they will rely too much on the DSS and not enough on their own training as to what questions to ask and what recommendations to make.

However, Canada seems to be moving toward taking more advantage of decision support systems across the realm of health care. For example, children who use prosthetic arms and legs answer a DSS-based questionnaire as to how they use their prostheses. The DSS even uses an animated puffin (PUFI) to offer encouragement, word clarification, and assurance to parents and children that they're "doing great." The DSS then aggregates the data so that clinicians can analyze how well the children are using their prosthetics and whether more training is required in proper

use. More than 12 hospital sites around the world are using this system, five in Canada, three in the United Kingdom, and the rest in Australia, Holland, Sweden, and Slovenia. Children's answers from around the world are added to the database, enabling clinicians to better advise children and parents on how to maximize the functionality of their prostheses.

At Toronto's University Health Network (UHN) made up of Toronto General Hospital, Toronto Western Hospital, and Princess Margaret Hospital, Katherine Henning, head of performance measurement, and project manager Janine Kaye, use a data warehouse to make sense of reams of data from an assortment of databases, including hospital records, pathology, pharmacy, physician order entry, and patient satisfaction. UHN has used a data warehouse since 2000 and has data as old as 1987. "We now have data coming in from as many as 15 transactional systems," says Kaye. "And we have about 40 people accessing that data through an Oracle reporting tool." Henning says that UHN only has about one-third of the data inputs they hope to have in the system. Next to be added to the data warehouse are nursing data and operating room data.

Beverly Delaney, director of administrative informational systems, says, "We use our decision support system (from Eclipsys) for all of our medical records reporting, for financial and performance analysis, for utilization management, for quality indicators, and essentially for any function that needs to look at integrated data. But the challenges we have faced in implementing all that have not been technical. We've rarely had a major technical issue. Most of our challenges have been cultural. . . . We've recently integrated with four other campuses. And most of them have long histories of doing things their own way. In the process, we've found that the ability and willingness of people to standardize their data is the biggest challenge. And they've got to be willing if a decision support tool is to ever be truly useful to everybody."

UHN is in the process of "Webifying" its DSS, to give users faster access to data through the intranet. In doing so, administrators also hope to give users multiple views of the same data, so that they can confirm for themselves what the data show; the various views of the same data should also help to show any inaccuracies in the data, leading to correcting data and to a better overall DSS.

In 2003 in Montreal, physicians begin using Pocket PCs with high-speed wireless network cards to access patient charts and send drug prescriptions electronically to pharmacies, where the prescriptions are automatically integrated into the pharmacy software. The system connects more than 30 physicians, 12 000 patients, and 31 pharmacies in Montréal. "We've tried to set it up so that no matter what pharmacy the patient visited, the system would be able to retrieve electronic prescriptions and send information about prescriptions dispensed," says Dr. Robyn Tamblyn, director of the MOXXI project. Patients can pick at a moment's notice which pharmacy they go to. And because it is electronic, pharmacists do not receive illegible handwritten prescriptions, but instead receive encrypted documents with all of the information they need. Of course, to facilitate this system, Quebec had to pass legislation making digital signatures legal.

CASE STUDY QUESTIONS:

1. What problems are hospitals and physicians encountering in diagnosing diseases and prescribing medications? What management, organization, and technology factors are responsible for these problems?

2. Are DSS appropriate solutions? Why or why not? What management, technology, and organization issues are involved in the use of these systems?

3. What obstacles prevent computer systems from improving the medical industry? How can these obstacles be removed?

Sources: Kirsten C. Somoza, "A Computerized Cardiac Teletriage Decision Support System: Effects on Nurse Performance," **http://hot.carleton.ca/hot-topics/articles/cardiac-teletriage** (accessed October 7, 2009); Andy Shaw, "Organizations Work to Improve Coding of Clinical Data," **www.canhealth.com/nov03.html** (accessed May 8, 2007); Neil Zeidenberg, "New Software Tracks How Children Use Their Prosthesis over Time," **www.canhealth.com/nov03.html** (accessed May 8, 2007); Andy Shaw, "Decision Support Systems Can Help Hospitals Reduce Costs and Improve Patient Care," **www.canhealth.com/nov03.html** (accessed May 8, 2007); Neil Zeidenberg, "Wireless Handheld Computers Enable Doctors to Prescribe at Point of Care," **www.canhealth.com/nov03.html** (accessed May 8, 2007).

CHAPTER 15

Managing Knowledge

LEARNING OBJECTIVES

After reading this chapter, you will be able to answer the following questions:

1. What is the role of knowledge management and knowledge management programs in business?

2. What types of systems are used for enterprise-wide knowledge management, and how do they provide value for businesses?

3. What are the major types of knowledge work systems, and how do they provide value for firms?

4. What are the business benefits of using intelligent techniques for knowledge management?

OPENING CASE

Content Management for the Royal Canadian Mint: How to Maximize Your Web Presence

The Royal Canadian Mint (RCM) does not just produce coins for Canada; it manufactures coins on contract for many other countries, too. The Mint also manufactures commemorative Canadian collector coins, a fine jewellery and watch collection, and a variety of customized products including medals and tokens, selling these products through a variety of channels. The Mint recognized the need to market online through an e-commerce site and also recognized the need to integrate the diverse content found in its legacy ERP systems.

Operating since 1908 and employing more than 700 people today, the Mint is intended to be a profit-making Crown corporation. Toward this end, the Mint employs a network of dealers and distributors around the world.

Once management decided on a Web site not only to promote its products but also to enhance the efforts of its sales force, the challenges were all too apparent. The site not only had to be

technically sophisticated so that it could produce personalized content for a variety of visitors and administer product catalogues but also had to integrate with the order fulfillment systems that were on a variety of platforms. To process orders and have sophisticated reporting requirements fulfilled as well, the Web site would need to link with legacy systems. And, oh yes, the system had to operate in both English and French.

"We wanted every visitor to the Mint's site to become a customer by offering them a comfortable shopping experience with rich search offerings and intuitive transactional processing capabilities," said Diane Plouffe Reardon, executive director of communications at the Mint. Until this project, the Mint had used outsourcers to create, maintain, and host its Web site, first developed in 1995. But working with outsourcers meant updates were costly and seldom done in a timely manner.

Content management is a substantial market, with about $1.16 billion in

software globally and an extra $2.9 billion in services, according to the Gartner Group. As part of its traditional strategy of buying companies to acquire their technology, in 2001 Microsoft bought NCompass, a Vancouver-based Web content management company. NCompass' main product is Resolution, which has been rolled into Microsoft's Content Management Server.

Realizing it could not redevelop its Web site on its own, the Mint worked with Proximi-T, an IT consulting firm to network with other vendors, primarily Microsoft, and develop an enterprise solution to manage the content of the redesigned Web site. Using Microsoft BizTake Server 2000, the Mint was able to use XML to extract and convert detailed product information. Today, visitors access personalized pages that deliver only content that is based on their preferences. Microsoft's content management tools let nontechnical writers and staff update online content easily.

The Mint's Web site, even before being converted to the new, user-friendly edition, held 4000 pages, half in English and half in French. "Prior to the use of Web content management software, every page was hard-coded in HTML," says Michael Toope, Web site coordinator. "Even fixing a typo required the work of a programmer." Mint staff also had to pick up orders manually online, but today the orders are fed directly into an order-entry system.

Sources: Grace Casselman, "Growing Like a Weed," **www.backbonemag.com/Magazine/E+Trends_07060601.asp** (accessed May 8, 2007); "Case Study: The Royal Canadian Mint," **www.microsoft.com/canada/casestudies/royal_canadian_mint.mspx?pf=true** (accessed October 7, 2009); and "The Royal Canadian Mint" home page, **www.mint.ca** (accessed June 8, 2009).

The Royal Canadian Mint's experience shows how organizational performance can benefit by making organizational knowledge more easily available. By organizing its knowledge about how to buy from the Mint, whether the buyer is a Canadian individual or a foreign government, the Mint has increased its efficiency and ability to serve customers.

The chapter-opening diagram calls attention to important points raised by this case and this chapter. The Mint is highly customer-focused. Much of the essential information and knowledge that should face the customer was not easily accessible because it was stored in many different documents and legacy systems. Delays in accessing vital information created inefficiencies that impaired the Mint's business performance, including its response to customers. In order to benefit from enterprise content management technology, the Mint had to integrate its Web site and Web store with its other legacy systems. This took a great deal of time and effort. By making content management user-friendly and efficient, the new system has made the Mint much more efficient and profitable.

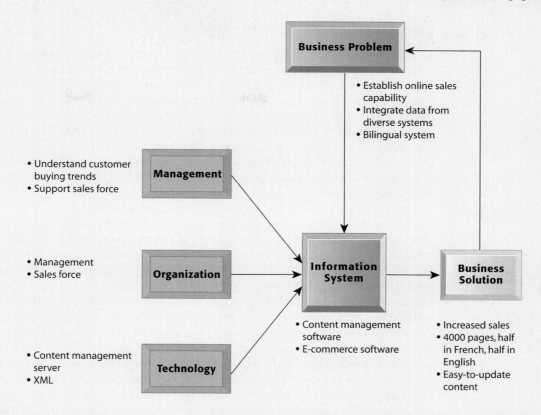

15.1 The Knowledge Management Landscape

Knowledge management and collaboration systems are among the fastest-growing areas of corporate and government software investment. Sales of enterprise content management software for knowledge management are expected to grow 15 percent annually through 2012. The past decade has likewise shown an explosive growth in research on knowledge and knowledge management in the economics, management, and information systems fields.

Knowledge management and collaboration are closely related. Knowledge that cannot be communicated and shared with others is nearly useless. Knowledge becomes useful and actionable when shared throughout the firm. As we described in Chapter 2, collaboration systems include Internet-based collaboration environments like Google Sites and IBM's Lotus Notes, social networking, e-mail and instant messaging, cell phones and wireless handhelds, wikis, and virtual worlds. In this chapter, we will be focusing on knowledge management systems, always mindful of the fact that communicating and sharing knowledge are increasingly important.

We live in an information economy in which the major source of wealth and prosperity is the production and distribution of information and knowledge. A large percentage of the Canadian labour force consists of knowledge and information workers and perhaps an even greater percentage of Canada's gross domestic product comes from the knowledge and information sectors, such as banking and finance, accounting, insurance, and publishing.

Knowledge management has become an important theme at many large business firms as managers realize that much of their firm's value depends on the firm's ability to create and manage knowledge. Studies have found that a substantial part of a firm's stock market value is related to its intangible assets, of which knowledge is one important component, along with brands, reputations, and unique business processes. Well-executed knowledge-based projects have been known to produce extraordinary returns on investment although knowledge-based investments are difficult to measure (Gu and Lev, 2001; Blair and Wallman, 2001).

Important Dimensions of Knowledge

There is an important distinction between data, information, knowledge, and wisdom. Chapter 1 defines **data** as streams of raw facts representing events occurring in organizations or the physical environment before they have been organized and arranged into a form that people can understand and use. To turn data into useful information, a firm must expend resources to organize data into categories of understanding, such as monthly, daily, regional, or store-based reports of total sales. To transform information into **knowledge,** a firm must expend additional resources to discover patterns, rules, and contexts where the knowledge works. Finally, **wisdom** is thought to be the collective and individual experience of applying knowledge to the solution of problems. Wisdom involves where, when, and how to apply knowledge.

Knowledge is both an individual attribute and a collective attribute of the firm. Knowledge is a cognitive, even a physiological, event that takes place inside peoples' heads. It is also stored in libraries and records, shared in lectures, and stored by firms in the form of business processes and employee know-how. Knowledge residing in the minds of employees that has not been documented is called **tacit knowledge** while knowledge that has been documented is called **explicit knowledge.** Knowledge can reside in e-mail, voice mail, graphics, and unstructured documents as well as structured documents. Knowledge is generally believed to have a location, either in the minds of humans or in specific business processes. Knowledge is "sticky" and not universally applicable or easily moved. Finally, knowledge is thought to be situational and contextual. For example, you must know when to perform a procedure as well as how to perform it. Table 15-1 reviews these dimensions of knowledge.

Another way to categorize knowledge is to view knowledge management as either static or dynamic. Static knowledge management refers to the knowledge involved being always available; it can be accessed, retrieved, used, and then re-accessed. Static knowledge management is best supported by electronic document management systems and tagging. Dynamic knowledge management, on the other hand, refers to knowledge transfer and knowledge sharing. Dynamic knowledge management is best supported by discussion forums, virtual communities, and email. See Section 15.2 for the types of systems that best support static and dynamic knowledge management.

We can see that knowledge is a different kind of firm asset from, say, buildings and financial assets; that knowledge is a complex phenomenon; and that there are many aspects

Data

Knowledge

Wisdom

Tacit knowledge

Explicit knowledge

TABLE 15-1 Important dimensions of knowledge.

KNOWLEDGE IS A FIRM ASSET	Knowledge is an intangible asset.
	The transformation of data into useful information and knowledge requires organizational resources.
	Knowledge is not subject to the law of diminishing returns as are physical assets, but instead experiences network effects as its value increases as more people share it.
KNOWLEDGE HAS DIFFERENT FORMS	Knowledge can be either tacit or explicit (codified).
	Knowledge involves know-how, craft, and skill.
	Knowledge involves knowing how to follow procedures.
	Knowledge involves knowing why, not simply when, things happen (causality).
KNOWLEDGE HAS A LOCATION	Knowledge is a cognitive event involving mental models and maps of individuals.
	There is both a social and an individual basis of knowledge.
	Knowledge is "sticky" (hard to move), situated (enmeshed in a firm's culture), and contextual (works only in certain situations).
KNOWLEDGE IS SITUATIONAL	Knowledge is conditional: Knowing when to apply a procedure is just as important as knowing the procedure (conditional).
	Knowledge is related to context: You must know how to use a certain tool and under what circumstances.

to the process of managing knowledge. We can also recognize that knowledge-based core competencies of firms—the two or three things that an organization does best—are key organizational assets. Knowing how to do things effectively and efficiently in ways that other organizations cannot duplicate is a primary source of profit and competitive advantage that cannot be purchased easily by competitors in the marketplace.

For instance, having a unique build-to-order production system constitutes a form of knowledge and perhaps a unique asset that other firms cannot copy easily. With knowledge, firms become more efficient and effective in their use of scarce resources. Without knowledge, firms become less efficient and less effective in their use of resources and ultimately fail.

Organizational Learning and Knowledge Management Like humans, organizations create and gather knowledge using a variety of organizational learning mechanisms. Through collection of data, careful measurement of planned activities, trial and error (experiment), and feedback from customers and the environment in general, organizations gain experience. Organizations that learn then adjust their behaviour to reflect that learning by creating new business processes and by changing patterns of management decision making. This process of change is called **organizational learning.** Arguably organizations that can sense and respond to their environments rapidly will survive longer than organizations that have poor learning mechanisms.

The Knowledge Management Value Chain

Knowledge management refers to the set of business processes developed in an organization to create, store, transfer, and apply knowledge. Knowledge management increases the ability of the organization to learn from its environment and to incorporate knowledge into its business processes. Figure 15-1 illustrates the five value-adding steps in the knowledge management value chain. Each stage in the value chain adds value to raw data and information as they are transformed into usable knowledge.

In Figure 15-1, information systems activities and related management and organizational activities are separated, with information systems activities on the top of the graphic

Organizational learning
Knowledge management

FIGURE 15-1 The knowledge management value chain.

Knowledge management today involves both information systems activities and a host of enabling management and organizational activities.

and management and organizational activities below. One apt slogan of the knowledge management field is, "Effective knowledge management is 80 percent managerial and organizational, and 20 percent technology."

In Chapter 1, we define *organizational and management capital* as the set of business processes, culture, and behaviour required to obtain value from investments in information systems. In the case of knowledge management, as with other information systems investments, supportive values, structures, and behaviour patterns must be built to maximize the return on investment in knowledge management projects. In Figure 15-1, the management and organizational activities in the lower half of the diagram represent the investment in organizational capital required to obtain substantial returns on the information technology (IT) investments and systems shown in the top half of the diagram.

Knowledge Acquisition Organizations acquire knowledge in a number of ways, depending on the type of knowledge they seek. The first knowledge management systems sought to build corporate repositories of documents, reports, presentations, and best practices. These efforts have been extended to include unstructured documents (such as e-mail). In other cases, organizations acquire knowledge by developing online expert networks so that employees can "find the expert" in the company who has the knowledge in his or her head.

In still other cases, firms must create new knowledge by discovering patterns in corporate data or by using knowledge workstations where engineers can discover new knowledge. These various efforts are described throughout this chapter. A coherent and organized knowledge system also requires systematic data from the firm's transaction processing systems that track sales, payments, inventory, customers, and other vital data, as well as data from external sources such as news feeds, industry reports, legal opinions, scientific research, and government statistics.

Knowledge Storage Once they are discovered, documents, patterns, and expert rules must be stored so they can be retrieved and used by employees. Knowledge storage generally involves the creation of a database. Document management systems that digitize, index, and tag documents according to a coherent framework are large databases adept at storing collections of documents. Expert systems also help corporations preserve the knowledge that is acquired by incorporating that knowledge into organizational processes and culture. Each of these is discussed later in this chapter.

Management must support the development of planned knowledge storage systems, encourage the development of corporate-wide schemas for indexing documents, and reward employees for taking the time to update and store documents properly. For instance, it would reward the sales force for submitting names of prospects to a shared corporate database of prospects where all sales personnel can identify each prospect and review the stored knowledge.

Knowledge Dissemination Portal, e-mail, instant messaging, wiki, social network, and search engine technology have added to an existing array of collaboration technologies and office systems for sharing calendars, documents, data, and graphics (see Chapter 7). Contemporary technology seems to have created a deluge of information and knowledge. How can managers and employees discover, in a sea of information and knowledge, that which is really important for their decisions and their work? Here, training programs, informal networks, and shared management experience communicated through a supportive culture help managers focus their attention on the important knowledge and information.

Knowledge Application Regardless of what type of knowledge management system is involved, knowledge that is not shared and applied to the practical problems facing firms and managers does not add business value. To provide a return on investment, organizational knowledge must become a systematic part of management decision making and become situated in decision support systems (described in Chapter 14). Ultimately, new knowledge must be built into a firm's business processes and key application systems, including enterprise applications for managing key internal business processes and relationships with customers and suppliers. Management supports this process by creating—based on new knowledge—new business practices, new products and services, and new markets for the firm.

Building Organizational and Management Capital: Collaboration, Communities of Practice, and Office Environments In addition to the activities we have just described, managers can help by developing new organizational roles and responsibilities for the acquisition of knowledge, including the creation of chief knowledge officer executive positions, dedicated staff positions (knowledge managers), and communities of practice. **Communities of practice (COPs)** are informal social networks of professionals and employees within and outside the firm who have similar work-related activities and interests. The activities of these communities include self- and group education, conferences, online newsletters, and day-to-day sharing of experiences and techniques to solve specific work problems. Many organizations, such as IBM and the World Bank, have encouraged the development of thousands of online communities of practice. These communities of practice depend greatly on software environments that enable collaboration and communication.

COPs can make it easier for people to reuse knowledge by pointing community members to useful documents, creating document repositories, and filtering information for newcomers. COP members act as facilitators, encouraging contributions and discussion. COPs can also reduce the learning curve for new employees by providing contacts with subject matter experts and access to a community's established methods and tools. Finally, COPs can act as a spawning ground for new ideas, techniques, and decision-making behaviour.

Types of Knowledge Management Systems

There are essentially three major types of knowledge management systems: enterprise-wide knowledge management systems, knowledge work systems, and intelligent techniques. Figure 15-2 shows the knowledge management system applications for each of these major categories.

Enterprise-wide knowledge management systems are general-purpose firm-wide efforts to collect, store, distribute, and apply digital content and knowledge. These systems include capabilities for searching for information, storing both structured and unstructured data, and locating employee expertise within the firm. They also include supporting technologies such as portals, search engines, collaboration tools (e-mail, instant messaging, wikis, blogs, and social bookmarking) and learning management systems.

The development of powerful networked workstations and software for assisting engineers and scientists in the discovery of new knowledge has led to the creation of knowledge work systems such as computer-aided design (CAD), visualization, simulation, and virtual

Communities of practice (COPs)
Enterprise-wide knowledge management systems

FIGURE 15-2   Major types of knowledge management systems.

Enterprise-Wide Knowledge Management Systems	Knowledge Work Systems	Intelligent Techniques
General-purpose, integrated, firmwide efforts to collect, store, disseminate, and use digital content and knowledge	Specialized workstations and systems that enable scientists, engineers, and other knowledge workers to create and discover new knowledge	Tools for discovering patterns and applying knowledge to discrete decisions and knowledge domains
Enterprise content management systems Collaboration tools Learning management systems Knowledge network systems	CAD 3-D virtualization Virtual reality Investment workstations	Data mining Neural networks Expert systems Case-based reasoning Fuzzy logic Genetic algorithms Intelligent agents

There are three major categories of knowledge management systems, and each can be broken down further into more specialized types of knowledge management systems.

reality systems. **Knowledge work systems (KWS)** are specialized systems built for engineers, scientists, and other knowledge workers charged with discovering and creating new knowledge for a company. We discuss knowledge work applications in detail in Section 15.3.

Knowledge management also includes a diverse group of **intelligent techniques,** such as data mining, expert systems, neural networks, fuzzy logic, genetic algorithms, and intelligent agents. These techniques have different objectives, from a focus on discovering knowledge (data mining and neural networks), to distilling knowledge in the form of rules for a computer program (expert systems and fuzzy logic), to discovering optimal solutions for problems (genetic algorithms). Section 15.4 provides more detail about these intelligent techniques.

15.2 Enterprise-Wide Knowledge Management Systems

Firms must deal with at least three kinds of knowledge. Some knowledge exists within the firm in the form of structured text documents (reports and presentations). Decision makers also need knowledge that is semistructured, such as e-mail, voice mail, chat room exchanges, videos, digital pictures, brochures, or bulletin board postings. In still other cases, there is no formal or digital information of any kind, and the knowledge resides in the heads of employees. Much of this knowledge is tacit knowledge that is rarely written down. Enterprise-wide knowledge management systems deal with all three types of knowledge.

Enterprise Content Management Systems

Businesses today need to organize and manage both structured and semistructured knowledge assets. **Structured knowledge** is explicit knowledge that exists in formal documents, as well as in formal rules that organizations derive by observing experts and their decision-making behaviours. But, according to experts, at least 80 percent of an organization's business content is semistructured or unstructured—information in folders, messages, memos, proposals, e-mails, graphics, electronic slide presentations, and even videos created in different formats and stored in many locations.

Enterprise content management systems help organizations manage both types of information. These systems have capabilities for knowledge capture, storage, retrieval, distribution, and preservation to help firms improve their business processes and decisions. These systems include corporate repositories of documents, reports, presentations, and best practices, as well as capabilities for collecting and organizing semistructured knowledge such as e-mail (see Figure 15-3). Major enterprise content management systems also

Knowledge work systems (KWS)

Intelligent techniques

Structured knowledge

Enterprise content management systems

FIGURE 15-3   An enterprise content management system.

An enterprise content management system has capabilities for classifying, organizing, and managing structured and semistructured knowledge and making it available throughout the enterprise.

enable users to access external sources of information, such as news feeds and research, and to communicate via e-mail, chat/instant messaging, discussion groups, and videoconferencing. Open Text Corporation (ranked Canada's leading software company in 2009), EMC (Documentum), IBM, and Oracle Corporation are leading vendors of enterprise content management software.

Bell Canada, with 28 million customer connections including telephone services, wireless communications, high-speed Internet, digital television and Voice over Internet protocol, needed to establish a centralized, Web-based library to hold more than half a million records to simplify compliance with the regulations of government departments and regulatory agencies including the Canadian Radio-television and Telecommunications Commission (CRTC), the Competition Bureau, and the Privacy Commissioner of Canada (Bell Canada, 2006). Bell Canada chose Open Text's LiveLink application to make compilation of needed information for compliance much more efficient and much more effective (see Figure 15-4).

A key problem in managing knowledge is the creation of an appropriate classification scheme, or **taxonomy,** to organize information into meaningful categories so that it can

Taxonomy

FIGURE 15-4   Open Text LiveLink ECM integrated knowledge management system.

Open Text's LiveLink ECM enterprise solution combines document management, knowledge management, business intelligence, and portal technologies and can be used for managing semistructured as well as structured knowledge.

be easily accessed. Once the categories for classifying knowledge have been created, each knowledge object needs to be "tagged," or classified, so that it can be easily retrieved. Enterprise content management systems have capabilities for tagging, interfacing with corporate databases where the documents are stored, and creating an enterprise portal environment for employees to use when searching for corporate knowledge.

Firms in publishing, advertising, broadcasting, and entertainment have special needs for storing and managing unstructured digital data such as photographs, graphic images, video, and audio content. For example, Coca-Cola must keep track of all the images of the Coca-Cola brand that have been created in the past at all of the company's worldwide offices, to prevent both redundant work and variation from a standard brand image (see the chapter-ending case study). **Digital asset management systems** help companies classify, store, and distribute these digital objects.

Knowledge Network Systems

Knowledge network systems, also known as *expertise location and management systems,* address the problem that arises when the appropriate knowledge is not in the form of a digital document but instead resides in the memory of expert individuals in the firm. Knowledge network systems provide an online directory of corporate experts in well-defined knowledge domains and use communication technologies to make it easy for employees to find the appropriate expert in a company. Some knowledge network systems go further by systematizing the solutions developed by experts and then storing the solutions in a knowledge database as a best practices or frequently asked questions (FAQ) repository (see Figure 15-5). AskMe and Tacit Software are leading knowledge network system vendors.

Digital asset management systems
Knowledge network systems

FIGURE 15-5   An enterprise knowledge network system.

A knowledge network maintains a database of firm experts, as well as accepted solutions to known problems, and then facilitates the communication between employees looking for knowledge and experts who have that knowledge. Solutions created in this communication are then added to a database of solutions in the form of FAQs, best practices, or other documents.

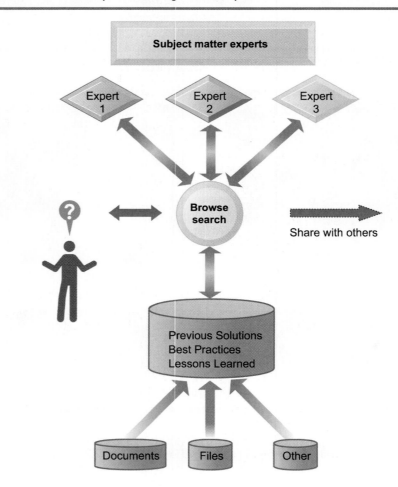

Intec Engineering Partnership, a project management company with more than 500 employees worldwide serving the global oil and gas industry, uses the AskMe enterprise knowledge network system. Using the system, an Intec engineer with a question could access relevant documents, Web links, and answers to previous related questions by initiating a keyword search. If no answer was found, that person could post a general question on a Web page for categories, such as Pipeline or Subsea, for other engineers accessing that page to answer. Alternatively, the person could review the profiles of all company engineers with relevant expertise and send a detailed e-mail query to experts who might have the answer. All questions and answers are automatically incorporated into the knowledge database.

Collaboration Tools and Learning Management Systems

The major enterprise content management systems include powerful portal and collaboration technologies. Enterprise knowledge portals can provide access to external sources of information, such as news feeds and research, as well as to internal knowledge resources along with capabilities for e-mail, chat/instant messaging, discussion groups, and video-conferencing.

Companies are starting to use consumer Web technologies such as blogs, wikis, and social bookmarking for internal use to foster collaboration and information exchange between individuals and teams. Blogs and wikis help capture, consolidate, and centralize this knowledge for the firm. Collaboration tools from commercial software vendors, such as Microsoft SharePoint and Lotus Connections, also offer these capabilities along with secure online collaborative workspaces.

Wikis, which we introduced in Chapters 2 and 7, are inexpensive and easy to implement. Wikis provide a central repository for all types of corporate data that can be displayed in a Web browser, including electronic pages of documents, spreadsheets, and electronic slides, and can embed e-mail and instant messages. Although users are able to modify wiki content contributed by others, wikis have capabilities for tracking these changes and tools for reverting to earlier versions. A wiki is most appropriate for information that is revised frequently but must remain available perpetually as it changes.

The Window on Management describes some of these corporate uses of Web 2.0 tools. As you read this case, try to identify the problem these companies were facing, what alternative solutions were available to management, and how well the chosen solution worked.

Social bookmarking makes it easier to search for and share information by allowing users to save their bookmarks to Web pages on a public Web site and tag these bookmarks with keywords. These tags can be used to organize and search for the documents. Lists of tags can be shared with other people to help them find information of interest. The user-created taxonomies created for shared bookmarks are called **folksonomies.** Delicious and Digg are two popular social bookmarking sites. The Window on Technology on page 471 describes this technology and its uses for knowledge management.

Companies need ways to keep track of and manage employee learning and to integrate it more fully into their knowledge management and other corporate systems. A **learning management system (LMS)** provides tools for the management, delivery, tracking, and assessment of various types of employee learning and training.

Contemporary LMS support multiple modes of learning, including CD-ROM, downloadable videos, Web-based classes, live instruction in classes or online, and group learning in online forums and chat sessions. The LMS consolidates mixed-media training, automates the selection and administration of courses, assembles and delivers learning content, and measures learning effectiveness.

For example, the Credit Union Institute of Canada (CUIC) uses Docent Inc.'s enterprise suite as the infrastructure for its e-learning solution. With more than 650 credit union members spread across the nation, organizing a solution was no simple task. But the solution delivers e-learning to member credit unions and/or their employees, so that if a local credit union decides not to offer education and training through the learning management system, a local credit union employee can still take advantage of the system to receive training.

Social bookmarking

Folksonomies

Learning management system (LMS)

WINDOW ON MANAGEMENT

Managing with Web 2.0

Who's blogging? It's not just twenty-somethings who want to chronicle their experiences, vent about consumer products, or put out a political message. Today's blogger might very well be an employee at IBM, Intel, Canadian Automobile Association, or any number of companies that have embraced Web 2.0 tools. Blogs, wikis, and social networking are emerging as powerful tools to boost communication and productivity in the corporate workforce. McKinsey & Co. consultants reported that approximately one-third of the top executives it polled use Web 2.0 tools or plan to deploy them.

Web 2.0 tools have made inroads into the business world because the software that supports them is generally inexpensive and user-friendly. A manager who wants to communicate with his or her team via a blog or have the progress of a project documented on a wiki can institute the technology without help from the IT department and without superiors worrying about high costs.

Canadian Online Pharmacy and Drugstore has an up-to-date blog. A previous edition of this text found a blog by CAA's CEO. Today that blog cannot be found. Various reasons have been cited for Canadian companies' unwillingness to post corporate blogs. These include the possibility of liability or disclosure in violation of securities regulations and laws. Yet our neighbours to the South appear to have no trouble in blogging on their corporate Web sites.

At Sun Microsystems, management instructed its engineers to create wiki pages that described their projects. Once the engineers were comfortable with the technology, it was easier for them to transition to using wikis for the company's formal software documentation. The use of wikis also spread to meeting notes, project plans, and software reports, resulting in a total fourfold increase in the amount of documented information at Sun.

At IBM, more than 26 000 employees have created blogs on the company's network to post about technology and the work they are doing. Project team members use wikis to store information and share memos. IBM's Wiki Central manages over 20 000 company wikis with more than 125 000 participants. The company created a wiki to help 50 of its experts on law, economics, government, and technology to collaborate on an intellectual property manifesto that serves as the foundation of its new patent policy.

Web 2.0 tools are particularly valuable at IBM, where 42 percent of the workforce operates remotely, either from home or from client offices. Brian Goodman, who is the Connecticut-based manager of a software development team with members in New York and Massachusetts, says that the wikis give him "a single view of the projects and their status" without bombarding each worker every day with an instant message.

IBM employees engage in social networking internally through its corporate directory, BluePages, which is edited by employees and serves as a sort of internal corporate MySpace. The directory contains basic information on 400 000 employees and is accessed 6 million times daily. Employees have control of most of the content on their individual entries and can post their own photos and résumés to their corporate "profiles."

IBM provides social networking capabilities to other companies through its IBM Lotus Connections software. Lotus Connections includes capabilities for user profiles, blogs, social bookmarking, and supporting communities of practice. Although some businesses block employee access to Facebook and other public networking sites, a number of businesses use them for limited purposes. Recruiters at Microsoft and Starbucks have used LinkedIn to search for potential job candidates. The Vancouver Police Service uses Second Life, a virtual reality Web site, for initial screening of some of its applicants, including meeting the applicants in Second Life's Web space.

Many companies and services also use RSS feeds (see Chapter 7) to notify the public of corporate events and news. Yet Twitter seems to be the latest Web 2.0 technology being used by many companies to publicize news and product offerings as a new marketing channel. The list of Canadian companies that are tweeting (sending messages using Twitter) include media companies (*The Globe and Mail*, CBC, and Canoe), technology companies such as Open Text, financial institutions such as RBC, and retailers such as lululemon. Other Canadian companies that are tweeting are WestJet, 1-800-Got-Junk, and even Toronto's Sick Kids Hospital. Twitter messages from these companies can notify "followers" of sales on flights or clothing, updates to software, and breaking news, as well as changes in the prime rate.

Two of the biggest challenges for companies using Web 2.0 technologies are convincing workers to embrace these tools and regulating their use. IBM reminds employees to remember the rules of privacy, respect, and confidentiality in its corporate code of conduct and does not allow any anonymous online communication. Companies using public social networking sites need to worry more about security and regulatory compliance because communications occur with parties outside the corporation. Employees chatting about their jobs could reveal sensitive information.

Some companies, such as Nokia and Frankfurt-based investment bank Dresdner Kleinwort, started wiki or blog implementations with a small group of employees. Once other managers and employees saw the business benefits, ease of use, and versatility of the tools, their departments were quick to adopt the technology.

1. How do Web 2.0 tools help companies manage knowledge, coordinate work, and enhance decision making?

2. What business problems do blogs, wikis, and other social networking tools help solve?

3. Describe how a company such as Air Canada or Sobeys would benefit from using Web 2.0 tools internally.

4. What challenges do companies face in spreading the use of Web 2.0? What issues should managers be concerned with?

Go to Sun Microsystems' Blogs home page at **http://blogs.sun.com** and click on a tab for a search word or phrase. Read at least two blog postings about your selected word or phrase. Answer the following questions:

1. What is the name of the tag you selected?

2. Who is the intended audience of these tags? Are they different audiences?

3. What subjects do the blog postings address?

4. Visit several more blogs in Sun's directory. If you were a Sun employee, do you think you would find the existence of these blogs helpful? Why or why not? Do you think there is value in blog entries that discuss the author's personal life instead of work-related matters?

Sources: Paul McDougall, "The 'TLA Wiki' and Other Tips to Spark Enterprise 2.0 Efforts," *InformationWeek*, June 16, 2008; Judith Lamont, "Social Networking: KM and Beyond," *KM World*, June 2008; Michael Totty, "Social Studies," *The Wall Street Journal*, June 18, 2007; William M. Bulkeley, "Playing Well with Others," *The Wall Street Journal*, June 18, 2007; Vauhini Vara, "Wikis at Work," *The Wall Street Journal*, June 18, 2007; Dan Carlin, "Corporate Wikis Go Viral," *BusinessWeek*, March 12, 2007; and David Forde, "Which Companies Are Using Twitter?" **http://profectio.com/which-companies-are-using-twitter** (accessed June 9, 2009).

15.3 Knowledge Work Systems

The enterprise-wide knowledge systems we have just described provide a wide range of capabilities that can be used by many if not all the workers and groups in an organization. Firms also have specialized systems for knowledge workers to help them create new knowledge and to ensure that this knowledge is properly integrated into the business.

Knowledge Workers and Knowledge Work

Knowledge workers, a term we introduced in Chapter 1, include researchers, designers, architects, scientists, and engineers who primarily create knowledge and information for the organization. Knowledge workers usually have high levels of education and memberships in professional organizations and are often asked to exercise independent judgment as a routine aspect of their work. For example, knowledge workers create new products or find ways of improving existing ones. Knowledge workers perform three key roles that are critical to the organization and to the managers who work within the organization:

- Keeping the organization current in knowledge as it develops in the external world—in technology, science, social thought, and the arts

- Serving as internal consultants regarding the areas of their knowledge, changes taking place, and opportunities

- Acting as change agents, evaluating, initiating, and promoting change projects

Requirements of Knowledge Work Systems

Most knowledge workers rely on office systems, such as word processors, voice mail, e-mail, videoconferencing, and scheduling systems, which are designed to increase worker productivity in the office. However, knowledge workers also require highly specialized knowledge work systems with powerful graphics, analytical tools, and communications and document management capabilities.

These systems require great computing power to handle the sophisticated graphics or complex calculations necessary for knowledge workers such as scientific researchers, product designers, and financial analysts. Because knowledge workers are so focused on knowledge in the external world, these systems also must give a knowledge worker quick and easy access to external databases. They typically feature user-friendly interfaces that enable users to perform needed tasks without having to spend a great deal of time learning how to use

FIGURE 15-6 Requirements of knowledge work systems.

Knowledge work systems require strong links to external knowledge bases in addition to specialized hardware and software.

the system. Knowledge workers are highly paid—wasting a knowledge worker's time is simply too expensive. Figure 15-6 summarizes the requirements of knowledge work systems.

Knowledge workstations often are designed and optimized for the specific tasks to be performed; so, for example, a design engineer requires a different workstation setup than a financial analyst. Design engineers need graphics with enough power to handle three-dimensional (3D) CAD systems. However, financial analysts are more interested in access to a myriad of external databases and optical disk technology for efficiently storing and accessing massive amounts of financial data.

Examples of Knowledge Work Systems

Major knowledge work applications include CAD systems, virtual reality systems for simulation and modelling, and financial workstations. **Computer-aided design (CAD)** automates the creation and revision of designs, using computers and sophisticated graphics software.

Computer-aided design (CAD)

Using a more traditional physical design methodology, each design modification requires a mould to be made and a prototype to be tested physically. That process must be repeated many times, which is a very expensive and time-consuming process. Using a CAD workstation, the designer need only make a physical prototype toward the end of the design process because the design can be easily tested and changed on the computer. The ability of CAD software to provide design specifications for the tooling and manufacturing processes also saves a great deal of time and money while producing a manufacturing process with far fewer problems.

Computer-aided design (CAD) systems improve the quality of product design by performing much of the design and testing work on the computer.

For example, architects from Skidmore, Owings, & Merrill LLP used a 3D design program called Revit to work out the creative and technical details of the design for the Freedom Tower at the site of the former World Trade Center. The software enabled the architects to strip away the outer layer to manipulate the shape of the floors. Changes appeared immediately in the entire model, and the software automatically recalculated the technical details in the blueprints.

Virtual reality systems have visualization, rendering, and simulation capabilities that go far beyond those of conventional CAD systems. They use interactive graphics software to create computer-generated simulations that are so close to reality that users almost believe they are participating in a real-world situation. In many virtual reality systems, the user dons special clothing, headgear, and equipment, depending on the application. The clothing contains sensors that record the user's movements and immediately transmit that information back to the computer. For instance, to walk through a virtual reality simulation of a house, you would need garb that monitors the movement of your feet, hands, and head. You also would need goggles containing video screens and sometimes audio attachments and feeling gloves so that you can be immersed in the computer feedback.

Virtual reality systems

WINDOW ON TECHNOLOGY

Sharing Knowledge with Social Bookmarking

Most Web users know the value of bookmarks, which allow Web surfers to store and annotate links to useful Web sites. Bookmarks make it much easer to re-locate information. But they are tied to a single machine and Web browser, so you cannot bring them with you or share them easily with people in other locations.

Enter social bookmarking. Instead of storing bookmarks on desktops, users store them on shared sites, where they can be accessed from any location with Web access and also shared with other people. The shared sites can be sites for bookmarking pages on the public Web or internal corporate sites for bookmarking pages on the corporate intranet.

The bookmarks are "tagged" with keywords to help organize and classify them. Other people can use these tags to find bookmarks relevant to their interests that may help them find information more easily, including new sources of information that might be missed by search engines.

For example, suppose you are on a corporate team doing research on wind power. If you did a Web search and found relevant Web pages on wind power, you would click on a bookmarking button on the social networking site and create a tag identifying each Web document in such a way that it would be linked to wind power. You can click on the "tags" button at the social networking site to see a list of all the tags you created and select the documents you need.

Some even use these tags to identify other users with similar interests. Because social bookmarking sites indicate the author of each bookmark and provide access to that person's other bookmarked resources, users can make social connections with other individuals interested in a particular topic. This process allows like-minded individuals to find one another and create new communities of users.

It could be said that social bookmarking creates a network of resources and connections that represents the interests and judgments of a community of users.

Web-based social bookmarking sites are on the rise, including Del.icio.us (pronounced "delicious"), which was acquired by Yahoo! in 2005. Del.icio.us is targeted at individual consumers, but there are other social bookmarking sites offering services to academic and business users. Academics use CiteULike.org to share and store academic papers while medical researchers and practitioners use Connotea.org to track references. Visitors to social bookmarking sites can search for resources by keyword, person, or popularity and see the public bookmarks, tags, and classification schemes that registered bookmark users have created.

IBM developed Dogear, a social bookmarking service for businesses. It includes a user authentication feature, which is important for ensuring only selected employees collaborate. Dogear allows users in a business to search and bookmark information on either the public Web or an internal corporate intranet. Users can decide whether to make all their tagged bookmarks public or only selected bookmarks. (The rest are kept private.) In addition to facilitating document sharing, Dogear connects people in large organizations who would otherwise never meet and promotes information sharing between individuals in a team. According to David Millen, manager of IBM's Collaborative User Experience group, social bookmarking "allows you to see who is interested in the topics you're interested in." If you think a particular person's bookmarks are especially useful, you can subscribe to those bookmarks. Dogear users can subscribe to particular tags and have newly tagged items delivered automatically.

There are downsides. Public social bookmarking sites provide no oversight about how resources are organized or tagged. In some instances, this will lead to inconsistent or disorganized uses of tags. For example, if a user saves a bookmark for a site with information about wind power, but tags the site only with the term *wind power* and not with the terms *alternative energy* or *renewable energy*, that information might never be found by someone looking for information about wind power as a source of alternative energy. Social bookmarking reflects the values of a community of users, so there is always a chance they will present a skewed view of a particular topic.

To Think About

1. What are the advantages and disadvantages of using social bookmarking for knowledge management?

2. What management, organization, and technology issues should be addressed when considering whether to use social bookmarking for knowledge management at a business?

3. Should there be different standards for posting bookmarks to public Web pages at a public Web site versus posting bookmarks to internal corporate Web pages on a corporate social bookmarking site?

MIS in Action

Visit the social bookmarking site Del.icio.us (**http://Del.icio.us**), and search for bookmarks on a topic of your choice, such as

global warming, bird flu, ethanol, or open source. Then answer the following questions:

1. How easy was it to find bookmarks about your topic? How many bookmarks did you find?

2. Compare these bookmarks to the results of a search on your topic of choice using Google, Yahoo!, or another search engine. Which tools were the most useful in pointing you to good information?

3. Would you use Del.icio.us to find information for a research paper or business presentation? Why or why not?

Sources: Michael Totty, "Information Found—and Shared," *The Wall Street Journal*, September 11, 2006; Shamus McGillicudy, "Social Bookmarking: Pushing Collaboration to the Edge," SearchCIO.com, June 21, 2006; and Vauhini Vara, "Offices Co-opt Consumer Web Tools Like 'Wikis' and Social Networking," *The Wall Street Journal*, September 12, 2006.

CAD systems improve the quality and precision of product design by performing much of the design and testing work on the computer.

Virtual reality is just starting to provide benefits in educational, scientific, and business work. The Canadian Air Force has access to ultra-realistic threat simulation to help pilots train for warfare. Ottawa-based PRIOR Data Services Ltd. developed tactical engagement display software for the Canadian Forces' Surface Threat Electronic Warfare System (STEW) at the air base in Cold Lake, Alberta. The system provides realistic ground threat radar signals for the air crew's electronic warfare effects and reaction training. The system is made up of five threat emitters that can be reconfigured to replicate a range of threat systems. The system is responsive to jamming and manoeuvres, and automatically records the engagement for later playback and debriefing (Balfour, 1999). Virtual reality applications developed for the Web use a standard called **Virtual Reality Modelling Language (VRML).** VRML is a set of specifications for interactive, 3D modelling on the World Wide Web that can organize multiple media types, including animation, images, and audio to put users in a simulated real-world environment. VRML is platform-independent, operates over a desktop computer, and requires little bandwidth.

DuPont, the Wilmington, Delaware, chemical company, created a VRML application called HyperPlant that enables users to access 3D data over the Internet using Web browser software. Engineers can go through 3D models as if they were physically walking through a plant, viewing objects at eye level. This level of detail reduces the number of mistakes they make during construction of oil rigs, oil plants, and other structures.

The financial industry is using specialized **investment workstations** to leverage the knowledge and time of its brokers, traders, and portfolio managers. Firms such as TD Canada Trust and Assante have installed investment workstations that integrate a wide range of data from both internal and external sources, including contact management data, real-time and historical market data, and research reports. Previously, financial professionals had to spend considerable time accessing data from separate systems and piecing together the information they needed. By providing one-stop information more quickly and with fewer errors, the workstations streamline the entire investment process from stock selection to updating client records. Table 15-2 summarizes the major types of knowledge work systems.

15.4   Intelligent Techniques

Virtual Reality Modelling
Language (VRML)
Investment workstations

Artificial intelligence and database technology provide a number of intelligent techniques that organizations can use to capture individual and collective knowledge and to extend their knowledge base. Expert systems, case-based reasoning, and fuzzy logic are used for

TABLE 15-2   Examples of knowledge work systems.

KNOWLEDGE WORK SYSTEM	FUNCTION IN ORGANIZATION
CAD/CAM (computer-aided manufacturing)	Provides engineers, designers, and factory managers with precise control over industrial design and manufacturing
Virtual reality systems	Provide drug designers, architects, engineers, and medical workers with precise, photorealistic simulations of objects
Investment workstations	High-end PCs used in financial sector to analyze trading situations instantaneously and facilitate portfolio management

capturing tacit knowledge. Neural networks and data mining are used for **knowledge discovery.** They can discover underlying patterns, categories, and behaviours in large data sets that could not be discovered by managers alone or simply through experience. Genetic algorithms are used for generating solutions to problems that are too large and complex for human beings to analyze on their own. Intelligent agents can automate routine tasks to help firms search for and filter information for use in electronic commerce, supply chain management, and other activities.

Data mining, which we introduced in Chapter 6, helps organizations capture undiscovered knowledge residing in large databases, providing managers with new insight for improving business performance. It has become an important tool for management decision making, and we provide a detailed discussion of data mining for management decision support in Chapter 14.

The other intelligent techniques discussed in this section are based on **artificial intelligence (AI)** technology, which consists of computer-based systems (both hardware and software) that attempt to emulate human behaviour. These systems would be able to learn languages, accomplish physical tasks, use a perceptual apparatus, and emulate human expertise and decision making. Although AI applications do not exhibit the breadth, complexity, originality, and generality of human intelligence, they play an important role in contemporary knowledge management.

Capturing Knowledge: Expert Systems

Expert systems are an intelligent technique for capturing tacit knowledge in a very specific and limited domain of human expertise. These systems capture the knowledge of skilled employees in the form of a set of rules in a software system that can be used by others in the organization. The set of rules in the expert system adds to the memory, or stored learning, of the firm.

Expert systems lack the breadth of knowledge and the understanding of fundamental principles of a human expert. They typically perform very limited tasks that can be performed by professionals in a few minutes or hours, such as diagnosing a malfunctioning machine or determining whether to grant credit for a loan. Problems that cannot be solved by human experts in the same short period of time are far too difficult for an expert system. However, by capturing human expertise in limited areas, expert systems can provide benefits, helping organizations make high-quality decisions with fewer people. Today, expert systems are widely used in business in discrete, highly structured decision-making situations.

How Expert Systems Work   Human knowledge must be modelled or represented in a way that a computer can process. Expert systems model human knowledge as a set of rules that collectively are called the **knowledge base.** Expert systems have from 200 to many thousands of these rules, depending on the complexity of the problem. These rules are much more interconnected and nested than in a traditional software program (see Figure 15-7).

The strategy used to search through the knowledge base is called the **inference engine.** Two strategies are commonly used: forward chaining and backward chaining (see Figure 15-8).

Knowledge discovery
Artificial intelligence (AI)
Expert systems
Knowledge base
Inference engine

FIGURE 15-7   Rules in an expert system.

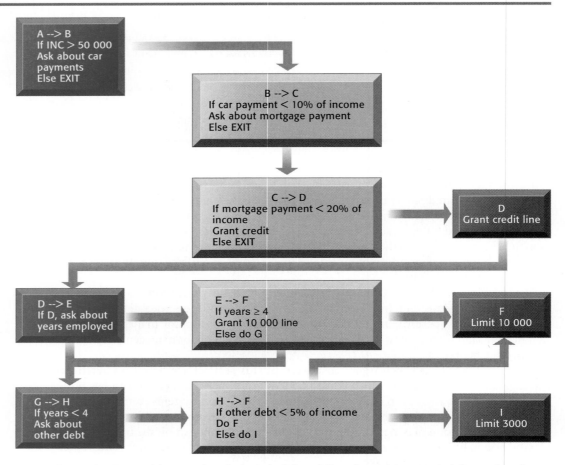

An expert system contains a number of rules to be followed. The rules are interconnected; the number of outcomes is known in advance and is limited; there are multiple paths to the same outcome; and the system can consider multiple rules at a single time. The rules illustrated are for simple credit-granting expert systems.

FIGURE 15-8   Inference engines in expert systems.

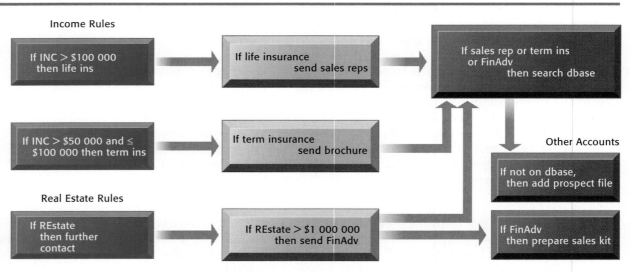

An inference engine works by searching through the rules and "firing" those rules that are triggered by facts gathered and entered by the user. Basically, a collection of rules is similar to a series of nested IF statements in a traditional software program; however, the magnitude of the statements and degree of nesting are much greater in an expert system.

In **forward chaining,** the inference engine begins with the information entered by the user and searches the rule base to arrive at a conclusion. The strategy is to fire, or carry out, the action of the rule when a condition is true. In Figure 15-8, beginning on the left, if the user enters a client's name with income greater than $100 000, the engine will fire all rules in sequence from left to right. If the user then enters information indicating that the same client owns real estate, another pass of the rule base will occur and more rules will fire. Processing continues until no more rules can be fired.

In **backward chaining,** the strategy for searching the rule base starts with a hypothesis and proceeds by asking the user questions about selected facts until the hypothesis is either confirmed or disproved. In our example, in Figure 15-8, ask the question, "Should we add this person to the prospect database?" Begin on the right of the diagram, and work toward the left. You can see that the person should be added to the database if a sales representative is sent, term insurance is granted, or a financial advisor visits the client.

Examples of Successful Expert Systems Expert systems provide businesses with an array of benefits including improved decisions, reduced errors, reduced costs, reduced training time, and higher levels of quality and service. Here are several examples:

The Learning Edge, a Toronto-based company, developed the IBM AS/400 Development Software Advisor as a marketing aid to help IBM's prospective customers better understand their application development needs and options. First the expert system gathers environmental and business process information; then it analyzes the data and recommends a programming language.

Countrywide Funding Corporation in Pasadena, California, uses an expert system to improve decisions about granting loans. This loan-underwriting firm employs about 400 underwriters in 150 offices around the country.

The company developed a PC-based expert system in 1992 to make preliminary creditworthiness decisions on loan requests. The company had experienced rapid, continuing growth and wanted the system to help ensure consistent, high-quality loan decisions. Countrywide's Loan Underwriting Expert System (CLUES) has about 400 rules. Countrywide tested the system by sending every loan application handled by a human underwriter to CLUES as well. The system was refined until it agreed with the underwriters in 95 percent of the cases.

Countrywide does not rely on CLUES to reject loans because the expert system cannot be programmed to handle exceptional situations, such as those involving a self-employed person or complex financial schemes. An underwriter must review all rejected loans and makes the final decision. Nevertheless, CLUES has other benefits. Traditionally, an underwriter could handle six or seven applications a day. Using CLUES, the same underwriter can evaluate at least 16 per day. "Countrywide illustrates the importance of managers and common sense in the use of expert systems. Countrywide made millions of faulty subprime mortgages in 2007 not because of the CLUES system, but because managers relaxed proper mortgage standards."

Con-Way Transportation built an expert system called Line-haul to automate and optimize planning of overnight shipment routes for its nationwide freight-trucking business. The expert system captures the business rules that dispatchers follow when assigning drivers, trucks, and trailers to transport 50 000 shipments of heavy freight each night across 25 states and Canada and when plotting their routes. Line-haul uses data on daily customer shipment requests, available drivers, trucks, trailer space, and weight stored in an Oracle database. The expert system uses thousands of rules and 100 000 lines of program code written in C^{++} to crunch the numbers and create optimum routing plans for 95 percent of daily freight shipments.

Con-Way dispatchers tweak the routing plan provided by the expert system and relay final routing specifications to field personnel responsible for packing the trailers for their nighttime runs. Con-Way recouped its $3.6 million investment in the system within two years by reducing the number of drivers, packing more freight per trailer, and reducing damage from rehandling. The system also reduces dispatchers' arduous nightly tasks (Pastore, 2003).

Although expert systems lack the robust and general intelligence of human beings, they can provide benefits to organizations if their limitations are well understood. Only

Forward chaining
Backward chaining

certain classes of problems can be solved using expert systems. Virtually all successful expert systems deal with problems of classification in limited domains of knowledge where there are relatively few alternative outcomes and these possible outcomes are all known in advance. Expert systems are much less useful for dealing with unstructured problems typically encountered by managers.

Many expert systems require large, lengthy, and expensive development efforts. Hiring or training more experts may be less expensive than building an expert system. Typically, the environment in which an expert system operates is continually changing so that the expert system must also continually change. Some expert systems, especially large ones, are so complex that in a few years the maintenance costs equal the development costs.

Organizational Intelligence: Case-Based Reasoning

Expert systems primarily capture the tacit knowledge of individual experts, but organizations also have collective knowledge and expertise that they have built up over the years. This organizational knowledge can be captured and stored using case-based reasoning. In **case-based reasoning (CBR),** descriptions of past experiences of human specialists, represented as cases, are stored in a database for later retrieval when the user encounters a new case with similar parameters. The system searches for stored cases with problem characteristics similar to the new one, finds the closest fit, and applies the solutions of the old case to the new case. Successful solutions are tagged to the new case, and both are stored together with the other cases in the knowledge base. Unsuccessful solutions also are appended to the case database along with explanations as to why the solutions did not work (see Figure 15-9).

Case-based reasoning (CBR)

FIGURE 15-9   How case-based reasoning works.

Case-based reasoning represents knowledge as a database of past cases and their solutions. The system uses a six-step process to generate solutions to new problems encountered by the user.

Expert systems work by applying a set of IF-THEN-ELSE rules extracted from human experts. Case-based reasoning, in contrast, represents knowledge as a series of cases, and this knowledge base is continuously expanded and refined by users. You will find case-based reasoning in diagnostic systems in medicine or customer support where users can retrieve past cases whose characteristics are similar to the new case. The system suggests a solution or diagnosis based on the best-matching retrieved case.

Fuzzy Logic Systems

Most people do not think in terms of traditional IF-THEN rules or precise numbers. Humans tend to categorize things imprecisely using rules for making decisions that may have many shades of meaning. For example, a company can be *large, medium,* or *small* in size. Temperature can be *hot, cold, cool,* or *warm.* These categories represent a range of values.

Fuzzy logic is a rule-based technology that can represent this type of imprecision by creating rules that use approximate or subjective values. It can describe a particular phenomenon or process linguistically and then represent that description in a small number of flexible rules. Organizations can use fuzzy logic to create software systems that capture tacit knowledge where there is linguistic ambiguity.

Let us look at the way fuzzy logic would represent various temperatures in a computer application to control room temperature automatically. The terms (known as *membership functions*) are imprecisely defined so that, for example, in Figure 15-10, cool is between 45 degrees and 70 degrees, although the temperature is most clearly cool between about 60 degrees and 67 degrees. Note that *cool* is overlapped by *cold* or *norm*. To control the room environment using this logic, the programmer would develop similarly imprecise definitions for humidity and other factors, such as outdoor wind and temperature. The rules might include one that says: "If the temperature is *cool* or *cold* and the humidity is low while the outdoor wind is high and the outdoor temperature is low, raise the heat and humidity in the room." The computer would combine the membership function readings in a weighted manner and, using all the rules, raise and lower the temperature and humidity.

Fuzzy logic provides solutions to problems requiring expertise that is difficult to represent in the form of crisp IF-THEN rules. In Japan, Sendai's subway system uses fuzzy logic controls to accelerate so smoothly that standing passengers need not hold on. Mitsubishi Heavy Industries in Tokyo has been able to reduce the power consumption of its air conditioners by 20 percent by implementing control programs in fuzzy logic. The autofocus

Fuzzy logic

FIGURE 15-10 Fuzzy logic for temperature control.

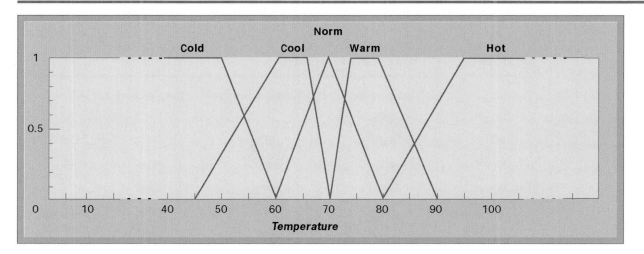

The membership functions for the input called *temperature* are in the logic of the thermostat to control the room temperature. Membership functions help translate linguistic expressions such as *warm* into numbers that the computer can manipulate.

device in cameras is possible only because of fuzzy logic. In these instances, fuzzy logic allows incremental changes in inputs to produce smooth changes in outputs instead of discontinuous ones, making it useful for consumer electronics and engineering applications.

Management has also found fuzzy logic useful for decision making and organizational control. In Canada, researchers are using fuzzy logic systems to estimate declining fish populations so that fisheries management can take action where appropriate; other Canadian researchers are working on fuzzy logic systems to help with forestry resource management by taking current geographic information system data and projecting it into the future. A Wall Street firm created a system that selects companies for potential acquisition, using the language stock traders understand. A fuzzy logic system has been developed to detect possible fraud in medical claims submitted by health care providers anywhere in the United States.

Neural Networks

Neural networks are used for solving complex, poorly understood problems for which large amounts of data have been collected. They find patterns and relationships in massive amounts of data that would be too complicated and difficult for a human being to analyze. Neural networks discover this knowledge by using hardware and software that parallel the processing patterns of the biological or human brain. Neural networks "learn" patterns from large quantities of data by sifting through data, searching for relationships, building models, and correcting over and over again the model's own mistakes.

A neural network has a large number of sensing and processing nodes that continuously interact with each other. Figure 15-11 represents one type of neural network comprising an input layer, an output layer, and a hidden processing layer. Humans "train" the network by feeding it a set of training data for which the inputs produce a known set of outputs or conclusions. This helps the computer learn the correct solution by example. As the computer is fed more data, each case is compared with the known outcome. If it differs, a correction is calculated and applied to the nodes in the hidden processing layer. These steps are repeated until a condition, such as corrections being less than a certain amount, is reached. The neural network in Figure 15-11 has learned how to identify a fraudulent credit card purchase. Also, self-organizing neural networks can be trained by exposing them to large amounts of data and allowing them to discover the patterns and relationships in the data.

While expert systems seek to emulate or model a human expert's way of solving problems, neural network developers claim that they do not program solutions and do not aim to solve specific problems. Instead, neural network designers seek to put intelligence into the hardware in the form of a generalized capability to learn. In contrast, the expert system is highly specific to a given problem and cannot be retrained easily.

Neural networks

FIGURE 15-11 How a neural network works.

A neural network uses rules it "learns" from patterns in data to construct a hidden layer of logic. The hidden layer then processes inputs, classifying them based on the experience of the model. In this example, the neural network has been trained to distinguish between valid and fraudulent credit card purchases.

Input Layer   **Hidden Layer**   **Output Layer**

Data
- Age
- Income
- Purchase history
- Frequency of purchases
- Average purchase size

Results

Valid purchase

Fraudulent purchase

Neural network applications in medicine, science, and business address problems in pattern classification, prediction, financial analysis, and control and optimization. In medicine, neural network applications are used for screening patients for coronary artery disease, for diagnosing patients with epilepsy and Alzheimer's disease, and for performing pattern recognition of pathology images. The financial industry uses neural networks to discern patterns in vast pools of data that might help predict the performance of equities, corporate bond ratings, or corporate bankruptcies. Visa International uses a neural network to help detect credit card fraud by monitoring all Visa transactions for sudden changes in the buying patterns of cardholders.

There are many puzzling aspects of neural networks. Unlike expert systems, which typically provide explanations for their solutions, neural networks cannot always explain why they arrived at a particular solution. Moreover, they cannot always guarantee a completely certain solution, arrive at the same solution again with the same input data, or always guarantee the best solution. They are very sensitive and may not perform well if their training covers too little or too much data. In most current applications, neural networks are best used as aids to human decision makers instead of substitutes for them.

Genetic Algorithms

Genetic algorithms are useful for finding the optimal solution for a specific problem by examining a very large number of possible solutions for that problem. They are based on techniques inspired by evolutionary biology, such as inheritance, mutation, selection, and crossover (recombination).

A genetic algorithm works by representing information as a string of 0s and 1s. The genetic algorithm searches a population of randomly generated strings of binary digits to identify the right string representing the best possible solution for the problem. As solutions alter and combine, the worst ones are discarded, and the better ones survive to go on to produce even better solutions.

In Figure 15-12, each string corresponds to one of the variables in the problem. One applies a test for fitness, ranking the strings in the population according to their level of desirability as possible solutions. After the initial population is evaluated for fitness, the algorithm then produces the next generation of strings, consisting of strings that survived the fitness test plus offspring strings produced from mating pairs of strings, and tests their fitness. The process continues until a solution is reached.

Genetic algorithms

FIGURE 15-12 The components of a genetic algorithm.

		Length	Width	Weight	Fitness
1 1 0 1 1 0	1	Long	Wide	Light	55
1 0 1 0 0 0	2	Short	Narrow	Heavy	49
0 0 0 1 0 1	3	Long	Narrow	Heavy	36
1 0 1 1 0 1	4	Short	Medium	Light	61
0 1 0 1 0 1	5	Long	Medium	Very light	74
A population of chromosomes			**Decoding of chromosomes**		**Evaluation of chromosomes**

This example illustrates an initial population of "chromosomes," each representing a different solution. The genetic algorithm uses an iterative process to refine the initial solutions so that the better ones, those with the higher fitness, are more likely to emerge as the best solution.

Genetic algorithms are used to solve problems that are very dynamic and complex, involving hundreds or thousands of variables or formulas. The problem must be one where the range of possible solutions can be represented genetically and criteria can be established for evaluating fitness. Genetic algorithms expedite the solution because they are able to evaluate many solution alternatives quickly to find the best one. For example, General Electric engineers used genetic algorithms to help optimize the design for jet turbine aircraft engines, where each design change required changes in up to 100 variables. The supply chain management software from i2 Technologies uses genetic algorithms to optimize production-scheduling models incorporating hundreds of thousands of details about customer orders, material and resource availability, manufacturing and distribution capability, and delivery dates.

Hybrid AI Systems

Genetic algorithms, fuzzy logic, neural networks, and expert systems can be integrated into a single application to take advantage of the best features of these technologies. These systems are called **hybrid AI systems.** Hybrid applications in business are growing. In Japan, Hitachi, Mitsubishi, Ricoh, Sanyo, and others are starting to incorporate hybrid AI in products such as home appliances, factory machinery, and office equipment. Matsushita has developed a "neurofuzzy" washing machine that combines fuzzy logic with neural networks. Nikko Securities has been working on a neurofuzzy system to forecast convertible-bond ratings.

Intelligent Agents

Intelligent agent technology helps businesses navigate through large amounts of data to locate and act on information that is considered important. **Intelligent agents** are software programs that work in the background without direct human intervention to carry out specific, repetitive, and predictable tasks for an individual user, business process, or software application. The agent uses a limited built-in or learned knowledge base to accomplish tasks or make decisions on the user's behalf, such as deleting junk e-mail, scheduling appointments, or travelling over interconnected networks to find the cheapest airfare to St. John's.

There are many intelligent agent applications today in operating systems, application software, e-mail systems, mobile computing software, and network tools. For example, the wizards found in Microsoft Office software tools have built-in capabilities to show users how to accomplish various tasks, such as formatting documents or creating graphs, and to anticipate when users need assistance.

Of special interest to business are intelligent agents for cruising networks, including the Internet, in search of information. Chapter 7 describes how shopping bots can help consumers find products they want and assist them in comparing prices and other features.

Many complex phenomena can be modelled as systems of autonomous agents that follow relatively simple rules for interaction. **Agent-based modelling** applications have been developed to model the behaviour of consumers, stock markets, and supply chains and to predict the spread of epidemics (Samuelson and Macal, 2006).

Procter & Gamble used agent-based modelling to improve coordination among different members of its supply chain in response to changing business conditions (see Figure 15-13). It modelled a complex supply chain as a group of semiautonomous "agents" representing individual supply chain components, such as trucks, production facilities, distributors, and retail stores. The behaviour of each agent is programmed to follow rules that mimic actual behaviour, such as "order an item when it is out of stock." Simulations using the agents enable the company to perform what-if analyses on inventory levels, in-store stockouts, and transportation costs.

Using intelligent agent models, P&G discovered that trucks should often be dispatched before being fully loaded. Although transportation costs would be higher using partially loaded trucks, the simulation showed that retail store stockouts would occur less often, thus reducing the amount of lost sales, which would more than make up for the higher distribution costs. Agent-based modelling has saved P&G $300 million annually on an investment of less than 1 percent of that amount (Anthes, 2003).

Hybrid AI systems
Intelligent agents
Agent-based modelling

FIGURE 15-13   Intelligent agents in P&G's supply chain network.

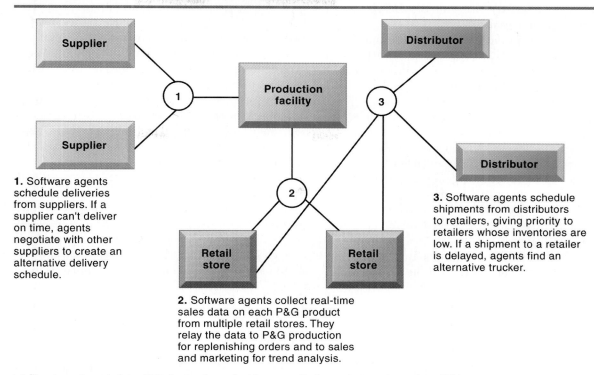

1. Software agents schedule deliveries from suppliers. If a supplier can't deliver on time, agents negotiate with other suppliers to create an alternative delivery schedule.

2. Software agents collect real-time sales data on each P&G product from multiple retail stores. They relay the data to P&G production for replenishing orders and to sales and marketing for trend analysis.

3. Software agents schedule shipments from distributors to retailers, giving priority to retailers whose inventories are low. If a shipment to a retailer is delayed, agents find an alternative trucker.

Intelligent agents are helping P&G shorten the replenishment cycles for products such as a box of Tide.

SUMMARY

1. ***What is the role of knowledge management and knowledge management programs in business?***

    Knowledge management is a set of processes to create, store, transfer, and apply knowledge in the organization. Much of a firm's value depends on its ability to create and manage knowledge. Knowledge management promotes organizational learning by increasing the ability of the organization to learn from its environment and to incorporate knowledge into its business processes. There are three major types of knowledge management systems: enterprise-wide knowledge management systems, knowledge work systems, and intelligent techniques.

2. ***What types of systems are used for enterprise-wide knowledge management, and how do they provide value for businesses?***

    Enterprise-wide knowledge management systems are firm-wide efforts to collect, store, distribute, and apply digital content and knowledge. Enterprise content management systems provide databases and tools for organizing and storing structured documents and tools for organizing and storing semistructured knowledge, such as e-mail or rich media. Knowledge network systems provide directories and tools for locating firm employees with special expertise who are important sources of

tacit knowledge. Often these systems include group collaboration tools (including wikis and social bookmarking), portals to simplify information access, search tools, and tools for classifying information based on a taxonomy that is appropriate for the organization. Enterprise-wide knowledge management systems can provide considerable value if they are well designed and enable employees to locate, share, and use knowledge more efficiently.

3. ***What are the major types of knowledge work systems, and how do they provide value for firms?***

    Knowledge work systems (KWS) support the creation of new knowledge and its integration into the organization. KWS require easy access to an external knowledge base; powerful computer hardware that can support software with intensive graphics, analysis, document management, and communications capabilities; and a user-friendly interface. Computer-aided design (CAD) systems and virtual reality systems, which create interactive simulations that behave like the real world, require graphics and powerful modelling capabilities. KWS for financial professionals provide access to external databases and the ability to analyze massive amounts of financial data very quickly.

4. *What are the business benefits of using intelligent techniques for knowledge management?*

Artificial intelligence lacks the flexibility, breadth, and generality of human intelligence, but it can be used to capture, codify, and extend organizational knowledge. Expert systems capture tacit knowledge from a limited domain of human expertise and express that knowledge in the form of rules. Expert systems are most useful for problems of classification or diagnosis. Case-based reasoning represents organizational knowledge as a database of cases that can be continually expanded and refined.

Fuzzy logic is a software technology for expressing knowledge in the form of rules that use approximate or subjective values. Fuzzy logic has been used for controlling physical devices and is starting to be used for limited decision-making applications.

Neural networks consist of hardware and software that attempt to mimic the thought processes of the human brain. Neural networks are notable for their ability to learn without programming and to recognize patterns that cannot be easily described by humans. They are being used in science, medicine, and business to discover patterns in massive amounts of data.

Genetic algorithms develop solutions to particular problems using genetically based processes such as fitness, crossover, and mutation. Genetic algorithms are beginning to be applied to problems involving optimization, product design, and monitoring industrial systems where many alternatives or variables must be evaluated to generate an optimal solution.

Intelligent agents are software programs with built-in or learned knowledge bases that carry out specific, repetitive, and predictable tasks for an individual user, business process, or software application. Intelligent agents can be programmed to navigate through large amounts of data to locate useful information and in some cases act on that information on behalf of the user.

Key Terms

Agent-based modelling, 480
Artificial intelligence (AI), 473
Backward chaining, 475
Case-based reasoning (CBR), 476
Communities of practice (COPs), 463
Computer-aided design (CAD), 470
Data, 460
Digital asset management systems, 466
Enterprise content management systems, 464
Enterprise-wide knowledge management systems, 463
Expert systems, 473
Explicit knowledge, 460

Folksonomies, 467
Forward chaining, 475
Fuzzy logic, 477
Genetic algorithms, 479
Hybrid AI systems, 480
Inference engine, 473
Intelligent agents, 480
Intelligent techniques, 464
Investment workstations, 472
Knowledge, 460
Knowledge base, 473
Knowledge discovery, 473
Knowledge management, 461

Knowledge network systems, 466
Knowledge work systems (KWS), 464
Learning management system (LMS), 467
Neural networks, 478
Organizational learning, 461
Social bookmarking, 467
Structured knowledge, 464
Tacit knowledge, 460
Taxonomy, 465
Virtual Reality Modelling Language (VRML), 472
Virtual reality systems, 471
Wisdom, 460

Review Questions

1. *What is the role of knowledge management and knowledge management programs in business?*

- *Define knowledge management, and explain its value to businesses.*
- *Describe the important dimensions of knowledge.*
- *Distinguish between data, knowledge, and wisdom and between tacit knowledge and explicit knowledge.*
- *Describe the stages in the knowledge management value chain.*

2. *What types of systems are used for enterprise-wide knowledge management, and how do they provide value for businesses?*

- *Define and describe the various types of enterprise-wide knowledge management systems, and explain how they provide value for businesses.*
- *Describe the role of the following in facilitating knowledge management: portals, wikis, social bookmarking, and learning management systems.*

3. *What are the major types of knowledge work systems, and how do they provide value for firms?*

- *Define knowledge work systems, and describe the generic requirements of knowledge work systems.*
- *Describe how the following systems support knowledge work: CAD, virtual reality, and investment workstations.*

4. *What are the business benefits of using intelligent techniques for knowledge management?*

- *Define an expert system, describe how it works, and explain its value to business.*
- *Define case-based reasoning, and explain how it differs from an expert system.*
- *Define a neural network, and describe how it works and how it benefits businesses.*
- *Define and describe fuzzy logic, genetic algorithms, and intelligent agents. Explain how each works and the kinds of problems for which each is suited.*

Discussion Questions

1. *Knowledge management is a business process, not a technology. Discuss your opinion.*

2. *Describe various ways that knowledge management systems could help firms with sales and marketing or with manufacturing and production.*

Collaboration and Teamwork: Rating Knowledge Network Systems

With a group of classmates, select two knowledge network system products, such as AskMe Enterprise and Tacit ActiveNet. Compare their features and capabilities. To prepare your analysis, use articles from computer magazines and the Web sites for the knowledge network software vendors. If possible, use electronic presentation software to present your findings to the class. If possible, use Google Sites to post links to Web pages, team communication announcements, and work assignments; to brainstorm; and to work collaboratively on project documents. Try to use Google Docs to develop a presentation of your findings for the class.

 Visit the MyMISLab Web site at **www.pearsoned.ca/mymislab**. This online homework and tutorial system puts you in control of your own learning with study and practice tools directly correlated to this chapter's content.

Learning Track Module

The following Learning Track provides content relevant to topics covered in this chapter:

1. Challenges of Knowledge Management Systems

HANDS-ON MIS   Projects

The projects in this section give you hands-on experience designing a knowledge portal, applying collaboration tools to solve a customer retention problem, using an expert system or spreadsheet tools to create a simple expert system, and using intelligent agents to research products for sale on the Web.

Management Decision Problems

1. U.S. Pharma Corporation, a fictional company, is headquartered in New Jersey but has research sites in Germany, France, the United Kingdom, Switzerland, and Australia. Research and development of new pharmaceuticals is the key to ongoing profits, and U.S. Pharma conducts research on and tests thousands of possible drugs. The company's researchers need to share information with others within and outside the company, including the U.S. Food and Drug Administration, Health Canada, the World Health Organization, and the International Federation of Pharmaceutical Manufacturers & Associations. Also critical is access to health information sites and to industry conferences and professional journals. Design a knowledge portal for Pharma's researchers. Include in your design specifications relevant internal systems and databases, external sources of information, and internal and external communication and collaboration tools. Design a home page for your portal.

2. Sprint Nextel has the highest rate of customer churn (the number of customers who discontinue a service) in the cell phone industry, amounting to 2.45 percent. In the first quarter of 2008 alone, 1.1 million customers switched from Sprint to another cell phone carrier. Management wants to know why so many

customers are leaving Sprint and what can be done to woo them back. Are customers deserting because of poor customer service, uneven network coverage, or the cost of Sprint cell phone plans? How can the

company use tools for online collaboration and communication to help find the answer? What management decisions could be made using information from these sources?

Improving Decision Making: Building a Simple Expert System for Retirement Planning

Software skills: Spreadsheet formulas and IF function or expert system tool
Business skills: Benefits eligibility determination

Expert systems typically use a large number of rules. This project has been simplified to reduce the number of rules, but it will give you experience working with a series of rules to develop an application.

When employees at your company retire, they are given cash bonuses. These cash bonuses are based on the length of employment and the retiree's age. To receive a bonus, an employee must be at least 50 years of age and have worked for the company for five years. The following table summarizes the criteria for determining bonuses.

Length of Employment	Bonus
<5 years	No bonus
5–10 years	20 percent of current annual salary
11–15 years	30 percent of current annual salary
16–20 years	40 percent of current annual salary
20–25 years	50 percent of current annual salary
26 or more years	100 percent of current annual salary

Using the information provided, build a simple expert system. Find a demonstration copy of an expert system software tool on the Web that you can download. Alternatively, use your spreadsheet software to build the expert system. (If you are using spreadsheet software, we suggest using the IF function so you can see how rules are created.)

Improving Decision Making: Using Intelligent Agents for Comparison Shopping

Software skills: Web browser and shopping bot software
Business skills: Product evaluation and selection

This project will give you experience using shopping bots to search online for products, find product information, and find the best prices and vendors.

You have decided to purchase a new digital camera. Select a digital camera you might want to purchase, such as the Canon PowerShot SD 950 or the Olympus Stylus 1200. To purchase the camera as inexpensively as possible, try

several of the shopping bot sites, which do the price comparisons for you. Visit My Simon (**www.mysimon.com**), BizRate.com (**www.bizrate.com**), and Google Product Search (**www.google.com/products**). Compare these shopping sites in terms of their ease of use, number of offerings, speed in obtaining information, thoroughness of information offered about the product and seller, and price selection. Which site or sites would you use and why? Which camera would you select and why? How helpful were these sites for making your decision?

CASE STUDY Innovation and Collaboration at Coca-Cola: It's the Real Thing

The Coca-Cola Company is the largest manufacturer, distributor, and marketer of nonalcoholic beverages, concentrates, and syrups in the world. Coca-Cola owns and maintains more than 450 brands, including Coke, Fanta, Sprite, Minute Maid, and Dasani water, some of which were obtained through acquisitions. The company's corporate headquarters are in Atlanta, Georgia, but Coke has operations in more than 200 countries worldwide.

Much of the company's success is a result of its highly recognizable and trusted brand. The Coca-Cola brand is often considered to be the most valuable brand in the world. The brand also holds a unique and important place in American culture. The Coca-Cola brand gives the company a large competitive advantage in the nonalcoholic beverage market.

Coca-Cola sells both its own beverages and concentrates and syrups to its bottling companies. Healthy partnerships with bottlers are critical to the financial well-being of the company. Of the 53 billion beverages consumed each day, 1.5 billion of those bear the Coke trademark. The company earned $35 billion in revenue in 2007, with more than 70 percent coming from outside the United States.

However, Coca-Cola's continued success is not a foregone conclusion. Threats to Coke's future profitability include growing health concerns regarding sweetened beverages and their implications for obesity, water scarcity in multiple regions worldwide, potential inability to expand into developing areas, ongoing relationships with bottling partners, and unfavourable economic conditions around the world.

New CEO Muhtar Kent, who took the chief executive position in July 2008, faces all of these challenges as he takes over from prior CEO Neville Isdell. Kent worked closely with Isdell on many initiatives and appears poised to steer the company through difficult times. Coke has held up better than many companies during the economic downturn, but profits have been tougher to come by in North America.

Even in periods of strong economic growth, the nonalcoholic beverage market is fast-moving, fad-driven, commodity-influenced, and difficult to control for very long. In order to maintain its status as a titan within this treacherous market, Coca-Cola must continue to use its brands, its financial strength, its strong distribution system, and its global reach to remain competitive and foster growth. Another critical objective for the company is to focus on innovation and collaboration with its customers, employees, and partners. For a global company like Coke, this objective is especially important and requires a considerable investment of time, energy, and resources.

For Coke, some of the changes that most effectively fostered innovation and collaboration have come in the form of new information systems. One prominent example involved an overhaul to the company's "digital asset management." As Coke continued to expand its global presence, a growing amount of digital content was scattered in an unorganized fashion. Employees had to spend considerable time searching through a growing mountain of content regarding market demographics, sales figures, images, videos, and cultural information and grapple with disorganized record keeping.

Coke's strength is built on images, messages, and marketing savvy, but sales and marketing teams around the globe lacked simple access to this information. So Coke used IBM's Content Manager software to create an online image library and digital archive containing images, documents, and videos, accessible by all employees via a standardized platform through the Web.

The company and its bottlers have all made a concerted effort to upgrade their infrastructure to reach their goal of more effective collaboration. In March 2008, Coca-Cola Enterprises (CCE), the company's largest bottling company, announced it would begin using Microsoft collaboration tools, including SharePoint Online for ad hoc team collaboration and content management, LiveMeeting for Web conferencing, and Office Communications Server Online for unified communications. Until then, the company had used nonintegrated collaboration tools. The integrated Microsoft products enhance

communication and collaboration across the company. Executives are able to broadcast live video to all of the company's knowledge workers. Employees can schedule LiveMeeting Web conferences using Microsoft Outlook or engage in a chat session using Office Communicator's instant messaging tool and turn it into a phone call. SharePoint provides a platform for a new intranet featuring industry news, video and audio content, executive blogs, and employee polls. CCE eventually wants to extend collaboration capabilities to mobile devices used by its 30 000 employees who stock trucks and replenish vending machines.

Coke continued efforts to foster innovation via information technology by developing the Common Innovation Framework: a system that allows Coca-Cola employees worldwide to search for and apply concepts to all of Coke's 2800 beverages. The system combines project management and business intelligence and is geared toward developing products and marketing them in a consistent and successful way across all of Coke's properties.

The system is used to develop new beverages, design new equipment, and create packaging concepts for new and established products. The goal of the system is to make the beverage and brand concepts that contributed to the success of certain products readily available to marketers and developers throughout the global enterprise, so that those concepts can be included in future products as well.

Coke Zero is an example of how the Common Innovation Framework is fuelling innovation and collaboration at the company. Coke Zero is a recent smash hit for the company. It is marketed as a diet cola without the bitter aftertaste. The Common Innovation Framework allowed managers and personnel in disparate areas of the company and various regions (finance, legal, marketing, R&D) to view the practices that made it successful in other countries and apply those concepts to future products. Japan is regarded as the most cutting-edge country when it comes to what will be popular; the Common Innovation Framework lets development teams in the United States and Europe see what is popular in Japan and allows them to carry those trends over in their own markets.

Coke's partnership with its bottlers is important to its success, but sometimes the relationship between the bottlers and the parent company can be strained. Coke relies mostly on independent, local bottlers, which is a boon to the communities in which the bottlers are located. Coke has significant investments in many bottling companies and even owns some bottlers outright. But because Coke owns a controlling stake in only a fraction of the total number of bottlers it uses for its products, it can be a challenge to get all of the approximately 300 bottling companies Coke deals with onto the same platform for the purpose of sharing information.

Coke's Project Scale was implemented to standardize the way Coke communicates with its bottlers and vice versa. Coke surveyed its largest bottlers and discovered that 90 percent of their business practices were shared and that most bottlers had planned software upgrades in the upcoming several years. So Coke developed the Coke One bottler model, based on version 6.0 of SAP's ERP platform. Coke

One supports 650 business processes common to all bottlers, which were eager to implement the model because they were hoping to upgrade their software anyway.

Coke hoped that the end result of the program would be better communication between the parent company and its bottlers, and by the same token, a more streamlined supply chain and a more cordial relationship between them. Some larger bottlers struck their own partnership with other technology companies as CCE did when it opted out of Coke One. But for smaller bottlers, the program represents readily available intellectual property and opportunities to get better deals, faster implementation of new processes, and higher capability. Project Scale has generally been regarded as a success since its implementation.

The fickle tastes of consumers represent an ongoing challenge for Coca-Cola as it continues to pursue growth and profitability. To that end, the company created Mycokerewards.com, a social network that acquires members by appealing to their tastes in sports, music, entertainment, and beverages. The site is an interactive showcase for Coke products and a place where drinkers of any Coke-trademarked beverage can redeem points for items that interest them in addition to networking with other Coke drinkers with similar interests.

Coke is also innovating within existing social networks like Facebook to market their products. Burn Energy Drinks, a Coke brand developed by Coca-Cola Europe, launched a groundbreaking application, Burn Alter Ego, which combines existing Facebook friendships, avatar mashup photo technology, and party storytelling. The application allows users to develop a virtual persona that has a "nightlife" that is entirely separate from their own. The more you use your character, the more options you have in customizing your avatar. The application is supposed to add excitement and randomness to existing friendships, and in the process, the developers hope, create more buzz surrounding Burn Energy Drinks.

All of these initiatives to foster innovation and richer collaboration between Coca-Cola employees figure to help the company remain competitive going forward. But competing industry giant Pepsico has gained market share while Coke has lost ground in the past few years. Like Coca-Cola, it has expanded into faster-growing markets for non-carbonated beverages and health drinks, and it is a formidable challenger. Other smaller companies like Cadbury Schwepps threaten to chip away at Coke's dominance in the market. The company believes that Coke's investment in innovation and collaboration should stand the company in good stead in the years to come.

CASE STUDY QUESTIONS:

1. Analyze Coca-Cola and its business strategy using the value chain and competitive forces models.

2. What is the relationship of collaboration and knowledge management to Coca-Cola's business strategy?

3. How is Coca-Cola using knowledge management systems to execute its business model and business strategy?

4. Why is Coca-Cola's relationship with its bottlers so important? What is Coke doing to improve its ability to collaborate with its bottlers?

5. What are Coca-Cola's prospects for success in the future? Will information systems make a difference? Why or why not?

Sources: Mary Hayes Weier, "Coke Exploits Collaboration Technology to Keep Brand Relevant," *InformationWeek*, July 19, 2008; Betsy McKay, "Can New CEO Put Fizz Back in Coke?" *The Wall Street Journal*, June 30, 2008; Theresa Lagos, "Coca-Cola Enterprises Leads in Global Collaboration and Next-Generation Business Processes with Cisco Technologies," Reuters.com, April 10, 2008; and "Our Company— Innovation," **www.coca-colathecompany.com** (accessed August 2008).

Part IV CANADIAN CASE STUDY:
Second Life: A New Generation of Online Application

Imagine you are a business student attending a British Columbia university, majoring in management information systems. Now imagine that you enjoy logging on to a site known as Second Life (**www.secondlife.com**) to play around in a virtual animated environment. Your interests, in addition to business, are criminal justice and law enforcement.

While dabbling one afternoon in Second Life, you meet three other animated characters, who it turns out are actually members of Vancouver's Police Department. They are in fact recruiting for new skilled technology workers to join the Vancouver Police Department. You decide to talk with these police characters and apply for one of these new-generation police positions.

Actually, that is happening now. Second Life is a sophisticated, online three-dimensional virtual world. It is customizable; users can register for free and create their own characters, known as avatars; there are no assigned roles for these avatars. Your avatar can represent you physically—or not. Your avatar may even be an animal or a metaphysical character or dragon—or almost anything else. You can customize the height, weight, skin colour, hair colour—almost any physical characteristic of your avatar—and name it with a pseudonym that represents whatever your desire is. Avatars can walk, run, dance, jump, fly, and even teleport to different environments, or properties, in Second Life. They can meet other avatars, interact, play, build, date, buy, and sell.

Buy and sell? What can they buy and sell? Users who register for free have a limited choice of clothes for their avatars. If you pay for a premium membership (approximately $12 per month), you have access to more costumes and accessories (boots, purses, bookbags, etc.) and can even buy virtual real estate to build your own nightclub, gym, coffee house, school, resort, hotel, or even home on. Trade is made in Linden dollars. Why Linden dollars? Linden Lab developed Second Life, so it called its virtual currency Linden dollars (L$). Premium users receive a one-time grant in Linden dollars of L$1250 plus a weekly stipend of L$300. It takes about 212 L$ to make CDN $1, as of July 2009 (but all L$ are measured only in U.S. dollars, so L$260 equals approximately US $1). There are even systems for converting Linden dollars to real-world U.S. dollars.

Let us look deeper at what Second Life is and then at what it represents for the future of online applications and electronic commerce. Second Life requires a fairly fast computer with a fairly fast graphics card and a broadband Internet connection. Second Life was originally an undeveloped environment or grid, the equivalent of a wilderness waiting to be developed by users. Users who register (and are known as members or residents) download the Second Life user software and can then begin their Second Life travels. Users can also create multiple accounts, appearing as various avatars; there is an additional premium for these multiple accounts. A single avatar's appearance can change dramatically as users can change their avatars whenever they wish.

In Second Life, members develop their own "content" or environment and retain intellectual property rights to their creations in the real world. The content varies from the costumes members can purchase to virtual shopping malls and gaming platforms. In addition to selling products, services are also available, such as classes in a variety of disciplines. Other members then buy this content, for example an avatar costume, for L$; the creator receives payment in L$, which can eventually be converted to real-world cash. A small percentage of residents actually earn income from the Second Life economy, from a few hundred to even several thousand dollars a month. A larger percentage make enough L$ to offset most of their own L$ expenditures. It is amusing that the Linden currency has drawn interest in economic circles regarding the possibility of taxing income earned in Linden dollars.

Second Life has a three-dimensional modelling tool enabling residents to create virtual landscapes, buildings, vehicles, furniture, costumes, machines—almost anything the mind can invent. There is also a standard library of gestures and sounds that avatars can make. Second Life also has its own scripting language, LSL, to add behaviours to objects, such as opening doors when approached. Creators of objects and behaviours can mark them as "no copy," "no mod" (cannot be modified by another), or "no trans" (meaning no transfer to another avatar). Residents are even recording music and uploading the files to Second Life so other residents can enjoy the music.

Residents of Second Life can also buy real estate in 65,536 square metre (16 acre) parcels, which are termed *islands*, and develop their islands as they see fit. Premium members can buy land up to 512 square metres without paying an additional fee. Larger areas require the payment of additional premiums that can range from US $5 per month to US $295 per month to own an island. This real estate can be sold to other residents for a profit—of course, in L$. Some private islands, governed by residents, have covenants, limiting resale or commercial activity, or having other restrictions.

Warning: There is adult content in Second Life; some islands are set up as brothels or pot shops. Mature content is separated from underage users; interestingly, for the underage crowd, there is a Teen Second Life. Teen Second Life was created in 2005 to permit teenagers to play in Second Life without having to falsify their personal information. Teen Second Life requires a valid cell phone number with SMS enabled (for the first-time logon validation message) but no longer requires a parent's credit card number.

To communicate in a text-based mode, residents can use local chat or global instant messaging. Chatting is used for public, but local, conversation that can be heard within 25 virtual metres, with the ability to whisper (heard only within 18 virtual metres) or shout (heard up to 96 virtual metres). Instant messaging is used for private conversations between only two avatars or the members of a group. Second Life even permits voice communication.

Avatars can walk or run, but they can also fly up to 170 virtual metres above their current terrain, or even higher. Avatars can ride in vehicles, even buying their own vehicles. Avatars can even teleport directly to a specific location. Interestingly, an avatar can create a "personal landmark," sort of a home base, and teleport back to it at any time, even giving the landmark to another avatar.

The technology driving Second Life is very advanced. Using various server farms, Second Life stores data about its residents and their accounts, the products and services that have been created, the geography of Second Life (real estate owned by residents), all of which are known as "assets." Occasionally, the servers are overloaded, and Second Life slows down, with some environments temporarily crashing. Linden Lab uses open-standards technologies, permitting users to create and improve software for the use of Linden Lab and Second Life. There are viewers, that is, client software, for Microsoft Windows, Mac OS X, and most versions of Linux for viewing the site that incorporates all of this technology.

Enough about how Second Life works. How did it get started? What makes it so important for commerce?

In 2003, Philip Rosedale, the former chief technology officer at Real Networks, created Second Life as part of his Linden Lab, the company he founded in 1999. Rosedale's investors included top technology gurus, such as Mitch Kapor, the creator of Lotus, Pierre Omidyar, the founder of eBay, Jeff Bezos, the founder of Amazon.com, and Ray Ozzie, who is Microsoft's chief technology architect; interestingly, they can all be found in

Second Life as avatars; Kapor also serves on Linden Lab's board of directors.

What makes Second Life so important? Its economy and its residents provide a real marketplace for real-world companies. How does that happen, and how are real-world companies and other organizations using Second Life?

In July 2008, Second Life had more than 14 million members representing more than 100 countries, 1.1 million of whom had logged on in the last 30 days. More than 40 000 users are logged on at almost any point during the day and into the night. More than 20 000 new members join Second Life every day. More than US $1.5 million is spent on Second Life in a 24-hour period, with more than L$ 200 000 being traded in a 24-hour period. In June 2008, almost 400 000 residents spent Linden dollars on the Grid. The Second Life economy has L$ 2.6 billion in circulation. The sheer volume of this virtual market has attracted a number of commercial, governmental, and not-for-profit organizations to try to use this market to further their goals.

As we saw at the beginning of this discussion, the Vancouver Police Department is recruiting on Second Life and held an information session for potential recruits in June 2007 on Second Life. After the information session, the Police Department received three résumés by e-mail and actually decided to interview a candidate who had attended the information session while in Italy.

Hewlett-Packard, Microsoft, and other technology companies are conducting initial interviews and participating in job fairs online at Second Life. Of course, follow-up interviews are held in person. Certain online etiquette applies, even for avatars, during job interviews. Communication is by instant messaging, with real-world information, such as names, being exchanged. One candidate for a Hewlett-Packard job was a man, whose avatar was female, but he felt that the Hewlett-Packard representative understood he was a man since he told the representative his real-world name. Gaffes such as having your avatar run into a wall or present a beer rather than a résumé to the interviewer are usually laughed off by both the resident and the interviewer since both know that the Second Life technology can occasionally be tricky to manoeuvre.

Canada Post has set up a retail area in Second Life. The retailers represented in Maple Grove are all in the Lookbook catalogue, a catalogue of Canadian catalogues published by Canada Post twice a year to showcase its retailer partners. Maple Grove and its stores are located on Second Life "land"—basically, a server—acquired by Canada Post from Second Life owner Linden Research Inc. The retailers do not pay to lease their virtual storefronts, but they do pay Canada Post a monthly maintenance fee. Maple Grove includes both U.S. and Canadian retailers that participate in the Lookbook catalogue.

The virtual stores are not transaction-enabled in the Second Life environment, but visitors can click on selected items in Maple Grove's stores to be delivered to a retailer's e-commerce site. "There are hundreds of thousands of Canadians in Second Life," says Laurene Cihosky, senior vice president for Canada Post's direct marketing division. "We want Maple Grove to be a place where they are comfortable to visit because it has a uniquely Canadian feel."

Governmental agencies also take an interest in this online world. Sweden recently became the first country to open an embassy in Second Life. The purpose of the online embassy is to promote Sweden's image and culture. The Government of Ontario is using Second Life for recruiting.

Second Life is being used as a giant virtual classroom for major colleges and universities, including Harvard, Princeton, Stanford, Loyalist College and Mohawk College (both located in Ontario), Queensland University in Australia, Thompson Rivers University in British Columbia, and a large number of universities and colleges from Europe (many from the United Kingdom) and the United States. In Canada, Great Northern Way Campus is a collaboration between four Canadian schools: the University of British Columbia, Simon Fraser University, British Columbia Institute of Technology, and Emily Carr Institute of Art and Design. This campus has a real-world presence just east of Vancouver. In Second Life, however, the campus erected a new virtual campus with a state-of-the-art virtual building on a Second Life island. Courses are offered through this online campus for the Masters in Digital Media program.

Late in 2006, a new trend occurred in Second Life. Large consortia of educational institutions purchase islands and then divide the "land" into smaller parcels to rent to colleges, universities, and educational projects and libraries. Land can be rented for as little as $200 per year with permission to use common space for larger events. Some of these universities even host advertising for positions for faculty in Second Life.

Corporations doing business in Second Life include Microsoft, Warner Brothers, Nike, Major League Baseball, Dell, Adidas, General Motors and Circuit City. An avatar can buy a pair of Nike shoes and wear them; Nike hopes, of course, that the real-world resident will also buy a pair of its shoes, so Second Life is basically another marketing and promotion channel.

In the movie *Field of Dreams*, the phrase "If you build it, they will come," achieved cultural recognition. In terms of Second Life, this has certainly been true. Online users by the millions have flocked to create the virtual environment that is Second Life. For each of the online locations created by schools, organizations, and corporations, it is apparent they believe that if they build their Second Life environment, not only will Second Life avatars come, but so will their real-world counterparts flock to these organizations' real-world counterparts.

To date, there has been no publicly available research to show that this is true, that companies and other groups hosting a Second Life presence are increasing sales or memberships. Some users who pay for premium membership resent those who ride their efforts for free without paying the premium. So it remains to be seen exactly how and how much Second Life will change the way we do business and receive education. But as the first such online environment with such a high volume of activity, it is possible that Second Life will present a new way of doing business.

CASE STUDY QUESTIONS

1. Do you think Second Life is a new way of doing business? Why or why not?

2. Do you think Second Life will survive and thrive, or do you think other similar online sites will catch up and pass Second Life?

3. Why would companies and other organizations choose to host a Second Life presence? How would a company make that decision? Who would be assigned to work on creating and maintaining the company's presence on Second Life?

4. How can organizations use data they collect in Second Life about visitors to their area of Second Life? Is Second Life a worthwhile use of organizational resources?

Sources: Wency Leung, "Recruiting Real Talent in a Virtual World," *The Globe and Mail*, July 16, 2007; "Pontiac Second Life Case Study," A Media Circus, **http://amediacirc.us/2007/02/29/pontiac-second-life-case-studyraw-notes** (accessed October 7, 2007); "Second Life," **http://en.wikipedia.org/wiki/Second_Life** (accessed July 15, 2007); Bob Rankin, "What Is Second Life?" **http://askbobrankin.com/what_is_second_life.html** (accessed October 7, 2009); Second Life home page, **www.secondlife.com** (accessed July 22, 2007); Sim Teach home page, **http://simteach.com/wiki/index.php?title=Institutions_and_Organizations_in_SL#UNIVERSITIES.2C_COLLEGES_.26_SCHOOLS** (accessed July 22, 2007); "Economic Statistics," **www.secondlife.com/whatis/economy_stats.php** (accessed July 22, 2007); "Visiting Second Life's Virtual World," *CBC News in Review* (February 2007).

References

Chapter 1

"Activision Uses LifeSize HD Video to Accelerate Game Development." **www.lifesize.com/files/Activision_ Case_Study.pdf** (accessed July 26, 2009).

Brynjolfsson, Erik and Lorin M. Hitt. "Beyond Computation: Information Technology, Organizational Transformation, and Business Performance." *Journal of Economic Perspectives,* 14(4) (2000).

Brynjolfsson, Erik. "The IT Productivity Gap." *Optimize* Magazine (July 2003).

Davern, Michael J. and Robert J. Kauffman. "Discovering Potential and Realizing Value form Information Technology Investments." *Journal of Management Information Systems,* 16(4) (Spring 2000).

Deutsch, Claudia. "Still Brown, but Going High Tech." *The New York Times* (July 12, 2007).

EMarketer. "Canada Online: Users and Usage." **www.emarketer .com/Reports/All/Emarketer_2000602.aspx** (2006).

Filipponio, Frank. "Toyota Aims to Sell 10.4M Vehicles in 2009." **www.autoblog.com/2007/08/22/toyotal-aims-to-sell-10- 4m-vehicles-in-2009/print** (accessed July 26, 2009).

Fratto, Mike. "High-Def Conferencing at a Low Price." *InformationWeek* (July 14, 2008).

Friedman, Thomas. *The World Is Flat.* New York: Farrar, Straus, and Giroux (2006).

Kolbasuk McGee, Marianne. "Looking into the Work-Trend Crystal Ball." *InformationWeek* (June 24, 2008).

Krapf, Eric. "What's Video Good For?" *InformationWeek* (July 1, 2008).

Laudon, Kenneth C. *Computers and Bureaucratic Reform.* New York: Wiley (1974).

Lohr, Steve. "As Travel Costs Rise, More Meetings Go Virtual." *The New York Times* (July 22, 2008).

"LTL's High-Tech Infusion." *UPS Compass* (Spring 2007).

Pew Internet and American Life. "Internet Activities." (2008). **www.pewinternet.org,** (accessed September 20, 2008).

Potterf, Katheryn. "Ready to Roll." *Profit Magazine* (May 26, 2008).

Rapoza, Jim. "Videoconferencing Redux." *eWeek* (July 21, 2008).

"RCGA Case Study." **www.martron.com** (accessed June 1, 2007).

"RCGA Cuts Costs and Improves Customer Service with Microsoft® .NET-based Online Tournament Program, April 21, 2005, **www.microsoft.com/canada/casestudies/ rcga.mspx?pf=true** (accessed September 3, 2009).

Rowley, Ian. "No Traffic Ahead for Toyota." *BusinessWeek* (February 6, 2006).

———. "Triumphs & Trip-Ups in 2004." *Baseline Magazine* (December 20, 2004).

Schwartz, Karen D. "Videoconferencing on a Budget." *eWeek* (May 29, 2008).

"Stephen Ross Fired as RCGA Executive Director." March 9, 2007, **www.fairwaysgolf.ca/news.php?id=290&what= news** (accessed September 3, 2009).

Teece, David. *Economic Performance and Theory of the Firm: The Selected Papers of David Teece.* London: Edward Elgar Publishing (1998).

United Parcel Service. "Powering Up the Supply Chain." *UPS Compass,* (Winter 2008). **www.ups.com** (accessed July 26, 2008).

Verisign. "Domain Name Industry Brief." (June 2008). **www.verisign.com** (accessed October 2, 2008).

Chapter 2

"Air Canada Selects Maintenix for Fleetwide Implementation." Reuters (April 15, 2008).

Chang, Richard. "Nano's Price Is Under Pressure." *The New York Times* (August 10, 2008).

Duvall, Mel. "Kia Motors America: Lemon Aid." *Baseline Magazine* (June 2005).

"Hudson's Bay Company Creates an Award-Winning Inventory Solution." **www.xtremeretail.com/studies/hbcfinal.pdf** (accessed September 3, 2009).

"Hudson's Bay Company Gains More Accurate Business Snapshot of its Zellers Operations with Microsoft SQL Server 2000 Reporting Services." **www.microsoft.com/ canada/casestudies/hbc.mspx** (accessed September 3, 2009).

"Maintenix Product Overview." **www.mxi.com** (accessed September 24, 2009).

Meckbach, Greg. "Air Canada to Overhaul Maintenance Software." *ComputerWorld Canada* (April 18, 2008).

Patrick, Ryan. "HBC Puts LID Technology on Zellers Inventory." IT World Canada. **www.itworldcanada.com/ Mobile/ViewArticle.aspx?title=&id=idgml-2726a919- 81bd-4628&s=395692** (accessed September 3, 2009).

SAP. "Alcan Packaging Implements mySAP SCM to Increase Shareholder Value." **www.mysap.com** (accessed August 20, 2005).

SAP AG. "Air Liquide." (2007).

Simons, Craig. "Kia Makes U.S. Inroads and Builds for Future Growth." Cox News Service (March 14, 2006).

Sutton, Neil. "HBC Puts IT Smarts into Its Merchandising Strategy." IT Business Canada. **www.itbusiness.ca,it/ client/en/Home/News.asp?id=40143&bsearch=True** (accessed September 3, 2009).

Trivedi, Gunjan. "Driving Down Cost." *CIO Asia* (February 2008).

www.kia.com (accessed June 18, 2006).

www.tatapeoplescar.com (accessed July 31, 2008).

Weill, Peter and Jeanne W. Ross. *IT Governance.* Boston: Harvard Business School Press (2004).

Chapter 3

"About 7-Eleven." **www.7-eleven.com/about/history.asp** (accessed May 11, 2007).

Alter, S. and Ginzberg, M. "Managing Uncertainty in MIS Implementation." *Sloan Management Review*, 20(1) (1978): 23–31.

"Amazon Adds Groceries to Its Site." *The Wall Street Journal* (June 15, 2006).

Associated Press. "eBay Rethinks Its Ways as It Enters Middle Age." (accessed via **CNN.com** June 18, 2007).

Barnes, Brooks. "Warner Tries a New Tactic to Revive Its DVD Sales." *The New York Times* (May 26, 2008).

Benderoff, Eric. "Web Sites Begin to Pay for Content." *The Baltimore Sun* (January 31, 2007).

Coase, Ronald H. "The Nature of the Firm." (1937) In Putterman, Louis and Randall Kroszner, *The Economic Nature of the Firm: A Reader*, Cambridge University Press, 1995.

Crane, Mary. "Child's Play? Amazon Takes On Toys." **Forbes.com** (July 5, 2006).

Drucker, Peter. "The Coming of the New Organization." *Harvard Business Review* (January–February 1988).

Flynn, Laurie J. "EBay Is Planning to Emphasize Fixed-Price Sales Format over Its Auction Model." *The New York Times* (August 20, 2008).

Holahan, Catherine. "eBay's Changing Identity." *BusinessWeek* (April 23, 2007).

———. "Google and YouTube: A Catch-22." *BusinessWeek* (January 26, 2007).

———. "Upload Video, Download Cash on YouTube?" *Business Week* (January 30, 2007).

Iansiti, Marco and Roy Levien, "Strategy as Ecology." *Harvard Business Review* (March 2004).

Jensen, Michael C., and William H. Meckling. "Theory of the Firm: Managerial Behavior, Agency Costs, and Ownership Structure." *Journal of Financial Economics* 3 (1976).

Keyes, James. "Data on the Fly." *Baseline* (August 2005).

Koch, Christopher. "Who's Mining the Store?" *CIO* (May 15, 2005).

Kolb, D.A., and A. L. Frohman. "An Organization Development Approach to Consulting." *Sloan Management Review* 12, no. 1 (Fall 1970).

Laudon, Kenneth. "A General Model of the Relationship Between Information Technology and Organizations." Center for Research on Information Systems, New York University. Working paper, National Science Foundation (1989).

Leavitt, Harold J. "Applying Organizational Change in Industry: Structural, Technological, and Humanistic Approaches." In *Handbook of Organizations*, edited by James G. March. Chicago: Rand McNally (1965).

LeClaire, Jennifer. "YouTube.com Stirs Napster Memories in Digital Movie Era." *TechNewsWorld* (February 5, 2007).

Luftman, Jerry, *Managing the Information Technology Resource: Leadership in the Information Age,* Englewood Cliffs, NJ: Prentice Hall (2003).

Marlin, Steven. "The 24-Hour Supply Chain." *InformationWeek* (January 26, 2004).

Mintzberg, Henry. *The Structuring of Organizations.* Englewood Cliffs, NJ: Prentice Hall (1979).

Neumeister, Larry. "Hollywood Asks YouTube: Friend or Foe?" *The New York Times* (January 15, 2007).

———. "Viacom Alleges YouTube Copyright Infringement." *USA Today* (May 27, 2008).

Oracle Corporation. "Streamlining Convenience." 2006 Shared Strategy Study and "7-Eleven Inc." **www.oracle.com** (accessed July 15, 2006).

Pasha, Shaheen. "Amazon Has New Stories to Tell." CNN Money (August 22, 2005).

Porter, Michael. *Competitive Advantage.* New York: Free Press (1985).

Porter, Michael E. "Strategy and the Internet." *Harvard Business Review* (March 2001).

Rivlin, Gary. "A Retail Revolution Turns 10." *The New York Times* (July 10, 2005).

Sandoval, Greg. "Does YouTube Have a Control Problem?" CNET News (February 5, 2007).

———. "Strategy and the Internet." *Harvard Business Review* (March 2001).

Steller, Brian. "Now Playing on YouTube: Clips with Ads." *The New York Times* (August 16, 2008).

Stone, Brad. "Buy.com Deal with Ebay Angers Sellers." *The New York Times* (July 14, 2008).

———. "EBay's Leader Moves Swiftly on a Revamping." *The New York Times* (January 24, 2008).

———. "Profit Climbs for eBay, but Auction Growth Is Slowing." *The New York Times* (July 17, 2008).

Stross, Randall. "Trying to Get a Read on Amazon's Books." The New York Times (February 12, 2006).

Sullivan, Laurie. "Fine-Tuned Pricing." *InformationWeek* (August 15–22, 2005).

Tedeschi, Bob. "Making Several Stops at Shops Online, but Paying All at Google." The New York Times (July 17, 2006).

Williamson, Oliver E. *The Economic Institutions of Capitalism.* New York: Free Press (1985).

Chapter 4

"About CAAST." **www.caast.com/about/default.asp?load=content** (accessed June 1, 2007).

Ball, K., "Situating Workplace Surveillance: Ethics and Computer Based Performance Monitoring. . . . Goes High Tech?" *Urban Geography* 23(3) (2001).

Brewin, Bob. "National Health Records Network to Hook Up with Google, Microsoft." **govexec.com** (March 27, 2008).

Brown Bag Software vs. Symantec Corp. 960 F2D 1465 (Ninth Circuit, 1992).

Business Software Alliance. "Global Piracy 2008" **http://global.bsa.org/globalpiracy2008/studies/globalpiracy2008.pdf** (2009).

Canadian Press. "U of M Students Disciplined for Cyberbullying." *The Globe and Mail* (March 30, 2009).

Canadian Standards Association International "Your Guide to the CSA's Privacy Code" **www.media-awareness.ca/english/resources/educational/handouts/privacy/csa_privacy_code_guide.cfm** (accessed October 7, 2009).

Carr, David F. and Sean Gallagher. "BofA's Direct-Deposit Debacle." *Baseline* (May 15, 2002).

Charkes, Juli S. "Cracking Down on the Cyberbully." *The New York Times* (March 30, 2008).

Chickowski, Ericka. "Are Google's Security Practices Up to Snuff?" **Baselinemag.com** (May 23, 2008).

Eckler, Rebecca. "The Joy of Socks." *Macleans*, March 5, 2007, **www.macleans.ca/homepage/magazine/article.jsp?content=20070305_103060_103060** (accessed August 3, 2009).

Evans, Bob. "More Opinions on Wal-Mart's Flexible Scheduling." *InformationWeek* (April 17, 2007).

———. "Wal-Mart's Latest 'Orwellian' Technology Move: Get over It." *InformationWeek* (April 6, 2007).

Gerencher, Kristen. "As More of Our Health Records Move Online, Privacy Concerns Grow." **FoxBusiness.com** (March 26, 2008).

Gonsalves, Chris. "Google, Microsoft Take Health Care IT Pulse." **Baselinemag.com** (March 31, 2008).

———. "Securing, Digitizing Medical Records Remain Priorities in Healthcare IT." **Baselinemag.com** (February 26, 2008).

Harris, Lissa. "Google Health Heads to the Hospital." *Technology Review* (May 28, 2008).

"Jeffrey Skoll." *Forbes*, **www.forbes.com/lists/2006/10/PB9U.html** (accessed August 3, 2009).

Jezovit, Andrea. "Welcome to Web 3.0." *Canadian Business Online*, June 18, 2007, **www.canadianbusiness.com/technology/trends/article.jsp?content=20070618_85496_85496** (accessed August 3, 2009).

Kiwi Commons. "Canadian Bill Proposed to Make Cyberbullying a Crime." (May 6, 2009), **www.kiwicommons.com/2009/05/Canadian-bill-proposed-to-make-cyberbullying-a-crime** (accessed July 26, 2009).

Labossiere, Danielle. "The Hidden Cost of Piracy in Canada." *The Globe and Mail* (May 5, 2006).

Lawton Christopher, and Ben Worthen. "Google to Offer Health Records on the Web." *The Wall Street Journal* (February 28, 2008).

Leishman, Joan. "Cyber-Bullying." CBC News, **www.cbc.ca/news/background/bullying/cyber_bullying.html** (accessed July 26, 2009).

Maag, Christopher. "When the Bullies Turned Faceless." *The New York Times* (December 16, 2007).

Maher, Kris. "Wal-Mart Seeks New Flexibility in Worker Shifts." *The Wall Street Journal* (January 3, 2007).

Martin, Nick. "U of M Probes Cyberbullying on Student Site." *The Winnipeg Free Press* (March 1, 2007).

Media Awareness Network. "Cyberbullying and the Law Fact Sheet. **www.media-awareness.ca/english/resources/educational/teaching_backgrounders/cyberbullying/cyberbullying_law2_h4.cfm?RenderforPrint=1** (accessed July 26, 2009).

"Missouri: Cyberbullying Law Is Signed." The Associated Press (July 1, 2008).

O'Connell, Vanessa. "Retailers Reprogram Workers in Efficiency Push." *The Wall Street Journal* (September 10, 2008).

"Preying on Patients." *MarketWatch* (June 19, 2008).

Rifkin, Jeremy. "Watch Out for Trickle-Down Technology." *The New York Times* (March 16, 1993).

Shaw, Gillian. "Majority of Canadian Kids Say Cyberbullying Seen as "Cool." *The Vancouver Sun* (February 25, 2009).

"Sixth Annual BSA—IDC Global Software Piracy Study." **http://global.bsa.org/globalpiracy2008/studies/globalpiracy2008.pdf**.

Sophos PLC. "*Security Threat Report//Q1 08.*" (2008 and 2009).

Steinhauer, Jennifer. "Woman Indicted in MySpace Suicide Case." *The New York Times* (May 16, 2008).

"Stuart MacDonald." **www.stuartmacdonald.ca** (accessed August 3, 2009).

"Tech Data Canada Equips Its Resellers and Employees with Tools to Help Fight Software Piracy." **www.microsoft.com/canada/casestudies/techdata.mspx** (accessed June 1, 2007).

"Tech Data Ranks 109th on 2007 Fortune 500." **www.portfolio.com/resources/company-profiles/TECD/press/2007/04/16/tech-data-ranks-109th-on-2007-fortune-500r** (accessed June 1, 2007).

The Canadian Alliance Against Software Theft. "Canadians Find Falsified Resumes a Bigger Offence than Using Pirated Software, **www.caast.com/resources/2006_national_study.pdf** (accessed June 1, 2007).

"To Trust or Not to Trust Personal Health Records?" *MarketWatch* (March 26, 2008).

U.S. Department of Health, Education, and Welfare, *Fair Information Practices* (1973).

"Welcome to Tech Data." **www.techdata.com/content/cen/about/companyinfo.main.aspx** (accessed July 23, 2009).

www.kronos.com (accessed July 15, 2008).

Chapter 5

Bernard, Rob. "Microsoft's Green Growth." *eWeek* (April 7, 2008).

Blau, John D. "BCE to Sell Stake in Canadian IT Service Provider CGI," *Infoworld*, (December 19, 2005), **www.infoworld.com/article/05/12/19/HNbcestake_1.html?IP%20TELEPHONY** (accessed February 13, 2009).

Carlton, Jim. "IT Managers Make a Power Play." *The Wall Street Journal* (March 27, 2007).

———. "IT Managers Find Novel Ways to Cool Powerful Servers." *The Wall Street Journal* (April 10, 2007).

Carr, David F. "Scaling Up or Scaling Out?" *Baseline* (January 2008).

Carr, Nicholas, *The Big Switch: Rewiring the World, from Edison to Google* (W.W. Norton, 2008).

CGI, "CGI Provides HR Self-Service Solution to Bell Canada's Employees, **www.cgi.com/web/en/library/ case_studies/71182.htm** (accessed February 13, 2009).

Chabrow, Eric. "The Wild, Wild Cost of Data Centers." *CIO Insight* (May 2008).

Claburn, Thomas. "Amazon's S3 Cloud Service Turns into a Puff of Smoke." *InformationWeek* (July 28, 2008).

———. "Open Source Developers Build on Amazon Web Services." **TechWeb.com** (January 12, 2007).

Cone, Edward. "Amazon at Your Service." *CIO Insight* (January 7, 2007).

Evans Data Corporation. "MySQL Gains 25% Market Share of Database Usage, Latest Evans Data Survey Shows." **www.evansdata.com/press/viewRelease.php** (March 22, 2007).

Ferguson, Scott. "Cooling the Data Center." *eWeek* (June 9, 2008).

Gartner Research. "Worldwide Outsourcing Market to Grow 8.1 Percent in 2008." (January 2008).

Gartner Research. "Worldwide PC Shipment to Grow 11 percent in 2008." (March 25, 2008).

"Green IT Comes of Age: Data Centres that Use 60 percent Less Power." **www.biggerthinking.com/en/efficient_ data_centres.aspx** (accessed February 13, 2009).

Greene, Jay. "Google and Salesforce: A Tighter Bond." *BusinessWeek* (April 15, 2008).

Hamm, Steve. "A Big Sales Job for Salesforce.com." *BusinessWeek* (September 24, 2007).

Hamm, Steve. "Google Apps as Tools for Outsourcers." **www.businessweek.com/globalbiz/blog/globespotting/ archives/2007/11/google_apps_as.html** (accessed October 15, 2009)

Hayes Weier, Mary. "Salesforce, Google Show Fruits of Their Collaboration. "*InformationWeek* (April 21, 2008).

Hof, Robert, D. "So You Wanna Be a Web Tycoon? Amazon Can Help." **www.webworkerdaily.com** (accessed January 24, 2007).

Hoover, J. Nicholas and Richard Martin. "Demystifying the Cloud." *InformationWeek* (June 23, 2008).

Hoover, J. Nicholas. "Ahead in the Cloud: Google, Others Expand Online Services." *InformationWeek* (April 14, 2008).

Hoover, J. Nicholas. "Service Outages Force Cloud Adopters to Rethink Tactics."*InformationWeek* (August 18–25, 2008).

Intel, 2004. Updated by the authors.

King, Rachael. "How Cloud Computing is Changing the World." *BusinessWeek* (August 4, 2008).

Kolbasuk McGee, Marianne. "Data Center Electricity Bills Double." *InformationWeek* (February 17, 2007).

Kolbasuk McGee, Marianne. "Salesforce as B-to-B Broker." *InformationWeek* (December 10, 2007).

Kurzweil, Ray. "Exponential Growth an Illusion?: Response to Ilkka Tuomi." KurzweilAI.net, September 23, 2003.

Lyman, P., and Varian, H. "How Much Information" *The Journal of Electronic Publishing* (December 2003).

Merrill Lynch. "The Cloud Wars: $100+ billion at stake." Merrill Lynch Report, August 5, 2008.

Metrics 2.0. "Worldwide PC Shipments to Reach 334 Million in 2010." **Metrics2.com** (accessed October 2, 2008).

Mintz, Jessica. "Amazon's Hot New Item: Its Data Center." Associated Press (February 1, 2008).

Ogg, Erica. "IDC Lowers IT Spending Forecast for 2009." CNET. **http://news.cnet.com/8301-1001_3-10095258-92.html** (November 12, 2008).

Ortutay, Barbara. "Analysts: Global Tech Spending to Retreat in 2009." Associate Press. **www.wtop.com?nid=108&sid= 1474899** (January 13, 2009).

Pallatto, John and Clint Boulton. "An On-Demand Partnership." *eWeek* (April 21, 2008).

Preimesberger, Chris. "Perils in the Cloud." *eWeek* (August 4, 2008).

Pritchett, Jennifer. "Queen's University Saving Green by Going Green." *The Kingston Whig Standard* (November 21, 2007).

Rasmussen, Neil. "White Paper #114: Implementing Energy Efficient Data Centers." W. Kingston, RI: American Power Conversion (2006). **http://forms.theregister.co.uk/misc/ oracle_resources?paper=779.**

Rivlin, Gary. "Software for Rent." *The New York Times* (November 13, 2007).

Salesforce.com, Report on Form 10-K for the fiscal year ended January 31, 2008, filed with the SEC on February 29, 2008.

Stango, Victor. "The Economics of Standards Wars." *Review of Network Economics* 3, Issue 1 (March 2004).

VMware, "VMware Virtual Desktop Infrastructure Connects Bell Canada for Optimized Customer Care," 2006, **www.vmware.com/files/pdf/customers/06Q3_cs_ vmw_Bell_Canada_English.pdf** (accessed February 13, 2009).

Weier, Mary Hayes. "Salesforce.com" and Marianne Kolbasuk McGee, "Salesforce as B-to-B Broker," *InformationWeek* (December 10, 2007).

Weill, Peter, Mani Subramani and Marianne Broadbent. "Building IT Infrastructure for Strategic Agility." *Sloan Management Review* 44, no. 1 (Fall 2002).

Woodie, Alex. "Global IT Spending Will be Up, Down, Forrester Says." IT Jungle (January 19, 2009). **www.itjungle.com/tfh/tfh011909-story02.html** (accessed October 7, 2009).

Chapter 6

Brunelli, Mark. "Oracle Database 10g Powers Growing MySpace.com Competitor." **SearchOracle.com** (January 31, 2007).

Carr, David F. "Inside MySpace.com." *Baseline Magazine* (January 16, 2007).

DeCarlo, Scott, and Brian Zajac. "HSBC Tops Forbes List of World's Largest Companies." *Forbes* (April 2, 2008).

Gartner Inc. "Dirty Data' is a Business Problem, not an IT Problem, Says Gartner." Sydney, Australia (March 2, 2007).

Gartner Research, "Gartner Says More than 25 Percent of Critical Data Used in Large Corporations Is Flawed" press release (2007), **www.gartner.com/press_releases/asset_74687_11.html** (accessed December 18, 2009).

Government Technology. "Case Study: Royal Canadian Mounted Police." **www.govtech.net/digitalcommunities/studies/sybase_RCMPv2.pdf** (accessed April 10, 2007).

Hewitt, Pat. "MySpace Social Networking Site Launches Canadian Version in English, French." *RedOrbit News* (May 14, 2007).

Jedras, Jeff. "Mining Gold from Data Silos." *Computer World Canada* (November 10, 2006).

Kavur, Jennifer. "RCMP Push National Police Data-Sharing Project." *Computer World Canada* (August 18, 2008).

Martinez, Joel. "Deconstructing MySpace.com Part 1—Social Networking Database." **www.communitymx.com** (accessed June 2, 2008).

Microsoft. "The Royal Canadian Mounted Police: Microsoft Software Helps Solve Crimes." **www.microsoft.com/canada/casestudies/rcmp.mspx** (accessed April 10, 2007).

"The IBM Retail Data Warehouse: Harnessing the Power of Information." **http://download.boulder.ibm.com/ibmdl/pub/software/data/sw-library/industry-models/brochure/IBM_Retail_Models.pdf** (accessed April 5, 2009).

"2005 Computerworld Honors Case Study: CADVIEW." **www.cwhonors.org/laureates/government/20055332.pdf** (accessed April 10, 2007).

Chapter 7

"BBBank eG," **www.webspy.com/resources/testimonials.aspx** (accessed April 26, 2009).

Berners-Lee, Tim, James Hendler, and Ora Lassila" The Semantic Web." *Scientific American Magazine* (May 17, 2001). **www.scientificamerican.com/article.cfm?id=the-semantic-web.**

Blackman, Andrew. "Foul Sents," *The Wall Street Journal,* March 26, 2007.

Boulton, Clint. "Google Apps Go to School." *eWeek* (April 21, 2008).

———. "Google Tucks Jotspot into Apps." *eWeek* (March 3, 2008).

———. "Microsoft Marks the Spot." *eWeek* (May 5, 2008).

Burrows, Peter. "The FCC, Comcast, and Net Neutrality." *BusinessWeek* (February 26, 2008).

Corbin, Kenneth. "Time Warner Cable Broadband Pricing Fight Rages." **www.internetnews.com/infra/print.php/3815591** (accessed October 7, 2009).

Dornan, Andy. "Is Your Network Neutral?" *InformationWeek* (May 18, 2008).

E-spionage Threat." *BusinessWeek* (April 10, 2008) and "An Evolving Crisis." *BusinessWeek* (April 10, 2008).

Edwards, John. "How to Get the Most from Unified Communications." *CIO* (February 8, 2008).

Gohring, Nancy. "Over 50 Percent of Companies Fire Workers for E-mail, Net Abuse," InfoWorld, February 28, 2008.

Guth, Robert A., Ben Worthen, and Charles Forelle. "Microsoft to Allow Software Secrets on Internet." *The Wall Street Journal* (February 22, 2008).

Helft, Miguel. "Ad Accord for Yahoo! and Google." *The New York Times* (June 13, 2008).

———. "Google and Salesforce Join to Fight Microsoft." *The New York Times* (April 14, 2008).

"HMV Group to Open Canada's Largest Dedicated Music, DVD Store" **www.hmvgroup.com/media/view.jsp?id=1007** (accessed April 24, 2009).

Hoover, J. Nicholas. "Microsoft-Yahoo! Combo Would Involve Overlap—and Choices." *InformationWeek* (February 18, 2008).

http://news.netcraft.com/archives/2009/06/17/june_2009_web_server_survey.html, and the changes are as of Netcraft June 2009 survey.

Jackson, Brian. "Montreal Man Arrested in Bell Canada Data Theft Case." *ITBusiness Canada,* **www.itbusiness.ca/it/client/en/Home/DetailNewsPrint.asp?id=47156** (accessed April 30, 2009).

Jackson, Maggie. "May We Have Your Attention, Please?" *BusinessWeek* (June 23, 2008).

Jones, K.C. "Piracy Becomes Focus of Net Neutrality Debater." *InformationWeek* (May 6, 2008).

Kessler, Andy. "The War for the Web." *The Wall Street Journal* (May 6, 2008).

Kulash, Jr., Damian. "Beware of the New New Thing." *The New York Times* (April 5, 2008).

Lohr, Steve. "Video Road Hogs Stir Fear of Internet Traffic Jam." *The New York Times* (March 13, 2008).

———. "Yahoo! Offer is Strategy Shift for Microsoft." *The New York Times* (February 2, 2008).

Markoff, John. "Competing as Software Goes to Web." *The New York Times* (June 5, 2007).

McKay, Lauren. "All Talk." *Customer Relationship Management Magazine* (June 2008).

Pallatto, John, and Boulton, Clint. "An On-Demand Partnership." *eWeek* (April 21, 2008).

Preston, Rob. "Meter Is Starting to Tick on Internet Access Pricing." *InformationWeek* (June 9, 2008).

Spencer, Jane. "How a System Error in Pakistan Shut YouTube." *The Wall Street Journal* (February 26, 2008).

Stern, Josh. "Investigating the Exaflood." *Convergence Magazine* (2008). **http://magazines.humber.ca/convergence2008/exaflood.html** (accessed April 26, 2009).

Strauss, Marina. "Virgin's Withdrawal Music to HMV's Ears." *The Globe and Mail* (June 29, 2005).

Turner, S. Derek. "Give Net Neutrality a Chance." *BusinessWeek* (July 12, 2008).

"Virgin Megastores USA Turns Up the Volume with Unified Communications." **www.microsoft.com** (accessed June 19, 2008).

Wegert, Katherine. "Workers Can Breach Security Knowingly or Not," Dow Jones News Service, June 24, 2007.

White, Bobby. "The New Workplace Rules: No Video-Watching." *The Wall Street Journal* (March 4, 2008).

Wiens, Jordan. "With Security, More Is Better." *InformationWeek* (March 10, 2008).

Wilson, Tim. "Canadian IT Exec Accused of Stealing Customer Database." **www.darkreading.com/shared/printableArticleSrc.jhtml?articleID=212201246** (accessed October 7, 2009).

Chapter 8

"Air Canada to Offer In-Flight WiFi," United Press International, **www.upi.com/Business_News/2008/09/09/Air-Canada-to-offer-in-flight-WiFi/UPI-26991221016927/print** (accessed September 23, 2009).

Bartholomew, Doug. "Canadian Networking Firm Derives Gains from I.T. Controls." *Baseline Magazine* (March 16, 2007), **www.baselinemag.com/c/a/Projects-Processes/Canadian-Networking-Firm-Derives-Gains-From-IT-Controls** (accessed October 15, 2009).

Boucher Ferguson, Renee. "Outages Hit Online Apps." *eWeek* (February 18, 2008).

Brewin, Bob. "All Aboard with Wi-Fi on Via Rail Canada," *Computerworld Canada* (July 10, 2003), **www.computerworld.com/printthis/2003/0,4814,82940,00.html** (accessed September 23, 2009).

Canadian Internet Policy and Public Interest Clinic. "Identity Theft: Introduction and Background." **www.cippic.ca/documents/bulletins/introduction.pdf** (March 2007).

Carruthers, Sean. "Forest Hills Cuts the Cords," November 6, 2003, **www.hubacanada.com/story_10783_4** (accessed September 26, 2005).

Cavusoglu, Huseyin, Birendra Mishra, and Srinivasan Raghunathan. "A Model for Evaluating IT Security Investments." *Communications of the ACM* 47, no. 7 (July 2004).

CBC News, August 18, 2003, **www.cbc.ca/news/background/poweroutage.**

———. August 20, 2003. **www.cbc.ca/news/background/poweroutage.**

Clark, Nicola and David Jolly. "French Bank Says Rogue Trader Lost $7 Billion". *The New York Times* (January 25, 2008).

Cleary, Brian. "Employee Role Changes and SocGen: Good Lessons from a Bad Example." **SCMagazineUS.com** (April 1, 2008).

"Computerworld: Free Hot Spots Pay Dividends," October 22, 2003, **www.bmannconsulting.com/node/614** (accessed September 23, 2009).

de Teran, Natasha. "Market Targets Loopholes in Equity Derivatives." **Financialnews-US.com** (March 28, 2008).

Dunn, John E. "Wi-Fi Networks Still Insecure in London's City," Techworld,com, **www.itworldcanada.com/a/Enterprise-Infrastructure/4de93aab-8968-47ce-9611-05566a5ad095.html** (accessed July 16, 2007).

E-spionage Threat." *BusinessWeek* (April 10, 2008) and "An Evolving Crisis." *BusinessWeek* (April 10, 2008).

Eaton, Brian. "Ottawa—A Hospital Built for Mesh," IT World Canada , August 2, 2005, **www.techworld.com/features/index.cfm?featureID=1607** (accessed September 23, 2009).

Ferguson, Renee Boucher. "Outages Hit Online Apps," *eWeek* (February 18, 2008).

Gauthier-Villars, David and Stacy Meichtry. "Kerviel Felt out of His League." *The Wall Street Journal* (January 31, 2008).

Gauthier-Villars, David, and Carrick Mollenkamp. "The Loss Where No One Looked." *The Wall Street Journal* (January 28, 2008).

Gauthier-Villars, David, Carrick Mollenkamp, and Alistair Macdonald. "French Bank Rocked by Rogue Trader." *The Wall Street Journal* (January 25, 2008).

Gilbert, Alorie. "Salesforce.com Users Lament Ongoing Outages." cnet News.com (February 1, 2006).

Grow, Brian, Keith Epstein, and Chi-Chu Tschang. "The New E-spionage Threat." *BusinessWeek* (April 15, 2008).

Hamilton Tyler. "Wi-Fi 'Hotspots' Coming to a Coffee Shop Near You," Toronto Star, February 18, 2005, **www.thestar.com/NASApp/cs/ContentServer?pagename=thestar/Layout/Article_Type1&c=Article&cid=1108806612792&call_pageid=968350072197&col=Columnist971715454851&DPL=IvsNDS%2f7ChAX&tacodalogin=yes** (accessed September 24, 2005).

Hoover, J. Nicholas. "Service Outages Force Cloud Adopters to Rethink Tactics." *InformationWeek* (August 18/25, 2008).

Hurst, Andrew, and Thierry Leveque. "SocGen Under Pressure as Rogue Trader Released." Yahoo! News (January 28, 2008).

Jackson, Brian. "Montreal Man Arrested in Bell Canada Data Theft Case," ITBusiness Canada, **www.itbusiness.ca/it/client/en/Home/DetailNewsPrint.asp?id=47156** (accessed April 30, 2009).

Judge, Peter. "Converged Softphone Cuts Bill," September 8, 2005, **www.itworldcanada.com/a/search/e10c3e79-22ad-4c3d-a8d4-47e0c1dc6123.html** (accessed September 24, 2005).

Kirk, Jeremy. "MySpace Users Struggle to Overcome Cybervandalism." *PC World* (June 30, 2008).

Laton McCartney, "Salesforce.com: When On-Demand Goes Off," *Baseline Magazine*(January 7, 2007).

Lombardi, Rosie. "Canadian Researchers Uncover New 'Wireless' Possibilities," July 29, 2005, **www.itworldcanada.com/a/search/a8dd82dc-62b6-46d1-846f-6a50e74b24bf.html** (accessed September 24, 2005).

Martin, Richard. "RIM Service Outage Leads to 'BlankBerrys' and Questions." *Information Week* (April 23, 2007).

McCartney, Laton. "Salesforce.com: When On-Demand Goes Off." *Baseline Magazine* (January 7, 2007).

McLean, Dan. "Bluetooth and WiFi, Meet WiMax Technology," August 4, 2005, **www.itworldcanada.com/a/search/6fa973d9-511a-4d6c-a3e3-c9209578f0df.html** (accessed September 24, 2005).

Mitchell, Dan. "It's Here: It's There; It's Spyware." *The New York Times* (May 20, 2006).

Pallatto, John. "Rare Database Bug Causes Salesforce.com Outage." *eWeek* (December 22, 2005).

———. "Salesforce.com Confirms 'Minor' CRM Outage." *eWeek* (January 6, 2006).

Parasie, Nicolas. "SocGen Discloses More Detail, Chronology of Alleged Fraud." **MarketWatch.com** (January 27, 2008).

Perez, Juan Carlos. "Facebook Stamps Out Malware Attack." *PC World* (August 8, 2008).

Richardson, Robert. "2007 CSI Computer Crime and Security Survey." Computer Security Institute (2007).

Sage, Adam. "Ex-SocGen Risk Auditor Calls Systems a Sham." *The Times* (February 7, 2008).

"Secure Voice and Data over Wi-Fi Moves Baycrest to Switch to Aruba," April 2004, **www.arubanetworks.com/pdf/baycrest_cs.pdf** (accessed September 24, 2005).

Shore, Randy. "WiFi Could Pose Threat during Vancouver Olympics," **http://www.canada.com/topics/news/national/story.html?id=207f6d54-68fc-40da-8ae3-dc9f057c2f54&k=25065** (accessed September 23, 2009).

Smith, Heather and Gregory Viscusi. "SocGen Threatened to Fire Kerviel in 2005, Court Document Says." **Bloomberg.com** (March 25, 2008).

Smith, Randall and Kate Kelly. "Once Again, the Risk Protection Fails." *The Wall Street Journal* (January 25, 2008).

Snyder, Bill. "Salesforce.com Outage Strikes Again." **TheStreet.com** (January 6, 2006).

Sophos plc. "Security Threat Report//Q1 08." (2008).

Stinnissen, Arni K, "Computer Crime, Search and Seizure." (April 11, 2001) **http://privacy.openflows.org/powerpoint/computercrime/sld003.htm** (accessed May 2, 2002).

Symantec Corporation. "Symantec Internet Threat Security Report." (March 2007).

"Trader Says SocGen Bosses Had to Know." *The New York Times*, (January 29, 2008).

Watson Goepel Maledy, LLP, "About Us," **www.wgmlaw.com** (accessed April 28, 2009).

Webroot, "Case Study: Watson Goepel Maledy LLP," **www.webroot.com/shared/pdf/Webroot_WatsonGoepel_CaseStudy_Email.pdf** (accessed April 28, 2009).

White, Bobby. "A Question of Priorities." *The Wall Street Journal* (July 30, 2007).

"Wi-Fi Arrest Highlights Security Dangers," **http://news.zdnet.com/2102-1009_22=5112000.html** (accessed July 16, 2007).

"Wireless Internet in Via 1 Class," **www.viarail.ca/wirelessinternet/en_index.html** (accessed September 24, 2005).

Chapter 9

Fulcher, Jim. "Rise of User-Friendly Devices Propels Strategic Use of Wireless Technology." *Manufacturing Business Technology* (February 18, 2007).

"Hats-Off: Dorfman Pacific Implements Symbol Enterprise Mobility Solution for Paperless Warehouse Operations." **www.symbol.com** (accessed September 13, 2006).

Hammer, Michael. "Process Management and the Future of Six Sigma." *MIT Sloan Management Review* 43, no.2 (Winter 2002).

Kempfer, Lisa, M. "Hats Off to Wireless." *Material Handling Management* (January 2007).

Lombardi, Rosie. "From Paper Trail to Patient Care," **www.itworldcanada.com/a/E-Government/78a168dc-e318-4702-ada5-0c93c482afca.html** (accessed April 17, 2007).

McDougall, Paul. "In Depth: When Outsourcing Goes Bad." *InformationWeek* (June 19, 2006).

Overby, Stephanie. "Big Deals, Big Savings, Big Problems." *CIO Magazine* (February 1, 2006)

———. "Simple Successful Outsourcing." *CIO Magazine* (October 1, 2005).

TGX Medical Systems, **www.tgxmedical.com/products_and_services/alex_gold.asp** (accessed April 17, 2007).

"The Ottawa Hospital Pandemic Influenza Plan Rough Draft #2, June 29, 2007, **www.champlainhealthworkers.ca/doc.aspx?id=61** (accessed May 27, 2009).

"The Ottawa Hospital Launches an Instrument Tracking System," **www.summitconnects.com/In_the_News/ARCHIVE/2005_10.htm** (accessed September 24, 2009).

Wailgum, Thomas. "How to Take Your Warehouse Wireless." *CIO Magazine* (February 1, 2007).

———. "Wireless—Five Steps to a Successful Wireless Rollout." *CIO Magazine* (February 1, 2007).

Chapter 10

"About EI: Clients," **www.eidenai.ca/EI/SiteContent/About/Clients** (accessed April 19, 2007).

"American Airlines Cargo to Join Unisys-Operated Cargo Portal Services." *Logistics Management* (May 2, 2005).

Barki, Henri, Suzanne Rivard, and Jean Talbot. "An Integrative Contingency Model of Software Project Risk Management" *Journal of Management Information Systems* 17(4) (Spring 2001).

Bartholomew, Doug. "Second Opinions." *Baseline Magazine* (March 2006).

Bartholomew, Doug and Chris Gonsalves. "CDC Issues Pandemic Systems Plan." *Baseline Magazine* (April 2008).

Beazley, Doug. "Gun Files Easy to Hack: *The Edmonton Sun* (March 10, 2006).

Brabston, Mary, Robert Zmud, and John Carlson. "Strategic Vision for Information Technology." In *Strategic Information Technology: Opportunities for Competitive Advantage*, Ed. Raymond Papp, Hershey, PA: Idea Group Publishing (2000).

"Cargo Portal Services Launches Two New Services." *Enterprise Networks and Servers* (October 2004).

"Case Study: A Billion Dollar Boondoggle." **www.maxwideman.com/papers/boondoggle/intro.htm.**

CBC News. "Canadian Corporate Takeovers That Made News." **www.cbc.ca/news/background/mergers** (accessed April 20, 2007).

CBC News. "Gun Registry Cost Soars to $2 Billion." (February 13, 2004).

CBC News. "Implementing the *Firearms Act*—the Rising Cost." (June 19, 2006).

Chabrow, Eric. "IT Plays Linchpin Role in High-Stakes M&As." *InformationWeek* (June 26, 2006).

Concours Group. "Delivering Large-Scale System Projects" (2000).

Dizard III, Wilson P. "CDC Weaving National Information Web." *Government Computer News* (April 3, 2006).

"EI Case Studies: Lemontonic," **www.eidenai.ca/EI/SiteContent/CaseStudies/Pages/LemontonicCaseStudy.html** (accessed April 19, 2007).

Fichman, R.G. "Real Options and IT Platform Adoption: Implications for Theory and Practice." *Information Systems Research*, 15(2) (2004).

Gefen, D. and C. Ridings. "Implementation Team Responsiveness and User Evaluation of CRM: A Quasi-Experimental Design Study of Social Exchange Theory." *Journal of Management Information Systems*, Special Issue on ERP, 19(1) (2002).

Iversen, J.H., L. Mathiassen, and P. A. Nielsen, "Managing Risks in Software Process Improvement: An Action Research Approach" *MIS Quarterly*, 28(3) (2004).

Jackson, Dale. "You Can't Beat Barbarians, So Why Not Join the Invasion? A Money Manager Assesses Valuations to Predict Targets." **http://ctv2.theglobeandmail.com/servlet/story/LAC.20070410.RPRIVATE10/business/Business/Business/&id=LAC_20070410_RPRIVATE10** (accessed October 7, 2009).

Jeffery, M., & Leliveld, I. Practices in IT Portfolio Management. *MIT Sloan Management Review*. 45(3) (2004).

Keen, Peter G.W. "Information Systems and Organizational Change." *Communications of the ACM* 24(1) (1981).

Laudon, Kenneth C. "CIOs Beware: Very Large Scale Systems." Center for Research on Information Systems, New York University Stern School of Business, working paper (1989).

Laudon, Kenneth C. and Carol Guercio Traver. *E-Commerce: Business, Technology, Society*, 5th edition. Upper Saddle River, NJ: Prentice-Hall (2009).

"Lemontonic Appoints Kaleil Isaza Tuzman to Board," **www.newswire.ca/releases/archive/February2005/24/c7770.html?view=print** (accessed April 19, 2007).

"Lemontonic: The Revolution of Life Online," **www.lemontonic.com** (accessed April 19, 2007).

Levinson, Meridith. "When Failure Is Not an Option." *CIO Magazine* (June 1, 2006).

Lombardi, Rosie. "From Paper Trail to Patient Care," **www.itworldcanada.com/a/E-Government/78a168dc-e318-4702-ada5-0c93c482afca.html** (accessed April 17, 2007).

McFarlan, F.W. "Portfolio Approach to Information Systems." *Harvard Business Review*, 59(5) (1981).

McGrath, Rita, and Ian MacMillan. "Assessing Technology Projects Using Real Options Reasoning" *Research Technology Management* 43(4) (2000).

McIlmurray, Spencer. "M&A Survival Kit: Relearning Enterprise Addition and Subtraction." *CIO Magazine* (October 24, 2006).

Moore, Nick. "The New Role of the CIO in M&A Due Diligence." *Software Mag.com* (July 2006).

"Multi-carrier Web-Based Booking for Air Cargo." **www.unisys.com/transportation/clients/featured__case__studies/northwest__airlines_c0___united__irlines__and__air__canada__case__study.htm** (accessed May 22, 2005).

"Online Daters Get Up Close and Personal at Microsoft .NET-based Lemontonic.com," **www.microsoft.com/canada/casestudies/lemontonic.mspx** (accessed September 24, 2009).

Peffers, K. and C. Gengler. "How to Identify New High-Payoff Information Systems for the Organization." *Communications of the ACM* (January 2003).

Rockart, J., "Chief Executives Define Their Own Information Needs." *Harvard Business Review* (March/April 1979).

Rockart, J.F. and M.E. Treacy. "The CEO Goes on-Line." *Harvard Business Review* (January–February 1982).

Ryan, S.D., Harrison, D.A., and Schkade, L.R. "Information-Technology Investment Decisions: When Do Costs and Benefits in the Social Subsystem Matter?" *Journal of Management Information Systems*, 19 (2002).

Schmidt, R. Lyytinen, K. Keil, M., Cule, P. "Identifying Software Project Risks: An International Delphi Study." *Journal of Management Information Systems*, 17(4), (Spring 2001).

Speier, C. and Morris, M. "The Influence of Query Interface Design on Decision Making Performance." MIS Quarterly, 27(3) (2003).

"The Ottawa Hospital Launches an Instrument Tracking System," **www.summitconnects.com/In_the_News/ARCHIVE/2005_10.htm** (accessed September 24, 2009).

"The Ottawa Hospital Pandemic Influenza Plan Rough Draft #2, June 29, 2007, **www.champlainhealthworkers.ca/doc.aspx?id=61** (accessed May 27, 2009).

TGX Medical Systems, **www.tgxmedical.com/products_and_services/alex_gold.asp** (accessed April 17, 2007).

Xia W., and G. Lee, "Grasping the Complexity of IS Development Projects." *Communications of the ACM* (2004).

Chapter 11

Albright, Evan. "Colgate-Palmolive Takes Control of Global IT with SAP RPM." *SAPNetWeaver Magazine* (October 2008).

Bloomberg News. "New Products and Demand in Emerging Markets Fatten Profits at P&G. and Colgate." *The New York Times* (January 31, 2007).

"Canada: Internet Usage, Broadband, and Telecommunication Reports." **Internetworldstats.com** (June 2009).

Carey, David. "Surviving the ERP Journey." *CIO Canada* (May 1, 2001).

Colgate-Palmolive, Inc. Form 10K, filed with the Securities and Exchange Commission for the fiscal year ending December 31, 2007, filed February 28, 2008.

Conrath, Chris. "SAP Is Sold on the Internet." *Network World Canada* (July 28, 2000).

Corbett, Sara. "Can the Cellphone Help End Global Poverty?" *The New York Times Magazine* (April 13, 2008).

Cook, Curtis, and Michelle Schoffro. "SAP Not Just for Big Companies." *Canada Computes* (October 9, 1999).

Davison, Robert. "Cultural Complications of ERP." *Communications of the ACM* 45, no. 7 (July 2002).

Dubowski, Stefan. "Book Retailer Spins Its Tale of SAP Tips." *ComputerWorld Canada*, June 10, 2005, **www.itworldcanada.com/a/search/6edebed9-0d6c-**

4909-b41a-204441899dcc.html (accessed October 7, 2009).

Ferraro, Nicole. "Africa's Portal to the Internet." *InformationWeek* (February 4, 2008).

Kelly, David A. "Managing in a Global Economy: SeverStal." *Profit Magazine* (February 2008). **www.severstal.com/eng** (accessed June 28, 2008).

Liang, Huigang, Yajiong Xue, William R. Boulton, and Terry Anthony Byrd. "Why Western Vendors Don't Dominate China's ERP Market." *Communications of the ACM* 47, no. 7. (July 2004).

Maxwell, Rebecca. "Rayovac Gets a Charge from Accelerated SAP." *ComputerWorld Canada* (September 10, 2000).

Mearlan, Lucas. "Sobeys Says Goodbye to SAP." *ComputerWorld Online* (February 2, 2001).

"mySAP.com to Power Canada's National Newspaper. *The Globe and Mail*." SAP Press Release, **www.sap.com** (accessed August 13, 2001).

"Nestlé Group in 2005: Record Sales and Profits—Higher Dividend Proposed." **www.nestle.com** (February 23, 2006).

Roche, Edward Mozley. "Managing Information Technology in Multinational Corporations." Upper Saddle River, NJ: Prentice Hall PTR, Upper Saddle River, NJ, (1992).

SAP Canada Web site, **www.sap.com/Canada/company** (accessed October 1, 2005).

SAP Web site, **www.sap.com** (accessed October 1, 2005).

"SeverStal Boosts Stake in Canada's High River Gold Ltd. **www.tradingmarkets.com/print.site/news/Stock%20News/2039414** (accessed September 25, 2009).

Steinert-Threlkeld, Tom. "Nestlé Pieces Together Its Global Supply Chain." *Baseline Magazine* (January 20, 2006).

The Associated Press. "Nestle Reports 14 Percent Rise in Sales." **MSNBC.com** (April 25, 2006).

Thomson, Inc. "SAP xApp Resource and Portofolio Management and SAP Consulting Enable Enterprise Wide Strategic and Operational R&D Portfolio Management." SAP White Paper, **sap.com** (accessed October 15, 2008).

Top 20 Countries—Internet Usage." **Internetworldstats.com** (May 2008).

ZDNet Australia. "Effective Management of Multiple Projects With SAP xApp Resource and Portfolio Management." (August 28, 2007).

Chapter 12

"Allan." **www.rhcapitalpartners.com/news_06_07allan.html** (accessed June 3, 2009).

"The Allan Candy Company Limited." *BusinessWeek*, **www.investing.businessweek.com/businessweek/research/stocks/private/snapshot.asp?privcapid=347209007** (accessed June 3, 2009).

"Allan Candy Sweetens Sales, Streamlines IT Using Microsoft Dynamics GP." **http://www.microsoft.com/canada/casestudies/allan_candy.mspx** (accessed September 30, 2009).

Allan Candy Company. "Our History." **www.allancandy.com/node/20** (accessed September 30, 2009).

Greenfield, Dave. "CRM 2.0." *eWeek* (June 16, 2008).

i2. The Supply Chain Company. **www.i2.com**.

Kerr, John. "Procter & Gamble Takes Inventory Up a Notch." *Supply Chain Management Review* (February 13, 2008).

Lau, Kathleen. "The Sweet Business of Making Candy." *Computerworld Canada* (May 22, 2009).

Lee, H.L., V. Padmanabhan, and S. Wang, "The Bullwhip Effect in Supply Chains." *Sloan Management Review* (Spring 1997).

McLaughlin, Kevin. "Partners Still Hung Over from Symantec ERP Upgrade." ChannelWeb (March 2, 2007).

Optiant. "Optiant Announces Multi-Echelon Inventory Optimization Enterprise Agreement with P&G" (October 17, 2007). **www.optiant.com** (accessed July 17, 2008).

"Our History." Allan Candy Company. **www.allancandy.com/node/20** (accessed (September 30, 2009).

Overby, Stephanie. "Can't We All Just Get Along?" *CIO Australia.* (March 10, 2004).

———. "SAP Chosen by Novartis as a Major Building Block." *EETimes* (June 16, 2003).

Songini, Marc L. "ERP Rollout Continues to Weigh Down Symantec." *Computerworld* (February 5, 2007).

———. "ERP Rollout Weighs Symantec Down." *Computerworld* (February 12, 2007).

———. "ERP Rollout Whacks Symantec's Bottom Line." *Computerworld* (January 31, 2007).

Walsh, Lawrence. "Symantec's Midnight at the Oasis." *Baseline Magazine* (March 31, 2008).

Chapter 13

Aspan, Maria. "How Sticky Is Membership on Facebook? Just Try Breaking Free." *The New York Times* (February 11, 2008).

———. "Quitting Facebook Gets Easier." *The New York Times* (February 13, 2008).

Bellman, Eric and Tariq Engineer. "India Appears Ripe for Cellphone Ads." *The Wall Street Journal* (March 10, 2008).

Carr, Jim. "Facebook Privacy Flap Should Spark Concern for Business." **SCMagazineUS.com** (March 26, 2008).

Claburn, Thomas. "Social Networks Find Ways to Monetize User Data." *InformationWeek* (November 10, 2007).

Cohen, Adam. "One Friend Facebook Hasn't Made Yet: Privacy Rights." *The New York Times* (February 18, 2008).

eMarketer, "Mobile Advertising: After the Growing Pains." **www.emarketer.com/Reports/All/Emarketer_2000452.aspx**.

Internet World Stats. **www.internetworldstats.com/am/ca.htm.**

"J&R Electronics Migrating to Blue Martini E-Commerce Platform." *Internetretailer.com* (November 8, 2006).

"J&R Electronics Taps Loyalty Lab's On-Demand Suite for First Shopper Loyalty Program." *Rtmilestones.com* (accessed May 1, 2007).

"J&R Music Turns to Toy." *Adweek* (August 19, 2008). **www.jr.com** (accessed August 28, 2008).

Krauss, Alan. "Piggybacking on Facebook." *The New York Times* (February 20, 2008).

McCartney, Laton. "Mid-Market Case: J&R Electronics Pumps Up the Volume." *Baseline Magazine* (March 13, 2007).

Needleman, Sarah. "Blogging Becomes a Corporate Job: Digital 'Handshake'?" *The Wall Street Journal* (May 31, 2005).

Nexon Corporation. **www.nexon.com** (accessed June 4, 2009).

"Nexon Vancouver Shutters Office." **www.techvibes.com/blog/nexon-vancouver-shutters-office** (accessed October 4, 2009).

"Online Extra: Stonyfield Farm's Blog Culture." *BusinessWeek* (May 2, 2005).

Richmond, Riva. "Some Facebook Applications Thrive, Others Flop." *The Wall Street Journal* (June 16, 2008).

Rothenberg, Randall. "Facebook's Flop." *The Wall Street Journal* (December 14, 2007).

Statistics Canada, "E-Commerce: Shopping on the Internet." *The Daily* (November 17, 2008) **www.statcan.gc.ca/daily-quotidien/081117/dq081117a-eng.htm**.

Stone, Brad. "In Facebook, Investing In a Theory." *The New York Times* (October 4, 2007).

"Stonyfield Farm's Chief Blogger Leaves." *Backbone Corporate Blogging Survey* (March 24, 2006). **www.stonyfieldfarms.com** (accessed September 12, 2006).

Swisher, Kara. "Playing with Others." *The Wall Street Journal* (June 9, 2008).

Tucows Blog Site. **http://blog.tucows.com/blog** (accessed May 6, 2007).

Vara, Vauhini. "Facebook CEO Seeks Help as Site Grows Up." *The Wall Street Journal*, March 5, 2008.

Wingfield, Nick. "Korea's Nexon Bets on Sales of Virtual Gear for Free Online Games." *The Wall Street Journal* (May 23, 2008).

Chapter 14

Bailey, Jeff. "Bumped Fliers and Plan B," *The New York Times* (May 30, 2007).

"Case Study: Libro Financial Group Uses Covarity to Deliver Superior Customer Service While Driving Process Efficiencies and Improving Risk Management Controls." **www.covarity.com/content/pressrelease/case-study-libro-financial-group-uses-covarity-deliver-superior-customer-servic** (accessed October 7, 2009).

"Credit Valley Hospital: Hospital Delivers Better Business Insight with PerformancePoint Server 2007," **www.microsoft.com/canada/casestudies/cvh052008.mspx** (accessed October 7, 2009).

Foust, Dean and Bachman, Justin. "You Think Flying Is Bad Now . . . ," *BusinessWeek* (May 28, 2008).

Hansell, Saul. "How Wall Street Lied to Its Computers." *The New York Times* (September 18, 2008).

Information Builders Inc. "Information Builders Underwrites New Enterprise Reporting System for National Life." **www.informationbuilders.com** (accessed August 7, 2005).

John, K., L. Lang, and J. Netter, "The Voluntary Restructuring of Large Firms in Response to Performance Decline." *Journal of Finance* 47 (3) (1992).

Kaplan R.S. and Norton D.P. "The Balanced Scorecard: Measures That Drive Performance." *Harvard Business Review* (Jan–Feb 1992).

LaPlante, Alice. "Travel Problems? Blame Technology," **InformationWeek.com** (June 11, 2007).

Libro Financial Group, **www.libro.ca.**

Maxcer, Chris. "Rohn and Haas: Dashboards to the Rescue." *SAP NetWeaver Magazine* 3 (2007). **http://office.microsoft.com/en-us/performancepoint/FX101680481033.aspx** (accessed October 7, 2009).

Oracle Corporation. "Pharmacia Gains Discipline and Improves Corporate Performance Management Thanks to a Comprehensive, Strategic View of Research Operations." **www.oracle.com** (accessed August 31, 2003).

Shaw, Andy. "Organizations Work to Improve Coding of Clinical Data," **www.canhealth.com/nov03.html** (accessed May 8, 2007).

Simon, H.A. *The New Science of Management Decision.* New York: Harper & Row (1960).

Somoza, Kirsten C. "A Computerized Cardiac Teletriage Decision Support System: Effects on Nurse Performance," **http://hot.carleton.ca/hot-topics/articles/cardiac-teletriage** (accessed October 7, 2009).

Sorenson, Chris. "Air Canada Warned Against Bumping Passengers," The Toronto Star, December 20, 2007.

"The Unfriendly Skies," USA Today, June 4, 2008.

www.canhealth.com/nov03.html (accessed May 8, 2007).

Zeidenberg, Neil. "New Software Tracks How Children Use Their Prosthesis over Time," **www.canhealth.com/nov03.html** (accessed May 8, 2007).

Chapter 15

Anthes, Gary H. "Agents Change." *Computerworld* (January 27, 2003).

Balfour, Gail, "Canadian Forces Train for Combat with Virtual Reality." Channelworld India (July 15, 1999) **www.itworldcanada.com/news/canadian-forces-train-for-combat-with-virtual-reality/135128** (accessed October 15, 2009).

Bell Canada. "Bell Canada Signs Seven-Year Contract with Large Canadian Financial Institution for a Fully Outsourced Internet Protocol-Based Contact Centre Solution" (April 27, 2006). **www.bell.ca/enterprise/EntNews_newsLetter_May2006_8.page** (accessed October 15, 2009).

Blair, Margaret M., and Steven Wallman. "Unseen Wealth." Brookings Institution Press (2001).

Bulkeley, William, M. "Playing Well with Others." *The Wall Street Journal* (June 18, 2007).

Carlin, Dan. "Corporate Wikis Go Viral." *BusinessWeek* (March 12, 2007).

Casselman, Grace. "Growing Like a Weed," **www.backbonemag.com/Magazine/E+Trends_07060601.asp** (accessed May 8, 2007).

"Economic Statistics." **www.secondlife.com/whatis/economy_stats.php** (accessed July 22, 2007.

Forde, David. "Which Companies Are Using Twitter?" **http://profectio.com/which-companies-are-using-twitter** (accessed June 9, 2009).

Gu, Feng, and Baruch Lev. "Intangible Assets. Measurements, Drivers, Usefulness." **http://pages.stern.nyu.edu/~blev/** (2001).

Hayes Weier, Mary. "Coke Exploits Collaboration Technology to Keep Brand Relevant." *InformationWeek* (July 19, 2008).

Lagos, Theresa. "Coca-Cola Enterprises Leads in Global Collaboration and Next-Generation Business Processes With Cisco Technologies." **Reuters.com** (April 10, 2008).

Lamont, Judith. "Social Networking: KM and Beyond." *KM World* (June 2008).

Leung, Wency. "Recruiting Real Talent in a Virtual World." *The Globe and Mail* (July 16, 2007).

McDougall, Paul. "The 'TLA Wiki' and Other Tips to Spark Enterprise 2.0 Efforts." *InformationWeek* (June 16, 2008).

McGillicudy, Shamus. "Social Bookmarking: Pushing Collaboration to the Edge." **SearchCIO.com** (June 21, 2006).

McKay, Betsy. "Can New CEO Put Fizz Back In Coke?" *The Wall Street Journal* (June 30, 2008).

"Our Company—Innovation." **www.coca-colathecompany.com** (accessed August 2008).

Pastore, Richard. "Cruise Control." *CIO Magazine* (February 1, 2003).

"Pontiac Second Life Case Study." A Media Circus home page, **http://amediacirc.us/2007/02/29/pontiac-second-life-case-studyraw-notes/** (accessed October 7, 2009).

Rankin, Bob. "What Is Second Life?" **http://askbobrankin.com/what_is_second_life.html** (accessed October 7, 2009).

Samuelson, Douglas A. and Charles M. Macal. "Agent-Based Simulation." OR/MS Today (August 2006).

Second Life home page. **www.secondlife.com** (accessed July 22, 2007).

"Second Life." **http://en.wikipedia.org/wiki/Second_Life** (accessed July 15, 2007).

Sim Teach home page, **http://simteach.com/wiki/index .php?title=Institutions_and_Organizations_in_ SL#UNIVERSITIES.2C_COLLEGES_.26_SCHOOLS** (accessed July 22, 2007).

Totty, Michael. "Information Found—and Shared." *The Wall Street Journal* (September 11, 2006).

———. "Social Studies." *The Wall Street Journal* (June 18, 2007).

Vara, Vauhini. "Offices Co-opt Consumer Web Tools Like 'Wikis' and Social Networking." *The Wall Street Journal* (September 12, 2006).

———. "Wikis at Work." *The Wall Street Journal* (June 18, 2007).

"Visiting Second Life's Virtual World." *CBC News in Review* (February 2007).

Glossary

2.5G networks Interim networks that provide data transmission rates ranging from 60 to 354 Kbps, enabling cell phones to be used for Web access, music downloads, and other broadband services; to be followed by 3G networks.

3G networks Cellular networks based on packet-switched technology with speeds ranging from 144 Kbps for mobile users to over 2 Mbps for stationary users, enabling users to transmit video, graphics, and other rich media, in addition to voice.

acceptable use policy (AUP) Defines acceptable uses of the firm's information resources and computing equipment, including desktop and laptop computers, wireless devices, telephones, and the Internet, and specifies consequences for noncompliance.

acceptance testing Provides the final certification that the system is ready to be used in a production setting.

access control Policies and procedures a company uses to prevent improper access to systems by unauthorized insiders and outsiders.

accountability The mechanisms for assessing responsibility for decisions made and actions taken.

accumulated balance digital payment systems Systems enabling users to make micropayments and purchases on the Web, accumulating a debit balance on their credit card or telephone bills.

agency theory Economic theory that views the firm as a nexus of contracts among self-interested individuals who must be supervised and managed.

agent-based modelling Modelling complex phenomena as systems of autonomous agents that follow relatively simple rules for interaction.

agile development Rapid delivery of working software by breaking a large project into a series of small sub-projects that are completed in short periods of time using iteration and continuous feedback.

Ajax Technique for creating interactive Web applications capable of updating the user interface without reloading the entire browser page.

analog signal A continuous waveform that passes through a communications medium; used for voice communications.

analytical CRM Customer relationship management applications dealing with the analysis of customer data to provide information for improving business performance.

antivirus software Software designed to detect, and often eliminate, computer viruses from an information system.

application controls Specific controls unique to each computerized application that ensure that only authorized data are completely and accurately processed by that application.

application server Software that handles all application operations between browser-based computers and a company's back-end business applications or databases.

artificial intelligence (AI) The effort to develop computer-based systems that can behave like humans, with the ability to learn languages, accomplish physical tasks, use a perceptual apparatus, and emulate human expertise and decision making.

attribute A piece of information describing a particular entity.

authentication The ability of each party in a transaction to ascertain the identity of the other party.

authorization management systems Systems for allowing each user access only to those portions of a system or the Web that person is permitted to enter, based on information established by a set of access rules.

authorization policies Determine differing levels of access to information assets for different levels of users in an organization.

automation Using the computer to speed up the performance of existing tasks.

autonomic computing Effort to develop systems that can manage themselves without user intervention.

backward chaining A strategy for searching the rule base in an expert system that acts like a problem solver by beginning with a hypothesis and seeking out more information until the hypothesis is either proved or disproved.

balanced scorecard method Framework for operationalizing a firm's strategic plan by focusing on measurable financial, business process, customer, and learning and growth outcomes of firm performance.

bandwidth The capacity of a communications channel as measured by the difference between the highest and lowest frequencies that can be transmitted by that channel.

banner ad A graphic display on a Web page used for advertising. The banner is linked to the advertiser's Web site so that a person clicking on it will be transported to the advertiser's Web site.

behavioural models Descriptions of management based on behavioural scientists' observations of what managers actually do in their jobs.

benchmarking Setting strict standards for products, services, or activities and measuring organizational performance against those standards.

best practices The most successful solutions or problem-solving methods that have been developed by a specific organization or industry.

biometric authentication Technology for authenticating system users that compares a person's unique characteristics such as fingerprints, face, or retinal image, against a stored set profile of these characteristics.

blade server Entire computer that fits on a single, thin card (or blade) and that is plugged into a single chassis to save space, power, and complexity.

blog Popular term for Web log, designating an informal yet structured Web site where individuals can publish stories, opinions, and links to other Web sites of interest.

blogosphere Totality of blog-related Web sites.

Bluetooth Standard for wireless personal area networks that can transmit up to 722 Kbps within a 10-metre area.

botnet A group of computers that have been infected with bot malware without users' knowledge, enabling a hacker to use the amassed resources of the computers to launch distributed denial-of-service attacks, phishing campaigns, or spam.

broadband High-speed transmission technology. Also designates a single communications medium that can transmit multiple channels of data simultaneously.

bugs Software program code defects.

bullwhip effect Distortion of information about the demand for a product as it passes from one entity to the next across the supply chain.

business continuity planning Planning that focuses on how the company can restore business operations after a disaster strikes.

business driver A force in the environment to which businesses must respond and that influences the direction of business.

business ecosystem Loosely coupled but interdependent networks of suppliers, distributors, outsourcing firms, transportation service firms, and technology manufacturers.

business functions Specialized tasks performed in a business organization, including manufacturing and production, sales and marketing, finance and accounting, and human resources.

business intelligence Applications and technologies to help users make better business decisions.

business model An abstraction of what an enterprise is and how the enterprise delivers a product or service, showing how the enterprise creates wealth.

business processes The unique ways in which organizations coordinate and organize work activities, information, and knowledge to produce a product or service.

business process management Methodology for revising the organization's business processes to use business processes as fundamental building blocks of corporate information systems.

business process re-engineering The radical redesign of business processes, combining steps to cut waste and eliminating repetitive, paper-intensive tasks in order to improve cost, quality, and service and to maximize the benefits of information technology.

business-to-business (B2B) electronic commerce Electronic sales of goods and services among businesses.

business-to-consumer (B2C) electronic commerce Electronic retailing of products and services directly to individual consumers.

bus topology Network topology linking a number of computers by a single circuit with all messages broadcast to the entire network.

cable Internet connections Internet connections that use digital cable lines to deliver high-speed Internet access to homes and businesses.

call centre An organizational department responsible for handling customer service issues by telephone and other channels.

CA*net The national backbone for Canada with one "drop" per province.

capital budgeting The process of analyzing and selecting various proposals for capital expenditures.

carpal tunnel syndrome (CTS) Type of RSI in which pressure on the median nerve through the wrist's bony carpal tunnel structure produces pain.

case-based reasoning (CBR) Artificial intelligence technology that represents knowledge as a database of cases and solutions.

cell phone A device that transmits voice or data, using radio waves to communicate with radio antennas placed within adjacent geographic areas called *cells*.

change agent In the context of implementation, the individual acting as the catalyst during the change process to ensure successful organizational adaptation to a new system or innovation.

change management Managing the impact of organizational change associated with an innovation, such as a new information system.

chat Live, interactive conversations over a public network.

chief information officer (CIO) Senior manager in charge of the information systems function in a firm.

chief knowledge officer (CKO) Senior executive in charge of an organization's knowledge management program.

chief privacy officer (CPO) Employee responsible for ensuring the organization complies with existing data privacy laws.

chief security officer (CSO) Employee who heads the formal security function for an organization and is responsible for enforcing the firm's security policy.

choice Simon's third stage of decision making wherein the individual selects among the various solution alternatives.

churn rate Measurement of the number of customers who stop using or purchasing products or services from a company. Used as an indicator of the growth or decline of a firm's customer base.

classical model of management Traditional description of management that focused on its formal functions of planning, organizing, coordinating, deciding, and controlling.

click fraud Fraudulently clicking on an online ad in pay-per-click advertising to generate an improper charge per click.

clicks-and-mortar Business model where the Web site is an extension of a traditional bricks-and-mortar business.

clickstream tracking Tracking data about customer activities at Web sites and storing them in a log.

client The user point of entry for the required function in client/server computing. Normally a desktop computer, workstation, or laptop computer.

client/server and architecture computing A model for computing that splits processing between clients and servers on a network, assigning functions to the machine most able to perform the function.

cloud computing Web-based applications that are stored on remote servers and accessed via the "cloud" of the Internet using a standard Web browser.

coaxial cable A transmission medium consisting of thickly insulated copper wire; can transmit large volumes of data quickly.

collaborative filtering Tracking users' movements on a Web site, comparing the information gleaned about a user's behaviour against data about other customers with similar interests to predict what the user would like to see next.

communities of practice Informal social networks of professionals and employees within and outside the firm who have similar work-related activities and interests.

competitive forces model Model used to describe the interaction of external influences, specifically threats and opportunities, that affect an organization's strategy and ability to compete.

complementary assets Additional assets required to derive value from a primary investment.

component-based development Building large software systems by combining pre-existing software components.

computer abuse The commission of acts involving a computer that may not be illegal but are considered unethical.

computer-aided design (CAD) Information system that automates the creation and revision of designs using sophisticated graphics software.

computer-aided software engineering (CASE) Automation of step-by-step methodologies for software and systems development to reduce the amount of repetitive work the developer needs to do.

computer crime The commission of illegal acts through the use of a computer or against a computer system.

computer forensics The scientific collection, examination, authentication, preservation, and analysis of data held on or retrieved from computer storage media in such a way that the information can be used as evidence in a court of law.

computer hardware Physical equipment used for input, processing, and output activities in an information system.

computer literacy Knowledge about information technology, focusing on understanding how computer-based technologies work.

computer software Detailed, preprogrammed instructions that control and coordinate the work of computer hardware components in an information system.

computer virus Rogue software program that attaches itself to other software programs or data files in order to be executed, often causing hardware and software malfunctions.

computer vision syndrome (CVS) Eyestrain condition related to computer display screen use; symptoms include headaches, blurred vision, and dry and irritated eyes.

consumer-to-consumer (C2C) electronic commerce Consumers selling goods and services electronically to other consumers.

controls All of the methods, policies, and procedures that ensure protection of the organization's assets, accuracy and reliability of its records, and operational adherence to management standards.

conversion The process of changing from the old system to the new system.

cookies Tiny files deposited on computer hard drives when visiting certain Web sites. Used to identify the visitor and track visits to the Web site.

co-optation Bringing the opposition into the process of designing and implementing a solution without giving up control of the direction and nature of the change.

copyright A statutory grant that protects creators of intellectual property against copying by others for any purpose for a minimum of 50 years.

core competency Activity at which a firm excels as a world-class leader.

core systems Systems that support functions that are absolutely critical to the organization.

cost transparency The ability of consumers to discover the actual costs merchants pay for products.

counterimplementation A deliberate strategy to thwart the implementation of an information system or an innovation in an organization.

critical success factors (CSFs) A small number of easily identifiable operational goals shaped by the industry, the firm, the manager, and the broader environment that are believed to assure the success of an organization. Used to determine the information requirements of an organization.

cross-selling Marketing complementary products to customers.

C-SOX Act passed by Parliament that imposes responsibility on companies and their managements to safeguard the accuracy and integrity of financial information that is used internally and released externally.

culture The set of fundamental assumptions about what products the organization should produce, how and where it should produce them, and for whom they should be produced.

customer decision-support system (CDSS) System to support the decision-making process of an existing or potential customer.

customer lifetime value (CLTV) Difference between revenues produced by a specific customer and the expenses for acquiring and servicing that customer minus the cost of promotional marketing over the lifetime of the customer relationship, expressed in today's dollars.

customer relationship management systems Information systems that track all the ways in which a company interacts with its customers and analyze these interactions to optimize revenue, profitability, customer satisfaction, and customer retention.

customization The modification of a software package to meet an organization's unique requirements without destroying the packaged software's integrity.

cybervandalism Intentional disruption, defacement, or destruction of a Web site or corporate information system.

data Streams of raw facts representing events occurring in organizations or the physical environment before they have been organized and arranged into a form that people can understand and use.

data administration A special organizational function for managing the organization's data resources, concerned with information policy, data planning, maintenance of data dictionaries, and data quality standards.

database A group of related files.

database (rigorous definition) A collection of data organized to service many applications at the same time by storing and managing data so that they appear to be in one location.

database administration Refers to the more technical and operational aspects of managing data, including physical database design and maintenance.

database management system (DBMS) Special software to create and maintain a database and enable individual business applications to extract the data they need without having to create separate files or data definitions in their computer programs.

database server A computer in a client/server environment that is responsible for running a DBMS to process SQL statements and perform database management tasks.

data cleansing Activities for detecting and correcting data in a database or file that are incorrect, incomplete, improperly formatted, or redundant. Also known as data scrubbing.

dataconferencing Teleconferencing in which two or more users are able to edit and modify data files simultaneously.

data definition DBMS capability that specifies the structure and content of the database.

data dictionary An automated or manual tool for storing and organizing information about the data maintained in a database.

data-driven DSS A system that supports decision making by allowing users to extract and analyze useful information that was previously buried in large databases.

data entry operators Staff whose main job is to enter data into information systems.

data flow diagram (DFD) Primary tool for structured analysis that graphically illustrates a system's component process and the flow of data between them.

data governance Policies and processes for managing the availability, usability, integrity, and security of the firm's data.

data inconsistency The presence of different values for same attribute when the same data are stored in multiple locations.

data manipulation language A language associated with a database management system that end users and programmers use to manipulate data in the database.

data mart A small data warehouse containing only a portion of the organization's data for a specified function or population of users.

data mining Analysis of large pools of data to find patterns and rules that can be used to guide decision making and predict future behaviour.

data quality audit A survey and/or sample of files to determine accuracy and completeness of data in an information system.

data redundancy The presence of duplicate data in multiple data files.

data visualization Technology for helping users see patterns and relationships in large amounts of data by presenting the data in graphical form.

data warehouse A database, with reporting and query tools, that stores current and historical data extracted from various operational systems that is consolidated for management reporting and analysis.

data workers People such as secretaries or bookkeepers who process the organization's paperwork.

decisional roles Mintzberg's classification for managerial roles wherein managers initiate activities, handle disturbances, allocate resources, and negotiate conflicts.

decision-support systems (DSS) Information systems at the organization's management level that combine data and sophisticated analytical models or data analysis tools to support semistructured and unstructured decision making.

deep packet inspection (DPI) Technology for managing network traffic by examining data packets, sorting out low-priority data from higher-priority, business-critical data, and sending packets in order of priority.

demand planning Determining how much product a business needs to make to satisfy all its customers' demands.

denial of service (DoS) attack Flooding a network server or Web server with false communications or requests for services in order to crash the network.

Descartes' rule of change A principle that states that if an action cannot be taken repeatedly, then it is not right to be taken at any time.

design Simon's second stage of decision making wherein the individual conceives of possible alternative solutions to a problem.

digital asset management systems Classify, store, and distribute digital objects such as photographs, graphic images, video, and audio content.

digital certificate An attachment to an electronic message to verify the identity of the sender and to provide the receiver with the means to encode a reply.

digital chequing Systems that extend the functionality of existing chequing accounts so they can be used for online shopping payments.

digital dashboard Displays all of a firm's key performance indicators as graphs and charts on a single screen to provide one-page overview of all the critical measurements necessary to make key executive decisions.

digital divide Large disparities in access to computers and the Internet among different social groups and different locations.

digital firm Organization where nearly all significant business processes and relationships with customers, suppliers, and employees are digitally enabled and key corporate assets are managed through digital means.

digital goods Goods that can be delivered over a digital network.

Digital Millennium Copyright Act (DMCA) A U.S. law that adjusts copyright laws to the Internet Age by making it illegal to make, distribute, or use devices that circumvent technology-based protections of copyrighted materials.

digital subscriber line (DSL) A group of technologies providing high-capacity transmission over existing copper telephone lines.

digital wallet Software that stores credit card, electronic cash, owner identification, and address information and provides this data automatically during electronic commerce purchase transactions.

direct cutover A risky conversion approach where the new system completely replaces the old one on an appointed day.

disaster recovery planning Planning for the restoration of computing and communications services after they have been disrupted.

disintermediation The removal of organizations or business process layers responsible for certain intermediary steps in a value chain.

disruptive technologies Technologies with a disruptive impact on industries and businesses, rendering existing products, services, and business models obsolete.

distributed database A database that is stored in more than one physical location. Parts or copies of the database are physically stored in one location, and other parts or copies are stored and maintained in other locations.

distributed denial-of-service (DDoS) attack Numerous computers inundating and overwhelming a network from numerous launch points.

documentation Descriptions of how an information system works from either a technical or end-user standpoint.

domain name English-like name that corresponds to the unique 32-bit numeric Internet Protocol (IP) address for each computer connected to the Internet.

domain name system (DNS) A hierarchical system of servers maintaining a database enabling the conversion of domain names to their numeric IP addresses.

domestic exporter Form of business organization characterized by heavy centralization of corporate activities in the home country of origin.

downtime Period of time in which an information system is not operational.

drill down The ability to move from summary data to lower and lower levels of detail.

DSS database A collection of current or historical data from a number of applications or groups. Can be a small PC database or a massive data warehouse.

DSS software system Collection of software tools that are used for data analysis, such as OLAP tools, data-mining tools, or a collection of mathematical and analytical models.

due process A process in which laws are well known and understood and there is an ability to appeal to higher authorities to ensure that laws are applied correctly.

dynamic pricing Pricing of items based on real-time interactions between buyers and sellers that determine what an item is worth at any particular moment.

e-government Use of the Internet and related technologies to digitally enable government and public sector agencies' relationships with citizens, businesses, and other arms of government.

efficient customer response system System that directly links consumer behaviour back to distribution, production, and supply chains.

electronic billing and presentation payment systems Systems used for paying routine monthly bills that allow users to view their bills electronically and pay them through electronic funds transfers from banks or credit card accounts.

electronic business (e-business) The use of the Internet and digital technology to execute all the business processes in the enterprise. Includes e-commerce as well as processes for the internal management of the firm and for coordination with suppliers and other business partners.

electronic commerce The process of buying and selling goods and services electronically involving transactions using the Internet, networks, and other digital technologies.

electronic data interchange (EDI) The direct computer-to-computer exchange between two organizations of standard business transactions, such as orders, shipment instructions, or payments.

e-mail The computer-to-computer exchange of messages.

employee relationship management (ERM) Software dealing with employee issues that are closely related to CRM, such as setting objectives, employee performance management, performance-based compensation, and employee training.

encryption The coding and scrambling of messages to prevent their being read or accessed without authorization.

end-user development The development of information systems by end users with little or no formal assistance from technical specialists.

end-user interface The part of an information system through which the end user interacts with the system, such as online screens, links, and commands.

end users Representatives of departments outside the information systems group for whom applications are developed.

enterprise applications Systems that can coordinate activities, decisions, and knowledge across many different functions, levels, and business units in a firm. Include enterprise systems, supply chain management systems, and knowledge management systems.

enterprise content management systems Systems that help organizations manage structured and semistructured knowledge, providing corporate repositories of documents, reports, presentations, and best practices and capabilities for collecting and organizing e-mail and graphic objects.

enterprise portal Web interface providing a single entry point for accessing organizational information and services, including information from various enterprise applications and in-house legacy systems so that information appears to be coming from a single source.

enterprise software Set of integrated modules for applications such as sales and distribution, financial accounting, investment management, materials management, production planning, plant maintenance, and human resources that allow data to be used by multiple functions and business processes.

enterprise systems Integrated enterprise-wide information systems that coordinate key internal processes of the firm.

enterprise-wide knowledge management systems General-purpose, firm-wide systems that collect, store, distribute, and apply digital content and knowledge.

entity A person, place, thing, or event about which information must be kept.

entity-relationship diagram A methodology for documenting databases illustrating the relationship between various entities in the database.

ergonomics The interaction of people and machines in the work environment, including the design of jobs, health issues, and the end-user interface of information systems.

ethical "no free lunch" rule Assumption that all tangible and intangible objects are owned by someone else, unless there is a specific declaration otherwise, and that the creator wants compensation for this work.

ethics Principles of right and wrong that can be used by individuals acting as free moral agents to make choices to guide their behaviour.

evil twin Wireless network that pretends to be legitimate to entice participants to log on and reveal passwords or credit card numbers.

exchanges Third-party Internet marketplaces that are primarily transaction-oriented and that connect many buyers and suppliers for spot purchasing.

executive support systems (ESS) Information systems at the organization's strategic level designed to address unstructured decision making through advanced graphics and communications capabilities.

expert systems Knowledge-intensive computer programs that capture the expertise of humans in limited domains of knowledge.

explicit knowledge Knowledge that has been documented.

Extensible Markup Language (XML) General-purpose markup language that describes the structure of a document and supports links to multiple documents, allowing data to be manipulated by the computer. Used for both Web and non-Web applications.

external integration tools Project management technique that links the work of the implementation team to that of users at all organizational levels.

extranet Private intranet that is accessible to authorized outsiders.

Fair Information Practices (FIP) A set of principles originally set forth in the United States in 1973 that governs the collection and use of information about individuals and forms the basis of most North American and European privacy laws.

fault-tolerant computer systems Systems that contain extra hardware, software, and power supply components that can back up a system and keep it running to prevent system failure.

feasibility study As part of the systems analysis process, the way to determine whether the solution is achievable, given the organization's resources and constraints.

feedback Output that is returned to the appropriate members of the organization to help them evaluate or correct input.

fibreoptic cable A fast, light, and durable transmission medium consisting of thin strands of clear glass fibre bound into cables. Data are transmitted as light pulses.

field A grouping of characters into a word, a group of words, or a complete number, such as a person's name or age.

file transfer protocol (FTP) Tool for retrieving and transferring files from a remote computer.

file A group of records of the same type.

firewall Hardware and software placed between an organization's internal network and an external network to prevent outsiders from invading private networks.

folksonomies User-created taxonomies for classifying and sharing information.

foreign key Field in a database table that enables users to find related information in another database table.

formal control tools Project management technique that helps monitor the progress toward completion of a task and fulfillment of goals.

formal planning tools Project management technique that structures and sequences tasks, budgeting time, money, and technical resources required to complete the tasks.

forward chaining A strategy for searching the rule base in an expert system that begins with the information entered by the user and searches the rule base to arrive at a conclusion.

fourth-generation language A programming language that can be employed directly by end users or less-skilled programmers to develop computer applications more rapidly than conventional programming languages.

franchiser Form of business organization in which a product is created, designed, financed, and initially produced in the home country but, for product-specific reasons, relies heavily on foreign personnel for further production, marketing, and human resources.

fuzzy logic Rule-based AI that tolerates imprecision by using nonspecific terms called *membership functions* to solve problems.

Gantt chart Visually represents the timing, duration, and resource requirements of project tasks.

general controls Overall control environment governing the design, security, and use of computer programs and the security of data files in general throughout the organization's information technology infrastructure.

genetic algorithms Problem-solving methods that promote the evolution of solutions to specified problems using the model of living organisms adapting to their environment.

geographic information system (GIS) System with software that can analyze and display data using digitized maps to enhance planning and decision making.

global culture The development of common expectations, shared artifacts, and social norms among different cultures and peoples.

global positioning system (GPS) Worldwide satellite navigational system.

Golden Rule Ethical principle that states "Do unto others as you would have them do unto you."

graphical user interface (GUI) The part of an operating system users interact with that uses graphic icons and the computer mouse to issue commands and make selections.

green computing The responsible use of computers that minimizes the impact of computers on the environment (e.g., power consumption, recycling capability).

grid computing Applying the resources of many computers in a network to a single problem.

group decision-support system (GDSS) An interactive computer-based system to facilitate the solution to unstructured problems by a set of decision makers working together as a group.

hacker A person who gains unauthorized access to a computer network for profit, criminal mischief, or personal pleasure.

hertz Measure of frequency of electrical impulses per second, with 1 hertz equivalent to 1 cycle per second.

high-availability computing Tools and technologies, including backup hardware resources, to enable a system to recover quickly from a crash.

hotspot A specific geographic location in which an access point provides public Wi-Fi network service.

hubs Very simple devices that connect network components, sending a packet of data to all other connected devices.

hybrid AI systems Integration of multiple AI technologies into a single application to take advantage of the best features of these technologies.

Hypertext Markup Language (HTML) Page description language for creating Web pages and other hypermedia documents.

Hypertext Transfer Protocol (HTTP) The communications standard used to transfer pages on the Web. Defines how messages are formatted and transmitted.

identity theft Theft of key pieces of personal information, such as credit card or social insurance numbers, in order to obtain merchandise and services in the name of the victim or to obtain false credentials.

Immanuel Kant's categorical imperative A principle that states that if an action is not right for everyone to take, it is not right for anyone.

implementation Simon's final stage of decision making wherein the individual puts the decision into effect and reports on the progress of the solution.

inference engine The strategy used to search through the rule base in an expert system; can be forward or backward chaining.

information Data that have been shaped into a form that is meaningful and useful to human beings.

information asymmetry Situation where the relative bargaining power of two parties in a transaction is determined by one party in the transaction possessing more information essential to the transaction than the other party.

information density The total amount and quality of information available to all market participants, consumers, and merchants.

information policy Formal rules governing the maintenance, distribution, and use of information in an organization.

information requirements A detailed statement of the information needs that a new system must satisfy; identifies who needs what information, and when, where, and how the information is needed.

information rights The rights that individuals and organizations have with respect to information that pertains to themselves.

information system Interrelated components working together to collect, process, store, and disseminate information to support decision making, coordination, control, analysis, and visualization in an organization.

information systems department The formal organizational unit that is responsible for the information systems function in the organization.

information systems literacy Broad-based understanding of information systems that includes behavioural knowledge about organizations and individuals using information systems as well as technical knowledge about computers.

information systems managers Leaders of the various specialists in the information systems department.

information systems plan A road map indicating the direction of systems development: the rationale, the current situation, the management strategy, the implementation plan, and the budget.

information technology (IT) All the hardware and software technologies a firm needs to achieve its business objectives.

information technology (IT) infrastructure Computer hardware, software, data, storage technology, and networks providing a portfolio of shared IT resources for the organization.

informational roles Mintzberg's classification for managerial roles wherein managers act as the nerve centres of their organizations, receiving and disseminating critical information.

informed consent Consent given with knowledge of all the facts needed to make a rational decision.

input The capture or collection of raw data from within the organization or from its external environment for processing in an information system.

instant messaging Chat service that allows participants to create their own private chat channels so that a person can be alerted whenever someone on his or her private list is online to initiate a chat session with that particular individual.

intangible benefits Benefits that are not easily quantified; they include more efficient customer service or enhanced decision making.

intellectual property Intangible property created by individuals or corporations that is subject to protections under trade secret, copyright, and patent law.

intelligence The first of Simon's four stages of decision making wherein the individual collects information to identify problems occurring in the organization.

intelligent agents Software programs that use a built-in or learned knowledge base to carry out specific, repetitive, and predictable tasks for an individual user, business process, or software application.

intelligent techniques Methods that include data mining, expert systems, neural networks, fuzzy logic, genetic algorithms, and intelligent agents.

internal integration tools Project management technique that ensures that the implementation team operates as a cohesive unit.

international information systems architecture The basic information systems required by organizations to coordinate worldwide trade and other activities.

Internet Global network of networks using universal standards to connect millions of different networks.

Internet Protocol (IP) address Four-part numeric address indicating a unique computer location on the Internet.

Internet service provider (ISP) A commercial organization with a permanent connection to the Internet that sells temporary connections to subscribers.

Internet telephony Technologies that use the Internet Protocol's packet-switched connections for voice service.

Internet2 Research network with new protocols and transmission speeds that provides an infrastructure for supporting high-bandwidth Internet applications.

interorganizational system Information system that automates the flow of information across organizational boundaries and links a company to its customers, distributors, or suppliers.

interpersonal roles Mintzberg's classification for managerial roles wherein managers act as figureheads and leaders for the organization.

intranet An internal network based on Internet and World Wide Web technology and standards.

intrusion detection systems Tools to monitor the most vulnerable points in a network to detect and deter unauthorized intruders.

investment workstations Powerful desktop computers for financial specialists, which are optimized to access and manipulate massive amounts of financial data.

IT governance Strategy and policies for using information technology within an organization, specifying the decision rights and accountabilities to ensure that information technology supports the organization's strategies and objectives.

iterative A process of repeating over and over again the steps to build a system.

Java Programming language that can deliver only the software functionality needed for a particular task, such as a small applet downloaded from a network; can run on any computer and operating system.

joint application design (JAD) Process to accelerate the generation of information requirements by having end users and information systems specialists work together in intensive interactive design sessions.

just-in-time strategy Scheduling system for minimizing inventory by having components arrive exactly at the moment they are needed and finished goods shipped as soon as they leave the assembly line.

key field A field in a record that uniquely identifies instances of that record so that it can be retrieved, updated, or sorted.

keylogger Spyware that records every keystroke made on a computer to steal personal information or passwords or to launch Internet attacks.

key performance indicators Measures proposed by senior management for understanding how well the firm is performing along specified dimensions.

knowledge Concepts, experience, and insight that provide a framework for creating, evaluating, and using information.

knowledge- and information-intense products Products that require a great deal of learning and knowledge to produce.

knowledge base Model of human knowledge that is used by expert systems.

knowledge discovery Identification of novel and valuable patterns in large databases.

knowledge management The set of processes developed in an organization to create, gather, store, maintain, and disseminate the firm's knowledge.

knowledge management systems Systems that support the creation, capture, storage, and dissemination of firm expertise and knowledge.

knowledge network system Online directory for locating corporate experts in well-defined knowledge domains.

knowledge work systems Specialized systems built for engineers, scientists, and other knowledge workers charged with discovering and creating new knowledge for a company.

knowledge workers People such as engineers or architects who design products or services and create knowledge for the organization.

learning management system (LMS) Tools for the management, delivery, tracking, and assessment of various types of employee learning.

legacy system A system that has been in existence for a long time and that continues to be used to avoid the high cost of replacing or redesigning it.

legitimacy The extent to which one's authority is accepted on grounds of competence, vision, or other qualities. Making judgments and taking actions on the basis of narrow or personal characteristics.

liability The existence of laws that permit individuals to recover the damages done to them by other actors, systems, or organizations.

Linux Reliable and compactly designed operating system that is an offshoot of UNIX and that can run on many different hardware platforms and is available free or at very low cost.

local area network (LAN) A telecommunications network that requires its own dedicated channels and that encompasses a limited distance, usually one building or several buildings in close proximity.

mainframe Largest category of computer, used for major business processing.

maintenance Changes in hardware, software, documentation, or procedures to a production system to correct errors, meet new requirements, or improve processing efficiency.

malware Malicious software programs such as computer viruses, worms, and Trojan horses.

managed security service providers (MSSPs) Companies that provide security management services for subscribing clients.

management information systems (MIS) (1) The study of information systems focusing on their use in business and management. (2) A specific category of information system serving middle management. MIS provide middle managers with reports on the organization's current performance to monitor and control the business and predict future performance.

management-level systems Information systems that support the monitoring, controlling, decision-making, and administrative activities of middle managers.

managerial roles Mintzberg's taxonomy for the expectations of activities that managers should perform in an organization.

man-month The traditional unit of measurement used by systems designers to estimate the length of time to complete a project. Refers to the amount of work a person can be expected to complete in a month.

market entry costs The costs merchants must pay simply to bring their goods to market.

marketspace A marketplace extended beyond traditional boundaries and removed from a temporal and geographic location.

mashup Composite software application that depends on high-speed networks, universal communication standards, and open source code.

mass customization The capacity to offer individually tailored products or services using mass production resources.

megahertz A measure of cycle speed or the pacing of events in a computer; one megahertz equals one million cycles per second.

menu costs Merchants' costs of changing prices.

metric A standard measurement of performance.

metropolitan area network (MAN) Network that spans a metropolitan area, usually a city and its major suburbs. Its geographic scope falls between a WAN and a LAN.

microbrowser Web browser software with a small file size that can work with low-memory constraints, tiny screens of handheld wireless devices, and low bandwidth of wireless networks.

micropayment Payment for a very small sum of money, usually less than $10.

microprocessor Very-large-scale integrated circuit technology that integrates the computer's memory, logic, and control on a single chip.

microwave A high-volume, long-distance, point-to-point transmission in which high-frequency radio signals are transmitted through the atmosphere from one terrestrial transmission station to another.

middle management People in the middle of the organizational hierarchy who are responsible for carrying out the plans and goals of senior management.

mid-range computer Middle-size computer that is capable of supporting the computing needs of smaller organizations or of managing networks of other computers.

minicomputer Middle-range computer used in systems for universities, factories, or research laboratories.

MIS audit Audit that identifies all the controls that govern individual information systems and assesses their effectiveness.

mobile commerce (m-commerce) The use of wireless devices, such as cell phones or handheld digital information appliances, to conduct both business-to-consumer and business-to-business e-commerce transactions over the Internet.

mobile wallets (m-wallets) Applications that store m-commerce shoppers' personal information and credit card numbers to expedite the purchase process.

moblog Specialized blog featuring photos with captions posted from mobile phones.

model An abstract representation that illustrates the components or relationships of a phenomenon.

model-driven DSS Primarily stand-alone system that uses some type of model to perform "what-if" and other kinds of analyses.

modem A device for translating a computer's digital signals into analog form for transmission over ordinary telephone lines or for translating analog signals back into digital form for reception by a computer.

module A logical unit of a program that performs one or several functions.

Moore's law Assertion that the number of components on a chip doubles each year.

MP3 (MPEG3) Compression standard that can compress audio files for transfer over the Internet with virtually no loss in quality.

multicore processor Integrated circuit to which two or more processors have been attached for enhanced performance, reduced power consumption, and more efficient simultaneous processing of multiple tasks.

multimedia The integration of two or more types of media such as text, graphics, sound, voice, full-motion video, or animation into a computer-based application.

multinational Form of business organization that concentrates financial management and control out of a central home base while decentralizing most other applications.

multiplexing Ability of a single communications channel to carry data transmissions from multiple sources simultaneously.

multitiered (N-tier) client/server architecture Client/server network in which the work of the entire network is balanced over several different levels of servers.

nanotechnology Technology that builds structures and processes based on the manipulation of individual atoms and molecules.

natural language Nonprocedural language that enables users to communicate with the computer using conversational commands resembling human speech.

net marketplaces Digital marketplaces based on Internet technology linking many buyers to many sellers.

netbook Small, low-cost, lightweight subnotebook optimized for wireless communication and Internet access.

network The linking of two or more computers to share data or resources, such as a printer.

network economics Model of strategic systems at the industry level based on the concept of a network where adding another participant entails zero marginal costs but can create much larger marginal gains.

network interface card (NIC) Expansion card inserted into a computer to enable it to connect to a network.

networking and telecommunications technology Physical devices and software that link various computer hardware components and transfer data from one physical location to another.

network managers Staff who manage the organization's networks.

network operating system (NOS) Special software that routes and manages communications on the network and coordinates network resources.

neural networks Hardware and/or software that attempt to emulate the processing patterns of the biological brain.

nonobvious relationship awareness (NORA) Technology that can find obscure hidden connections between people or other entities by analyzing information from many different sources to correlate relationships.

normalization The process of creating small, stable data structures from complex groups of data when designing a relational database.

object Software building block that combines data and the procedures acting on the data.

object-oriented DBMS An approach to data management that stores both data and the procedures acting on the data as objects that can be automatically retrieved and shared; the objects can contain multimedia.

object-oriented development Approach to systems development that uses the object as the basic unit of systems analysis and design. The system is modelled as a collection of objects and the relationship between them.

object-oriented programming An approach to software development that combines data and procedures into a single object.

object-relational DBMS A database management system that combines the capabilities of a relational DBMS for storing traditional information and the capabilities of an object-oriented DBMS for storing graphics and multimedia.

offshore outsourcing Outsourcing systems development work or maintenance of existing systems to external vendors in another country.

on-demand computing Firms offloading peak demand for computing power to remote, large-scale data processing centres, investing just enough to handle average processing loads and paying for only as much additional computing power as the market demands. Also called *utility computing*.

online analytical processing (OLAP) Capability for manipulating and analyzing large volumes of data from multiple perspectives.

online processing A method of collecting and processing data in which transactions are entered directly into the computer system and processed immediately.

online stored value payment systems Systems enabling consumers to make instant online payments to merchants and other individuals based on value stored in a digital document.

online transaction processing Transaction processing mode in which transactions entered online are immediately processed by the computer.

open source software Software that provides free access to its program code, allowing users to modify the program code to make improvements or fix errors.

operating system Software that manages the resources and activities of the computer.

operational CRM Customer-facing applications, such as sales force automation, call centre and customer service support, and marketing automation.

operational-level systems Information systems that monitor the elementary activities and transactions of the organization.

operational management People who monitor the day-to-day activities of the organization.

opt-in Model of informed consent permitting prohibiting an organization from collecting any personal information unless the individual specifically takes action to approve information collection and use.

opt-out Model of informed consent permitting the collection of personal information until the consumer specifically requests that the data not be collected.

organization (behavioural definition) A collection of rights, privileges, obligations, and responsibilities that are delicately balanced over a period of time through conflict and conflict resolution.

organization (technical definition) A stable, formal, social structure that takes resources from the environment and processes them to produce outputs.

organizational and management capital Investments in organization and management such as new business processes, management behaviour, organizational culture, or training.

organizational impact analysis Study of the way a proposed system will affect organizational structure, attitudes, decision making, and operations.

organizational learning Creation of new standard operating procedures and business processes that reflect an organization's experience.

output The distribution of processed information to the people who will use it or to the activities for which it will be used.

outsourcing The practice of contracting computer centre operations, telecommunications networks, or applications development to external vendors.

packet switching Technology that breaks messages into small, fixed bundles of data and routes them in the most economical way through any available communications channel.

paradigm shift Radical reconceptualization of the nature of the business and the nature of the organization.

parallel strategy A safe and conservative conversion approach where both the old system and its potential replacement are run together for a time until everyone is assured that the new one functions correctly.

particularism Making judgments and taking action on the basis of narrow or personal characteristics, in all its forms (religious, nationalistic, ethnic, regionalistic, geopolitical position).

partner relationship management (PRM) Automation of the firm's relationships with its selling partners using customer data and analytical tools to improve coordination and customer sales.

patches Small pieces of software that repair software flaws without disturbing the proper operation of the software.

patent A legal document that grants the owner an exclusive monopoly on the ideas behind an invention for between 17 and 20 years; designed to ensure that inventors of new machines or methods are rewarded for their labour while making widespread use of their inventions.

peer-to-peer Network architecture that gives equal power to all computers on the network; used primarily in small networks.

personal area network (PAN) Computer network used for communication among digital devices (including telephones and PDAs) that are close to one person.

personal digital assistant (PDA) Small, pen-based, handheld computer with built-in wireless telecommunications capable of entirely digital communications transmission.

personalization Ability of merchants to target marketing messages to specific individuals by adjusting the message for a person's name, interests, and past purchases.

PERT chart Network diagram depicting project tasks and their interrelationships.

pharming Phishing technique that redirects users to a bogus Web page, even when an individual enters the correct Web page address.

phased approach strategy Introduction of a new system in stages either by functions or by organizational units.

phishing Form of spoofing involving setting up fake Web sites or sending e-mail messages that resemble those of legitimate businesses that ask users for confidential personal data.

pilot study A strategy to introduce a new system to a limited area of the organization until it is proven to be fully functional; only then can the conversion to the new system across the entire organization take place.

pivot table Spreadsheet tool for reorganizing and summarizing two or more dimensions of data in a tabular format.

podcasting Publishing audio broadcasts via the Internet so that subscribing users can download audio files onto their personal computers or portable music players.

pop-up ads Ads that open automatically and do not disappear until the user clicks on them.

portal Web interface for presenting integrated personalized content from a variety of sources. Also refers to a Web site service that provides an initial point of entry to the Web.

portfolio analysis An analysis of the portfolio of potential applications within a firm to determine the risks and benefits, and to select among alternatives for information systems.

post-implementation audit Formal review process conducted after a system has been placed in production to determine how well the system has met its original objectives.

predictive analysis Use of data-mining techniques, historical data, and assumptions about future conditions to predict outcomes of events.

price discrimination Selling the same goods, or nearly the same goods, to different targeted groups at different prices.

price transparency The ease with which consumers can find out the variety of prices in a market.

primary activities Activities most directly related to the production and distribution of a firm's products or services.

primary key Unique identifier for all the information in any row of a database table.

privacy The claim of individuals to be left alone, free from surveillance or interference from other individuals, organizations, or the state.

private exchange Another term for a private industrial network.

private industrial networks Web-enabled networks linking systems of multiple firms in an industry for the coordination of trans-organizational business processes.

process specifications Information that describes the logic of the processes occurring within the lowest levels of a data flow diagram.

processing The conversion, manipulation, and analysis of raw input into a form that is more meaningful to humans.

procurement Sourcing goods and materials, negotiating with suppliers, paying for goods, and making delivery arrangements.

product differentiation Competitive strategy for creating brand loyalty by developing new and unique products and services that are not easily duplicated by competitors.

production The stage after the new system is installed and the conversion is complete; during this time, the system is reviewed by users and technical specialists to determine how well it has met its original goals.

production or service workers People who actually produce the products or services of the organization.

profiling The use of computers to combine data from multiple sources and create electronic dossiers of detailed information on individuals.

program-data dependence The close relationship between data stored in files and the software programs that update and maintain those files. Any change in data organization or format requires a change in all the programs associated with those files.

programmers Highly trained technical specialists who write computer software instructions.

programming The process of translating the system specifications prepared during the design stage into program code.

project Planned series of related activities for achieving a specific business objective.

project management Application of knowledge, tools, and techniques to achieve specific targets within a specified budget and time period.

protocol A set of rules and procedures that govern transmission between the components in a network.

prototype The preliminary working version of an information system for demonstration and evaluation purposes.

prototyping The process of building an experimental system quickly and inexpensively for demonstration and evaluation so that users can better determine information requirements.

P3P (Platform for Privacy Preferences) Industry standard designed to give users more control over personal information gathered on Web sites they visit.

public key encryption Uses two keys: one shared (or public) and one private.

public key infrastructure (PKI) System for creating public and private keys using a certificate authority (CA) and digital certificates for authentication.

pull-based model Supply chain driven by actual customer orders or purchases so that members of the supply chain produce and deliver only what customers have ordered.

pure-play Business models based purely on the Internet.

push-based model Supply chain driven by production master schedules based on forecasts or best guesses of demand for products, where products are "pushed" to customers.

query languages Software tools that provide immediate online answers to requests for information that are not predefined.

radio frequency identification (RFID) Technology using tiny tags with embedded microchips containing data about an item and its location to transmit short-distance radio signals to special RFID readers that then pass the data on to a computer for processing.

rapid application development (RAD) Process for developing systems in a very short time period by using prototyping, fourth-generation tools, and close teamwork among users and systems specialists.

rationalization of procedures The streamlining of standard operating procedures, eliminating obvious bottlenecks, so that automation makes operating procedures more efficient.

rational model Model of human behaviour based on the belief that people, organizations, and nations engage in basically consistent, value-maximizing calculations.

real options pricing models Models for evaluating information technology investments with uncertain returns by using techniques for valuing financial options.

record A group of related fields.

recovery-oriented computing Computer systems designed to recover rapidly when mishaps occur.

referential integrity Rules to ensure that relationships between linked database tables remain consistent.

relational DBMS A type of logical database model that treats data as if they were stored in two-dimensional tables. It can relate data stored in one table to data in another as long as the two tables share a common data element.

repeating data groups Unnormalized data wherein there can be multiple records associated with multiple records from another table.

repetitive stress injury (RSI) Occupational disease that occurs when muscle groups are forced through repetitive actions with high-impact loads or thousands of repetitions with low-impact loads.

request for proposal (RFP) A detailed list of questions submitted to vendors of software or other services to determine how well the vendor's product can meet the organization's specific requirements.

resource allocation The determination of how costs, time, and personnel are assigned to different phases of a systems development project.

responsibility Accepting the potential costs, duties, and obligations for the decisions one makes.

richness Measurement of the depth and detail of information that a business can supply to the customer as well as information the business collects about the customer.

ring topology A network topology in which all computers are linked by a closed loop in a manner that passes data in one direction from one computer to another.

risk assessment Determining the potential frequency of the occurrence of a problem and the potential damage if the problem were to occur. Used to determine the cost/benefit of a control.

risk aversion principle Principle that one should take the action that produces the least harm or incurs the least cost.

router Specialized communications processor that forwards packets of data from one network to another network.

routines Precise rules, procedures, and practices that have been developed to cope with expected situations.

RSS Technology using aggregator software to pull content from Web sites and feed it automatically to subscribers' computers.

SaaS (Software as a Service) Services for delivering and providing access to software remotely as a Web-based service.

safe harbour Private self-regulating policy and enforcement mechanism that meets the objectives of government regulations but does not involve government regulation or enforcement.

scalability The ability of a computer, product, or system to expand to serve a larger number of users without breaking down.

scope Measure that defines what work is and is not included in a project.

scoring model A quick method for deciding among alternative systems based on a system of ratings for selected objectives.

search costs The time and money spent locating a suitable product and determining the best price for that product.

search engine A tool for locating specific sites or information on the Internet.

search engine marketing Use of search engines to deliver in their results sponsored links, for which advertisers have paid.

Secure Hypertext Transfer Protocol (S-HTTP) Protocol used for encrypting data flowing over the Internet; limited to individual messages.

Secure Sockets Layer (SSL) Enables client and server computers to manage encryption and decryption activities as they communicate with each other during a secure Web session.

security Policies, procedures, and technical measures used to prevent unauthorized access, alteration, theft, or physical damage to information systems.

security policy Statements ranking information risks, identifying acceptable security goals, and identifying the mechanisms for achieving these goals.

Semantic Web Ways of making the Web more "intelligent," with machine-facilitated understanding of information so that searches can be more intuitive and effective; can be executed using intelligent software agents.

semistructured decisions Decisions in which only part of the problem has a clear-cut answer provided by an accepted procedure.

senior management People occupying the topmost hierarchy in an organization who are responsible for making long-range decisions.

sensitivity analysis Models that ask "what-if" questions repeatedly to determine the impact of changes in one or more factors on the outcomes.

server Computer specifically optimized to provide software and other resources to other computers over a network.

service-level agreement (SLA) Formal contract between customers and service providers that defines the specific responsibilities of the service provider and the level of service expected by the customer.

service-oriented architecture Software architecture of a firm built on a collection of software programs that communicate with each other to perform assigned tasks to create a working software application.

service platform Integration of multiple applications from multiple business functions, business units, or business partners to deliver a seamless experience for the customer, employee, manager, or business partner.

shopping bot Software with varying levels of built-in intelligence to help electronic commerce shoppers locate and evaluate products or services they might wish to purchase.

six sigma A specific measure of quality, representing 3.4 defects per million opportunities; used to designate a set of methodologies and techniques for improving quality and reducing costs.

smart card A credit-card-size plastic card that stores digital information and that can be used for electronic payments in place of cash.

smartphone Wireless phone with voice, text, and Internet capabilities.

sniffer Type of eavesdropping program that monitors information travelling over a network.

social bookmarking Capability for users to save their bookmarks to Web pages on a public Web site and tag these bookmarks with keywords to organize documents and share information with others.

social engineering Tricking people into revealing their passwords or other information by pretending to be legitimate users or members of a company in need of information.

social networking sites Online communities for expanding users' business or social contacts by making connections through their mutual business or personal connections.

social shopping Use of Web sites featuring user-created Web pages to share knowledge about items of interest to other shoppers.

sociotechnical design Design to produce information systems that blend technical efficiency with sensitivity to organizational and human needs.

sociotechnical view Seeing systems as composed of both technical and social elements.

software localization Process of converting software to operate in a second language.

software package A prewritten, precoded, commercially available set of programs that eliminates the need to write software programs for certain functions.

spam Unsolicited commercial e-mail.

spamming Form of abuse in which thousands and even hundreds of thousands of unsolicited e-mail and electronic messages are sent out, creating a nuisance for both businesses and individual users.

spoofing Attempts by hackers to hide their true identities by using fake e-mail addresses or masquerading as someone else; may involve redirecting a Web link to an address different from the intended one, with the site masquerading as the intended destination.

spyware Technology that aids in gathering information about a person or organization without their knowledge.

star topology A network topology in which all computers and other devices are connected to a central host computer. All communications between network devices must pass through the host computer.

storage area network (SAN) A high-speed network dedicated to storage that connects different kinds of storage devices, such as tape libraries and disk arrays, so they can be shared by multiple servers.

storage technology Physical media and software governing the storage and organization of data for use in an information system.

stored value payment systems Systems enabling consumers to make instant online payments to merchants and other individuals based on value stored in a digital account.

strategic transitions A movement from one level of sociotechnical system to another. Often required when adopting strategic systems that demand changes in the social and technical elements of an organization.

structure chart System documentation showing each level of design, the relationship among the levels, and the overall place in the design structure; can document one program, one system, or part of one program.

structured Refers to the fact that techniques are carefully drawn up, step by step, with each step building on the previous one.

structured decisions Decisions that are repetitive, routine, and have a definite procedure for handling them.

structured design Design where techniques are carefully drawn up, step by step, with each step building on a previous one.

structured knowledge Knowledge in the form of structured documents and reports.

Structured Query Language (SQL) The standard data manipulation language for relational database management systems.

supply chain Network of organizations and business processes for procuring materials, transforming raw materials into intermediate and finished products, and distributing the finished products to customers.

supply chain execution systems Systems to manage the flow of products through distribution centres and warehouses to ensure that products are delivered to the right locations in the most efficient manner.

supply chain management Integration of supplier, distributor, and customer logistics requirements into one cohesive process.

supply chain management systems Information systems that automate the flow of information between a firm and its suppliers in order to optimize the planning, sourcing, manufacturing, and delivery of products and services.

supply chain planning systems Systems that enable a firm to generate demand forecasts for a product and to develop sourcing and manufacturing plans for that product.

support activities Activities that make the delivery of a firm's primary activities possible. Consist of the organization's infrastructure, human resources, technology, and procurement activities.

switch Device to connect network components that has more intelligence than a hub and can filter and forward data to a specified destination.

switching costs The expense a customer or company incurs in lost time and expenditure of resources when changing from one supplier or system to a competing supplier or system.

syndicators Businesses aggregating content or applications from multiple sources, packaging them for distribution, and reselling them to third-party Web sites.

systems analysis The analysis of a problem that the organization will try to solve with an information system.

systems analysts Specialists who translate business problems and requirements into information requirements and systems, acting as liaison between the information systems department and the rest of the organization.

systems design The result of systems analysis that details how a system will meet the information requirements as determined by the systems analysis.

systems development The activities that go into producing an information systems solution to an organizational problem or opportunity.

systems life cycle A traditional methodology for developing an information system that partitions the systems development process into formal stages that must be completed sequentially with a very formal division of labour between end users and information systems specialists.

systems operators Staff who actually operate computers hands-on for tasks such as keeping systems running, changing paper on massive, high-speed printers, and loading hard drives.

system testing Testing the functioning of the information system as a whole in order to determine if discrete modules will function together as planned.

T lines High-speed data lines leased from communications providers, such as T1 lines (with a transmission capacity of 1.544 Mbps) or T3 lines.

T1 lines Cable with a fixed connection that is used for high-capacity Internet connections, typically at 1.544 Mbps.

tacit knowledge Expertise and experience of organizational members that has not been formally documented.

tangible benefits Benefits that can be quantified and assigned a monetary value; they include lower operational costs and increased cash flows.

taxonomy Method of classifying things according to a predetermined system.

technology standards Specifications that establish the compatibility of products and the ability to communicate in a network.

technostress Stress induced by computer use; symptoms include aggravation, hostility toward humans, impatience, and enervation.

Telnet Network tool that allows someone to log on to one computer system while doing work on another.

testing The exhaustive and thorough process that determines whether the system produces the desired results under known and possible conditions.

test plan Plan prepared by the development team in conjunction with users; it includes all of the preparations for the series of tests to be performed on the system.

text mining Discovery of patterns and relationships from large sets of unstructured data.

token Physical device similar to an identification card that is designed to prove the identity of a single user.

topology The way in which the components of a network are connected.

total cost of ownership (TCO) Designates the total cost of owning technology resources, including initial purchase costs, the cost of hardware and software upgrades, maintenance, technical support, and training.

total quality management (TQM) A concept that makes quality control a responsibility to be shared by all people in an organization.

touch point Method of firm interaction with a customer, such as telephone, e-mail, customer service desk, conventional mail, or point-of-purchase.

trade secret Any intellectual work or product used for a business purpose that can be classified as belonging to that business, provided it is not based on information in the public domain.

transaction costs Costs incurred when a firm buys on the marketplace what it cannot make itself.

transaction cost theory Economic theory stating that firms grow larger because they can conduct marketplace transactions internally more cheaply than they can with external firms in the marketplace.

transaction processing systems (TPS) Computerized systems that perform and record the daily routine transactions necessary to conduct the business; they serve the organization's operational level.

transborder data flow The movement of information across international boundaries in any form.

Transmission Control Protocol/Internet Protocol (TCP/IP) Dominant model for achieving connectivity among different networks. Provides a universally agreed-on method for breaking up digital messages into packets, routing them to the proper addresses, and then reassembling them into coherent messages.

transnational Truly global form of business organization with no national headquarters; value-added activities are managed from a global perspective without reference to national borders, optimizing sources of supply and demand and local competitive advantage.

Trojan horse A software program that appears legitimate but contains a second hidden function that may cause damage.

tuple A row or record in a relational database.

twisted wire A transmission medium consisting of pairs of twisted copper wires; used to transmit analog phone conversations but can be used for data transmission.

unified communications Method that integrates disparate channels for voice communications, data communications, instant messaging, e-mail, and electronic conferencing into a single experience where users can seamlessly switch back and forth between different communication modes.

Unified Modelling Language (UML) Industry standard methodology for analysis and design of an object-oriented software system.

unified threat management (UTM) Comprehensive security management tool that combines multiple security tools, including firewalls, virtual private networks, intrusion detection systems, and Web content filtering and anti-spam software.

uniform resource locator (URL) The address of a specific resource on the Internet.

unit testing The process of testing each program separately in the system. Sometimes called *program testing*.

UNIX Operating system for all types of computers, which is machine independent and supports multiuser processing, multitasking, and networking. Used in high-end workstations and servers.

unstructured decisions Nonroutine decisions in which the decision maker must provide judgment, evaluation, and insights into the problem definition; there is no agreed-upon procedure for making such decisions.

user–designer communications gap The difference in backgrounds, interests, and priorities that impede communication and problem solving among end users and information systems specialists.

user interface The part of the information system through which the end user interacts with the system; type of hardware and the series of on-screen commands and responses required for a user to work with the system.

utilitarian principle Principle that assumes one can put values in rank order and understand the consequences of various courses of action.

utility computing Model of computing in which companies pay only for the information technology resources they actually use during a specified time period. Also called *on-demand computing* or *usage-based pricing*.

value chain model Model that highlights the primary or support activities that add a margin of value to a firm's products or services where information systems can best be applied to achieve a competitive advantage.

value web Customer-driven network of independent firms who use information technology to coordinate their value chains to collectively produce a product or service for a market.

virtual company Organization using networks to link people, assets, and ideas to create and distribute products and services without being limited to traditional organizational boundaries or physical location.

virtualization Presentation of a set of computing resources so that they can all be accessed in ways that are not restricted by physical configuration or geographic location.

virtual private network (VPN) A secure connection between two points across the Internet to transmit corporate data. Provides a low-cost alternative to a private network.

Virtual Reality Modelling Language (VRML) A set of specifications for interactive three-dimensional modelling on the World Wide Web.

virtual reality systems Interactive graphics software and hardware that create computer-generated simulations that provide sensations that emulate real-world activities.

virtual world Computer-based simulated environment intended for its users to inhabit and interact via graphical representations called *avatars*.

Voice over IP (VoIP) The delivery of voice information using the Internet Protocol (IP).

war driving Technique in which eavesdroppers drive by buildings or park outside and try to intercept wireless network traffic.

Web 2.0 Second-generation, interactive Internet-based services that enable people to collaborate, share information, and create new services online, including mashups, blogs, RSS, and wikis.

Web 3.0 Future vision of the Web where all digital information is woven together with intelligent search capabilities; includes efforts to achieve a semantic Web.

Web browser An easy-to-use software tool for accessing the World Wide Web and the Internet.

Web bugs Tiny graphic files embedded in e-mail messages and Web pages that are designed to monitor online Internet user behaviour.

Web masters Staff who are responsible for the organization's Web site.

Web mining Discovery and analysis of useful patterns and information from the World.

Web site A collection of Web pages that includes a home page.

Web server A computer that uses Web server software to house and deliver Web pages for a Web site.

Web services Set of universal standards using Internet technology to integrate different applications from different sources without time-consuming custom coding. Used for linking different systems of different organizations or different systems within the same organization.

wide area network (WAN) Telecommunications network that spans a large geographical distance. May consist of a variety of cable, satellite, and microwave technologies.

widget Small software programs that can be added to Web pages or placed on the desktop to provide additional functionality.

Wi-Fi Standards for Wireless Fidelity, relating to the 802.11 family of wireless networking standards.

wiki Collaborative Web site where visitors can add, delete, or modify content, including the work of previous authors.

WiMax Popular term for IEEE Standard 802.16 for wireless networking over a range of up to 50 kilometres with a data transfer rate of up to 75 Mbps. Stands for *Worldwide Interoperability for Microwave Access*.

Windows Microsoft family of operating systems for both network servers and client computers. The most recent version is Windows 7.

Wintel PC Any computer that uses Intel microprocessors (or compatible microprocessors) and the Windows operating system.

wireless portals Portals with content and services optimized for mobile devices to steer users to the information they are most likely to need.

wireless sensor networks (WSNs) Networks of interconnected wireless devices with built-in processing, storage, and radio frequency sensors and antennas that are embedded into the physical environment to provide measurements of many points over large spaces.

wisdom The collective and individual experience of applying knowledge to the solution of problems.

workflow management The process of streamlining business procedures so that documents can be moved easily and efficiently from one location to another.

World Wide Web A system with universally accepted standards for storing, retrieving, formatting, and displaying information in a networked environment.

worms Independent software programs that propagate themselves to disrupt the operation of computer networks or destroy data and other programs.

XML (eXtensible Markup Language) General-purpose language that describes the structure of a document and supports links to multiple documents, allowing data to be manipulated by the computer. Used for both Web and non-Web applications.

Photo and Screen Shot Credits

Index

Name Index

Organization Index

Subject Index